Four British Women Novelists: Anita Brookner, Margaret Drabble, Iris Murdoch, Barbara Pym

THE MAGILL BIBLIOGRAPHIES

The American Presidents, by Norman S. Cohen, 1989
Black American Women Novelists, by Craig Werner, 1989
Classical Greek and Roman Drama, by Robert J. Forman, 1989
Contemporary Latin American Fiction, by Keith H. Brower, 1989
Masters of Mystery and Detective Fiction, by J. Randolph Cox, 1989
Nineteenth Century American Poetry, by Philip K. Jason, 1989
Restoration Drama, by Thomas J. Taylor, 1989
Twentieth Century European Short Story, by Charles E. May, 1989
The Victorian Novel, by Laurence W. Mazzeno, 1989
Women's Issues, by Laura Stempel Mumford, 1989
America in Space, by Russell R. Tobias, 1991
The American Constitution, by Robert J. Janosik, 1991
The Classical Epic, by Thomas J. Sienkewicz, 1991
English Romantic Poetry, by Bryan Aubrey, 1991
Ethics, by John K. Roth, 1991
The Immigrant Experience, by Paul D. Mageli, 1991
The Modern American Novel, by Steven G. Kellman, 1991
Native Americans, by Frederick E. Hoxie and Harvey Markowitz, 1991
American Drama: 1918-1960, by R. Baird Shuman, 1992
American Ethnic Literatures, by David R. Peck, 1992
American Theatre History, by Thomas J. Taylor, 1992
The Atomic Bomb, by Hans G. Graetzer and Larry M. Browning, 1992
Biography, by Carl Rollyson, 1992
The History of Science, by Gordon L. Miller, 1992
The Origin and Evolution of Life on Earth, by David W. Hollar, 1992
Pan-Africanism, by Michael W. Williams, 1992
Resources for Writers, by R. Baird Shuman, 1992
Shakespeare, by Joseph Rosenblum, 1992
The Vietnam War in Literature, by Philip K. Jason, 1992
Contemporary Southern Women Fiction Writers, by Rosemary M. Canfield Reisman and Christopher J. Canfield, 1994
Cycles in Humans and Nature, by John T. Burns, 1994
Environmental Studies, by Diane M. Fortner, 1994
Poverty in America, by Steven Pressman, 1994
The Short Story in English: Britain and North America, by Dean Baldwin and Gregory L. Morris, 1994

Four British Women Novelists:
Anita Brookner, Margaret Drabble, Iris Murdoch, Barbara Pym

*An Annotated and Critical
Secondary Bibliography*

George Soule

Magill Bibliographies

The Scarecrow Press, Inc.
Lanham, Md., & London
and
Salem Press
Pasadena, Calif., & Englewood Cliffs, N.J.
1998

SCARECROW PRESS, INC.

Published in the United States of America
by Scarecrow Press, Inc.
4720 Boston Way
Lanham, Maryland 20706

4 Pleydell Gardens
Kent CT20 2DN, England

Copyright © 1998 by George Soule

British Library Cataloguing in Publication Information Available

Library of Congress Cataloging-in-Publication Data

Soule, George, 1930–
     Four British women novelists : Anita Brookner, Margaret Drabble,
     Iris Murdoch, Barbara Pym : an annotated and critical bibliography /
     George Soule.
          p.   cm. — (Magill bibliographies)
     Includes index.
     ISBN 0-8108-3505-3 (cloth : alk. paper)
     1. English fiction—Women authors—History and criticism—
Bibliography.   2. Women and literature—Great Britain—
History—20th century—Bibliography.   3. English fiction—20th
century—History and criticism—Bibliography.   4. Brookner, Anita
—Criticism and interpretation—Bibliography.   5. Drabble, Margaret,
1939–   —Criticism and interpretation—Bibliography.   6. Murdoch,
Iris—Criticism and interpretation—Bibliography.   7. Pym, Barbara
—Criticism and interpretation—Bibliography.   I. Title.
II. Series.
Z2014.F4S68   1998
[PR888.W6]
016.823'914099287—dc21   98-5992
                                                                   CIP

To Carolyn and Kate,
who enjoy these stories as much as I do.

Contents

Contents

Contents

Acknowledgments

For their help in preparing this bibliography I wish to thank the staff of the Lawrence McKinley Gould Library of Carleton College, especially Michael Current, Associate Librarian for Interlibrary Services; Nancy Casper, Interlibrary Services Assistant; Kathy Schwartz, Loan Services Assistant; Terry Metz, Associate Librarian for Systems Support and Instruction; and Ann Niles, Associate Librarian. I would also like to thank Carleton College's Academic Computing staff, in particular Andrea Nixon, and the Carleton College English Department.

I started this project knowing I could use the Minitex Library Information Network, funded by the Minnesota Legislature through the Minnesota High Education Coordinating Board. I am grateful to all these bodies. I would also like to thank the staff of the periodicals department of the Rølvaag Library of St. Olaf College for their help and my good friends Lois and Charles Messner for reading and summarizing a number of articles written about Iris Murdoch in French.

I am happy to acknowledge the debt I owe those who compiled earlier bibliographies of these authors' work, especially the Modern Language Association's International Bibliography. I am particularly indebted to Cheryl K. Bove and John Fletcher for *Iris Murdoch: A Descriptive Primary and Annotated Secondary Bibliography* (1994).

Many thanks to my wife Carolyn, who urged me to take on this project and who encouraged me all along the way.

Introduction

This bibliography will help researchers, general readers, students, and teachers to find what has been written about four contemporary British women novelists: Anita Brookner, Margaret Drabble, Iris Murdoch, and Barbara Pym. So much has been written about British women novelists that this volume could only accommodate the criticism of these four; I regret not being able to include such writers as Muriel Spark, Angela Carter, A. S. Byatt, and Fay Weldon.

This bibliography can be used in several ways. Readers wanting to survey what has been said about a particular author can read through the appropriate section to discover what have been the critics' favorite topics. Those wanting help in finding specific kinds of criticism and information can turn to the "General Studies" of an author for accounts of all or part of her career. Each "General Studies" section lists (alphabetically by author) the books and articles that deal significantly with more than one novel by that author. Each entry summarizes the author's general ideas and lists which of her works are specifically noted in the "Criticism of Individual Novels" sections.

To find what has been said about particular titles, readers can go directly to these "Criticism of Individual Novels" sections. For each author, the novels are listed in order of their first publication. I note when the American title of a novel differs from the original British title and, for Barbara Pym, when dates of composition are very different from dates of publication. Under each title, readers will find (organized alphabetically by author) a list of books and articles that deal primarily with that novel or that make significant remarks about it. Some entries are quite brief, for they may note only salient and unique comments on the novel in question without attempting to summarize the author's overall argument. Users of this book are urged to turn from such entries to the entry for the book or article under "General Studies." All entries carry full bibliographical descriptions, so that researchers will not have to page back and forth to locate the information they want. "Bibliographical Studies" and "Other Works" sections provide other kinds of useful information.

I have tried to make clear who is saying what. Unless it is specified differently, the ideas in each annotation are those of the author of the article or book being annotated. One exception is with interviews. Even though these are indexed by the name of the interviewer, the ideas expressed generally belong to the novelist, not to the interviewer.

This is a critical bibliography. Although I do not try to grade each item, I do make a number of explicit critical judgments, especially about particularly fine articles and books. In addition, I make many judgments implicitly: a long and detailed summary usually implies that an item is worth a substantial amount of attention. Although some of my remarks will seem idiosyncratic to some readers, I hope my judgments will guide readers to worthwhile and useful material.

Though it is critical, this bibliography is not selective. It covers almost all the criticism of these four novelists that has been written from the beginnings of their career until to the end of 1996. There are a few later entries. In order to keep this book within manageable size, I have omitted for the most part all of the following: very short pieces or very brief notices in longer works; most treatments in standard handbooks and general surveys; introductions and afterwords; material designed for school use; material not in English (though I have included a few articles written in French about Iris Murdoch); articles in popular magazines and newspapers; dissertation abstracts. I have usually not listed book reviews in standard literary journals. An exception has been made for novels published since 1988. For these works, I have included reviews from *The New York Times Book Review*, *The New York Review of Books*, *London Review of Books*, *The Times Literary Supplement*, and several other publications.

I have omitted material which does not deal with novels: that is, commentary on these authors' works of children's literature, poetry, short stories, drama, opera, literary criticism, philosophy, art history, politics, history, and the like. I have had to omit a very small number of specialized items which Carleton College's excellent interlibrary loan system (which draws upon the resources of the University of Minnesota) could not obtain for me.

Reading these novels has given me a great deal of pleasure. In addition, they have taught me about art, about how people live, about the range of ideas people can entertain, and about what possibilities life holds or does not hold. I think these authors are great artists. This bibliography will help make these novels more delightful and more accessible to a growing number of readers.

George Soule

Anita Brookner

General Studies

Baxter, Gisèle Marieks. "Cultural Experiences and Identity in the
Early Novels of Anita Brookner." *English* 42 (Summer, 1993):
125-139.
Baxter discusses the similarities of three central characters of
early Brookner novels: Ruth of *A Start in Life*, Kitty of
Providence, and Edith of *Hotel du Lac*. These women were born
of childish, European parents. They themselves seem childish as
they try to escape their heritage by their ultimately unsuccessful
attempts to be accepted by one kind of traditional English world.
Interestingly, this world is not that of the gentry; the men they
seek represent the financially secure ideal of the Thatcher era.
Baxter points out that these women attempt to belong by
dressing appropriately (but they get clothes subtly wrong) and by
cooking (the only times they cook are for the men they want).
These women complicate their lives by trying to use formulae
from literature to apply to live by. By the end of the novels, they
have not succeeded in joining English society, but they find they
have been true to their true identities. They find they have the
strength to live on, even though they know they will never be in
the inner circle. Baxter provides detailed analyses of each of the
three novels.

Bradbury, Malcolm. *The Modern British Novel.* London: Martin
Secker & Warburg, 1993.
Minimal comments. Brookner is part of a trend for British
authors to write on European subjects. Her heroines are thought-
ful and ironic; her restraint and precision remind the author of
Henry James.

Burchfield, Robert. "Two Kinds of English? Jeffrey Archer and Anita
Brookner." In *The State of the Language*, edited by Christopher

Ricks and Leonard Michaels. Berkeley: University of California Press, 1990.
A linguist compares a best-selling author's prose to Brookner's. Brookner's grammar and usage are more exact than his; she uses more foreign words (especially French ones) but fewer slang expressions; and she uses the subjunctive more often.

Fisher-Wirth, Ann. "Hunger Art: The Novels of Anita Brookner." *Twentieth Century Literature* 41 (Spring, 1995): 1-15.
A valuable article. Fisher-Wirth admires Brookner's novels but is repelled by what seems to be their message: nice girls finish last. Brookner women seem to exist by their own choice within a patriarchal structure that excludes them. They not only accept this structure, but endorse it. They are humiliated, and their self-knowledge is about the depths to which they can sink. They are deprived of parents; what sexual experiences they have result in pain. Fisher-Wirth treats *Hotel du Lac*, *A Friend from England*, *Latecomers*, *A Closed Eye*, *Fraud*, and *A Family Romance*.
Brookner's novels are really more universal than this. Brookner treats, not just women's neuroses, but a universal tragic situation. Behind all of her fables is the scene in *Latecomers* in which Fibich realizes all his pain comes from his separation from his mother. Fisher-Wirth goes on to suggest that in *A Closed Eye*, Brookner articulates a particularly feminine way of dealing with this universal condition. Harriet rejects conventional happiness and starves for starvation's sake; emotional hunger feeds her as life will not. She moves into a feminine "wild zone" of madness or vision. *A Family Romance* shows that even life's winners have this hunger.

Galef, David. "You Aren't What You Eat: Anita Brookner's Dilemma." *Journal of Popular Culture* 28 (Winter, 1994): 1-7.
Food and love are often associated, no more so than in Brookner's novels. Her women grow up starved for affection, yet try to feed others. As in the novels of Barbara Pym, the underlying pattern in Brookner is often this: a self-denying mother feeds an ungrateful son. Sometimes feeding their male friends expresses the women's mastery, sometimes their revenge. But most often they fail to win their man. Why do they not change? Altering the

habits of a lifetime is difficult. Galef comments on *A Start in Life, Providence, Hotel du Lac,* and *A Misalliance.*

Guppy, Shusha. "The Art of Fiction XCVIII: Anita Brookner." *Paris Review* 29 (Fall, 1987): 147-169.
This excellent interview occurred just before *A Friend from England* was published. Guppy summarizes Brookner's life and describes the author in her London apartment. Brookner talks about her youth in a traditional Jewish London home, about her characters (in particular the problem female authors have drawing male characters), about her themes and their moral aspects, about authors who have influenced her, about existentialism and the perils of romanticism, and about her distrust of radical feminism.

Haffenden, John. "Anita Brookner." In *Novelists in Interview.* London: Methuen, 1985.
A raw and revealing interview just before the publication of *Hotel du Lac.* Brookner talks about her parents, hints at a great passion gone wrong, and calls herself a miserable and lonely person. Although she first wrote fiction to counteract her sense of powerlessness, the therapy has not been successful. She distances herself from feminism. Her attraction to eighteenth century reason is related to her novels' wit.

Hosmer, Robert E., Jr. "Paradigm and Passage: The Fiction of Anita Brookner." In *Contemporary British Women Writers: Narrative Strategies.* New York: St. Martin's Press, 1993.
Brookner's central characters (and Brookner herself) are in the tradition of the exile figure, from the Bible, through Anglo-Saxon poetry, to our day. Although Hosmer's definition of the exile's experience is vague, it yields valuable insights into Brookner's novels and enables him to make persuasive distinctions among them. Hosmer also speculates intelligently on the relation of her novels to Brookner's private life.

Kenyon, Olga. *Women Novelists Today: A Survey of English Writing in the Seventies and Eighties.* New York: St. Martin's Press, 1988.
In her introduction, Kenyon sketches the new freedom of contemporary women novelists and the kinds of recent criticism

which promote that freedom. In contrast, Brookner's female characters feel limited in an old-fashioned way. Appropriately, Brookner's plots resemble those of traditional romances— "women's novels." Such novels show implicitly how a patriarchal culture can impose restrictions without women knowing it. Brookner's novels differ from nineteenth century novels and from recent popular romances in that her heroines are painfully aware of their limitations. They know that for some inexplicable reason they will not assert themselves enough to win the men they want. Kenyon's arguments are sometimes schematic and hard to follow, but hers is a representative reading of Brookner's early work. She appends a short list of feminist writing and general literary criticism.

_____. *Women Writers Talk: Interviews with Ten Women Writers.* New York: Carroll & Graf, 1990.
Brookner describes her family, her life as an art historian, and her way of writing (she seldom revises). Her theme is often the perils of romantic love and hope; she has begun to write more about men. In this interview, Brookner talks at length about *Family and Friends* and replies to her critics. Short descriptive bibliography of works of feminism and literary criticism.

Kurz, Helga. "The Impossibility of Female Friendship: A Study of Anita Brookner's Female Characters." *Arbeiten aus Anglistik und Amerikanistik* 15 (1990): 13-25.
In novels told from a first-person perspective, Brookner creates two kinds of women: her central spinster heroines, who are complex and detached, and other women, who are predictable and unimaginative. Brookner implies that real friendship between women is impossible. Her heroines can make only small talk with other women; they retreat to their solitary homes when they can. They find literature gives them no help in understanding other women. Any hope that the heroines can change is destroyed at the end of their novels, often by an apparently insignificant other woman. The problems of these heroines seem to be Brookner's own and limit the worth of the novels. Kurz looks specifically at *A Start in Life, Providence, Look at Me, Hotel du Lac, A Misalliance,* and *A Friend from England.*

McGuirk, Carol. "Drabble to Carter: Fiction by Women, 1962-1992." In *The Columbia History of the British Novel*, edited by John Richetti. New York: Columbia University Press, 1994.
McGuirk finds that many women writers of this era have a number of traits in common. Their early lives were disrupted by World War II. They are concerned to distance themselves both from mass culture and high culture. Their novels are not dramatic; they are often uneventful and end awkwardly. They center on women, especially women in competition. Brookner fits this definition well. McGuirk comments on *Brief Lives*.

Sadler, Lynn Veach. *Anita Brookner*. Boston: Twayne, 1990.
Sadler's book devotes a chapter to each of Brookner's first seven novels. Her informal introduction and her concluding chapter express her annoyance with Brookner's heroines: they are so alienated, so constrained by honor, and so lonely that they cannot act the way a healthy and educated woman should. In Chapter One, she surveys what little is known of Brookner's life and discusses the range of her reading of fiction. The analyses of individual novels point out similarities among the themes and characters and explain many parallels with other French and English novels. Sadler regularly arranges characters in a continuum from good to bad and laments Brookner's ignorance of a middle way. Sadler's insistent reproaches of Brookner and her heroines weaken an admirably detailed and insightful book.

Schofield, Mary Anne. "Spinster's Fare: Rites of Passage in Anita Brookner's Fiction." In *Cooking by the Book*. Bowling Green, Ohio: Bowling Green State University Popular Press, 1989.
Schofield outlines the stages of female development as expressed in the rituals of cooking and uses this outline to illuminate Brookner's early novels through *A Misalliance*. Schofield adds a final stage for contemporary women: learning to do without the male, to become aggressive and independent, and to enjoy cooking spinster's meals. This interesting essay sometimes distorts the novels to fit its simple theory.

Skinner, John. *The Fictions of Anita Brookner: Illusions of Romance*. New York: St. Martin's Press, 1992.

A study of Brookner's first nine novels arranged in three groups of
three.   In his introductory chapter, Skinner discusses the sharply
differing critical views of Brookner's novels.   He then promises to
discuss four groups of writers to whom Brookner has been compared: nineteenth-century French novelists, some classic English
and American writers, contemporary women novelists, and
writers of popular romances.   He discusses romanticism as it
appears in Brookner's intellectual background and in her
nonfiction writings.   Although he acknowledges that Brookner
creates memorable characters, his central concerns are the
structures and themes of her work.

Although he says he will postpone until his final chapter any
consideration of her heroines as semi-autobiographical, his accounts of individual novels are filled with such speculations. He
also discusses the implications of the works of art reproduced on
Brookner's dust jackets and paperback covers. In his final chapter, Skinner provides a fascinating discussion of how Brookner's
plots fit the categories of modern narrative theory. He then asks
two questions: To what extent should readers view Brookner's
novels as autobiographical? How reliable are Brookner's own
autobiographical remarks? Some critical terms are not clearly
defined.

Soule, George. "Anita Brookner." In *Magill's Survey of World Literature, Supplement,* edited by Frank N. Magill.   Tarrytown,
N.Y.: Marshall Cavendish, 1995.
A survey of Brookner's life and achievements. Specific analyses
of *A Start in Life, Look at Me,* and *Hotel du Lac.*

Stetz, Margaret Diane. "Anita Brookner: Woman Writer as Reluctant
Feminist." In *Writing the Woman Artist: Essays on Poetics,
Politics, and Portraiture,* edited by Suzanne W. Jones. Philadelphia: University of Pennsylvania Press, 1991.
Stetz explains clearly how Brookner disagrees with an orthodox
feminist. Though both decry women who use feminine wiles to
get what they want, Brookner regards these women not as
culturally determined creatures, but as facts of life.   At times
Brookner is dazzled by such women and even envies them.   To
Brookner, women are not sisters but antagonists.   Even so, Stetz
believes that Brookner's novels exhibit an important kind of

feminism. She argues brilliantly that Brookner's heroines must come to terms with their mothers to achieve contentment, and she argues less persuasively that Brookner depends greatly on the models of female authors, especially Virginia Woolf. An important article.

Watson, Daphne. *Their Own Worst Enemies: Women Writers of Women's Fictions*. London: Pluto Press, 1995.
In Chapter 2, Watson treats both Brookner and Barbara Pym. Brookner's early novels were promising because they contained humor and irony. In *Hotel du Lac*, irony and other devices suggested that the narrator was distant from Edith Hope and judged her as limited and self-deluded. But subsequent novels show that Brookner shares Edith's attitudes, for she has become just as formulaic and fraudulent as romance writers and blockbuster authors like Jackie Collins. Like Pym, she appeals to a middle-class audience. Her characters are one-dimensional. Like Pym's heroines, they are "weak, exploitative, insensitive, vain, self-important." They waste themselves pursuing men when they could have had rewarding relationships with women.

Waugh, Patricia. "Anita Brookner." In *Feminine Fictions: Revisiting the Postmodern*. London: Routledge, 1989.
Waugh deals with how Brookner's early novels show, perhaps uncritically, that women are trapped in infantile roles. They yearn, not for an autonomous self, but for romantic fulfillment in marriage. Waugh provides useful insights into the dynamics of Brookner's fiction.

Criticism of Individual Novels.

A Start in Life (in the U.S., *The Debut*), 1981.

Baxter, Gisèle Marie. "Clothes, Men, and Books: Cultural Experiences and Identity in the Early Novels of Anita Brookner." *English* 42 (Summer, 1993): 125-139.
Ruth resembles the heroines of *Providence* and *Hotel du Lac* in many ways. She tries to apply literature to her life. She hopes to

attract a man who will enable her to join traditional English society. She expresses her love by cooking for him. By the end, she affirms her identity; she accepts the fact that she will never be accepted.

Guppy, Shusha. "The Art of Fiction XCVIII: Anita Brookner." *Paris Review* 29 (Fall, 1987): 147-169.
Brookner describes how she wrote this novel out of personal despair. She wanted to analyze her life.

Sadler, Lynn Veach. *Anita Brookner*. Boston: Twayne, 1990.
In Chapter 2, Sadler summarizes the story and points out many ways in which Ruth Weiss's life parallels Brookner's own life and the lives of characters in novels by Honoré de Balzac, Gustave Flaubert, Margaret Drabble, and Barbara Pym. Sadler also shows how the lives of other characters in the novel echo Ruth's life. Sadler's analysis is incisive, but naïvely judgmental: Ruth allows herself to be deluded by literature's happy endings, but does not learn the positive lessons literature can teach. Like Pym's heroines, Ruth is passive and seems to lack the energy to create a life that Brookner's readers can find satisfactory.

Schofield, Mary Anne. "Spinster's Fare: Rites of Passage in Anita Brookner's Fiction." In *Cooking by the Book*. Bowling Green, Ohio: Bowling Green State University Popular Press, 1989.
Schofield's outline of the stages of female initiation illuminates a great many stages in Brookner's account of Ruth's cooking and Ruth's life. The theory is less convincing when it deals with Ruth's return from Paris to London.

Skinner, John. *The Fictions of Anita Brookner: Illusions of Romance*. New York: St. Martin's Press, 1992.
Skinner groups this with Brookner's next two novels because each is directly linked with a specific work of French fiction. In this case, it is Honoré de Balzac's *Eugénie Grandet*; Skinner discusses how the career of Ruth Weiss parallels that of Balzac's heroine and how Brookner allows Ruth to make significant deviations at decisive moments. Skinner also explains how food in this novel suggests love and discusses how Brookner undercuts the conventions of romance potboilers.

Waugh, Patricia. *Feminine Fictions: Revisiting the Postmodern.*
London: Routledge, 1989.
Ruth suffers from her relation to her mother, for she represses her
own needs and fears success in the male world.

Providence, 1982.

Baxter, Gisèle Marie. "Clothes, Men, and Books: Cultural Experiences and Identity in the Early Novels of Anita Brookner."
English 42 (Summer, 1993): 125-139.
Kitty resembles the heroines of *A Start in Life* and *Hotel du Lac* in
that she tries to understand life through literary texts and in that
she wants to be accepted by traditional English people. She tries
to dress correctly, but does not quite succeed. She seems stronger
at the end of the novel.

Guppy, Shusha. "The Art of Fiction XCVIII: Anita Brookner." *Paris
Review* 29 (Fall, 1987): 147-169.
Brookner agrees that this novel parallels *Adolphe* by the French
author Benjamin Constant (1767-1830). The heroines of both
novels judge men badly.

Hosmer, Robert E., Jr. "Paradigm and Passage: The Fiction of Anita
Brookner." In *Contemporary British Women Writers: Narrative
Strategies.* New York: St. Martin's Press, 1993.
Exile for Kitty Maule is many things. It means being divided between her French heritage, as represented by her grandparents,
and her life in England. Hosmer details how her divisions influence how she dresses, speaks, and behaves. As an exile, Kitty
hopes for love, but she loves a man whose belief in providence
makes clear her own exile from any kind of God. A valuable
analysis.

Sadler, Lynn Veach. *Anita Brookner.* Boston: Twayne, 1990.
In Chapter 3, Sadler calls Kitty Maule's situation ironic: she is an
academic expert on Romanticism, yet she is deceived by the
dreams evoked by romantic novels and cannot learn the lessons
this literature teaches. She does not realize that Maurice Bishop,
the romantic figure she loves, is a fraud. Brookner probably

intended Kitty to be a stronger woman than Ruth Weiss in *A Start in Life*, but Kitty does not realize she could assert herself for reasons other than simply to please a man. Sadler points out many parallels between Kitty's situation and those of other characters, parallels the reader sees but which Kitty in her obtuseness cannot.

Schofield, Mary Anne. "Spinster's Fare: Rites of Passage in Anita Brookner's Fiction." In *Cooking by the Book*. Bowling Green, Ohio: Bowling Green State University Popular Press, 1989.
Schofield uses food to illustrate the stages of female initiation. Kitty flees from the food lovingly forced on her at home but fails to nourish her lover Maurice. Later, Kitty learns to nourish herself, and at a final dinner with Maurice discovers she cannot be nourished by another person.

Skinner, John. *The Fictions of Anita Brookner: Illusions of Romance.* New York: St. Martin's Press, 1992.
This novel shares many things with *A Start in Life:* unmarried heroines with non-English parents, the heroines' academic achievements, and their love for unattainable men. Skinner discusses how Brookner uses food and clothing significantly. His main emphases are on how the structures both novels show two circles of hope and disillusion and on how *Providence* draws upon and departs from its particular French model, Constant's *Adolphe*.

Soule, George. "Anita Brookner." In *Magill's Survey of World Literature, Supplement*, edited by Frank N. Magill. Tarrytown, N.Y.: Marshall Cavendish, 1995.
Brief analysis of a typical Brookner heroine.

Look at Me, 1983.

Haffenden, John. "Anita Brookner." In *Novelists in Interview*. London: Methuen, 1985.
Brookner says she regrets this depressing novel.

Kenyon, Olga. *Women Writers Talk: Interviews with Ten Women Writers*. New York: Carroll & Graf, 1990.
Brookner despises Frances for being stupid.

Sadler, Lynn Veach. *Anita Brookner*. Boston: Twayne, 1990.
   In Chapter 4, Sadler says that Frances differs from Brookner's
   previous heroines. Although she is a loser in the game of romance, she is no sexual innocent. This novel is different because
   Brookner discusses a writer's life and craft, especially how writers
   are driven by their memories. Sadler points out many parallels
   among the characters of this story and those of other Brookner
   novels. Here too there is a difference: the foil characters in this
   novel present different ways of living; there is even a happy family that represents a middle ground Brookner's heroines never
   achieve. Sadler calls Brookner a conservative feminist and notes
   that here Brookner treats men sympathetically for the first time.

Schofield, Mary Anne. "Spinster's Fare: Rites of Passage in Anita
   Brookner's Fiction." In *Cooking by the Book*. Bowling Green,
   Ohio: Bowling Green State University Popular Press, 1989.
   Female cooking rituals help explain this novel. Although Frances
   never outgrows her love of nursery food, as she expands her social
   world she comes to like exotic restaurant meals. She does not
   cook for the man she loves and loses. At the end, she is alone, but
   she takes control of her household and does not cook. Schofield
   may bend her thesis to describe this conclusion as positive.

Skinner, John. *The Fictions of Anita Brookner: Illusions of Romance*.
   New York: St. Martin's Press, 1992.
   Skinner finds this novel's connection to French literature in
   fictional works by André Gide and Marcel Proust. Skinner
   emphasizes Brookner's employment of first-person narration.
   Although this technique has some limitations and causes
   inconsistencies, it adds a new dimension to Brookner's fiction.
   The narrator is both a naïve diarist and a self-conscious novelist.
   The novelist Frances Hinton reflects on her motives for writing:
   she wants to say "Look at me" and wants satirical revenge. She
   also reveals an ability to repress her own erotic experience and her
   speculations about that of other people.

Soule, George. "Anita Brookner." In *Magill's Survey of World Lit-
   erature, Supplement*, edited by Frank N. Magill. Tarrytown,
   N.Y.: Marshall Cavendish, 1995.
   Brief analysis focused on the ending of the novel.

Stetz, Margaret Diane. "Anita Brookner: Woman Writer as Reluctant
  Feminist." In *Writing the Woman Artist: Essays on Poetics,
  Politics, and Portraiture,* edited by Suzanne W. Jones. Philadelphia: University of Pennsylvania Press, 1991.
  Stetz thinks that one of Brookner's narrative patterns as most
  clearly revealed in this novel. Frances's gift for writing was
  inspired and encouraged by her mother and left her when her
  mother died. Frances contemplates writing shallow, satiric,
  revengeful fiction until her mother's influence frees her to write
  compassionately.

Waugh, Patricia. *Feminine Fictions: Revisiting the Postmodern.*
  London: Routledge, 1989.
  Waugh sees Frances's problems in psychological terms. Like
  many women, Frances is painfully and childishly obsessed by the
  memory of her mother. She thinks a particular man will cure her
  problems, but her immature yearning for romance drives him
  away.

Hotel du Lac, 1984.

Baxter, Gisèle Marie. "Clothes, Men, and Books: Cultural Experiences and Identity in the Early Novels of Anita Brookner."
  English 42 (Summer, 1993): 125-139.
  Edith is like the heroines of *A Start in Life* and *Providence* in that
  she looks at her life through literature, apparently through the
  kind of popular romantic fiction she writes. Like the others, she is
  attracted to men like David and Mr. Neville who represent aspects
  of traditional English life. Like the others, she cooks, but only for
  the man she wants. But she cannot belong. Her clothes and her
  hairstyles reflect her self-consciousness and lack of confidence.
  But the true literary subtext of Edith's life is not the romance
  heroine she creates, but Virginia Woolf. She is often compared to
  Woolf and even dresses like her; the novel has echoes of *To the
  Lighthouse.* By the end of the novel, Edith finds she possesses the
  strength and sense of identity of a Woolf-like figure. She understands her position at the margins of English life. She is an
  independent female artist; she has a room of her own.

Fisher-Wirth, Ann. "Hunger Art: The Novels of Anita Brookner." *Twentieth Century Literature* 41 (Spring, 1995): 1-15.
Edith begins to resist the dilemma in which most Brookner women find themselves. She refuses to define herself as someone who is not made for love.

Guppy, Shusha. "The Art of Fiction XCVIII: Anita Brookner." *Paris Review* 29 (Fall, 1987): 147-169.
Brookner emphasizes that in this novel as in life, hares always win out over tortoises. She says that at the end of the novel Edith's relation to David is without hope and that Edith should have married one of the two men who wanted to marry her. In fact, Brookner says she changed her mind about having Edith marry Philip Neville as she finished the novel. Interesting, but perhaps misleading, comments.

Haffenden, John. "Anita Brookner." In *Novelists in Interview.* London: Methuen, 1985.
Brookner is pleased that this novel is less overtly autobiographical than her earlier ones. Very interesting remarks on how readers should regard Edith at the end of the novel, in particular on how she revised her final telegram.

Hosmer, Robert E., Jr. "Paradigm and Passage: The Fiction of Anita Brookner." In *Contemporary British Women Writers: Narrative Strategies.* New York: St. Martin's Press, 1993.
Edith Hope is another Brookner exile. Although she yearns for home and marriage as depicted in the romance novels she writes, she is alienated by birth from the English world. Moreover, she describes herself as having been exiled from England during the period of the novel's action. Yet she has energy that will save her: physical energy, which she shows by her incessant walking, and mental energy, which she shows in her lucid introspection. Hosmer neatly points out how the novel's other characters illuminate Edith's predicament by contrast. Unlike other Brookner heroines, Edith makes some progress. Hosmer thinks that, although at the end of the novel Edith is still an exile, she is now one by choice. She has not compromised her integrity. A valuable analysis.

Kenyon, Olga. *Women Novelists Today: A Survey of English Writing in the Seventies and Eighties.* New York: St. Martin's Press, 1988.

Brookner's emphasis on the hotel building itself is a feminine device. Although she invokes the conventions of women's novels in Edith's books, Brookner gives the reader a skillful and ironic perspective on romance conventions in her story of Edith's life. Sexy, greedy women like the Puseys may be empty and vapid, but that is little consolation to Edith, whose Victorian ideals will not allow her a real-life romantic ending.

_____. *Women Writers Talk: Interviews with Ten Women Writers.* New York: Carroll & Graf, 1990.

Brookner says she planned to end this novel happily with love triumphant. The novel's setting is a real hotel in Switzerland where Brookner has stayed, and Brookner says she resembles Edith Hope in that both are lonely, perceptive observers.

Sadler, Lynn Veach. *Anita Brookner.* Boston: Twayne, 1990.

In Chapter 5, Sadler provides a detailed and sympathetic analysis of what she considers a better novel than Brookner's earlier fictions. It is wittier, more precise in its descriptions, and somehow more healthy. Edith, for all her mousy and Barbara Pym-like qualities, is a strong person underneath, given to self-knowledge, and able to see jokes about herself. Unlike other Brookner heroines, she has several men to choose from—though there is no satisfactory choice. Sadler emphasizes how Edith's reflections on the difference between romance fiction and real life are more telling than similar reflections in the earlier novels. Sadler also treats in precise detail how the other characters provide comments on Edith's problems, especially how Edith's father once provided the wisdom that Edith continues to need. Brookner's plot is more full of suspense and drama than usual. An economical, precise, and valuable essay.

Schofield, Mary Anne. "Spinster's Fare: Rites of Passage in Anita Brookner's Fiction." In *Cooking by the Book.* Bowling Green, Ohio: Bowling Green State University Popular Press, 1989.

Edith feeds her married lover, but she discovers that what is important is to feed herself. The failures of all the female guests at Hotel du Lac are caused by men and are expressed by their unwholesome eating habits.

Skinner, John. *The Fictions of Anita Brookner: Illusions of Romance.* New York: St. Martin's Press, 1992.
Skinner brings various kinds of contemporary criticism to bear on this novel, which he considers her best. Although the novel draws affectionately upon the conventions of popular romances, it explains them and undercuts them at the same time. He discusses the novel's complicated time scheme, by which Edith's successive love affairs are told concurrently. He explains at length the novel's equally complicated point of view, its mixture of first-person letters and third-person narration. The novel's confusions, secrets, and misunderstandings often make readers unsure what to believe; Skinner takes what may be Brookner's awkwardness, especially in Chapter 1, as evidence of an intentional strategy. He also uses contemporary feminist and psychological ideas to explain Edith's anxieties, her love of silence, and her emphasis on Jennifer's physical opulence. A difficult, sometimes debatable, but always valuable essay.

Soule, George. "Anita Brookner." In *Magill's Survey of World Literature, Supplement.* Tarrytown, N.Y.: Marshall Cavendish, 1995.
Brief analysis.

_____. "Hotel du Lac." In *Masterplots II: Women's Literature,* edited by Frank N. Magill. Pasadena, Calif.: Salem Press, 1995.
Edith's story says a lot about the nature of fiction and the relation of an author to his or her story. Soule stresses Edith's statement that she believes in romance endings. The novel's point of view is complicated by the letters Edith edits for her lover's consumption and by the fact that many or all of them are never sent. The novel has a dreamlike quality, with odd, monstrous, and even (in the case of Neville) satanic characters. Neville and Edith spend a day on a ship of fools; Neville, Mrs. Pusey, and Jennifer suggest Milton's Satan, Sin, and Death.

Stetz, Margaret Diane. "Anita Brookner: Woman Writer as Reluctant Feminist." In *Writing the Woman Artist: Essays on Poetics,*

Politics, and Portraiture, edited by Suzanne W. Jones. Philadelphia: University of Pennsylvania Press, 1991.
Stetz finds significant parallels with Virginia Woolf's *The Voyage Out,* though Edith escapes the fate of Woolf's heroine.

Watson, Daphne. *Their Own Worst Enemies: Women Writers of Women's Fictions.* London: Pluto Press, 1995.
In Chapter 2, Watson treats both Brookner and Barbara Pym. Brookner's early novels were promising because they contained humor and irony. At the end of *Hotel du Lac,* Watson wonders how the reader is asked to view Edith. Is she too happy in her unhappy state to want to change? Are readers asked to feel compassion for this self-deluded woman? Irony and other devices imply that the narrator is distant from Edith and judges her as limited. Yet later novels suggest that Brookner thinks Edith is correct in her attitudes.

Waugh, Patricia. *Feminine Fictions: Revisiting the Postmodern.* London: Routledge, 1989.
Waugh criticizes Edith (and by implication Brookner) for thinking that her own needs and her inevitable frustrations typify the innate condition of women. Waugh gives precise attention to Edith's reaction to the other women in the novel.

Family and Friends, 1985.

Kenyon, Olga. *Women Novelists Today: A Survey of English Writing in the Seventies and Eighties.* New York: St. Martin's Press, 1988.
Mimi is an example of a Brookner heroine who cannot push herself forward. Kenyon analyzes how the novel focuses upon the contrasts among family members: two are flashy, selfish, and greedy, whereas two are obedient and unfulfilled. Kenyon thinks Brookner's writing is itself repressed.

_____. *Women Writers Talk: Interviews with Ten Women Writers.* New York: Carroll & Graf, 1990.
Brookner says this is the only one of her novels (through *Latecomers* of 1988) she truly likes. This interview deals with *Family*

and Friends as a fictionalized account of tensions between control and freedom within Brookner's own family.   Interesting biographical connections.

MacLaine, Brent. "Photofiction as Family Album: David Galloway, Paul Theroux, and Anita Brookner." *Mosaic: A Journal for the Interdisciplinary Study of Literature* 24 (Spring, 1991): 131-149.
MacLaine's provocative essay surveys novels in which photographs play important roles, usually by reminding narrators of public moments in the past and of the stories that lie behind the pictures. MacLaine thinks these remembered images can lead to Wordsworthian, yet post-Romantic "spots of time." *Family and Friends* provides one example. Brookner "unfreezes" her photographs as motion pictures often do. By looking at wedding photos, Sofka begins to feel that her world is coming apart, but the narrator discovers new connections.

Sadler, Lynn Veach. *Anita Brookner.* Boston: Twayne, 1990.
In Chapter 6, Sadler says that, though it echoes her previous concerns, this novel extends the range of Brookner's fiction by focusing on an entire family. Sadler emphasizes Sofka Dorn, the fullest portrait of a mother in Brookner's works, her two daughters, and especially her sons. These men also represent something new for Brookner: fully developed male characters. Even though each is composed of contradictory traits, they provide a sharp contrast: Frederick, the passive and easily controlled voluptuary, and Alfred, a good and hard-working man with literary dreams. The fates of both pairs of sons and daughters are not so neatly plotted as in her earlier novels: the good and the bad end up differently, but the bad do not necessarily win. Sadler also comments on the novel's odd point of view. An very useful essay.

Schofield, Mary Anne. "Spinster's Fare: Rites of Passage in Anita Brookner's Fiction." In *Cooking by the Book.* Bowling Green, Ohio: Bowling Green State University Popular Press, 1989.
The rites of female initiation through cooking, which Schofield finds in Brookner's earlier novels, are significantly absent from this book, perhaps because it treats families and not individual women.

Skinner, John. *The Fictions of Anita Brookner: Illusions of Romance.*
New York: St. Martin's Press, 1992.
Skinner discusses the reliability of the narrator and notes
Brookner's variations on her usual themes and devices. He thinks
that Brookner points to postmodern narrative devices when she
uses certain critical terms. He analyzes the novel's iconographical
tendencies. Readers are asked to visualize some characters in
Family and Friends as figures of myth or as more recent stereotypes. Skinner is most valuable when he discusses the novel's
most obvious structural device: the series of family photographs
on which the narrator bases her comments.

A Misalliance [in the U.S.: *The Misalliance*], 1986.

Galef, David. "You Aren't What You Eat: Anita Brookner's
Dilemma." *Journal of Popular Culture* 28 (Winter, 1994): 1-7.
Food and love are often associated in Brookner's novels. Her
women grow up starved for affection, yet try to feed others. Even
after her divorce, Blanche continues to cook. Mousie and Sally
cannot cook; their ineptitude is part of their attraction.

Guppy, Shusha. "The Art of Fiction XCVIII: Anita Brookner." *Paris
Review* 29 (Fall, 1987): 147-169.
Brookner says this novel avoids the determinism of her earlier
works and is full of sentiment. She defends Blanche from the
charge of being boring.

Sadler, Lynn Veach. *Anita Brookner.* Boston: Twayne, 1990.
In Chapter 7, Sadler judges the central character and finally finds
her wanting. She asks how any woman can be so self-effacing as
Blanche, how Blanche at the moment of asserting some independence can welcome back her erring husband. Sadler places
Blanche at one end of a continuum of female characters which
runs from good women like her to predators like Sally Beamish
and Blanche's husband's mistress, Mousie. She analyzes how
Blanche's world, like that of other Brookner heroines, is shaped by
her reading: Mousie was a character from the kind of story
Blanche did not read. This novel also reminds us that Brookner is
an art historian, for Blanche tries to understand her life by

deciphering paintings from London's National Gallery. Whereas earlier Brookner novels imply that selfish, predatory persons always win in life and good persons like Blanche always lose, this novel suggests that the bad are sometimes defeated. Sadler makes perceptive remarks on the place of children in Brookner's world. Despite some narrow judgments, a useful essay.

Schofield, Mary Anne. "Spinster's Fare: Rites of Passage in Anita Brookner's Fiction." In *Cooking by the Book*. Bowling Green, Ohio: Bowling Green State University Popular Press, 1989.
Although after her divorce Blanche sticks to ritual cooking, her heart is not in it. She is pathetic as she looks about for others to nourish (Sally, Elinor). She does not progress to valuing her single life, to cooking spinster's meals, until she has been welcomed into the world of mature women by Mrs. Duff.

Skinner, John. *The Fictions of Anita Brookner: Illusions of Romance*. New York: St. Martin's Press, 1992.
Skinner emphasizes how Brookner's career as an art historian is evident in this novel. When Blanche visits public art galleries, she divides the images she sees there into two groups. One is pagan, young, uninhibited, predatory, and associated with the Mediterranean sun, whereas the other is Christian, saintly, virginal, and full of suffering. This polarity, much like others found in Brookner's novels, permeates the novel, as "good" characters like Blanche and her friend Patrick Fox are victimized by "bad" pagans like Sally Beamish. Skinner points out that Brookner's portrait of Patrick's problems looks forward to similar portraits in later novels. At the end of the novel, Blanche despairs and then is seemingly reborn. When her husband returns to frustrate her plans for a vacation in the sun, Skinner regards it as a defeat. He also notes that Brookner's heroines are getting older.

Soule, George. "The Misalliance." In *Masterplots II: Women's Literature*, edited by Frank N. Magill. Pasadena, Calif.: Salem Press, 1995.
This novel is a psychological and realistic study of a divorced and lonely middle-aged woman. Its third-person point of view brings the reader close to Blanche's efforts to fill her day without creating inappropriate attachments, or *misalliances*. Blanche understands

her plight by making figures in paintings into symbols: both Sally and Mousie are identified with happy, selfish pagan excess, while Blanche resembles a martyred saint: innocent, dutiful, and altruistic. Soule stresses that this is Blanche's symbolic pattern, not the novel's. By the end, Blanche frees herself from her pattern of symbols by refusing to act like a martyr.

A Friend from England, 1987.

Fisher-Wirth, Ann. "Hunger Art: The Novels of Anita Brookner." *Twentieth Century Literature* 41 (Spring, 1995): 1-15.
One of Brookner's most painful novels. At first reading it may seem that, unlike other Brookner heroines, Rachel has escaped being caught in the structure of a patriarchal society. But on re-reading, Fisher-Wirth is convinced that Rachel should be seen as yearning to be included in the Livingstone household, as beloved as their daughter Heather. Rachel's essential desolation is revealed by her sex life: she walks the street in search of one-night stands. Heather's relationship in Italy is a wholesome one.

Guppy, Shusha. "The Art of Fiction XCVIII: Anita Brookner." *Paris Review* 29 (Fall, 1987): 147-169.
In references to this then forthcoming novel, Brookner says she now feels that people become happy by their boldness. She describes the heroine as emancipated, yet defeated by innocence.

Plante, David. "They Won Their Life on the Football Pools." *The New York Times Book Review*, March 20, 1988, 9, 11.
Brookner's heroines usually feel alienated from English society because of their continental origins. Here, although Rachel is English, she is also an alien. Her attitude toward the Livingstones is confused: she dislikes Heather for her protected English existence, but nevertheless she fights to prevent Heather from damaging that life. Rachel herself must remain stubbornly alone.

Sadler, Lynn Veach. *Anita Brookner*. Boston: Twayne, 1990.
In Chapter 8, Sadler focuses on the narrator of this first-person novel, Rachel Kennedy, who divides people in the usual Brookner way. On one hand, there is Rachel as she describes herself:

independent, adventurous, experienced, and anti-romantic. On
the other hand are the Livingstones: innocent, warm, loving,
romantic, ceremonial. But Brookner is distinct from her narrator.
Rachel is inconsistent, for she has had romantic dreams, and she
basks in the comfort of the Livingstone's home. Sadler shows how
Rachel's conflicting values lead her to envy the happiness of the
Livingstone's daughter, who seems to have it all: marriage, love,
children. Sadler also shows how in this novel, although she
paints some scathing portraits of feminists, Brookner presents a
convincing portrait of the condition of contemporary women. A
very useful essay.

Skinner, John. *The Fictions of Anita Brookner: Illusions of Romance.*
New York: St. Martin's Press, 1992.
This novel reprises many of Brookner's earlier themes and devices, though this time by means of a somewhat unreliable first-
person narrator.   Rachel Kennedy divides people into anti-
romantic, liberated, rational feminists (like herself) and romantic,
conventional, protected, and very often happy women and their
families (like Heather Livingstone and her parents). But the way
Rachel narrates her story makes the reader sometimes feel that she
is unreliable and almost psychotic in her obsession with Heather.
The reader also wonders if some of Rachel's condescending
opinions are Brookner's own. Skinner discusses this novel's debts
to Jane Austen and Henry James.

Stetz, Margaret Diane. "Anita Brookner: Woman Writer as Reluctant
Feminist." In *Writing the Woman Artist: Essays on Poetics,
Politics, and Portraiture,* edited by Suzanne W. Jones. Philadel-
phia: University of Pennsylvania Press, 1991.
Stetz sees significant parallels with Virginia Woolf's *The Voyage
Out.*

Latecomers, 1988.

Bawer, Bruce. "Doubles and More Doubles." *The New Criterion* 7
(April, 1989): 67-74.
Bawer compares Brookner to Paul Auster, Ann Beattie, and
Bobbie Ann Mason. This is an unhappy novel that evokes the

impoverished lives of its lonely characters. Toto is a surrogate of the author.

Dinnage, Rosemary. "Exiles." *The New York Review of Books*, June 1, 1989, 34-36.
Dinnage reviews Brookner's career and distinguishes American reactions (how British!) from British ones (how continental!). She then maps Brookner territory in London: not the usual sad bed-sitting rooms of Kentish Town, but more affluent and upholstered flats in places like St. John's Wood. *Latecomers* is Brookner's best novel, for it departs from her usual formula to show how major characters, despite their early traumas, find ways to live moderately well. Hartman and Fibich are particularly moving as they grow old in different ways.

Duchêne, Anne. "Coming Through." *The Times Literary Supplement*, August 12, 1988, 891.
Duchêne admires *Latecomers* for its wider than usual range of characters and for its moving treatment of important themes: growing old, the painful relations of adults and children, and the quiet strength of friendship. She admires the dignity of the two central male characters.

Fisher-Wirth, Ann. "Hunger Art: The Novels of Anita Brookner." *Twentieth Century Literature* 41 (Spring, 1995): 1-15.
What makes Brookner a tragic novelist, not just a chronicler of female neuroses, can be seen in Fibich's visit to the continent. Even though he is rejuvenated by the visit, he is shattered when he remembers the moment when he parted from his mother. This primal and universal moment is literally the moment of loss for every human being, and it lies behind the sense of loss most Brookner characters experience.

Hosmer, Robert E., Jr. "Paradigm and Passage: The Fiction of Anita Brookner." In *Contemporary British Women Writers: Narrative Strategies*. New York: St. Martin's Press, 1993.
The central male characters are both a special kind of exile: Jews who got out of Hitler's Germany. By putting the past behind him, Hartman creates a good life in his business and at home. In contrast, Fibich even in middle age is estranged from English life and

from his son Toto. The introspective Fibich tries to heal his wounds by returning to boyhood scenes in East Berlin. There he finds peace when he decides not to seek his father anymore, but to be a father himself. Hosmer thinks that Brookner finally shows two exiles who find the joys of life. A persuasive analysis.

Leavitt, David. "`Look! We Have Come Through.'" *The New York Times Book Review*, April 2, 1989, 3.
Brookner's novels are not mere tissues of feminine delicacy; rather, they display power struggles and serious inequities. Here Brookner departs from her usual formula and shows how damaged persons of very different temperaments can come through to modest triumphs. Even the selfish Toto's terrorizing his parents can bring some joy.

Skinner, John. *The Fictions of Anita Brookner: Illusions of Romance*. New York: St. Martin's Press, 1992.
Relationships here are highly patterned: two contrasting men have two contrasting wives; each couple has two contrasting children, one male and one female. In the beginning, Brookner's arrangement into chapters is just as schematic. But she transcends her patterns by focusing on male characters and by creating a moving story of how they eventually (as "latecomers") achieve a kind of repose. She also breaks new ground in her occasionally savage wit. Skinner points out many narrative hints that Brookner does not follow up, possibly for personal reasons.

Sudrai, Jean. "Goings and Comings." *The Yale Review* 79 (Spring, 1990): 414-438.
Sudrai discusses how differently the two exiled men and their wives face their isolation and fears. The couples end the novel with different kinds of limited triumphs—one of joy, the other of love.

Lewis Percy, 1989.

Birch, Diana. "Looking for Magic." *London Review of Books*, September 14, 1989, 19.

Brookner's novels are as little like fairy tales as possible. Even though Lewis has an innocent dream of awakening Tissy as a Sleeping Beauty, it backfires: although they marry, she becomes a feminist. Yet the novel's ending seems like a fairy-tale. Lewis had to abandon his dreams to be rewarded.

Lopate, Phillip. "Can Innocence Go Unpunished?" *The New York Times Book Review*, March 11, 1990, 10.
Lewis Percy is a warmer and more hopeful exploration of Brookner's usual moral question: how can innocence thrive in the world? Lopate marvels at how a female novelist can enter sympathetically into a male's contest with a female character. Brookner departs from her early novels, for even though the book's final twist may be excessive, readers can accept that innocence may be given a second chance for happiness.

Skinner, John. *The Fictions of Anita Brookner: Illusions of Romance*. New York: St. Martin's Press, 1992.
Lewis Percy is a male version of Brookner's earlier heroines who, though timid academics, envision life in the terms of romantic literature. Brookner sabotages Lewis's heroic fantasies in a way than makes him resemble Don Quixote. Lewis's fantasies are mainly sexual and center on women, his hum-drum wife Tissy and the exotic Emmy. Skinner reads the end of the novel in two ways. When Emmy joins Lewis to escape to America after Tissy left him, this may be the crowning event of his process of spiritual rebirth. More probably, it is an ironic portent of further disasters. Though it is hard to pin down exactly how Brookner employs her third-person point of view, the novel offers such a devastating critique of female behavior (including that of Tissy's newfound feminism) that a happy ending is hard to accept.

Symons, Julian. "Parsons Green Pursuits." *The Times Literary Supplement*, August 25, 1989, 917.
Symons praises the characterization and scenes of the first half of this novel, especially a passage which describes the innocent Lewis in a Paris salon. In later chapters, however, Brookner views Lewis without irony as he becomes both dull and ridiculous. The airport ending is a mistake. Even so, Brookner's attempt has been worth the effort.

Updike, John. "Nice Tries." *The New Yorker*, May 1, 1989, 111-114.
Despite first impressions, the novel's female characters are the
center of the author's attention. Brookner gives to her characters
the love they cannot give each other.

Brief Lives, 1990.

Duguid, Lindsay. "The Downward Drag and Loss of Allure." *The
Times Literary Supplement*, August 24, 1990, 889.
Whereas John Aubrey's seventeenth-century book with the same
title recounts the public lives of men, Brookner's novel deals with
the private lives of women. Duguid evokes the contrasts in Fay's
character: although she is gentle and is generally nice to people,
she is capable of spite and is confident in her judgments. Now
that Brookner is herself older, the women she writes about are
also older. Brookner shows these women living apart from men;
Duguid focuses on a hilarious and touching restaurant scene late
in the novel. Brookner's famous style is notable for its elegant
descriptions of colors and textures.

Kornblatt, Joyce Reiser. "A Grudge Against Their Lovers." *The New
York Times Book Review*, July 21, 1991, 14.
Kornblatt admires Brookner's treatment of Fay, who only wishes
to be normal and calm—and to be taken seriously by her lovers.
The novelist understands Fay's fascination with the flamboyant
and selfish Julia and sympathizes with Fay's quiet and largely successful determination to grow old with dignity and without
bitterness.

McGuirk, Carol. "Drabble to Carter: Fiction by Women, 1962-1992."
In *The Columbia History of the British Novel*, edited by John
Richetti. New York: Columbia University Press, 1994.
This novel presents a powerful portrait of sorrow. Fay only
realizes her emotional ties to people after they die.

Soule, George. "Brief Lives." In *Masterplots II: Women's Literature*,
edited by Frank N. Magill. Pasadena, Calif.: Salem Press, 1995.
An analysis of the novel's point of view and its theme (Fay's unsuccessful pursuit of happiness). Julia plays a shifting role in

Fay's imagination and comes to embody an unflinching and disillusioned gaze at the truth.

Symons, Julian. "Dirty Jokes." *London Review of Books*, September 13, 1990, 16.
The opening chapter artfully sets up the story of Fay and Julia. Although male characters are secondary, they are wonderfully realized; the same is true of Julia's hangers-on. Brookner's real subject is the onset of old age for women, and Fay is admirable in her happiness.

A Closed Eye, 1991.

Annan, Gabriele. "Still Life." *The New York Review of Books*, May 14, 1992, 25-26.
The title refers to a passage from Henry James and tells readers about the novel's central character. Harriet lives with her eyes half closed to the joys and horrors of life. Even her young friend Lizzie finds that she lies to her in the end. But Lizzie and Harriet are both like other Brookner women (and unlike most modern heroines), for they resist change. Their problems as not so much social as existential: their sense of futility and helplessness proceeds from a numbing depression. As she evokes these states of near helplessness, Brookner treats readers to witty dissections of secondary characters, marvelous evocations of London neighborhoods, and precise associations of menus with the people who serve them.

Armstrong, Isobel. "Choosing What to Know." *The Times Literary Supplement*, August 23, 1991, 20.
In Harriet, Brookner evokes her usual character (the mild traditional woman who yearns for a man she cannot have) and sets up her usual parallels and oppositions. But the novel judges Harriet more severely than usual: she lacks warmth, she spoils her daughter, and she almost succeeds in repressing these truths.

Casey, Constance. "One Name Must Never Be Mentioned." *The New York Times Book Review*, April 12, 1992, 12-13.

Harriet's eyes are open, not closed, to what happens to her and the other characters. Casey worries that Harriet is always passive, except for two occasions: once when she is pregnant and once when she loves the caddish Jack. Brookner's vision is not happy.

Fisher-Wirth, Ann. "Hunger Art: The Novels of Anita Brookner." *Twentieth Century Literature* 41 (Spring, 1995): 1-15.
By the end of this novel, Harriet does not attempt to be happy. She is starving for starvation's sake; her emotional hunger feeds her the way that usual happiness will not. Harriet moves from her loss into a feminine "wild state" which is either mad or visionary.

Parrinder, Patrick. "Dreams of Avarice." *London Review of Books*, August 29, 1991, 18.
Harriet gets material wealth but denies her daughter essential experience. Harriet sees Imogen's death as a sacrifice. Brookner's plot is unconvincing, and her style is almost a parody.

Fraud, 1992.

Bayley, John. "Living with a Little Halibut." *London Review of Books*, October 8, 1992, 12-13.
Brookner's treatment of Anna Durant is an example of art giving interest to a character who would be banal in real life. Readers will be more sympathetic to Mrs. Marsh, who echoes our muted dislike for the novel's heroine. Bayley compares Brookner to Henry James in the way she formulates mysteries without solving them. As in other novels, Bayley relishes Brookner's switch from delicate analyses of central characters to nicely malicious treatments of their antagonists—in this case the brash Vicki. He also finds Brookner's characters somewhat unrealistic in that they appear to harbor the author's own thoughts at some times but not at others.

Fisher-Wirth, Ann. "Hunger Art: The Novels of Anita Brookner." *Twentieth Century Literature* 41 (Spring, 1995): 1-15.
Perhaps, unlike other Brookner heroines, Anna breaks free. Fisher-Wirth does not think so.

Hegi, Ursula. "The Curse of Being a Good Woman." *The New York Times Book Review*, January 10, 1993, 7.

Fraud is a study of what happens when parents dominate their daughters, not only Anna but her French friend Marie-France. Brookner provides many different perspectives on Anna. Hegi finds the ending abrupt and therefore unconvincing.

Rodd, Candace. "Drawing-room Despair." *The Times Literary Supplement*, August 21, 1992, 17.

Rodd defends Brookner from accusations that she tells the same story in every novel and defines Brookner's effect as disturbing and soothing at the same time. She describes Anna with sympathy as a woman who has a strong heart, who desires strongly, and who has the strength to set her dream aside. Even though at the end of the novel the reader wishes Anna well, it is the old, kindly yet pragmatic Mrs. Marsh who engages our affections.

A Family Romance [in the U.S.: *Dolly*], 1993.

Fisher-Wirth, Ann. "Hunger Art: The Novels of Anita Brookner." *Twentieth Century Literature* 41 (Spring, 1995): 1-15.

Brookner's unsatisfied heroines find that their emotional hunger can feed the soul better than life's pleasures. This novel shows that even one of life's winners feels this hunger too.

Foster, Aisling. "Brookner Country." *The Times Literary Supplement*, June 25, 1993, 22.

Brookner shows the strong bonds women can forge, despite occasional misunderstandings. Even though she lives more flamboyantly, does Dolly end up as repressed as Jane? Or is the energetic Dolly the true heroine of the novel?

Kino, Carol. "She Married Well-Off Uncle Hugo." *The New York Times Book Review*, February 20, 1994, 12.

Kino admires the first two-thirds of this novel, which deals not only with Dolly and Jane's relationship but also with Jane's maturing as a writer. It is Dolly and her husband Hugo, not her parents, who inspire Jane's erotic imagination. After the deaths of her parents, both Jane and the novel go downhill. Jane becomes set in her opinions, turning into an aging bore.

A Private View, 1994.

Clee, Nicholas. "Closed Circuit." *The Times Literary Supplement,* June 17, 1994, 22.
Clee praises the effects of Brookner's prose rhythms. He thinks George Bland's story is not convincing because the novelist's own sympathies do not extend past his world. Although the novel exhibits Brookner's usual virtues, Clee predicts that the novelist's detractors will find their opinions confirmed.

Dinnage, Rosemary. "The Downhill Slope." *The New York Review of Books,* January 12, 1995, 20-21.
Brookner the novelist is like Gwen John the painter: she has a "palette of finely related grays." In this novel, as in *Latecomers,* she excels at describing the friendship of heterosexual men. Dinnage is not sure if Bland's interest in Katy is convincing, or if he would have been better off marrying her.

Lee, Hermione. "Déjà View." *The New Yorker,* January 30, 1995, 89-91.
Lee sympathizes with Brookner's detractors, but confesses her addiction. She calls George Bland's attraction to Katy sado-masochistic and thinks that *A Private View* is more strange and forlorn than usual.

Simon, Linda. "Oh, to Do Something Shocking." *The New York Times Book Review,* January 8, 1995, 9.
Bland is another version of Brookner's usual central character. Even though Katy is the target of his rage, he thinks that this vulgar woman may liberate him. She may give him the strength to reinvent himself, to do something shocking, to feel more fully alive. As usual in Brookner, the plan does not work. As usual, readers will be dismayed at the character's lack of imagination.

Wood, James. "Aspic of the Novel." *New Republic,* April 24, 1995, 41-42.

When Wood calls this one of Brookner's better novels, he is not saying much. He thinks that her prose is antiquated and that her characters are caricatures. They not only are dull, but they possess sufficient self-knowledge to tell readers about their dullness. Worse yet, Brookner grossly oversimplifies her moral categories. The result is a whine.

Incidents in the Rue Laugier, 1995.

Mantel, Hilary. "Mother of Invention." *The New York Times Book Review*, January 14, 1996, 25.
When Brookner explores Maud's world, she discerns, not only its underlying despair, but many nuances of feeling. Maud's telling her mother of her marriage wonderfully mixes comedy and pathos. Mantel thinks the first two-thirds of this novel is brilliant, but when Maud moves to London, both she and the novel itself lose power.

Wood, Gaby. "An Elegant Muteness." *The Times Literary Supplement*, June 2, 1995, 21.
This novel reads like the winding-down of a melancholy life. Maud's languor is matched by Brookner's, as her writing becomes lazy and repetitive. A genuinely gloomy book.

Altered States, 1996.

Atkins, Lucy. "A View of the Glacier." *The Times Literary Supplement*, June 21, 1996, 25.
Brookner leaves her readers uncertain about how guilty Alan is in his wife's breakdown. Though he lacks some moral and spiritual qualities, he is not a monster, a man doomed to wander. In this novel, Brookner gives form to the absence at the core of most of her central characters: Sarah, though perhaps not believable, embodies absence, a fabulous vision that will never materialize. When Alan searches for Sarah, he searches for a fiction within a fiction.

Soule, George. "Altered States." In *Magill's Literary Annual, 1998*, edited by Frank N. Magill. Pasadena, Calif.: Salem Press, 1998.
In Brookner's terms, Sarah is this novel's hare and Alan is in part its tortoise. Read as a realistic novel, *Altered States* may have flaws: Alan seems too feminine, Sarah is too vaguely drawn, and some situations are contrived. But as a story about the impact of a sexual obsession on a man's life, the novel has much to offer. Alan's obsession with Sarah makes him do cruel things to his wife, but ultimately it leads him through its torture to a kind of equilibrium. At the end, he can deal with Sarah as an equal and make her do a charitable act. Sarah acknowledges his change when she briefly seems human and smiles. With his hard-won wisdom, Alan begins to understand what the other people in his life were really like.

Visitors, 1997.

Kemp, Peter. "More of the Same." *The Sunday Times Books*, June 8, 1997, 9.
Kemp dismisses this novel as typical Brookner. An antiquated style signals antiquated subject matter. As usual, the lair of a mouse-like character, Thea May, is invaded by a seeming predator, Steve. In this case, Steve turns out to be "gently bred" and mouse-like himself.

Other Works

Hotel du Lac was filmed in 1986. As an art historian, Brookner has written a number of books, including: *Watteau* (Feltham: Hamlyn Publishing Group, 1967); *The Genius of the Future: Studies in French Art Criticism* (London: Phaidon, 1971); *Greuze: The Rise and Fall of an Eighteenth-Century Phenomenon* (London: Paul Elek, 1972); *Jacques-Louis David* (London: Oxford University Press, 1974); and *Soundings* (London: Harvill Press, 1997). She has written many articles, introductions, and reviews.

Margaret Drabble

General Studies

Allan, Tuzyline Jita. *"The Middle Ground*: Determinism in a Changing World." In *Womanist and Feminist Aesthetics: A Comparative Review.* Athens: Ohio University Press, 1995.
Allan sees Drabble's feminism as a development from Virginia Woolf's and criticizes it from a womanist (black feminist) point of view. Drabble's early novels show women trapped in a patriarchal world. From *A Needle's Eye* on, Drabble's vision has included a masculine point of view, but her women are still trapped. *The Middle Ground*, which Allan analyzes at length, shows Drabble's attempt to bridge the gaps between races and sexes. From a womanist perspective, her efforts are not satisfactory.

Beards, Virginia K. "Margaret Drabble: Novels of a Cautious Feminist." *Critique* 15, no. 1 (1973): 35-47. Reprinted in *Contemporary Women Novelists*, edited by Patricia Meyer Spacks. Englewood Cliffs, N.J.: Prentice-Hall, 1977.
A dated but useful article giving a feminist perspective on what Beards sees as Drabble's pessimistic assessment of women's hopes. The analyses are often forced, but the remarks on *The Waterfall* are challenging.

Boch, Gudrun. "Survival in a 'Dying Tradition': The Novels of Margaret Drabble." In *Essays on the Contemporary British Novel*, edited by Hedwig Bock and Albert Wertheim. Munich: Max Hueber, 1986.
Drabble is a traditional novelist who is earnestly interested in serious moral questions. Boch surveys Drabble's characters and themes through *The Middle Ground*, with special emphasis on *The Needle's Eye*.

Bradbury, Malcolm. *The Modern British Novel.* London: Secker & Warburg, 1993.

Brief references set the novels through *The Gates of Ivory* in context. In Bradbury's list of the most important British novels since 1976, Drabble is well represented.

Burkhart, Charles. "Arnold Bennett and Margaret Drabble." In *Margaret Drabble: Golden Realms*, edited by Dorey Schmidt. No. 4 in *Living Author Series*. Edinburg, Tex.: Pan American University, 1982.
This important essay uses Drabble's biography of Bennett to discuss how the two authors are similar in themes, style, and popular appeal. Burkhart's main purpose is to evaluate Drabble's work. Her early, more personal novels contain much bathos and sentimentality. Although her later and longer novels show an admirable treatment of "the question of England," they have too much journalistic detail, too many obvious symbols, and too many odd authorial intrusions. Drabble should learn from Bennett to return to a more personal way of writing novels.

Campbell, Jane. "'Both a Joke and a Victory': Humor as Narrative Strategy in Margaret Drabble's Fiction." *Contemporary Literature* 32 (Spring, 1991): 75-99.
Humor is everywhere in Drabble's work. In the early novels, readers are sometimes confused by the mixture of humor and sympathy. In later novels, the humor ranges from light to the very dark (in *A Natural Curiosity*). Some novels like *The Radiant Way* have comparatively little humor. In general, readers are not encouraged to approve of characters who cannot laugh or who use humor aggressively or for the wrong reasons. Throughout her career, Drabble's humor has often served her self-reflexive tendencies. Her narrators joke about fiction and provide conscious fictional clichés, or they disappoint readers with open endings. Characters who think they can plot their lives are usually made to look foolish. Narrators even make jokes at their own expense. A valuable survey.

_____. "Margaret Drabble and the Search for Analogy." In *The Practical Vision: Essays in English Literature in Honor of Flora Roy*, edited by Campbell and James Doyle. Waterloo, Ontario, Canada: Wilfred Laurier University Press, 1978.

Although Drabble is a realist, she gives significance to her details in many ways. In her early novels, Drabble scatters allusions to novels of the past. Characters themselves are conscious of literary analogies to their lives. In *The Waterfall*, Jane agonizes because, although she cannot tell her story with a traditional plot, she cannot give up such plots of rescue and salvation. Drabble's later novels are different. Her themes concern fate and luck; the rescue plot is gone. None of her characters are professionally literary. In both *The Needle's Eye* and *The Realms of Gold*, Drabble manages her plot to provide the analogies which literary references provided earlier.

Connor, Steven. *The English Novel in History 1950-1995*. London: Routledge, 1996.
Discusses *Jerusalem the Golden*, *The Ice Age*, and *Radiant Way* at length. Refers to *The Middle Ground*, *A Natural Curiosity*, and *The Gates of Ivory*.

Cooper-Clark, Diana. "Margaret Drabble: Cautious Feminist." *Atlantic Monthly*, November, 1980, 69-75. Reprinted in *Critical Essays on Margaret Drabble*, edited by Ellen Cronan Rose. Boston: G. K. Hall, 1985, and in *Interviews with Famous Novelists*. New York: St. Martin's Press, 1986.
This interview covers many of Drabble's interests: the opening of possibilities for contemporary women, her moral imperatives, her kind of feminism, the joys of motherhood, her male characters, and her opinions of Jane Austen, George Eliot, William Wordsworth, and Arnold Bennett.

Creighton, Joanne V. "An Interview with Margaret Drabble." In *Margaret Drabble: Golden Realms*, edited by Dorey Schmidt. No. 4 in *Living Author Series*. Edinburg, Tex.: Pan American University, 1982.
In a 1979 interview, Drabble comments briefly on individual novels, her love of the poetry of William Wordsworth, her religion, and her faith in England. She explains her use of an intrusive narrator. She says that as she writes she does not know how her novels will end because her main characters have a degree of autonomy.

_____. *Margaret Drabble.* London: Methuen, 1985.
A well-written and useful guide. In her preface and introduction, Creighton sums up Drabble's appeal and gives succinct accounts of her life, her literary career, and the authors who influenced her. One great influence was her teacher at Cambridge, F. R. Leavis. Creighton thinks Drabble is popular because her novels are both traditional and innovative and because readers are captivated by her narrative voice. Creighton focuses on problems raised by Drabble's manipulation of points of view. Even though she employs an omniscient narrator in her later "state of Britain" novels, Drabble's attitudes are hard to pin down. In her central chapters, Creighton discusses the separate novels through *The Middle Ground.* She sees that Drabble's interest have broadened over the years from the problems of individual women to matters of the community.

Crosland, Margaret. *Beyond the Lighthouse: English Women Novelists in the Twentieth Century.* London: Constable, 1981.
Crosland makes only brief remarks on this novel. Drabble's heroines are self-indulgent, and her novels offer most women little help.

Cunningham, Gail. "Patchwork and Patterns: The Condition of England in Margaret Drabble's Later Novels." In *The British and Irish Novel Since 1960,* edited by James Acheson. New York: St. Martin's Press, 1991.
Cunningham divides Drabble's career up to 1991 into three parts. The early novels are neatly patterned and focus on one intelligent, educated young woman. The next group comprises novels which treat social and political themes; women are not their exclusive focus. In her third stage beginning with *The Middle Ground,* Drabble does not give up such themes but returns to a specific feminine perspective and finds deeper and less pleasant patterns in individuals and society. Cunningham discusses *The Millstone, The Middle Ground, The Radiant Way,* and *A Natural Curiosity* at some length.

_____. "Women and Children First: The Novels of Margaret Drabble." In *Twentieth Century Women Novelists,* edited by Thomas F. Staley. Totowa, N.J.: Barnes & Noble Books, 1982.

Drabble the critic can be seen in her literary allusions, especially in her titles. Even though she does not appear to be a doctrinaire feminist, female concerns are at the heart of her work. These concerns are often seen against a background of nineteenth century literature. Cunningham illustrates the changes in Drabble's work by discussing *The Millstone* and *The Realms of Gold*.

Drabble, Margaret. "Mimesis: The Representation of Reality in the Post-War Novel." *Mosaic: A Journal for the Interdisciplinary Study of Literature* 20 (Winter, 1987): 1-14.
A lecture delivered by Drabble in 1985. Taking Eric Auerbach's *Mimesis* as her starting point, Drabble discusses the changing nature of what it is possible for novelists, especially female novelists, to describe. She thinks Doris Lessing has led the way in trying to represent reality honestly, but even she has failed. Because she herself is fascinated by the details of everyday life, she includes many facts, even irrelevant ones, in her novels. She often gives facts symbolic overtones. Postwar novelists like herself are very aware that they do this.

Eifrig, Gail. "The Middle Ground." In *Margaret Drabble: Golden Realms*, edited by Dorey Schmidt. No. 4 in *Living Author Series*. Edinburg, Tex.: Pan American University, 1982.
Efrig places Drabble's career in the history of English fiction by women. Virgina Woolf asked how and when women's novels would enter the mainstream of fiction. Drabble's work answers this question, for, especially in her later novels, she connects women's issues with larger concerns.

Elkins, Mary Jane. "Facing the Gorgon: Good and Bad Mothers in the Late Novels of Margaret Drabble." In *Narrating Mothers: Theorizing Maternal Subjectivities*, edited by Brenda O. Daly and Maureen T. Reddy. Knoxville: University of Tennessee Press, 1991.
A somewhat forced thesis. Elkins argues that Drabble's novels from *The Realms of Gold* on evade some important feminist issues. Drabble divides her most important female characters into Good Mothers and Bad Mothers. The bad are credible figures: isolated, unsupported, imprisoned in one way or another, and living on the verge of madness. The Good Mothers, however, are

not convincing, for they give the wrong impression of women's lot. Readers know these lucky women are clearly exceptions to the usual truths. Drabble seems to admit as much, for their happy endings are undercut.

Firchow, Peter. "Margaret Drabble." In *The Writer's Place: Interviews on the Literary Situation in Contemporary Britain.* Minneapolis: University of Minnesota Press, 1974.
Drabble speaks about F. R. Leavis (she shared his concerns, but he had a destructive influence on writers) and about Jane Austen (another bad influence, one who had bad attitudes toward social justice). She describes who inspired her to write (Angus Wilson, Saul Bellow, and Simone de Beauvoir) and how she begins a novel (the ideas and the characters come first).

Fox-Genovese, Elizabeth. "The Ambiguities of Female Identity: A Reading of the Novels of Margaret Drabble." *Partisan Review* 46, no. 2 (1979), 234-248.
A serious challenge to Drabble's art by a noted Marxist historian who judges the novelist according to a fairly specific feminist program. Fox-Genovese thinks Drabble's vision is limited because double. On one hand, readers hear the self-conscious, literary author; on the other, an individual, subjective female voice. One result of this dualism is that Drabble's values are not clear. What her characters can provide is chatter: meaningless conversation and long lists that promise more meaning than they deliver. Moreover, her women achieve only personal happiness. This satisfaction comes too often, Fox-Genovese complains, at the expense of other women. As a result, Drabble gives little sense that individual women's fates are linked with any moral or social purpose.

Gullette, Margaret Morganroth. "Ugly Ducklings and Swans: Margaret Drabble's Fable of Progress in the Middle Years." *Modern Language Quarterly* 44 (September, 1983): 285-304. Reprinted with minor changes in *Safe at Last in the Middle Years: The Invention of the Midlife Progress Novel: Saul Bellow, Margaret Drabble, Anne Tyler, John Updike.* Berkeley: University of California Press, 1988.

Gullette's thesis is very interesting: Drabble's novels have as their deep structure a myth of growth and ascension. For Drabble's heroines, being lucky is the norm; her novels are comic in structure. The duckling-to-swan transformation is a symbol for several different kinds of change, the steps of which Gullette details. The heroines of later novels change into calm and powerful women of middle age. *The Waterfall, Jerusalem the Golden, The Ice Age, The Realms of Gold,* and *The Middle Ground* are treated in detail.

Hannay, John. *The Intertexuality of Fate: A Study of Margaret Drabble.* Columbia: University of Missouri Press, 1986.
Despite its awkward title, this is an interesting book of myth-criticism. In his Introduction, Hannay says that real life and the plots of stories are not necessarily at odds. In real life, people feel that *fate* is present when events appear to imitate the patterns (or *intertexts*) of stories they have read. Characters in realistic fiction like Drabble's can have similar feelings. (Hannay refers here to Sophia's theories in *The Millstone.*) When Drabble refers to other stories, these references are not decorative allusions, but guides to the intertexts or myths which shape the heart of the novel. In fact, the main characters are often aware of these stories. Drabble and her characters often mention fate when they want to draw attention to intertexts; accidents and coincidences are often signs that an intertext is influencing the action.
  Hannay considers three of the intertexual patterns Drabble uses most in chapters on *The Waterfall, The Needle's Eye,* and *The Ice Age.* He thinks considering intertexts can solve many of the problems critics of Drabble have been worrying about. For example, *The Middle Ground* may suffer because it lacks a pervasive intertext. In his conclusion, Hannay discusses what "fate" means to Drabble and makes interesting comments on *Jerusalem the Golden* and *The Realms of Gold.*

————. "Margaret Drabble: An Interview." *Twentieth Century Literature: A Scholarly and Critical Journal* 33 (Summer, 1987): 129-149.
Information on Drabble's life in the mid-1980's. She worries about having too many literary references. She is interested, not in the long-term literary perspective, but in portraying life as it is now, both in Britain and in the world. She wants to write about

how people really act; she is not interested in creating role models. Specific remarks on *The Needle's Eye*, *The Ice Age*, and *The Middle Ground*.

_____. "Margaret Drabble: The Paradox of Grace." *Contemporary Literature* 26 (Summer, 1985): 239-242.
A review of Mary Hurley Moran's *Margaret Drabble: Existing Within Structures* which contrasts it with Valerie Grosvenor Myer's *Margaret Drabble: Puritanism and Permissiveness*. Hannay thinks both books deal with the paradox of suffering and renewal, but Myer concentrates too much on suffering and Moran too much on renewal. Moran hints at, but does not explore, a topic that Hannay finds more promising: the way Drabble's characters use literary patterns to imagine their lives.

Hardin, Nancy S. "An Interview with Margaret Drabble." *Contemporary Literature* 14 (Summer, 1973): 273-295.
A diffuse interview. Drabble has been influenced by the writings of John Bunyan. Interesting remarks on *The Millstone*, *The Waterfall*, and *The Needle's Eye*.

Harper, Michael F. "Margaret Drabble and the Resurrection of the English Novel." *Contemporary Literature* 23 (Spring, 1982): 145-168. Reprinted in *Critical Essays on Margaret Drabble*, edited by Ellen Cronan Rose. Boston: G. K. Hall, 1985.
An important article. Encouraged by Drabble herself, critics have often called her novels old-fashioned in their realism and omniscient narrators. But the novels actually are contemporary departures from the critics' modernist values. Like other artists of her time, Drabble knows that each human being lives in a separate reality. But this insight does not drive her to celebrate anarchy or suffer despair. Drabble's novels shows how we construct fragile but satisfying communities. Short but insightful analyses of *A Summer Bird-Cage*, *The Millstone*, *Jerusalem the Golden*, *The Waterfall*, and *The Realms of Gold*.

Higdon, David Leon, "The Sense of Tradition in Margaret Drabble's Novels." *Conference of College Teachers of English Studies* 50 (September, 1985): 25-31.

Discusses the importance to Drabble's novels of various kinds of literary references.

Hutchinson, Mary Anne.   "Margaret Drabble," revised by George Soule.   In *Cyclopedia of World Authors*, rev. 3rd ed., edited by Frank N. Magill. Pasadena, Calif.: Salem Press, 1997.
Hutchinson provides a brief overview, with recent biographical information.

Irvine, Lorna.   "No Sense of an Ending: Drabble's Continuous Fictions."   In *Critical Essays on Margaret Drabble*, edited by Ellen Cronan Rose. Boston: G. K. Hall, 1985.
Irvine surveys one of the most important considerations in Drabble criticism.   She reviews recent theories of how female novelists tell their stories and then looks at Drabble's novels to see what characteristically female features they exhibit, especially in their endings. Irvine finds that, even though Drabble is interested in the apocalyptic thinking that informs the catastrophic closure of many novels written by men, her usual ending is open.   It is affirmative and implies that life goes on.   (Her concern for motherhood and children is clearly related to this sense.) When Drabble ends a novel more traditionally, the ending is so neat that it calls attention to the artifice of closure.   The firmly closed stories told by the characters themselves make an ironic contrast to the main open-ended narrative. Irvine surveys the endings of all the novels through *The Middle Ground*.

Kenyon, Olga.   *Women Novelists Today: A Survey of English Writing in the Seventies and Eighties*.   New York: St. Martin's Press, 1988.
Although Drabble writes in the conservative and realistic tradition, her themes are new. Like contemporary sociologists, Drabble portrays how educated women experience the conflict between living a full life and being a mother. She focuses with frankness on women's biological, even gynecological concerns, as well as on problems of sexual inhibition. Specific comments on *The Realms of Gold*, *The Ice Age*, and *Middle Ground*.

_____. *Women Writers Talk: Interviews with Ten Women Writers*. New York: Carroll & Graf, 1990.

Drabble thinks that the themes of her generation of women novelists emerged when they discovered how difficult it was to have both children and a career. Even so, not all have discarded romantic themes. Her own major influence has been William Wordsworth, who expresses the worth of every human being and the dignity of humble work. She is not interested in simple storytelling but uses stories to explore characters and ideas. Novelists who talk to readers in a postmodern manner assume that these readers are as intelligent as they are. The interview focuses on *The Radiant Way* and has interesting remarks on symbols in *The Realms of Gold*.

Korenman, Joan S. "The Liberation of Margaret Drabble." *Critique: Studies in Modern Fiction* 21, no. 3 (1980): 61-72.
Drabble's themes have grown larger. Her early novels show the problems of young women (frigidity, identity, careers) and often end by suggesting some kind of secular salvation. *The Waterfall* represents the culmination of these novels, when Jane achieves a kind of grace when she experiences a sexual breakthrough. Later novels do not ignore earlier concerns, but ask bigger questions. If a woman got all she wanted, would she be happy? Does life have meaning for women and for men? Korenman comments on *The Needle's Eye*, *The Realms of Gold*, and *The Ice Age*.

Lambert, Ellen Z. "Margaret Drabble and the Sense of Possibility." *University of Toronto Quarterly* 49 (Spring, 1980): 228-251. Reprinted in *Critical Essays on Margaret Drabble*, edited by Ellen Cronan Rose. Boston: G. K. Hall, 1985.
A charming and eloquent essay. A reader enjoys Drabble novels not so much because of their realism as because of the idea of possibility they communicate. Even though her heroines are not innocent or complacent, they are eager and full of hope. Lambert discusses *A Summer Bird-Cage*, *Jerusalem the Golden*, and *The Realms of Gold*.

Lay, Mary M. "Temporal Ordering in the Fiction of Margaret Drabble." *Critique: Studies in Modern Fiction* 21, no. 3 (1980): 73-84.
Novelists have many ways of treating time. When the amount of time spent by characters performing fictional acts approximates

the time it take to read about them, we have what Lay calls "the fictional present." Drabble not only employs this fictional present, but in *The Needle's Eye*, *The Realms of Gold*, and *The Ice Age* she presents fictional presents happening simultaneously to different people in different places. The differences in her presentations of time provide a key to the differences among these novels. A convincing argument about how Drabble creates her fictional worlds.

Le Franc, Bolivar. "An Interest in Guilt." *Books and Bookmen* 14 (September, 1969): 20-21.
Despite Drabble's saying she is not a feminist writer, Le Franc finds that she is very feminine in her subject matter and her style. Her women may appear sophisticated, but they are really vulnerable and childlike. Drabble's heroines feel guilt and fear sex, most noticeably in *The Waterfall*. Drabble prefers the density of that novel and of *Jerusalem the Golden* to the stylistic thinness of her early novels.

Levitt, Morton P. "The New Victorians: Margaret Drabble as Trollope." In *Margaret Drabble: Golden Realms*, edited by Dorey Schmidt. No. 4 in *Living Author Series*. Edinburg, Tex.: Pan American University, 1982.
Drabble is admired because she has rejected the modern experiments of Joyce and Woolf in order to write novels in the Victorian mode. Yet Victorian ways of storytelling cannot represent the uncertainties of the contemporary world. In particular, Drabble's omniscience dominates her characters so that even though they suffer from contemporary woes, they do not resemble free human beings. Even when she appears to experiment with postmodern devices in later novels, her omniscient presence dominates. In short, her narrative methods parody and undercut her subject matter. Specific comments on *The Waterfall*, *Realms of Gold*, and *The Ice Age*.

Libby, Marion Vlastos. "Fate and Feminism in the Novels of Margaret Drabble." *Contemporary Literature* 16 (Spring, 1975): 175-192.
Libby reads the novels through *The Needle's Eye* as showing Drabble's own development. The novelist in her first four novels shows her heroines as struggling against fate as it works through the restraints of a patriarchal society. *The Millstone* is the best,

for Rosamund achieves professional independence and loves her baby. *The Waterfall* is the worst because Jane is passive. Perhaps, Libby speculates, Drabble has had to confront her own passivity before she could create Rose in *The Needle's Eye*, a woman of beauty and strength who employs her will against fate even when she returns to her husband at the end. Libby hopes Rose will leave him soon. A dated and programmatic argument.

McCulloch, Joseph. "Dialogue with Margaret Drabble." In *Under Bow Bells: Dialogues with Joseph McCulloch.* London: Sheldon Press, 1974.
A transcript of a lunch-time dialogue in a City of London church. Drabble agrees with McCulloch that ours is an analytical age; in contrast to those alive a century ago, people today are much less sure about spiritual matters. The novel is a good medium for exploring ideas in the hope of arriving at truth. The discussants agree that many people want the assurance of a divine love as immediate and unconditional as a mother's love for her children. Drabble confesses her need for God, but says she cannot find Him.

McGuirk, Carol. "Drabble to Carter: Fiction by Women, 1962-1992." In *The Columbia History of the British Novel*, edited by John Richetti. New York: Columbia University Press, 1994.
McGuirk finds that many women writers of this era have a number of traits in common. Their early lives were disrupted by World War II. They are concerned to distance themselves both from mass culture (such as Charles's television programs in *The Radiant Way*) and high culture. Their novels are not dramatic; they are often uneventful and end awkwardly. They center on women, especially women in competition (such as in *A Summer Bird-Cage*). In her later novels, Drabble describes women's friendships.

Madison, Beth. "Mr. Bennett, Mrs. Woolf, and Mrs. Drabble." *West Virginia University Philological Papers* 34 (1988): 118-127.
In 1920 Virginia Woolf attacked the conventions of novels by Arnold Bennett for not being adequate to express the new age. Drabble's relation to earlier modernist conventions is similar, except that she does not reject them. She appropriates them to her

own use. Madison illustrates her thesis by a discussion of *The Middle Ground*.

Manheimer, Joan. "Margaret Drabble and the Journey to the Self." *Studies in the Literary Imagination* 11 (Fall, 1978): 127-143. Reprinted in *British Novelists Since 1900*, edited by Jack I. Biles. New York: AMS Press, 1987.
Although Drabble's heroines have to struggle with society, they also must contend with other women. Her typical heroine must lose her mother or escape from her in order to achieve anything. Manheimer surveys the early novels and finds that Jane in *The Waterfall* makes the most progress. *The Realms of Gold*, however, is an unconvincing failure.

Mayer, Suzanne H. "Margaret Drabble's Short Stories: Worksheets for Her Novels." In *Margaret Drabble: Golden Realms*, edited by Dorey Schmidt. No. 4 in *Living Author Series*. Edinburg, Tex.: Pan American University, 1982.
Drabble's short stories can illuminate her novels, particularly *Jerusalem the Golden* and *The Realms of Gold*.

Milton, Barbara. "An Interview with Margaret Drabble." *Paris Review* 20 (Fall-Winter, 1978): 40-65.
No extensive focus on any one novel. Drabble tells about her childhood, about how she writes and how her characters develop. Her heroines are George Eliot, Mrs. Gaskell, and George Sand. She thinks her novels are funny. She finds it hard to write about stupid people and about men. Her novels "explore new territory" and thus have a moral function. We probably do not have as much free will as we think. Coincidences may very well be part of a larger pattern we do not see at present. Drabble says she has a mystic sense that some day that pattern will become clear.

Moran, Mary Hurley. *Margaret Drabble: Existing Within Structures*. Carbondale: Southern Illinois University Press, 1983.
A clear but oversimplified survey of the world of Drabble's fiction through *The Middle Ground*. Moran thinks that Drabble's basic vision is bleak, as dark as that of her most pessimistic characters. The oppressions of both nature and family are discussed in separate chapters. Yet the imagination and its expression in

literature allow human beings a few redeeming moments of
intense joy.

_____. "Spots of Joy in the Midst of Darkness." In *Margaret
Drabble: Golden Realms*, edited by Dorey Schmidt. No. 4 in
Living Author Series. Edinburg, Tex.: Pan American University,
1982.
A shorter version of Moran's argument in *Margaret Drabble:
Existing Within Structures*.

Murphy, Brenda. "Women, Will, and Survival: The Figure in
Margaret Drabble's Carpet." *South Atlantic Quarterly* 82 (Winter,
1983): 38-50.
In this valuable article, Murphy adopts Drabble's division of
women into high-powered, independent, and amoral carnivores
and their herbivore victims. In her first five novels, Drabble
searches for a moral response to this opposition. In *The Waterfall*,
the struggle is within the heroine herself.

Myer, Valerie Grosvenor. *Margaret Drabble: Puritanism and
Permissiveness*. New York: Barnes & Noble Books, 1974.
Myer distributes her insights into the specific novels through *The
Needle's Eye* throughout this book, whose general thesis is that all
Drabble's early heroines are trying to escape from their puritanical
backgrounds and to discover how to live in a permissive society.
Although they never completely escape, each manages to make
some adjustment to her world. In a second section, Myer dis-
cusses the significance of the pervasive strains of imagery Drabble
employs and her emphasis on the importance of community.

_____. *Margaret Drabble: A Reader's Guide*. New York: St.
Martin's Press, 1991.
Although these essays on individual novels (through *A Natural
Curiosity*) are not always well organized, they are valuable. Myer
usefully identifies literary and historical allusions, sets the novels
against their differing literary backgrounds, and surveys critical
opinion about them. Myer stresses Drabble's puritan heritage and
her spiritual dimension. She notes that Drabble became a novelist
in the same year (1963) that saw the beginnings of both the permissive society and feminism.

Nicolaisen, W. F. H. "'What a Name. Stephen Halifax': Onomastic Modes in Three Novels by Margaret Drabble." *Literary Onomastics Studies* 10 (1983): 269-283.

A brief look at Drabble's use of first and last names. Nicolaisen concludes that she supplies a sufficiently great variety to avoid confusion and that she and her characters are aware of the power of names themselves and the way they are used. Specific comments on *A Summer Bird-Cage* and *The Waterfall*.

Parker, Gillian, and Janet Todd. "Margaret Drabble." In *Women Writers Talking*, edited by Janet Todd. New York: Holmes & Meier, 1983.

A very informative interview. Drabble talks about the female tradition in the novel in English (not only is there female content, but there is a female sentence). She lists the novelists who have influenced her: Austen, Eliot, Woolf (only recently), Lessing, and Mary McCarthy. She begins writing her novels with ideas, not characters; her characters do have a life of their own, and Drabble does not always understand them. (She dislikes critics who tell her what her heroines should have done.) Her prose reads like the spoken voice. Especially in her later novels she is concerned with problems of social justice, but not to the extent of denouncing Britain. Specific remarks on *The Waterfall, The Needle's Eye, The Radiant Way,* and *The Middle Ground.*

Pearson, Carol, and Katherine Pope. *The Female Hero in American and British Literature.* New York: R. R. Bowker, 1981.

In their exposition of what the female hero is like, the authors make reference to *The Millstone, Jerusalem the Golden, The Realms of Gold,* and *The Ice Age.*

Pickering, Jean. "Margaret Drabble's Sense of the Middle Problem." *Twentieth Century Literature* 30 (Winter, 1984): 475-483.

On the basis of an interview with Drabble, Pickering provides important insights into the way her novels were written and structured. In the cases of *The Needle's Eye, The Realms of Gold,* and *The Ice Age,* each began with an idea which in turn informed the novel's crisis. Drabble conceives of her characters as leading full lives outside of fiction, lives which continue after the novel is over. She presents the reader with the intersections of their lives as they move toward these crises. Though the endings of the novels may not be satisfying in a traditional way, they are the logical product of the crises in which Drabble is most interested. Pickering's observations also illuminate *The Middle Ground*.

Poland, Nancy. "Margaret Drabble: 'There Must Be a Lot of People Like Me.'" *Midwest Quarterly* 16 (April, 1975): 255-267.
A chatty interview in which Poland gives biographical details and Drabble expresses herself on women's changing roles. Drabble says that she is a moral writer, not because she teaches, but because she explores contemporary issues and asks the reader to think. Why is she popular? There seem to be many other people who worry about the same things she does. Brief remarks on *The Waterfall* (Brontë-like) and *The Needle's Eye* (Simon is based on a real person).

Preussner, Dee. "Talking with Margaret Drabble." *Modern Fiction Studies* 25 (Winter, 1979): 563-577.
Drabble on Doris Lessing: She likes her middle novels the best. She has more faith than Lessing in the structures of a democratic society and, now that she has children, more faith in the joys of domestic life. She also thinks that she is more conventional than Lessing in matters of the spirit; she does not believe in gurus or in extrasensory perception. Compared to men, women writers are at a disadvantage, for if they have children, it is not as easy to travel widely. Drabble comments at length on *The Needle's Eye*.

Rose, Ellen Cronan, ed. *Critical Essays on Margaret Drabble.* Boston: G. K. Hall, 1985.
A very important collection of essays. In her useful introduction, Rose surveys the development of serious critical concern with Drabble's novels, especially feminist concern. She charts Drabble's own changes as well. Specific essays on *The Millstone, The Waterfall, The Realms of Gold, The Ice Age,* and *The Middle Ground.* Extensive bibliography.

_____. *Equivocal Figures: The Novels of Margaret Drabble.* Totowa, N.J.: Barnes & Noble Books, 1980.
A survey of Drabble's novels through *The Ice Age.* Rose fits the novels into an evolving conceptual scheme which she draws from

such feminist writers as Simone de Beauvoir, Mary Daly, and Adrienne Rich. Her scheme often works well, especially with Drabble's earlier novels. As the book goes on, the details of the novels fade into the background, and by the end Rose's book is openly personal and polemical. See discussions of separate novels. Bibliography.

_____. "The Sexual Politics of Narration: Margaret Drabble's Feminist Fiction." *Studies in the Novel* 20 (Spring, 1988): 86-99. Rose's persuasive thesis is that Drabble, despite the broadening of her themes after *The Needle's Eye*, remains a feminist novelist. We know Drabble continues to oppose patriarchal views because she refuses to impose traditional structures on unstructured reality. In fact, Drabble implies that she chronicles only some of the stories that could be told about her characters' independent lives. Rose gives lucid and valuable explanations of the differences between feminist and patriarchal assumptions about fiction. She comments at length on *The Waterfall*, *The Realms of Gold*, and *The Middle Ground*.

Roxman, Susanna. *Guilt and Glory: Studies in Margaret Drabble's Novels 1963-80*. Stockholm: Almquist & Wiksell International, 1984.
Roxman discusses the novels through *The Middle Ground* from several perspectives: their literary backgrounds, their rendering of philosophical issues like the roles of fate and chance, and their expressive use of images. But despite this book's somewhat fragmented organization (it was a thesis), Roxman succeeds in making explicit some of Drabble's implicit themes.

Rozencwajg, Iris. "Interview with Margaret Drabble." *Women's Studies* 6 (1979): 335-347.
Drabble supplies some details on how she started to write. She admires George Eliot and Doris Lessing, but is baffled by Iris Murdoch. She thinks Henry James was wrong to address his novels to a small number of elite readers. She has hoped to have a wider audience, but fears she has failed. Clara in *Jerusalem the Golden* may be a tough survivor, but she is Drabble's least favorite heroine, perhaps because Clara is elitist.

Rubenstein, Roberta. "Fragmented Bodies/Selves/Narratives: Margaret Drabble's Postmodern Turn." *Contemporary Literature* 35 (Spring, 1994): 136-155.
Drabble's fictional worlds become darker as she matures. Later works are fragmented in several senses. They show more images of the fragmented human body and of political and social division. Moreover, the narratives themselves are fragmented in decidedly postmodern ways. Rubenstein treats *The Radiant Way* and *A Natural Curiosity* briefly and then treats *The Gates of Ivory* in depth. A very important article, especially on the last of these works.

Ruderman, Judith. "An Invitation to a Dinner Party: Margaret Drabble on Women and Food." In *Margaret Drabble: Golden Realms*, edited by Dorey Schmidt. No. 4 in *Living Author Series*. Edinburg, Tex.: Pan American University, 1982.
Women's attitudes toward preparing food are always significant in Drabble's novels. The responsibility to prepare meals can be a source of bondage or of power. Refusing to prepare food can be a sign of selfishness. But as Drabble develops into a social novelist, parties become central to her fiction, culminating with Kate's preparations at the end of *The Middle Ground*.

Sadler, Lynn Veach. *Margaret Drabble*. Boston: Twayne, 1986.
An introductory survey of Drabble's career as a writer. In Chapter 1, Sadler provides biographical details, and in her final chapter she summarizes the changes in Drabble's reputation. In between, she treats the novels through *The Middle Ground* roughly in chronological order, though *The Garrick Year* is discussed after *The Needle's Eye*. Sadler summarizes plots and characters and identifies themes. The short essays "Males in Drabble's Novels" and "Drabble on Marriage" appear at the end of Chapters 5 and 6. See entries under individual novels.

Sage, Lorna. "Female Fictions: The Women Novelists." In *The Contemporary English Novel*, edited by Malcolm Bradbury and David Palmer. New York: Holmes & Meier, 1980.
Like Iris Murdoch, Drabble writes novels that have ties to the nineteenth century. Characters' appearances and inner lives are

defined by their homes. Sage thinks Drabble's technique of listing details is monotonous and her characters shallow.

Satz, Martha. "Less of a Woman as One Gets Older: An Interview with Margaret Drabble." *Southwest Review* 70 (Spring, 1985): 187-197.
Interview. Women have advantages as writers, for they are more in touch with emotions and social life. Drabble opposes feminists who look down on motherhood. The problems which most interest her now concern old age and what people can hope for. Specific remarks on *The Ice Age* and *The Middle Ground*.

Schmidt, Dorey, ed. *Margaret Drabble: Golden Realms.* No. 4 in *Living Author Series.* Edinburg, Tex.: Pan American University, 1982.
A collection of fourteen essays on Drabble, listed separately here. Bibliography supplements that of Robert J. Stanton in *A Bibliography of Modern British Novelists*.

Seiler-Franklin, Carol. *Boulder-pushers: Women in the Fiction of Margaret Drabble, Doris Lessing and Iris Murdoch.* Berne, Switzerland: Peter Lang, 1979.
Seiler-Franklin asks how women writers portray women of various kinds. Like the rest, Clara in *Jerusalem the Golden* breaks away from her puritanical upbringing. At the end, she is passive but greedy and will survive. Frances in *The Realms of Gold* is one of the few women who are really successful at an occupation. She will not let her children get in the way of her success. Though she is independent, she depends on the admiration of others. Frances is the exception, rather than the rule, and Seiler-Franklin thinks she is too fortunate.
   Rosamund of *The Millstone* is a pure scholar and achieves real independence only when her pregnancy and the birth of her daughter force her into the real world. Jane in *The Waterfall* is a type of creative woman. She is saved, not so much by a man, but by learning to accept her own sexuality. In *The Needle's Eye*, Rose may be seen as representing housewives, for she is neither a professional or an artist. She is trapped in a bad marriage and willingly surrenders herself for the sake of her children.

Showalter, Elaine. *A Literature of Their Own: British Women Novelists from Brontë to Lessing.* Princeton, N.J.: Princeton University Press, 1977.

Showalter calls Drabble the most traditional of contemporary writers, for Drabble's heroines through *The Needle's Eye* usually acknowledge their limitations and their submission to men. Children are their consolation prize, but Drabble seems to suggest that she knows these women are not victorious. Specific remarks on *The Millstone* and *The Needle's Eye.*

Sizemore, Christine Wick. *A Female Vision of the City: London in the Novels of Five British Women.* Knoxville: University of Tennessee Press, 1989.

Twentieth century women writers have imagined London though a typically female image, that of a network. Different writers imagine that network differently. Drabble sees London as a web of streets and of personal relations, a place where women can make connections and achieve freedom. Sizemore comments on most of Drabble's novels, but focuses on *The Middle Ground* and *The Radiant Way*, with shorter treatments of *The Needle's Eye*, *The Realms of Gold*, and *The Ice Age.* A very interesting thesis worked out in detail.

Stovel, Nora F. "`A Feminine Ending?': Symbolism as Closure in the Novels of Margaret Drabble." *English Studies in Canada* 15 (March, 1989): 80-93.

Drabble's novels seem inconclusive to many readers. Unlike traditional novels, they end without the story being neatly tied up. Drabble gives such endings, Stovel thinks, for several reasons. Ideologies make conclusive endings easy, but she does not believe in any. That includes feminism, and Stovel surveys feminist objections to her novels. Moreover, Drabble cannot shape her novels because they are autobiographical.

Even though Drabble's narratives do not end conclusively, a final symbol gives a sense of closure to each novel. These symbols often look in several directions, suggesting the unity of the ideal and the real, the figurative and the literal, the optimistic and the pessimistic. They often help sum up the novel. Their optimistic side echoes the structural feature of Drabble's novels, a turning point in which negation gives way to affirmation and vision. Stovel's survey of the final symbols of the novels through *The Radiant Way* is too brief, but it provides a starting point for analysis.

_____. "From Wordsworth to Bennett: The Development of Margaret Drabble's Fiction." *International Fiction Review* 15 (Summer, 1988): 130-140.
Drabble wrote two major critical works in two decades, one on William Wordsworth in 1966 and the second on Arnold Bennett in 1974. Her differing critical discussions provide insights into the differences between the novels she wrote in each decade. Wordsworth and the heroines of her first-person novels through *The Waterfall* all explore their individual visions, often using images drawn from natural scenery, and all find they must deal with an oppressive society.
On the other hand, Drabble's novels of the 1970's resemble Bennett's. These third-person novels treat individuals who live within a larger and more diverse society and who deal with political and economic issues. Society itself is seen as evolving. Instead of natural scenery in these novels, we more often encounter man-made constructions. *Jerusalem the Golden* is somewhat of an exception. Drabble's novels of the 1980's appear to continue her practices of the 1970's.

_____. *Margaret Drabble, Symbolic Moralist.* Mercer Island, Wash.: Starmont House, 1989.
This valuable study treats individual novels through *The Radiant Way.* In her introductory chapter, Stovel argues that Drabble is a moralist, particularly with relation to the conflicting concerns of professional mothers. As an artist, Drabble uses symbols (such as a golden world) to communicate her moral concerns. Not only is Drabble the narrator a symbolist, but so are each of her heroines. Drabble's themes and her symbols develop as she progresses as a novelist. Stovel thinks that each Drabble novel has a turning point where pessimism gives way to some degree of optimism. Bibliography.

_____. "Margaret Drabble's Golden Vision." In *Margaret Drabble: Golden Realms*, edited by Dorey Schmidt. No. 4 in

Living Author Series. Edinburg, Tex.: Pan American University, 1982.
Too often Drabble is seen as only a realist. Actually, her novels are full of natural symbolism. Stovel examines Drabble's visions of an ideal world in *Jerusalem the Golden* and *Realms of Gold*.

Taylor, D. J. *After the War: The Novel and English Society Since 1945*. London: Chatto & Windus, 1993.
Taylor treats Drabble briefly in his survey of British fiction since World War II. She figures as an example of an author who harbors liberal assumptions and biases. Taylor is particularly severe on *The Millstone*.

Todd, Richard. "The Presence of Postmodernism in British Fiction: Aspects of Style and Selfhood." In *Approaching Postmodernism*, edited by Douwe Fokkema and Hans Bertens. Amsterdam: John Benjamins, 1986.
Todd locates Drabble on a spectrum of postmodernism displayed by the British novel since the 1950's. He finds a specific postmodern passage in *The Realms of Gold*.

Waugh, Patricia. *Feminine Fictions: Revisiting the Postmodern*. London: Routledge, 1989.
Drabble is among a group of writers who may appear to have only old-fashioned modern and realist assumptions, but really are aware of postmodern conditions. Drabble's heroines are of two types: They either attempt to drown their subjective selves, or they move from a sense of separateness toward establishing connections with other people. Waugh discusses *The Millstone* and *The Waterfall* at some length.

Whitehill, Sharon. "Two for Tea: An Afternoon with Margaret Drabble." *Essays in Literature* 11 (Spring, 1984): 61-75.
A pleasant interview. Drabble reports that she now enjoys reading D. H. Lawrence and that she thinks her novels are funny, though some readers do not. She begins to work with a theme or a problem, not a plot. Interesting comments on *The Realms of Gold* and *The Middle Ground*.

Whittier, Gayle. "Mistresses and Madonnas in the Novels of Margaret Drabble." In *Gender and Literary Voice*, edited by Janet Todd. Vol. 1, n.s., in *Women & Literature*. New York: Holmes & Meier, 1980.

A very valuable analysis of some basic tensions as viewed by Drabble and of the patterns that her heroines' experience. The nineteenth century novel routinely contrasts madonnas (women as mothers) and mistresses (women as objects of erotic desire). Drabble views this division from a woman's point of view and adds another tension, that between motherhood and a career. The problems of combining motherhood and work are explicit in *The Garrick Year*; the energizing effects of pregnancy on a woman's work are noted in *The Millstone* and *The Waterfall*. But Drabble's main concern is with motherhood itself. Whittier constructs a pattern or archetype which most of Drabble's mothers/heroines experience. First, conception, which is casual or accidental; a woman may be in need of something, but she enters the pattern unknowingly. This sexual phase often inhibits her creativity.

Second, during pregnancy she is awakened to the feelings and fears of common humanity; this time may be a creative one for her work. Next, the birth of the baby is a time of rebirth, a mysterious transformation for the woman. Motherhood comes next and is not sentimentalized. The woman now is vulnerable to what may happen to her child; the mother is a gambler who risks everything. In later novels such as *The Realms of Gold*, Drabble's heroines appear to resolve the conflict between motherhood and erotic love.

Zeman, Anthea. *Presumptuous Girls: Women and Their World in the Serious Woman's Novel*. London: Weidenfeld & Nicolson, 1977.

A broad survey of women's issues and the themes of female novelists since Jane Austen. Drabble deals with the marriage market in *A Summer Bird-Cage*, with growing old in *The Realms of Gold*, and with sexual love in *The Waterfall*.

Criticism of Individual Novels

A Summer Bird-Cage, 1963.

Allan, Tuzyline Jita.   "*The Middle Ground*: Determinism in a
    Changing World." In *Womanist and Feminist Aesthetics: A
    Comparative Review.* Athens: Ohio University Press, 1995.
    Drabble's early novels show women caught in the definitions of a
    patriarchal world. Sarah values her looks more than her brains
    and prepares herself for marriage.

Beards, Virginia K.   "Margaret Drabble: Novels of a Cautious
    Feminist." *Critique* 15, no. 1 (1973): 35-47. Reprinted in *Con-
    temporary Women Novelists,* edited by Patricia Meyer Spacks.
    Englewood Cliffs, N.J.: Prentice-Hall, 1977.
    Beards's feminist reading sees Sarah and other women as re-
    pressed by men in their choice of study, in their career options,
    and in marriage.

Campbell, Jane.   "`Both a Joke and a Victory': Humor as Narrative
    Strategy in Margaret Drabble's Fiction." *Contemporary Litera-
    ture* 32 (Spring, 1991): 75-99.
    In Drabble's novels, readers should suspect characters who lack
    humor. Stephen may be a satirist, but he is not funny and lacks
    compassion. In contrast, Louise can finally laugh at herself.

Creighton, Joanne V. *Margaret Drabble.* London: Methuen, 1985.
    In her chapter "Bird-cages," Creighton is critical of some ways
    Drabble has concocted her story to avoid important issues, but
    feels she captures what it is like to leave a university and enter the
    adult world. Creighton points out that Drabble leads readers to
    distance themselves from Sarah's judgments expressed in the first
    person.

Davidson, Arnold E.   "Pride and Prejudice in Margaret Drabble's *A
    Summer Bird-Cage*." *Arizona Quarterly* 38 (Winter, 1982): 303-
    310.
    Sarah Bennett recalls Elizabeth Bennet. Davidson looks at the
    parallels between this novel and Jane Austen's *Pride and
    Prejudice,* and finds that Drabble reverses Austen in many ways.

There is not universally acknowledged truth in Drabble. Sarah must learn both assertiveness and pride. Austen would have disapproved of Sarah's vanity about her own body and of the way the Bennett sisters regard Daphne. Most important, whereas in Austen the relation of the sisters to men is primary and their relation to each other is secondary, in Drabble the reverse is true. At the heart of *A Summer Bird-Cage* is the story of Sarah and Louise getting together. Davidson thinks that Drabble and Austen would agree that Louise had to get over much false pride to make this happen.

Harper, Michael F. "Margaret Drabble and the Resurrection of the English Novel." *Contemporary Literature* 23 (Spring, 1982): 145-168. Reprinted in *Critical Essays on Margaret Drabble*, edited by Ellen Cronan Rose. Boston: G. K. Hall, 1985.
Sarah's problems are postmodern ones: she knows she cannot easily enter new social worlds, and she finds she cannot write a modern realistic novel. Her insights make clear why Stephen, the successful satirist, is hateful.

Irvine, Lorna. "No Sense of an Ending: Drabble's Continuous Fictions." In *Critical Essays on Margaret Drabble*, edited by Ellen Cronan Rose. Boston: G. K. Hall, 1985.
Sarah thinks her brother-in-law will write a traditional novel with a cataclysmic conclusion. *A Summer Bird-Cage* itself ends inconclusively, with Sarah calling the reader's attention to the fact she is writing her own ongoing story.

Lambert, Ellen Z. "Margaret Drabble and the Sense of Possibility." *University of Toronto Quarterly* 49 (Spring, 1980): 228-251. Reprinted in *Critical Essays on Margaret Drabble*, edited by Ellen Cronan Rose. Boston: G. K. Hall, 1985.
Sarah is the first of Drabble's heroines to radiate a sense of life's possibilities. She knows she is lucky in that she is both intelligent and beautiful, much more so than the dreary Daphne. Although she has a moral sense, Sarah is happy in her good fortune. Lambert thinks Drabble excels in rendering Sarah's sense of her exuberant identity.

McGuirk, Carol. "Drabble to Carter: Fiction by Women, 1962-1992."
    In *The Columbia History of the British Novel*, edited by John
    Richetti. New York: Columbia University Press, 1994.
    Many women writers of this era center their stories on women,
    especially women in competition. Here Sarah competes with
    Louise and Daphne. She is blinded by her pride, her feelings of
    superiority, and her narcissistic regard for her own beauty.

Myer, Valerie Grosvenor. *Margaret Drabble: Puritanism and
    Permissiveness*. New York: Barnes & Noble Books, 1974.
    Sarah is a typical early Drabble heroine. In contrast to her amoral
    sister, Sarah is restrained by her puritan conscience.

_____. *Margaret Drabble: A Reader's Guide*. New York: St.
    Martin's Press, 1991.
    Myers alludes to autobiographical elements in the novel and sets it
    in the context of other works by women. Many literary allusions
    are identified and explained. Sarah's problems anticipate those of
    Drabble's later heroines and have no easy solutions.

Nicolaisen, W. F. H. "`What a Name. Stephen Halifax': Onomastic
    Modes in Three Novels by Margaret Drabble." *Literary Onomas-
    tics Studies* 10 (1983): 269-283.
    Comments on the significance of proper names. Some character's
    names have little content, while others (like "Stephen Halifax")
    are objects of speculation.

Rose, Ellen Cronan. *Equivocal Figures: The Novels of Margaret
    Drabble*. Totowa, N.J.: Barnes & Noble Books, 1980.
    In her first chapter, Rose sees Sarah as exhibiting the problems of
    the young girl as described by Simone de Beauvoir in *The Second
    Sex*. Sarah is fascinated by the adult world where a woman has
    her role defined by men. She is drawn to its attractions—includ-
    ing sex. At the same time she wishes to retain her girlish auton-
    omy. The other female characters represent other responses to
    this dilemma. Because the novel is told in the first person, Rose is
    not sure if we are to assume Drabble fully understands the
    problems she presents.

Roxman, Susanna. *Guilt and Glory: Studies in Margaret Drabble's Novels 1963-80*. Stockholm: Almquist & Wiksell International, 1984.

Although this novel may echo Henry James's *The Portrait of a Lady* and may owe ideas to Simone de Beauvoir's *The Second Sex* (1949), its major source is George Eliot's *Middlemarch*. Both tell of two sisters. Both Eliot's Dorothea and Drabble's Louise marry wealthy, inhibited, unhappy, ugly men. Both women go to Rome and are seen standing next to works of art. Louise's lover resembles Dorothea's second husband, Will. Roxman points out interesting parallels, but does not discuss the obvious differences. The novel does not provide a very edifying discussion of moral ideas. People are divided into categories, and the carnivores seem fated to eat the herbivores. Some retribution seems to be visited on Louise for her carnivorous activities, but she is happy in the end.

Sadler, Lynn Veach. *Margaret Drabble*. Boston: Twayne, 1986.

In Chapter 2, Sadler provides a plot-summary of the novel, identifies its themes. She evokes its central character and discusses its critical reception.

Stovel, Nora. *Margaret Drabble, Symbolic Moralist*. Mercer Island, Wash.: Starmont House, 1989.

The conflicts of the novel are obvious: marriage vs. career, carnivores vs. herbivores, sister vs. sister. Stovel persuasively demonstrates that the novel develops these conflicts with an intricate web of symbols: birds (in bird-cages), beasts, and flowers. If Sarah's conscious use of symbols is somewhat schematic, Drabble's own attitude is ironic, for Sarah does not decipher her symbols's ultimate meanings. Louise has her own set of symbols, and in order for them to reconcile it is necessary for each sister to understand the other's symbolism.

Zeman, Anthea. *Presumptuous Girls: Women and Their World in the Serious Woman's Novel*. London: Weidenfeld & Nicolson, 1977.

Zeman compares this novel to those written by women in earlier eras. Now that more women are better educated, Drabble can show an educated young women who challenges the assumption that women must marry. Although she knows she cannot be a

complete woman if she stays to teach at her university, Sarah
worries because she cannot find models of happy marriages.

The Garrick Year, 1964.

Allan, Tuzyline Jita.   "*The Middle Ground*: Determinism in a
Changing World."   In *Womanist and Feminist Aesthetics: A
Comparative Review*. Athens: Ohio University Press, 1995.
Drabble's early novels show women caught in the definitions of a
patriarchal world. Emma rebels against the requirements of being
a wife and mother by her freakish behavior.   But she ends by
affirming her traditional position. A womanist critic objects.

Beards, Virginia K.   "Margaret Drabble: Novels of a Cautious
Feminist."   *Critique* 15, no. 1 (1973): 35-47.   Reprinted in
Contemporary Women Novelists, edited by Patricia Meyer Spacks.
Englewood Cliffs, N.J.: Prentice-Hall, 1977.
A feminist reading.   Even though readers are charmed by
Emma's odd personality, they soon see that Emma is subjugated
by her husband and frustrated by her babies.   Although she is
sexually frigid and is imprisoned by the traditional idea that
women do not enjoy sex, she secretly wonders if this has to be so.

Creighton, Joanne V. *Margaret Drabble*. London: Methuen, 1985.
In her chapter "Bird-cages," Creighton evokes Emma's neurotic
personality which alternately charms and repels the reader. What
does Drabble want the reader to feel?   Even when at the end
Emma reaches some accommodation with her lot, Drabble gives
us no real resolution.

Irvine, Lorna.   "No Sense of An Ending: Drabble's Continuous
Fictions."   In *Critical Essays on Margaret Drabble*, edited by
Ellen Cronan Rose.   Boston: G. K. Hall, 1985.
Although Emma is threatened by climactic events at the end of the
novel, we are assured that, because she is a mother, she will
endure.

Myer, Valerie Grosvenor.   *Margaret Drabble: Puritanism and
Permissiveness*. New York: Barnes & Noble Books, 1974.

When Emma judges herself as shallow, we know she has a residue of the puritanical values she seems to have rebelled against.

_____. *Margaret Drabble: A Reader's Guide.* New York: St. Martin's Press, 1991.
When serialized on the radio, this novel made Drabble famous. Myer supplies social and geographical background and biographical parallels. She gives a useful summary of the story (the ending seems arbitrary) and its characters, especially Emma.

Preussner, Dee. "Patterns in *The Garrick Year.*" In *Margaret Drabble: Golden Realms,* edited by Dorey Schmidt. No. 4 in *Living Author Series.* Edinburg, Tex.: Pan American University, 1982.
An important metaphor by which to interpret this novel is the theater. Emma is an actor playing various limited roles rather than a participant in life's dramas. Even motherhood does not free her to live fully, as symbolized by the currents of the Wye River. Even though she is attracted to stories that progress to conclusions, her own life's pattern is circular. A convincing reading of this novel.

Rose, Ellen Cronan. *Equivocal Figures: The Novels of Margaret Drabble.* Totowa, N.J.: Barnes & Noble Books, 1980.
In her first chapter, Rose sees Emma as exhibiting the problems of the young girl as described by Simone de Beauvoir in *The Second Sex.* Readers should see Emma's marriage as like Louise's in *A Summer Bird-Cage.* Like both Louise and Sarah, Emma has not reconciled being an adult woman with her desire to remain a girl. Rose analyzes in detail Emma's problems, such as anorexia and her related dislike of sex. Rose reads her fear of drowning as fear of sexual yielding. Because the novels are told in the first person, Rose is not sure if Drabble fully understands the problems she presents.

Roxman, Susanna. *Guilt and Glory: Studies in Margaret Drabble's Novels 1963-80.* Stockholm: Almquist & Wiksell International, 1984.
Roxman's discussions tell us little about this novel. Her comparison of Drabble's Emma to Gustave Flaubert's Emma Bovary is

unconvincing. The novel explores the moral problems of female submission and male privilege, and the heroine thinks some of her sufferings are the result of retribution.

Sadler, Lynn Veach. *Margaret Drabble*. Boston: Twayne, 1986.
Sadler treats this novel out of chronological order. In Chapter 6, she treats Emma's unhappy marriage as representative of most marriages in Drabble novels. Emma's problems stem from her parents; they have left her a dissatisfied person. Marriage does not change her, for she still yearns for the excitement of the single life. Paradoxically, she also yearns to give her life shape. In the course of the novel, in particular after her daughter's brush with death, she begins to shed tears for other people and even has hopes of loving her husband.

Stovel, Nora F. "`A Feminine Ending?': Symbolism as Closure in the Novels of Margaret Drabble." *English Studies in Canada* 15 (March, 1989): 80-93.
Drabble provides symbolic closure to her novels with equivocal final symbols. Here the snake in the garden suggests the mixed nature of the future Emma will experience.

_____. *Margaret Drabble, Symbolic Moralist*. Mercer Island, Wash.: Starmont House, 1989.
Stovel provides a later version of "Staging a Marriage: Margaret Drabble's *The Garrick Year*." At the heart of the novel is the opposition of the theater (illusion, role-playing, self-deception) and the River Wye (the reality of passion, sexual and maternal).

_____. "Staging a Marriage: Margaret Drabble's *The Garrick Year*." *Mosaic: A Journal for the Interdisciplinary Study of Literature* 17 (Spring, 1984): 161-174.
A detailed and persuasive analysis of the patterns of this novel. Stovel fills in the biographical background to the novel (including rare remarks about Drabble's unpublished undergraduate thesis) and then demonstrates the novel's artistry. At the center is Emma's relation to the theater. Emma has only contempt for it, though paradoxically she is a role-player herself and is easily influenced by life's dramas. In fact, she often miscasts herself in the roles she chooses in life, such as that of a mistress. Her crises (her

and David's infidelities, the near-drowning) seem to jolt her into some kind of reality. Stovel compares the end of this novel to that of *The Needle's Eye*; in both cases she doubts the marriage will last.

Whittier, Gayle. "Mistresses and Madonnas in the Novels of Margaret Drabble." In *Gender and Literary Voice*, edited by Janet Todd. No. 1, n. s., in *Women & Literature*. New York: Holmes & Meier, 1980.

This novel shows how women are torn between their desires for a career and their desires for marriage and motherhood. Emma shows part of the usual Drabble pattern. Here as elsewhere in Drabble, mothers are seen as particularly sexy, and mothers are vulnerable to accidents that befall their children.

The Millstone [in the U.S.: *Thank You All Very Much*], 1965.

Allan, Tuzyline Jita. "*The Middle Ground*: Determinism in a Changing World." In *Womanist and Feminist Aesthetics: A Comparative Review*. Athens: Ohio University Press, 1995.

Drabble's early novels show women caught in the definitions of a patriarchal world. Rosamund, entrapped by biology, tries to conceal her female characteristics.

Beards, Virginia K. "Margaret Drabble: Novels of a Cautious Feminist." *Critique* 15, no. 1 (1973): 35-47. Reprinted in *Contemporary Women Novelists*, edited by Patricia Meyer Spacks. Englewood Cliffs, N.J.: Prentice-Hall, 1977.

A strained feminist reading. Beards thinks Drabble is admirable in that in this novel she considers alternatives to the ordinary lives of women, lives outside of marriage and patriarchal dominance. Rosamund strives for achievement like a man and is successful.

Bromberg, Pamela S. "The Development of Narrative Technique in Margaret Drabble's Novels." *Journal of Narrative Technique* 16 (Fall, 1986): 179-191.

This novel poses a problem. If Rosamund is an unreliable narrator, how can the reader be sure what ultimately is true? Readers ask many questions: By the end, has Rosamund changed? Is this

a story of feminist triumph or of arrested development? Bromberg
thinks that these ambiguities are a major flaw in the novel.

Butler, Colin. "Margaret Drabble: *The Millstone* and Wordsworth.
English Studies 59 (1978): 353-360.
In a closely argued attack, Butler examines this novel and Drabble's critical study of Wordsworth and finds that the same attitudes
underlie each. Drabble oversimplifies the poet and ignores his
transcendental and social dimensions. *The Millstone* suffers because Rosamund is a superficial character. She is right to reject
the vanities of London. But she retreats into love for her daughter
and does not develop her sympathies into social concerns.

Creighton, Joanne V. *Margaret Drabble*. London: Methuen, 1985.
In her chapter "Bird-cages," Creighton again asks how much
distance there is between Rosamund, the first-person narrator, and
Drabble, the ultimate narrator. She concludes that this problem
causes readers to be drawn to speculate on Rosamund's unconscious motives and problems, especially on her attitudes to her
parents and to George. Different readers will see different degrees
of distance.

Cunningham, Gail. "Patchwork and Patterns: The Condition of
England in Margaret Drabble's Later Novels." In *The British and
Irish Novel Since 1960*, edited by James Acheson. New York: St.
Martin's Press, 1991.
Cunningham discusses this as a typical early Drabble novel. It
centers on one young, educated woman, and it shows a pattern in
her life. There is a pattern too in Drabble's religious, literary, and
cultural references.

_____. "Women and Children First: The Novels of Margaret
Drabble." In *Twentieth Century Women Novelists*, edited by
Thomas F. Staley. Totowa, N.J.: Barnes & Noble Books, 1982.
Cunningham says this novel provides a representative display of
Drabble's early themes and concerns. Rosamund is a privileged
product of her parents' and her university's liberal but impersonal
values. Conceiving a child brings her out of her isolation. Not
only does she give life to another human being, but she needs the

help of strangers. Rosamund comes to recognize this and to acknowledge deep feeling for her daughter.

Firchow, Peter E. "Rosamund's Complaint: Margaret Drabble's *The
Millstone* (1966)." In *Old Lines, New Forces: Essays on the
Contemporary British Novel, 1960-1970*, edited by Robert K.
Morris. Rutherford, N.J.: Fairleigh Dickinson University Press,
1976.
Firchow's well-written essay reviews Drabble's career through the
mid-1970's and then treats *The Millstone* as a representative
novel. He sees Rosamund as an unflinchingly honest woman
who, through her experiences of pregnancy and motherhood, must
face some central problems of living in the modern welfare state.
Machines are everywhere in this novel, and the biggest machine is
the National Health Service. Rosamund discovers that the natural
impulses of human love are the most powerful ones, though the
range of her love is limited to her baby.

Hardin, Nancy S. "Drabble's *The Millstone*: A Fable for Our Times."
Critique 15, no. 1 (1973): 22-34.
Rosamund's story is one to inspire contemporary women. She is
young, intelligent, and independent, and is also a hard-working
scholar. Like many contemporary women, she is suspicious of sex
and fears it. When she finds she is pregnant, she does not
compromise her integrity, for she will do without a husband and
succeed as a single mother. She matures. After the baby is born,
she learns to love her. Hardin works out Drabble's explicit and
implicit comparisons to the heroine of the Elizabethan poet
Samuel Daniel's "The Complaint of Rosamund."

Harper, Michael F. "Margaret Drabble and the Resurrection of the
English Novel." *Contemporary Literature* 23 (Spring, 1982):
145-168. Reprinted *Critical Essays on Margaret Drabble*, edited
by Ellen Cronan Rose. Boston: G. K. Hall, 1985.
When Lydia rejects a real-life accident as too unrealistic for fiction, Harper illuminates the incident as showing how far Drabble
has come from modernism. Rosamund, on the other hand, accepts the unrealistic but real accident of conception.

Libby, Marion Vlastos. "Fate and Feminism in the Novels of Margaret
    Drabble" *Contemporary Literature* 16 (Spring, 1975): 175-192.
    Rosamund fights against a patriarchal society and wins. She
    achieves professional independence and loves her baby.

Myer, Valerie Grosvenor. *Margaret Drabble: Puritanism and Per-
    missiveness.* New York: Barnes & Noble Books, 1974.
    Rosamund is a perfect example of an early Drabble heroine, for
    she has inherited both the strengths and the limitations of her par-
    ents' liberal Victorian non-conformist traditions. She is industri-
    ous, ambitious, self-conscious, and abstinent. When she conceives
    a child, she regards it as a punishment and tries to face her
    responsibilities. By the end of the novel, she has softened her
    heart toward her baby. Myer thinks this novel is a success.

————————. *Margaret Drabble: A Reader's Guide.* New York: St.
    Martin's Press, 1991.
    Rosamund, an upper-middle-class socialist, is shocked when her
    pregnancy introduces her to the real world of babies and the lower
    classes. Myer discusses the problem of how we are to take
    Rosamund, the first-person narrator, for critics disagree on
    whether Drabble identifies with her or is distanced from her.
    Myer fills in biographical and social backgrounds and identifies
    the sources of many allusions and quotations.

Pearson, Carol, and Katherine Pope. *The Female Hero in American
    and British Literature.* New York: R. R. Bowker, 1981.
    The authors cite Rosamund as showing specific details of the
    female quest. Rosamund as a girl was imprisoned by society's
    expectations. She departs on her journey as a fallen woman and
    does not let having a baby stop her quest. She is liberated when
    she returns home to a loving community with her daughter.

Rose, Ellen Cronan. *Equivocal Figures: The Novels of Margaret
    Drabble.* Totowa, N.J.: Barnes & Noble Books, 1980.
    In her first chapter, Rose sees Rosamund as exhibiting the prob-
    lems of the young girl as described by Simone de Beauvoir in *The
    Second Sex.* Like Drabble's earlier heroines, Rosamund wishes to
    avoid not only adult sexuality but also love and responsibility.
    Rose has her own reading of the end of the novel. Although

having a baby forces Rosamund briefly out of isolation, she remains alone. She does not even love her child. Because the novel is told in the first person, Rose is not sure if we are to assume Drabble fully understands the problems she presents.

Roxman, Susanna. *Guilt and Glory: Studies in Margaret Drabble's Novels 1963-80.* Stockholm: Almquist & Wiksell International, 1984.
Roxman considers the sources advanced by Nancy Hardin (Samuel Daniel's "The Complaint of Rosamund") and Colin Butler (Wordsworth in general), and she judges them to be unconvincing. Rosamund has been raised with puritanical moral ideals, and as a result she questions her own privileged status. She cannot enjoy her blessings. She carries out her ideal of independence to extreme lengths; she regards her baby's illness as retribution for her unjust advantages. Roxman discusses alternative explanations of what Drabble may mean.

Sadler, Lynn Veach. *Margaret Drabble.* Boston: Twayne, 1986.
In Chapter 3, Sadler discusses Drabble's attitude to this early work, summarizes the plot, and evokes Rosamund's character. She sees Rosamund as independent, lonely, ungenerous, and rigid, though at the end she has achieved professional success and has begun to love at least her daughter.

Showalter, Elaine. *A Literature of Their Own: British Women Novelists from Brontë to Lessing.* Princeton, N.J.: Princeton University Press, 1977.
Rosamund feels trapped in specifically female humiliations, but pregnancy helps educate her.

Spitzer, Susan. "Fantasy and Femaleness in Margaret Drabble's *The Millstone.*" *Novel* 11 (Spring, 1978): 227-246. Reprinted in *Critical Essays on Margaret Drabble*, edited by Ellen Cronan Rose. Boston: G. K. Hall, 1985.
An interesting psychoanalytical reading of the novel. Spitzer argues that we should not think that Rosamund ever comes to terms with her problems. Even though she gains some self-knowledge, Rosamund persists in many unconscious self-deceptions to the end. She childishly desires to have her baby by

herself and simultaneously to remain a young girl, hating all aspects of adult female sexuality. Spitzer goes on to speculate that the novel's first-person narration may obscure Drabble's own confusion on these matters.

Stovel, Nora F. "`A Feminine Ending?': Symbolism as Closure in the Novels of Margaret Drabble." *English Studies in Canada* 15 (March, 1989): 80-93.
Drabble gives closure to her novels by providing equivocal final symbols. Here Octavia, who had been viewed as a millstone, is transformed into a pearl. This suggests how Rosamund's love has changed how she regards her daughter.

_____. *Margaret Drabble, Symbolic Moralist.* Mercer Island, Wash.: Starmont House, 1989.
This novel's theme concerns, not illegitimacy, but childbirth and its effects on Rosamund. Stovel sums up the central opposing symbols as the Ivory Tower (where Rosamund the literary professional lives alone without love) and the Marketplace (the world of ordinary people and the National Health Service, which she must enter). When Rosamund feels passion for her ill baby, she has begun to adapt to the real world. Stovel explains the ambiguous symbol of the millstone itself.

Taylor, D. J. *After the War: The Novel and English Society Since 1945.* London: Chatto & Windus, 1993.
This novel displays all the usual (and contradictory) liberal attitudes toward class, wealth, status, and achievement.

Waugh, Patricia. *Feminine Fictions: Revisiting the Postmodern.* London: Routledge, 1989.
Rosamund yearns for a modern sense of wholeness and tries to deny her female qualities in favor of masculine rationality and objectivity. By the end of the novel, she has begin to connect with other people, in this case her infant daughter.

Whittier, Gayle. "Mistresses and Madonnas in the Novels of Margaret Drabble." In *Gender and Literary Voice*, edited by Janet Todd. No. 1, n.s., in *Women & Literature.* New York: Holmes & Meier, 1980.

Rosamund exemplifies part of Drabble's usual pattern, for pregnancy and motherhood energize her work.

Jerusalem the Golden, 1967.

Beards, Virginia K.   "Margaret Drabble: Novels of a Cautious Feminist."   *Critique* 15, no. 1 (1973): 35-47.   Reprinted in *Contemporary Women Novelists*, edited by Patricia Meyer Spacks. Englewood Cliffs, N.J.: Prentice-Hall, 1977.
This novel shows how society causes women to have trouble finding a career.   Clara is not so sexually inhibited as most women; she finds she must (and can) manipulate men to get what she wants. Really, she wins very little.

Blodgett, Harriet.   "Enduring Ties: Daughters and Mothers in Contemporary English Fiction by Women."   *South Atlantic Quarterly* 80 (Autumn, 1981): 441-453.
This article uses eight female authors to make a superficial survey the state of mother-daughter relationships. *Jerusalem the Golden* shows that daughters can successfully rebel and find salvation in London.   Even so, Clara gains an understanding of her mother and of her hometown.

Burkhart, Charles.   "Arnold Bennett and Margaret Drabble."   In *Margaret Drabble: Golden Realms*, edited by Dorey Schmidt. No. 4 in *Living Author Series*.   Edinburg, Tex.: Pan American University, 1982.
This novel owes much to Bennett in its central character, its theme, and its style.   Burkhart likes the account of Clara's childhood but thinks the novel suffers because it offers the fraudulent Denhams as an ideal.   Drabble's style suffers as well.

Connor, Steven.   *The English Novel in History 1950-1995*. London: Routledge, 1996.
In Chapter 2, Connor sees this work as a "condition of England novel," for it shows in significant detail Clara's often difficult cultural journey from the unsophisticated North to the worldly London.

Creighton, Joanne V. *Margaret Drabble*. London: Methuen, 1985.
In her chapter "Golden Realms," Creighton groups this novel with
two later novels, *The Needle's Eye* and *The Realms of Gold*. In
them, Drabble gradually broadens her theme and writes somewhat
traditional novels of characters in society using a third-person
point of view. In this novel, the narrator not only sympathizes
with Clara but also judges her, though the exact nature of the final
judgment is open to debate.

Edwards, Lee R. "Jerusalem the Golden: A Fable for Our Times."
Women's Studies 6, no. 3 (1979): 322-334.
Contemporary writers have difficulties with their heroines. They
cannot reward them in the old-fashioned way with marriage to a
handsome man. But they know that in real life the new kind of
assertive and intelligent women often must pay for their freedom.
In *Jerusalem the Golden*, Drabble provides a story to satisfy
modern readers. Clara is liberated and selfish; she demands a
golden world. She is ready for it when it appears in the form of
the Denhams, first the female Clelia, then the male Gabriel. In
her affair with Gabriel, Drabble allows Clara to avoid any version
of the usual female responsibilities. Clara even grows, for when
at the end she finds that she is the logical product of her mother's
repressed hopes, her past is exorcised. She has the energy to resist
being a victim, and ends the story with a sense of life's possibilities. Edwards implies this fable may be self-indulgent.

Gardiner, Judith Kegan. "The Heroine as Her Author's Daughter." In
Feminist Criticism: Essays on Theory, Poetry, and Prose, edited
by Cheryl L. Brown and Karen Olson. Metuchen, N.J.: Scarecrow
Press, 1978.
Women in the contemporary world must reject both their mothers
and their mothers' way of life in order to find true identity. This
pattern is found in many novels, including *Jerusalem the Golden*.
When Clara reads her mother's girlhood notebooks, she somehow
finds her identity and can leave home with her lover.

_____. "A Wake for Mother: The Maternal Deathbed in Women's
Fiction." *Feminist Studies* 4 (June, 1978): 164-165.
In recent fiction we find a new myth for women. Men, like Oedi-
pus, symbolically kill their fathers to take their places, but

contemporary female fictional characters kill their mothers so as not to become like them. Gardiner explores a daughter's search for identity in five novels by seeing how the each heroine lives through and expresses four aspects of mother-daughter relations. Like others, Clara's love exists side by side with rage against her mother and struggles against her. Both women are strong; Clara resembles her mother in her need to dominate. Even so, like other heroines, Clara exemplifies young women's tendency not to separate themselves as completely from their parents as men do. Clara never feels far from her mother, and when at the end she finds her mother's mementos, she knows she is descended from her. Some other aspects of typical relations, particularly those involving sex roles, are less clear in this novel, though her mother's death does allow Clara to resume her sex life. In all this, Gardiner does not ask us to approve of Clara.

Gullette, Margaret Morganroth.   "Ugly Ducklings and Swans: Margaret Drabble's Fable of Progress in the Middle Years." *Modern Language Quarterly* 44 (September, 1983): 285-304. Reprinted with minor changes in *Safe at Last in the Middle Years: The Invention of the Midlife Progress Novel: Saul Bellow, Margaret Drabble, Anne Tyler, John Updike.* Berkeley: University of California Press, 1988.
Clara is a perfect example of the way Drabble's basic myth operates. We do not suffer with Clara as an ugly duckling because the account of her childhood is only remembered. Like most swans, Clara has her doubts about her transformation, as does Drabble herself at the end.

Harper, Michael F.   "Margaret Drabble and the Resurrection of the English Novel." *Contemporary Literature* 23 (Spring, 1982): 145-168. Reprinted in *Critical Essays on Margaret Drabble*, edited by Ellen Cronan Rose. Boston: G. K. Hall, 1985.
Clara hates her own world of Northam. When she wonders what happens inside the houses she sees on her first trip to Paris, we understand that she wants not just to travel but to inhabit different worlds. She is shocked by the wonderful new world of the Denhams, but she learns to live in it. We should approve her change. Only readers who are bound by modernist and realist conventions of characters will be against it. A provocative reading.

Irvine, Lorna. "No Sense of An Ending: Drabble's Continuous
Fictions." In *Critical Essays on Margaret Drabble*, edited by
Ellen Cronan Rose. Boston: G. K. Hall, 1985.
Although the hymn she loves celebrates the apocalypse of Revela-
tion, Clara's own life will go on. The last sentences suggest that
Clara will not submit to the usual endings of fiction.

Johnston, Sue Ann. "The Daughter as Escape Artist." *Atlantis: A
Women's Studies Journal* 9 (Spring, 1984): 10-22.
Johnston tries to fit this novel (and two others) into an interesting
theory of how women must both break free from their mothers and
somehow come to terms with them. Johnston's theoretical
concerns sometimes distort her comments on *Jerusalem the
Golden*, but she makes valuable observations. She stresses how
much Clara thinks about and fears her mother throughout the
book: her thoughts about her hometown are really thoughts about
mother. Clara tries to separate herself from her mother, first by
constructing a purely negative image of her, and then by finding
attractive surrogate mothers such as Mrs. Denham. (Johnston
thinks Clelia also functions as a mother-figure.)
    Clara also tries to escape by breaking sexual taboos. Having an
affair with a married man is such a breaking, though sleeping
with Gabriel is also a way of bonding with her surrogate family.
Clara's breaking her ties to her mother causes her to think that her
pleasures have brought retribution. When she returns home, her
discovery that her mother was a complex human being does not
lead to a reconciliation. Nevertheless, it changes Clara. She can
accept Northam and feel compassion for her mother. Her fantasy
of the future (a hazy union with Gabriel and Clelia, a combination
of sex and maternal affection) may be silly, but she has achieved
separateness and is now better prepared to love herself and others.
Johnston's reading of the end of this novel is unique.

Lambert, Ellen Z. "Margaret Drabble and the Sense of Possibility."
University of Toronto Quarterly 49 (Spring, 1980): 228-251. Re-
printed in *Critical Essays on Margaret Drabble*, edited by Ellen
Cronan Rose. Boston: G. K. Hall, 1985.
Here is another of Drabble's energetic and hopeful heroines,
though Clara, coming from the lower middle class in the north of
England, is less lucky than some of the others. Clara is conscious

of her own luck and development. She realizes how lucky she is in finding the Denhams. Yet love eludes her, perhaps because she has had to work so hard to get close to it.

Le Franc, Bolivar. "An Interest in Guilt." *Books and Bookmen* 14 (September, 1969): 20-21.
Drabble thinks this novel has a cold density. Clara expresses the novelist's worst side.

Myer, Valerie Grosvenor. *Margaret Drabble: Puritanism and Permissiveness.* New York: Barnes & Noble Books, 1974.
Clara is a typical early heroine, for she rebels against her grim puritanical family and background. Yet she cannot divest herself of some puritan traits; she is energetic and hard-working, cheap and ungenerous. Her admiration for the Denhams shows she can be deceived by false gold. She has few moral scruples. Myers finds it hard to praise the resolution Clara achieves and thinks that Drabble may have been confused.

_____. *Margaret Drabble: A Reader's Guide.* New York: St. Martin's Press, 1991.
A very helpful essay. Myer identifies important literary and philosophical allusions and discusses some literary parallels at length: Thackeray's *Vanity Fair*, Christina Rossetti's "Goblin Market," and most important Evelyn Waugh's *Brideshead Revisited.* Myer focuses on the novel's main problem: What are we to think of Clara and her fascination with the Denhams? Is the Denhams' house a new Jerusalem or just a fashionable, charming place? Is Clara ultimately a social success or a moral failure? Myer surveys the novel's major critics and comes down on Clara's side, though with reservations.

Pearson, Carol, and Katherine Pope. *The Female Hero in American and British Literature.* New York: R. R. Bowker, 1981.
In developing their theory of the female heroine, the authors cite Clara as a woman who finds it difficult to escape from her mother. When she does escape, she continually fears that she will have to return home and become like her mother. As with other heroines, she is liberated by her mother's approaching death and by discovering that her mother once had youthful dreams.

Raban, Jonathan. *The Technique of Modern Fiction: Essays in Practical Criticism*. London: Edward Arnold, 1968.
Raban quotes the passage describing Clara at Le Bourget airport and finds that Drabble employs two different styles. When Clara is thinking, Drabble employs many dependent clauses. When Clara is acting, Drabble uses coordination, parenthetical remarks, and strings of phrases. These constructions suggest that all of Clara's actions are equally important or unimportant—something Clara herself thinks is true.

Rose, Ellen Cronan. *Equivocal Figures: The Novels of Margaret Drabble*. Totowa, N.J.: Barnes & Noble Books, 1980.
Rose admires this novel as being a great step forward in Drabble's career as a novelist. Drabble is autobiographical here, but achieves control by employing a third-person narrator to achieve distance and by creating patterns of images and literary allusions. For her plot and to some extent for her theme, she took several Arnold Bennett novels as her models. Rose thinks that Clara differs from Bennett characters in that, unlike Bennett's Hilda Lessways but like Drabble's own earlier heroines, Clara does not really change. Though she seems somewhat free at the end, she is really imprisoned by what she has made of herself.

_____. "Margaret Drabble: Surviving the Future." *Critique* 15, no. 1 (1973): 5-20.
Drabble's short story "A Voyage to Cythera" helps us read this novel. In both fictions, a woman feels the lure of a romantic world full of passion. At the end, Clara still feels the lure of a life of tenderness and intrigue. But like the heroine of the short story, Clara is not completely victorious. She too is essentially excluded from the warmth of real passion.

Roxman, Susanna. *Guilt and Glory: Studies in Margaret Drabble's Novels 1963-80*. Stockholm: Almquist & Wiksell International, 1984.
Like others, Roxman sees Arnold Bennett's novels behind *Jerusalem the Golden*, and a de Maupassant story as well. But Roxman sees Thackeray's *Vanity Fair* as a more important source, both in strains of images (gold and glittering) and in central characters. Both authors are finally somewhat ambiguous in the judgments of

their heroines. Roxman finds the novel suggests the importance of privilege in society, but, since Clara remains unpunished for any of her shortcomings, a reader will find little moralizing in the novel.

Sadler, Lynn Veach. *Margaret Drabble*. Boston: Twayne, 1986.
In Chapter 2, Sadler summarizes the plot and discusses the characters. The Denhams are wonderful, but flawed; Phillipa is enigmatic. Clara lacks morals and, in spite of using many men, is not very sexual. She ends up well. She is less rigid than before and still energetic.

Stovel, Nora F. "`A Feminine Ending?': Symbolism as Closure in the Novels of Margaret Drabble." *English Studies in Canada* 15 (March, 1989): 80-93.
Drabble gives closure to her novels by providing equivocal final symbols. Here Clara misinterprets the golden Jerusalem as referring to a terrestrial paradise and at the end of the novel still embraces a gilded world.

_____. "`A Great Kick at Misery': Lawrence's and Drabble's Rebellion Against the Fatalism of Bennett." In *D. H. Lawrence's Literary Inheritors*, edited by Keith Cushman and Dennis Jackson. New York: St. Martin's Press, 1991.
Critics have noted that D. H. Lawrence's *The Lost Girl* attacks the Victorian values of Arnold Bennett's *Anna of the Five Towns*. Stovel argues that in *Jerusalem the Golden* Drabble joins this attack but differs from Lawrence in significant ways. Stovel explores the similarities these novels share: in all three, a heroine grows up in the misery of the industrial midlands in an atmosphere of puritanical repression. Bennett's Anna submits to her constraints, but both Lawrence and Drabble create heroines who rebel and escape repression in order to search for new and satisfying freedoms. Lawrence and Drabble differ what freedom is. Alvina in *The Lost Girl* achieves happiness through sex; she is happy to be dominated by her Italian lover. Clara's state at the end of her novel is more unsettled, but she is not under any man's thumb.

_____. *Margaret Drabble, Symbolic Moralist.* Mercer Island, Wash.: Starmont House, 1989.
Stovel echoes some of the material in the article above. At the end, Clara has not so much triumphed as alienated the reader by her bad behavior during her second visit to Paris. Her return to London is a return to a superficial life. At one point, however, Clara seems to understand her limitations. Stovel is persuasive when she points out the unappealing sides of the Denhams' supposedly golden household.

_____. "Margaret Drabble's Golden Vision." In *Margaret Drabble: Golden Realms*, edited by Dorey Schmidt. No. 4 in *Living Author Series*. Edinburg, Tex.: Pan American University, 1982.
Stovel sees a vision of a golden world at the heart of this novel. Clara yearns for a golden Jerusalem in society; Stovel points out that Clara gets her idea from a bad translation of a hymn, corrected in later editions. Stovel also maintains that Clara is wrong to think she has found this golden world in London. Far from triumphing, by denying her childhood roots Clara becomes hardened by her experiences. Stovel notes that in her biography of Arnold Bennett, Drabble recounts that as an adult she once saw her hometown of Sheffield as golden, much as the older Clara briefly finds Northam less ugly than before.

The Waterfall, 1969.

Beards, Virginia K. "Margaret Drabble: Novels of a Cautious Feminist." *Critique* 15, no. 1 (1973): 35-47. Reprinted in *Contemporary Women Novelists*, edited by Patricia Meyer Spacks. Englewood Cliffs, N.J.: Prentice-Hall, 1977.
The most interesting of Beards's analyses. Jane discovers and represents women's tragic state in ways that contradict patriarchal ideas about what women want. She moves from a loveless and debilitating marriage to a state of bondage to the man who liberated her from frigidity. Jane is not fulfilled but lonely. Drabble may imply that happiness is not possible.

Berg, Temma F. "From Pamela to Jane Gray: or, How Not to Become
the Heroine of Your Own Text." *Studies in the Novel* 17
(Summer, 1985): 115-137.

A very detailed argument full of convincing parallels.
Contemporary women do not need to give up reading traditional
and phallocentric novels, but they can learn to read old novels in
new ways. Women can learn to do this from fictional women who
have revised the texts they have read. Despite how critics have
read the novel in the past, Richardson's *Pamela* reinterpreted the
Cinderella story: Pamela really seduces Mr. B. *Jane Eyre* in turn
revises Pamela's story. Rochester reads it and agrees; at the end of
the book he and Jane are equals in reciprocal happiness, though
unfortunately Rochester's emasculation has been the price.

Drabble's Jane Gray sees Rochester as a victim and rewrites her
story so that the heroine can have her hero intact. Though Jane
seems passive, she is actually powerful as an author and will not
give the story a traditional ending. Unlike Rochester, her James is
not a reader; he feels no guilt. Yet he and Jane are equals, for
they each awake each other, Jane from frigidity, James from a
coma. Yet even though James may escape Rochester's fate,
Drabble sees both him and Jane as helpless. So Drabble's and
Jane's revision of the story has, not the usual happy ending, but a
postmodern conclusion which implies ongoing suffering.

Bergmann, Harriet F. "'A Piercing Virtue': Emily Dickinson in Margaret Drabble's *The Waterfall*. *Modern Fiction Studies* 36
(Summer, 1990): 181-193.

Because this novel's epigraph is from Emily Dickinson, Bergman
compares Jane to the character of the American poet as seen in
her poetry. Both Jane and Emily have a Calvinistic sense of
doom, but neither has a traditional religious faith. Both are artists
and have an unusual ability to distance themselves from themselves. Not only do they realize they will not attain their desires,
but they actively choose to renounce worldly satisfaction. They
differ in that Jane seems to accept her femaleness more explicitly
than does Dickinson, but in different ways both seem to be in control of their lives.

Bromberg, Pamela S. "The Development of Narrative Technique in Margaret Drabble's Novels." *Journal of Narrative Technique* 16 (Fall, 1986): 179-191.

This novel marks a turning in Drabble's career. Where before her novels were deterministic and centered on the psychology of the heroine, this novel strikes out in the direction of self-reflexiveness and experimentation. The story is told in traditional fashion in the third person and in a feminist way in the first person. This first-person narrative is Jane's attempt to tell the truth about life for a woman in her time, a truth that cannot be told in the old forms. A tidy ending is typical of older novels, but this novel has no traditional ending.

Creighton, Joanne V. *Margaret Drabble*. London: Methuen, 1985.

In her chapter "Bird-cages," Creighton groups this book with Drabble's first three novels, for all are first-person narratives that raise the question of how much distance a reader senses between the heroine and Drabble herself. *The Waterfall* is unusually complex. Creighton finds that Jane and Drabble both discover postmodern attitudes toward fiction.

_____. "The Reader and Modern and Post-Modern Fiction." *College Literature* 9 (Fall, 1982): 216-230.

An admirable and important article in which Creighton first explains how earlier theory (the New Criticism) was closely related to works of modernist fiction (such as Woolf's *To the Lighthouse*). In a similar way, recent reader-response theory shares assumptions with postmodern fiction. As reader-response criticism stresses what New Critics ignored, so postmodern novels like *The Waterfall* reintroduce the reader into the work of art. Like John Fowles's *The French Lieutenant's Woman*, *The Waterfall* seems to be a traditional story for its first fifty pages until the author then shatters any illusion. But in Drabble, the reader gets not just two different endings (as in Fowles), but two quite different explanations of what happens to Jane.

Although the third-person story is shaped by the conventions of romance, Jane's first-person story is not necessarily any more truthful. It is often self-justifying, playfully obscure, and inconsistent; Jane shows obvious blind spots. Moreover, Jane asserts in the first person that her romantic fantasy with James is very real indeed. Readers are puzzled. Should they be content simply to experience the flow of words? Should they try to fill in gaps to construct some sort of unity? Would this unity be the same for all readers? Creighton thinks that attempts to find unity will fail.

_____. "Reading Margaret Drabble's *The Waterfall.*" In *Critical Essays on Margaret Drabble*, edited by Ellen Cronan Rose. Boston: G. K. Hall, 1985. A reprint of part of the author's "The Reader and Modern and Post-Modern Fiction." *College Literature* 9 (Fall, 1982): 216-230.
Readers of this novel must wonder what to believe—the third-person narrative which we discover was written and edited by Jane? Jane's first-person narrative in which she herself creates fantasies and undercuts them? Or Drabble, the elusive implied author? Is Jane psychotic or devious? The novel as a whole resists neat summation; the gaps in its narrative invite the readers to speculate. Arguing against other recent critics (Libby, Beards, and Rose), Creighton thinks that Jane's life as we see it has no more closure than the novel itself. She thinks that by the end of the book Drabble probably admires Jane's resilience and what progress she has made.

_____. "Sisterly Symbiosis: Margaret Drabble's *The Waterfall* and A. S. Byatt's *The Game. Mosaic: A Journal for the Interdisciplinary Study of Literature* 20 (Winter, 1987): 15-29.
Creighton begins with the fact that Drabble and the novelist A. S. Byatt are sisters and then uses psychological theories to illuminate their novels and to speculate on their lives. Creighton focuses specifically on *The Waterfall* and Byatt's *The Game*. Both novels deal with the necessity female artists feel to be aggressive and to escape from traditional structures. Both novels also deal with sisterly relations (antagonistic and reciprocal) as well as with female oedipal problems. In *The Waterfall*, Jane makes Lucy and James into surrogate and pre-oedipal parents before making her oedipal switch from female to male. Creighton thinks that Drabble sees the situation from only one sister's point of view and minimizes the consequences; Byatt, however, tells the painful story from both sides.

Cushman, Keith. "Dabbling in the Tradition: *The Waterfall* and *The Mill on the Floss*." In *The Modernists: Studies in a Literary Phenomenon: Essays in Honor of Harry T. Moore*. Rutherford, N.J.: Fairleigh Dickinson University Press, 1987.

A neat and thorough analysis of the similarities between this novel and George Eliot's. Like other Drabble novels, *The Waterfall* derives significance from parallels and allusions to master-pieces of English literature. Here the basic groupings of characters have much in common. Jane is like Maggie Tulliver, except Jane goes to bed with her lover. Both cousins are named Lucy, but Drabble updates her woman by making her promiscuous. Stephen and Philip resemble James and Malcolm, and both sets of parents are very respectable. Fate and determinism play large roles in each novel. A central contrast is in the place of water: Maggie drowns, but Jane's waterfall is her liberation. These obvious parallels make a significant contrast between Eliot's moral certainties and Drabble's modern ambiguities.

Emmitt, Helen V. "'Drowned in a Willing Sea': Freedom and Drowning in Eliot, Chopin, and Drabble." *Tulsa Studies in Women's Literature* 12 (Fall, 1993): 315-332.

Emmitt makes several very interesting points when she compares Jane to two nineteenth century heroines: Maggie from George Eliot's *The Mill on the Floss* and to Edna from Kate Chopin's *The Awakening*. Both earlier heroines found marriage, the fate society and literature prescribed for them, to be unsuitable. Both died by drowning in manners that were satisfying in fantasy and in literature.

For Jane Gray, on the other hand, drowning came by a water-fall, a symbolic rendering of an orgasm. Jane passively achieves what Maggie and Edna could not achieve: a world of complete love. But Jane's story does not end there; Drabble shows her heroine breaking her ties to the past. After the car crash, Jane rejects the role literature would give her and fends for herself by herself. Drabble gives her the first-person voice the earlier hero-ines did not have. When she and James visit Goredale Scar, the reader may think this natural feature is another symbol, but Jane, who now lives in the real world, does not: it is what it is.

Frye, Joanne S. *Living Stories, Telling Lives: Women and the Novel in Contemporary Experience.* Ann Arbor: University of Michigan Press, 1986.
Brief remarks on Drabble's use of both first- and third-person narratives. Readers can sense Jane's problems.

Fuoroli, Caryn. "Sophistry or Simple Truth?: Narrative Technique in Margaret Drabble's *The Waterfall*." *Journal of Narrative Technique* 11 (Spring, 1981): 110-124.
A critical and detailed view of the way Drabble handles the shifts in point of view. In this novel's early sections, Drabble the author keeps her distance from Jane, but later on the author and Jane become confused. Jane raises many questions which are simply dropped; Drabble provides no perspective on what is happening. Fuoroli thinks that Drabble's lack of control makes this novel less valuable than what its early sections promise.

Gilligan, Carol. *In a Different Voice.* Cambridge: Harvard University Press, 1982.
In Chapter 5, "Women's Rights and Women's Judgment," Gilligan discusses how college-age women try to deal with important moral dilemmas. She compares this novel to George Eliot's *The Mill on the Floss* to delineate the responses women have when women's rights conflict with moral responsibilities. One kind of response is evasion: women sacrifice themselves or they drift irresponsibly. Jane's initial passiveness in *The Waterfall* is an example of drifting. But Jane is too truthful to deny her responsibility for long. Like the college women Gilligan interviewed, Jane takes responsibility, asserts her integrity. Like other women, she faces the charge of selfishness when she stands up for her individual rights. Jane shows that this charge, one which tormented Maggie in Eliot's novel, can torment her as well. One of her answers is to try to create a new morality to condone what she is doing. Gilligan's chapter is not a full interpretation, but it clarifies the novel's moral issues.

Greene, Gayle. "Margaret Drabble's *The Waterfall*: New System, New Morality." *Novel: A Forum on Fiction* 22 (Fall, 1988): 45-65. Reprinted in *Writing the Woman Artist: Essays on Poetics,*

Politics, and Portraiture, edited by Suzanne W. Jones. Philadelphia: University of Pennsylvania Press, 1991.
Jane should be seen not only as a lover but also as a female writer who uses ways of writing to move toward a new way for women to live. Green thinks that this novel owes a debt to Doris Lessing's *The Golden Notebook* and points out many useful parallels between the two. More important, Greene enlists many contemporary critics to help her make the contrast between the old kind of story Jane writes in the third person and the new kind of story she writes in the first. The old story is full of literary allusions and poetic figures of speech; its characters are conventional (the dominant man, the passive woman), its closure strong, its moral firm: adultery is punished by death. Although Jane's new story analyzes and criticizes the old one, it is not satisfactory either. By the end, Jane seems to merge her stories and get at least some of what she wants. Her puns suggest a new story of mutual passion, a love that neither binds or destroys.

Gullette, Margaret Morganroth. "Ugly Ducklings and Swans: Margaret Drabble's Fable of Progress in the Middle Years." *Modern Language Quarterly* 44 (September, 1983): 285-304. Reprinted with minor changes in *Safe at Last in the Middle Years: The Invention of the Midlife Progress Novel: Saul Bellow, Margaret Drabble, Anne Tyler, John Updike.* Berkeley: University of California Press, 1988.
Drabble's basic myth of transformation applies even here. Although Jane is trapped in many ways, her imagination is free.

Hannay, John. *The Intertexuality of Fate: A Study of Margaret Drabble.* Columbia: University of Missouri Press, 1986.
The intertext of this novel is tragic romance. In the third-person story Jane writes, its conventions show clearly: the passive heroine, the influence of fate, the allusions to other tragic lovers. At first the reader only suspects that the author is doctoring reality in a conventional way. The reader knows this for sure when the romantic story is subverted and commented on by Jane in a first-person narrative, supposedly a more realistic device. Jane thereby claims that her first-person account is realistic and true because she has openly rejected the intertext of romance. Yet realism to Jane is more extravagant than fiction: she claims she and James

were fated to love. Jane denies romantic formulae only to reassert them in a realistic context.

What then does Hannay think about Jane? She cannot escape the intertext, either in her writing or in her life. Readers may see Jane and James's love as bondage and Jane as infantile and neurotic. But life will not conform to Jane's intertext. The car crash could have ended a tragic romance, but it does not, and even Jane cannot give in to her intertext, either in the first or in the third person. Hannay analyzes the rest of the novel as showing Jane's vacillations between affirming tragic romance, denying it, and imagining other, more satisfying intertexts. A stimulating and challenging chapter.

Hardin, Nancy S. "An Interview with Margaret Drabble." *Contemporary Literature* 14 (Summer, 1973): 273-295.
Drabble says she feels guilty about writing this novel, for not everyone can be lucky enough to feel their life has been changed by sexual love. She did not set out to write in both the first- and third-person perspectives.

Harper, Michael F. "Margaret Drabble and the Resurrection of the English Novel." *Contemporary Literature* 23 (Spring, 1982): 145-168. Reprinted in *Critical Essays on Margaret Drabble*, edited by Ellen Cronan Rose. Boston: G. K. Hall, 1985.
Jane lives in many different worlds and seeks to find some kind of unity. She is painfully aware of being alone and worries that nobody else resembles her. But like a novelist, she begins to trust that she can at least partially enter into the world of another person. Jane's problems lies at the heart of Drabble's own as a postmodern novelist.

Irvine, Lorna. "No Sense of An Ending: Drabble's Continuous Fictions." In *Critical Essays on Margaret Drabble*, edited by Ellen Cronan Rose. Boston: G. K. Hall, 1985.
Unlike the heroines of Drabble's earlier novels, Jane discusses the problems of endings in general and specifically the possibility of giving her own story either a morally or aesthetically satisfactory one. Yet Jane rejects closure for her story. By doing this, she rejects death and fate and affirms her freedom to choose.

Kelly, Darlene. "'Either Way, I stand Condemned': A Woman's Place
in Margaret Atwood's *The Edible Woman* and Margaret Drabble's
The Waterfall." *English Studies in Canada* 21 (September, 1995):
320-332.
Kelly finds that both novels show that, at least in the 1960's,
women could find satisfaction neither in marriages nor in affairs.
In Atwood's novel, marriage is even more repellent than in Drabble's. Even though Drabble has said that Jane is saved by her affair with James, Kelly thinks that Drabble's opinion is undermined
by the novel itself. Even though Jane and James continue to have
trysts, their sublime experience in Yorkshire is shown to be
hollow by the bitter mixture of whiskey and chalk that James
drinks afterwards.

Levitt, Morton P. "The New Victorians: Margaret Drabble as
Trollope." In *Margaret Drabble: Golden Realms*, edited by Dorey
Schmidt. No. 4 in *Living Author Series*. Edinburg, Tex.: Pan
American University, 1982.
Drabble's narratives are usually Victorian in their use of omnis-
cience. This novel seems at first to be different, for it changes
abruptly from the third- into the first-person perspective. But
Jane's first-person narrative is not convincing, for it shifts into the
narrator's third-person voice.

Libby, Marion Vlastos. "Fate and Feminism in the Novels of Margaret
Drabble" *Contemporary Literature* 16 (Spring, 1975): 175-192.
In this novel, Drabble reaches a low point. Jane does not fight
patriarchal society. She is passive and self destructive. She
allows herself to become a sex-object. Drabble sometimes seems
to endorse Jane's attitude.

Manheimer, Joan. "Margaret Drabble and the Journey to the Self."
Studies in the Literary Imagination 11 (Fall, 1978): 127-143.
Reprinted in *British Novelists Since 1900*, edited by Jack I. Biles.
New York: AMS Press, 1987.
As opposed to earlier heroines, Jane achieves a kind of
independence. Her "rescue" by James is pure fantasy, but the act
of telling her story is not. She has escaped, but perhaps only to a
neurotic life.

Myer, Valerie Grosvenor. *Margaret Drabble: Puritanism and Permissiveness*. New York: Barnes & Noble Books, 1974.
Jane is like other early Drabble heroines, for she rejects her puritan heritage, yet cannot escape it. Jane is particularly aware of what she is doing, and worries about her adultery. She may see James's love as her salvation, but it is her corruption as well.

_____. *Margaret Drabble: A Reader's Guide*. New York: St. Martin's Press, 1991.
Myer as usual discusses Drabble's literary allusions, from Virgina Woolf and Thomas Hardy to John Bunyan. She also relates the book's division into first- and third-person narration to the differing influences of Woolf and Arnold Bennett. She is most interested in Jane Gray's first person story of her marriage, adultery, and deliverance. Jane's narrative reflects self-consciously on storytelling (especially on the endings of stories) and employs symbols in greater numbers than had been usual for Drabble. The waterfall itself is a both a female sexual symbol and a symbol of spiritual rebirth. In her adultery with the somewhat satanic James, Jane experiences Eve's fortunate fall into a kind of salvation.

Nicolaisen, W. F. H. "'What a Name. Stephen Halifax': Onomastic Modes in Three Novels by Margaret Drabble." *Literary Onomastics Studies* 10 (1983): 269-283.
Drabble uses names significantly in this novel. We never learn Jane's maiden name, though her married name gains significance by being the same as an executed Queen. Nicolaison analyzes Jane's naming of her second child "Bianca."

Parker, Gillian, and Janet Todd. "Margaret Drabble." In *Women Writers Talking*, edited by Janet Todd. New York: Holmes & Meier, 1983.
Drabble says that feminists do not like this novel because it implies (rightly) that she thinks that the passion of heterosexual love is important.

Peel, Ellen. "Subject, Object, and the Alternation of First- and Third-Person Narration in Novels by Alther, Atwood, and Drabble:

Toward a Theory of Feminist Aesthetics." *Critique: Studies in Contemporary Fiction* 30 (Winter, 1989): 107-122.
Peel speculates that one structural feature of many *feminist* novels is the alternation of first- and third-person narration. She thinks that this alteration shows a feminist (and perhaps only contemporary feminist) sense of woman's double role as an active subject and as a passive object of male eyes. Peel compares Jane in *The Waterfall* to the heroines of several other novels with alternating narration and finds that, more than the others, Jane grows into a kind of mental health. A sign of this health is the way her third-person or objective narrator grows closer to her first-person or subjective one. The ending of the novel is not conclusive because Jane is finally healthy.

Rabinowitz, Nancy S.   "Talc on the Scotch: Art and Morality in Margaret Drabble's *The Waterfall.*"   *International Journal of Women's Studies* 5 (May-June 1982): 236-245.
Jane (like Drabble herself) acknowledges the force of the moral patterns of traditional Victorian novels like George Eliot's *The Mill on the Floss.* She experiences a sublime moment in nature and recognizes the pull of tragic endings. But, although she does not reject these forces, she (like Drabble) undercuts them. She achieves a degree of happiness, not so much by means of her affair with James, but from the active independence readers see at the end of the novel.

Regan, Nancy.   "A Home of One's Own: Women's Bodies in Recent Women's Fiction."   *Journal of Popular Culture* 11 (Spring, 1978): 772-788.
In many works of fiction, houses are symbolic of the human body. Significantly, at the beginning of this novel Jane owns her house (she is ultimately in control of her body), but is a sloppy housekeeper (she is not at ease within it). Later, Jane is saved by mutual seduction. Regan approves of *The Waterfall* as envisioning a happiness that involves a compromise of individuality and thinks that Jane comes closer than most heroines to having a happy sex life.

Rose, Ellen Cronan.   *Equivocal Figures: The Novels of Margaret Drabble.*   Totowa, N.J.: Barnes & Noble Books, 1980.

An important and challenging discussion. Drabble returns to Simone de Beauvoir's question in *The Second Sex*: Can one be both a female and an autonomous person? Rose thinks Drabble shows how a woman can be both. By her liaison with James, Jane discovers her full and passive sexuality. By actively switching her narrative back and forth from first to third person, Jane shows how she can express her active side as well. Like Doris Lessing in *The Golden Notebook*, Drabble in this novel writes both about being a woman and about being a woman artist. By the end, as Jane becomes less and less divided as a person, first and third persons merge. Rose brilliantly sums up her argument by close analyses of the novel's last pages and sentences.

_____. "Feminine Endings—And Beginnings." *Contemporary Literature* 21 (Winter, 1980): 81-99.
An adaptation of material from *Equivocal Figures*.

_____. "The Sexual Politics of Narration: Margaret Drabble's Feminist Fiction." *Studies in the Novel* 20 (Spring, 1988): 86-99.
Rose's thesis is that Drabble's structures are feminist ones that work against the imposing of patriarchal structures on experience. Here Jane frees herself from the tyranny of the various closures of romance to try to tell her story honestly.

Roxman, Susanna. *Guilt and Glory: Studies in Margaret Drabble's Novels 1963-80*. Stockholm: Almquist & Wiksell International, 1984.
Though Jane as a modern woman differs greatly from Maggie Tulliver, *The Mill on the Floss* by George Eliot lies explicitly behind this novel. Jane is a fatalist and carries self-denial to extremes. Later on when she finds sexual happiness and freedom, she worries about the privileges she has received. Perhaps, she thinks, the car crash and even the possibility of blood clots are retribution. Roxman finds it difficult to say what Drabble thinks on these issues. In a later chapter, Roxman analyzes twenty passages in which Drabble employs images of water and other liquids, not just as suggestive descriptions but as tropes. Although most authors use fire to talk about love, Drabble employs liquid metaphors and similes to connote love and lovemaking. Roxman

makes comparisons to Jane Austen, to Matthew Arnold, and to the seventeenth century poet Henry Vaughan.

Rubenstein, Roberta. "Margaret Drabble's *The Waterfall*: The Myth of Psyche, Romantic Tradition, and the Female Quest." In *Margaret Drabble: Golden Realms*, edited by Dorey Schmidt. No. 4 in *Living Author Series*. Edinburg, Tex.: Pan American University, 1982.

A closely argued and important essay in which the author uses myth to interpret a novel many readers have found puzzling. Rubenstein sees Drabble making parallels with classical myths (especially Cupid and Psyche) and legends (Tristan and Iseult) to explain Jane Gray's experience in her real contemporary world. The parallels to Jane's story are not mathematically exact, but illuminating. Jane herself is conscious of how her struggles have a mythic, even sacred dimension as she sacrifices herself to her lover James, who releases her from her prison of frigidity. After the accident, she performs the tasks of Psyche for James/Eros. Her reward is not undying love, but a new, stronger self, one who tells her story in the first person. But critics and readers ask: How are we to regard the heroine at the end of the novel? Is she limited? selfish? Rubenstein thinks Drabble leaves us with a paradox: contemporary women are torn between desire and the need for autonomy. Perhaps, Rubenstein suggests, this dilemma is resolved by Kate in *The Middle Ground*.

Sadler, Lynn Veach. *Margaret Drabble*. Boston: Twayne, 1986.

In Chapter 4, Sadler labels Jane as helpless. Jane is even called repulsive for the unhealthy passiveness she shows at the beginning of the novel. She misuses literary references to excuse her behavior and is not a good mother. Toward the end of the novel, Jane changes for the better: she acts and feels somewhat free.

Skoller, Eleanor Honig. "The Progress of a Letter: Truth, Feminism, and *The Waterfall*." In *Critical Essays on Margaret Drabble*, edited by Ellen Cronan Rose. Boston: G. K. Hall, 1985.

A difficult essay in which Skollar argues that although feminists often naïvely want to render women's experience directly, this is impossible. Drabble has usually been read naïvely as well; this novel, for example, can be seen as a sophisticated modern tale of adultery. But Drabble is really experimenting with how women's experience can be approached with words. Interesting discussions of how *The Waterfall's* characters match up with royal pretenders from British history and of how the so-called feminine endings of novels are related to the feminine endings in poetry.

Soule, George. "The Waterfall." In *Cyclopedia of Literary Characters II*, edited by Frank N. Magill. Pasadena, Calif.: Salem Press, 1990.

A survey of this novel's characters.

Spivak, Gayatri Chakravorty. "Feminism and Critical Theory." In *For Alma Mater: Theory and Practice in Feminist Scholarship*, edited by Paula A. Treichler and Cheris Kramarae. Urbana: University of Illinois Press, 1985.

As part of a general discussion of literary theory, Spivak cites *The Waterfall* as example of a woman's novel that manages to avoid issues of class and race. The whole novel is told from and takes place in a privileged world. Jane's attitudes are prejudiced and her shifts of points of view enable her to avoid many issues. Although Spivak wonders if the narrator is ironic, she asserts, as she did in her earlier article, that Drabble does not consider the stories of lower class people worth telling.

_____. "Three Feminist Readings: McCullers, Drabble, Habermas." *Union Seminary Quarterly Review* 35 (Fall/Winter 1979-1980): 15-34.

Spivak argues that it is necessary to carry on feminist, racial, and class struggles in daily lives. Drabble's novel is useful, not because she treats these matters seriously, but because it manifests the kind of female passivity to avoid and the atmosphere of class privilege to be criticized. Even though Jane shows some sympathy for a lower-class boy in her father's school, she herself is of such high status that she has had her poetry read on the BBC. The social class to which Jane belongs contains the only people Drabble thinks are worth writing about.

Stovel, Nora F. "`A Feminine Ending?': Symbolism as Closure in the Novels of Margaret Drabble." *English Studies in Canada* 15 (March, 1989): 80-93.

Jane consciously considers how to end her novel traditionally. She (and Drabble) gives closure by providing the equivocal final symbol of Goredale Scar. Its suggestions echo the novel's other symbols, and its two waterfalls suggest two ongoing loves, though with no hint of the commitments that end traditional love stories.

_____. *Margaret Drabble, Symbolic Moralist.* Mercer Island, Wash.: Starmont House, 1989.

Stovel is an accomplished guide through this complex novel, in which symbols become a tool for exploring the psyche. Stovel identifies water (and waterfalls) as the central symbol of love. Flowers suggest love's powers as does the kiss that awakens the sleeping princess. After the car crash, these symbols are reversed; Jane feels dry, flowers wilt, love dies. But then Jane as princess awakens James from a coma. Love revives, and Drabble's symbols recover their original force.

Walker, Nancy. "Women Drifting: Drabble's *The Waterfall* and Chopin's *The Awakening.*" *Denver Quarterly* 17 (Winter, 1983): 88-96.

The central characters in both novels see themselves as different from most women, for they drift without much regard for what will happen to them. Jane differs from Chopin's Edna in that she pays some attention to society's rules. Her story ends differently as well, as is appropriate for someone living in the Twentieth Century.

Waugh, Patricia. *Feminine Fictions: Revisiting the Postmodern.* London: Routledge, 1989.

The third-person narration presents Jane's story as a quest for the romantic whole self, but in the first person Jane is critical. By the end of the novel, Waugh thinks Jane begins to give over her role as victim.

Whittier, Gayle. "Mistresses and Madonnas in the Novels of Margaret Drabble." In *Gender and Literary Voice*, edited by Janet Todd. No. 1, n.s., in *Women & Literature.* New York: Holmes & Meier, 1980.

Jane exemplifies (in a somewhat disjointed order) most parts of Drabble's archetype of motherhood, a pattern that involves risk and suffering in all its stages. Her children's father is absent; Jane as a mother is sexually attractive to James, even though (or perhaps because) their sex violates a taboo; interestingly, when she is sexually active, she is not creative. Yet their love cannot last; when Jane finally must choose, she chooses her children. James is a St. Joseph figure: not a real husband, but a needed surrogate. After his accident, he resembles the children in other Drabble novels, for the heroine nurses him to health. His problem is that he interfered with Drabble's myth of maternity.

Wyatt, Jean. "Escaping Literary Designs: The Politics of Reading and Writing in Margaret Drabble's *The Waterfall*." *Perspectives on Contemporary Literature* 11 (1985): 37-45.
A lucid analysis of this novel using contemporary theory. Wyatt thinks that when Jane Gray interprets her fictional experience through the plots of nineteenth century novels like *Jane Eyre*, she typifies the way real women often see their real experiences. In her third-person narrative, Jane excludes everything that does not contribute to the story of romantic love; the images and symbols she uses are also borrowed from older romantic novels. But Jane fights back when she turns to the first person. Her narrative now is much more random; she includes un-romantic details; she avoids old-fashioned closure. Her act of writing becomes the way she gets away from romantic feelings, and Drabble makes the reader do the same. Then Drabble seems to ask: is there such a thing as authentic love? The answer is complex. Jane ends up coping well with the real world in which love, though it is not now the only force, still has some power.

Zeman, Anthea. *Presumptuous Girls: Women and Their World in the Serious Woman's Novel*. London: Weidenfeld & Nicholson, 1977. Zeman prizes Drabble for her frankness about sex and love. One frank admission is that the advances of medical science are not really important. Drabble's account of erotic love dispels the evasions of romance novels.

The Needle's Eye, 1972.

Creighton, Joanne V. *Margaret Drabble*. London: Methuen, 1985.
In her chapter "Golden Realms," Creighton sees this novel as ostensibly told in a traditional omniscient-narrator, third-person fashion. It asks if people can remake themselves and answers that neither Rose or Simon can. But traditional narrative methods are made complex because we see so much of Rose through Simon's biased eyes; readers eventually see that she is not so wonderful as he thinks. Ultimately, the novel is only marginally traditional because its third-person narrator does not display a clear set of values. Drabble suggests that there are no solutions to Rose's and Simon's problems.

Davidson, Arnold E. "Parables of Grace in Drabble's *The Needle's Eye*." In *Margaret Drabble: Golden Realms*, edited by Dorey Schmidt. No. 4 in *Living Author Series*. Edinburg, Tex.: Pan American University, 1982.
Sets the novel's realistic action against the parable suggested in its title: how can a rich man enter heaven? Drabble's story is more complicated than that of her artistic ancestor, John Bunyan of *A Pilgrim's Progress*. Drabble asks: Should one seek God's grace if it will hurt others? Both Rose and Simon try to do good but do not completely succeed. Yet even though the end of the novel is not clear, there may be some hope. Although Rose and Simon have not obtained grace, they are striving for it.

Dixson, Barbara. "Patterned Figurative Language in *The Needle's Eye*." In *Margaret Drabble: Golden Realms*, edited by Dorey Schmidt. No. 4 in *Living Author Series*. Edinburg, Tex.: Pan American University, 1982.
Critics find this complex novel hard to sum up. Drabble controls its various personal and social threads by a pattern of figurative language. Dixson examines how all the traditional sacred and secular implications of Rose's name are appropriate to her character, as are the suggestions of other plant names and of gardens in general. Rose herself is a realistic character as well; she wavers between being a flawed human person and being what her name symbolizes. She may think she has lost God's grace, but that does not mean that she really has.

Gussow, Mel. "Margaret Drabble: A Double Life." *The New York Times Book Review*, October 9, 1977, 7, 40-41.
An interview. Drabble began work on this novel when she was asked to write an article on child custody.

Hannay, John. *The Intertexuality of Fate: A Study of Margaret Drabble*. Columbia: University of Missouri Press, 1986.
Hannay's reading is antifeminist. The intertext of this novel, the story of returning to one's origins and one's fate, is not so clearly apparent as is the intertext of *The Waterfall*. Simon and Rose are only intermittently aware of the stories that shape their lives. When Simon thinks he is being drawn back to his mother, he refuses, thereby (like Clara in *Jerusalem the Golden*) enacting the opposite tragic story of refusal. Rose initially rejects her parents and her home by marrying Christopher. She then rejects Christopher as well to build a new home in an unfashionable section of North London. But she does return home to confront her parents and to confront the intertexts by John Bunyan that had shaped her decisions. Her final move is to accept her return, not to her literal home, but to a life of married strife that resembles the home she grew up in. Hannay's reading is at odds with those critics who consider Rose's return to her husband a betrayal of womanhood.

————. "Margaret Drabble: An Interview." *Twentieth Century Literature: A Scholarly and Critical Journal* 33 (Summer, 1987): 129-149.
At the end, although Rose won, she recognized her husband's equal rights. Besides, Christopher is not such a bad man. Drabble wants to describe how people act, not to create role models.

Hardin, Nancy S. "An Interview with Margaret Drabble." *Contemporary Literature* 14 (Summer, 1973): 273-295.
Rose will lose whether she returns to her husband or not; she chooses the harder alternative. Drabble thinks she might have ended the novel differently if she had not still been living with her first husband.

Irvine, Lorna. "No Sense of An Ending: Drabble's Continuous Fictions." In *Critical Essays on Margaret Drabble*, edited by Ellen Cronan Rose. Boston: G. K. Hall, 1985.

The novel shows us many epiphanies almost achieved. Rose longs for epiphanies, for absolute endings, to be saved or damned. But she ultimately exercises her free choice to return to an inconclusive life.

Klein, Norma. "Real Novels about Real Women." *Ms.* 1, September, 1972, 7-8.
In the third issue of this famous magazine, Drabble is said to deal with what all young women are concerned about. Klien praises Drabble for drawing self-confident, proud, and tough women. They want love and marriage, but on their own terms—terms which can include careers. But Drabble goes astray in *The Needle's Eye*, especially when Rose returns to her husband.

Korenman, Joan S. "The Liberation of Margaret Drabble." *Critique: Studies in Modern Fiction* 21, no. 3 (1980): 61-72.
Like other later Drabble novels, this shows men as well as women asking new questions about the meaning of life.

Lay, Mary M. "Margaret Drabble's *The Needle's Eye*: Jamesian Perception of Self." *College Language Association Journal* 28 (September, 1984): 33-45.
Lay compares the characters and relationships of this novel to those in Henry James's *The Ambassadors*. Simon, Rose, and James's Lambert Strether all change in the course of the novel, but then return to earlier commitments. These returns should not be viewed as defeats, for all have become survivors who have gained perspective. Rose may feel that she has corrupted herself, but both novels imply that nobody achieves complete freedom and joy.

_____. "Temporal Ordering in the Fiction of Margaret Drabble." *Critique: Studies in Modern Fiction* 21, no. 3 (1980): 73-84.
Lay examines how Drabble presents her readers with the simultaneous fictional presents of both Rose and Simon. Early in the novel, they are apart and isolated. Later they appear together in a single fictional present. Toward the end, as they begin to resolve their problems, Drabble presents time in its durational aspect.

Libby, Marion Vlastos. "Fate and Feminism in the Novels of Margaret Drabble" *Contemporary Literature* 16 (Spring, 1975): 175-192.

Rose is Drabble's most admirable heroine. In her own way, she is strong and beautiful as she opposes the pressures of a patriarchal society. She creates her own identity. Unlike Simon, she can act. Libby is disappointed when Rose returns to her husband, but views that, not as a betrayal of ideals, but as an act of will. Even so, Libby hopes Rose will leave her husband soon.

Little, Judy. "Imagining Marriage." In *Portraits of Marriage in Literature*, edited by Anne C. Hargrove and Maurine Magliocco. Macomb, Ill.: Essays in Literature, 1984.

Drabble, among a few other novelists like Doris Lessing and Iris Murdoch, seems to imagine working marriages that survive the death of traditional romantic passion. The end of this novel may seem to some as a betrayal of feminist ideals. But when Rose returns to Christopher, Drabble shows the reader such a marriage, for Rose recognizes her husband's existence as a separate person and his love for their children.

Mannheimer, Monica. "The Search for Identity in Margaret Drabble's *The Needle's Eye*." *Dutch Quarterly Review of Anglo-American Letters* 5 (1975): 24-38.

Both Rose and Simon have crises which force them to understand what their childhoods did to them and why they have made important decisions. But despite their understandings, neither can escape his or her fate. Simon remains with his unloved wife, and Rose sacrifices herself when she returns to her husband. Mannheimer calls this a novel about defeat. In a postscript, Drabble herself argues against the defeatist label. The characters, she says, are not defeated, for they continually struggle on, seeking identity more than freedom. They may not be happy, but they experience moments of happiness.

Murphy, Brenda. "Women, Will, and Survival: The Figure in Margaret Drabble's Carpet." *South Atlantic Quarterly* 82 (Winter, 1983): 38-50.

In terms taken from *A Summer Bird-Cage*, Rose looks like a herbivore but really is a carnivore. Unlike earlier carnivores, she learns how to balance saving her own soul with acknowledging her duty to others. It is difficult for her to renounce part of her individuality, but in doing so she gains as well as loses.

Myer, Valerie Grosvenor. *Margaret Drabble: Puritanism and Permissiveness.* New York: Barnes & Noble Books, 1974.
Rose is like other heroines of early Drabble novels, for she flees from the evangelism she learned at home only to embrace puritan ideas about the wickedness of riches. Simon agrees with Rose's scruples. But Myer challenges many readings of this novel when she argues that, unlike other heroines, Rose is sexually responsive. She is particularly responsive to Christopher, a sexy and powerful man, and she returns to him and to her children. Christopher, if fact, provides a resolution to the book's rejection of strict puritanism when he combines money-making with care for his family.

_____. *Margaret Drabble: A Reader's Guide.* New York: St. Martin's Press, 1991.
Drabble's wider themes bring with them a looser style and idioms from the north of England. The literary background of this novel includes works by Doris Lessing, Charles Dickens, Elizabeth Gaskell, and Julian of Norwich; most important is the Bible, the Gospel of Matthew in particular. Myers disagrees with the criticism of many feminists that Rose betrays herself by returning to an abusive husband. Myer sees this novel as exploring the paradoxes of a theological feminism in which Rose is a Christ-like figure. An important argument.

Parker, Gillian, and Janet Todd. "Margaret Drabble." In *Women Writers Talking*, edited by Janet Todd. New York: Holmes & Meier, 1983.
Drabble says that Rose's decisions are valid. The stone lions at the novel's end are real; she discovered them at the Alexandra Palace in North London as she was completing the novel.

Pickering, Jean. "Margaret Drabble's Sense of the Middle Problem." *Twentieth Century Literature* 30 (Winter, 1984): 475-483.
This novel began with Drabble's interest in child custody cases. The crisis of the completed book takes place when Simon realizes that what Christopher really wants is to get his children back, not Rose's money.

Preussner, Dee. "Talking with Margaret Drabble." *Modern Fiction Studies* 25 (Winter, 1979): 563-577.

Drabble believes in the parable of the needle's eye: you cannot be both good and rich. Rose can not fully participate in her lower-class community, for she can come and go as she pleases. Rose finds out that the greatest sin is withdrawing from your family. Drabble says she had Henry James's *The Portrait of a Lady* in mind as she wrote this novel, for in both cases rich heroines have great opportunities but make wrong decisions.

Rose, Ellen Cronan. *Equivocal Figures: The Novels of Margaret Drabble.* Totowa, N.J.: Barnes & Noble Books, 1980.
In a clear and discerning but ultimately polemical analysis, the author points out that Drabble's omniscient narrator here has two centers of consciousness. One is male. Although Simon gives evidence of many patriarchal ideas, he is much more sympathetic than most men to Rose's very feminine problems. In the end, he interprets Rose as a secular saint who gives her wealth to charity and denies herself when she returns to her ex-husband for the sake of their children.

But Rose is really more complicated. At first she stands against the patriarchal demands of the law when she decides to give her children to her ex-husband. Then she breaks free from old-fashioned Christian ways of thinking when she rejects the ideas of John Bunyan. But when she does deny herself, she finds not liberation but oppression again. The author thinks that the confusions of the novel's ending are signs that Drabble herself has taken a step backward in what had been her progress toward the true doctrines of feminist philosophy by which literature should be judged.

_____. "Margaret Drabble: Surviving the Future." *Critique* 15, no. 1 (1973): 5-20.
Drabble's short story "A Voyage to Cythera" helps us read this novel. Like the heroine of that story, Simon's past incapacitates him from understanding another person. Simon cannot see that Rose is an ordinary woman, not a symbol. At the story's crisis, Rose decides to be a mother, not a martyr.

_____. "The Sexual Politics of Narration: Margaret Drabble's Feminist Fiction." *Studies in the Novel* 20 (Spring, 1988): 86-99.

Drabble's structures are feminist ones that oppose imposing patriarchal structures on experience. For example, in this novel we find two different versions of Rose's return to her husband.

Roxman, Susanna. *Guilt and Glory: Studies in Margaret Drabble's Novels 1963-80.* Stockholm: Almquist & Wiksell International, 1984.
Roxman lucidly and brilliantly sorts out the moral problems of this novel. Rose acts morally throughout as she renounces her social privileges because they are wrong. Simon, coming from a lower class, naturally hates privilege and admires Rose for this act. Although Christopher comes from an even less privileged family than does Simon, he ruthlessly pursues money and its powers. After Rose and Christopher realize their values are completely different, they divorce. Rose then makes the moral decision to give their children to Christopher because if she got custody, it would be because women are traditionally favored in divorce cases.
In a later section, Roxman makes an important distinction between two kinds of ethics. For Rose, it is most important to do right; that is, the intentions behind an act are very much more important than that act's actual consequences. Christopher, a character much misunderstood by critics, has utilitarian morals, according to which an act is judged by its consequences. Part of what he wants for their children is their material good. Even so, Roxman detects that Drabble gives the edge of sympathy to Rose.

Ruderman, Judith. "An Invitation to a Dinner Party: Margaret Drabble on Women and Food." In *Margaret Drabble: Golden Realms,* edited by Dorey Schmidt. No. 4 in *Living Author Series.* Edinburg, Tex.: Pan American University, 1982.
Two dinner parties are important. Julie's party is a failure because her guests are bored. In contrast, Diana's party is a success because it introduces Simon to Rose.

Sadler, Lynn Veach. *Margaret Drabble.* Boston: Twayne, 1986.
In Chapter 5, Sadler provides more than her usual useful introductory comments. Here she analyzes this novel by comparing it in detail to John Bunyan's *Pilgrim's Progress* and *Grace Abounding.* The comparison illuminates Rose's quest and the novel's ending,

which also reminds Sadler of the theme of resignation in Wordsworth's later poetry.

Sale, Roger. *On Not Being Good Enough: Writings of a Working Critic.* New York: Oxford University Press, 1979.
Drabble is a more important presence in this novel than her characters. Sale responds to her intelligence, her sympathies, and her brilliance but wonders how the novel holds together. Drabble has not cared enough about her characters to look closely at their situations.

Showalter, Elaine. *A Literature of Their Own: British Women Novelists from Brontë to Lessing.* Princeton, N.J.: Princeton University Press, 1977.
Rose's return to Christopher mirrors Drabble's own masochistic resignation to women's destiny. Showalter sees hope that Drabble will realize that she has outgrown traditional attitudes.

Sizemore, Christine Wick. *A Female Vision of the City: London in the Novels of Five British Women.* Knoxville: University of Tennessee Press, 1989.
Women novelists and female characters give us our vision of the city in the twentieth century. Rose, a woman, sees London as a holy city and her neighborhood as a web of relationships. Simon, a man, does not.

Stovel, Nora F. "`A Feminine Ending?': Symbolism as Closure in the Novels of Margaret Drabble." *English Studies in Canada* 15 (March, 1989): 80-93.
Drabble gives closure to her novels by providing equivocal final symbols, here the stone lions at the gateway to Rose's future.

_____. *Margaret Drabble, Symbolic Moralist.* Mercer Island, Wash.: Starmont House, 1989.
This novel's meaning is best approached by examining its central opposition of law to love. On the side of law are the parable of the needle's eye, renunciation, sacrifice, rocks, and the character of Simon. On the side of love are the parable of the talents, flowers, community, marriage, Christopher, and his making money to help his children. Rose is torn between these forces, her mind having

been tainted by her Calvinist nurse. The result is repression. But though Simon admires it, Rose lays her nurse's influence aside and returns to Christopher and family and love. Stovel discusses several reasons why some readers have objected to this ending, but insists it is the proper one.

Whittier, Gayle. "Mistresses and Madonnas in the Novels of Margaret Drabble." In *Gender and Literary Voice*, edited by Janet Todd. No. 1, n.s., in *Women & Literature*. New York: Holmes & Meier, 1980.
Drabble extends her myth of motherhood into the middle years. The conflict between love and other activities has lessened. But the conflict between sex and motherhood continues; Rose declines to sleep with Simon, but sleeps with her child. Now lovers like Simon must be willing to be interim fathers for existing children.

The Realms of Gold, 1975.

Atwood, Margaret. "Margaret Atwood Talks to Margaret Drabble." *Chatelaine* 60 (April, 1987): 73, 124, 126, 130.
The famous Canadian novelist quizzes Drabble on her opinions and personal life. Atwood calls attention to the scope, including politics, of *The Radiant Way*. Drabble says she admires Margaret Thatcher for her confidence and for keeping the issue of her gender out of politics. Drabble also remembers her discovery that it was hard work to combine raising children and writing novels.

Bromberg, Pamela S. "'Death and Love': *Memento Mori* in Margaret Drabble's *The Realms of Gold*." In *The Symbolism of Vanitas in the Arts, Literature, and Music: Comparative and Historical Studies*, edited by Liana DeGirolami Cheney. Lewiston, N.Y.: Edwin Mellen Press, 1992.
A very interesting reading of the novel in the context of earlier literature and Christian symbolism. Drabble's earlier novels appear to accept the Christian duality between mind and body. *The Realms of Gold* recalls in particular the contempt of body and flesh that readers find in *Hamlet* and other Elizabethan and Jacobean dramas. We see everywhere a consciousness of the bones beneath the flesh, especially the visible teeth of the human skull.

The Ollerenshaw's family disease is a despair caused by such puritanical preoccupations; in this novel Stephen dies of it. His death may make Frances's triumph less than total, but she does reject puritanism to accept her mortality and affirm the values of life and love. Some bits of bone/teeth are transformed by daughters and by lovers into symbols of love.

_____. "Romantic Revisionism in Margaret Drabble's *Realms of Gold.*" In *Margaret Drabble: Golden Realms*, edited by Dorey Schmidt. No. 4 in *Living Author Series*. Edinburg, Tex.: Pan American University, 1982.
A brilliant discussion of how Drabble's reading of Wordsworth shapes the significance of the novel. Bromberg sets the lives of four characters against Wordsworth's own. Three of the four (David, Janet, and Stephen) represent three unsatisfactory responses. Frances's development not only parallels Wordsworth's, but changes its pattern to respond more fully and more happily to her century. She discovers her own "spots of time" or powerful memories and uses them to achieve a happiness based both on love and community and on her acceptance of mortality.

Creighton, Joanne V. *Margaret Drabble*. London: Methuen, 1985.
In her chapter "Golden Realms," Creighton interestingly links Drabble's intrusive third-person narration to the novel's double nature. It sometimes seems a traditional story told in the tradition of Henry Fielding and William Makepeace Thackeray. But often the virtuosity of its omniscience becomes so self-conscious that it becomes a postmodern novel. The reader soon sees that the stories told by the characters themselves, especially stories of golden realms, are shaped by their tellers. Creighton insists on the novel's complexity in other ways. For example, Frances worries about Darwinian evolution and fate, both in general and in her family. The narrator playfully gives Frances and Karel the happy ending of a traditional novel, though this ending also seems to echo that of E. M. Forster's *Howard's End*.

Cunningham, Gail. "Women and Children First: The Novels of Margaret Drabble." In *Twentieth Century Women Novelists*, edited by Thomas F. Staley. Totowa, N.J.: Barnes & Noble Books, 1982.

Cunningham explicates the significance of the title's allusion to Keats. Drabble's treatment of Frances's mature problems is itself mature. The crisis of the novel occurs at Aunt Con's funeral, and its resolution lies in the subsequent harmony and happiness. Not all characters (like Stephen and his baby) are lucky enough to be part of this harmony.

Davis, Cynthia A. "Unfolding Form: Narrative Approach and Theme in *The Realms of Gold*." *Modern Language Quarterly* 40 (December, 1979): 390-402. Reprinted in *Critical Essays on Margaret Drabble*, edited by Ellen Cronan Rose. Boston: G. K. Hall, 1985.
Drabble's narrator is self-conscious and somewhat intrusive, but she is not playing postmodern games. This novel does refer to the world outside of art. By means of images (especially crater images), parallel scenes, and varied responses to the same event, Drabble creates a world in which different characters have complementary but different ways of seeing life. Though the novel does not have any simple theme, it finds constant elements in life: fate, death, and love.

Eis, Jacqueline. "The Omniscient Narrator in *The Realms of Gold*." *San Jose Studies* 8, no. 2 (1982): 101-107.
Drabble is not a forceful omniscient narrator and does not judge her characters.

Gullette, Margaret Morganroth. "Ugly Ducklings and Swans: Margaret Drabble's Fable of Progress in the Middle Years." *Modern Language Quarterly* 44 (September, 1983): 285-304. Reprinted with minor changes in *Safe at Last in the Middle Years: The Invention of the Midlife Progress Novel: Saul Bellow, Margaret Drabble, Anne Tyler, John Updike*. Berkeley: University of California Press, 1988.
Drabble's basic myth of transformation is here seen in Frances's achievements. She wills her own change into a powerful and gregarious woman.

Gussow, Mel. "Margaret Drabble: A Double Life." *The New York Times Book Review*, October 9, 1977, 7, 40-41.

An interview. Drabble says that this novel began with her reading accounts of old ladies dying alone in cottages.

Harper, Michael F. "Margaret Drabble and the Resurrection of the English Novel." *Contemporary Literature* 23 (Spring, 1982): 145-168. Reprinted in *Critical Essays on Margaret Drabble*, edited by Ellen Cronan Rose. Boston: G. K. Hall, 1985.
A short but important treatment. This novel comments on Drabble's position as a postmodern novelist. When she reconstructs the life of Tizouk, Frances too is a creator of imaginative fictions. Harper thinks this novel makes plain Drabble's break with modernism in other ways as well. The story is full of startling coincidences. The omniscient narrator enters many minds, who in turn construct different fictional worlds. Even so, there is a sense of family among them, and their communion gives the novel its hope.

Higdon, David Leon. "Margaret Drabble's *The Realms of Gold*: `Its Lines Were the Lines of Memory.'" In *Shadows of the Past in Contemporary British Fiction*. Athens: University of Georgia Press, 1985.
The Keats poem alluded to in the title is about the excitement of discovery. Although Frances makes many archeological discoveries like Tizouk, she avoids some of the unpleasant parts of these ancient cultures. She is also tormented by personal matters. She realizes she dislikes being apart from Karel, the man she loves; she knows she has avoided professional risks; her family has been scandalized by her aunt's death. These torments make her realize the value of love and family and family history, however imperfect they are. The other major characters in the book (Stephen, David, and Janet) dramatize aspects of Frances's character and potential fates.

Irvine, Lorna. "No Sense of An Ending: Drabble's Continuous Fictions." In *Critical Essays on Margaret Drabble*, edited by Ellen Cronan Rose. Boston: G. K. Hall, 1985.
Characters like Stephen get satisfaction for apocalyptic endings, but not so Frances. Despite what she knows of the horrors of history, she remains committed to process. Irvine identifies three

times in which the narrator enters Frances's story to make a similar point and tells the reader what will happen in the future.

Kaplan, Carey. "A Vision of Power in Margaret Drabble's *The Realms
of Gold.*" *Journal of Women's Studies in Literature* 1 (Summer,
1979): 233-242. Reprinted in *Critical Essays on Margaret
Drabble*, edited by Ellen Cronan Rose. Boston: G. K. Hall, 1985.
A very interesting example of using image-patterns to explore the
meaning of a novel. Just as critics find phallic imagery in Hem-
ingway's novels, so Kaplan finds womb-like images all through
The Realms of Gold: craters, excavations, ditches, even a cavity in
Frances's tooth. To be creative, these voids must be fertilized and
nurtured. Some characters like Stephen do not succeed; others
like Frances give birth both physically (her children) and mentally
(the city of Tizouk). Men like David and Karel can create as well.
By her womb imagery, Drabble plays down the father's role in
conception or inspiration and emphasizes the dangers and pains of
birth and the importance of nurturing both children and ideas.

Kenyon, Olga. *Women Novelists Today: A Survey of English Writing
in the Seventies and Eighties.* New York: St. Martin's Press,
1988.
Kenyon sees an analogy between Frances's archeological discoveries and an artist's creations. Drabble widens her scope in this
novel to include a great variety of people, including some who
suffer for the pains of this world and others like Frances who are
more optimistic.

_____. *Women Writers Talk: Interviews with Ten Women Writers.*
New York: Carroll & Graf, 1990.
Frances's luck in finding gold bars is a symbol of the creative
process. Drabble intends her title to be optimistic.

Korenman, Joan S. "The Liberation of Margaret Drabble." *Critique:
Studies in Modern Fiction* 21, no. 3 (1980): 61-72.
Like other later Drabble novels, this shows men as well as women
asking questions about the meaning of life. Frances understands
Stephen's suicide, but backs away from dwelling on the truths that
caused his despair. The happy ending does not obscure the
novel's strain of pessimism.

Lambert, Ellen Z. "Margaret Drabble and the Sense of Possibility." *University of Toronto Quarterly* 49 (Spring, 1980): 228-251. Reprinted in *Critical Essays on Margaret Drabble*, edited by Ellen Cronan Rose. Boston: G. K. Hall, 1985.

Frances is another of Drabble's hopeful heroines, but she is older than the others and has gained a lot of the things she worked for. She is different also in that she desires things for others as well as for herself; she cries tears of despair at their fates. Janet Bird is in many ways Frances's opposite, yet she has her moments of hope as well.

Lay, Mary M. "Temporal Ordering in the Fiction of Margaret Drabble." *Critique: Studies in Modern Fiction* 21, no. 3 (1980): 73-84.

In a greater than usual portion of this novel, Drabble's characters are portrayed in their fictional presents as if these moments happened simultaneously. In this way, Drabble emphasizes their isolation. The only time a great number of them converge in one fictional present is at Aunt Connie's funeral. The novel is also marked by more authorial intrusion than usual and by a great slowing down of time when we listen to Frances think.

Levitt, Morton P. "The New Victorians: Margaret Drabble as Trollope." In *Margaret Drabble: Golden Realms*, edited by Dorey Schmidt. No. 4 in *Living Author Series*. Edinburg, Tex.: Pan American University, 1982.

Even though Drabble appears to employ a typically postmodern intrusiveness, this technique is really just a part of her Victorian omniscient storytelling. So too are her use of coincidence (the lost and found post card) and her final summary of her characters' fates.

Little, Judy. *Comedy and the Woman Writer: Woolf, Spark, and Feminism*. Lincoln: University of Nebraska Press, 1983.

In her pages on Drabble, Little summarizes many points made in her article "Humor and the Female Quest."

_____. "Humor and the Female Quest: Margaret Drabble's *The Realms of Gold*." *Regionalism and the Female Imagination* 4, no. 2 (1978): 44-52.

Little distinguishes two poles of woman's humor in this novel. Janet's few humorous remarks are wry, resistant, or attacking. Frances, on the other hand, is sometimes playful, sometimes celebratory, sometimes mocking at dangers. Their different styles are appropriate to their different roles in the dominant myth of the novel. In contrast to male quest myths, in Drabble we get variations on the story of Demeter and Persephone. Janet is clearly a Persephone, seduced by glitter into the Hades of marriage; the world she experiences is full of hellish images. Demeter in the form of Frances (she *is* a professional digger under the ground) can only partially rescue her, as in the ancient story. Frances is also a Persephone figure, but one who has triumphed over despair and has emerged as a strong, happy, and fulfilled woman. Little makes interesting points, but her overall argument is not fully convincing.

_____. "Margaret Drabble and the Romantic Imagination: *The Realms of Gold.*" *Prairie Schooner* 55 (Spring-Summer, 1981): 241-252.
This novel shows the influence of some major ideas of the Romantic writers. Frances acknowledges the effect that landscape has on the mind, especially the depressing effect of the north of England. Like Romantic poets, Frances is also aware that the imagination can create, for her imagination can be said to have created Tizouk. Other characters, like Janet and Stephen, are not so forceful; their imaginations are not strong enough to create. Frances, however, briefly wonders whether creating golden worlds is worthwhile, whether or not human dreams are futile. She is revived by remembering past examples of the effects of imagination, and the novel reunites her with her lover. Both of them know that in a tragic world they are the lucky survivors.

Manheimer, Joan. "Margaret Drabble and the Journey to the Self." *Studies in the Literary Imagination* 11 (Fall, 1978): 127-143. Reprinted in *British Novelists Since 1900*, edited by Jack I. Biles. New York: AMS Press, 1987.
Manheimer judges this novel by non-literary standards. Drabble here betrays of the ideals of independence displayed by Jane in *The Waterfall*. Although the narrator's many intrusions show

that Drabble herself has achieved freedom, her character Frances does not convince.

Murphy, Brenda. "Women, Will, and Survival: The Figure in Margaret Drabble's Carpet." *South Atlantic Quarterly* 82 (Winter, 1983): 38-50.

In Murphy's terms (borrowed from *A Summer Bird-cage*), Frances is Drabble's reaffirmation of the carnivore, a high-powered woman who is destined to survive. Janet Bird, on the other hand, is a pure herbivore.

Myer, Valerie Grosvenor. *Margaret Drabble: A Reader's Guide*. New York: St. Martin's Press, 1991.

A loosely organized collection of helpful material. Myers notes the opinions of many critics and recommends some of them. In the background she sees Virginia Woolf's *Mrs. Dalloway*, Shakespeare's *Antony and Cleopatra*, and several English Romantic poets. The fates of two male characters recall the story of Empedocles. Myers treats Frances, her depression and salvation, but has more to say about Janet and David, especially on what Drabble told her about what was cut from the novel before publication.

Parker, Gillian, and Janet Todd. "Margaret Drabble." In *Women Writers Talking*, edited by Janet Todd. New York: Holmes & Meier, 1983.

Drabble finds Frances to be a good role model. She admires the character's energy and determination; Frances is selfish, but you have to be selfish. But Frances has been lucky.

Pearson, Carol, and Katherine Pope. *The Female Hero in American and British Literature*. New York: R. R. Bowker, 1981.

In describing the female hero, the authors cite Frances often. She is initially imprisoned because society provides women with no model for what women should do after their children are grown. Yet she gets courage from a memory: beautiful, surviving newts in a backyard. She manages to become reconciled with her family by finding a substitute mother in Aunt Con and returns home to a life with her lover and friends.

Pickering, Jean. "Margaret Drabble's Sense of the Middle Problem."
Twentieth Century Literature 30 (Winter, 1984): 475-483.
The crisis of this novel is the death of Aunt Connie.

Quinn, Joseph A. "Christianity and Secularism in the Later Margaret
Drabble." *University of Windsor Review* 18 (Fall-Winter, 1984):
67-75.
Drabble's later novels show characters who search for life's
meaning. Though some feel a need for God, most find a kind of
salvation in human love. Drabble's omniscient narrator makes
readers feel distant from these sufferings as they watch characters
struggling to live lives they cannot control. In this novel, Frances
explicitly says she cannot aspire to God's love, but she finds
salvation in Karel's love. Other characters do not get this far.
Quinn compares this novel to one with more religious tendencies,
The Ice Age.

Rigney, Barbara Hill. *Lilith's Daughters: Women and Religion in
Contemporary Fiction.* Madison: University of Wisconsin Press,
1982.
Frances is a contemporary Eve figure, not a temptress or an sub-
missive female, but a woman who claims power. She imagined
Tizouk, and it existed. Frances provides a positive role model.

Rose, Ellen Cronan. *Equivocal Figures: The Novels of Margaret
Drabble.* Totowa, N.J.: Barnes & Noble Books, 1980.
Rose finds the plot of this novel irrelevant and reads it in the con-
text of Adrienne Rich's ideas about mothers and daughters and
Mary Daly's concept of "Gyn/ecology." Frances's happiness at the
end is purely private. The novel's many coincidences show that
Drabble herself knew she was writing only a pleasing fiction.

_____. "The Sexual Politics of Narration: Margaret Drabble's
Feminist Fiction." *Studies in the Novel* 20 (Spring, 1988): 86-99.
Rose's thesis is that Drabble's structures are feminist ones that
oppose imposing patriarchal structures on experience. For example, this novel suggests that its characters have many untold
stories. Even as we have it, the novel is not so much Frances's
story as the chronicle of her family.

Rowe, Margaret M. "The Uses of the Past in Margaret Drabble's *The
  Realms of Gold*." In *Margaret Drabble: Golden Realms*, edited
  by Dorey Schmidt. No. 4 in *Living Author Series*. Edinburg,
  Tex.: Pan American University, 1982.
  Rowe strains the parallels with Keats's sonnet, but her essay is
  otherwise persuasive. Frances Wingate changes the way she
  thinks about the past as an archeologist. More importantly, she
  comes to think differently about her family's own past. Her
  schematic and mechanistic views give way to organic and complex ones.

Roxman, Susanna. *Guilt and Glory: Studies in Margaret Drabble's
  Novels 1963-80*. Stockholm: Almquist & Wiksell International,
  1984.
  This novel is filled with literary allusions, but Roxman examines
  only tenuous parallels with *Wuthering Heights* (Drabble echoes
  some of Brontë's names) and a few more convincing ones in the
  writings and life of the ancient Greek philosopher Empedocles.
  This novel's treatment of privilege focuses on the forces of
  heredity and landscape. Privileged people also are lucky in being
  alive, in love, and successful. Frances visits Adra, an African
  nation which seems fated to prosper. In contrast, people like Janet
  seem doomed to be oppressed. In a later section, Roxman
  discusses in admirable complexity the relation of each the novel's
  dominant images of earth, fire, and water to the treatment of time
  in each of its four sections. These relations are in turn
  significantly connected to various images of death and the
  conceptions of fate and privilege which Drabble also explores.

Ruderman, Judith. "An Invitation to a Dinner Party: Margaret
  Drabble on Women and Food." In *Margaret Drabble: Golden
  Realms*, edited by Dorey Schmidt. No. 4 in *Living Author Series*.
  Edinburg, Tex.: Pan American University, 1982.
  Women are characterized by their appetites. Frances's lust for life
  shows in her love for food; Another character's problems are
  revealed in her anorexia. Although critics have objected to the
  great number of pages devoted to Janet Bird's dinner party, the
  party is significant. When the electricity goes off, the guests for a
  while are magically united.

Sadler, Lynn Veach. *Margaret Drabble*. Boston: Twayne, 1986.
     In Chapter 7, Sadler treats this novel by summarizing its plot with
     a running commentary. She sees the theme as the importance of
     coming to terms with the past: personal, familial, and general.
     Feminists may object to Frances finding happiness in the love of a
     man and to several of the male characters being good persons.
     Sadler implies her own objections to the convenient coincidences
     that are needed to make the happy ending.

Sale, Roger. "The Realms of Gold." *Hudson Review* 28 (Winter,
     1975-76): 616-628.
     A collective review of a number of novels. Sale thinks *The
     Realms of Gold* is superlative. Even though it seems to wander in
     Janet's and David's stories, he sees that it fits together. Sale likes
     the joyous ending.

Sharpe, Patricia. "On First Looking into *The Realms of Gold.*"
     Michigan Quarterly Review 16 (Spring, 1977), 225-231.
     Sharpe criticizes Valerie Grosvenor Myer's *Margaret Drabble:
     Puritanism and Permissiveness* for assuming that free sexual re-
     sponse is always a good thing. Frances is sexually well adjusted.
     But Drabble wants the reader to see that Frances's happy survival
     is just another turn that lives can take. Sharpe defends the happy
     ending: Drabble is challenging her solemn readers by implying
     that sometimes life can work out well.

Sizemore, Christine Wick. *A Female Vision of the City: London in
     the Novels of Five British Women*. Knoxville: University of Ten-
     nessee Press, 1989.
     Twentieth century women novelists and their female characters
     give us positive visions of cities. David, a male geologist, does
     not appreciate cities. In contrast, Frances creates the civilization
     of Tizouk out of her female imagination and even reestablishes a
     network of human relations in an English village.

Stovel, Nora F. "'A Feminine Ending?': Symbolism as Closure in the
     Novels of Margaret Drabble." *English Studies in Canada* 15
     (March, 1989): 80-93.

Drabble gives closure to her novels by providing equivocal final symbols. Here Stovel says that a piece of yellow glass is suggestive—her least convincing example to prove her general theory.

_____. *Margaret Drabble, Symbolic Moralist.* Mercer Island, Wash.: Starmont House, 1989.

This novel pits the forces of gold and life against those of lead and death. Lead is most obvious in a suicide's coffin, but the forces of death appear in the form of the Holocaust and in the fossils that Frances's geologist cousin discovers. Frances is allied with gold and life, but even she has problems with death. In her depression she questions the value of her accomplishment, of all human achievement. And her golden city of Tizouk was not a utopia. When she tries to return to her roots, she discovers that her home territory in England is squalid. But Frances finds elements of good in her ancestry and native country. With the help of her lover, she makes an accommodation to the mixture of gold and lead that makes up the world. Frances's acceptance allows Drabble to give the novel a happy ending, full of symbolic flora and fauna.

_____. "Margaret Drabble's Golden Vision." In *Margaret Drabble: Golden Realms*, edited by Dorey Schmidt. No. 4 in *Living Author Series.* Edinburg, Tex.: Pan American University, 1982.

This novel answers *Jerusalem the Golden.* Like Clara, Frances rejects her home, but Frances seeks for a golden age in the past. Eventually she discovers her golden world in her family's part of rural England.

Updike, John. "Drabbling in the Mud." *The New Yorker*, January 12, 1976, 88-90.

Updike does not like the way Drabble tells this novel. He objects to the narrator's casual admission of ignorance, her slack organization, her dependence on coincidence, and her inclusion of episodes that do not seem relevant. As a loosely related series of essays, the novel is more interesting. The novel is at its best in scenes when a woman finds herself alone and when shallow conversation overlays some deeper meaning about the way human beings are related to nature.

Whitehill, Sharon. "Two for Tea: An Afternoon with Margaret
    Drabble." *Essays in Literature* 11 (Spring, 1984): 61-75.
    Drabble says she had intended to give Frances, Janet, and David
    one-third of the novel each, but she changed her mind when she
    had trouble writing about David.

Whittier, Gayle. "Mistresses and Madonnas in the Novels of Margaret
    Drabble." In *Gender and Literary Voice*, edited by Janet Todd.
    No. 1, n.s., in *Women & Literature*. New York: Holmes & Meier,
    1980.
    Drabble extends her treatment of motherhood into middle age.
    Frances experiences little conflict with her career.   Like other
    lovers, Karel must be a good substitute father; he often seems to
    need mothering himself. The risks children run in other novels
    are magnified by Stephen and his baby.   On the other hand,
    Frances manages to integrate motherhood and eros, though with
    mild incestuous overtones.

Zeman, Anthea. *Presumptuous Girls: Women and Their World in the
    Serious Woman's Novel*. London: Weidenfeld & Nicholson, 1977.
    Drabble thinks that a middle-aged heroine can escape the prob-
    lems of growing old. Zeman disagrees.

The Ice Age, 1977.

Burkhart, Charles.   "Arnold Bennett and Margaret Drabble."   In
    Margaret Drabble: Golden Realms, edited by Dorey Schmidt.
    No. 4 in *Living Author Series*.   Edinburg, Tex.: Pan American
    University, 1982.
    A passage from this novel provides an example of how brilliantly
    Drabble has broadened her concerns in her later novels.

Connor, Steven. *The English Novel in History 1950-1995*. London:
    Routledge, 1996.
    In Chapter 2, Connor says that this novel not only announces that
    it will be a "condition of England" novel by anatomizing the
    nation's sickness, it has a story that promises to do that. Anthony
    Keating's career (Oxford to the BBC to property development)
    mirrors the cultural shifts that have occurred. Yet the novel falls

short of its promise. Passages of Dickensian prophetic rant clash with the banality of the realistic story. Symbols like the cold and imprisonment (the narrowing and restraint of the nation's vitality) and birds (first the death, then the birth of hope) are substitutes for real detail. The end of the novel suggests that England cannot be imagined.

Creighton, Joanne V. *Margaret Drabble*. London: Methuen, 1985.
In her chapter "Urban Ground," Creighton considers this novel together with *The Middle Ground*. Both widen Drabble's focus to include much of life in the contemporary city. Drabble's characters, like Drabble herself, are middle-aged but not at all settled. Their unease reflects the condition of Britain itself, as Malcolm Bradbury does in *The History Man* and as John Fowles does in *Daniel Martin*. Creighton calls *The Ice Age* a masculine novel: it is clearly plotted and seems to comes to a definite ending. The novel is set against the real boom and bust in the property market in the 1970's. Despite its breadth, Creighton does not think the novel answers many of the questions it raises.

Elkins, Mary Jane. "Facing the Gorgon: Good and Bad Mothers in the Late Novels of Margaret Drabble." In *Narrating Mothers: Theorizing Maternal Subjectivities*, edited by Brenda O. Daly and Maureen T. Reddy. Knoxville: University of Tennessee Press, 1991.
Elkins divides Drabble's women into Good Mothers who win and Bad Mothers who do not. Alison is an exception: a Good Mother who loses.

Gardiner, Judith Kegan. "Evil, Apocalypse, and Feminist Fiction." *Frontiers: A Journal of Women Studies* 7 (1983): 74-80.
An interesting and complex argument which uses four contemporary novels to discuss how women view the good and evil in the public and private spheres. Like Lessing and two American novelists, Drabble in *The Ice Age* sees the public world, in Britain or under totalitarianism, as one of male-dominated class oppression. Jane's adolescent rebellion is silly and ineffective, for nothing can change. In the private realm, the battle is feminine, one between mother and daughters. The villains are mothers who reject and daughters who irresponsibly blame, and the heroines

are responsible mothers. The inconsistencies of these views are reflected in the inconsistencies and evasions of the narrative voice in this novel. These observations suggest that women shape their fictions by a myth which is radically different myth from that employed by male writers. The female myth centers on struggles between women, especially between mothers and daughters, for autonomy.

Gindin, James. "Three Recent British Novels and an American Response." *Michigan Quarterly Review* 17 (Spring, 1978): 223-246.
At her best, Drabble provides a summary of bleak historical trends in England. But this novel is deeply flawed. Although Anthony Keating seems to offer hope, the materials of the novel provide no justification. The novel's last fifty pages are fantasy.

Gussow, Mel. "Margaret Drabble: A Double Life." *The New York Times Book Review*, October 9, 1977, 7, 40-41.
An interview. In her 1970's novels, Drabble says she is less interested in her inner life and more interested in how society works. For her novels, she reads newspapers and does research: perhaps she is somewhat of a journalist. *The Ice Age* took form after she read a book on the property boom in England, a commercial development that was not necessarily a bad thing. She did not want to write a "woman's novel" but found she could not write well about a male character who was directly involved in business manipulations. The term "ice age" is a metaphor for economic depression. But Americans should not be fooled by British complaining into thinking that Britain will not recover.

Hannay, John. *The Intertexuality of Fate: A Study of Margaret Drabble*. Columbia: University of Missouri Press, 1986.
Hannay explains that the intertext for this novel is the story of the Providential ordering of the events of this world. The way Providence works is mysterious, but the novel opens with a sense of national gloom related to the guilt of the central male character and ends with his private renewal in prison. This progress is the sign of the Providential intertext. But is Anthony's renewal related to what happens to the English nation? Other characters do not follow this pattern. But other patterns do not explain national

events very well either, and Drabble raises the possibility of a Providential renewal of the nation. But this intertext does not work in a realistic mode; it remains only a hope. An interesting account of a difficult novel to sum up.

_____. "Margaret Drabble: An Interview." *Twentieth Century Literature: A Scholarly and Critical Journal* 33 (Summer, 1987): 129-149.
Interesting discussion about Drabble's suggestions of fate in general and Alison's fate in particular. Was her fate a trial? A joke? Drabble says that the characters in this novel are odd and that all were based on people she knew. She admits she cannot create a good working class character, particularly a male.

Hansen, Elaine Tuttle. "The Uses of Imagination: Margaret Drabble's *The Ice Age*." In *Critical Essays on Margaret Drabble*, edited by Ellen Cronan Rose. Boston: G. K. Hall, 1985.
That this bleak novel is male-centered does not mean that Drabble endorses the masculine imagination. Rather, as Hansen proves in a brilliant analysis of the novel's opening paragraph, Drabble the narrator distances herself from the mind of Anthony Keating. Drabble also implicitly criticizes his masculine money-making activities by occasional short paragraphs and by the way she concludes narrative sections with withering ironies. Anthony's becoming a spy is just another masculine wrong turn; Drabble does not endorse his religious conversion in prison. Although there is no central female character in this novel, in different ways both Maureen and Alison provide positive models for new ways for women to accept freedom and responsibilities.

Irvine, Lorna. "No Sense of An Ending: Drabble's Continuous Fictions." In *Critical Essays on Margaret Drabble*, edited by Ellen Cronan Rose. Boston: G. K. Hall, 1985.
This novel's pervasive sense of ruin seems to demand an ending of apocalyptic closure. But even so, the major characters persevere, or at the worst are left in a kind of suspended animation.

Joseph, Gerhard. "The *Antigone* as Cultural Touchstone: Matthew Arnold, Hegel, George Eliot, Virginia Woolf, and Margaret

Drabble." *Publications of the Modern Language Association of America* 96 (January, 1981): 22-35.
Matthew Arnold dismissed the conflict in Sophocles's *Antigone* as irrelevant to his era. But Joseph thinks that Drabble in *The Ice Age* finds the story relevant to her times. Anthony's exchange of his own life for Jane's is Antigone-like, an irrational and existential act of self-assertion. The author's many references to Sophocles's play prove that Drabble's parallels are conscious. Joseph calls this novel the "Dover Beach" for our day.

Kenyon, Olga. *Women Novelists Today: A Survey of English Writing in the Seventies and Eighties.* New York: St. Martin's Press, 1988.
Even though Drabble uses realism to evoke English society in the mid-1970's, she also employs symbolism. She creates full characters and pessimistically views them as caught in a dying world.

Korenman, Joan S. "The Liberation of Margaret Drabble." *Critique: Studies in Modern Fiction* 21, no. 3 (1980): 61-72.
Like other later Drabble novels, *The Ice Age* shows men as well as women asking new questions about the meaning of life. Does Anthony's faith suggest Drabble is turning to religion? The novel is ambiguous.

Lay, Mary M. "Temporal Ordering in the Fiction of Margaret Drabble." *Critique: Studies in Modern Fiction* 21, no. 3 (1980): 73-84.
The treatment of time in this novel is appropriate to its frozen world. To a greater extent than in any previous novel, Drabble shows isolated characters in simultaneous fictional presents. They are mainly static; they resist choosing to act, and when they do, their actions come to nothing. At the end when Anthony Keating withdraws from this world, he has no fictional present.

Levitt, Morton P. "The New Victorians: Margaret Drabble as Trollope." In *Margaret Drabble: Golden Realms*, edited by Dorey Schmidt. No. 4 in *Living Author Series*. Edinburg, Tex.: Pan American University, 1982.
In spite of bad times, Drabble seems to see the possibilities of change for women, for men, and for Britain in general. But her

omniscient narrative voice dominates the novel and is at odds with her theme. Her vision of the books of the future (like that being written by Anthony Keating in prison) is chilling.

Murphy, Brenda. "Women, Will, and Survival: The Figure in Margaret Drabble's Carpet." *South Atlantic Quarterly* 82 (Winter, 1983): 38-50.
In Murphy's borrowed terms, Alison begins as a typical Drabble high-powered woman, a carnivore. But the world turns her into a herbivore.

Myer, Valerie Grosvenor. *Margaret Drabble: A Reader's Guide.* New York: St. Martin's Press, 1991.
Myer describes the setting: the bad winter that began with the oil crisis of 1973. In a loosely organized essay, Myer says that the novel is based on religion (in particular on Boethius's *Consolations of Philosophy*), that it concerns economic depression (especially with property developers), and that Drabble shows a growing tendency to include news and historical summaries in her fiction. Drabble alludes to the Bible, Claude Levi-Strauss, Dickens's *Little Dorrit*, William Blake, *Macbeth*, and *Antony and Cleopatra*. Myer thinks that, although Drabble's subject matter is all of England, she is successful only with middle-class characters.

Pearson, Carol, and Katherine Pope. *The Female Hero in American and British Literature.* New York: R. R. Bowker, 1981.
Female heroes must slay many dragons. One such obstacle is the requirement that a woman be perfect. The authors cite Alison as an example of one woman who is rejected because she is viewed as perfect.

Pickering, Jean. "Margaret Drabble's Sense of the Middle Problem." *Twentieth Century Literature* 30 (Winter, 1984): 475-483.
The crisis of this novel occurs when Alison confronts her daughter Jane and tells her that she (Jane) is responsible for what has happened to herself.

Quinn, Joseph A. "Christianity and Secularism in the Later Margaret Drabble." *University of Windsor Review* 18 (Fall-Winter, 1984): 67-75.

An important article from a religious perspective. In Anthony,
Drabble has created her most religious character. Quinn analyzes
Anthony's first and last scenes, both of which contain symbolic
birds, the last of which Anthony sees as God's messenger.
Drabble's narrator shares some of Anthony's concerns, but
ironically undercuts his final vision. This irony coupled with the
narrator's constant shifting from mind to mind has several effects.
Though Anthony, like other characters, has little control over the
materials of his life, he tries to shape them into a meaningful
pattern. The reader, looking down from the narrator's distance,
sees that Anthony's pattern is no more valid than other patterns.
Even so, Drabble implies some sort of mystical communion
among the characters who share similar conditions.

Rose, Ellen Cronan. *Equivocal Figures: The Novels of Margaret
Drabble*. Totowa, N.J.: Barnes & Noble Books, 1980.
Rose illuminates Anthony's progress to religion by quoting John
Milton's "Lycidas," but insists that a feminist analysis would be
very different. The trouble is that Drabble does not (or does not
yet) endorse such feminist views. At best, Drabble's novels of the
1970's resemble the "equivocal figures" her title: depending on
your point of view, you can read them as endorsing traditional and
patriarchal values or as leaning towards the feminist values Rose
herself has discovered.

Roxman, Susanna. *Guilt and Glory: Studies in Margaret Drabble's
Novels 1963-80*. Stockholm: Almquist & Wiksell International,
1984.
This novel's moral problems turn on issues of privilege, especially
economic privilege. England's financial woes are in some sense
the result of its past excess.

Sadler, Lynn Veach. *Margaret Drabble*. Boston: Twayne, 1986.
In Chapter 7, Sadler again makes a running commentary as she
summarizes the story. The novel's theme is what can be done
when you are a middle-aged failure, either as a person or as a nation. Anthony copes moderately well. He is a good man; he respects the lower classes. Even his religious faith is consistent.
Alison is a much different story. She cannot cope, and Sadler
thinks Drabble's treatment of her is a weakness in the novel. In

Chapter 3, Sadler admires Len's and (especially) Maureen's independence.

Satz, Martha. "Less of a Woman as One Gets Older: An Interview with Margaret Drabble." *Southwest Review* 70 (Spring, 1985): 187-197.
Drabble says she structured this novel around the idea of society as a web of interconnected groups after she reread George Eliot's *Middlemarch*.

Sizemore, Christine Wick. *A Female Vision of the City: London in the Novels of Five British Women*. Knoxville: University of Tennessee Press, 1989.
Women novelists in the twentieth century give us visions of the civilization of the city. In this novel, female characters appreciate London and its neighborhoods. Male characters, however, are determined to destroy London's fabric by tearing it down and developing it. Only Anthony once had a feminine vision of the city.

Stovel, Nora F. " 'A Feminine Ending?': Symbolism as Closure in the Novels of Margaret Drabble." *English Studies in Canada* 15 (March, 1989): 80-93.
Drabble gives closure to her novels by providing equivocal final symbols. In this novel, the image of a bird in flight suggests different kinds of hope for Anthony and for Britain.

_____. *Margaret Drabble, Symbolic Moralist*. Mercer Island, Wash.: Starmont House, 1989.
This novel uses the collapse of Britain's property market as a symbol of the nation's spiritual bankruptcy. Images of glaciers (from the Ice Age) are everywhere, creating prisons, both literal and figurative. These images are part of an apocalyptic storm, a vision of the forces destroying the England of idyllic countryside and cathedral towns. Everywhere people are murdered, mutilated, handicapped, diseased, or imprisoned. England itself has become exploited, ravaged, dug up, walled up. Its new buildings are phallic monuments to commercial success. Walachia's totalitarian state and Anthony's imprisonment symbolize what is happening to Britain's spirit. Tiny gleams of hope may come from Anthony and

Alison's moment before a storm and from Anthony's spiritual
renewal at the end.

The Middle Ground, 1980.

Allan, Tuzyline Jita.   "*The Middle Ground*: Determinism in a
    Changing World."   In *Womanist and Feminist Aesthetics: A
    Comparative Review*. Athens: Ohio University Press, 1995.
    Allan sets this novel against a background of Virginia Woolf's life
    and ideas. Drabble has come a long way from Woolf. She has a
    university education and sexual freedom. Whereas Woolf's *Mrs.
    Dalloway's* England is colonial yet homogenous, in *The Middle
    Ground* Drabble's England is postcolonial. Throughout the novel
    and especially in its final *Dalloway*-like party, races, classes, and
    sexes mix with something like equality. Drabble in fact is con-
    cerned with building bridges. Kate's slow understanding of her
    Iraqi boarder shows sensitivity. Allan brilliantly analyzes an ex-
    change between Kate and Hugo that echoes one between Clarissa
    Dalloway and Peter Walsh, an exchange in which a woman and a
    man begin to communicate.
        But Drabble's optimism is undermined by her nihilistic idea of
    fate, which to her means the luck of birth. What seems from one
    perspective to be bridge-building in society can seem from another
    perspective to be mere role-playing. To a womanist critic like
    Allan, Kate (and others like Evelyn) suffer from postfeminist
    trauma. Trapped by their neuroses, these women feel excessive
    guilt. Trapped by deterministic ideas, Drabble can make only
    incomplete efforts to make connections between cultures and
    between the sexes.

Bromberg, Pamela S.   "Narrative in Drabble's *The Middle Ground*:
    Relativity Versus Teleology."   *Contemporary Literature* 24
    (Winter, 1983): 463-479.
    A lucid and persuasive exposition of why some readers objected to
    this novel and why they are wrong. They expected Drabble to go
    on writing novels structured to show women growing up, but what
    they found is an unstructured novel without a feminist slant.
    Bromberg sees *The Middle Ground* as the culmination of tenden-
    cies in Drabble's novels of the 1970's. Instead of presenting a

story of one woman developing through a long time span, Drabble now presents a synchronic picture of a group over a short period of time, here about two months.

Kate is not a usual fictional character, for she is presented as having a life outside of what Drabble tells us, and we are presented with some details which may not be relevant to the main concerns of the novel. Drabble may confuse the reader by presenting many different points of view. In fact, Bromberg thinks that Hugo's attempt at writing a novel about Kate forms the center of the novel. Although Kate's life often seems to be preparing for novelistic crises, these crises do not occur. Kate gets through her problems by accepting in an undramatic moment the diversity and uncertainty of life. Her final party will celebrate the friendships and family ties based on these principles.

Burkhart, Charles. "Arnold Bennett and Margaret Drabble." In *Margaret Drabble: Golden Realms*, edited by Dorey Schmidt. No. 4 in *Living Author Series*. Edinburg, Tex.: Pan American University, 1982.
Burkhart dislikes Drabble's heavy-handed later style. Here she overuses metaphors derived from sewage.

Campbell, Jane. "'Both a Joke and a Victory': Humor as Narrative Strategy in Margaret Drabble's Fiction." *Contemporary Literature* 32 (Spring, 1991): 75-99.
In her work as a journalist, Kate misuses humor. But she changes, and at the end her laughter is shared.

_____. "Reaching Outwards: Versions of Reality in *The Middle Ground*." *Journal of Narrative Technique* 14 (Winter, 1984): 17-32.
Even though she realizes that patterns can be forced, Drabble searches for a new sort of form in this novel. Campbell thinks Drabble has created a satisfying form out of formlessness. She does so by emphasizing relativity rather than avoiding it. She provides varied perspectives through her many points of view and by her many literary parallels. Her narrator makes many comments on the problem. In particular, Drabble shows how difficult it is for Hugo to write a truthful yet organized novel about Kate.

In the end, the novel is shaped by a sense of people moving ahead in hope.

Connor, Steven. *The English Novel in History 1950-1995*. London: Routledge, 1996.
In Chapter 2, Connor says that novels like *The Middle Ground* not only show England at a specific time in its history, but are an examples of its decline.

Creighton, Joanne V. *Margaret Drabble*. London: Methuen, 1985.
In her chapter "Urban Ground," Creighton compares this novel to *The Ice Age*. Though alike in focusing on the state of Britain, this is a "feminine" novel. That is, it has little action and does not come to a strong conclusion. Its title is suggestive. The central characters are in the middle of life; the ground of London is shifting; below this ground are sewers, literal and metaphorical; Britain is somewhat in the middle of a larger world. In spite of these interesting ingredients, Creighton finds the novel deficient in intensity. In drawing parallels between the fictitious Kate and Drabble herself, Creighton sees the author as in transition, open to new directions. Creighton hopes Drabble in the future will be able to evoke the broad range of British culture and at the same time deal more deeply with personal and feminist concerns.

Cunningham, Gail. "Patchwork and Patterns: The Condition of England in Margaret Drabble's Later Novels." In *The British and Irish Novel Since 1960*, edited by James Acheson. New York: St. Martin's Press, 1991.
Unlike Drabble's early novels, *The Middle Ground* and its heroine declare themselves against trying to find patterns in the jumble of London and life. Kate does discover some small patterns and senses a large pattern when she gets an aerial view of the city.

Eifrig, Gail. "The Middle Ground." In *Margaret Drabble: Golden Realms*, edited by Dorey Schmidt. No. 4 in *Living Author Series*. Edinburg, Tex.: Pan American University, 1982.
Even though this novel has been criticized for lacking action and plot, Efrig sees it as actively concerned with the past and future of Kate, of Drabble the novelist, and of Britain. It asks how human goodness can survive in a world of violence. Kate's final party is

an answer, especially the bay tree she buys for it that symbolizes the enduring qualities of the nation.

Elkins, Mary Jane. "Alenoushka's Return: Motifs and Movement in Margaret Drabble's *The Middle Ground*." In *Critical Essays on Margaret Drabble*, edited by Ellen Cronan Rose. Boston: G. K. Hall, 1985.

This novel is about searching for meaning in life. But, because it provides little forward-moving action, readers must discover this theme in the parallels and patterns provided by digressions, by embedded fairy tales, and by the slow revelations of family histories. Common negative elements can be discerned as well: compulsively neat women descend from nervous collapse into repression; babies are dead, lost, or denied. Yet Kate, like other Drabble heroines, will be kept from failure by her virtues: energy, warmth, spontaneity, and lust for life's diversity.

Greene, Gayle. "Bleak Houses: Doris Lessing, Margaret Drabble, and the Condition of England." *Forum for Modern Language Studies* 28 (October, 1992): 314-319.

Green discusses two pairs of novels to illustrate the changes in "condition of England" novels from the 1970's to the 1980's. Each pair contains one novel by Drabble and one by Lessing. Lessing's *The Summer Before Dark* is bleak; its heroine, like England, has little of value left—but the heroine does end with an affirmation of motherhood. In *The Middle Ground*, Kate is similarly disillusioned at first, both about her personal life and about England. Her dreams of happiness and social justice have proved false. Yet with the help of her love and compassion for her family and friends, Kate can feel hope for herself and her nation. Houses are often used by both writers as metaphors for the personal lives they contain and for England itself. Drabble contrasts this pair of novels to a later pair: Lessing's *The Good Terrorist* and Drabble's *The Radiant Way*.

Gullette, Margaret Morganroth. "Ugly Ducklings and Swans: Margaret Drabble's Fable of Progress in the Middle Years." *Modern Language Quarterly* 44 (September, 1983): 285-304. Reprinted with minor changes in *Safe at Last in the Middle Years: The Invention of the Midlife Progress Novel: Saul Bellow,*

Margaret Drabble, Anne Tyler, John Updike. Berkeley: University of California Press, 1988.

In this novel, we see only the final stages of Drabble's basic myth. Kate is a swan—a woman of maturity, achievement, and calm—who simply becomes more swanlike. Unlike many of Drabble's heroines, she does not need to return to her roots. In fact, when she does revisit her home, she finds nothing there from which to learn.

Hannay, John. "Margaret Drabble: An Interview." *Twentieth Century Literature: A Scholarly and Critical Journal* 33 (Summer, 1987): 129-149.

Drabble makes interesting remarks on this novel. When she wrote it, she wanted to portray Britain as it was at that moment. Perhaps it could be called a documentary. Its plotlessness can be seen in Kate, who seems to wish for a big event to happen but chooses easier options. When Drabble thinks of the party echoing *Mrs. Dalloway* at the end, she realizes that she could not really resolve the novel.

Hoffmann, Anne Golomb. "Acts of Self-Creation: Female Identity in the Novels of Margaret Drabble." In *Faith of a (Woman) Writer*, edited by Alice Kessler-Harris and William McBrien. Westport, Conn.: Greenwood Press, 1988.

Hoffman sees Drabble working through personal concerns in her novels. The early rather melodramatic novels pictured young women either entrapped by marriage (*The Garrick Year*) or escaping that trap only to become isolated (*The Millstone*). In her later novels and in *The Middle Ground* in particular, Drabble broadens her picture of women (from film star to social worker) and the greater range of possibilities they enjoy. She stresses the experience of motherhood and female friendship. Like Woolf, the later Drabble disdains traditional plots and concentrates on life's great web of connections, such as those Kate senses when she gets an aerial view of London from a hospital room. Drabble's narrator does not sum up this vision. She is not an omniscient narrator but a privileged onlooker.

Irvine, Lorna. "No Sense of An Ending: Drabble's Continuous Fictions." In *Critical Essays on Margaret Drabble*, edited by Ellen Cronan Rose. Boston: G. K. Hall, 1985.

Irvine thinks this novel specifically connects sexuality and the endings of fictions—men preferring the climactic, women the continuous. Both Kate and Evelyn are survivors. The growing tree Kate selects for her party suggests her unknown future.

Kenyon, Olga. *Women Novelists Today: A Survey of English Writing in the Seventies and Eighties.* New York: St. Martin's Press, 1988.
Like Virginia Woolf in *Mrs. Dalloway,* Drabble here takes her heroine though a short period of London life. Drabble evokes a wide range of experiences and characters by means of a loose structure which enables her to include disconnected episodes from newspapers and television. Kenyon thinks Drabble has tried to include too much material.

Madison, Beth. "Mr. Bennett, Mrs. Woolf, and Mrs. Drabble." *West Virginia University Philological Papers* 34 (1988): 118-127.
Drabble adapts modernist conventions to the postmodern situation in several ways. Like characters in Joyce's *Ulysses,* Drabble's characters roam around one city during a short period of time. In *Ulysses,* they walk, but in Drabble, they travel by almost every possible conveyance. Much time is spent in transit, and this time is usually filled with tension. Secondly, although like modernist writers Drabble provides many different moments from different subjective perspectives, she modifies the effect of these moments by her disturbingly intrusive narrator. And where a modernist uses images to flesh out characterization or amplify meaning, Drabble's images of mutilation and sewage function mainly to give an unpleasant evocation of urban life.

Murphy, Brenda. "Women, Will, and Survival: The Figure in Margaret Drabble's Carpet." *South Atlantic Quarterly* 82 (Winter, 1983): 38-50.
Kate is a typical Drabble high-powered woman—a carnivore. She has midlife crises, but she survives by virtue of her self-interest. Although the novel raises some ambiguities, Drabble seems to admire Kate's success.

Myer, Valerie Grosvenor. *Margaret Drabble: A Reader's Guide.* New York: St. Martin's Press, 1991.

A loosely organized but valuable essay. Myer criticizes Drabble for being unable to describe accurately working-class lives (like that of the young Kate) and for patronizing other such characters. The disparate story-lines are connected by several devices. The novel shows many characters interpreting their experience through filters and frames: the media, codes of dress and manners, intellectual concepts. Many characters see that the optimistic egalitarian ideals of the 1960's have failed but are unsure what lies ahead. A system of images pervades the novel: physical and mental health are threatened by images of violence, sickness, dirt, and excrement. Drabble's strength is that she brings together mundane facts and spiritual concerns.

Parker, Gillian, and Janet Todd. "Margaret Drabble." In *Women Writers Talking*, edited by Janet Todd. New York: Holmes & Meier, 1983.
Drabble says this is a state of London novel. It is also about feminism.

Pickering, Jean. "Margaret Drabble's Sense of the Middle Problem." *Twentieth Century Literature* 30 (Winter, 1984): 475-483.
A very interesting reading. Pickering says that Drabble here overtly employs a tactic she has often suggested before. The narrator tells us that she is just reporting the sometimes superficial facts of the real stories that lie beneath the surface, stories of characters who have lives independent of this novel. These facts do not necessarily cohere to form a unified vision. The narrator disclaims responsibility for the conclusions the reader draws. Kate herself draws similar conclusions about her own life. When she revisits the scenes of her childhood, she (unlike some earlier Drabble characters) finds no continuity with the present, nor can she imagine a pattern extending into her future. So Kate decides not to look for patterns in her life, but to go ahead with life itself. Hence her happy party, with its diverse and inclusive guest list.

Quinn, Joseph A. "Christianity and Secularism in the Later Margaret Drabble." *University of Windsor Review* 18 (Fall-Winter, 1984): 67-75.
Brief remarks. Quinn finds several kinds of religious feeling in *The Ice Age* but none in *The Middle Ground*. Kate drifts though

life, not deeply touched by anything. Readers are so distanced from her that they do not care.

Rose, Ellen Cronan. "Drabble's *The Middle Ground*: `Mid-Life' Narrative Strategies." *Critique: Studies in Contemporary Fiction* 23 (Spring, 1982): 69-82.
Kate expects her life to unfold in units and thinks that her Iraqi boarder Mujid will bring her to her next stage. But she discovers that events refuse to fall into significant patterns, much the same thing Hugo discovers when he tries to write a novel. Part way through, even Drabble's narrator abandons interpretation and provides readers only with documents. By the end, Kate sees Mujid, not as a step in her development, but as an individual. She moves forward in hopeful anticipation, much like a character in a soap opera.

_____. "The Sexual Politics of Narration: Margaret Drabble's Feminist Fiction." *Studies in the Novel* 20 (Spring, 1988): 86-99.
Rose's thesis is that Drabble's structures are feminist ones that do not impose patriarchal structures on experience. Here neither the narrator nor Kate herself can find narrative patterns in her life. Many details are left to speak for themselves.

Rose, Phyllis. "Margaret Drabble." In *The Writing of Women: Essays in Renaissance*. Middletown, Conn.: Wesleyan University Press, 1985.
A revised version of her *New York Times Book Review* article.

_____. "Our Chronicler of Britain." *The New York Times Book Review*, September 7, 1980, 1, 32-33.
In the future, readers will turn to novels like this to find out what life was like in Britain in 1980. Britain, in fact, is the central character. Although the novel is an experiment, it does not succeed. Transitions are awkward, there is little action, there are too many facts, and it ends with no sense of hope.

Roxman, Susanna. *Guilt and Glory: Studies in Margaret Drabble's Novels 1963-80*. Stockholm: Almquist & Wiksell International, 1984.

There is much discussion of fate in this novel, though Roxman thinks Drabble now thinks more of statistical probability. Kate often feels fated, and many supposed accidents turn out to be less than accidental. Nevertheless, many people do seem to escape their seemingly fated conditions, and at the end Kate feels free to face the future. In a later section, Roxman deals with the dominant cluster of images in the novel: dirt, disease, disease-carrying animals and insects, garbage, excrement, and sewers. These images exist mainly as concrete descriptions, not tropes. Unlike Dickens when he uses such images, Drabble does not appear to be condemning squalor. Roxman analyzes twenty passages, and concludes that these images suggest that England is diseased in many ways, physical and moral. It is significant that as a part of her looking to the future, Kate cleans her house.

Rubenstein, Roberta. "From Detritus to Discovery: Margaret Drabble's *The Middle Ground.*" *Journal of Narrative Technique* 14 (Winter, 1984): 1-16.
Rubenstein explores Drabble's echoes of Virginia Woolf's *Mrs. Dalloway.* In particular, as other characters in Woolf's novel serve to emphasize aspects of Clarissa Dalloway, so do characters like Evelyn make clear aspects of Kate. Although Drabble's narrator is more intrusive, both novels end with parties celebrating the renewal of their heroines. Many insights here, but Rubenstein's loosely-organized argument is sometimes strained.

_____. "Margaret Drabble's *The Waterfall*: The Myth of Psyche, Romantic Tradition, and the Female Quest." In *Margaret Drabble: Golden Realms*, edited by Dorey Schmidt. No. 4 in *Living Author Series.* Edinburg, Tex.: Pan American University, 1982.
The Middle Ground may resolve the question with which *The Waterfall* ends: how can women escape being torn between desire and the need for autonomy?

Ruderman, Judith. "An Invitation to a Dinner Party: Margaret Drabble on Women and Food." In *Margaret Drabble: Golden Realms*, edited by Dorey Schmidt. No. 4 in *Living Author Series.* Edinburg, Tex.: Pan American University, 1982.

This novel displays guilt for enjoying good food when many people go hungry. Yet at the end, Kate's party is seen as an admirable and necessary human activity, one by which she creates moments of harmony in a chaotic world.

Sadler, Lynn Veach. *Margaret Drabble*. Boston: Twayne, 1986.
In Chapter 7, Sadler echoes many of the ideas of "'The Society We Have': The Search for Meaning in Drabble's *The Middle Ground*." Drabble is annoying when she intrudes so often and when she refuses to draw conclusions or to order her material. Yet the book has energy and intelligence.

_____. "'The Society We Have': The Search for Meaning in Drabble's *The Middle Ground*." *Critique: Studies in Contemporary Fiction* 23 (Spring, 1982): 83-92.
Although this novel includes much simple reporting and is full of lists, Drabble gives Kate's life shape in several ways. Kate finds she must acknowledge her ties to the past. Kate finds value in her relations with her children and in her responsibilities to her extended family. The book shows both sorts of relations in its many social occasions, especially in its anticipated final party.

Satz, Martha. "Less of a Woman as One Gets Older: An Interview with Margaret Drabble." *Southwest Review* 70 (Spring, 1985): 187-197.
In an interview, Drabble describes the problems she had weaving the parts of this unstructured novel together. The novel implies that Drabble is through coping with ideologies.

Sizemore, Christine Wick. *A Female Vision of the City: London in the Novels of Five British Women*. Knoxville: University of Tennessee Press, 1989.
Drabble uses the image of a network to describe London and fills in the outlines of that vision in great detail. Both Kate and Evelyn see the variety and jumble of the city. Evelyn sees good in bad people and bad areas. At one point Kate gets an aerial view of the streets of the city and at another ponders its vast network of sewers. These physical networks parallel the networks of human relations both women affirm, though sometimes with reluctance.

Stovel, Nora F. "`A Feminine Ending?': Symbolism as Closure in the Novels of Margaret Drabble." *English Studies in Canada* 15 (March, 1989): 80-93.
Drabble gives closure to her novels by providing equivocal final symbols. Here a bay tree has both optimistic and pessimistic suggestions.

_____. *Margaret Drabble, Symbolic Moralist.* Mercer Island, Wash.: Starmont House, 1989.
The central symbol of this novel is London's sewer system. It suggests the cesspool of society, Kate's subconscious life, and the complexity of the narrative itself. The vision of London as cesspool is closely related to unpleasant images of excrement, insects, parasites, poison, disease, and maimed people. The novel's tone changes when Kate exchanges her worm's-eye view of London for an aerial view. When she looks out of a high window, she sees an optimistic pattern of death and rebirth, destruction and reconstruction. Kate celebrates with a party which is full of obvious symbols.

Whitehill, Sharon. "Two for Tea: An Afternoon with Margaret Drabble." *Essays in Literature* 11 (Spring, 1984): 61-75.
Drabble says that the plot of this novel is a failure. But she adds that this is what the novel us about: the impossibility of imposing plots on life.

The Radiant Way, 1987.

Annan, Gabriele. "Worriers." *The New York Review of Books*, February 4, 1988, 17-18.
Drabble chronicles the early eighties, displaying her usual precise description and insight as well as a talent for horror. If her characters do not live as fully as Virginia Woolf would have wished, their story is readable. Perhaps Drabble is an Edwardian novelist.

Atwood, Margaret. "Margaret Atwood Talks to Margaret Drabble." *Chatelaine* 60 (April, 1987): 73, 124, 126, 130.
The famous Canadian novelist quizzes Drabble on her opinions and personal life. Atwood calls attention to the scope, including

politics, of *The Radiant Way*. Drabble says she admires Margaret Thatcher for her confidence and for keeping the issue of her gender out of politics. Drabble also remembers her discovery that it was hard work to combine raising children and writing novels.

Campbell, Jane. "`Both a Joke and a Victory': Humor as Narrative Strategy in Margaret Drabble's Fiction." *Contemporary Literature* 32 (Spring, 1991): 75-99.
There is less laughter than usual in this novel, perhaps because it is not a hopeful book. The narrator may be having fun with the expectations of some readers when she does not resolve various plots in the usual ways.

Connor, Steven. *The English Novel in History 1950-1995*. London: Routledge, 1996.
In Chapter 2, Connor deals with this "condition of England" novel at length. Liz and Charles once shared the postwar ideal of England's having a common culture. This ideal ("The Radiant Way") is undermined by Thatcher's economic policies and, in the novel, by the violence of severed heads, by the miners' strike, and by Liz's discoveries about sexual molestation. The nation is now divided; the condition is bleak.

Cunningham, Gail. "Patchwork and Patterns: The Condition of England in Margaret Drabble's Later Novels." In *The British and Irish Novel Since 1960*, edited by James Acheson. New York: St. Martin's Press, 1991.
In contrast to Drabble's intelligently pattered early novels, *The Radiant Way* shows that simple patterns do not explain private or public life in the 1980's. Some deeper patterns do emerge. This novel (improbably) has many echoes of Jane Austen.

Greene, Gayle. "Bleak Houses: Doris Lessing, Margaret Drabble, and the Condition of England." *Forum for Modern Language Studies* 28 (October, 1992): 314-319.
Green discusses two pairs of novels—one each by Drabble and Lessing—to illustrate the changes in "condition of England" novels from the 1970's to the 1980's. Both novels of the first pair, which included *The Middle Ground*, ended with an affirmation. Lessing's radically nihilistic *The Good Terrorist* and Drabble's

The Radiant Way make up the second, and much more bleak, pair. The dissolution of Liz's marriage parallels the failure of the hopes liberals once had for England. Liz's return to her past unearths only horrors; Britain's economic system hold little hope.

Kenyon, Olga. *Women Writers Talk: Interviews with Ten Women Writers.* New York: Carroll & Graf, 1990.
Drabble says that this novel is not a "woman's book." It began when Drabble asked what went wrong in England in the 1980's. Drabble thinks that, although politically pessimistic, the novel shows how individuals of all classes can live good lives.

McGuirk, Carol. "Drabble to Carter: Fiction by Women, 1962-1992." In *The Columbia History of the British Novel*, edited by John Richetti. New York: Columbia University Press, 1994.
Although Drabble's first novel, *A Summer's Bird-Cage*, depicts women in competition, her later novels shows women's friendships. Esther is a woman outside the norm.

Marsh, Kelly A. "The Neo-Sensational Novel: A Contemporary Genre in the Victorian Tradition." *Philological Quarterly* 74 (Winter, 1995): 99-123.
Marsh first defines the Victorian sensational novel. Beneath the surface of a respectable and even fashionable society lies a scandalous *secret*, often one of sexual irregularities and which involves hidden networks of people and chains of past events. The novels are set in the present, describe bizarre events, and draw upon journalistic sources. Though some critics see these novels as conservative, they were often radical in questioning women's roles and bourgeois values.
The Radiant Way and *A Natural Curiosity* (Marsh treats them together) are part of this tradition. Liz is a member of London's elite; the novels have many very odd happenings, like Jilly Fox's murder. Liz's past holds many secrets, mainly sexual in one way or another. Like the heroine of a Victorian sensational novel, Liz reacts to learning her secrets with overpowering emotional sensations. In fact, even though she is a psychiatrist, Liz had denied until then the full emotional impact of her past. (Alix's investigations into the murderer's childhood provide a parallel.) Drabble may seem postmodern when she intrudes into her narrative, but

the force of neo-sensationalist fiction is against postmodernism. Postmodernists think that morality and ethics are socially constructed, but neo-sensationalist novels like Drabble's imply that truth exists and that human beings can find at least part of it through sensation.

Myer, Valerie Grosvenor. *Margaret Drabble: A Reader's Guide.* New York: St. Martin's Press, 1991.

Drabble splits her concerns into those of three central female characters. Myer is good on this novel's mixed genre. This is a state of England novel; it asks "What is England like in the 1980's?" With her satire of Alix and Brian, Drabble makes clear that the old liberal attitudes do not work. It is also a "two nations" novel, contrasting sophisticated London with the depressing workaday north. In telling Liz's story, Drabble goes more deeply into sexual problems and family matters than in earlier novels. Claudio's artistic origins are in magic realism. Myers notes the rich background of art history references and explicates some of them.

Rubenstein, Roberta. "Fragmented Bodies/Selves/Narratives: Margaret Drabble's Postmodern Turn." *Contemporary Literature* 35 (Spring, 1994): 136-155.

Drabble's later works show images of the fragmented human body and of political and social divisions. Moreover, the narratives themselves are fragmented in decidedly postmodern ways. In this novel, bodies are decapitated, the social world seems to be falling apart, and the self-conscious narrator presents disjointed stories.

_____. "Sexuality and Intertextuality: Margaret Drabble's *The Radiant Way.*" *Contemporary Literature* 30 (Spring, 1989): 95-112.

Drabble uses intertextuality to make significant allusions to other novelists and adapts several classical stories in order to examine women's lives. References to Virginia Woolf point out several similar themes. References to the Minotaur and its labyrinth suggest problems in female sexual development. And references to the Medusa stories suggest not only women's power but also the radiance of the sun. The three friends are revealed as women who can be illuminated and hence can bond at the end of the novel.

Sizemore, Christine Wick. *A Female Vision of the City: London in the Novels of Five British Women*. Knoxville: University of Tennessee Press, 1989.
Like other women novelists of the twentieth century, Drabble's novels provide a vision of the city. In this novel, London is not so radiant as before. But its three major female characters react to the city with love, though in different ways. Esther is conscious of decay and ugliness. Alix sees the networks of relationships in lower-class neighborhoods but also the horrors that await people like Jilly Fox. Liz sees connections with the past, often focusing on architectural detail. The novel's title may be an ironic reference to a geometrical utopian city envisioned by Le Corbusier.

Stovel, Nora F. "'A Feminine Ending?': Symbolism as Closure in the Novels of Margaret Drabble." *English Studies in Canada* 15 (March, 1989): 80-93.
Drabble gives closure to her novels by providing equivocal final symbols, here a sun which may be rising or setting.

_____. *Margaret Drabble, Symbolic Moralist*. Mercer Island, Wash.: Starmont House, 1989.
Critics applaud this "state of England" novel, but complain that nothing happens. Stovel contends that although the important happenings of the novel are not easily identified, they are signaled by symbols. Though the symbol of "the radiant way" once motivated its characters, the novel's main vision is communicated by demonic symbols: werewolves, devils, murders, severed heads. The turning point occurs when, after Jilly's and Claudio's deaths, the three central women turn to their private affairs and begin new lives. Yet a symbolic minotaur remains for Liz, having been heralded by many images of mazes and labyrinths. Liz's quest is to discover the secret of her father's life and death. Only when she has remembered his actions can she join the other two women in a garden symbolic of hope for the future.

Updike, John. "Seeking Connections in an Insecure Country." *The New Yorker*, November 16, 1987, 153-159.
Updike praises Drabble's intelligence, her sympathy, and her sense of diversity and connectedness. But he does not find Drabble's portrayal of female friendship convincing, nor her portrayal

of Esther. In addition he finds the novel too diffuse and at times banal.

A Natural Curiosity, 1989.

Campbell, Jane. "`Both a Joke and a Victory': Humor as Narrative Strategy in Margaret Drabble's Fiction." *Contemporary Literature* 32 (Spring, 1991): 75-99.
This novel's humor is dark, but surprisingly, it is more humorous than *The Radiant Way*. But readers laugh at the incompetence of "experts," at forbidden subjects, and at surprising turns in the story. Moreover, Drabble's language here is at its most exuberant.

Connor, Steven. *The English Novel in History 1950-1995*. London: Routledge, 1996.
Drabble's trilogy is a "condition of England novel." It contains many events and many perspectives, mirroring the looseness of lived history.

Cunningham, Gail. "Patchwork and Patterns: The Condition of England in Margaret Drabble's Later Novels." In *The British and Irish Novel Since 1960*, edited by James Acheson. New York: St. Martin's Press, 1991.
Drabble's early novels found patterns in a single young woman's life. In *A Natural Curiosity*, Drabble reveals deeper and more grim psychotic patterns in both individual lives and the life of Britain. Repeated references to Celtic and Roman times suggest the timelessness of barbarism. Characters in the present respond by trying to leave Britain. The novel's positive values are located in the north and in the friendship of three middle-aged women.

Elkins, Mary Jane. "Facing the Gorgon: Good and Bad Mothers in the Late Novels of Margaret Drabble." In *Narrating Mothers: Theorizing Maternal Subjectivities*, edited by Brenda O. Daly and Maureen T. Reddy. Knoxville: University of Tennessee Press, 1991.
Drabble usually divides her females into good and bad mothers. In this novel, Drabble uniquely forgives some bad mothers.

Marsh, Kelly A. "The Neo-Sensational Novel: A Contemporary Genre in the Victorian Tradition." *Philological Quarterly* 74 (Winter, 1995): 99-123.
In her interesting analysis, Marsh treats this novel and *The Radiant Way* together. See the summary under *The Radiant Way*.

Myer, Valerie Grosvenor. *Margaret Drabble: A Reader's Guide.* New York: St. Martin's Press, 1991.
Alix's odd interest in the murderer Paul Whitmore is central to this novel. Drabble contrasts the moral and ordered world in which most people live with the violent and sexual jungle that lies just beyond it. This novel's ideas about sex, particularly Liz's ideas about children and sex, have caused critics to wonder about Drabble's attitudes.

Rubenstein, Roberta. "Fragmented Bodies/Selves/Narratives: Margaret Drabble's Postmodern Turn." *Contemporary Literature* 35 (Spring, 1994): 136-155.
Like Drabble's other later works, this novel shows many images of the fragmented human body and of political and social division. The narrative itself is fragmented in a postmodern way.

_____. "Severed Heads, Primal Crimes, Narrative Revisions: Margaret Drabble's *A Natural Curiosity.*" *Critique: Studies in Contemporary Fiction* 33 (Winter, 1992): 95-105.
Rubenstein asks why this novel and its predecessor provide so many images of decapitation and dismemberment. In both novels, these images show human barbarity and depravity. Alix investigates social depravity in the case of Paul Whitmore, the imprisoned murderer from *The Radiant Way.* She thinks she can explain him by the way he grew up, especially by the influence of his horrible mother. Liz probes psychic and family depths, generating more sympathy for Paul. She also discovers that her mother bore an illegitimate daughter and that her father abused children, including herself. But these discoveries do not lead Liz (or the novel) to firm conclusions. Her half sister turns out well; her father was not really that bad. In a television interview, she tentatively defends deviant sexual practices. Not only does *A Natural Curiosity* not offer solutions, but Rubenstein thinks it obscures the issues.

The Gates of Ivory, 1991.

Annan, Gabriele. "Numbers Game." *The New York Review of Books*, May 28, 1992, 15-16.
Annan reviews the trilogy and comments on how Drabble now extends her concerns to the whole world. Drabble renders her London people well but is not so interesting about East Asia. Besides these two worlds, Annan identifies a third force in the novel: a strain of meditative reflections and portentous questions which lead nowhere. Drabble's problem is how to write about multitudes and about individuals at the same time. She may think she is writing a new sort of novel here, but Tolstoy did it earlier and more successfully in *War and Peace*. An illuminating review.

Ashton, Rosemary. "From Bayswater to Bangkok." *The Times Literary Supplement*, October 4, 1991, 27.
Ashton thinks that this very ambitious novel is sometime contrived. Though Drabble distinguishes between "good time" in London and "bad time" in East Asia, the novel's final London traffic jam suggests that the West is on the edge of "bad time" as well. The novel's London scenes are not funny enough, but Drabble is not somber enough in the Thailand and Cambodia portions.

Connor, Steven. *The English Novel in History 1950-1995*. London: Routledge, 1996.
Drabble's trilogy is a "condition of England novel." It contains many events and many perspectives, mirroring the looseness of lived history.

Lesser, Wendy. "Fiction in Review." *Yale Review* 80 (July, 1992): 198-208.
Lesser expresses her displeasure with this novel. Drabble is an irritatingly intrusive narrator. Her mounds of information and political ideas are not integrated into the novel's story. Conrad's old-fashioned storytelling dealt better with exotic cultures.

Rubenstein, Roberta. "Fragmented Bodies/Selves/Narratives: Margaret Drabble's Postmodern Turn." *Contemporary Literature* 35 (Spring, 1994): 136-155.

An important article on this challenging novel. Like Drabble's other late novels, *The Gates of Ivory* is filled with images of the fragmented and suffering human body: severed heads, skulls, finger bones, not to mention cancer and complications from menstruation. The consciousness of many characters are similarly fragmented, as are families and the political and social structures of the world itself. Even so, the novels central characters yearn for the modern world and value what they hope are their meaningful friendships. Drabble's scope is wide indeed.

To tell of these things, Drabble's narration is necessarily postmodern. Events in the almost plotless story are often arbitrary, disconnected, impossible of interpretation. Hence Drabble provides many lists, including one of possible fates for a character. As narrator, Drabble self-consciously refers to other fictions, notably Shakespeare's *Coriolanus* and Joseph Conrad's *Heart of Darkness,* and ends the novel with a bibliography. Unlike other postmodern narrators, she apologizes for the limitations of fiction itself. Traditional narrative techniques are inadequate, and there is neither time nor space to record all the world's untold stories.

Simon, Linda. "Rambo, Rimbaud, Which is Best?" *The New York Times Book Review,* May 10, 1992, 8.
The best review of this book. Simon sums up the questions Drabble asks: What can we do about the world's problems? What kind of narrative is appropriate? What kind can help? *The Gate of Ivory* is not so much a novel as a meditation on our world. Stephen Cox asks what kind of story can make sense of it and finds no answers. Neither does Liz. Are stories of Rambo or stories by Rimbaud most meaningful? Miss Porntip does not care about stories, for she is perfectly suited to postmodernism. In a way, so is this novel. Its characters do not move us, and the novel itself implies that old-fashioned characters have gone the way of old-fashioned stories.

Sutherland, John. "Drabble's Progress." *London Review of Books,* December 5, 1991, 18.
Sutherland gives the novel but one paragraph. A facile overview.

The Witch of Exmoor, 1996.

Duchêne, Anne. "A Fable of Fairness." *The Times Literary Supplement*, October 11, 1996, 26.
This novel is a muddled fairy-tale, unsteady in its tone. Sometimes Drabble and her heroine Frieda are very close; sometimes Drabble is an intrusive narrator. The novel is concerned with the idea of a just society and its impossibility. There is a suggestion that the next generation will do better.

Truax, Alice. "Dangerous Games." *The New Yorker*, November 3, 1997, 107-108.
Drabble's novel is about the game of power in families, in politics, and in fiction. The children play it upstairs. Adults play it in life; Frieda's children and their spouses have all they need for the good life but plot for more. Drabble plays it in her novel, for by the end readers may sympathize with the two young people and hope for them. To what end is Drabble manipulating her readers?

Waugh, Theresa. "A Hermit with a Handful." *The Spectator*, October 19, 1996, 46-47.
An appreciative review that contrasts the marvelous Frieda with her horrible children. The children and their spouses are greedy and corrupt, the products of privilege. Waugh thinks Drabble belabors the theme of justice and wishes the book were longer.

Bibliographical Studies

Korenman, Joan S. "A Margaret Drabble Bibliography." In *Critical Essays on Margaret Drabble*, edited by Ellen Cronan Rose. Boston: G. K. Hall, 1985.

Martin, Gyde-Christine. "Margaret Drabble: A Bibliography." *Bulletin of Bibliography* 45 (March, 1988): 21-32.
Supplements Stanton.

Packer, Joan Garrett. *Margaret Drabble: An Annotated Bibliography*. New York: Garland, 1988.

Schmidt, Dorey. "A Bibliography Update." In *Margaret Drabble: Golden Realms*. No. 4 in *Living Author Series*. Edinburg, Tex.: Pan American University, 1982.
Updates Stanton.

Stanton, Robert J. *A Bibliography of Modern British Novelists*. Troy, N.Y.: Whitson, 1978.

Other Works

Drabble has written several plays and screenplays. She has published a few short stories and a great many essays and introductions. She has also published a critical study of *Wordsworth* (New York: Arco, 1969) and two biographies: *Arnold Bennett* (New York: Knopf, 1974) and *Angus Wilson* (London: Secker & Warburg, 1995). She has edited the fifth edition of *The Oxford Companion to English Literature* (Oxford: Oxford University Press, 1985) and is the author of the illustrated volume *A Writer's Britain* (New York: Knopf, 1979). A motion picture, *A Touch of Love*, was made of *The Millstone* in 1965.

Iris Murdoch

General Studies

Allen, Brooke. "The Drawing-room Comedy of Iris Murdoch." *New Criterion* 15 (September, 1996): 66-73.
Even though Murdoch novels have serious themes, many readers enjoy them as drawing-room comedies. Her characters are drawn from upper-middle-class society, the world in which such comedy thrives. Almost everyone has enough money, learns Latin and Greek, and drinks too much whiskey. Murdoch's limited optimism often informs the novels' happy endings (which resemble those in Shakespeare). Parts of *Under the Net* and *The Black Prince* recall P. G. Wodehouse. Allen treats *Jackson's Dilemma* at some length.

Allen, Diogenes. "Two Experiences of Existence: Jean-Paul Sartre and Iris Murdoch." *International Philosophical Quarterly* 14 (June, 1974): 181-187.
A scene from *The Unicorn* challenges Roquentin's nausea in *La Nausée*. Allen prefers Murdoch's way of describing the human situation.

Allen, Walter. *The Modern Novel in Britain and the United States.* New York: E. P. Dutton, 1964.
Allen treats Murdoch briefly together with John Wain, Kingsley Amis, and William Golding. Murdoch is potentially a great novelist, but her work is obscure, especially *The Severed Head. The Bell* is her best; Allen praises the complex character of Michael. Yet how can a reader tell what is symbolic and what is not?

_____. *Tradition and Dream.* London: Hogarth Press, 1964.
Reprints his remarks from *The Modern Novel in Britain and the United States.*

Allsop, Kenneth. *The Angry Decade*. New York: The British Book
    Centre, 1958.
    In Part 2, Allsop groups Murdoch with such novelists as Amis and
    Wain. In his chatty essay, he praises Murdoch's comic scenes, her
    great range, her style, and her sympathy, though he finds her
    symbolism puzzling. In *Under the Net*, he likes the evocation of
    Jake's London. *The Flight from the Enchanter* is incoherent.

Atlas, James. "The Abbess of Oxford." *Vanity Fair*, March, 1988,
    70, 76, 80, 82, 86.
    Anecdotes and some reflections on her work.

Baldanza, Frank. *Iris Murdoch*. New York: Twayne, 1974.
    An important and very useful book. Baldanza's first chapter and
    his Conclusion give an excellent overview of Murdoch's career
    through 1973. He considers how best to label her novels
    (philosophical? intellectual? comic?) before locating them in the
    realist tradition of the eighteenth and nineteenth century English
    novel. Her plots are traditional, usually turning on erotic entan-
    glements and surprising twists. (Perhaps her force comes from
    the tension between her desire to write such plots and her natural
    tendency to write allegory.) Baldanza often focuses on Murdoch's
    sensational scenes, judging some to be more effective than others.
    Her most typical character is an upper-middle-class male
    professional, but we often meet adolescent girls, exotic Eastern
    Europeans, male homosexuals, as well as powerful, tyrannical,
    even satanic figures.
    Baldanza calls her technique that of "transcendental realism," a
    kind of story that begins realistically, but soon introduces outra-
    geous or fantastic elements. Often her plots display a contrast
    between a saint-like person and an artist or between an "alien
    god" figure and others who think he embodies their suppressed
    desires. In Murdoch's later novels, Baldanza finds suggestions of
    Platonic love. He also surveys her essays and comments on what
    her manuscripts reveal. Other chapters deal with all the novels
    through *The Black Prince*. Baldanza occasionally judges the
    novels only from the perspective of realism and therefore finds
    objectionable her overtly symbolic characters, her improbable
    happenings, and the novels' melodrama.

_____. "Iris Murdoch and the Theory of Personality." *Criticism: A Quarterly for Literature and the Arts* 7 (Spring, 1965): 176-189.

Murdoch objects to theories of personality by philosophers like Sartre. Like great novelists of the past, Murdoch thinks human beings are separate, unique, eccentric, and free, and she wants to create such characters living in a messy, contingent world. Since each human being is separate, a person has a moral duty to try to understand and love these separate beings. Murdoch's novels also imply a non-religious transcendental reality, which includes real evil. Her novels are not easily summarized. Each part must be considered with every other part before a work's total meaning can be understood. Baldanza makes brief comments on many novels and then analyzes *A Severed Head* in detail. A good summary of Murdoch's ideas.

Bell, Pearl K. "Games Writers Play." *Commentary* 71 (February, 1981): 69-73.

To Murdoch, fiction is a game, her characters chessmen. Her plots are implausible, and her novels lack moral discernment. Readers may be amused, but they are not moved.

Bellamy, Michael O. "An Interview with Iris Murdoch." *Contemporary Literature* 18 (Spring, 1977): 129-140.

In this July, 1976, interview, Murdoch expresses ideas about nineteenth century novelists (they could be optimistic because they wrote in a unified civilization), about D. H. Lawrence (he was propagandistic), about her temperament (she is not a pessimist; most events are comic), and about the novel (it is an open form, though her own plots may be too powerful), religion (she has Buddhist tendencies but now feels close to Christianity), literary theory (beware!), morality (it lies in *not* imposing form on others), and romantic love (it is an occasion for creating myths). She favors the advances women are making in education and in contributing to society. Although because she identifies with men she has many male narrators, she points out that many women talk in her novels. Real people are very odd, though they manage to disguise their oddities. They make myths about themselves, then are dominated by these myths and select other people to play roles in them. Novels can show how this process works.

Murdoch adroitly parries many of the interviewer's leading questions.

Berthoff, Warner. "Fortunes of the Novel: Muriel Spark and Iris Murdoch." *Massachusetts Review: A Quarterly of Literature, the Arts and Public Affairs* 8 (Spring, 1967): 301-332. Reprinted in *Fictions and Events: Essays in Criticism and Literary History.* New York: E. P. Dutton, 1971.
Unlike most other British writers, Murdoch has not been inhibited by the dream of writing a masterpiece. Her novels are often deficient in imagination, and her observations and descriptions are not always precise. But despite her flaws she has many virtues. She seems to have become a novelist to deal with topics that philosophers had given up on, such as love and communication between human beings. Her novels show the encounters of people dealing with these problems, inadequately for the most part. Her characters at first simply fail to understand; then they act upon misunderstandings, fail disastrously, learn something, and then recover and act again. Although they do not usually find a resolution, they may gain some degree of freedom and love. Berthoff analyzes *The Red and the Green* in detail.

Bigsby, Christopher. "Interview with Iris Murdoch." In *The Radical Imagination and the Liberal Tradition: Interviews with English and American Novelists*, edited by Christopher Bigsby and Heide Ziegler. London: Junction Books, 1982.
Murdoch talks about philosophy, about those who influenced what she thinks, and about politics, morality, and religion. She discusses the problem of free characters at length. Even though a novel must have authority and structure, characters within that structure can seem to be free, to have inner lives. Interesting remarks on *The Sandcastle, A Fairly Honorable Defeat, The Black Prince*, and *The Sea, The Sea*.

_____. "The Uneasy Middleground of British Fiction." *Granta* 3 (1980): 137-149.
Murdoch can be located in the middle ground of British fiction, between cozy, conservative writers and experimental ones. She is liberal, but not wholly rationalist. Interesting remarks on *The Black Prince*.

Biles, Jack I. "An Interview with Iris Murdoch." *Studies in the Literary Imagination* 12 (Fall, 1978): 115-125. Reprinted in *British Novelists Since 1900*. New York: AMS Press, 1987.
Murdoch does not promote her philosophical ideas in her novels. She identifies with male narrators because they can best embody the human condition; she is not interested in the "female predicament." Even though she is careful about symbols and about the suggestions of her characters' names, people often see symbolic meanings that are not there. Characters often create symbols that are not those of the novel as a whole. Interesting brief remarks on *The Black Prince*.

Bloom, Harold, ed. *Iris Murdoch*. New York: Chelsea House, 1986.
An anthology of criticism of most Murdoch novels published through 1986. Each article deals with general issues as well as with specific novels. Bloom calls Murdoch an original religious story teller and Britain's most eminent novelist, though her mixture of realism and fantasy is not completely successful. The editor's introduction treats *The Good Apprentice* at length.

_____. *The Western Canon: The Books and School of the Ages*. New York: Harcourt Brace, 1994.
Bloom calls Murdoch a descendant of George Eliot. He places two of Murdoch's novels on his list of the essential books of the Western canon: *Bruno's Dream* and *The Good Apprentice*.

Borklund, Elmer. "(Jean) Iris Murdoch." In *Contemporary Novelists*, 2d ed., edited by James Vinson. New York: St. Martin's Press, 1972.
A reader must know something about Murdoch's philosophical ideas to make sense of most of her novels. She is a pessimist, for she sees human beings as accidental creatures, blinded by self, roaming in a contingent universe. He outlines Murdoch's characteristic plot and makes brief comments on her novels through *The Black Prince*.

Bove, Cheryl K. "Americas and Americans in Iris Murdoch's Novels." In *Encounters with Iris Murdoch*, edited by Richard Todd. Amsterdam: Free University Press, 1988.

Bove argues that in Murdoch's novels the United States is regularly associated with violent forces, evil people, failed artists, bad
scholarship, and bad theory. In the discussion that followed this
paper, Murdoch disagreed somewhat, saying that some references
are jokes and citing several good characters who are Americans or
who go to America: Ludwig in *An Accidental Man* and Anne in
Nuns and Soldiers. Her personal feelings toward the United
States are mainly affectionate.

_____. *A Character Index and Guide to the Fiction of Iris
Murdoch*. New York: Garland, 1986.
An annotated list of characters, animals, places, and historical
references in Murdoch's novels and plays through 1985. Bove
groups the references to each work together and within that group
lists items alphabetically. An index lists *all* items alphabetically.
Bove's introduction provides a useful and lucid summary of
Murdoch's ideas about art and morals. Life has no ultimate point;
human beings are naturally selfish and can overcome their selfishness only by a loving and accurate attention to what is outside
them, including other people. Art has several roles; the novel can
show by its characterizations what other people are like. Unfortunately, the characters in most modern novels do not exhibit the
rich interior lives that real people experience.

_____. "New Directions: Iris Murdoch's Latest Women." In
Critical Essays on Iris Murdoch, edited by Lindsey Tucker. New
York: G. K. Hall, 1992.
Murdoch has been criticized for writing novels which employ a
male point of view and whose female characters are mainly weak
victims. Murdoch defends herself by denying there are many
ultimate differences between the sexes; she creates many androgynous characters. Moreover, what some call weak characters, she
would say are "good." Nevertheless, Bove says that two late
novels show a change. Murdoch's looser plots do not call for a
first-person male narrator. Their centers of consciousness are
scattered, with the result that much of the novel is told through
female minds. Bove discusses *The Book and the Brotherhood* and
The Message to the Planet.

_____. *Understanding Iris Murdoch.* Columbia: University of South Carolina Press, 1993.
This lucid handbook for college students covers Murdoch's works through 1989. Bove analyzes the novels, some briefly, some at length. In Chapter 1, she summarizes Murdoch's life, sets her in the tradition of English realist novelists, and discusses her important ideas: Platonism, Simone Weil's theory of attention, egotism and its effects, failures of communication, and attempts to find the good. Chapter 2 summarizes Murdoch's philosophical works. Bove's conclusion gives a brief and very useful summary of Murdoch's ideas. Bibliography.

Bradbury, Malcolm. "'A House Fit for Free Characters': Iris Murdoch and *Under the Net.*" In *Possibilities: Essays on the State of the Novel.* London: Oxford University Press, 1973. Reprinted in *No, Not Bloomsbury.* New York: Columbia University Press, 1988.
Bradbury first presents a succinct and evocative overview of Murdoch's fictional world and various responses to it. At its heart, he sees a conflict between two realities: the reality of the social world of independent beings and the reality of a world of mystery and symbolism. She writes against symbolic fiction, but her own novels are often symbolically ordered, as illustrated by an episode from *The Red and the Green.* Bradbury thinks Murdoch mediates this conflict by saying that love, a moral impulse toward the good, can be apprehended in particulars. Bradbury discusses *Under the Net* at length, adding to his earlier ideas.

_____. *The Modern British Novel.* London: Secker & Warburg, 1993.
In his overview, Bradbury treats Murdoch sympathetically and emphasizes her departures from realism.

Brans, Jo. *Listen to the Voices: Conversations with Contemporary Writers.* Dallas: Southern Methodist University Press, 1988.
"Virtuous Dogs and a Unicorn" is an account of an interview with Murdoch. The dogs in her novels, like the fragile Zed in *The Philosopher's Pupil*, are often figures of virtue. She thinks much contemporary philosophy distorts moral concerns: morals are not a matter of taste. Religion is the deep aspect of life; the concept of grace has meaning. She is pleased that Lisa and Danby end

happily in *Bruno's Dream*. She defends Tallis's dirty kitchen in *A Fairly Honorable Defeat*.

Bronzwaer, W. J. M. *Tense in the Novel: An Investigation of Some Potentialities of Linguistic Criticism*. Gronigen, the Netherlands: Wolters-Noordhoff, 1970.
This book is written for the specialist, but in Chapter 4 Bronzwaer makes his seemingly narrow linguistic investigations into *The Italian Girl* relevant to Murdoch's deepest concerns. He asks important questions about Murdoch's fiction. Do Murdoch's symbols leads us to transcendence or are they merely confused or expressive? Are Murdoch characters opaque like other human beings or simply unpredictable? Are her melodramatic plots evocative of life's density or are they pointless? Are the novels escape reading, or do they answer the assertions of logical positivists? Bronzwaer's answers uphold the worth of Murdoch's fictions.

Brooks-Davies, Douglas. *Fielding, Dickens, Gosse, Iris Murdoch, and Oedipal* Hamlet. New York: St. Martin's Press, 1989.
Brooks-Davies thinks that Murdoch had a *Hamlet* period, a time in which a number of her novels were influenced by that play. He notes the influence in *The Good Apprentice*, *Henry and Cato*, and *Nuns and Soldiers*, and discusses *The Black Prince* at length from a psychologist's perspective.

Burgess, Anthony. *The Novel Now: A Student's Guide to Contemporary Fiction*. London: Faber & Faber, 1967.
Brief notes on *The Bell*, *The Red and the Green*, *A Severed Head*, and *The Sandcastle*.

Burke, John J., Jr. "Canonizing Iris Murdoch." *Studies in the Novel* 19 (Winter, 1987): 486-494.
A survey of books by Dipple, Hague, Todd, Conradi, and Bloom. Even though critics and others cannot agree on what future readers will think are Murdoch's greatest virtues, she should be canonized as one of the greatest novelists of the last half of the twentieth century.

Byatt, A. S. *Degrees of Freedom: The Novels of Iris Murdoch.* New York: Barnes & Noble Books, 1965. Expanded ed. London: Vintage, 1994.

Byatt reviews Murdoch's ideas about crystalline and journalistic novels and about character. She asks how much freedom characters have in Murdoch's novels through *The Unicorn.* In her last chapter, Byatt looks at individual novels and at Murdoch's work as a whole. Although she finds many virtues, she concentrates on Murdoch's faults. Murdoch's prose is sometimes inflated and lazy. In spite of her ideas, in some novels her overall plan and her symbols predominate over the development of interesting characters. The 1994 expanded edition reprints the original and adds other items: a foreword; the entire text of Byatt's *Iris Murdoch* (1976); a review by Michael Levenson of a book by Byatt; and Byatt's own reviews of *The Time of the Angels, The Nice and the Good, Bruno's Dream, The Black Prince, Henry and Cato, The Sea, The Sea, Nuns and Soldiers, The Good Apprentice,* and *The Book and the Brotherhood.*

_____. *Iris Murdoch.* Harlow, Essex, England: Longman Group, 1976. Reprinted in part in *Iris Murdoch,* edited by Harold Bloom. New York: Chelsea House, 1986. Reprinted (with a 1986 postscript) as Chapter 19 in *Degrees of Freedom* [expanded edition]. London: Vintage, 1994.

In this brilliant and very short pamphlet, Byatt presents an overview of Murdoch's achievement and of her relation to other novelists. Murdoch's philosophical writings are the key to understanding her novels. Byatt lucidly and succinctly explains Murdoch's analysis of the inadequacies of two modern concepts of character and the kinds of novel these concepts produce: the crystalline novel and the journalistic novel. Byatt also explains what Murdoch means by virtue, the Good, freedom, love, attention, and contingency, and why the novelist has such an important job. In her comments on individual novels, Byatt shows how they can be understood by reference Murdoch's central ideas, ideas she has adapted from Sartre and from her husband, John Bayley. Byatt discusses why some readers have trouble reading Murdoch and explains her own reservations. Byatt's 1986 postscript treats *Nuns and Soldiers, The Good Apprentice, The Sea, The Sea,* and *The Philosopher's Pupil.* Byatt notes Murdoch's longer and looser structures, the increase in "peripheral people" and in the density of social structures in her novels, and her deepening concern with magic and religion.

_____. "People in Paper Houses: Attitudes to 'Realism' and 'Experiment' in English Postwar Fiction." In *The Contemporary English Novel*, edited by Malcolm Bradbury and David Palmer. New York: Holmes & Meier, 1980.

Although Murdoch has moved toward realism, not only do her characters seem fictive to the reader, they appear to view themselves in the light of Victorian and modernist novels. Murdoch's plots are similarly derivative, often from Shakespeare. Murdoch shows both an awareness of the problems of realism and an attachment to its values. Brief discussions of *Under the Net* and *The Black Prince*.

Cavaliero, Glen. *The Supernatural and English Fiction*. New York: Oxford University Press, 1995.

In Chapter 6, Cavaliero provides a brief but illuminating discussion of this difficult subject. Murdoch mixes naturalistic detail and bizarre yet explicable happenings with inexplicable, preternatural events. One example of such an event is Ann's talk with Jesus in *Nun's and Soldiers*; she could be said to have imagined it, except that it left a real mark on her. Cavaliero finds the key to Murdoch's use of the paranormal in Chapter 17 of *The Nice and the Good*, where she speaks of the mysterious agencies of the human mind. He discusses *The Unicorn* and *The Sea, The Sea* at length. Although Murdoch acknowledges supernatural powers may be evil, she thinks they are most often a force for the good.

Church, Margaret. "Social Consciousness in the Works of Elizabeth Bowen, Iris Murdoch, and Mary Lavin." *College Literature* 7 (Spring, 1980): 158-163.

Church generalizes from an essay Murdoch published in 1959 to assert that Murdoch thinks socialism provides the best way to realize the Good. Annette in *Flight from the Enchanter* shows the value Murdoch places on personal freedom. An essay of limited value.

Cohan, Steven. "From Subtext to Dream Text: The Brutal Egoism of Iris Murdoch's Male Narrators." *Women and Literature* 2 (1982): 222-242. Reprinted in *Men and Women*, edited by Janet Todd. New York: Holmes & Meier, 1981.

When Murdoch routinely employs male characters to embody the general human condition and female characters to represent the mysterious other, she may be satirizing contemporary culture for what it will accept. Nevertheless, her first-person male narrators seem to be literally male, and often Murdoch seems limited by the conventions of narrative from judging them explicitly enough. We can see, however, from the judgments made clear in *The Sea, The Sea* that these men aggressively and even brutally impose their fantasies on women. Cohan also discusses *A Severed Head, The Black Prince*, and *A Word Child* and refers to *The Italian Girl* in passing.

Colley, Mary. "Iris Murdoch—The `Good' Novelist." *Contemporary Review* 261 (December, 1992): 319-322.

In a slight essay, Colley focuses on structure, particularly that of openings, in Murdoch's novels. Murdoch does not introduce the reader gently to her characters, but demands and gets total participation. Like Anthony Trollope, Murdoch often shows different people in different places at the same time. Colley illustrates her points with references, especially to *The Book and the Brotherhood* and *A Message to the Planet*.

Conradi, Peter. *Iris Murdoch: The Saint and the Artist*. New York: St. Martin's Press, 1986.

In his preface, Conradi identifies the novels written between 1970 and 1985 as Murdoch's finest and proposes to read her early works in the light of their achievement. In the introduction, he argues that critics are wrong to impose Murdoch's early critical and philosophical ideas on her fiction. Nevertheless, he reviews these ideas and finds helpful several of the contrasts she makes: artist/saint and (especially) existentialist/mystic. Such contrasts should not be material for debate, for Murdoch explores the middle ground between these extremes, and her fiction tries to combine the virtues of each. In later chapters, Conradi continues his general argument while treating Murdoch's novels through *The Philosopher's Pupil*. In Chapter 3, he contrasts two of

Murdoch's best critics, Dipple and Sage, and concludes that neither sees the whole picture: Murdoch is both a stern puritan moralist and a cheerful, worldly writer who values pleasure and common sense.

In Chapter 4, Conradi discusses Murdoch's use of Plato and Freud. Many of her characters are unenlightened and unconscious, doomed to live within the same myths, to repeat the same patterns in their lives. Some move away from patterns, beyond control, beyond myth, into the world's flux. Art enacts a battle between its erotic sources in the unconscious and freedom and true love for others. In Chapter 6, Conradi discusses moments of enlightenment or the sublime and distinguishes between positive and negative sublimes. Murdoch differs from Sartre, who recognizes (as nausea) only the negative sublime. Murdoch's positive sublime is often imaged the immersion in water (suggesting immersion in the love of the world's various ingredients), hence the importance of swimming and ordeals by water in her novels. In his conclusion, Conradi defends Murdoch against her critics and asks readers not to try to force her novels into her theories. There is an appendix on Murdoch and Romanticism.

_____. "Iris Murdoch and Dostoevsky." In *Encounters with Iris Murdoch*, edited by Richard Todd. Amsterdam: Free University Press, 1988. Reprinted in *Dostoevskii and Britain*. Oxford: Berg Publishers Limited, 1995.

Conradi calls both religious novelists. Both doubt God's existence but are fascinated by the example of Christ. Both fear that the decline of organized religion will cause moral anarchy. In Dostoevsky, anarchy is dramatized as murder and the rape of children; in Murdoch, we find incest, adultery, and theft. Both authors are also interested in the unconscious and sadomasochistic behavior. Both authors think that good people are selfless, but both see how easily egotistical people can parody that selflessness. Conradi also sees similarities in the authors' techniques. Both employ doubled characters; both present scenes, often public, in which characters are humiliated and embarrassed in the extreme; both show a realism that can be termed Gothic; both create moments that are simultaneously painful and funny. Following this paper, John Bayley comments that in major writers like Murdoch and Fyodor Dostoevski, readers do not sense an individual personality.

Conradi and Murdoch make specific remarks on *Under the Net*, *Flight from the Enchanter*, *A Severed Head*, and *The Philosopher's Pupil*.

_____. "The Metaphysical Hostess: The Cult of Personal Relations in the Modern English Novel." *ELH* 48 (Summer, 1981): 427-453.
An important argument. Conradi identifies "the metaphysical hostess" as a type of character to be found in twentieth century fiction both as a organizing principle and as a cultural symptom. This figure is usually an unsatisfied upper-middle-class matron who promotes intimate relations; she longs to bring other characters together, often at parties in drawing rooms, to promote civilized reconciliations in a world botched by men. The roots of this figure go back to Bloomsbury and beyond; they supply a kind of religious authority in a age without religion. Good examples are E. M. Forster's Mrs. Wilcox (*Howard's End*) and Mrs. Moore (*A Passage to India*) and Virginia Woolf's Mrs. Dalloway and Mrs. Ramsay (*To the Lighthouse*). Murdoch has many such figures, to name a few: Anna in *Under the Net*, Kitty in *A Word Child*, and Antonia in *A Severed Head*. But, Conradi asks, are these characters only dehumanized symbols, surrogates for the author? In Murdoch's novels, he answers, they can be both semidivine figures of reconciliation *and* free human characters who can be viewed without undue reverence.

_____. "Platonism in Iris Murdoch." In *Platonism and the English Imagination*, edited by Anna Baldwin and Sarah Hutton. New York: Cambridge University Press, 1994.
Murdoch's Platonism is part of her revolt against existentialism and dominant Anglo-Saxon philosophies. As it was revolutionary for Plato in his day, for Murdoch to argue for the soul is revolutionary in hers. Her use of Plato differs from that of modern philosophers: where they emphasize Plato's aesthetics, she stresses his patience with the flux of experience. In morality, Murdoch uses Plato's myth of the cave to describe a person's escape from egotistical fantasy. (Murdoch distrusts psychiatrists because they encourage self-centeredness. Conradi looks briefly at psychologists in *A Severed Head*, *The Sacred and Profane Love Machine*, and *The Good Apprentice*.) She endorses Plato's concept of Eros;

sexual energy can move a person away from fantasies. Art can also move people away from the self to the good. Conradi thinks Murdoch has changed from writing schematic novels to writing works in which myth is subordinate to character. Conradi discusses *Under the Net*, *The Bell*, *Bruno's Dream*, and *The Black Prince*.

Crawford, Fred. "Iris Murdoch: Murmurs of Maternal Lamentation." In *Mixing Memory and Desire: The Waste Land and British Novels*. University Park: Pennsylvania State University Press, 1982.

Crawford identifies many allusions to Eliot's poem in Murdoch's novels. Less convincingly, he finds many parallel situations as well. Murdoch disagrees with many of Eliot's ideas, especially his misogyny. As is the case with most postwar British writers, Murdoch has not been influenced by Eliot very much.

Crosland, Margaret. *Beyond the Lighthouse: English Women Novelists in the Twentieth Century*. New York: Taplinger, 1981.

Crosland gives a brief and appreciative survey of the novels through *An Accidental Man*. Murdoch intrigues us by giving us different sorts of reality, by mixing normal characters with very odd ones, and by displaying the varieties of love, especially homosexuality.

Culley, Ann. "Theory and Practice: Characterization in the Novels of Iris Murdoch." *Modern Fiction Studies* 15 (Autumn, 1969): 335-345.

Culley reviews Murdoch's ideas about the many failures of characterization in twentieth century novels and about what characters in novels should be like. They should resemble real individual human beings: opaque, singular, and free. Murdoch admits her characters do not always live up to her ideals.

Cunneen, Sally. "Ingmar Bergman Crossed with Charlie Chaplin? What Iris Murdoch Doesn't Know." *Commonweal*, November 9, 1979, 623-626.

Murdoch agrees with James in *The Sea, The Sea*: good exists, but most people are too egotistical to perceive it. Murdoch's novels are comic as she shows her self-centered protagonists humbled.

But how can we laugh at the triumph of evil? Cunneen thinks Murdoch knows that laughter keeps readers from exaggerating their own importance. Although Murdoch does not acknowledge positive possibilities for the human race, her novels point in that direction.

Davies, Alistair, and Peter Saunders. "Literature, Politics, and Society." In *Society and Literature, 1945-1970,* edited by Alan Sinfield. New York: Holmes & Meier, 1983.
In their sketch of British cultural life since 1945, the authors group Murdoch with Angus Wilson in questioning liberal traditions and the influence of Bloomsbury. In *Flight from the Enchanter*, immoral and energetic people from Eastern Europe challenge English civil servants, who are unwilling or unable to resist.

Dawson, S. W. "New Scrutinies, I: Iris Murdoch: or, Anyone for Incest?" *The Human World* 2 (1971): 57-61.
Dawson makes a case against Murdoch. From the beginning, her limitations have included a whimsical sentimentality like that found it women's magazines. She has a predilection for farce, especially incestuous bedroom farce. Readers are not touched by her characters, whom she manipulates to fit into her contrived narrative schemes. Critics are beginning to think her novels are trivial.

Dick, Bernard. "The Novels of Iris Murdoch: A Formula for Enchantment." *Bucknell Review: A Scholarly Journal of Letters, Arts and Science* 14 (May, 1966): 66-81.
Murdoch shows self-deluding characters who surrender their personalities to other characters who have charismatic force. These enchanters are not really so powerful; their force has been given them by the deluded people themselves. Delusion is not love. Real love can only come from disenchantment. Dick makes brief comments on Murdoch's first seven novels.

Dipple, Elizabeth. *Iris Murdoch: Work for the Spirit.* London: Methuen, 1982.
A very important work, though perhaps one that emphasizes one side of Murdoch's vision too strongly. Dipple explains in her

preface that she will concentrate on Murdoch's later works which
show the presence of Platonic thought. In her introduction,
Dipple investigates why readers find Murdoch's novels difficult.
Beneath their realistic surface of mainly bourgeois life are intima-
tions of another consistent world. Characters yearn for different
transcendencies—innocence, love, God. Although their intima-
tions never materialize, Dipple thinks the characters do learn
about virtue and holiness, qualities best described by the Platonic
concept of the Good. Throughout her book, though Dipple is
generous to all aspects of Murdoch's world, she locates Murdoch's
essential message in this concept.

In Chapter 2, Dipple identifies and analyzes several of
Murdoch's near-saints, characters who are as good as humans can
be. To differing degrees, they have conquered their own self-
centered ego and can look at the world without illusion. Because
they are not obsessed, they cannot be heroic; they remain minor
characters in their novels. Nevertheless they exhibit in purer form
the tendency of almost all Murdoch characters to yearn for truth
and the good. Dipple sets Murdoch's novels in the context of
nineteenth century fiction (in which the hero's triumph was an
affirmation of moral good) and that of the twentieth century.
Especially in postmodern fiction, there is no moral hero; the only
heroes are the writers themselves, who communicate their self-
centered virtuosity to similarly egotistic readers.

In Chapter 3, Dipple first explains that Murdoch's realism is
not narrowly positivistic or ideological. (Many critics have
wrongly tried to define her by ideology.) On the contrary, her
characters have autonomy; they are "accidental," not kept in order
by their author's controlling doctrines or narrow conceptions of
what is real. Yet, paradoxically, Murdoch does have an ideology,
for many of her characters point to "the Good," some of them
unconsciously. To defend Murdoch against unsympathetic
readers, Dipple discusses two such unconsciously good characters:
Hugo from *Under the Net* and Ann from *An Unofficial Rose*. In
fact, almost all of Murdoch's characters have some impulse toward
the good, even though they can never achieve it. Here Murdoch
differs from Plato, who thought a few wise persons could do so.
The best Murdoch's characters can do is renounce all the images
of their culture and view life as a blank. Dipple discusses these
ideas at length with reference to *The Time of the Angels*. Yet

despite this theory, Murdoch's novels abound in the joys of the world itself.

In Chapter 4, Dipple focuses on how Murdoch's style evokes these joys as it becomes more and more descriptive. Dipple offers a brilliant analyses of the various ingredients of Murdoch's world: her cross-references, her recurring objects (rocks, kites, porcelain) and symbols (birds, fish, the sea), and her stable of recurring character types. In their obsessions and neuroses, Murdoch's characters reveal their author's interest in Freud. Like men in Plato's cave, all of them seem to see only the shadows of the full richness of the real world. Yet most yearn for something; most use their resources to enter on a quest, a quest which is never completed. Dipple praises Murdoch's enthralling descriptions of violent acts and her vivid and unsettling depiction of the physical world. Murdoch's various kinds of closure remind readers of the unpredictability of real people. Art is important in Murdoch's world. Its images and structures are magical. Although this magic can be dangerously self-deceptive and fantastic, images and magic help the mind move toward Murdoch's transcendent good. Indeed, for Murdoch art is superior to philosophy. The great artist enacts the Apollo/Marsyas myth; as he moves toward truth by the destruction of self, he suffers great pain (Marsyas is flayed alive in the story). Dipple discusses Murdoch's use of this myth in *A Fairly Honorable Defeat* (briefly) and in *The Black Prince* (at length).

In subsequent chapters, Dipple treats, sometimes briefly and sometimes at length, all of Murdoch's novels through *Nuns and Soldiers*. At the end of Chapter 5, Dipple argues that *The Nice and The Good* represents the beginning of Murdoch's mature style. It and later novels show realistically human characters who act with freedom, rather than being forced into allegorical frameworks. Murdoch's intellectual influences are still present (Plato, Buddhism, Shakespeare, Wittgenstein, and others), but they do not control the characters. As a result, the later novels are harder to understand than Murdoch's earlier ones. Dipple more and more identifies a bleak Buddhist vision as Murdoch's ultimate message. Her happy endings and happy characters are either unsatisfactory or ironic. Bibliography.

_____. "The Green Knight and Other Vagaries of the Spirit; or, Tricks and Images for the Human Soul; or, the Uses of Imaginative Literature." In *Iris Murdoch and the Search for Human Goodness*, edited by Maria Antonaccio and William Schweiker. Chicago: University of Chicago Press, 1996.

Murdoch's novels call for multiple readings and multiple interpretations to begin to understand what they say about the human soul. This is particularly true of *The Book and the Brotherhood*, *The Message to the Planet*, and *The Green Knight*. Dipple comments at some length on each novel, being careful to use ideas expressed in *Metaphysics as a Guide to Morals*, but not to be bound by them. She finds that each novel contains "a single complex character [who] carries an enormous weight of metaphoric power beyond the boundaries of the possible."

_____. *The Unresolvable Plot: Reading Contemporary Fiction.* New York: Routledge, 1989.

In Chapter 9, Dipple proves that, even though Murdoch has been called old-fashioned, her recent novels are experimental. She illustrates Bakhtin's idea of polyphonic fiction in *The Philosopher's Pupil* and *The Good Apprentice*. Even though they appear to be conventional stories, neither are formally unified, and both seem ambiguous.

Dollimore, Jonathan. "The Challenge of Sexuality." In *Society and Literature, 1945-1970.* New York: Holmes & Meier, 1983.

In his survey of attitudes toward sex since World War II, Dollimore remarks on Murdoch's treatment of homosexuality (especially in *A Fairly Honorable Defeat*) and of the inadequacies of marriage.

Dunbar, Scott. "On Art, Morals and Religion: Some Reflection on the Work of Iris Murdoch." *Religious Studies* 14 (December, 1978): 515-524.

In this discussion of *The Sovereignty of the Good*, Dunbar comments on two novels in which characters approach the Good and God. In *The Bell*, Dora experiences transcendence through the beauty of art at the National Gallery. In *The Unicorn*, Effingham's ego is laid aside in the bog.

Elson, John. "Iris Murdoch." *Contemporary Review* 247 (December, 1985): 311-315.

A sympathetic overview of Murdoch's career and the reception of her novels to 1985. Elson praises her for the serious questions she asks (what is inherently valuable?) and for deepening conventional moral responses. Her characters hold philosophic views but are not caricatures.

Emerson, Donald. "Violence and Survival in the Novels of Iris Murdoch." *Transactions of the Wisconsin Academy of Sciences, Arts, and Letters* 57 (1969): 21-28.

Emerson surveys Murdoch's theories and practices and zeroes in on two themes in four novels: *Under the Net*, *The Bell*, *An Unofficial Rose*, and *The Time of the Angels*. Violence can take the form of outward acts (such as murder) or inward conditions (such as enslavement). Survival is not always possible for Murdoch's characters, nor do they always desire it. Some of those who survive do so from ignorance.

Felheim, Marvin. "Symbolic Characterization in the Novels of Iris Murdoch." *Texas Studies in Literature and Language* 2 (Spring, 1960): 189-197.

In each of her early novels, Murdoch creates a pair of female characters to carry the novel's meaning. These women are passionate and energetic; at first they may be victims, but many eventually emerge as fulfilled persons. Because they function as symbols, they often seem puzzling. But they are realistic characters as well; they serve as bridges between the reality of contemporary England and Murdoch's ideas. Felheim treats *Under the Net*, *The Flight from the Enchanter*, *The Sandcastle*, and *The Bell*.

Fletcher, John. "`Cheating the Dark Gods': Iris Murdoch and Racine." *International Fiction Review* 6 (Winter, 1979): 75-76.

Modernist writers like James Joyce used old stories to structure their works. Writers like Murdoch (who is postmodern in this respect) evoke the literature of the past in a less slavish way. Fletcher discusses Murdoch's use of Racine in *A Severed Head*.

_____. "Iris Murdoch." In *British Novelists Since 1980, Part 2: H-Z*, edited by Jay L. Halio. Vol. 14 of *Dictionary of Literary Biography*. Detroit: Gale Research, 1983.

Fletcher deals with the reservations some critics have had about Murdoch's novels. He provides biographical detail, emphasizing the importance of her marriage to John Bayley. Fletcher comments on each novel through *Nuns and Soldiers*, paying special attention to *Under the Net* and *The Sea, The Sea*.

_____. "Iris Murdoch: The Foreign Translations." In *Encounters with Iris Murdoch*, edited by Richard Todd. Amsterdam: Free University Press, 1988.

A survey of translations through 1987. Fletcher describes some of the books, gives examples of print runs, and appends an alphabetical list of novels and their translations and a handy table. Murdoch comments on some textual alterations in American editions and on the problems of translating the novels' titles.

_____. "Iris Murdoch, Novelist of London." *International Fiction Review* 17 (Winter, 1990): 9-13.

Fletcher lists the addresses where Murdoch has lived in London. London plays many roles in the novels: sometimes it is simply a setting, but other times it is integral to the action. Although the city has changed since Murdoch began to picture it, much of it remains. Most of her London scenes are set in Hammersmith, Kensington, Chelsea, Westminster, and the City, mainly in the portions of these districts that are close to the Thames. This river can be said to dominate the geography of many novels. Fletcher discusses four novels in which London is most important: *Under the Net*, *Bruno's Dream*, *A Fairly Honorable Defeat*, and *A Word Child*.

_____. "Rough Magic and Moral Toughness: Iris Murdoch's Fictional Universe." In *The British and Irish Novel Since 1960*, edited by James Acheson. New York: St. Martin's Press, 1991.

An illuminating reading of many of Murdoch's most important novels. Characters show how illusions and selfishness lead to fantasy, self-pity, and despair. In contrast, Murdoch herself appears to have learned from Wittgenstein that people can aspire to the Good as they look toward a transcendent perfection. Yet Murdoch is not sentimental; violence in her novels calls attention to her paradoxes, contradictions, and ironies. When she mystifies, it is not to befuddle the reader, but to intensify her story. Her happy endings exact a price and are thereby bittersweet at best. In politics, even though she has shown sympathy to the left, her hard-nosed moral ideas (for example, on abortion) make her lean to the right. Fletcher makes useful remarks on *Henry and Cato*, *An Accidental Man*, *The Sacred and Profane Love Machine*, and *A Word Child*; he makes longer comments on the novels he thinks are her greatest: *A Fairly Honorable Defeat* and *The Black Prince*.

Fogarty, Margaret E. "The Fiction of Iris Murdoch: Amalgam of Yeatsian and Joycean Motifs." In *Literary Interrelations: Ireland, England and the World II: Comparison and Impact*, edited by Wolfgang Zach and Heinz Kosok. Tübingen, Germany: Gunter Narr, 1987.
Although it is not commonly acknowledged, Murdoch's work is Irish at its source. This can be seen by noting the many allusions she makes to the works of James Joyce and W. B. Yeats and the many symbols and images she shares with these authors. Like Yeats, Murdoch quests for universal archetypes and is enthralled by symbols. Fogarty looks closely at *Under the Net* and *The Black Prince*, but her comparisons are not always convincing.

Fraser, G. S. "Iris Murdoch: The Solidity of the Normal." In *International Literary Annual* II, edited by John Wain. London: John Calder, 1959.
A lucid and stylish look at Murdoch's first four novels. Fraser discusses how each shows social values (or does not show them). He makes appreciative remarks about Murdoch's craftsmanship, descriptions, intensity, and humor.

_____. *The Modern Writer and His World: Continuity and Innovation in Twentieth-Century English Literature*. Rev. ed. London: André Deutsch, 1964. Reprint. Westport, Conn.: Greenwood Press, 1975.
In Chapter 11, Fraser makes brief comments on Murdoch's career through *The Bell* (his favorite). He then surveys objections to

Murdoch's work: it is too intellectual, too philosophic, too improbable. He generalizes about her themes.

Ganner-Rauth, H. "Iris Murdoch and the Brontë Heritage." *Studies in English Literature* 58 (1981): 61-74.
Surveys the Brontë influence on *The Unicorn* and *The Sacred and Profane Love Machine*. Brief notes on *The Italian Girl* and *The Time of the Angels*.

German, Howard. "Allusions in the Early Novels of Iris Murdoch." *Modern Fiction Studies* 15 (Autumn, 1969): 361-377.
Murdoch's many allusions are not extended or perfect parallels. German identifies clusters of allusions in her first five novels.

_____. "The Range of Allusions in the Novels of Iris Murdoch." *Journal of Modern Literature* 2 (September, 1971): 57-85.
Murdoch makes many allusions in her novels, allusions to literary works, biographies, and myths. Because most allusions are covert, they can easily be missed by a casual reader. These allusions are not just to English sources; they connect Murdoch to a wide range of cultures. Although Murdoch repeats herself in different novels, each novel has its own cluster of dominant allusions, and a specific allusion may suggest one thing in one novel and quite a different thing in another. German analyzes in detail the allusions in *An Unofficial Rose*, *The Unicorn*, *The Italian Girl*, *The Red and the Green*, and *The Time of the Angels*. A very useful source of information and suggestions.

Gerstenberger, Donna. *Iris Murdoch*. Lewisburg, Pa.: Bucknell University Press, 1975.
Even though this book forms part of an "Irish Writers Series," Gerstenberger admits that Murdoch is primarily an English writer. In Chapter 1, she generalizes about the novelist's themes and characters and comments briefly on the novels through *Bruno's Dream*, noting whatever allusions to Irish material she can find. Chapter 2 concerns Murdoch's one Irish novel, *The Red and the Green* (the chapter is reprinted in *Iris Murdoch*, edited by Harold Bloom; New York: Chelsea House, 1986). In Chapter 3, Gerstenberger concludes that, although it is hard to discern specifically Irish traits in Murdoch's novels, her Irish characters

are consistent. They are usually lower-class servants of British middle-class masters. They are simple, delightful, sexy, warm, and often thieving. Is Murdoch a snob? Gerstenberger tries not to say so.

Gindin, James. "Comedy in Contemporary British Fiction." *Papers of the Michigan Academy of Science, Arts, and Letters* 44 (1959): 389-397.
Gindin distinguishes a group of British novelists in 1959 from those of the preceding generation. They do not satirize the follies of a meaningless world. They are not experimental. They use comedy was a way of commenting on all of British society. Compared to Kingsley Amis, Murdoch relies more on farce.

_____. "Ethical Structures in John Galsworthy, Elizabeth Bowen, and Iris Murdoch." In *Forms of Modern Fiction*, edited by Alan Warren Friedman. Austin: University of Texas Press, 1975.
In Murdoch's early novels, characters create codes to live by. When the codes fail, the characters are left with simple existence. In *The Flight from the Enchanter*, Murdoch seems to prefer those who escape enchantment and do not bully others. In *A Severed Head*, however, her sympathies seem to be with the powerful Honor Klein. In her later novels, she is more consistent, and she draws characters who try to do good things. Can they succeed? Murdoch seems to think that sometimes they can. In fact, her novels are intended to do good: literature can have an ethical function.

_____. "Images of Illusion in the Work of Iris Murdoch." *Texas Studies in Literature and Language* 2 (Spring, 1960): 180-188.
Murdoch's characters face illusions; an image connected with a specific illusion forms part of the title of each of her first four novels. Each novel has a God-like character whose wisdom is false and whose advice is bad. Gindin also comments on Murdoch's symbols: houses and other man-made structures, gardens, fish, lizards, dogs. He treats specifically *Under the Net, The Flight from the Enchanter, The Sandcastle*, and *The Bell*.

_____. *Postwar British Fiction*. Berkeley: University of California Press, 1962.

The chapter on Murdoch adds comments on *A Severed Head* to his article "Images of Illusion in the Work of Iris Murdoch."

Glover, Stephen. "Iris Murdoch Talks to Stephen Glover." *New Review* 3 (November, 1976): 56-59.
Miscellaneous opinions on the novel and her novels. She invents the entire plot first, then writes two drafts. Dialogue is very important, but she only has two speech patterns: Oxford English and Irish. As a result, she makes alien characters sound Irish. She does not reread her novels. She recognizes her characters are mainly Oxford graduates or civil servants, but does not consider this a limitation. She is very interested in Buddhism and Hinduism. She is not a Christian, for she does not believe in a personal God, but she does feel close to both Catholic and Anglican traditions. Have her novels become less humorous over the years? No! They are funnier and better.

Gordon, David J. "Iris Murdoch's Comedies of Unselfing." *Twentieth Century Literature* 36 (Summer, 1990): 115-136.
This prize-winning essay has many brief references to many novels. Murdoch's stories are set in an almost ahistorical present. What matters is not the past or the future so much as a time-shattering event that creates a new consciousness. Her extravagant storytelling methods suggest that she sees truths past those that ordinary stories can convey. At the heart of Murdoch's work are several Platonic axioms: human beings are drawn to the Good and Truth; their egos often make them mistake apparent goods for the Good; Absolute Truth enjoins silence; most people live in need of a Truth they cannot reach.

Murdoch provides few truly Good characters, and they are usually marginal, silent, almost invisible; one exception is Tallis in *A Fairly Honorable Defeat*. To defeat the egotism that stands in the way of truth, Murdoch describes the painful process of "unselfing." The myth of the flaying of Marsyas tells of such pain. Gordon discusses how Murdoch both draws on Freud and disagrees with him. Instead of a mechanistic model to describe what directs human action, Murdoch invokes a combination of Necessity and Chance. Gordon also discusses her concept of contingency (important because life's contingencies destroy egotistic fantasies). He also stresses her humor and generous judgments.

Murdoch views most of her characters from a comic perspective as they struggle against their egos, rationalizing their errors and trying to be good.

_____. *Iris Murdoch's Fables of Unselfing*. Columbia: University of Missouri Press, 1995.

In his introduction, Gordon outlines Murdoch's ideas and influences. Chapter 1 deals with her ideas about language and freedom in relation to the ideas of Sartre, Wittgenstein, and Weil. Murdoch often uses words from a liberal humanistic vocabulary in special illiberal senses. In Chapter 2, Gordon describes the novels' different paths to the good. There are saints, like Tallis from *A Fairly Honorable Defeat*, and there are others who move toward the good through love or art. In both cases, the ego poses the greatest obstacle. Androgynous characters suggest the fusing of sex and spirit for which some characters wish.

In Chapter 3, Gordon discusses charismatic and demonic power-figures, characters often associated with Eastern Europe. In contrast to such figures, there are good characters who have a negative charisma. There also are in-between characters who do harm when they assume a role of power but cannot sustain it; these are chastised or, if Platonists, humiliated. Power figures cause suffering, which is in turn passed on to others; Murdoch opposes Christianity's romanticizing such suffering. (The suffering of Marsyas is different; his agony is his moment of contact with the divine.)

Murdoch's ideas about power cause problems to her in her role as an artist: how can she be against power and at the same time direct her plots? Gordon notes that she seems to be more tolerant of power in her later novels; she admits good magic into *The Sea, The Sea*. She often uses her artistic power cunningly. Twists of plots frustrate the plans of her characters. She employs two kinds of structural irony. In some novels, she creates two characters who have partially valid outlooks, yet mutually exclusive ones. Examples are Dora and Michael in *The Bell*. A second kind of structural irony comes from her fallible first-person narrators; they reveal themselves even as they tell their story.

In Chapter 4, Gordon explains Murdoch's challenge to Freudian concepts of motivation, causality, guilt, anxiety, and obsession. Unlike the characters of other novelists, her characters' stories do not end when they understand their own motives. Their destinies unfold, and they may humbly realize that their motives have been ineffective and unimportant in a world ruled by Chance and Necessity. Despite her tolerance and generosity, Murdoch is not a humanist; she does not advocate any happy middle way. Moments in her novels which suggest supernatural intervention are her way of showing her dissatisfaction with rationalist worldviews. Because the world is not ruled by motives and strict causality, her novels cannot be tragic. Murdoch calls them comic; Gordon calls them tragi-comic. He analyzes *The Nice and the Good* at length.

In Chapters 5 through 8, Gordon traces Murdoch's development and makes sketchy comments on individual novels. He divides the novels into three groups: Murdoch's apprenticeship (through *The Time of the Angels*); her major work (*The Nice and the Good* through *The Good Apprentice*); and her later work (beginning with *The Book and the Brotherhood*). Gordon's conclusion is titled "Murdoch's Ambitiousness." She has asked to be compared to the greatest of artists, and many critics think she deserves this comparison. Time will tell.

Goshgarian, Gary. "Feminist Values in the Novels of Iris Murdoch." *Revue des Langues Vivantes* 40 (1974): 519-527.
Even though she does not tell the usual feminist stories, Murdoch has feminist concerns. Many of her male characters construct fantasies about women, often exalting them as goddesses. Real women are not goddesses, but complete human beings; Murdoch's theories about the uniqueness of each human character apply to them. In particular, Goshgarian discusses *The Sandcastle*, *The Unicorn*, *A Severed Head*, and *An Unofficial Rose*.

Green, Arthur. "The Worlds of Iris Murdoch." *The Iris Murdoch Newsletter*, no. 10 (December, 1996): 1-6.
Despite what some critics have said, Iris Murdoch should be seen as an Anglo-Irish author. She sets several novels in Ireland; she has many Irish characters; she makes many Irish references. Green describes her family's Irish background in detail; she has taken names from her own family for some of her characters.

Griffin, Gabriele. *The Influence of the Writings of Simone Weil on the Fiction of Iris Murdoch.* San Francisco: Mellen Research University Press, 1993.

A rewarding book, to which a summary cannot do justice. In her introduction, Griffin focuses upon the influence on Murdoch not only of Weil's moral philosophy but also of her ideas about gender roles. Murdoch rejects both "masculine" linguistic analysis and existentialism, which takes the male experience as its norm. In successive chapters, Griffin considers Murdoch's use though *The Book and the Brotherhood* of Weil's ideas about "selflessness," "knowing the void," and "attention." In her conclusion, Griffin summarizes how the two women's ideas agree and how they differ in some respects. Griffin also deals with the direction Murdoch's work has taken.

Haffenden, John. *Novelists in Interview.* London: Methuen, 1985. An earlier version appeared in *Literary Review* 58 (April, 1983): 31-35.

Haffenden prefaces this important 1983 interview with examples of interesting opinions of Murdoch's work and a summary of what she has said about her concerns. In the interview, Murdoch discusses *The Philosopher's Pupil* at length and makes many general observations. She envies painters because she loves the visual world. There is water in every one of her novels; because she almost drowned once, she fears the sea. Her books are full of happiness, though many characters are tortured by remorse because their lives have taken wrong turns. People have secret dream-lives that novelists can use. Freud, who stole ideas from Plato, wrongly encourages a preoccupation with the self. A strong myth in a novel narrows its characters, as in *A Severed Head*, a novel that marked for her the end of one line of development. She does not worry any more about the tension between form and contingency.

Hague, Angela. *Iris Murdoch's Comic Vision.* Cranbury, N.J.: Associated University Presses, 1984.

A lucid and valuable book. In Chapter 1, Hague discusses theories of comedy from Freud to Northrop Frye and the nature of recent British comic novels. In Chapter 2, Hague considers Murdoch's kind of comedy, which is often dark and ironic.

Hague's subsequent chapters analyze three of Murdoch's novels as comedies: *An Accidental Man, The Black Prince,* and *The Sea, The Sea.*

Hall, James. "Blurring the Will: The Growth of Iris Murdoch." *ELH* 32 (June, 1965): 256-273.
In Murdoch's usual story, the struggle of egotistic and destructive activity with vulnerability may lead to some kind of private rebirth. Her characters are subordinate to her plot. Hall treats *Under the Net, The Sandcastle,* and *The Bell.* A difficult argument to follow.

_____. *The Lunatic Giant in the Drawing Room: The British and American Novel Since 1930.* Bloomington: Indiana University Press, 1968.
This volume contains an expanded version of his earlier article, "Blurring the Will."

Hall, William F. "*Bruno's Dream*: Technique and Meaning in the Novels of Iris Murdoch." *Modern Fiction Studies* 15 (Autumn, 1969): 429-443.
Murdoch's novels show a contest between the forces of form/ masculinity/consciousness and those of contingency/femaleness/ unconsciousness. In one group of novels, the main character tries to move from form to contingency: *A Severed Head, Under the Net, An Unofficial Rose, The Italian Girl, The Red and the Green.* In a second group, a young woman from the contingent world enters a world of form that has lost its energy; she first disrupts it and then tries to effect a reconciliation: *The Flight from the Enchanter, The Bell, The Sandcastle, The Unicorn* (a special case), *The Time of the Angels.* (Hall is confusing about which group *The Nice and the Good* belongs in.) Hall illustrates his theory by an analysis of *Bruno's Dream.*

_____. "'The Third Way': The Novels of Iris Murdoch." *Dalhousie Review* 46 (Autumn, 1966): 306-318.
A lucid exposition of Murdoch's ideas about modern philosophy and fiction. Neither the philosophers of existentialism or linguistic empiricism can account for a real person's experience of the real world. Like these philosophers, Murdoch knows the world is

formless and contingent, but she accepts this world. Likewise, whereas Jean-Paul Sartre sees love as the enslaving of one consciousness by another, Murdoch conceives of love as one person becoming aware that other different persons exist. (Hall calls this Murdoch's central theme.) Hall points out the nature of Murdoch's comic vision; he thinks that her characters' symbolic actions are more successful than her more obvious static symbols. He defines the pattern of the usual plot of her novels through *The Italian Girl*: An individual enters an enclosed and formal society dominated by a powerful God-like figure. This entrance begins to break down the form of that society to reveal human contingency; the God-like figure is revealed as less powerful. Some characters may learn Murdoch's central truth: that other people exist. Hall refers to many novels, specifically to *Under the Net* and *A Severed Head*.

Harding, D. W. "The Novels of Iris Murdoch." *Oxford Magazine* 2 (October 26, 1961): 34-35.
Harding attacks Murdoch's first four novels, especially *A Severed Head*. The ingredients of her novel (falling in love, bars, alcohol, mechanical contraptions) all appeal to the late-blooming, eternally adolescent, educated classes. Murdoch teaches them an air of superior detachment.

Hawkins, Peter. *The Language of Grace: Flannery O'Connor, Walker Percy, and Iris Murdoch*. Cambridge, Mass.: Cowley Publications, 1983.
Although Murdoch does not believe in God, she is concerned with spiritual matters. Her evocation of a nonreligious transcendence allows religious believers to read her novels in a religious way. In fact, Murdoch's Good may turn out to be God. Murdoch has philosophical ideas about art and about the mysteries of other people; Hawkins discusses how she frames these concepts in a vocabulary drawn from religion. He discusses *The Bell* in passing and *A Word Child* at length.

Hebblethwaite, Peter. "Feuerbach's Ladder: Leszek Kolakowskie and Iris Murdoch." *Heythrop Journal* 13 (April, 1972): 143-161.

This article deals, not with Murdoch's novels, but with her philosophical attempts in *The Sovereignty of Good* to breathe life into religious ideas by secularizing them.

Henry, Aline. "Le Symbolisme dans les Romans d'Iris Murdoch." In *Rencontres avec Iris Murdoch*. Caen, France: Centre de Recherches de Littérature et Linguistique des Pays de Langue Anglaise de l'Université de Caen, 1978. [In French.]
In varying degrees, Murdoch's novels are full of symbols. Her titles are often symbolic, as are her characters' names. Many characters are in themselves symbolic types: the enchanter, the lucid observer, twins or doubles, the child-woman, the outsider. Places are often symbolic: houses reflect their dwellers, caverns and holes represent steps toward reality or reveal characters' hidden desires. Psychoanalytic symbols are very important to Murdoch. Her training as a philosopher may provide her essential idea (different in manner from that of Sartre): the Good. Finally, Murdoch draws symbols from art: mainly from painting, but from music and literature as well. The evolution of her symbols parallels her own moral and philosophical evolution. Perhaps Murdoch counts too much on her readers' level of culture.

Heusel, Barbara. "An Interview with Iris Murdoch." *University of Windsor Review* 21 (Winter, 1988): 1-13.
In this 1987 interview, Murdoch resists various interpretations: she is not a satirist; Ireland has not influenced her deeply; defeating egotism is not masochistic; the idea of Bakhtinian carnival and the profanation of the sacred is not what she is about; she does not mock Christian utopias; she does not play tricks in her novels; she does not base characters on people she knows. Interesting specific remarks on *The Unicorn*, *The Good Apprentice*, and *The Philosopher's Pupil*.

_____. *Patterned Aimlessness: Iris Murdoch's Novels of the 1970s and 1980s*. Athens: University of Georgia Press, 1995.
Heusel investigates how Murdoch's novels synthesize many perspectives, including the philosophical. In Chapter 1, she analyzes Murdoch's philosophical position, mainly as it appears in *Metaphysics as a Guide to Morals*, and compares it to those of thinkers Murdoch dislikes (Jean-Paul Sartre, Friedrich Nietzsche, and

Jacques Derrida) and likes (Plato, Immanuel Kant, and Ludwig Wittgenstein). Murdoch opposes the idea of a personal God, but recognizes the human desire for one. She herself posits the idea of transcendent good and says that human love is an attentiveness to other people.

In Chapter 2, Heusel provides a lucid and valuable explanation of Murdoch's debt to Wittgenstein. Although Murdoch disagrees with him about some things, both she and Wittgenstein have similar ideas: the influence of teachers and mentors is often strong and can be good; scientific investigation is not the only road to truth; ordinary language can force people to misunderstand unfamiliar ideas; life's mysteries can be approached by playful language games and puzzles, by shifting perspectives, and by juxtapositions without explanation. Both are attracted by Buddhism. In Chapter 3, Heusel discusses Wittgenstein in relation to *A Word Child*, *Nuns and Soldiers*, and *The Sea, The Sea*. In Chapter 4, Heusel challenges Murdoch's protests that her novels have little to do with her philosophy. Heusel says the novels address questions of morality, and their characters often take philosophical stances. She surveys three of Murdoch's early philosophical texts for what they say about fiction.

In Chapter 5, Heusel uses Bakhtinian dialogic analysis to illuminate Murdoch's way of letting her characters express themselves in their own kinds of language, especially in *An Accidental Man*. In Chapter 6, Heusel examines Bakhtinian carnivalesque qualities in *The Philosopher's Pupil* and *The Black Prince*. In Chapter 7, she uses Bakhtinian ideas to examine *Nuns and Soldiers* and *The Message to the Planet* in order to find free female characters. In Chapter 8, she looks at the main characters of *A Word Child*, *The Black Prince*, *The Sea, The Sea*, and *Nuns and Soldiers*, and explains how they are free to impose patterns on chaotic reality, free to see themselves as heroic questers. In reality they make a variety of movements; some of these movements are circular, as described by metaphors of the cave, the labyrinth, and a network. These characters often experience cataclysmic change.

Chapter 9 provides an overview of Murdoch's fiction. Even though the world and the genre of each novel is different, Heusel identifies patterns that underlie the body of her work. One basic pattern is Platonic, especially an upward movement propelled by Eros from inside the Cave to the sunlight of the Good. Many of

the obsessed characters who climb toward the sun are male, perhaps because her readers are not ready to accept the value of
female obsessions.   These figures usually experience sudden
moments of surprising beauty often accompanied by suffering.
Murdoch also recognizes and even celebrates a downward movement into the dark caverns of the soul. A second basic pattern
comes from Wittgenstein, a movement to get under the net of
logical systems and illusions to discover the reality underneath.
Heusel also describes the novels by metaphors of geologic strata:
the modern world overlays the Christian world, which overlays
the ancient world and its ever-present gods; the underground is
literally present in *The Philosopher's Pupil*. Murdoch's patterns
are spatial: Heusel reproduces diagrams the author drew on her
manuscripts. In her conclusion, Heusel defends Murdoch, then
defines and praises her achievement.

Heyd, Ruth. "Interview with Iris Murdoch." *University of Windsor
Review* 1 (Spring, 1965): 138-143.
Heyd reproduces Murdoch's opinions after an interview with her.
Many Murdoch characters project their longings on other people;
some characters try to impose form on a muddled reality.
Murdoch thinks of freedom as conquering such obsessions, the
result of which is a "release of spirit." Withdrawing from the
world is not freedom, as the Abbess tells Michael in *The Bell*.
Søren Kierkegaard's concept of "the knight of faith" describes
some of her characters who may seem dull and ordinary, but who
ignore theory and possess a kind of certitude.

Hoffman, Frederick.   "Iris Murdoch: The Reality of Persons."
Critique: Studies in Contemporary Fiction 7 (Spring, 1964): 48-
57.
Murdoch's novels can be categorized on the basis of their
characters. In some, characters are subordinate to the pattern of
the novel; Hoffman discusses *Under the Net, The Flight from the
Enchanter*, and *The Sandcastle*. In others, characters are self-
conscious and somewhat free of the novels' patterns; Hoffman
discusses *The Bell* and makes very brief remarks on *A Severed
Head, An Unofficial Rose*, and *The Unicorn*.

_____. "The Miracle of Contingency: The Novels of Iris Murdoch." *Shenandoah* 17 (Autumn, 1965): 49-56. Reprinted as "The Italian Girl" in *Iris Murdoch*, edited by Harold Bloom. New York: Chelsea House, 1986.

Murdoch describes love as a slow meditative movement toward understanding of other persons. Hoffman sees this idea reflected in her fiction, particularly in the character of Edmund in *The Italian Girl*.

Holbrook, David. "The Charming Hate of Iris Murdoch." In *The Masks of Hate*. Oxford: Pergamon, 1972.

In Chapter 21, Holbrook says Murdoch plays a part in the dehumanization of culture. She does not care for her characters; her novels have a bad and inhumane influence. He particularly objects to Murdoch's and her characters' cool treatment of two incidents in her obscene and immoral novel *The Flight from the Enchanter*: Rosa's sexual encounters with the Polish brothers and Annette's being left, partially clothed, in a closet.

Hope, Frances. "The Novels of Iris Murdoch." In *On Contemporary Literature*, edited by Richard Kostelanetz. New York: Avon Books, 1964.

Hope surveys Murdoch's first five novels, and finds *A Severed Head* a worrying departure.

Hoskins, Robert. "Iris Murdoch's Midsummer Nightmare." *Twentieth Century Literature* 18 (July, 1972): 191-198.

Murdoch show Shakespeare's influence, not only in making many allusions to his plays, but in incorporating extended parallels. Hoskins demonstrates by comparing *A Fairly Honorable Defeat* to *A Midsummer Night's Dream*.

Jefferson, Douglas W. "Iris Murdoch: The Novelist and the Moralist." In *The Uses of Fiction: Essays on the Modern Novel in Honor of Arnold Kettle*, edited by Douglas W. Jefferson and Graham Martin. Milton Keynes, England: Open University Press, 1982.

Jefferson presents a paradox: Murdoch is not only a flamboyant, comic, bizarre novelist, but she is also a moral one. Many characters struggle to be good: Gunnar in *A Word Child*, Ludwig in *An Accidental Man*, and John Duncane in *The Nice and the Good*.

Jefferson says the latter is presented with a series of temptations worthy of Saint Anthony of Padua. Yet Murdoch the novelist is not so consistent as Murdoch the moralist. The novelist extends love to less-than-good characters, such as Randall in *An Unofficial Rose*. Sometimes her zest for novelty causes her to forget moral concerns. She extends the reader's sympathies to old people like Bruno and to homosexuals like Michael in *The Bell*, but sometimes, as in her presentation of Patricia in *The Black Prince*, she is not sympathetic at all.

_____. "Iris Murdoch and the Structures of Character." *Critical Quarterly* 26 (Winter, 1984): 47-58.
Although some of Murdoch's intellectual and artistic characters fulfill themselves by discovering things outside themselves, most of her characters develop in a machinelike fashion from one basic impulse or obsession. Jefferson refers to many novels and discusses four at length: *The Sacred and Profane Love Machine*, *A Word Child*, *An Accidental Man* (which he likes), and *The Sea, The Sea* (which he does not).

Johnson, Deborah. *Iris Murdoch*. Bloomington: Indiana University Press, 1987. Chapter 1 is reprinted in *Critical Essays on Iris Murdoch*, edited by Lindsey Tucker. New York: G. K. Hall, 1992. A brilliant and useful feminist and psychoanalytical study of novels through *The Good Apprentice*. In Chapter 1, Johnson examines Murdoch's practice of putting a first-person male narrator at the center of her plots. These men are single, articulate, gifted, artistic, and powerful; they are often frustrated and thereby impelled to rigorous self-examination. They are to some degree misogynistic; they see women, not as separate human beings, but as objects and obstacles. Johnson thinks that women read such stories by identifying both with the quester and with the feminine objects. Murdoch is aware of these problems and undermines male assumptions. Like other female writers, she mimics male attitudes, sometimes by playful repetition, in order to undermine male authority. Murdoch often reveals that men's quests are inadequate or illusory. She shows how a man's oedipal quest conflicts with a woman's oedipal attachments. She diffuses oedipal situations with comedy.

In Chapter 2, Johnson shows how the female author undermines her first-person male narrator in other ways. In *Under the Net*, *A Severed Head*, *The Sea, The Sea*, and *The Philosopher's Pupil*, the narrator's exaggerated language and his conventional poses and opinions imply a female author who suggests he is not understanding the true complexities of situation. In *The Black Prince*, the female author uses the male narrator to veil herself and the horrors of her true subject matter.

In Chapter 3, Johnson discusses Murdoch's third-person narratives, which she thinks are less successful than the first-person ones. In them readers find a clash of voices that suggests the instability of narrative authority. Johnson is critical of the way Murdoch's omniscient narrators render women's love in terms appropriate to magazine romances. She also worries about Murdoch's plots. Female characters are often in unhappy predicaments: imprisoned, enslaved, their talents uncultivated, their love defeated. In the claustrophobic novels published between 1963 and 1966, the detached author seems to collude with harsh, patriarchal plots to provide a vision of hell. Allusions to Tennyson suggest that women have been *textualized*; that is, they have been reduced to myth. Culturally induced female misery is only briefly revealed, as if the author is trying to escape her own dread. Even though in later novels women are more free, the treatment of Dora in *The Bell* points to what Johnson thinks is a fundamental split in Murdoch's attitude toward women.

In Chapter 4, Johnson considers Murdoch's use of myth and symbol and argues that they should be read in a double-voiced way; that is, they should be read with a feminist subtext. Johnson provides an example by analyzing at length two symbols from *The Bell*. She also shows that when Murdoch employs her favorite myth of Plato's cave in fiction, two readings are possible: the orthodox public male reading and a private female poetic reading. In the feminist reading, the Cave is not a place of illusion but a womblike place of truth, of female eroticism, and of creativity. Johnson discusses many cavelike structures in the novels (*The Nice and the Good*, *The Sea, The Sea*, *Nuns and Soldiers*, and *The Philosopher's Pupil*) and adds that for many female characters their cave is their place of imprisonment or even their own bodies.

In Chapter 5, Johnson discusses the novels' endings. What some critics find unsatisfying is actually Murdoch undercutting conventional endings to call attention to their strong element of wish fulfillment. Murdoch herself is split between her masculine, philosophical, cerebral side that likes to wrap up a novel neatly and her feminine, poetic, emotional side that knows that the world is unstable and cannot be so easily summarized. She shows her feminine side when she ends a novel without full closure (as in *The Sea, The Sea*), when she makes improbabilities overwhelm any pretenses to realism (as in *A Severed Head*), or when she indicates by subtle verbal clues that the story is being artfully drawn to a close (as in *The Bell* or *The Nice and the Good*).

Kane, Richard C.   "Didactic Demons in Contemporary British Fiction."   *University of Mississippi Studies in English* 8 n.s. (1990): 36-57.
An article apparently written before his book on Murdoch, Spark, and Fowles was published. A number of contemporary British novelists mix the demonic with moral concerns. In these stories, powerful demonic enchanters can teach painful moral lessons to weaker characters, just as enchanting novelists can teach their readers. Kane analyzes *A Severed Head* at length.

_____. *Iris Murdoch, Muriel Spark, and John Fowles: Didactic Demons in Modern Fiction*.   Rutherford, N.J.: Fairleigh Dickinson University Press, 1988.
These authors mix the demonic with moral concerns.   Kane devotes chapters to *The Flight from the Enchanter*, *A Severed Head*, and *The Unicorn*.

Karl, Frederick R. *The Contemporary English Novel*. Rev. ed. New York: Farrar, Straus & Giroux, 1972.
In the course of his survey, Karl describes Murdoch's work unflatteringly. Although he concedes she is intelligent and talented, he is upset by her mixture of comedy, the burlesque, and seriousness. Her characters can be divided into the fixed and the flexible. Her best novels are *A Severed Head*, *An Unofficial Rose*, and *The Unicorn*.

Kemp, Peter. "The Fight Against Fancy: Iris Murdoch's *The Red and the Green*." *Modern Fiction Studies* 15 (Autumn, 1969): 403-415.

Murdoch's novels show a group of semi-allegorical characters patterned around a central philosophical idea. To live morally, she insists, a person must escape patterns and pay imaginative attention to the real contingent world. But she herself is guilty of creating fantasy; her principles are at odds with her practice. In light of these ideas, Kemp analyzes *The Red and the Green*.

Kennard, Jean E. "Iris Murdoch: The Revelation of Reality." In *Number and Nightmare: Forms of Fantasy in Contemporary Fiction*. Hamden, Conn.: Archon Books, 1975.

A lucid, compact, and valuable essay, with comments on many of the novels through *A Fairly Honorable Defeat*. To Murdoch, the real world is contingent and unfathomable. But most of her characters live in fantasy worlds, worlds which often take the shape of webs of interconnected persons. In her novels' usual pattern, people *do* escape personal fantasies and communal webs, often by means of sensational scenes that surprise both the characters and the reader. Often breaking away takes the form of breaking bonds with a twin. The result is the characters' discovery of an amazing new reality. Through loving attention they may come to know the uniqueness of others.

Kennard identifies three kinds of passages in which Murdoch renders the wonders of reality. There are scenes of true enchantment, always very simply rendered. There are scenes in which simple things seem miraculous. There are "technical scenes" in which, by the clarity and precision of detail, Murdoch makes readers see what extraordinary things are happening. Murdoch also uses fantasy in the novels to suggest the mysteriousness of reality. Kennard calls this method "super-realism," a kind of exaggeration to make the reader understand that the real world is very strange.

Kenney, Alice P. "Mistress of Creation." *Mythlore* 11 (Summer, 1984): 18-20, 45.

In contrast to some ancient creation myths, many modern writers emphasize that *women* have creative powers. In *A Severed Head*, Murdoch creates a powerful figure in Honor Klein. At first Martin adores her as a mother/warrior goddess; later he sees her simply as a strong woman. Even though these modern writers do not always discuss the social barriers female artists face in expressing their creativity, their examples encourage all women.

Kenyon, Olga. *Women Novelists Today: A Survey of English Writing in the Seventies and Eighties.* New York: St. Martin's Press, 1988.

Although Kenyon's essay is badly organized and awkward, it touches on many important aspects of Murdoch's fiction: her characters' unique obsession with the Good; her curious mixture of realism and fantasy; her sense of the comic absurdity of all humans; and the importance of love's energy, of magic, and of mystical experience in her novels. Kenyon stresses Murdoch's choice of male narrators, how they experience erotic love and how much they find they must learn. Kenyon also notes what some have thought to be limitations, especially the absence of mothers and of close female friends in the novels. She provides very short discussions, mainly of female characters, in *The Black Prince, The Sea, The Sea, Nuns and Soldiers, The Philosopher's Pupil,* and *The Good Apprentice.*

_____. *Women Writers Talk: Interviews with Ten Women Writers.* New York: Carroll & Graf, 1990.

In this interview conducted by David Gerard, Murdoch makes remarks about her ideas (she feels close to Christianity but does not believe in Christian dogma), on studying philosophy (it teaches how to think clearly), on existentialism (she disagrees with its idea of total freedom), and on the novel (great novels are funny).

Kermode, Frank. "The House of Fiction: Interviews with Seven English Novelists." *Partisan Review* 30 (Spring, 1963): 61-82. Reprinted in *The Novel Today,* edited by Malcolm Bradbury. London: Fontana/Collins, 1977.

Murdoch clarifies her distinction between crystalline and journalistic novels. She thinks giving a great deal of attention to form may keep a novelist from delving into painful subjects. She is fascinated by the mechanics of a car slipping into a river or a bell being raised from a lake.

_____. "Iris Murdoch." In *Modern Essays*. London: Fontana/ Collins, 1971.
When Murdoch insists that her characters must be free and thinks that only love can connect them to their mysterious otherness, these ideas link her to Bloomsbury writers. Readers sense that much is going on beneath the surface; each novel contains the ghost of a major novel.

Khanna, Urmilla. "Iris Murdoch and Shakespeare." *Yearly Review* [University of Delhi] (December, 1991): 17-28.
Khanna discusses the reasons for Murdoch's high regard for Shakespeare and surveys her use of Shakespeare (especially Sonnet 144) since Richard Todd wrote *The Shakespearean Interest*. Brief remarks on *The Sea, The Sea, The Philosopher's Pupil, The Book and the Brotherhood*, and *The Good Apprentice*.

Kogan, Pauline. "Beyond Solipsism: A Study of Iris Murdoch's Novels." *Literature and Ideology* 1 (1969): 47-69.
A severe criticism of Murdoch's reactionary work from a Marxist perspective.

Kriegel, Leonard. "Iris Murdoch: Everybody Through the Looking-glass." In *Contemporary British Novelists*, edited by Charles Shapiro. Carbondale: Southern Illinois University Press, 1965.
Murdoch will probably not fulfill her early promise. She lacks sensuousness and rage; she is insular; she is missing the vision of a writer like D. H. Lawrence. Kriegel likes *Under the Net* the best. In *Flight from the Enchanter*, Mischa is unreal; the novel is too symbolic and too playful. In *An Unofficial Rose*, neither Hugh or Randall is credible. *The Unicorn* does not move because it manipulates its readers by symbols. In contrast, *The Italian Girl* is moderately successful, and *The Bell* is a good novel. It is intense; its symbol works; Dora is a good character. A thin argument.

Kuehl, Linda. "Iris Murdoch: The Novelist as Magician/The Magician aas Artist." *Modern Fiction Studies* 15 (Autumn, 1969): 347-360. Reprinted in *Contemporary Women Novelists*, edited by Patricia Meyer Spacks. Englewood Cliffs, N.J.: Prentice-Hall, 1977.

A famous attack on Murdoch's novels, taking as representative examples *The Flight from the Enchanter*, *A Severed Head*, and *The Unicorn*. Kuehl concludes that Murdoch employs time-worn Gothic settings and melodramatic plots in service of her chosen genre: metaphysical fantasy. Her characters are stock types and can be divided into enchanters, their accomplices, and the enchanted. All are loaded with philosophic, mythic, and literary baggage. Murdoch is too obscure to be a novelist of ideas and too playful to be a novelist of character.

Leavis, L. R. "The Anti-Artist: The Case of Iris Murdoch." *Neophilologus* 72 (January, 1988): 136-154.
A heavily ironic and snide *ad hominum* attack on Murdoch's fiction. Despite her attempts to be a great novelist and despite the praise of her admirers, she is really not a novelist at all. Behind Leavis's mean-spirited diatribe are serious charges: compared to D. H. Lawrence, Murdoch creates characters that do not live and plots that are totally absurd. Her novels often resemble thrillers, detective fictions, or women's magazine stories. In short, they are lurid kitsch.

Le Gros, Bernard. "Roman et Philosophie chez Iris Murdoch." In *Rencontres avec Iris Murdoch*. Caen, France: Centre de Recherches de Littérature et Linguistique des Pays de Langue Anglaise de l'Université de Caen, 1978. [In French.]
Because of the recurrent patterns and untraditional allegorical elements in Murdoch's novels, Le Gros labels them "metaphysical novels." Murdoch the metaphysician relies on Plato's cave allegory and concludes that although human beings are prisoners in the cave, we have not lost our ideas of Love, Beauty, or the Good. Yet Murdoch is playful and likes to mystify the reader. Le Gros suggests that someone should investigate how she uses mystification as an element in her fiction.

Levidova, Inna. "Reading Iris Murdoch's Novels," translated by David Catin. *Soviet Literature* 10 (1977): 170-178.
Levidova describes Murdoch's reception in the Soviet Union and gives a sympathetic overview of Murdoch's career and themes, especially the possibility of moving from blindness to a new vision. She stresses Murdoch's skill as a story teller and the presence in

her work of concrete things: places, animals, trees. Realism can conflict with the harsh frames of Murdoch's plots. What is least characteristic of Murdoch is wishful thinking. Levidova singles *The Black Prince* out for special praise.

Lundin, Roger. "Murdoch's Magic: The Consolations of Fiction." *Christian Century*, May 18, 1988, 499-502.
Murdoch wants to salvage the legacy of Christianity through art. She and her characters attempt to get some of the benefits of Christianity without making any fundamental commitments. In this, she resembles thinkers like Reinhold Niebuhr who interpret Christianity through reigning intellectual fashions. The solace Murdoch's characters receive is grounded only on fantasy and desire. Lundin discusses *The Book and the Brotherhood* at length.

McCabe, Bernard. "The Guises of Love." *Commonweal*, December 3, 1965, 270-273.
A survey of Murdoch's novels. Her themes concern freedom and various forms of love. But the novels do not always perform what they promise; they have too many symbols; they are too manipulative. Murdoch's tone is too matronly. McCabe is particularly harsh toward *The Bell* and *The Red and the Green*.

McDowell, F. P. W. "'The Devious Involutions of Human Character and Emotions': Reflections of Some Recent British Novels." *Wisconsin Studies in Contemporary Literature* 4 (Autumn, 1963): 339-366.
In a review of British fiction, McDowell calls Murdoch brilliant, but complains that her symbols are not sufficiently consistent or precise. McDowell comments on *An Unofficial Rose* and *The Unicorn*.

McEwan, Neil. "Iris Murdoch's Contemporary World." In *The Survival of the Novel*. Totowa, N.J.: Barnes & Noble Books, 1981.
Although some critics call Murdoch old-fashioned, her novels depend for their effect on the tension between traditional and contemporary elements. McEwan discusses *The Bell*, *The Nice and the Good*, and *Henry and Cato*.

Maes-Jelinek, Hena.   "A House for Free Characters."   *Revue des Langues Vivantes* 29 (1963): 45-69.
A survey of Murdoch's first six novels. Maes has a simple thesis: Murdoch's characters do not guide their actions by conventional morality. Her survey shows how some of them achieve freedom by learning how to live without fantasy. She admires Murdoch, but thinks her novels are not sufficiently moving.

Magee, Brian.   "Philosophy and Literature: Dialogue with Iris Murdoch." In *Men of Ideas: Some Creators of Contemporary Philosophy.* New York: Viking Press, 1979.
An excellent interview in which Murdoch clarifies her ideas on the relations between philosophy and literature. She emphasizes that both activities involve a search for truth.

Majdiak, Daniel.   "Romanticism in the Aesthetics of Iris Murdoch." *Texas Studies in Literature and Language: A Journal of the Humanities* 14 (Summer, 1972): 359-375.
A long discussion of Murdoch's aesthetics which concludes that, despite her anti-Romanticism, she is a romantic in some ways. Majdiak illustrates this thesis by valuable short analyses of *The Time of the Angels* and *The Bell*.

Marget, Madeline.   "The Water is Deep: Iris Murdoch's `Utterly Demanding Present.'" *Commonweal*, June 14, 1991, 399-402.
Murdoch denies God but demonstrates his presence. Marget finds dramatic action, water symbolism, and distinctive structures in three novels: *The Philosopher's Pupil, The Nice and the Good,* and *Bruno's Dream.*

Martin, Graham.   "Iris Murdoch and the Symbolist Novel." *British Journal of Aesthetics* 5 (July, 1965): 296-300.
Murdoch is unusual in that even though her instinct is to write "crystalline" or tightly plotted novels, she is not a social novelist. She cannot communicate the complex characters and the web of institutions, habits, and traditions which older novelists revealed. The roots of Murdoch's characters are not in society but in their inner lives. Thus even though her best novels can be called crystalline, her characters have inner lives that resist allegory. Martin discusses *The Unicorn* at length.

Martz, Louis. "Iris Murdoch: The London Novels." In *Twentieth Century Literature in Retrospect*, edited by Reuben A. Brower. Cambridge, Mass.: Harvard University Press, 1971. Reprinted in *Iris Murdoch*, edited by Harold Bloom. New York: Chelsea House, 1986.

Murdoch resembles Dickens in her love of London, as shown by the particularity with which many of its neighborhoods are described. For Murdoch's characters, their love of place is related to their capacity for love of other persons. Although some novels are located in London without much sense of place, in *Under the Net, Bruno's Dream*, and *A Fairly Honorable Defeat* London is not only vividly present but thematically significant.

Massie, Allan. *The Novel Today*. London: Longman House, 1990.

Murdoch is treated briefly. Massie thinks Murdoch's characters are unrealistic when they speak freely of their repressed emotions. She is by turns realistic, melodramatic, improbable, macabre, and illuminating.

Mehta, Ved. "Onward and Upwards with the Arts: A Battle Against the Bewitchment of Our Intelligence." *The New Yorker*, December 9, 1961, 59-159. Reprinted in *The Fly and the Fly Bottle: Encounters with British Intellectuals*. London: Weidenfeld & Nicolson, 1963.

In his survey of British intellectuals, especially those at Oxford, Mehta visits Murdoch briefly. She looks like St. Joan and remembers Wittgenstein. She seems to Mehta more intuitive than analytic. In *The New Yorker*, the passage on Murdoch begins on page 108; in *The Fly and the Fly Bottle*, on page 53.

Meidner, Olga M. "The Progress of Iris Murdoch." *English Studies in Africa* 4 (March, 1961): 17-38.

An interesting and valuable, if somewhat jumbled and judgmental, evaluation of Murdoch's first four novels. Meidner values *Under the Net* highly, but thinks that in her next three novels, Murdoch goes downhill. Her prose gets more drab, in part because she employs less and less figurative language. She seems less assured. Even though her intellect seems to be winning out over intuition, her narrators become more detached, indecisive, and pessimistic. Meidner makes detailed comments on *Under the*

Net, The Flight from the Enchanter, The Sandcastle, and *The Bell.*

Mettler, Darlene D. *Sound and Sense: Musical Allusion and Imagery in the Novels of Iris Murdoch.* New York: Peter Lang, 1991.
Murdoch has some background in music and shows considerable familiarity with it. Mettler examines allusions to music and musical imagery in eight of Murdoch's novels: *The Bell, The Time of the Angels, The Nice and the Good, A Fairly Honorable Defeat, The Black Prince, The Sea, The Sea, Nuns and Soldiers,* and *The Philosopher's Pupil.* (She makes brief allusions to several others.) In Chapter 2, Mettler reviews theories about the relationship of music and literature. Some of Mettler's comparisons are strained, but she makes many interesting interpretations.

Meyers, Jeffrey. "The Art of Fiction CXVII: Iris Murdoch." *Paris Review* 115 (Summer, 1990): 206-225.
Murdoch provides some biographical details and talks at length about how she composes a novel: one great problem is when, after starting to write, you should begin to plot out a novel's overall structure. A good story is essential to a novel. She is attracted to Buddhism. She praises John Cowper Powys for treating sex better than did D. H. Lawrence. She enjoyed A. S. Byatt's *Possession.* Her favorite fictional characters are Achilles and Mr. Knightley.

_____. "An Interview with Iris Murdoch." *Denver Quarterly* 26 (Summer, 1991): 102-111.
Meyers elicits details of Murdoch's early life, but Murdoch parries his questions about literary influences. She expresses opinions on Ireland (the IRA are very bad), Communism (she is glad she knew the Party from within), homosexuality (she hates anti-gay prejudice). She values most religions, though not literal beliefs; she considers herself a Christian Buddhist, still within the Anglican Church.

Miles, Rosalind. *The Fiction of Sex: Themes and Functions of Sex Differences in the Modern Novel.* London: Vision Press, 1974.
Miles describes how novelists of the nineteenth and twentieth centuries treat sexual differences. In Chapter 4, Annette in *The Flight from the Enchanter* is an example of a female imprisoned

in many roles.   In Chapter 5, Miles discusses working-class characters: Mrs. Carberry in *An Accidental Man* is not successful; Pattie in *The Time of the Angels* is an excellent study of the psychology of service.   Murdoch's dazzling effects may obscure both her naturalism and her kind of satire (which mixes laughter and love).   Because Murdoch shows so many ways that love is imperfect, readers sometimes wonder how it can exist at all.

Morin, Michele.   "Passion et Salut dans l'Oeuvre d'Iris Murdoch."   In *Rencontres avec Iris Murdoch*.   Caen, France: Centre de Recherches de Littérature et Linguistique des Pays de Langue Anglaise de l'Université de Caen, 1978.   [In French.]
According to Plato, the forces of Eros drive people toward Beauty. The same forces or passions cause Murdoch characters to strive for a transcendent absolute Truth or Good.   Passions come in four varieties: amorous, religious, artistic, and moral.   Although not logically impossible, salvation through religion usually fails, because the self and its fantasies create obstacles.   Atheism may be the ideal religion.   Unlike religion, love requires another human as an intermediary, but the intrusion of self again makes perfect love almost impossible.   Artistic passion must distinguish between good art and bad art; even with good art, it is difficult to conquer the self.   Because words hide ultimate reality more than they revel it, music is closer to Truth than is literature.   Moral passion can reach the Good only by complete self-abnegation, which is impossible.   As a result, the passions can hope to achieve, not salvation, but only the intuition of salvation.   Morin refers briefly to *The Bell*, *The Red and the Green*, *The Time of the Angels*, *The Black Prince*, *The Nice and the Good*, and *Bruno's Dream*.

Morrell, Roy.   "Iris Murdoch: The Early Novels."   *Critical Quarterly* 9 (Autumn, 1967): 272-282.
Many of Murdoch's characters are isolated in their private worlds; some emerge to recognize the separateness of other people. Morrell comments on *Under the Net*, *The Sandcastle*, and *The Bell*.

Moss, Howard.   "Narrow Escapes: Iris Murdoch."   *Grand Street* 6 (Autumn, 1986): 228-240.

This rambling review-essay contains valuable criticism. Moss
discusses the monster/magicians at the center of two novels: *The
Philosopher's Pupil* and *The Sea, The Sea*: Rozanov and Charles
Arrowby. These characters inspire devotion in others. They
themselves try to possess persons they cannot possess; they learn
that youth and the past cannot be recaptured. Both stories have
magical houses and take place against a background of water.
Animals and natural enigmas like stars and rocks convey a sense
of mysterious forces beyond what the characters understand.
Moss also comments on *Nuns and Soldiers* and *The Good
Apprentice*, and discusses Murdoch's Jewish characters. His
summary: Murdoch's novels show a mind too inventive to stop.

Murdoch, Iris. "Against Dryness: A Polemical Sketch." *Encounter* 16
(January, 1961): 16-20. Reprinted in *Iris Murdoch*, edited by
Harold Bloom. New York: Chelsea House, 1986.
Perhaps Murdoch's most famous essay. Our contemporary conception of personality is too shallow: we see a human being as a
solitary, totally free individual, educable by using theories of
materialistic behaviorism. As a result, contemporary novels do
not depict individuals struggling in society but fall into two unsatisfactory types. The *crystalline* novel provides a "dry," short, self-
contained allegorical view of the human condition; it does not
have characters like those in nineteenth century novels. The
journalistic novel is its opposite: large, detailed, seemingly
documentary, not so much shapeless as formed by fantasy.
Murdoch calls for novels that will portray the complexity of the
moral concerns, the opacity of the human character, and density
and contingencies of human life. Such novels will be eloquent;
they will invigorate without consoling.

_____. "Iris Murdoch Answers Our Questions." *Iris Murdoch
News Letter*, no. 5 (Summer, 1991): 1.
Murdoch describes the care she takes with her titles, specifically
The Message to the Planet, *The Philosopher's Pupil*, *Nuns and
Soldiers*, and *The Good Apprentice*. She lists the foreign coun-
tries she has visited and notes her special affinity for Russia,
India, and Japan.

Murray, William M. "A Note on the Iris Murdoch Manuscripts in the University of Iowa Libraries." *Modern Fiction Studies* 15 (Autumn, 1969): 445-448.

The library has two holograph manuscript copies of each of the following: *Under the Net, The Bell, A Severed Head* (the play), *An Unofficial Rose, The Unicorn, The Red and the Green, The Time of the Angels,* and *Bruno's Dream.* The library also has some working papers for *A Severed Head* (the novel) and *An Unofficial Rose.*

Nettell, Stephanie. "An Exclusive Interview." *Books and Bookmen* 11 (September, 1966): 14, 15, 66.

Murdoch protests that she is not a philosophical novelist. All novels are comic and should make readers laugh fairly often. Each of her novels has its unique atmosphere: fog is vital to *The Time of the Angels.* Murdoch tells about how she writes. Novels begin with a germ of an idea; she works out the plot before she begins to write. She would like to write a novel with a large cast of free characters, but myth takes over and limits her characters' freedom. She plans to keep on writing: "I should hate to be alive and not be able to write a novel."

Nussbaum, Martha C. "Love and Vision: Iris Murdoch on Eros and the Individual." In *Iris Murdoch and the Search for Human Goodness*, edited by Maria Antonaccio and William Schwelker. Chicago: University of Chicago Press, 1996.

In order to understand Murdoch, Nussbaum contrasts the attitudes of Plato and Dante toward the relationship of sexual love to the Good, and finds they are in conflict. Plato says that sexual desire increases the yearning for the Good; Dante thinks sex decreases such yearnings. Plato thinks that sexual love is a source of vision, whereas Dante thinks it impedes vision. To Plato, sexual love is present not only at the beginning of the journey to the good, but all along the way. To Dante, sexual desire must be purged before any vision can be achieved. Plato's lovers see each other as individual agents of the Good; for Dante, sexual love impedes attention to the qualities of its object.

Because Murdoch's writings can be cited to support both views, Nussbaum attempts to discover Murdoch's essential ideas about sexual love by analyzing *The Sacred and Profane Love Machine* and *The Black Prince*. She finds that Murdoch is more allied to Plato, and that she supplements that philosopher in that she does not avoid the particularities (including their odd bodies) of individual human beings. For Murdoch, art can best tell the whole truth about idiosyncratic and comic human beings. But Nussbaum finds some distaste in Murdoch's attitudes toward her characters and their sex lives. Murdoch provides a contrast to the Aristotelian James Joyce, who celebrates individuality and sex because he does not recognize any reason to ascend to any Platonic good. Yet Nussbaum detects some Aristotelian traces in Murdoch as well.

Oates, Joyce Carol. "Sacred and Profane Iris Murdoch." In *The Profane Art: Essays and Reviews*. New York: E. P. Dutton, 1983.
This chapter is a review of *The Sea, The Sea* with many references to other works. Murdoch's novels are filled with ideas, not human beings. At their best, equal forces of ideas do battle; the winner is the one most in tune with the impersonal universe. Individuals find it almost impossible to escape from their self-centered fantasies; they live in a world with other people in the same condition. Although this is a pessimistic view, it does not exclude comedy, and Murdoch's mission is to protect her readers from despair.

Obumselu, Ben. "Iris Murdoch and Sartre." *ELH* 42 (Summer, 1975): 296-317.
Murdoch's "aesthetic mysticism" is an attempt to bring back traditional values. She is wrong when she says that great art is dependent on realistic contingencies. Obumselu discusses *Under the Net*, *An Unofficial Rose*, and *The Unicorn*.

O'Connor, Patricia J. "Iris Murdoch: Philosophical Novelist." *New Comparison: A Journal of Comparative and General Literary Studies* 8 (Fall, 1989): 164-176.
Is Murdoch a "philosophical novelist"? In a plodding essay, O'Connor answers "yes." Sartre is such a novelist: his novels show how his philosophical ideas work in everyday life. In *Under the Net*, Murdoch too expresses ideas she has written about in philosophical terms. Jake is at first blinded by his own ego; at the end of the story, he knows he must pay attention to reality.

O'Connor, William Van. *The New University Wits and the End of Modernism.* Carbondale: Southern Illinois University Press, 1963.

In his essay "Iris Murdoch: The Formal and the Contingent," O'Connor offers superficial surveys of Murdoch's first five novels.

Packer, P. A. "The Theme of Love in the Novels of Iris Murdoch." *Durham University Journal* 38 (1977): 217-224.

An eloquent and evocative essay. Packer wittily reviews some objections to Murdoch's work, but then discusses her greatest strength: her treatment of the complexities of love, of the inner dramas of mental and psychological states her characters enjoy and suffer. For Murdoch, human love leads to her highest value, the Good. Packer illustrates the varieties of love with examples from *The Sandcastle*, *The Bell*, *The Nice and the Good*, *A Fairly Honorable Defeat*, and *Bruno's Dream*.

Parker, Peter, ed. *A Reader's Guide to the Twentieth Century Novel.* New York, Oxford University Press, 1995.

Plot summaries and brief assessments of *The Bell*, *A Fairly Honorable Defeat*, *The Sacred and Profane Love Machine*, and *The Sea, the Sea.*

Phillips, Diana. *Agencies of the Good in the Work of Iris Murdoch.* Frankfurt: Peter Lang, 1991.

A major study of Murdoch's ideas and their relation to five novels (*The Bell*, *The Unicorn*, *Bruno's Dream*, *A Fairly Honorable Defeat*, and *The Black Prince*) selected to represent stages in her development. Phillips does not praise these novels when they reflect Murdoch's philosophical ideas or criticize them when they do not. Rather, Phillips tries to show how the novels dramatize Murdoch's vision. Throughout, she relates Murdoch's ideas to those of other philosophers and makes illuminating comparisons to Murdoch's other novels. Chapter 1 deals with Murdoch's conception of the novel and especially with her attempt to create free and whole characters who seem to exist beyond their roles in a particular novel. In Chapter 2, Phillips defines Murdoch's philosophical position by discussing her objections to linguistic philosophy and to existentialism. In Murdoch's view, man is not simply a rational being living in a world of fact nor a neurotic inward-looking being cut off from the world. Man is a being capable of seeing beyond himself, capable of apprehending transcendent realties. These realities may be religious, though Murdoch prefers Platonic ones.

In Chapter 3, Phillips explains Murdoch's idea that love, death, and art are all "agencies of the Good." (Phillips here specifically discusses Murdoch's debts to Simone Weil and to Gabriel Marcel.) Love frees man from delusions and thereby helps him envision the Good. Far from encoding philosophy in her novels, she seeks to enhance philosophy by the vision of art. This book is made difficult for many readers by its untranslated French quotations and by its unusually long paragraphs. Bibliography.

_____. "The Challenge of the Past: Iris Murdoch and the Legacy of the Great Nineteenth-Century Novelists." *Caliban* 27 (1990): 73-81.

The twentieth century has produced novels in which lonely individual characters try to come to terms with their psyches against a schematic social background. Murdoch admires the novels of the nineteenth century because they give a truer picture of unique and mysterious human beings living in a complete society. Her novels have a strong moral influence.

Piper, William Bowman. "The Accommodation of the Present in Novels by Murdoch and Powell." *Studies in the Novel* 11 (Summer, 1979): 178-193.

A very interesting essay. Piper argues that the way a novelist presents the present is an important indication of what his or her novels are about. Anthony Powell's first-person narration in *A Dance to the Music of Time* firmly places most action in the past; his narrator is more interested in the pattern of the dance than individual acts, even acts of transforming importance. Murdoch is almost completely the opposite, especially in her first-person novels. Even though she must use the conventional past tense, she is most interested in rendering important and very intense collisions of individual characters *in the present*. She does not use the past tense to meditate; she hardly uses the future to look back. When there are surprises, they happen to the character and to the reader simultaneously. Piper makes specific comments on *A Severed Head*, *The Black Prince*, and *A Word Child*.

Poirier, Richard. "The Politics of Self-Parody." *Partisan Review* 35 (Summer, 1968): 339-353.
Poirier relates fiction to the politics of the Vietnam War. Along the way, he says that Murdoch, Jorge Luis Borges, John Barth all produce fictions that are self-parodies: that is, in some of their stories they make the formal properties of fiction the subject of fiction.

Punja, Prem Parkash. *The Novels of Iris Murdoch: A Critical Study.* Jalandar, India: ABS Publications, 1993.
A study of the novels through *The Good Apprentice.* Punja's chapters deal with Murdoch's life and critical reactions, her ideas about the novel, the adaptations of the Gothic (loosely defined), her good characters, her treatment of sexual relationships, and her treatment of religion, morality, and politics. Punja makes many comments on individual novels.

Rabinovitz, Rubin. "Iris Murdoch." In *Six Contemporary British Novelists,* edited by George Stade. New York: Columbia University Press, 1976. The first part of this essay is a reprint of his pamphlet *Iris Murdoch* (New York: Columbia University Press, 1968).
Rabinovitz discusses Murdoch's works individually through *The Sacred and Profane Love Machine.* He succinctly points out autobiographical elements in her novels as well as the presence of ideas from Sartre, Wittgenstein, Weil, Freud, Nietzsche, and others. Rabinovitz's brief analyses of Murdoch's early novels are valuable, but as he proceeds to later works they become more and more perfunctory.

Ramanathan, Suguna. "The Concept of Good in Four of Iris Murdoch's Later Novels." *Heythrop Journal* 28 (1987): 388-404.
An earlier version of her arguments in *Iris Murdoch: Figures of Good.* Here she deals mainly with *Henry and Cato, The Sea, The Sea, Nuns and Soldiers,* and *The Philosopher's Pupil.*

_____. *Iris Murdoch: Figures of Good.* London: Macmillan, 1990.
In her introduction, Ramanathan explains that the idea of goodness is central to Murdoch's thought, especially in seven of her

later novels. Each of these contains one character who embodies aspects of the Good. These characters are not central to the story or triumphant. In fact, they are marginal, powerless against the extraordinary force of selfish power. Murdoch's position can be called religious, for the Good is transcendent; her concepts are similar to Buddhist ideas, but more obviously related to Christian ones. Although Murdoch is not a Christian, Christ is usually for her a figure of perfect selfless love, an example of goodness. In the introduction, Ramanathan deals many novels in passing and with *A Fairly Honorable Defeat* in detail. Later chapters discuss *Henry and Cato*, *The Sea, The Sea*, *Nuns and Soldiers*, *The Philosopher's Pupil*, *The Good Apprentice*, *The Book and the Brotherhood*, and *Message to the Planet*. In her brief conclusion, she deals with the charge that Murdoch's characters are simply vehicles for ideas.

Randall, Julia. "Against Consolation: Some Novels of Iris Murdoch." *The Hollins Critic* 13 (February, 1976): 1-15.
A chatty and impressionistic tour of most of Murdoch's novels through *A Word Child*. Randall nicely summarizes Murdoch's skeptical outlook: Murdoch sympathizes with those who desire consolations, but ultimately is against consolation. Randall finds Murdoch's men convincing. Some characters (like Mischa from *The Flight from the Enchanter)* are fantastic, like dragons from the depths of the human psyche. Murdoch's usual form resembles romantic comedy and her view of life balances negative and positive. Randall likes *An Accidental Man*; its comic pattern is satisfying. She thinks *The Sacred and Profane Love Machine* and *An Unofficial Rose* are without hope. Perhaps because Murdoch writes comic fiction, her novels are forgettable.

Ratcliffe, Michael. *The Novel Today*. London: Longmans, Green, 1968.
In Chapter 3, Ratcliffe deals with Murdoch briefly. She admirably combines intelligence, imagination, and wit, with the ability to tell spellbinding stories. *The Bell* and *A Severed Head* are best; later novels (through *The Nice and the Good*) represent a decline.

Ricks, Christopher. "A Sort of Mystery Novel." *New Statesman*, October 22, 1965, 604-605.

A celebrated attack. In her essays, Murdoch champions free characters. In her novels, she exemplifies what she deplores: her characters are simply mechanical. Ricks discusses *The Red and the Green*.

Rippier, Joseph. *Some Postwar English Novelists.* Frankfurt: Diesterweg, 1965.
A helpful but superficial overview of the novels through *The Unicorn*.

Rose, W. K. "An Interview with Iris Murdoch." *Shenandoah* 19 (Winter, 1968): 3-22. Reprinted as "Iris Murdoch, Informally" in *London Magazine* 8 (June, 1968): 59-73.
A very interesting interview. Murdoch describes her work habits and lists the authors she re-reads: Dickens, Jane Austen, Tolstoy, Dostoevski, and Henry James (who has particularly influenced her). Though she is glad she was trained in analytical philosophy, she is a moral and political philosopher. Philosophy, especially metaphysics, is important in her novels, but not usually central. She uses symbols that come naturally, but is not a symbolist writer. She is not a Freudian. She wants to write "open" novels with free characters and accidental happenings, yet she often deals with the forceful and even enslaving powers (often sexual powers) that demonic or godlike characters have over their victims. When she was influenced by existentialism, her subject was freedom; now under Plato's influence, her subject is love. In particular, she likes *The Unicorn*, for it mixes sexual forces with spiritual and religious ones.

Roxmann, Susanna. "Contingency and the Image of the Net in Iris Murdoch, Novelist and Philosopher." *Edda*, no. 2 (1983): 65-70.
Roxmann finds that most authors use the metaphor of a net to suggest a trap. Murdoch sometimes uses the image this way (in *The Bell*, Catherine is trapped in a net). Most often, she uses it in a way derived from Wittgenstein and perhaps the philosopher Carl G. Hempel. As in *Under the Net*, a net can be a metaphor for theorizing and thus distorting reality, and Murdoch has several characters who do not want to recognize the contingency of reality.

Sage, Lorna.   "Female Fictions: The Women Novelists."   In *The Contemporary English Novel*, edited by Malcolm Bradbury and David Palmer. New York: Holmes & Meier, 1980.
Sage finds Murdoch's novels unsatisfying, for they appear to fight against the changing world. Yet in most novels discordant figures appear, characters who seem to be from another world; they have the openness most of the other characters lack. Other discordant characters are writers who attempt to write philosophy.

_____.   "The Pursuit of Imperfection."   *Critical Quarterly* 19 (Summer, 1977): 67-87.
Murdoch's novels are full of unrealistic characters in patterned plots, like the novels of Arnold Baffin in *The Black Prince*. Sage discusses *Henry and Cato*.

_____.   *Women and the House of Fiction: Post-War Women Novelists*. New York: Routledge, 1992.
In Chapter 3, Sage groups Murdoch with Margaret Drabble, Edna O'Brien, and Mary McCarthy as novelists who, like their predecessors in the nineteenth century, deal with ordinary life. Sage summarizes Murdoch's ideas and comments on some of her novels. *Under the Net* is a perverse novel of ideas. In *A Severed Head*, Honor is a fabrication. Sage thinks that in *The Red and the Green* Murdoch begins her mature work, for not only does it have many characters and a sprawling plot, but its descriptions of Dublin are well done. In her later novels, abstract issues are shown through a range of individualized characters who are inter-related, yet distinctly drawn. Murdoch places these characters in a convincing mass of local and contingent detail.

Schaumburger, Nancy.   "Interview with Dame Iris Murdoch."   *Iris Murdoch News Letter*, no. 9 (Autumn, 1995): 9-11.
Murdoch remarks on the roles Dickens, Kipling, and other writers have played in her life. She says she does not admire Wittgenstein any more. *The Book and The Brotherhood* is a novel she particularly likes.

Scholes, Robert.   *The Fabulators*.   New York: Oxford University Press, 1967.   Murdoch chapter reprinted in *Fabulation and Metafiction*. Urbana: University of Illinois Press, 1979.

In Chapter 5, Scholes defines allegory as a form of story that sees life through a filter of philosophy or theology. He goes on to distinguish Murdoch's kind of allegory from that created by earlier writers. In past, allegory revealed divine order; for contemporary writers like Murdoch, allegory reveals the order imposed by the human mind. Murdoch's world is full of meanings, but devoid of Meaning. Scholes analyzes *The Unicorn* at length.

Seiler-Franklin, Carol. *Boulder-pushers: Women in the Fiction of Margaret Drabble, Doris Lessing and Iris Murdoch.* Berne, Switzerland: Peter Lang, 1979.
How do women writers regard women? Seiler-Franklin surveys some of Murdoch's female characters. Gracie in *An Accidental Man* is a typical self-centered and greedy young woman; Dorina in the same novel is unstable and mad, dominated by her husband. Dora in *The Bell* shows the beginnings of maturity as she moves from dependence to independence. In *A Fairly Honorable Defeat*, Morgan is an intellectual who longs for freedom, but who accepts her place in society. Hilda in the same novel is a typical married housewife whose security is destroyed. Harriet in *The Scared and Profane Love Machine* is another subservient housewife whose dreams are shattered.

Shattock, Joanne. *The Oxford Guide to British Women Writers.* Oxford: Oxford University Press, 1993.
A brief notice gives an overview of Murdoch's works (including non-fiction) and suggestions for further reading.

Sinfield, Alan. "Varieties of Religion." In *Society and Literature, 1945-1970.* New York: Holmes & Meier, 1983.
In his survey of religious life in Britain after World War II, Sinfield refers briefly to *The Bell* and to *The Time of the Angels* in order to show how traditional Christianity has gone downhill.

Sizemore, Christine Wick. *A Female Vision of the City: London in the Novels of Five British Women.* Knoxville: University of Tennessee Press, 1989.
Twentieth century women writers such as Margaret Drabble imagine London though a typically female image: a network. In contrast, Murdoch sees London as a labyrinth, and her male

characters see it in a typically male way: organized around landmarks. Her early novels like *Bruno's Dream* are Dickensian in their affection for London, yet not sentimental like Dickens. Then in novels like *A Word Child*, Murdoch shows her ties to feminism as London becomes a labyrinth containing the Minotaur of egotism at its center. Men are egotistical and lonely, whereas female characters hold the threads of human attachment which will offer a way out. A further stage is found in *Nuns and Soldiers*: characters do not avoid confronting their selfishness. Sizemore refers to many novels in passing and analyzes these three novels in detail. Even though this essay is not tightly organized, it is valuable and suggestive.

Slaymaker, William E. "An Interview with Iris Murdoch." *Papers on Language and Literature: A Journal for Scholars and Critics of Language and Literature* 21 (Fall, 1985): 425-432.
An interview based on his 1982 article. Murdoch qualifies most of the ideas about freedom that Slaymaker advances: she has not become more deterministic. To see things clearly gives freedom. Good art takes people out of their fantasies. Religion can liberate people from selfishness and neurosis.

_____. "Myths, Mystery and the Mechanisms of Determinism: The Aesthetics of Freedom in Iris Murdoch's Fiction." *Papers on Language and Literature: A Journal for Scholars and Critics of Language and Literature* 18 (Spring, 1982): 166-180. Reprinted in *Critical Essays on Iris Murdoch*, edited by Lindsey Tucker. New York: G. K. Hall, 1992.
Slaymaker identifies freedom as one of Murdoch's central concerns and surveys how her ideas develop in her philosophical essays. She is not a determinist; she explains not only what forces limit human freedom but also how some freedom may be achieved. In contrast to her philosophical statements, her later novels imply that their characters have even less freedom than before. Slaymaker discusses *The Black Prince* at length and makes brief comments on the five novels that follow it.

Souvage, Jacques. "The Novels of Iris Murdoch." *Studia Germanica Gandensia* 4 (1962): 225-252.

A loosely organized overview of Murdoch's first five novels. Souvage stresses her ideas that morality and virtue involve realizing the existence of other people and that the world is a contingent, messy one inhabited by contingent, messy people. He praises the way plot and theme become more and more integrated in her works.

Spear, Hilda D. *Iris Murdoch*. New York: St. Martin's Press, 1995.
Spear gives succinct analyses of all Murdoch's novels in chronological order through *The Green Knight*. In her introduction, she provides an outline of Murdoch's life, but she observes that the novels are not very autobiographical (except for the dogs). They are not philosophical novels, though in them realistic characters live in worlds that have philosophical significance. Murdoch herself has moved from an interest in (and disagreement with) Sartre to an allegiance to aspects of Plato's thought, especially the concept of the Good. She is not religious, but a "fellow-traveler." Her question is: how can human beings have a concept of the Good in a world without a traditional God? As a novelist, she has been influenced by the Victorians (especially Henry James) and Shakespeare. She works out her plots before she begins to write. In her discussion of Murdoch's *Metaphysics as a Guide to Morals* in Chapter 7, Spears explains how Murdoch blends old myths with characters involved with contemporary moral concerns. In her conclusion (Chapter 8), Spear makes some judgments as she reviews quickly the history of the critical reception of Murdoch's novels.

Stettler-Imfeld, Barbara. *The Adolescent in the Novels of Iris Murdoch*. Zürich: Juris Druck & Verlag Zürich, 1970.
The introduction surveys classic and modern English novels and places Murdoch among those recent authors who view adolescents from the perspective of psychology. Murdoch's adolescents are not at the center of their novels, but are connected to the central adult characters. Some adolescents are warm-hearted and open; others are silent and secretive.
Stettler-Imfeld treats Annette in *Flight from the Enchanter*, Don and Felicity in *The Sandcastle*, Toby in *The Bell*, Miranda and Penn in *An Unofficial Rose*, Flora in *The Italian Girl*, Andrew in *The Red and the Green*, and Pierce and Barbara in *The*

Nice and the Good. She considers these characters with respect to the crises that propel them from childhood (new environments, problems in their parents' lives, first love); to their reactions and solutions (mental flight, symbolic actions, real actions); and to their ways of moving towards maturity (realistic and romantic love, struggles with adults). She then sets these figures in the worlds of the novels and of Murdoch's general ideas. This book is overly schematic, but Stettler-Imfeld provides many valuable insights into adolescent characters.

Stevenson, Randall. *The British Novel Since the Thirties*. Athens: University of Georgia Press, 1986.
Brief remarks on many novels. Stevenson says *A Fairly Honorable Defeat* has more realistic life than a Golding novel.

Stubbs, Patricia. "Two Contemporary Views on Fiction: Iris Murdoch and Muriel Spark." *English* 23 (Autumn, 1974): 102-110.
Murdoch's ideas about fiction do not correspond to her actual practices. She insists that novels must be rooted in the miscellaneous facts of real experience and in the complexities of unique characters; she argues against mythic, symbolic novels. In practice, her natural tendency is to write mythic novels, and her novels show a tension between fact and myth. Their plots are sometimes criticized for being too mythic and their characters unreal. Her theory is thus corrective: she values what is most foreign to her talent. Stubbs criticizes Murdoch for trying to do in fiction what is more appropriate to philosophy, especially when she tries to give new meaning to traditional religious ideas.

Sturrock, John. "Reading Iris Murdoch." *Salmagundi* 80 (Fall, 1988): 144-160.
A valuable survey full of unique insights. Murdoch became a novelist because she found Oxford philosophy severely limited. In contrast, her novels can show a concern for freedom, humanity, and moral questions. Her improbable plots impress readers with the strangeness of the world, its mysteries and accidents. Life in a Murdoch novel is intense; emotional disruptions lead to moral questionings, which in turn allow Murdoch to provide lessons in the nature of goodness. She defines bad love as the controlling and manipulative love of Palmer Anderson in *The Severed Head*

and Blaise in *The Sacred and Profane Love Machine*. She shows false freedom, as when Randall in *An Unofficial Rose* feels he can do anything. In contrast, Murdoch's highest values reside in attentiveness to others. Sturrock says that Murdoch's marvelous descriptions of processes are examples of this kind of attention: Rain's car slipping into a river in *The Sandcastle* and getting a cage out of a small room in *Under the Net*.

Sullivan, Zohreh Tawakuli. "The Contracting Universe of Iris Murdoch's Gothic Novels." *Modern Fiction Studies* 23 (Winter, 1977-78): 557-569. Reprinted in *Critical Essays on Iris Murdoch*, edited by Lindsey Tucker. New York: G. K. Hall, 1992. Murdoch increasingly demonizes the isolated, self-centered individual who craves power and order. Instead of trying to live in the true community of love and imagination, such persons attempt to make substitute communities based on work or on erotic relationships, often symbolized by dark rooms. Sullivan analyzes in detail three Gothic novels in which such false and inverted communities appear: *The Flight from the Enchanter*, *The Unicorn*, and *The Time of the Angels*. These novels help readers see clearly Murdoch's idea of evil.

_____. "Iris Murdoch and the Enchantment of Untruth." In *Essays on the Contemporary British Novel*, edited by Hedwig Bock and Albert Wertheim. Munich: Max Hueber Verlag, 1986. An interesting survey of Murdoch's fiction through *Nuns and Soldiers*. Sullivan groups Murdoch's novels in a unique way that brings out some characteristics of individual novels that could easily be overlooked. Her first three novels provide an overture to the rest of Murdoch's work, each novel prefiguring a number of others in a particularly significant way. *Under the Net* looks forward to *The Black Prince*, *A Word Child*, and *The Sea, The Sea*, in that all center on a single self-centered artist-protagonist. *The Flight from the Enchanter* prefigures other "closed," semi-allegorical novels such as *A Severed Head*, *The Unicorn*, *The Italian Girl*, and *The Time of the Angels*. These novels show a fascination with powerful demonic egoists. *The Sandcastle* is the first of Murdoch's "open," decentered novels, the others being *The Bell*, *An Unofficial Rose*, *The Red and the Green*, *The Nice and the Good*, *Bruno's Dream*, *An Accidental Man*, *The Sacred and*

Profane Love Machine, Henry and Cato, and *Nuns and Soldiers.*
A Fairly Honorable Defeat belongs in part to each of the last two
groups.

_____. "Women Novelists and Variations on the Uses of
Obscurity." *South Carolina Review* 16 (Fall, 1983): 51-58.
Early twentieth century women writers like Virginia Woolf
thought their art could be true to their experience only by being
private and obscure. Murdoch, like other women writers in later
years, try to write works which reflect both the tensions between
the private and public worlds and their connections. Sullivan
looks briefly at *The Sea, The Sea* to prove her point.

Swinden, Patrick. *Unofficial Selves.* New York: Barnes & Noble
Books, 1973.
In Chapter 7, Swinden discusses Murdoch's ideas about characters
and says that her novels do not necessarily reflect her theories. To
understand Murdoch, we must understand her pattern. Unlike
most other novelists, she writes stories in which connections
between characters are more important than motivations. Even
when a character has a purpose for an act, the consequences of
that act are often far different from those intended. Murdoch's
characters have a inner sense of identity like those of other novelists, but Murdoch's characters often construct fantasies they think
are real. They can only discover their identities by discarding the
roles they find themselves playing and by understanding the plots
in which these roles figure. Readers must come to understand a
novel's web of plots before they can understand its characters
(conventional novels work in the opposite direction). Murdoch's
novels are like games in which the pieces can fit together in many
ways, most of them false. At the end, readers (and some characters) may sense what a true arrangement might be. Ultimately,
Murdoch distinguishes between patterns that are products of
individual fantasies and patterns that are inherent in human acts
and relationships. Swinden applies his theories to *Under the Net*
and *A Fairly Honorable Defeat.*

Taylor, D. J. *After the War: The Novel and English Society Since
1945.* London: Chatto & Windus, 1993.

Taylor mentions Murdoch throughout his book. He says her spirituality is only loosely attached to definable beliefs.

Taylor, Jane. "Iris Murdoch Talks to Jane Taylor." *Books and Bookmen* 11 (April, 1971): 26-27.

A brief interview. Though Murdoch defends recent philosophers, she insists she is not a philosophical novelist, but a creator of realistic stories. She does not base her characters on people she knows, and she does not identify obsessively with any particular characters. She praises the virtues of magnanimity and humility.

Todd, Richard. *Iris Murdoch*. London: Methuen, 1984. Reprinted in part in *Iris Murdoch*, edited by Harold Bloom. New York: Chelsea House, 1986.

Todd's introduction succinctly sets Murdoch's novels and ideas in their contexts; he emphasizes how they refuse to fit into contemporary categories. What is constant in Murdoch's stories are characters with secret obsessions. Todd discusses four phases of Murdoch's career (through *The Philosopher's Pupil*) in four chapters and discusses each novel briefly. He considers the reception of her works and her theories of the novel.

_____. *Iris Murdoch: The Shakespearean Interest*. New York: Barnes & Noble Books, 1979. Chapter 2 is reprinted in *Critical Essays on Iris Murdoch*, edited by Lindsey Tucker. New York: G. K. Hall, 1992.

A difficult book with several very valuable ideas about Murdoch's fiction. In his introduction, Todd defines Murdoch's essential problem as how to be true to contingent reality while writing an ordered work of art. Shakespeare seems to resolve this dilemma. One way Murdoch tries to solve it is by using symbols and other artistic devices in ways that are significant, not in themselves, but in their contexts; they are part of the flow of contingent reality. Another way is by *plausibility*; she attempts to make improbable events acceptable in their context. Todd deals with several important objections to Murdoch's practices. He discusses how Shakespearean concepts have informed the novels through 1975, with emphasis on *The Nice and the Good, Bruno's Dream, A Fairly Honorable Defeat, An Accidental Man*, and *The Black Prince*.

In Chapter 2, Todd notes that Shakespeare combines believable characters with magical forms which are satisfying without offering false consolations. Although Murdoch admires this achievement, she knows she cannot imitate it totally. Nevertheless, she often has characters like Bradley Pearson in *The Black Prince* act in conformance to or comment upon Shakespearean patterns. In Chapter 3, Todd investigates Murdoch's attempt to emulate Shakespeare's *King Lear* in treating suffering and death with a consolation that is not false. He discusses *An Accidental Man*, *Bruno's Dream*, and *A Word Child*. In Chapter 4, Todd attempts unsuccessfully to relate the patterned endings of six Murdoch novels to the happy patterned endings of Shakespearean comedy by using categories from Northrop Frye's *A Natural Perspective*. The novels are *A Severed Head*, *An Unofficial Rose*, *The Nice and the Good*, *A Fairly Honorable Defeat*, *An Accidental Man*, and *The Sacred and Profane Love Machine*. He concludes that Murdoch seldom can avoid her fundamental problem.

In Chapter 5, Todd considers power figures in Shakespeare (Oberon, Prospero, and the Duke in *Measure for Measure)* and in Murdoch's novels, especially in *A Fairly Honorable Defeat* and *The Nice and the Good*. Some of Murdoch's characters break away from the enchantments of power figures; one power figure, John Ducane, becomes part of the novel's resolution. Todd concludes with a brief survey of some of Murdoch's theoretical writings. Even if it does not provide clear answers, Todd's book tackles important questions.

_____. "The Presence of Postmodernism in British Fiction: Aspects of Style and Selfhood." In *Approaching Postmodernism*, edited by Douwe Fokkema and Hans Bertens. Amsterdam: John Benjamins, 1986.
Todd locates Murdoch near John Fowles on a spectrum of kinds of postmodernism displayed by the British novel since the 1950's. The editorial apparatus of *The Black Prince* challenges the main text, and Murdoch seems to refer to her own concerns as a novelist in Bradley's theories about *Hamlet*.

Todd, Richard, ed. *Encounters with Iris Murdoch: Proceedings of an Informal Symposium on Iris Murdoch's Work Held at the Free*

University, Amsterdam, on 20 and 21 October 1986. Amsterdam: Free University Press, 1988.

At this conference, papers were presented by John Fletcher, Peter Conradi, W. Bronzwaer, Cheryl Bove, and Diana Phillips. Each paper was followed by Murdoch's response and a discussion. Participants included the persons listed above as well as John Bayley, James Brockway, Helen ten Holt, and the editor.

Tucker, Lindsey, ed. *Critical Essays on Iris Murdoch.* New York: G. K. Hall, 1992.

A collection of twelve important essays, most previously published as articles or parts of books. In the introduction, Tucker provides a succinct overview of Murdoch's philosophical and critical ideas. Then Tucker reviews how these ideas relate to Murdoch's novels. For example, like the crystalline novelists she criticizes, Murdoch uses myth. But for Murdoch, myth is the construction of obsessed and deluded minds; she does not recognize myth in the Jungian sense of basic human pattern. Tucker also focuses on Murdoch's debts to Freud and Plato. Both her idea of erotic energy and her kind of realism are particularly Platonic. Tucker provides a brief review of Murdoch scholarship and introduces her collection.

Turner, Jack. *Murdoch vs. Freud: A Freudian Look at an Anti-Freudian.* New York: Peter Lang, 1993.

A crude book that often becomes pure invective. In the introduction, Turner asks why Murdoch has such a strong aversion to Freud and psychoanalysis, even when she often makes use of Freudian ideas. He notes interestingly that Murdoch and Freud do not only disagree, but that they proceed from very different conceptual bases. Turner then criticizes Murdoch sharply from a simple Freudian basis. As a child rebels against its father, Murdoch rebels against Freud, against her own idolized (and castrated) father, and against her husband. Her novels show her own psychic battles under the guise of a confused religiosity. The novels attract readers because readers see such battles as their own. Although the novels seem to cohere satisfactorily, they ultimately fall apart. Murdoch mistakes Freud's superego for God. Turner continues his arguments in separate chapters on *Under the Net, A Severed Head, The Unicorn, A Fairly Honorable Defeat, The Sacred and Profane Love Machine, The Sea, The Sea,* and

The Good Apprentice. Chapter 9 offers brief remarks on *The Black Prince, A Word Child,* and *The Philosopher's Pupil.* No index.

Vance, Norman. "Iris Murdoch's Serious Fun." *Theology* 84 (November, 1981): 420-428.
Even though Murdoch's world does not admit God, her novels show an awareness of mysteries underlying everyday life. Persons who depend on normal civilized reason fare no better than philosophers and Freudians in understanding their world. Murdoch's positive force is the Good, which is attainable fleetingly thorough art. Vance makes brief remarks on some early novels, including *The Sandcastle.*

Wall, Stephen. "Aspects of the Novel, 1930-1960." In *The Twentieth Century,* edited by Bernard Bergonzi. Vol. 7 in *History of Literature in the English Language.* London: Barrie & Jenkins, 1970.
At the end of his essay, Wall treats Murdoch's novels through *Bruno's Dream.* Many of the ideas and techniques she first used in *Under the Net* are those she continues to use: fantastic happenings, strictly patterned relationships among unfathomable persons, mysterious authority figures, the notions of Wittgenstein. All her novels are love stories. Wall likes *The Bell* and *A Severed Head* best and looks at them briefly.

Weatherhead, A. Kingsley. "Backgrounds with Figures in Iris Murdoch." *Texas Studies in Literature and Language: A Journal of the Humanities* 10 (Winter, 1969): 635-648.
Weatherhead sees a pattern in the novels through *The Red and the Green*: A person leaves home or leaves the spell of a less than powerful enchanter in order to be free. But he or she falls under the spell of a more powerful enchanter, a figure who demands to be loved without hope of reciprocity. Even though the enchanted persons may leave their enchanters (often with violence), they do not usually settle down. Both the enchanter and the enchanted are defined by their background: their rooms, their clothes, and even their bodies. Weatherhead explains how these concepts illuminate *Under the Net, Flight from the Enchanter, An Unofficial Rose, The Unicorn,* and *The Red and the Green.*

West, Paul. *The Modern Novel*. London: Hutchinson, 1963.

In Part 2 of Volume 1, West treats Murdoch's first six novels briefly. He thinks she is over ingenious and too analytical. *The Bell* is too symbolic.

Whiteside, George. "The Novels of Iris Murdoch." *Critique: Studies in Contemporary Fiction* 6 (Spring, 1964): 27-47.

A dense, comprehensive, and valuable survey of Murdoch's first seven novels. Whiteside defies the genre of Murdoch's novels precisely: she is basically a realistic satirist (though some novels merit other terms). In her usual plot, a central character falls love (either protective or abject love) and dreams romantic dreams from which he or she must awake. These dreams take the form of projecting a personality on the object of love, a person who will not return that love. Unlike other writers of this century such as T. S. Eliot, Murdoch does not loathe the world of ordinary people. She satirizes it, yet is sympathetic toward it. Whiteside makes valuable comments on all of Murdoch's novels through *The Unicorn*.

Widmer, Kingsley. "The Wages of Intellectuality . . . and the Fictional Wages of Iris Murdoch." In *Twentieth Century Women Novelists*, edited by Thomas F. Staley. Totowa, N.J.: Barnes & Noble Books, 1982.

A difficult and evocative survey of Murdoch's novels through *A Word Child*. Widmer first identifies a self-destructive, English, middle-class, intellectual male as the usual target of Murdoch's satire and an enchanter as a staple figure of her fiction. He evokes Murdoch's complex ironies as he briefly discusses each novel. Early novels that depend on the trappings of Gothic melodrama are overdone; *A Severed Head* is a complex success. Some later novels have traditional niceness at their core, yet others are bleak. In general, Murdoch longs for traditional values, yet sets her stories in an existential world. She wagers that, in this world's muddles and in her own multiple ironies, the reader can find morality. Yet, because her characters never seem fully developed, what most readers find is only an intellectual game.

Wilkins, John. "Christ and Myth." *Frontier* (August, 1965): 219-221.
A report of a question and answer session at a conference in
Oxford. Do novelists need a mythological framework? Can
Christian myths do the job? Murdoch thinks many novelists like
herself and Dostoevsky do need to see life against a larger background. Jane Austen and Tolstoy do not. Using a myth poses the
danger of having it close your mind to fresh truths, making you a
slave to your own comfortable fantasy. Greek and Christian
myths have deep truths; one can not simply manufacture myths.
Christian myths can stimulate some novelists; others who look
back to pagan innocence prefer Greek myths. Murdoch says that
science fiction strikes her as very unimaginative and that science
can destroy the imagination.

Winsor, Dorothy A. "Iris Murdoch and the Uncanny: Supernatural
Events in *The Bell*." *Literature and Psychology* 30 (1980): 147-
154.
To Freud, the presence of the "uncanny" (his word for seemingly
supernatural events) signals the presence of the repressed and
primitive feelings of the child. Murdoch too knows that primitive
energies lie below both the conventional social world and the
world of organized religion. Supernatural or uncanny events in
her novels either tear the veil of convention away from reality or
signal the appearance of a new fantasy. Either way, the force of
the primitive is dangerous. Supernatural events in the novels may
express Murdoch's fear that human beings cannot sustain real
love. Winsor analyzes *The Bell* at length.

_____. "Iris Murdoch's Conflicting Ethical Demands: Separation
versus Passivity in *The Sacred and Profane Love Machine*."
Modern Language Quarterly: A Journal of Literary History 44
(December, 1983): 394-409. Reprinted in *Critical Essays on Iris
Murdoch*, edited by Lindsey Tucker. New York: G. K. Hall, 1992.
The ordered ideas of Murdoch's essays do not explain the moral
complexities of her fiction. Whereas the essays describe growing
out of childish self-absorption into an adult recognition that other
people exist, the novels present a world in which almost everyone
is trapped in childish fantasies and in which one merges with
other people only by dominating or by submitting. Goodness to
Murdoch lies in the second alternative: allowing yourself to be

destroyed in order to avoid destroying others. Winsor analyzes *The Sacred and Profane Love Machine* at length.

_____. "Solipsistic Sexuality in Iris Murdoch's Gothic Novels." *Renascence* 34 (Autumn, 1981): 52-63. Reprinted in *Iris Murdoch*, edited by Harold Bloom. New York: Chelsea House, 1986. Murdoch's three major experiments with Gothic material allow her to explore the relation between inner fantasy and outer reality, especially with regard to sexuality. Winsor treats how Murdoch's ideas change from *The Bell* to *The Unicorn* and *The Time of the Angels*. Winsor's arguments are often schematic and not fully convincing.

Wolfe, Peter. *The Disciplined Heart: Iris Murdoch and Her Novels*. Columbia: University of Missouri Press, 1966.
An early and valuable work. Wolfe's introduction and Chapter 2 locate Murdoch's philosophical and critical ideas in their contexts. His title refers to Murdoch's definition of love as a disciplined sense of the reality of other persons. Wolfe considers Murdoch's first eight novels, through *The Italian Girl*, in light of these ideas. Wolfe's conclusion summarizes his important ideas.

Criticism of Individual Novels

Under the Net, 1954.

Allen, Brooke. "The Drawing-room Comedy of Iris Murdoch." *New Criterion* 15 (September, 1996): 66-73.
In some ways, this novel owes more to P. G. Wodehouse than to Samuel Beckett.

Amis, Kingsley. *The Amis Collection: Selected Non-Fiction 1954-1990*. London: Hutchinson, 1990.
Includes an appreciative short review of this novel. Murdoch makes philosophical talk convincing and understandable. She succeeds in writing a novel from a first-person male point of view and in mixing funny and serious material.

Baldanza, Frank. *Iris Murdoch*. New York: Twayne, 1974.
  In Chapter 2, Baldanza provides a succinct and valuable analysis.
  The novel shows Murdoch's usual division of characters into artist
  (Jake) and saint (Hugo). Although its sources can be found in
  French fiction by such authors as Samuel Beckett and Raymond
  Queneau, Murdoch's themes go beyond existentialist negatives.
  After all his sexual and professional confusions, Jake learns from
  Hugo in Chapter 18 that other people's motives are not the same
  as his and also that other people make similar mistakes. At the
  novel's end, he and the other characters have learned to live lives
  which combine renunciation and a faith in living. Even though
  he thinks some incidents are much too improbable to be effective,
  Baldanza eloquently points out that Murdoch's tone is everywhere
  positive and fresh. Her inventiveness celebrates the marvels of the
  world.

Batchelor, Billie. "Revision in Iris Murdoch's *Under the Net*." *Books
  at Iowa* 8 (April, 1968): 30-36.
  Two sets of revisions on a holograph manuscript owned by the
  University of Iowa reveal many things. Murdoch composed her
  first draft quickly, making few revisions as she wrote. Then she
  revised extensively to make her prose more vivid, more clear, and
  more economical. She deleted a passage in which Jake offered to
  exchange Mars for the typescript of "The Wooden Nightingale."
  She changed Jake's name from Malone to Donaghue, perhaps to
  avoid a name just used by Samuel Beckett. Other major deletions
  treated Hugo's opposition to general theories, Jake and Lefty's
  discussion of socialism, and some matters concerning the hospital.
  Murdoch also deleted a final paragraph in which Jake prepares to
  take Mars for a walk. Batchelor thinks that this paragraph would
  have blunted the effect of the printed novel's ending.

Bove, Cheryl K. *Understanding Iris Murdoch*. Columbia: University
  of South Carolina Press, 1993.
  In Chapter 3, Bove says that a debate about language is at the
  heart of this novel. Speech is necessarily inaccurate; silence (or
  mime theater) is better. Some characters can be called good: Mrs.
  Tinckham and Hugo. The latter is selfless; he recognizes other
  people are separate beings; he is against theory.

Bradbury, Malcolm. "Iris Murdoch's *Under the Net.*" *Critical Quarterly* 4 (Spring, 1962): 47-54.
Part of this essay is reprinted as part of "`A House Fit for Free Characters': Iris Murdoch and *Under the Net*" in Bradbury's *Possibilities: Essays on the State of the Novel.* Oxford: Oxford University Press, 1973.
Bradbury sees the myth of Vulcan, Mars, and Venus behind this novel. He also discerns the influence of Henry James.

_____. "`A House Fit for Free Characters': Iris Murdoch and *Under the Net.*" In *Possibilities: Essays on the State of the Novel.* London: Oxford University Press, 1973.
Bradbury eloquently praises the ornate and speculative qualities of Murdoch's mind and praises this novel's social details. In spite of Murdoch's denials, Bradbury reasserts his belief that allusions to Vulcan, Mars, and Venus are important.

Burke, John Jr. "Murdoch, Sartre, and Song." *The Iris Murdoch Newsletter*, no. 3. (Summer, 1989): 4-5.
Anna's singing over the radio suggests she has broken Hugo's spell. But why does Jake ask to turn the radio off? Because Anna's song recalls a similar song in Sartre's *La Nausée*, Murdoch may be distancing herself from Sartre. In Sartre's novel, the song gives the hero faith in the power of art. In Murdoch's novel, the hero also prepares to write a novel, but in specifically moral ways. Anna's song reminds Jake of the kind of love he must set aside to pay attention to the world.

Byatt, A. S. *Degrees of Freedom: The Novels of Iris Murdoch.* New York: Barnes & Noble Books, 1965.
Murdoch simultaneously explores characters and the ideas they live by. In many ways Jake is a typical hero of his time: an outsider, a restless and inquisitive man who lives within himself and who shies away from work and intimacy. Byatt examines the social and political world he lives in, an unsatisfactory world torn apart by revolution and big business. By the end, Jake completes his two quests. He realizes his ideal Anna is but a song; the real Anna is a separate human being who is ultimately unknowable. He also recognizes Hugo's truths: that everything is particular and contingent and that fantasies of order are destructive. Jake can

now have a limited but real freedom of action. In Chapter 9, Byatt praises this novel for its balance of form and its free characters.

_____. *Iris Murdoch*. Harlow, Essex, England: Longman Group, 1976.
Byatt treats this novel at the beginning and end of Section II. It is a philosophical fable which criticizes the ideas of Sartre and deals with the dangers and importance of form. Unlike a Sartre hero, Jake discovers that the world is full of other people he can learn about.

_____. "People in Paper Houses: Attitudes to `Realism' and `Experiment' in English Postwar Fiction." In *The Contemporary English Novel*, edited by Malcolm Bradbury and David Palmer. New York: Holmes & Meier, 1980.
Brief discussion. This novel is a fable about realism as well as a comment on Wittgenstein and Sartre. Murdoch rewrites scenes from *La Nausée* to criticize Sartre's omitting some aspects of life.

Conradi, Peter. *Iris Murdoch: The Saint and the Artist*. New York: St. Martin's Press, 1986.
Although Conradi comments on this novel throughout his book, he focuses on it in Chapter 2. It is the most obviously philosophical of Murdoch's novels. Jake is an existentialist hero; ideas from Wittgenstein and Plato abound. Jake's unreliability as a narrator is part of the novel's pattern of copying, plagiarism, and theft. These motifs connect to Murdoch's insistence that art forms (here film in particular) do not tell the truth. Jake is also a picaresque hero, and his quest is to understand Hugo. Jake finally discovers Hugo's wisdom (which may be Murdoch's): one must distrust theories of order and unity, see the world's particulars afresh, and then love them. Unlike other critics, Conradi thinks the novel's conclusion is open-ended.

_____. "Iris Murdoch and Dostoevsky." In *Encounters with Iris Murdoch*, edited by Richard Todd. Amsterdam: Free University Press, 1988.
Hugo can be compared to Prince Myshkin in *The Idiot*. There are also parallels with *Notes from the Underground*.

Davis, Robert Murray. "On Editing Modern Texts: Who Should Do What, and to Whom?" *Journal of Modern Literature* 3 (April, 1974): 1012-1020.
  Davis lists many of the changes made in the American edition of this novel and the reasons American editors had for making them. Critics must quote from the English edition.

DeMott, Benjamin. "Dirty Words." *Hudson Review* 18 (Spring, 1965): 31-44.
  Hugo's distrust of language and praise of silence are ideas he shares with many other writers and their characters. In this novel, Hugo's ideas paralyze Jake until he can renew his faith. Murdoch wrote *Under the Net* out of resentment over nonwriters taking over language. Silence can be a strategy and a therapy.

Dipple, Elizabeth. *Iris Murdoch: Work for the Spirit.* London: Methuen, 1982.
  In Chapter 2, Dipple says that Hugo ranks only slightly below Murdoch's near-saints because his goodness is unconscious. In Chapter 3, Dipple outlines the allegorical scheme of the novel in which Hugo is a figure of renunciation, of withdrawal from the world. As such, he both inspires Jake and provides a contrast to him. In Chapter 4, she calls *Under the Net* a successful example of Murdoch's novels of trickery and plotting. The title refers to Wittgenstein's net of language by which people try to order the chaos of reality.

Emerson, Donald. "Violence and Survival in the Novels of Iris Murdoch." *Transactions of the Wisconsin Academy of Sciences, Arts, and Letters* 57 (1969): 21-28.
  The novel is lively and not grim. Appropriately, even though there is much violence, it is good-natured. Jake grows in understanding and survives into a new life.

Felheim, Marvin. "Symbolic Characterization in the Novels of Iris Murdoch." *Texas Studies in Literature and Language* 2 (Spring, 1960): 189-197.
  Murdoch often creates a pair of female characters (here Anna and Sadie) who carry the burden of a novel's meaning. Because they

function as symbols, they often seem puzzling. Sadie is an intellectual; Anna is the mystery for which Jake quests.

Fletcher, John. "Iris Murdoch, Novelist of London." *International Fiction Review* 17 (Winter, 1990): 9-13.
Much of the London described here is gone. The Viaduct Tavern still exists, as does Hammersmith Upper Mall.

Fogarty, Margaret E. "The Fiction of Iris Murdoch: Amalgam of Yeatsian and Joycean Motifs." In *Literary Interrelations: Ireland, England and the World II: Comparison and Impact*, edited by Wolfgang Zach and Heinz Kosok. Tübingen, Germany: Gunter Narr, 1987.
Murdoch's essential Irishness can be seen by the parallels between this novel and Joyce's *Portrait of the Artist as a Young Man* and by Murdoch's allusions to it. Jake is like Stephen. Both novels make much of silence, flight, enchantment, and birds.

Fraser, G. S. "Iris Murdoch: The Solidity of the Normal." In *International Literary Annual* II, edited by John Wain. London: John Calder, 1959.
This novel does not display any idea of a normal social community. Jake is not rebelling against society, but rather he is testing his personal ability to adapt. Fraser contrasts him to the rebellious hero of John Wain's *Hurry on Down*, who in the end desires some kind of society. Jake is tougher than Wain's hero—and funnier.

German, Howard. "Allusions in the Early Novels of Iris Murdoch." *Modern Fiction Studies* 15 (Autumn, 1969): 361-377.
In treating Hugo, Murdoch draws upon a life of Wittgenstein. Jake's adventures owe much to *The Aeneid*, especially in the Trojan horse/film set episode.

Gindin, James. "Images of Illusion in the Work of Iris Murdoch." *Texas Studies in Literature and Language* 2 (Spring, 1960): 180-188.
The image of the net suggests the traps and illusions that Jake faces on every side: ways of life and philosophical systems. In contrast to these illusions are natural things, like gardens and the

dog Mars. This novel's inadequate God-figures are Hugo and Mrs. Tinckham.

Goldberg, Gerald Jay. "The Search for the Artist in Some Recent British Fiction." *South Atlantic Quarterly* 62 (Summer, 1963): 387-401.
Goldberg sets *Under the Net* in the context of other contemporary novels which also record a central character's search for the truth about life. Jake is an isolated wanderer whose life is a private conversation. After talking with Hugo, he realizes that he had been seeing the world through the patterns of his own fantasy. In the future, he will try to find truth through writing.

Gordon, David J. *Iris Murdoch's Fables of Unselfing*. Columbia: University of Missouri Press, 1995.
In Chapter 3, Gordon notes two kinds of structural irony in this novel. Two opposing and partially valid approaches to life, Jake's and Hugo's, are shown, but not reconciled. Jake is an unreliable narrator, but Murdoch fails to maintain authorial distance from him. In Chapter 5, Gordon treats Jake and Hugo's friendship. Hugo combines elements of Sartre, Weil, and Wittgenstein into a character who is both enchanter and saint. Even though Hugo is against all theory, Jake the writer finds that theory is necessary.

Griffin, Gabriele. *The Influence of the Writings of Simone Weil on the Fiction of Iris Murdoch*. San Francisco: Mellen Research University Press, 1993.
Griffin refers to this novel several times. Jake's relation to Hugo is an obsession, for it is based on his own need. Murdoch's London is often Gothic. This novel's happy ending suggests that the young Murdoch still thought that moral self-improvement was possible.

Hague, Angela. "Picaresque Structure and the Angry Young Novel." *Twentieth Century Literature: A Scholarly and Critical Journal* 32 (Summer, 1986): 209-220.
Hague reviews the early criticism that mistakenly grouped Murdoch with such "angry" novelists as John Wain and Kingsley Amis.

Hall, James. "Blurring the Will: The Growth of Iris Murdoch." *ELH* 32 (June, 1965): 256-273.
Two metaphors control the action: property and the idyll in which communication is possible. At the end, there is no reconciliation, just a regrouping.

Hall, William F. "'The Third Way': The Novels of Iris Murdoch." *Dalhousie Review* 46 (Autumn, 1966): 306-318.
Hall think this novel presents Murdoch's ideas too allegorically to be effective. In Jake's world, Lefty embodies Sartrean political action and Hugo represents several strains of modern philosophical theory. Jake is torn between them; he rejects both to become an artist.

Heyd, Ruth. "Interview with Iris Murdoch." *University of Windsor Review* 1 (Spring, 1965): 138-143.
Jake is one of many obsessed Murdoch characters who try to impose form on a muddled reality.

Hoffman, Frederick. "Iris Murdoch: The Reality of Persons." *Critique: Studies in Contemporary Fiction* 7 (Spring, 1964): 48-57.
Murdoch's novels can be categorized on the basis of their characters. In some, characters are subordinate to the novel's pattern. For example, here Jake (anti-theory) is opposed to Hugo.

Hooks, Susan Luck. "Development of Identity: Iris Murdoch's *Under the Net*." *Notes on Contemporary Literature*, September, 1993, 6-8.
In a brief note, Hooks illuminates this novel by diagramming the four main characters as sides of a rectangle, the sides representing (roughly) creativity, theory, materialism, and beauty. Ideally, a person would balance these entities, and here each character seems to be moving toward balance. Most of the novel, however, dramatizes imbalance.

Hope, Frances. "The Novels of Iris Murdoch." In *On Contemporary Literature*, edited by Richard Kostelanetz. New York: Avon Books, 1964.

This work seems like a refusal to write a novel. It implies that life is simply a series of contingent adventures too fragmented to be pattered.

Johnson, Deborah. *Iris Murdoch*. Bloomington: Indiana University Press, 1987.
In Chapter 2, Johnson shows how the female author playfully and ironically undercuts the male narrator by showing him reacting to women in conventional ways taught him by the theater and by the cinema. Jake must revise his ways of reacting. In Chapter 5, Johnson speculates that Murdoch regards her novels as Hugo regards his fireworks: brilliant, enjoyable, but impermanent.

Kellman, Steven G. "Raising the Net: Iris Murdoch and the Tradition of the Self-Begetting Novel." *English Studies* 57 (February, 1976): 43-50. Revised version in *The Self-Begetting Novel*. London: Macmillan, 1980. Original version reprinted as "*Under the Net*: The Self-Begetting Novel" in *Iris Murdoch*, edited by Harold Bloom. New York: Chelsea House, 1986.
Kellman defines a "self-begetting novel" as one which tells of the rebirth of the protagonist as a novelist. Jake initially is a rootless, Frenchified, homeless writer who lives only within the constructs of his own mind. Jake gradually and consciously learns to accept the contingent world around him: Mrs. Tinckham's mess of a shop, a strange litter of kittens, and the power of song. As a result, he will stop translating second-rate French fiction and write a good novel himself. Kellman is convincing when he contrasts Jake to the central characters in novels by Sartre and James Joyce.

Kennard, Jean E. "Iris Murdoch: The Revelation of Reality." In *Number and Nightmare: Forms of Fantasy in Contemporary Fiction*. Hamden, Conn.: Archon Books, 1975.
In order to enter the real world, Jake has to escape from the fantasies of theory and from the magic of the mime theater. The rescue of Mars is one of Murdoch's "technical scenes," passages whose very precise details communicate how remarkable the world really is.

Kermode, Frank.   "The House of Fiction: Interviews with Seven
    English Novelists." *Partisan Review* 30 (Spring, 1963): 61-82.
    Reprinted in *The Novel Today*, edited by Malcolm Bradbury.
    London: Fontana/Collins, 1977.
    Murdoch says that Hugo is paralyzed by the problem of how
    theorizing divides people from real objects.

Leavis, L. R. "The Anti-Artist: The Case of Iris Murdoch." *Neophi-
    lologus* 72 (January, 1988): 136-154.
    In a heavily ironic attack on Murdoch and her novels, Leavis
    singles out this work as her best. Despite the author's manipula-
    tions, some of the characters seem authentic. It should be read as
    a "light comedy."

Maes-Jelinek, Hena.   "A House for Free Characters."   *Revue des
    Langues Vivantes* 29 (1963): 45-69.
    Murdoch characters do not live by conventional morality. Jake
    lives by his fantasies and thereby fails to understand Anna and
    Hugo. Finally he realizes that Hugo is not powerful, that life is
    not a continuous progression, that theories are futile, and that
    communication by words is limited. The novel suffers because its
    philosophical ideas are not closely integrated with its picaresque
    plot.

Martz, Louis.   "Iris Murdoch: The London Novels."   In *Twentieth
    Century Literature in Retrospect*, edited by Reuben A. Brower.
    Cambridge, Mass.: Harvard University Press, 1971. Reprinted in
    Iris Murdoch, edited by Harold Bloom.   New York: Chelsea
    House, 1986.
    Murdoch's evocation of London in this novel is like Dickens's in
    that many of the bombed out sights she describes have vanished as
    completely as those mentioned by the earlier novelist. Murdoch's
    descriptions are significant, for they remind us of Jake. Although
    his mind is full of undigested modern ideas, Jake's true self loves
    the city, and this love suggests his capacity to love other people.

Meidner, Olga M. "The Progress of Iris Murdoch." *English Studies in
    Africa* 4 (March, 1961): 17-38.
    Meidner thinks this is the best of Murdoch's first four novels. It is
    admirably varied; Murdoch's style is assured and poetic.   Its

conclusion is morally decisive. Perhaps low-life is treated too sentimentally.

Morrell, Roy. "Iris Murdoch: The Early Novels." *Critical Quarterly* 9 (Autumn, 1967): 272-282.
Here, as in a Sartre novel, characters bump into other characters; the difference is that in Murdoch these bumps make them human. Jake awakes from his isolation to recognize Hugo's and Anna's separateness.

Obumselu, Ben. "Iris Murdoch and Sartre." *ELH* 42 (Summer, 1975): 296-317.
In Sartre's *La Nausée*, the hero aspires to the formality of art. In contrast, Jake knows that Anna's formal song is nothing but enchantment, that form is only a man-made delusion. Obumselu criticizes Murdoch for her ideas.

O'Connor, Patricia J. "Iris Murdoch: Philosophical Novelist." *New Comparison: A Journal of Comparative and General Literary Studies* 8 (Fall, 1989): 164-176.
In *Under the Net*, Murdoch expresses ideas she has written about in philosophical terms. Jake is at first blinded by his own ego; by the end of the story, he knows he must pay attention to reality.

O'Connor, William Van. *The New University Wits and the End of Modernism.* Carbondale: Southern Illinois University Press, 1963.
In his essay "Iris Murdoch: The Formal and the Contingent," O'Connor says that this novel, unlike those by Amis and Wain to which it is compared, has a dreamlike atmosphere. Its satire is sympathetic. Some things Hugo says cannot be understood.

_____.   "Two Types of `Heroes' in Post-War British Fiction." *Publications of the Modern Language Association of America* 77 (March, 1962): 168-174.
O'Connor finds that many novels written in England after World War II have a new kind of hero. He is often a seedy young man with nothing conventionally heroic about him, only a distaste for humbug. He is the product of the clash between the newly educated lower classes and the old world of gentlemen. Jake in

Under the Net fits this definition. In later novels, Murdoch avoids
this kind of protagonist.

Porter, Raymond J. "Leitmotif in Iris Murdoch's *Under the Net*."
    Modern Fiction Studies 15 (Autumn, 1969): 379-385.
    This illuminating article argues that the story of Jake's develop-
ment is supported by several clusters of words and images.
Suggestions of enchantment, spells, dreams, and fairy tales often
attach to the characters (Anna and Hugo) who have the most
influence over Jake. Reflections in mirrors or water suggest the
difference between images and the real thing, between Jake's
illusions and reality. The change in Jake's ideas is suggested by
images of patterns being broken and by the renewing effects of
water, especially when characters swim in the Thames.

Punja, Prem Parkash. *The Novels of Iris Murdoch: A Critical Study*.
    Jalandar, India: ABS Publications, 1993.
    In Chapter 4, Punja identifies Hugo as one of Murdoch's truly
good characters. He is a socialist and pacifist who is indifferent to
material things. He tolerates a pauper like Jake; he sympathizes
with people and tries to avoid hurting them. He offers his body
for medical research. But in contrast to what happens in many
novels, Hugo is not rewarded for his goodness. In Chapter 5,
Punja notes that when Jake develops a capacity to feel for others,
he realizes that many of his judgments have been wrong.

Rabinovitz, Rubin. "Iris Murdoch." In *Six Contemporary British
    Novelists*, edited by George Stade. New York: Columbia Univer-
sity Press, 1976. The first part of this essay is a reprint of
Rabinovitz's pamphlet *Iris Murdoch* (New York: Columbia
University Press, 1968).
    Jake, whose adventures echo Murdoch's own life, tries to be a
solipsistic Sartrean hero, but accepts contingency by the end.
Hugo echoes Wittgenstein. Despite the echoes, the novel is very
original. A good discussion.

Rice, Thomas Jackson. "The Reader's *Flight from the Enchanter*." In
    Critical Essays on Iris Murdoch, edited by Lindsey Tucker. New
York: G. K. Hall, 1992.

A brilliant essay which compares *Flight from the Enchanter* to *Under the Net*. In his fictional novel "The Silencer," Jake the egotistical artist tried to impose a design on his readers; it is not clear if Jake ever escapes his egocentricity. The point of Murdoch's novel is that such designs falsify reality; its first-person point of view is appropriate to Jake's solipsism. In contrast, *Flight*'s non-artist characters (who are just as egotistic) do not impose designs; they feel they play roles in dramas imposed on them.

Rippier, Joseph. *Some Postwar English Novelists*. Frankfurt: Diesterweg, 1965.

A helpful but superficial overview of the early novels. *Under the Net* tells the story of Jake's drifting and his inconsequential adventures. At the end, he remains free.

Roxmann, Susanna. "Contingency and the Image of the Net in Iris Murdoch, Novelist and Philosopher." *Edda*, no. 2 (1983): 65-70.

Murdoch often uses the image of a net in a way derived from Wittgenstein and perhaps the philosopher Carl G. Hempel: a net is a metaphor for theorizing, for distorting reality. Jake may fight against the contingent world, but taken as a whole this novel is a gigantic image of concreteness and contingency.

Souvage, Jacques. "The Novels of Iris Murdoch." *Studia Germanica Gandensia* 4 (1962): 225-252.

Jake differs from the hero of Sartre's *La Nausée* in that he finds himself in society. The complexities of Murdoch's world can be seen in this novel's end: we get both Hugo's and Jake's point of view, but no resolution. The plot of *Under the Net* is not unified, for Jake is sometimes a moral man, sometimes a picaresque hero.

_____. "The Unresolved Tension: An Interpretation of Iris Murdoch's *Under the Net*." *Revue des Langues Vivantes* 26 (1966): 420-430.

This novel, like other early Murdoch novels, suffers from an unevenness of tone, a lack of unity. On one hand, it is a *bildungsroman*, the story of Jake's development as an artist through his friendship with Hugo and love for Anna. This Jake is a rounded character who eventually discovers his identity and his vocation.

In contrast, much of the plot is picaresque; Murdoch here is attracted by surface glitter and the fantastic. The Jake who is involved with stealing manuscripts or kidnapping dogs is only conventional.

Spear, Hilda D. *Iris Murdoch*. New York: St. Martin's Press, 1995.
Chapter 2 groups this novel with the three others published in the 1950's. In all four, isolated characters are often imprisoned while desiring freedom. Critics see them as reflecting philosophical ideas that interested Murdoch at the time. Jake seems like a Sartrean man until we realize he is only self-centered. Hugo, whose ideas may derive from Wittgenstein, explains the novel's central opposition: the flight for freedom is a flight toward theory and from truth. Truth can be sought only in restrictive and particular settings; truth-seekers try to crawl under the net of language to discover particularity. Some imprisonments, like Anna's in her theater, are retreats from truth. And Jake and Hugo must escape from the net of language to find the silence of truth. Jake, the first-person narrator, tells us that Hugo is central to the story, but he misunderstands Hugo completely (if we can believe Hugo). A difficult but helpful discussion.

Sturrock, John. "Reading Iris Murdoch." *Salmagundi* 80 (Fall, 1988): 144-160.
The key to virtue and freedom is attention. Sturrock sees this quality in Murdoch's description of getting a cage out of a small room.

Swinden, Patrick. *Unofficial Selves*. New York: Barnes & Noble Books, 1973.
In Chapter 7, Swinden says that this novel shows the working out of two errors. Jake commits his first error by believing in Hugo's ideas about silence. Jake comes to understand that when Anna lives in her mime theater under the net of language in silence and chaos, she is in the grip of Hugo's theory. Jake's second error is believing that because the patterns of his personal fantasies are false, all patterns are false. In fact, Jake eventually accepts his part in the pattern of his own life, a plot that he has created for himself. Other Murdoch characters understand this idea without Jake's clarity. A valuable explanation.

Todd, Richard. *Iris Murdoch*. London: Methuen, 1984.

In Chapter 2, Todd groups Murdoch's first four novels together in their concern for the implications of existentialism. *Under the Net* is a European novel, and Todd explains its many debts to other writers. Here Murdoch tries, for the most part successfully, to combine realism (especially in descriptions of London) with form. Jake, a man devoted to form and theory, must learn from Hugo, a man of truth and formlessness.

Tominga, Thomas T. "Wittgenstein and Murdoch on the 'Net' in a Taoist Framework." *Journal of Chinese Philosophy* 17 (June, 1990): 257-270.

Jake, Gellman, and Hugo are all philosophic types. Hugo thinks that because language falsifies experience, one should remain silent. This idea is one both Murdoch and Wittgenstein share with Taoism. Tominga discusses some differences between Wittgenstein and Murdoch.

Turner, Jack. *Murdoch vs. Freud: A Freudian Look at an Anti-Freudian*. New York: Peter Lang, 1993.

In Chapter 2 of this chaotic book of invective, Turner speculates that not only does Murdoch rebel against father figures and against scientific truth, but she projects her own horrible fantasies. The desirable Anna is the woman that the unattractive Murdoch wishes she could be.

Vickery, John B. "The Dilemmas of Language: Sartre's *La Nausée* and Iris Murdoch's *Under the Net*." *Journal of Narrative Technique* 1 (May, 1971): 69-76.

Vickery compares Sartre's novel to Murdoch's. Both writers seek to redefine how language works through similar central characters. Sartre's Roquentin comes to a philosophical impasse when he hopes to make language once again refer to things; his interest is phenomenological. Murdoch's Jake, on the other hand, lives with other people in a society which gradually corrects his mistakes. He adjusts to the way language works and aspires to creative work that will recognize the opacity of other people; his interest is epistemological. Vickery ties both works to Murdoch's ideas about crystalline novels and about Totalitarian (or Existential) Man.

Watson, George. "The Coronation of Realism." *The Georgia Review* 41 (Spring, 1987): 5-16.
   Watson argues that *Under the Net* and novels by Amis and Golding mark 1953 and 1954 as the start of a new era in English fiction. These novelists reject Joyce and Woolf: they blend somewhat radical politics with conservative, even old-fashioned techniques; their stories are comic and full of narrative events.

Weatherhead, A. Kingsley. "Backgrounds with Figures in Iris Murdoch." *Texas Studies in Literature and Language: A Journal of the Humanities* 10 (Winter, 1969): 635-648.
   In Murdoch's early novels, characters (often defined by their environment) fall under the spell of powerful enchanters but eventually reject them. Jake is first ensnared by Anna and her unreal golden world. He rejects her inadvertently, but his later rejection of the enchanter Hugo is deliberate. Weatherhead is unsure how to interpret Jake's situation at the end of the novel.

Whiteside, George. "The Novels of Iris Murdoch." *Critique: Studies in Contemporary Fiction* 6 (Spring, 1964): 27-47.
   Jake loves Hugo in that he projects his concept of a philosopher on Hugo and then falls under its spell. Hugo does not create Jake's illusion. Jake's search for Hugo reads like a parody of quests for fathers. When Jake finds out he is wrong, the spell is broken.

Widmann, R. L. "Murdoch's *Under the Net*: Theory and Practice of Fiction." *Critique: Studies in Modern Fiction* 10 (1968): 5-16.
   Widmann, after taking a swipe at A. S. Byatt, summarizes Murdoch's definition of a great novel, sets *Under the Net* against that definition, and finds it wanting. Its point is unclear. Murdoch's light treatment of Jake's immoral treatment of Finn is itself unethical. She is unconcerned that Jake does not grow up. Her characters are anything but "free," for there are signs that Murdoch knew their fates when she was writing her opening chapters. Thus, by her own definition, Murdoch is not a great novelist. Widmann notes that Murdoch successfully parodies the plot of many stories when hers ends with "boy-gets-dog."

Wolfe, Peter. *The Disciplined Heart: Iris Murdoch and Her Novels*. Columbia: University of Missouri Press, 1966.

Through comedy, this novel presents Murdoch's philosophical ideas about how theory must be avoided. The theories of many characters fail, and Hugo fails as a person as well. The novel's tone comes from Jake's knowing in retrospect that the world is chaotic, as dramatized by many surprises and plot reversals. The novel itself is not chaotic, for its climaxes come at regular intervals in Chapters 4, 8, 12, 16, and 20. Though Wolfe discusses the novel's flaws, he thinks it has many merits.

The Flight from the Enchanter, 1956.

Baldanza, Frank. *Iris Murdoch*. New York: Twayne, 1974.
    In Chapter 3, Baldanza explains that in this work Murdoch first employs many of the devices and characters which typify her novels. She presents a range of evil, from the simple and violent destructiveness of the Lusiewicz brothers to the sophisticated manipulations of Mischa Fox and Calvin Blick. In what may be a statement of theme, Blick explains that Mischa is not to be defined; he is simply a figure on which others project their desires. Baldanza analyzes the novel's many variations on the pattern of flight and quest, especially with regard to Rosa and Mischa. Annette is an early example of Murdoch's impetuous and amoral adolescent girl; her continual metamorphosis seems to echo Ovid's tale of Daphne. John Rainborough's story provides comic parallels to the novel's serious themes. Even though the novel ends with a few positive notes, its resolution is not so optimistic as that of *Under the Net*.

Bove, Cheryl K. "Americas and Americans in Iris Murdoch's Novels."
In *Encounters with Iris Murdoch*, edited by Richard Todd. Amsterdam: Free University Press, 1988.
    In Murdoch's novels, the United States is regularly associated with many bad things, including the arbitrary stipulations made by relief agencies such as SELIB.

————. *Understanding Iris Murdoch*. Columbia: University of South Carolina Press, 1993.
    In Chapter 8, Bove groups this work among Murdoch's "gothic" novels. In Mischa, Murdoch introduces her first enchanter, a

powerful figure who possesses Gothic characteristics and who
manipulates people who wish to be manipulated. Nina and the
Lusiewicz brothers are war victims, though the brothers themselves become abusers of sexual power.

Burgess, Anthony. *The Novel Now: A Student's Guide to Contemporary Fiction.* London: Faber & Faber, 1967.
Murdoch imposes enough of a pattern on her material to give
significance to Rainborough's career. But she does not order
many unexplained and uncontrolled (and often magical) events.

Byatt, A. S. *Degrees of Freedom: The Novels of Iris Murdoch.* New
York: Barnes & Noble Books, 1965.
This novel is dominated by images of pursuit, flight, capture, and
enchantment. Characters find not only that they are not free but
also that they are enslaved to one degree or another. (An exception is the detached, saintly Peter Saward.) In the social sphere,
characters are enslaved by factory jobs and by the international
agency SELIB. Nina, a perpetual serf, is an innocent victim; the
Lusiewicz brothers liberate themselves into a rootless freedom.
Rosa and Rainborough show different forms of personal enslavement. Even though she enjoys being an enchantress herself, Rosa
is in Mischa's power and for a while in that of the Lusiewicz
brothers as well. At the end, Rosa achieves a degree of freedom.
Unlike many critics, Byatt treats Mischa as a rounded character.
He is a man who has the power to kill, who is terrified by the
destructive sea, and who is detached from human beings, feeling
pity but not love for their blasted lives. A valuable essay in which
Byatt points out many illuminating parallels to other Murdoch
novels. In Chapter 9, Byatt criticizes Murdoch for allowing her
plan to predominate over her characters in this novel. Annette is
pure fantasy.

_____. *Iris Murdoch.* Harlow, Essex, England: Longman Group,
1976.
Byatt calls this a philosophical fable that begins with the Sartre's
ideas and moves beyond them. It shows how power enslaves in
many ways, including sexual ones, and how enslavement is
destructive. Mischa protects by enslaving and thus destroys what
he protects. Although Mischa's agent Calvin Blick argues that

human beings cannot escape their fantasies, the novel implies that an escape is possible.

Conradi, Peter. *Iris Murdoch: The Saint and the Artist*. New York: St. Martin's Press, 1986.
In Chapter 3, Conradi briefly discusses this comic and fantastic novel as showing a contrast between two characters. Mischa, the enchanter, is an artist-figure full of pity and destructiveness. His counterpart is the saintly Peter Saward, an ascetic and simple man who distrusts absolutist theories.

_____. "Iris Murdoch and Dostoevsky." In *Encounters with Iris Murdoch*, edited by Richard Todd. Amsterdam: Free University Press, 1988.
The fishbowl scene reminds Todd of a Dostoevskian fiasco of humiliation.

Davies, Alistair, and Peter Saunders. "Literature, Politics, and Society." In *Society and Literature, 1945-1970*, edited by Alan Sinfield. New York: Holmes & Meier, 1983.
Murdoch questions both liberal traditions and the influence of Bloomsbury. In *Flight from the Enchanter*, immoral and energetic people from Eastern Europe challenge English civil servants, who are unwilling or unable to resist.

Dipple, Elizabeth. *Iris Murdoch: Work for the Spirit*. London: Methuen, 1982.
In Chapter 5, Dipple calls this one of Murdoch's novels of trickery and plotting, the novel in which many of Murdoch's characteristic devices are first seen. Mischa is the enchanter, though the source of his power is obscure; Rosa is in flight from him. On a primitive level, the Polish brothers are enchanters as well. At the center of the novel are sexual conflicts and the contrast of Eastern and Western Europe, the latter being symbolized by machines. Dipple explains Mischa's three categories of women: unicorn, siren, and wise woman. Everyone looks to Mischa's party for salvation, but it becomes hellish. Annette is the first of Murdoch's many destructive adolescent girls. Dipple calls it is an energetic, but peculiar novel.

Felheim, Marvin. "Symbolic Characterization in the Novels of Iris Murdoch." *Texas Studies in Literature and Language* 2 (Spring, 1960): 189-197.
Murdoch often creates a pair of female characters who carry the burden of a novel's meaning. These women are passionate and energetic; at first they may be victims, but many eventually emerge as fulfilled persons. Because they function as symbols, they often seem puzzling. In this novel, both Annette and Rosa flee the enchanter and move toward freedom.

Fiedler, Leslie. "The Novel in the Post-Political World." *Partisan Review* 23 (Summer, 1956): 358-365.
After disparaging three novels by other authors, Fiedler finds in Murdoch's work a new beginning for the form. Murdoch knows that politics is gibberish. She comically disregards sentiment, sensibility, and realism. She stands against the conventional English novel's urbanity, good sense, and dissection of motives.

Fraser, G. S. "Iris Murdoch: The Solidity of the Normal." In *International Literary Annual* II, edited by John Wain. London: John Calder, 1959.
Like *Under the Net*, this novel has no sense of social norms against which its characters can be judged. All of the characters surprise; they can do anything at any time. Mischa is a cardboard character.

German, Howard. "Allusions in the Early Novels of Iris Murdoch." *Modern Fiction Studies* 15 (Autumn, 1969): 361-377.
Murdoch's allusions are not extended or perfect parallels. In this novel, they may make characters seem ambiguous or unrealistic. Many allusions to *Through the Looking-Glass* occur in reference to Annette and Rainborough (who resembles Humpty Dumpty). Annette is associated with the "Little Mermaid" story as well; other characters, especially Mischa, are connected to fables from Middle East, Balkan, and Norse sources.

Gerstenberger, Donna. *Iris Murdoch*. Lewisburg, Pa.: Bucknell University Press, 1975.
In Chapter 1, Gerstenberger says this novel opposes the liberal and deterministic assumptions of Britain's postwar welfare state.

It shows the predicament of its many alien characters, their displaced status emblematic of a more general estrangement from the world and from each other. Rosa's liberal stereotypes lead her to give herself to the Lusiewicz brothers. Even though Mischa is the enchanter, most characters refuse to see reality, thus enchanting themselves.

Gindin, James. "Images of Illusion in the Work of Iris Murdoch." *Texas Studies in Literature and Language* 2 (Spring, 1960): 180-188.
Illusions are connected with enchantment here; different people have different illusions. In contrast, there are natural things that cannot be possessed, like fish. This novel's bogus God-figure is Peter Saward.

Gordon, David J. *Iris Murdoch's Fables of Unselfing*. Columbia: University of Missouri Press, 1995.
In Chapter 5, Gordon says that this novel introduces the demonic enchanter to Murdoch's fiction, in this case an evil spreading from Central Europe to London. In another sense, it is other characters who create the enchanter in their own minds. The novel seems contrived and melodramatic. Peter Saward is the first of Murdoch's near-saints, a man who is not enchanted by Mischa and who is pointlessly good.

Griffin, Gabriele. *The Influence of the Writings of Simone Weil on the Fiction of Iris Murdoch*. San Francisco: Mellen Research University Press, 1993.
Griffin refers to this novel several times. Weil's idea of the deadening effect of working with machines is seen in Rosa's job. Nina is an example of an uprooted person (Weil stressed the "need for roots"). A clear case of the failure of attention takes place when Rosa does not listen to Nina.

Heyd, Ruth. "Interview with Iris Murdoch." *University of Windsor Review* 1 (Spring, 1965): 138-143.
Many characters in this novel can be termed obsessed as they project their longings and fears on Mischa.

Hoffman, Frederick. "Iris Murdoch: The Reality of Persons." *Critique: Studies in Contemporary Fiction* 7 (Spring, 1964): 48-57.

Murdoch's novels can be categorized on the basis of their characters. In some, characters are subordinate to the pattern of the novel. Here Mischa is the powerful enchanter who bends people to his will. Rosa is at first enchanted, but then frees herself, repudiates Mischa, and becomes an old-fashioned independent spirit who will run a woman's magazine.

Hope, Frances. "The Novels of Iris Murdoch." In *On Contemporary Literature*, edited by Richard Kostelanetz. New York: Avon Books, 1964.

Unlike *Under the Net*, this work is a novel with a real plot. Life is still complicated, but the novelist facing life resembles Saward facing his indecipherable script: you do the best you can.

Kane, Richard C. *Iris Murdoch, Muriel Spark, and John Fowles: Didactic Demons in Modern Fiction*. Rutherford, N.J.: Fairleigh Dickinson University Press, 1988.

Murdoch is one of several recent British writers who make moral statements by means of demonic elements. This novel shows the influence of Elias Canetti, who wrote on power and on the psychology of despots, and of Simone Weil, who wrote about the evil nature of power. Mischa Fox is the powerful and even demonic man; because he is a despot, as Canetti explains, he is secretive. He is an enchanter, for other characters fantasize about him. Kane discusses his power over Annette, Nina, Hunter, Calvin Blick, and most of all Rosa. Rosa is still under Mischa's spell when she befriends the Lusiewicz brothers. She enjoys her mastery over them. Then they turn the tables and master her; she is spellbound. Mischa breaks that spell, and Rosa flees from his enchantment to Peter Saward, one of the few persons who is not enchanted by Mischa. As the novel ends, the reader is not sure if Rosa is really free from her fantasies and enchantments.

Kennard, Jean E. "Iris Murdoch: The Revelation of Reality." In *Number and Nightmare: Forms of Fantasy in Contemporary Fiction*. Hamden, Conn.: Archon Books, 1975.

To suggest closeness to primitive reality, Murdoch often uses characters from Eastern Europe, here the Polish brothers. They are part of a larger web of dependency with Mischa at the center, a web that must be broken for characters to see matters clearly. One brother breaks the web, and so does Rosa. The moment when Hunter sees the photographs of Rosa and the brothers is one of Murdoch's moments of clarity and revelation. The netsuke pieces are some of Murdoch's miraculous objects.

Kuehl, Linda. "Iris Murdoch: The Novelist as Magician/The Magician as Artist." *Modern Fiction Studies* 15 (Autumn, 1969): 347-360. Reprinted in *Contemporary Women Novelists*, edited by Patricia Meyer Spacks. Englewood Cliffs, N.J.: Prentice-Hall, 1977.
In a notable attack, Kuehl calls this novel a grotesque joke.

Maes-Jelinek, Hena. "A House for Free Characters." *Revue des Langues Vivantes* 29 (1963): 45-69.
This novel is flawed by irrelevancies and by contrivance. Its characters are not fully drawn.

Malak, Amin. "George Orwell and Iris Murdoch: Patterns of Power." *International Fiction Review* 13 (Summer, 1986): 92-94.
George Orwell's *1984* and this novel are both concerned with power, Orwell in the political realm, Murdoch in the individual and ethical. In both novels, power is used to manipulate and violate others. Murdoch focuses on how powerful people inspire order and impose patterns of thought. Both novels employ similar images for similar effects: Big Brother's eye is everywhere; Mischa's eyes are odd, and Blick's camera is their extension. Both novels show power working through impersonal bureaucracies. In both, power is opposed by the forces of love and freedom.

Meidner, Olga M. "The Progress of Iris Murdoch." *English Studies in Africa* 4 (March, 1961): 17-38.
Moral themes predominate over character in this novel. It is not so good as *Under the Net* because Murdoch tries to present surrealistic events in a plain style. Her uses of figurative language are often striking but not satisfactory. The conclusion is morally ambiguous.

_____. "Reviewer's Bane: A Study of Iris Murdoch's *The Flight from the Enchanter*." *Essays in Criticism* 11 (October, 1961): 435-447.
This novel is a brilliant failure. It has interesting themes, especially the conflict between the English and people from the rest of Europe. But the novel confuses by mixing realistic characters with ones like Blick who are mainly symbols. It is unclear what the enchanter, Mischa, actually does. Even though he does not seem evil, he produces puzzling effects on many characters. Perhaps the key is simply that characters like Rosa and Hunter *think* he is powerful. Meidner thinks that Rainborough's courtship of Miss Casement is a parody. The Polish brothers are wonderful in their amorality. Annette is not successfully drawn. Meidner submitted these views to Murdoch for her comments.

Miles, Rosalind. *The Fiction of Sex: Themes and Functions of Sex Differences in the Modern Novel*. London: Vision Press, 1974.
In Chapter 4, Miles cites Annette as an example of a female imprisoned in a variety of conventional roles: a narcissistic adolescent, a cold mermaid-like young woman, a sophisticate. None of her roles does her much good.

O'Connor, William Van. *The New University Wits and the End of Modernism*. Carbondale: Southern Illinois University Press, 1963.
In his essay "Iris Murdoch: The Formal and the Contingent," O'Connor praises this novel's comic vitality. It is an allegory. Mischa represents the cruel absolutist state; *Artemis* represents liberal British opposition.

Punja, Prem Parkash. *The Novels of Iris Murdoch: A Critical Study*. Jalandar, India: ABS Publications, 1993.
In Chapter 3, Punja argues that this is a Gothic novel. It is not Gothic just because it has specifically Gothic details, for it owes more to *Through the Looking-Glass* and to *The Little Mermaid* than to Gothic stories. But its atmosphere is eerie, fairy-tale-like. There are many parallels with Middle-Eastern deities. Mischa is demonic and enslaves people like Nina. There are many odd women.

Rabinovitz, Rubin. "Iris Murdoch." In *Six Contemporary British Novelists*, edited by George Stade. New York: Columbia University Press, 1976. The first part of this essay is a reprint of Rabinovitz's pamphlet *Iris Murdoch* (New York: Columbia University Press, 1968).
Many refugees are spiritually as well as geographically uprooted. This, according to Simone Weil, causes spiritual lethargy. The cause of uprooting is power, and there is much power and enchantment of various sorts in this novel. Slaves often become enchanted voluntarily. The powerful Mischa is sad because he cannot dominate completely. Rosa escapes Mischa, but fails to love and help others.

Rice, Thomas Jackson. "The Reader's *Flight from the Enchanter*." In *Critical Essays on Iris Murdoch*, edited by Lindsey Tucker. New York: G. K. Hall, 1992.
A brilliant essay on this novel and *Under the Net*. In the earlier novel, Jake the egotistical artist tries to impose a design on his readers; Murdoch's point is that such designs falsify reality. In *Flight*, nonartist characters (who are just as egotistic) do not impose designs; rather, each feels that he or she plays a role in the design imposed on them, whether by Mischa or by SELIB. When they try to escape, they find that their flight is part of an even larger drama. Some, like Rainborough and Annette, discover their roles are not so important as they once thought. Others, like Peter from the beginning and Rosa eventually, discover that other people exist independently of their own egos and that with detachment one can understand what is happening in life. The same can be true of readers of Murdoch's fiction.

Rose, W. K. "An Interview with Iris Murdoch." *Shenandoah* 19 (Winter, 1968): 3-22. Reprinted as "Iris Murdoch, Informally" in *London Magazine* 8 (June, 1968): 59-73.
Revealing remarks about Mischa. He is made into a demon by other characters. Such demonic figures often possess energies that allow them to enslave their victims.

Souvage, Jacques. "The Novels of Iris Murdoch." *Studia Germanica Gandensia* 4 (1962): 225-252.

Mischa is a symbol of power, not a real person. All the other characters are held by a powerful enchanter of some sort. The pattern in most cases is one of attraction and then flight; Rosa in particular moves from illusion to realism. This novel shows a plot well integrated with its theme.

Spear, Hilda D. *Iris Murdoch*. New York: St. Martin's Press, 1995.
In Chapter 2, Speer links this novel with the three others published in the 1950's and discusses it very briefly. As in the others, many characters are in some way imprisoned. In this story, the enchanter Mischa Fox pulls strings to help Rosa dispel illusions and find a new kind of life. She breaks with the Lusiewicz brothers; later she sees that the mysterious Mischa himself is demystified.

Stettler-Imfeld, Barbara. *The Adolescent in the Novels of Iris Murdoch*. Zürich: Juris Druck & Verlag Zürich, 1970.
Annette's break from childhood is first a movement into a new world, from her finishing school into real life. She is still childish, self-centered, and aloof. Her acts are mainly symbolic; her love of mystery is symbolized by her fascination of with the reflections of crystals, mirrors, gems, and water. When she falls in love with Mischa, she becomes self-conscious, yearning, and even violent. She twice enters the water (a symbol of Mischa's world): she puts her arm in the fishbowl, and she jumps into the sea. Even after she hears the jaded Mischa's opinion of young girls, she does not realize he does not love her. When finally she does, she knows that she is not invulnerable, that nobody will protect her. She symbolically tries to sacrifice her jewels. Then she acts in a non-symbolic way: she attempts to commit suicide to revenge herself on those who have hurt her. She fails and decides not to die. When she goes off with her parents, she has begun to mature. Unlike some other adolescents in Murdoch, Annette does not influence the lives of adults very much.

Sullivan, Zohreh Tawakuli. "The Contracting Universe of Iris Murdoch's Gothic Novels." *Modern Fiction Studies* 23 (Winter, 1977-78): 557-569. Reprinted in *Critical Essays on Iris Murdoch*, edited by Lindsey Tucker. New York: G. K. Hall, 1992.

Sullivan briefly but tellingly restates many of the points of her earlier article. The Polish brothers are a more primitive version of Mischa; their enslavement of Rosa is a demonic parody of marriage, appropriate to a demonic world as defined by Northrop Frye.

_____. "Enchantment and the Demonic in Iris Murdoch: *The Flight from the Enchanter*." *Midwest Quarterly: A Journal of Contemporary Thought* 16 (April, 1975): 276-297. Reprinted as "The Demonic: *The Flight from the Enchanter*" in *Iris Murdoch*, edited by Harold Bloom. New York: Chelsea House, 1986.

In this brilliant and challenging analysis, Sullivan sees the elusive Mischa not only as a character with his own psychological peculiarities but also as the most powerful enchanter in a demonic world. In this novel and in others by Murdoch, what enchanters call love is really their imposition of form (and theory) on reality; they encourage fantasies to create destructive illusions in themselves and in others. To illustrate, Sullivan discusses the novel's opening chapter in which the reader sees Annette living in the fantasies from which she never escapes. Rainborough is enchanted by Agnes's feminine force. Although Peter Saward has obsessions, he is free from the demands of the ego and therefore is immune to Mischa's power. Not so Rosa. Sullivan sees her living in a demonic world in which she flees from Mischa's enchantment and in which she both enchants and is enchanted by the Polish brothers. When she awakens to her condition and all the destruction it creates, she is able to turn her back on Mischa. Even so, Sullivan does not think that at the end of the novel Rosa has left the demonic world of enchantment.

Todd, Richard. *Iris Murdoch*. London: Methuen, 1984.

In Chapter 2, Todd groups Murdoch's first four novels together in their concern for the implications of existentialism. This novel focuses on power relations. Although the central relation is between the fleeing Rosa and the enchanter Mischa, Rosa's relations with the Lusiewicz brothers raise similar problems. The chief fantasies of the novel are not the novelist's but those created by the characters themselves (mainly their fantasies about Mischa). Murdoch thus can portray the magic of relations within

a group. Savard is the only one not to invest Mischa with power.
Todd discusses Murdoch's debt to the novelist Eilas Canetti.

Weatherhead, A. Kingsley.   "Backgrounds with Figures in Iris
   Murdoch." *Texas Studies in Literature and Language: A Journal
   of the Humanities* 10 (Winter, 1969): 635-648.
   In Murdoch's early novels, characters (often defined by their
   environment) fall under the spell of powerful enchanters and
   eventually reject them. Here Rosa's rejection of Mischa is particularly sensational: she smashes his aquarium.

Whiteside, George. "The Novels of Iris Murdoch." *Critique: Studies
   in Contemporary Fiction* 6 (Spring, 1964): 27-47.
   An interesting reading. Rosa loves Mischa because she projects
   her vision of wisdom on him; she fears him because he seems to
   combine the wisdom of Hugo in *Under the Net* with power. Rosa
   finally realizes she has created her spell. Calvin Blick's very
   name suggests the power of a Calvinist view of sin and guilt.
   Murdoch implicitly satirizes the impotence of British liberal
   socialism (and its magazine *Artemis*) in the face of the power of
   Eastern Europe, as personified by Mischa and the Polish brothers.

Wolfe, Peter. *The Disciplined Heart: Iris Murdoch and Her Novels*.
   Columbia: University of Missouri Press, 1966.
   In Chapter 4, Wolfe investigates Murdoch's ideas about obstacles
   to freedom as they appear in this novel. Murdoch creates
   characters from a broad range of social groups; each character is
   isolated, but capable of causing pain to others. Mischa is an
   enchanter, yet willful and cold, a man without mutual relationships. Most of the others are enslaved to him and derive their
   identities from him: Rainborough, Nina, Annette, Hunter, and
   Rosa are discussed. The last three are lucky and escape. Rosa
   may be an unattractive character, but she has strength and grows
   morally. Wolfe points out parallels to many myths as well as
   allusions to Shelley's "Ode to the West Wind."

The Sandcastle, 1957.

Baldanza, Frank. *Iris Murdoch*. New York: Twayne, 1974.
In Chapter 4, Baldanza says that the novel's title suggests that romantic dreams, such as those of Mor and Rain, are both limited and destructive. The lovers' sensual indulgence is contrasted to the sane practicality of Mor's wife, Nan. Baldanza praises the novel's great scenes not only for being wonderfully told but also for their thematic significance. For example, when Rain's car sinks into the stream, it suggests the falseness of her relation to Mor. The ubiquitous gypsy woodcutter suggests life's mysteries, as do Mor's children.

Bigsby, Christopher. "Interview with Iris Murdoch." In *The Radical Imagination and the Liberal Tradition: Interviews with English and American Novelists*, edited by Christopher Bigsby and Heide Ziegler. London: Junction Books, 1982.
Murdoch says she did not amplify Nan enough. She could have described Nan's ideas and dreams.

Bove, Cheryl K. *Understanding Iris Murdoch*. Columbia: University of South Carolina Press, 1993.
In Chapter 7, Bove treats this novel very briefly. She stresses the importance of Bledyard and of what he tells other characters.

Burgess, Anthony. *The Novel Now: A Student's Guide to Contemporary Fiction*. London: Faber & Faber, 1967.
This story is contrived to make a point: ordinary people cannot deal with freedom.

Byatt, A. S. *Degrees of Freedom: The Novels of Iris Murdoch*. New York: Barnes & Noble Books, 1965.
In Chapter 4, Byatt explains how even this inferior novel enlarges on Murdoch's basic concerns. Mor thinks he is free to find happiness with Rain, but Bledyard explains that such freedom is a fantasy. Mor must learn that freedom is respect for the limitations of reality and for the separateness of other people, notably Nan and Rain. Nan herself is shocked into recognizing Mor's separate existence. Her endorsement of Mor's political ambitions is not a trap but an acceptance of him.

_____. *Iris Murdoch*. Harlow, Essex, England: Longman Group, 1976.
In *The Sandcastle* and other novels written at this time, Murdoch tries to emulate nineteenth century English novelists in creating characters who are not simply symbols but are free, complex, and even formless. Here Bledyard is particularly mysterious. He accuses Mor of not seeing other people as complex individuals.

Conradi, Peter. *Iris Murdoch: The Saint and the Artist*. New York: St. Martin's Press, 1986.
In Chapter 3, Conradi briefly criticizes this lightweight novel for dividing the reader's sympathies between Rain and Nan. Bledyard, this novel's saintly character, is charmless, Christlike, and puritanical. His opposition to representing the human face recalls Plato; it reminds readers that art objects are imperfect and that life's arrangements are the same.

Dick, Bernard. "The Novels of Iris Murdoch: A Formula for Enchantment." *Bucknell Review: A Scholarly Journal of Letters, Arts and Science* 14 (May, 1966): 66-81.
Rain enchants Mor, yet Rain is herself a fraud, for she is dominated by the memory of her father. Enchantment in this novel degenerates into mere infatuation.

Dipple, Elizabeth. *Iris Murdoch: Work for the Spirit*. London: Methuen, 1982.
In Chapter 2, Dipple calls Bledyard one of three characters in the novels who are almost saints. Even though he participates in the community, he sees through other characters' romantic and self-centered illusions and tells them the truth. His apparently rigid opinions on portrait painting echo Platonic arguments. In Chapter 5, Dipple treats Murdoch's first ten novels and categorizes this as one of her religious novels, one concerned with good and evil. Dipple thinks the novel fails because its three disparate elements do not cohere: Bledyard's seriousness, the shallow romance of Rain and Mor, and the hints of the supernatural in the gypsy, in Felicity's voodoo rites, and in her dog's ghost.

Felheim, Marvin. "Symbolic Characterization in the Novels of Iris Murdoch." *Texas Studies in Literature and Language* 2 (Spring, 1960): 189-197.
Murdoch often creates a pair of female characters who carry the burden of the novel's meaning. Here the contrasting pair are Nan (an older woman who dislikes flowers, a housewife who ties Mor to his home and job) and Rain (a younger, flower-loving artist, who gives Mor a chance to escape to France). All three characters grow as the novel progresses.

Fraser, G. S. "Iris Murdoch: The Solidity of the Normal." In *International Literary Annual* II, edited by John Wain. London: John Calder, 1959.
Unlike Murdoch's first two novels, *The Sandcastle* has a sense of social norms against which actions are judged. Mor's difficult situation may be symbolized by the episode of the stuck car, which suggests something about the intractability of life.

German, Howard. "Allusions in the Early Novels of Iris Murdoch." *Modern Fiction Studies* 15 (Autumn, 1969): 361-377.
Murdoch alludes to Boswell's *Life of Johnson*, the poetry of John Keats and Robert Browning, Sir Thomas Malory, *The Romance of the Rose*, and Celtic myths. George Sand's experiences and traits are attributed to Rain.

Gerstenberger, Donna. *Iris Murdoch*. Lewisburg, Pa.: Bucknell University Press, 1975.
In Chapter 1, Gerstenberger calls Mor a man who is too passive to act upon his ideas of life's possibilities. The novel has suggestions of things outside of the genre's conventions: the gypsy and the children's dreams.

Gindin, James. "Images of Illusion in the Work of Iris Murdoch." *Texas Studies in Literature and Language* 2 (Spring, 1960): 180-188.
The love of Mor and Rain is an illusion, as fragile as a sandcastle, as opposed to Demoyte's house, a symbol of the human tradition. As usual, gardens contribute to illusion; unusually, this novel's dog is an illusory one. Demoyte is this novel's untrustworthy God-figure.

Goshgarian, Gary. "Feminist Values in the Novels of Iris Murdoch." *Revue des Langues Vivantes* 40 (1974): 519-527.

Many of Murdoch's novels show men constructing fantasies about women, in particular exalting them as goddesses, not as real human beings. Here Mor pursues Rain as a holy grail, as a goddess who can bring him new life. But Rain, though talented, is only a somewhat ordinary young woman.

Gordon, David J. *Iris Murdoch's Fables of Unselfing*. Columbia: University of Missouri Press, 1995.

In Chapter 1, Gordon says Bledyard speaks for Murdoch in telling Mor that he is not selfless in his love and in telling Rain that images do not tell the truth. In Chapter 5, Gordon finds evidence of a new sensitivity in two scenes.

Griffin, Gabriele. *The Influence of the Writings of Simone Weil on the Fiction of Iris Murdoch*. San Francisco: Mellen Research University Press, 1993.

Griffin refers to this novel several times throughout her study. In order to emphasize that the individual self is not the center of the world, Murdoch often presents events, like the appearance of the gypsy, that have no rational explanation. Mor's regard for Rain shows how a self-centered person's love can be based on need, not on a knowledge of the other person. The raising of Rain's car shows one kind of Weilian attention.

Hall, James. "Blurring the Will: The Growth of Iris Murdoch." *ELH* 32 (June, 1965): 256-273.

Hall praises this novel highly. Mor and Rain experience an idyll together, but cannot translate it into the real world. The anxiety produced by their problem is expressed by the scene in which Rain's car slips into a river.

Hoffman, Frederick. "Iris Murdoch: The Reality of Persons." *Critique: Studies in Contemporary Fiction* 7 (Spring, 1964): 48-57.

Murdoch's novels can be categorized on the basis of their characters. In some, characters are subordinate to the pattern of the novel. The pattern here pits love against infatuation, the family against confusion. The ending is inconclusive.

Hope, Frances. "The Novels of Iris Murdoch." In *On Contemporary Literature*, edited by Richard Kostelanetz. New York: Avon Books, 1964.
This work is more conventional and realistic than Murdoch's first two novels. Rain's car slipping into the river may symbolize Mor's impending emotional disaster.

Johnson, Deborah. *Iris Murdoch*. Bloomington: Indiana University Press, 1987. Chapter 1 reprinted in *Critical Essays on Iris Murdoch*, edited by Lindsey Tucker. New York: G. K. Hall, 1992.
In Chapter 1, Johnson explains how Mor's male quest is undermined by a female author. It is clear that Mor does not understand Rain, his object; there are sides of her personality that Mor does not know. Although she may be an object in Mor's oedipal drama, she is the center of her own: her attachment to her dead father is strong.

Kennard, Jean E. "Iris Murdoch: The Revelation of Reality." In *Number and Nightmare: Forms of Fantasy in Contemporary Fiction*. Hamden, Conn.: Archon Books, 1975.
Mor's love for Rain is a fantasy. Many people tell him he does not see her as an individual. The episode in which Rain's car slides into the river is one of Murdoch's most memorable "technical scenes," scenes which in their precise detail make readers realize how extraordinary the world is.

Kermode, Frank. "The House of Fiction: Interviews with Seven English Novelists." *Partisan Review* 30 (Spring, 1963): 61-82. Reprinted in *The Novel Today*, edited by Malcolm Bradbury. London: Fontana/Collins, 1977.
Murdoch says she is fascinated by the mechanics of how a car slips into a river.

Leavis, L. R. "The Anti-Artist: The Case of Iris Murdoch." *Neophilologus* 72 (January, 1988): 136-154.
In a ironic and snide *ad hominem* attack on Murdoch's novels, Leavis calls this work a "pot-boiler." Murdoch borrows heavily from Hardy and Lawrence. Its romantic/tragic plot is suitable only for women's magazines.

Maes-Jelinek, Hena. "A House for Free Characters." *Revue des Langues Vivantes* 29 (1963): 45-69.
Murdoch characters do not live by conventional morality. Even though the major characters in this novel seem to be restrained by convention, they have their dreams of freedom. In the end, Mor cannot break loose from Nan, his unpleasant but powerful wife.

Meidner, Olga M. "The Progress of Iris Murdoch." *English Studies in Africa* 4 (March, 1961): 17-38.
This novel is not so good as *Under the Net* because its focus is narrow, its fantasy is uninteresting, and its dull prose shows little figurative language. Its ending is morally indecisive.

Morrell, Roy. "Iris Murdoch: The Early Novels." *Critical Quarterly* 9 (Autumn, 1967): 272-282.
Mor and Rain drift into private worlds without futures. Donald and Felicity are similarly isolated. The gypsy reminds them of the world's contingency and of the existence of other people.

Packer, P. A. "The Theme of Love in the Novels of Iris Murdoch." *Durham University Journal* 38 (1977): 217-224.
Packer discusses Murdoch's treatment of many varieties of love, including that of Mor and Rain. Even though both are unhappy in the end, both gain from their experience. Nan, too, is changed and becomes more vulnerable.

Punja, Prem Parkash. *The Novels of Iris Murdoch: A Critical Study.* Jalandar, India: ABS Publications, 1993.
In Chapter 4, Punja discusses Bledyard as a lonely and even mocked figure of goodness. He is benevolent, but he tells Mor the truth: Mor does not see the separate reality of either his wife or Rain. In Chapter 5, Punja comments that because Nan begins to understand Mor, she wins the marital war.

Raban, Jonathan. *The Technique of Modern Fiction: Essays in Practical Criticism.* London: Edward Arnold, 1968.
Raban focuses on the rose-garden scene and analyzes the precise symbolic significance of the garden's details (the flowers, the trees, the moon) and its antithesis, the house. The characters, especially Mor and Rain, are defined by their reactions to these

symbols.   Raban asks if Murdoch's characters are too strictly defined.

Rabinovitz, Rubin. "Iris Murdoch." In *Six Contemporary British Novelists*, edited by George Stade.   New York: Columbia University Press, 1976. The first part of this essay is a reprint of Rabinovitz's pamphlet *Iris Murdoch* (New York: Columbia University Press, 1968).
A brief treatment. As individuals should attend to others (Nan and Mor do not), so artists must be humble enough to attend to their subjects, as in Rain painting Demoyte. The novel lacks intensity.

Spear, Hilda D. *Iris Murdoch*. New York: St. Martin's Press, 1995.
In Chapter 2, Speer groups this novel with others of the 1950's in which many characters are imprisoned. In this case, they are shut up in the closed community of a boys' school. This novel's flight form reality is the love between Mor and Rain; it has the stability of a sandcastle. In the end, normality and family prevail in a story that Speer, in a brief discussion, finds too neat. She praises the theatricality of Rain's car sinking into the stream.

Stettler-Imfeld, Barbara.   *The Adolescent in the Novels of Iris Murdoch*. Zürich: Juris Druck & Verlag Zürich, 1970.
Felicity and Don have shared a secret, childish world of magic and private games. Felicity is haunted by the ghost of the family dog and tries to get rid of Rain by a ritual; Don is fascinated by gems. Their hope that the world will stay the same is shattered by the crises in their parents' lives. Don rejects magic and retreats into the mysteries of the jewelry shop and mountain climbing, then acts to confront his father by climbing the steeple. Felicity consoles herself with communing with the ghost of her dog and by practicing private magic rites, one of which seems to work. When their parents begin to pay attention to their children as individual near-adults and when Mor decides to stay home, the children rejoin the family circle, and Mor pays attention to their plans. In this novel, adolescents influence adults.

Sturrock, John. "Reading Iris Murdoch." *Salmagundi* 80 (Fall, 1988): 144-160.

People achieve freedom by attention to other people and to events outside themselves. Sturrock sees this quality of attention in Murdoch's descriptions of Rain's car slipping into the river and of the boys climbing the tower.

Todd, Richard. *Iris Murdoch*. London: Methuen, 1984.
    In Chapter 2, Todd groups Murdoch's first four novels together in their concern for the implications of existentialism. He considers this novel a mixed bag. Rain is a figure of power about whom other characters weave their private fantasies. Mor evades such self-knowledge, but is not well enough realized to satisfy. The gypsy reveals something about many of Murdoch's symbols: he is not significant in himself, but he is given different meanings by different characters.

Vance, Norman. "Iris Murdoch's Serious Fun." *Theology* 84 (November, 1981): 420-428.
    Mor shows the spiritual poverty of the intellectual left. Rain's car slipping into the water symbolizes the power of contingent events.

Whiteside, George. "The Novels of Iris Murdoch." *Critique: Studies in Contemporary Fiction* 6 (Spring, 1964): 27-47.
    Mor is the lover. His love of Rain is protective, not abject; he desires youth and freedom. This novel is too sympathetic to be called satiric, and Whiteside does not like it as much as other early Murdoch novels.

Wolfe, Peter. *The Disciplined Heart: Iris Murdoch and Her Novels*. Columbia: University of Missouri Press, 1966.
    In Chapter 5, Wolfe calls this work less symbolic and less witty than Murdoch's first two novels. *The Sandcastle* asks to what extent people can understand their choices and act on them. Rain, though she has known from childhood about the instability of human affairs, is an aggressive person and somewhat in control. The insensitive and selfish Nan is also fairly strong. But Mor is not. Wolfe divides the novel into two parts: its first half shows Mor's ineptitude as parent, husband, and politician, the second half his ineptitude as a lover. He is given conservative, prudent Apollonian advice by Bledyard and more Dionysian advice by Demoyte, but he follows neither for long. He is timid, indecisive,

and deceitful by turns. In the end, he decides to return to his family; the rebirth promised by his love for Rain will not occur. Wolfe thinks that with Felicity's occult rites Murdoch makes a playful attack on the rationalism of Western philosophy—for the rites do seem to work.

The Bell, 1958.

Baldanza, Frank. *Iris Murdoch*. New York: Twayne, 1974.

In Chapter 5, Baldanza calls this novel one of Murdoch's early masterpieces, a clearly told story containing a wide range of characters and filled with significant parallels and recurrent motifs. It has Murdoch's usual parade of sensational scenes, most of which evoke the novel's themes. Characters are defined by their attitudes toward religion; they range from the atheist journalist Noel Spens to the Abbess, a rock of spiritual strength.

Within the Imber community, the central contrast is between the two leaders, James and Michael. James believes in a simple moral code applicable without regard to the quirks of individuality. Michael not only acknowledges more ambiguity than does James, but his own life shows the complexities of moral issues. Although Murdoch seems to prefer Michael's views, the novel's complexities do not permit the issue to be resolved.

Two other characters provide extremes. Nick is evil, though Michael feels he could have been helped. Dora is a vulgar, sexy, superficial innocent. Even though she seems almost outside of religious categories, she alone has a vision (in the National Gallery), and she causes the old bell to ring. Baldanza suggests that the bell itself symbolizes many things, both religious and erotic.

Beams, David W. "The Fortunate Fall: Three Actions in *The Bell*." *Twentieth Century Literature: A Scholarly and Critical Journal* 34 (Winter, 1988): 416-433.

Beams is dissatisfied with all earlier readings of this novel because critics have not understood its allegory. He then offers his new and coherent interpretation. Dora's arrival at Imber Court represents the advent of New Testament grace in a place of Old Testament law. Beams looks at three actions and finds them all the same action, the drama of the central doctrine of Christianity: the Incarnation and Resurrection, otherwise known as the Fortunate Fall. These three actions are Dora's rescue of the butterfly, the release of the trapped bird, and the raising of the bell itself. The bell's message is that of the Annunciation. Water symbolizes the natural world, the place of baptism; the sun symbolizes grace. Beams makes much of Toby, who begins by symbolizing prelapsarian innocence, and Dora.

Bove, Cheryl K. *Understanding Iris Murdoch*. Columbia: University of South Carolina Press, 1993.

In Chapter 3, Bove says that members of the Imber community fail at the difficult task of loving one another, probably because they pay too much attention to rules. She sets the sermons of James and Michael at the opposite ends of a continuum of advice; at the center is the Abbess and her realistic advice to love one another. The two outsiders who raise the medieval bell, Toby and Dora, do so for differing motives. Of the two, it is Dora who learns the most from her experiences.

Burgess, Anthony. *99 Novels: The Best in English Since 1939*. New York: Summit Books, 1984.

A quick overview. The novel is simultaneously realistic and symbolic. The bell itself suggests many things, including both love and self-knowledge.

_____. *The Novel Now: A Student's Guide to Contemporary Fiction*. London: Faber & Faber, 1967.

Burgess praises this "poetic" novel for combining a realistic story with symbolism, in this case the ambiguous symbol of the bell.

Byatt, A. S. *Degrees of Freedom: The Novels of Iris Murdoch*. New York: Barnes & Noble Books, 1965.

In Chapter 5, Byatt objects that when Dora rings the old bell, Murdoch substitutes a symbolic act for something the novel should show. What does the bell symbolize? Byatt discusses its various meanings for various characters. Her main interest is in the two characters who actively explore their own limitations, Dora and Michael. Dora is trapped in a bad marriage; she is lured to Imber Court, a place that appears to limit her freedom even more. Her progress toward some kind of freedom begins in the National Gallery and ends when she leaves Imber. In her limited freedom, she learns to swim and to like Mozart.

Byatt thinks Michael an admirable study of a person caught in a spiritual fantasy, an attempt to impose a religious pattern on his life. Murdoch judges him with sympathy as she presents the stages of his making decisions on moral issues. He wrongly tries to escape responsibilities. Byatt analyzes the steps by which Michael tries to cope with his homosexuality and contrasts his sermon with the one preached by James. It is only after Nick dies that Michael sees he has been too self-centered. In Chapter 9. Byatt praises this novel for having both a meaningful plan and interesting characters. She objects to the bell symbol as "planted."

_____. *Iris Murdoch*. Harlow, Essex, England: Longman Group, 1976.

In *The Bell* and other novels written at this time, Murdoch tries to emulate nineteenth century English novelists in creating characters who are not simply symbols but free and even formless. The bell itself symbolizes art, and is one of many artworks in the novel. Characters try and fail to achieve the perfection of art in life. Yet they are true characters in that they are free to work out their destinies.

Conradi, Peter. *Iris Murdoch: The Saint and the Artist*. New York: St. Martin's Press, 1986.

In Chapter 5, Conradi notes the many similarities this novel has to *The Unicorn*: the remote enclosed settings, the spiritual environment and Platonic hints, the innocent outsiders who set out on rescue missions. Here Imber Court (whose geography is indebted to Plato and Dante) houses a neurotic group who suffer in different ways from spiritual pride. The central debate at Imber is summed up by a pair of sermons. James, this novel's absolutist saint, argues that everyone must aspire only to the best. Michael, this novel's artist-figure, urges tolerance and urges people to attempt what is possible in a limited world. The Abbess provides a balanced perspective which takes in both positions. Murdoch shows sympathy with Michael's position when the novel insists that many religious impulses have sources in erotic energies. At the center of the novel, Michael is one of three limited people who

have the novel's experiences of the sublime. (The others are Toby
and Dora.) Michael finds that he is not fit either for the religious
life or for the world. Nevertheless, he survives the destruction of
his dreams to play a non-heroic role. Although the ancient Bell is
consciously awkward and symbolizes different things to different
people, Conradi thinks it has an ambiguous force.

_____. "Platonism in Iris Murdoch." In *Platonism and the
English Imagination*, edited by Anna Baldwin and Sarah Hutton.
New York: Cambridge University Press, 1994.
Michael seeks to rise from his condition, but finds he must
descend into the contingent world.

Dipple, Elizabeth. *Iris Murdoch: Work for the Spirit.* London:
Methuen, 1982. Chapter 8 is reprinted in *Critical Essays on Iris
Murdoch*, edited by Lindsey Tucker. New York: G. K. Hall, 1992.
In Chapter 3, Dipple cites Dora's reaction to paintings in the
National Gallery and to the old bell itself as illustrations of
Murdoch's idea of the religious function of art. In Chapter 4,
Dipple treats *The Bell* with Murdoch's first ten novels and calls it
a religious work. Dipple thinks Murdoch successfully integrates
all her story's elements. The power of the past to poison the
present, as seen in Michael's life, is echoed by the bell itself. Its
original message of religious love, sullied even in the distant past,
rings hollow in the present world of sexual muddles. When he
learns this, Michael returns to the real world in which there are no
consolations.
    In Chapter 8, Dipple discusses *The Bell* in comparison to the
later *Henry and Cato*. Both novels contrast the sacred and profane. Michael and Cato have religious vocations (and suppressed
homosexual desires); Dora and Henry are both profane. Unlike
Brendan in *Henry and Cato*, James in *The Bell* proclaims a rule-
bound and destructive Christianity. Dipple finds the Imber
community itself to be torn by the tension between its regulations
born of high ideals and its self-centered members with their
repressed sexuality: Michael fights his homosexual impulses, and
the reader discovers that the pure Catherine desires Michael. Paul
tries fiercely to fabricate his own ideal. Outside the convent, only
the profane Dora is given true glimpses of the religious spirit, and

those are given only through art, through the pictures in the National Gallery and through the medieval bell itself.

Dunbar, Scott. "On Art, Morals and Religion: Some Reflection on the Work of Iris Murdoch." *Religious Studies* 14 (December, 1978): 515-524.
This essay is mainly a discussion of *The Sovereignty of the Good*. In *The Bell*, Dora experiences transcendence through the beauty of art at the National Gallery.

Emerson, Donald. "Violence and Survival in the Novels of Iris Murdoch." *Transactions of the Wisconsin Academy of Sciences, Arts, and Letters* 57 (1969): 21-28.
As appropriate to a novel with a serious tone, the violence here is serious, outwardly (suicide) and inwardly (betrayal). Survival is not a matter of a transforming moment, but of slow change. In the end, Michael and Dora have hope for the future.

Felheim, Marvin. "Symbolic Characterization in the Novels of Iris Murdoch." *Texas Studies in Literature and Language* 2 (Spring, 1960): 189-197.
In her early novels, Murdoch often creates a pair of female characters who carry the burden of the novel's meaning. These women at first may be victims, but many eventually emerge as fulfilled persons. Here the withdrawn, religious Catherine contrasts with Dora: youthful, imaginative, inquisitive, and eventually independent.

Fraser, G. S. "Iris Murdoch: The Solidity of the Normal." In *International Literary Annual* II, edited by John Wain. London: John Calder, 1959.
This novel shows two communities: the enduring convent and the amateurish construct of Imber Court. Michael's and Dora's journeys toward self-discovery involve understanding both communities. Dora in particular sees that Imber Court deserves some respect.

Gérard, Albert. "Iris Murdoch." *La Revue Nouvelle* 39 (June, 1964): 663-640. [In French.]

This novel's central character, the bell, is also the symbol which organizes the plot and makes concrete the work's theme of love. Although the Abbey represents the highest form of love, Murdoch's focus is on the lay community nearby and its praiseworthy, ridiculous, and pathetic aspirations to spiritual heights of which it is not capable. Its male and female members lose themselves in superficialities far removed from true love or charity. What is blamable is not human nature, but the prideful refusal of human beings to recognize its limits. The community members are so consumed by their utopian vision of their own salvation that they do not recognize the existence of other people. Murdoch therefore chooses Dora to be the novel's center of consciousness. Despite her limitations, Dora does know that other people exist. When the bell rises out of the water, Murdoch suggests that aspiration within limits is possible.

German, Howard. "Allusions in the Early Novels of Iris Murdoch." *Modern Fiction Studies* 15 (Autumn, 1969): 361-377.
Except for references to Dante's *Inferno*, this novel has few allusions.

Gindin, James. "Images of Illusion in the Work of Iris Murdoch." *Texas Studies in Literature and Language* 2 (Spring, 1960): 180-188.
Imber Court is a human contrivance. The new bell gives different illusions of individual salvation to different people; the old bell is only a curiosity. Michael and the Abbess are inadequate God-figures. In opposition to them are things of nature: the woods, birds, Murphy the dog. Dora survives, probably because she is formless, like natural things.

Gordon, David J. *Iris Murdoch's Fables of Unselfing*. Columbia: University of Missouri Press, 1995.
In Chapter 1, Gordon discusses the problem of unselfing in this novel. In Chapter 3, he cites Michael as one of Murdoch's characters who tries to play a role he cannot sustain and is chastised. Gordon sees structural irony in the contrast of Michael and Dora: each has a different sort of ordeal, valid but incomplete.

Griffin, Gabriele. *The Influence of the Writings of Simone Weil on the Fiction of Iris Murdoch*. San Francisco: Mellen Research University Press, 1993.
Griffin refers to this novel throughout her study. It is a tightly structured, "crystalline" work. Good people in Murdoch tend to be androgynous, like the Abbess. For Murdoch, Michael's dream is an aspect of the destabilized self. When Murdoch tells about this dream, she confuses the reader as to what is real in order to compel attention. The raising of the old bell shows attention to mechanical detail. Michael's failure to prevent Nick's suicide is a failure of attention.

Hall, James. "Blurring the Will: The Growth of Iris Murdoch." *ELH* 32 (June, 1965): 256-273.
Imber Hall is midway between the convent and the world. It is both a group of naïve religious people hoping to support one another and a community with sin and worldliness at its heart. The new bell represents the group's unrealizable hopes; the old bell suggests the continuity of human rebelliousness. It is the angry, rebellious, and questioning Dora who exposes the hypocrisy. Yet Murdoch suggests that there is value in trying for goodness.

Hawkins, Peter. *The Language of Grace: Flannery O'Connor, Walker Percy, and Iris Murdoch*. Cambridge, Mass.: Cowley Publications, 1983.
Murdoch often provides secular analogues for religious experience. Dora's experience in The National Gallery shows her a mystery and transports her into a "state of secular grace." Murdoch respects religion. The Imber group's aspirations fail, but they are not mocked. Even though at the end Michael feels betrayed by God, the mass exists for him.

Heusel, Barbara. *Patterned Aimlessness: Iris Murdoch's Novels of the 1970s and 1980s*. Athens: University of Georgia Press, 1995.
In Chapter 9, Heusel reproduces a sketch of Imber Abbey from Murdoch's manuscript. Its Renaissance architecture suggests both the consolations of religion and women's entrapment.

Heyd, Ruth. "Interview with Iris Murdoch." *University of Windsor Review* 1 (Spring, 1965): 138-143.
As the Abbess tells Michael, he is too obsessed by his guilt to give Nick the help he needs. James Tayper Pace is an example of Kierkegaard's "knight of faith," a man who seems dull and ordinary but who has a simple certitude.

Hoffman, Frederick.   "Iris Murdoch: The Reality of Persons." *Critique: Studies in Contemporary Fiction* 7 (Spring, 1964): 48-57.
Murdoch's novels can be usefully categorized on the basis of their characters. In some, characters are subordinate to pattern. In this novel, which Hoffman praises, characters are relatively free. Imber Court's formality is undercut by the weakness of the flesh and by the unique impulses of individual characters.

Hope, Frances. "The Novels of Iris Murdoch." In *On Contemporary Literature*, edited by Richard Kostelanetz. New York: Avon Books, 1964.
Hope praises this novel about the high cost of deception. At its heart is the contrast between James's and Michael's sermons. The novel implies that it is impossible to avoid human frailties by retiring from the world.

Johnson, Deborah. *Iris Murdoch*. Bloomington: Indiana University Press, 1987.
In Chapter 3, Johnson explores Murdoch's split feelings about women in her treatment of Dora. Even though Dora is a typical Murdoch woman imprisoned by her patriarchal husband, she is also a fresh and vital character. She is a "female text" living with her own pleasure, a text on which others read what they will. Yet Murdoch's omniscient comments almost agree with Michael's harsh and misogynistic ones. In Chapter 4, Johnson argues that Murdoch's symbols have a feminist subtext. Beneath the orthodox symbolic suggestions of Imber's fruit garden are implications of female sympathy (Dora for Catherine) and of thwarted female potential. The bell itself can mean different things to different characters. To Dora, ringing it is an act of self-assertion, a message of unexpressed female sexuality, that begins her own transformation. In Chapter 5, Johnson notes how in this novel

Murdoch undermines the usual kind of ending: subtle tense shifts move Dora out of the Imber story and into inconclusive real life.

Jones, Dorothy. "Love and Morality in Iris Murdoch's *The Bell*." *Meanjin Quarterly* 26 (March, 1967): 85-90.
An interesting and valuable article. Murdoch's central concern is the relation of formal patterns to contingency. In fiction, this relation is between myth and free, individual human characters. In this novel, Imber Court imposes patterns on its inmates, and individual inmates create their own patterns, patterns which are consoling and protective, but possibly dangerous. Michael considers himself a passive part of a divine pattern, a position which removes the need for moral decisions. When Michael ignores his anarchic animal passions, he makes a mistake that leads to Nick's suicide. Another good example of this contrast is the marriage of Paul (a patterned man) and Dora (who is as contingent as characters come). Dora resents being looked down upon by members of Imber Court, so she tries to impose her own pattern by raising the bell. The lifting of the bell symbolizes stirring of emotions in the subconscious.

After the community disbands, Dora and Michael emerge, Dora with new strength and Michael with a sense of his limitations. The Abbey itself intrigues. It is by definition a very patterned place, yet the nuns seem charming and wise. Jones thinks it differs from Imber Court in that its formality is flexible (as when a nun meets Toby inside the walls or when a nun saves Dora and Catherine from drowning). The nuns seem to be able to accommodate pattern and contingency, but they do not communicate to the world outside their walls.

Juillard, M. "Proper Nouns as Proper Style-Markers of Poetry and Prose." *Literary and Linguistic Computing* 5 (1990): 1-8.
Juillard compares Murdoch's proper nouns in *The Bell* to those in novels by Ian Fleming and John Wain. Murdoch uses proportionately more proper nouns than the other authors, but they are not so colorful. Murdoch's proper nouns mainly name places (the National Gallery) and things (*The Times*) with cultural significance and artists. Fleming's proper nouns have little relation to high culture, but name objects (like specific weapons and cars) and have metonymic overtones.

Kaehele, Sharon, and Howard German. "The Discovery of Reality in Iris Murdoch's *The Bell.*" *PMLA: Publications of the Modern Language Association of America* 82 (December, 1967): 554-563.
Murdoch creates credible characters, many of whom (like James) judge by absolute or overly simple standards. Such judgments hurt outsiders like Dora. Other characters, less afraid of the world's messiness, are less quick to judge. Like Michael, they try through love to understand the diversity of other people, though Michael himself fails to accept his love for Nick. This contrast between love and judgment is reflected in the two bells. The old bell's Latin motto proclaims love, whereas the plain, polished modern bell has a motto about judgment. The authors look at Dora and Michael in detail. Dora's selfish life begins to change when she has a vision of art's otherness in the National Gallery. Michael, who had yearned for absolute good, finds he needs to break out of this pattern and thereby gets a kind of freedom.

Kennard, Jean E. "Iris Murdoch: The Revelation of Reality." In *Number and Nightmare: Forms of Fantasy in Contemporary Fiction.* Hamden, Conn.: Archon Books, 1975.
Murdoch makes the point that there is some reality beyond the individual consciousness when Dora responds to a painting in the National Galley. Imber Court is one of Murdoch's webs in restraint of freedom. Both James and Michael reveal in their sermons the very different ways in which each is constrained. James preaches rules; he is restrained by convention. Michael's sermon turns on the self; he is restrained by neurosis. As various characters break free from the web, Murdoch characteristically sunders a pair of twins, Nick and Catherine. The raising of the bell is this novel's "technical scene," a passage whose detail is so precise as to make readers realize how remarkable the world is.

Kermode, Frank. "The House of Fiction: Interviews with Seven English Novelists." *Partisan Review* 30 (Spring, 1963): 61-82. Reprinted in *The Novel Today*, edited by Malcolm Bradbury. London: Fontana/Collins, 1977.
Murdoch is fascinated by the mechanics of a bell being raised from a lake.

Kimber, John. "The Bell: Iris Murdoch." *Delta* 18 (Summer, 1959): 31-34.

Kimber is not sure what *The Bell* is about. Perhaps its central concern is simply its characters' many problems of identity. Perhaps it asks what makes a good life. The novel has many flaws, the greatest of which are inconsistencies of tone and distance. Nevertheless, Kimber praises Murdoch for paying serious attention to individual consciousnesses and their relation to events.

Leavis, L. R. "The Anti-Artist: The Case of Iris Murdoch." *Neophilologus* 72 (January, 1988): 136-154.

In a heavily ironic and snide attack on Murdoch and her novels, Leavis gives *The Bell* moderate praise. Some characters do ring true, especially Michael. The raising of the bell belongs in a thriller.

McCabe, Bernard. "The Guises of Love." *Commonweal*, December 3, 1965, 270-273.

The Imber Court people try to live by rules but are helpless before reality. McCabe thinks Murdoch is too manipulative and that the bell symbol is too intrusive.

McCarthy, Margot. "Dualities in *The Bell* (Iris Murdoch)." *Contemporary Review* 213 (December, 1968): 313-317.

The novel is full of pairings of contrasted characters. The most important pair is Dora and Michael, but there are others: Noel and Paul, Nick and Toby, Nick and Catherine, Michael and James. McCarthy is most eloquent on the two bells. Gabriel, the old bell, sounds the raw force of life, the energetic and sensual unselfconscious pleasure in life itself. It is the fact of Incarnation; Gabriel is almost a person to Dora. The new bell is a ritualized acknowledgment of the fact, a subdued and restrained worship of a false god.

McEwan, Neil. "Iris Murdoch's Contemporary World." In *The Survival of the Novel*. Totowa, N.J.: Barnes & Noble Books, 1981.

Murdoch's novels depend for their effect on the tension between traditional and nontraditional elements. Most of the characters in this novel (except for Dora) seem to be old-fashioned ones drawn in an old-fashioned way. Their spiritual predicaments, however, are contemporary. And if the old bell is a symbol, it is an unorthodox one, for it figures differently in different characters' fantasies.

McGinnis, Robert M. "Murdoch's *The Bell*." *Explicator* 28 (September, 1969), Item 1.
    Murdoch's novel bears significant resemblances to Gerhart Hauptmann's *Die Versunkene Glocke*. Both novels contain two sermons and two bells, as well as other parallels. One of Hauptmann's bells is pagan, the other Christian.

Maes-Jelinek, Hena. "A House for Free Characters." *Revue des Langues Vivantes* 29 (1963): 45-69.
    Most of Murdoch's characters do not live by conventional morality. James Taper Pace proclaims the principle of conscious obedience to strict rules. Even though Michael Meade has the self-knowledge and sympathy to act freely, he is restrained by his frailty. Dora Greenfield is amoral, but enslaved by love. She gets a brief moment of power, and by the book's end she is free to learn.

Majdiak, Daniel. "Romanticism in the Aesthetics of Iris Murdoch." *Texas Studies in Literature and Language: A Journal of the Humanities* 14 (Summer, 1972): 359-375.
    Despite her anti-Romanticism, Murdoch is a romantic in some ways. In this novel, Michael must come to realize that his religious and sexual energies come from the same source. The bell itself is a Romantic symbol, though in an anti-Romantic way it is viewed differently by different characters such as Michael and Dora. The community here is a parody of the contemporary Anglican ideals of T. S. Eliot.

Meidner, Olga M. "The Progress of Iris Murdoch." *English Studies in Africa* 4 (March, 1961): 17-38.
    This novel contains admirable analyses of moral and intellectual issues. Its psychological analyses of some of its characters, notably Michael, are profound; Nick's sermon to Toby in Chapter 21 is effective. But it continues Murdoch's decline as a novelist in

many ways. Its style is prosaic; it contains much less figurative language than does *Under the Net*. Its form is simply a series of variations on a theme. Dora has no recognizable voice, and her motivations are not convincing. It is morally indecisive.

Mettler, Darlene D. *Sound and Sense: Musical Allusion and Imagery in the Novels of Iris Murdoch*. New York: Peter Lang, 1991.
This novel is full of musical sounds: a handbell's ringing, a madrigal, bird songs, jazz, plainsong, Bach, Mozart, and finally the sound of the old bell itself. Mettler speculates on the significance of each of these sounds to the plot of the novel and especially to the maturation of Dora. The simple dignity of the old bell's sound suggests truth, and it influences many people.

Morrell, Roy. "Iris Murdoch: The Early Novels." *Critical Quarterly* 9 (Autumn, 1967): 272-282.
Michael, like many of Murdoch's characters, is isolated, and he waits for a choice to be made for him. Dora is isolated and mischievous, until she realizes someone might be hurt by her tricks and lets the bell speak for itself. Dora is not inhibited by her limitations, but blunders on.

Packer, P. A. "The Theme of Love in the Novels of Iris Murdoch." *Durham University Journal* 38 (1977): 217-224.
Packer praises Murdoch's rendering the complexities of many varieties of love, including that of Michael's love for Nick. Even though this love is related to the Good, it does not open Michael's heart.

Phillips, Diana. *Agencies of the Good in the Work of Iris Murdoch*. Frankfurt: Peter Lang, 1991.
In Chapter 4, Phillips analyzes *The Bell*'s characters in detail. Though Michael wishes to be good, he is distracted by his loves and by the guilt and self-deception in which they involve him. Phillips considers the novel's two sermons: James urges innocence and rules; Michael stresses introspection. Both men eventually fail because their advice is not based on love. Even Michael's imperfect love could have saved Nick. At the end, Michael is not happy, but is learning to live without illusions. Phillips also analyzes other characters. Nick seems to have been the aggressor

with Michael. Catherine was forced into her role as saint. Although Toby experiences an epiphany of perfection in the nunnery garden, he soon is involved in the messy world again; Phillips wonders if he will turn out to be destructive. Dora, one of the novel's only generous characters, is awakened by two epiphanies: her vision of beauty in the National Gallery and her apprehension of the old bell's energy. At the end of this chapter, Phillips compares this novel to *The Unicorn*.

Punja, Prem Parkash. *The Novels of Iris Murdoch: A Critical Study.* Jalandar, India: ABS Publications, 1993.
In Chapter 3 on Murdoch's Gothicism, Punja evokes Imber Court's hellish atmosphere. It is a place of sexual perversion, suicide, and disintegrating relationships. In Chapter 6, Punja interprets Nick's and Catherine's motives. The novel shows the dangers of judging people cruelly by simplistic codes.

Rabinovitz, Rubin. "Iris Murdoch." In *Six Contemporary British Novelists*, edited by George Stade. New York: Columbia University Press, 1976. The first part of this essay is a reprint of Rabinovitz's pamphlet *Iris Murdoch* (New York: Columbia University Press, 1968).
The Imber group fails collectively, suggesting the failure of all established religious systems, and individually. Some characters fail by adhering to rules; others fail in love. Michael is far too immersed in his dream of destiny to respond to Nick's needs. Dora, a woman of simple goodness, is the only character to have a mystical experience, but it soon dissipates. The bells mean different things to different people, but they suggest eternity to those who are not too preoccupied with themselves to listen.

Sinfield, Alan. "Varieties of Religion." In *Society and Literature, 1945-1970*. New York: Holmes & Meier, 1983.
In his survey of religious life in Britain after World War II, Sinfield refers briefly to *The Bell* to show how Christianity has fallen victim to the inadequacies of traditional formulae. Here religion is revived in private terms, such as Dora's experience in the National Gallery.

Soule, George. *"The Bell."* In *Cyclopedia of Literary Characters, Revised Edition*, edited by Frank N. Magill. Pasadena, Calif.: Salem Press, 1998.
A survey of this novel's characters.

Souvage, Jacques. "The Novels of Iris Murdoch." *Studia Germanica Gandensia* 4 (1962): 225-252.
The bell is Murdoch's symbol of the moral life, although it is interpreted differently by different characters in keeping with their individual needs. Dora alone understands what the bell stands for in itself.

_____. "Symbol as Narrative Device: An Interpretation of Iris Murdoch's *The Bell*." *English Studies* 43 (April, 1962): 81-96.
The bell in this novel is an excellent symbol for Murdoch's moral vision; its meaning builds as the novel progresses. To Michael, its up-and-down motion symbolizes human limitations and therefore his own failings. Because Imber Court did not treat Nick and Dora charitably, they both enlist Toby to help destroy the community. The new bell resembles a postulant trying to enter the nunnery; the failure of the new bell symbolizes the failure of the community to achieve the Good Life.

Spear, Hilda D. *Iris Murdoch*. New York: St. Martin's Press, 1995.
In Chapter 2, Speer calls this the best of Murdoch's novels of the 1950's. Characters are fully drawn; they have independent lives which are not neatly tied up in the novel's ending. Their complex relations are the source of wonderfully dramatic moments. Dora is one of the central characters. Imprisoned in her marriage to Paul, she finds freedom and finally silence only in the confines of Imber Court. The novel's concern for love extends from the sensual to the spiritual; Michael's life illustrates the difficulty of reconciling these extremes.

Stettler-Imfeld, Barbara. *The Adolescent in the Novels of Iris Murdoch*. Zürich: Juris Druck & Verlag Zürich, 1970.
Toby's entrance into adolescence is complicated. An innocent, shy youth, he enters the new world of Imber Court to get guidance, but finds corruption instead. He also experiences love. Michael's gestures shatter his innocence, and he wonders whether

he too is homosexual. He sometimes retreats from these confusions by communing with Nick's dog or by swimming. He acts in ways that bring about some change in his condition: he dives into the lake, he climbs the nunnery wall, and he devotes himself to raising the old bell. When he feels sexual passion for Dora, whom he regards as Woman rather than as an individual woman, he is reassured. Still, he is confused about his loyalties and confesses all to James. His final act is to leave the Court. His presence has had the effect of pushing Michael toward self-knowledge.

Stewart, Jack F. "Dialectics in Murdoch's *The Bell*." *Research Studies* 48 (December, 1980): 210-217.
A dense, valuable article in which Stewart dialectically sets out Murdoch's dialectics by reading this novel in light of Murdoch's philosophical essays. The two sermons make clear by verbal parallels the distinction between James and Michael. James stands for self-forgetfulness, for seeing reality outside the self, for obeying rules. The bell speaks to him of candor and truthfulness. Michael, in contrast, stands for both self-knowledge and self-fulfillment. The bell, in its rising and falling motion, speaks to him of human imperfection.

In Murdoch's terms, James is an Ordinary Language Man, limited by convention from apprehending what other people are like. (Even though Dora seems to have learned from James in her experience in the National Gallery, he judges her harshly.) Michael is a Totalitarian Man, limited by his neuroses from acting correctly, particularly in the case of Nick. His spiritual aspirations are really the sublimation of his repressed desires. The opinions of James are closer to Murdoch's ideology, Michael's to her methodology. She uses the novel to test her ideas.

Todd, Richard. *Iris Murdoch*. London: Methuen, 1984.
In Chapter 2, Todd groups Murdoch's first four novels together in their concerns. In *The Bell*, Murdoch provides more details about her characters' early lives than before. This novel is organized around the repetition of patterns, notably one in which actions which have been hurtful in the past are repeated in the present.

Wall, Stephen. "The Bell in *The Bell*." *Essays in Criticism: A Quarterly Journal of Literary Criticism* 13 (July, 1963): 265-273.

What does the bell symbolize? The novel is not a simple allegory. The meaning of the bell shifts as it is interpreted by different characters. Dora throws herself at it with characteristic impulsiveness. To James, it is innocence; to Michael, it is subject to limitations. In short, the bell is a focal point for the novel, but not a center of meaning. Too great a focus on the bell might cause a reader to miss the novel's great moments, such as the autumnal afternoon as Dora leaves Imber Court.

Whiteside, George. "The Novels of Iris Murdoch." *Critique: Studies in Contemporary Fiction* 6 (Spring, 1964): 27-47.
The inhabitants of Imber Court are religious in a romantic, and therefore delusive way. Two examples of protective love are here. Paul wishes to protect Dora, but she eventually escapes. Michael's love for Nick is protective as well as homosexual. The young Nick, as the object of love's delusions, naturally tries to escape and betrays Michael. But at Imber Court, Nick does love Michael. Michael's foolish rejection and Nick's suicide make this novel almost tragic.

Winsor, Dorothy A. "Iris Murdoch and the Uncanny: Supernatural Events in *The Bell.*" *Literature and Psychology* 30 (1980): 147-154.
A very interesting analysis from the perspective of psychology. Like Freud, Murdoch knows that primitive energies lie below the conventional social world. Imber Court's geography and its repressive rules imply a desire to suppress man's primitive psychic nature. James suppresses it by convention; Michael by neurosis. In either case suppression leads to a failure to love. The old bell's possible supernatural power symbolizes both ancient sexual violence and art's ability to transform it into forms that take social norms into account. The nuns of the Abbey suggest that this transformation works in a celibate world. In the everyday world, only Dora seems transformed by her uncanny contact with the old bell. Ever so, her adjustment may not be successful. Supernatural events in the novels may express Murdoch's fear that human beings cannot sustain real love. Such supernatural or uncanny events either tear the veil of convention away from reality or signal the appearance of a new fantasy. Either way, the forces of

the primitive are dangerous. Murdoch implies that it may have
been better to repress them.

_____. "Solipsistic Sexuality in Iris Murdoch's Gothic Novels."
Renascence 34 (Autumn, 1981): 52-63.   Reprinted in *Iris
Murdoch*, edited by Harold Bloom. New York: Chelsea House,
1986.
Murdoch experiments with Gothic material to explore the relation
between inner fantasy and outer reality, especially with regard to
sexuality. Most characters in this novel deny their sexuality with
disastrous results. Only Dora seems to grow; her raising the old
bell is an act of defiance. Winsor suggests (unconvincingly) that
to the members of the Court, the Abbey represents primitive
sexuality. Even so, she thinks this novel is more optimistic than
Murdoch's other Gothic experiments.

Wolfe, Peter. *The Disciplined Heart: Iris Murdoch and Her Novels.*
Columbia: University of Missouri Press, 1966.
In Chapter 6, Wolfe reads this novel in an original and interesting
way. *The Bell* contains fuller characters than those Murdoch has
created earlier, characters whose histories we know much about.
In this way she gives a sense of life, not just as events in the
present, but also as a continuum. Murdoch further implies, as
Nietzsche asserted, that those who do not understand the past are
fated to repeat it. Imber Court is filled with people who want to
escape the usual anxieties of life; it is a halfway house between a
spiritual life (the Abbey) and the world. But the world cannot be
avoided.   The physical world is solidly present in Murdoch's
detailed descriptions, and the men and women in the court have
their human imperfections. Whatever the motives of Dora and
Toby may be, the bell they raise tolls a message of heterosexual
physical love.
As the novel unfolds, Dora makes some progress, perhaps
because she is never hindered by Christian theory.   Not so
Michael.   He preaches self-knowledge, but is deluded.   By
refusing to understand his homosexuality, he loses both human
and divine love. At the end, he seems shallow when he cannot
understand Catherine's love for him. Wolfe thinks that when the
bell destroys Imber Court, Murdoch is saying that in Britain there

is now no middle ground between the increasingly isolated Church and the world.

A Severed Head, 1961.

Arnold, David Scott. *Liminal Readings: Forms of Otherness in Melville, Joyce and Murdoch*. New York: St. Martin's Press, 1993.

Readers must be actively involved to discover the liberating experience this novel offers. Two readings are necessary to grasp its full irony. A reader first sees Martin as a naïve narrator involved in a series of comic episodes he cannot explain. Although he is fallible, he is not deceptive, for the reader senses Murdoch the novelist behind the story. For a long time, Martin does not understand the otherness of other people; finally, through Honor, he does. At the end, although the reader may wonder whether or not Martin has changed, the novel has a satisfying degree of closure. In a second reading, the reader accepts Martin as the retrospective author of the novel, an author fully conscious of the fallible Martin to whose story he gives a mythic dimension. Arnold provides many examples of the presence of Martin the retrospective author in the text. Arnold maintains that this device not only asks the reader to learn what Martin learns but also provides so many kinds of irony that the ending (intentionally on Murdoch's part) is full of ambiguities.

Baldanza, Frank. *Iris Murdoch*. New York: Twayne, 1974.

In Chapter 6, Baldanza sorts out this perplexing novel convincingly. He suggests many meanings for the title: a severed head may suggest Martin's moral incompleteness as well as Honor Klein's resemblance to a primitive object that utters prophecies. The novel's tightly organized plot, in which each major character consummates a sexual relation with almost every other major character, is not merely sensational. Many of the characters must learn to love the otherness of other people. This is especially true of Martin, this novel's version of Murdoch's bumbling male character, who begins the novel as a self-centered romantic hero like Joyce's Stephen Dedalus, and ends the novel, after a succession of shocks, as a more mature and powerful person.

Something like this can be said of his wife Antonia, who Baldanza thinks represents Murdoch's satire of a Bloomsbury woman. Alexander, who is trying to move as a sculptor from symbolism to a kind of realism, suggests the path Murdoch feels the novel should take. Honor Klein is this novel's "alien god" figure, for she combines intelligence and power with Semitic and oriental exotic qualities. Her judgment of Martin leads him away from romantic illusions and toward the maturity he possesses at the end of the novel. Murdoch's denouement is satisfying, even though it is not static or happy in any conventional sense.

——————————. "Iris Murdoch and the Theory of Personality." *Criticism: A Quarterly for Literature and the Arts* 7 (Spring, 1965): 176-189.
After summarizing Murdoch's ideas about personality, Baldanza illustrates these ideas by analyzing this novel. His analysis is reprinted with a few revisions in Chapter 6 of his book, *Iris Murdoch.*

——————. "The Manuscript of Iris Murdoch's *A Severed Head.*" *Journal of Modern Literature* 3 (February, 1973): 75-90.
Baldanza describes the working notes for this novel and its two manuscripts in the University of Iowa Library. These documents reveal what was discarded in the process of writing the novel: characters, events, and symbols that help us to understand the novel as published. Its setting was originally country houses, probably in Ireland. Georgie had a brother. Murdoch repeatedly noted a quote from Proust ("love is madness") and speculated that love prospers best between empiricists and idealists or dreamers. Several myths were emphasized, especially those of Eros/Psyche, Gyges/Candaules, and a Japanese legend about incest. For publication, Murdoch cut out many significant repetitions and echoes. Baldanza goes through the novel chapter by chapter and notes what she changed. Chapters 3, 6, and 30 were completely rewritten; he describes in detail the changes to the severed head image of Chapter 6.

Bove, Cheryl K. "Americas and Americans in Iris Murdoch's Novels." In *Encounters with Iris Murdoch,* edited by Richard Todd. Amsterdam: Free University Press, 1988.

In Murdoch's novels, the United States is regularly associated with bad theorists, such as the psychoanalyst Palmer Anderson.

_____. *Understanding Iris Murdoch.* Columbia: University of South Carolina Press, 1993.
In Chapter 7, Bove treats this novel briefly. Its complicated mingling of sexual partners is a satire on Freudianism. That the characters are childless reinforces the reader's impression of their moral sterility.

Burgess, Anthony. *The Novel Now: A Student's Guide to Contemporary Fiction.* London: Faber & Faber, 1967.
This novel's world is located outside of ordinary experience. The characters seem without free choice as they take part in a dance patterned by the author. Yet at the end, Martin yields.

Byatt, A. S. *Degrees of Freedom: The Novels of Iris Murdoch.* New York: Barnes & Noble Books, 1965.
In Chapter 6, Byatt is impressive as she reads this novel as commentary on Sartre and Freud. For the egocentric dramas those men find in life, Murdoch substitutes Martin's slow and comic progress toward truth. In the process, Byatt comments upon the rich meaning of the severed head symbol and upon the many sorts of love that do not succeed, especially Antonia's and Palmer's. It is Honor Klein who possesses truth: a loving respect for the unique other person. Martin finally learns that when he sees a transfigured telephone box and when he observes Honor's incest. At the ending, Martin and Honor are equals. Even though Byatt thinks the novel's ending is awkward, Martin may be the only Murdoch character to move into a freer world. In Chapter 9, Byatt says that, although this novel is neatly worked out, its characters are not realistic and lack warmth.

_____. *Iris Murdoch.* Harlow, Essex, England: Longman Group, 1976.
In *A Severed Head* and other novels written during the same years, Murdoch shows how many actions are driven by psychological forces the actors may not understand. Here the force is sado-masochistic sexuality. Byatt shows how Murdoch plays with different concepts of what a severed head may symbolize.

_____. "'The Omnipotence of Thought': Frazer, Freud and Post Modernist Fiction." In *Passions of the Mind: Selected Essays*. London: Chatto & Windus, 1991.

The section of this essay that deals with *A Severed Head* recapitulates Byatt's argument in *Degrees of Freedom*, though with some change in emphasis.

Cohan, Steven. "From Subtext to Dream Text: The Brutal Egoism of Iris Murdoch's Male Narrators." *Women and Literature* 2 (1982): 222-242. Reprinted in *Men and Women*, edited by Janet Todd. New York: Holmes & Meier, 1981.

Murdoch's first-person male narrators routinely try to impose their destructive fantasies upon women. Martin's oedipal fantasies on innocence are destroyed when Honor forces him to recognize the feminine other. Cohan thinks that because of the novel's first-person narration Murdoch does not make her judgment on Martin clear enough.

Conradi, Peter. *Iris Murdoch: The Saint and the Artist*. New York: St. Martin's Press, 1986.

In Chapter 4, Conradi sees Martin as changing by the end of the novel into a more realistic and less judgmental person, one who is not so caught up in his own illusions as before. Most of the characters live in a world moved by the desire for sex and power. Murdoch takes the mechanical repetitions at the heart of this world to absurd and comical lengths. The word "civilized" resounds through the novel, which can be read as a satire on Bloomsburian liberalism. The novel's title may refer to Murdoch's speculation how Sartre and Freud would interpret the head of Medusa.

_____. "Iris Murdoch and Dostoevsky." In *Encounters with Iris Murdoch*, edited by Richard Todd. Amsterdam: Free University Press, 1988.

Both writers worry about the moral anarchy that follows from the decline of organized religion. Both present doubled characters, and both create scenes of public and private humiliation. Conradi makes specific remarks on this novel.

_____. "Platonism in Iris Murdoch." In *Platonism and the English Imagination*, edited by Anna Baldwin and Sarah Hutton. New York: Cambridge University Press, 1994.
Murdoch distrusts psychologists because they encourage self-centeredness. Palmer is a demon.

Dick, Bernard. "The Novels of Iris Murdoch: A Formula for Enchantment." *Bucknell Review: A Scholarly Journal of Letters, Arts and Science* 14 (May, 1966): 66-81.
Palmer and Honor are enchanters playing the roles of Zeus and Hera. Honor is ultimately the more powerful one. Dick gives a strange reading of the novel's last scene between Honor and Martin.

Dipple, Elizabeth. *Iris Murdoch: Work for the Spirit*. London: Methuen, 1982.
In Chapter 5, Dipple groups this with Murdoch's first ten novels and characterizes it as one dependent on tricks and plotting. *A Severed Head* is a dazzling high comedy in which Murdoch satirizes psychoanalysis and the vanities of society. The head in the title and related images emphasize the divisions between the intellect and the body in this group of novels. Rosemary and Antonia are the first of what will become a common Murdoch type: a wealthy, self-centered, and rapacious middle-aged woman. Dipple's most useful point is that, whereas in other novels Murdoch uses mythological allusions to enhance the action, here such devices (and there are a great many) simply mask the characters' evil motives.

Fletcher, John. "'Cheating the Dark Gods': Iris Murdoch and Racine." *International Fiction Review* 6 (Winter, 1979): 75-76.
The moment when Martin realizes he loves Honor parallels the moment in a Racine play in which the hero or heroine realizes he or she is trapped and cannot escape a tragic ending. In both authors' works, characters eventually recognize that their fate has been determined. Fletcher illustrates his point by an analysis of *Andromache*.

German, Howard. "Allusions in the Early Novels of Iris Murdoch." *Modern Fiction Studies* 15 (Autumn, 1969): 361-377.

Murdoch's allusions in this novel are mainly oriental: objects, literature, myths, and philosophy (in a debased version).

Gordon, David J. *Iris Murdoch's Fables of Unselfing*. Columbia: University of Missouri Press, 1995.
In Chapter 1, Gordon argues that characters like Palmer who try to set people free are pseudo-healers. In Chapter 3, Gordon sees crude structural irony is Martin's first-person narrator. In Chapter 5, Gordon draws attention to Murdoch's first allusions to the Apollo/Marsyas myth.

Goshgarian, Gary. "Feminist Values in the Novels of Iris Murdoch." *Revue des Langues Vivantes* 40 (1974): 519-527.
Murdoch's feminist concerns are to show men constructing fantasies about women, in particular exalting them as goddesses. Martin views Honor as a powerful Medusa who can transform him. Honor, however, refuses to be an object of fantasy and wants love to be based on reality.

Gossman, Ann. "Icons and Idols in Murdoch's *A Severed Head*." *Critique: Studies in Modern Fiction* 18 (April, 1977): 92-98. Reprinted as "Icons and Idols in *A Severed Head*" in *Iris Murdoch*, edited by Harold Bloom. New York: Chelsea House, 1986.
Gossman notes how loving in this novel is often described by images of religious worship. Martin in particular worships his women by candlelight in dim rooms. These dim rooms resemble caves, which connect the actions of the novel to Murdoch's revision of Plato's cave myth in her essay *The Sovereignty of Good*. Prodded by Honor, Martin moves from total delusion to the beginnings of illumination. But like all but a few of Murdoch's characters, he does not become truly good or truly free.

Gregor, Ian. "Towards a Christian Literary Criticism." *The Month* 219 (April, 1965): 239-249.
Gregor comments on *A Severed Head* (and D. H. Lawrence's *Women in Love*) to make his point: although there is no Christian literary criticism, there are Christian literary critics of responses to novels. When Martin finds his world is empty, Honor makes

him aware of the dark gods. Here is where a Christian literary critic could begin to see Christ.

Griffin, Gabriele. *The Influence of the Writings of Simone Weil on the Fiction of Iris Murdoch*. San Francisco: Mellen Research University Press, 1993.

Griffin refers to this novel throughout. Murdoch undermines the centrality of the self with open endings like this novel's. She shows contradictions within the personality by having characters write multiple versions of a letter, as Martin does. Murdoch's feminism is qualified when she fails to show Honor having any women friends; Honor is an honorary male. Persons (like Honor) who are capable of real moral striving tend to be androgynous in Murdoch's novels. Very feminine characters like Georgie lack moral seriousness.

Hall, William F. "'The Third Way': The Novels of Iris Murdoch." *Dalhousie Review* 46 (Autumn, 1966): 306-318.

Very interesting comments. All the characters suffer, not because they are decadently modern, but because they still love in the old-fashioned infantile way and are unaware of it. They suffer because, though the old-fashioned Christian ideas no longer guide them, nothing has taken their place. Perhaps at the end some new spirit appears between Martin and Honor.

Harding, D. W. "The Novels of Iris Murdoch." *Oxford Magazine* 2 (October 26, 1961): 34-35.

This novel is witty and farcical, but the love between Martin and Honor is unintelligible.

Henkle, Roger B. "Signals of the Comic." In *The Psychoanalytic Study of Literature*, edited by Joseph Reppen and Maurice Charney. Hillsdale, N.J.: The Analytic Press, 1985.

Henkle uses this novel to discuss how a writer can make disturbing matter comic. From the beginning, Martin and Georgie's conversation locates the reader firmly and reassuringly in conventional life. The mysterious, dangerous, and uncomic figures of Palmer and Honor impinge on this conventional world. Murdoch keeps mystery from getting out of hand in many ways. Dangerous things are made into art; sacred things are made profane. Many characters lack a strong will. The author is clearly in control of all the events; Martin's life even reveals a pattern.

Heyd, Ruth. "Interview with Iris Murdoch." *University of Windsor Review* 1 (Spring, 1965): 138-143.
Many Murdoch characters are obsessed and self-deluded. Honor Klein is clearly one of Murdoch's favorites, for she conquers self-deception.

Hope, Frances. "The Novels of Iris Murdoch." In *On Contemporary Literature*, edited by Richard Kostelanetz. New York: Avon Books, 1964.
This novel contains little other than form. Hope thinks Murdoch is developing in the wrong direction.

Hoskins, Robert. "*Hamlet* and *A Severed Head*." *American Notes and Queries* 21 (September-October, 1981): 18-21.
Many critics have shown how Murdoch echoes Shakespeare. Here, although the consequences of his behavior are relatively trivial, Martin is Hamlet-like in his early passiveness, in his antic disposition, and in his later impulsive and violent behavior. Antonia acts Gertrude's part, and Georgie resembles Ophelia. Several allusions to *Hamlet* underline these parallels.

Johnson, Deborah. *Iris Murdoch*. Bloomington: Indiana University Press, 1987. Chapter 1 is reprinted in *Critical Essays on Iris Murdoch*, edited by Lindsey Tucker. New York: G. K. Hall, 1992.
In Chapter 1, Martin's male quest is undermined by the female author in several ways: she makes it comic, and she makes clear that he is mired in erotic self-deception. Honor may be the object of Martin's quest, but she is so powerful that the reader may think that *she* is the central quester. In Chapter 2, Johnson shows how Martin's first person urbane narration is undercut by a female presence in his words, a presence that suggests violence under the surface. In Chapter 5, Johnson cites Honor's return to Martin as an example of an improbable event that serves to undermine the conventional ending of a novel.

Kane, Patricia. "The Furnishings of a Marriage." *Notes on Contemporary Literature* 2 (1972): 4-5.

Martin shows his excessive love for his possessions by valuing them more highly than his wife and by referring to them by their full identifications, such as "*Waterford* glass." After Honor's love changes him, he stops using these labels.

Kane, Richard C. "Didactic Demons in Contemporary British Fiction." *University of Mississippi Studies in English* 8, n.s. (1990): 36-57.
Like other contemporary British novelists, Murdoch mixes the demonic with moral concerns. Martin begins this novel in an un-enlightened state. He thinks his relationships with two women, Georgie and Antonia, are well-defined. In Murdochian terms, he has no concept of their otherness until Antonia leaves him for Palmer. Even then, Martin lives in an enchanted world, serving them in what seems to be a genteel and civilized arrangement. Enter Honor Klein in a cloud of demonic imagery. She turns Martin into a demon himself; he takes her sword as a transfer of power and attacks her. She in turn is revealed as more human in her own obsession for Palmer. At the end, Martin and Honor approach each other as equals and without illusions.

_____. *Iris Murdoch, Muriel Spark, and John Fowles: Didactic Demons in Modern Fiction.* Rutherford, N.J.: Fairleigh Dickinson University Press, 1988.
Kane's chapter on this novel anticipates his article "Didactic Demons . . . ."

Kennard, Jean E. "Iris Murdoch: The Revelation of Reality." In *Number and Nightmare: Forms of Fantasy in Contemporary Fiction.* Hamden, Conn.: Archon Books, 1975.
Murdoch often presents Eastern Europeans as being closer than the English to primitive and instinctive humanity; such a character is Honor Klein. This novel's revelation scene occurs when Martin sees Honor and Palmer in bed. Such scenes awaken the reader to how surprising the real world can be.

Kenney, Alice P. "The Mythic History of *A Severed Head*." *Modern Fiction Studies* 15 (Autumn, 1969): 387-401.
An ingenious and impressive article. Kenney sets this novel in the context of post-war British history and historiography (Martin

is a military historian). More importantly, Kenney illuminates the novel by explaining many parallels between it and both ancient history and, especially, Celtic mythology. Many characters have their Greek and Roman parallels, especially as seen by the historian Edward Gibbon. (Palmer's psychoanalysis is viewed with the same contempt with which Gibbon viewed Christianity.) Much of what happens between Martin and Honor is illuminated by Celtic parallels as explained by Anne Ross in her book *Pagan Celtic Britain*. Honor is closely related to a female Celtic warrior divinity, Medb. When Honor shocks Martin from his narrow perspective, he begins to study anthropology and to understand Honor's point of view. She makes progress toward understanding him, and some kind of communication is finally achieved.

Kuehl, Linda. "Iris Murdoch: The Novelist as Magician/The Magician as Artist." *Modern Fiction Studies* 15 (Autumn, 1969): 347-360. Reprinted in *Contemporary Women Novelists*, edited by Patricia Meyer Spacks. Englewood Cliffs, N.J.: Prentice-Hall, 1977.
In a notable attack, Kuehl doubts that a romantic relation between Martin and Honor is possible. The novel should end with Martin impaled on Honor's sword.

Leavis, L. R. "The Anti-Artist: The Case of Iris Murdoch." *Neophilologus* 72 (January, 1988): 136-154.
A heavily ironic, snide *ad hominem* attack on Murdoch's novels. In contrast to a Lawrence novel, this farce shows squalid sex indulged in by puppet-like characters.

Maes-Jelinek, Hena. "A House for Free Characters." *Revue des Langues Vivantes* 29 (1963): 45-69.
Murdoch characters do not live by conventional morality. Here characters are restrained mainly by the web of their relationships. Martin is enslaved by Honor, the goddess. He changes when he loses his fantasies about other people and sees Honor as a woman.

Malcolm, Donald. "To Everyone, With Love." *The New Yorker*, May 6, 1961, 172-176.
A snide review that mocks the plot's intricacies and the way Murdoch ends her chapters.

Mettler, Darlene D. *Sound and Sense: Musical Allusion and Imagery in the Novels of Iris Murdoch*. New York: Peter Lang, 1991.
In Chapter 6, Mettler points out parallels with this novel and Richard Wagner's opera *Götterdämmerung*.

O'Connor, William Van. "Iris Murdoch: *A Severed Head*." *Critique: Studies in Modern Fiction* 5 (Spring-Summer, 1962: 74-77.
Murdoch's amoral characters have no true identities. Honor is a goddess from the dark, primeval side of man. She is the Goddess of Reality, Freud's Reality Principle, as she tells Martin this novel's truths. In the conclusion's Shakespeare-like sorting out of couples, Honor accepts Martin without promising him happiness.

_____. *The New University Wits and the End of Modernism*. Carbondale: Southern Illinois University Press, 1963.
The chapter "Iris Murdoch: The Formal and the Contingent" is a reprint of O'Connor's *Critique* article.

Pearson, Gabriel. "Iris Murdoch and the Romantic Novel." *New Left Review* 13-14 (January-April, 1962): 137-145.
Pearson discusses *A Severed Head* in light of Murdoch's "Against Dryness" and his theories about romantic art. In contrast to *The Bell*, which he likes, Person thinks *A Severed Head* is a failure. Its plot is mechanical; its settings are inconsistent; its characters do not live. Honor is a particular failure: a man-woman who combines Rebecca and Svengali, an empty fantasy. The nature of her power is simply asserted.

Piper, William Bowman. "The Accommodation of the Present in Novels by Murdoch and Powell." *Studies in the Novel* 11 (Summer, 1979): 178-193.
Murdoch gets intensity by rendering vivid actions in the present tense. The novel suffers because the action ends just when the interesting actions (Martin and Honor living together) could begin.

Punja, Prem Parkash. *The Novels of Iris Murdoch: A Critical Study*. Jalandar, India: ABS Publications, 1993.
In Chapter 5, Punja says this novel shows sexual relations in Western materialistic bourgeois society; with no family ties,

people simply try to satisfy themselves in relationships. Martin alone changes because he meets Honor, a teacher. Honor's reference to alchemy suggests that their love will give birth to the philosopher's stone.

Rabinovitz, Rubin. "Iris Murdoch." In *Six Contemporary British Novelists*, edited by George Stade. New York: Columbia University Press, 1976. The first part of this essay is a reprint of Rabinovitz's pamphlet *Iris Murdoch* (New York: Columbia University Press, 1968).

Murdoch makes use of Freud throughout this novel. In particular, she creates the psychoanalyst Palmer, whose message of freedom and moral anarchy is reflected in the plot. Murdoch deplores this anarchy; moreover, she implies that psychoanalysis encourages an excess of introspection, whereas what people need is attention to people outside themselves. Martin is impeded in his quest of maturity by too much rationality and too great a care for objects, not people. In his love for Honor, he grows up. But why should Honor love Martin? Rabinovitz does not find Honor convincing.

Rose, W. K. "An Interview with Iris Murdoch." *Shenandoah* 19 (Winter, 1968): 3-22. Reprinted as "Iris Murdoch, Informally" in *London Magazine* 8 (June, 1968): 59-73.

Revealing remarks about Honor Klein. She is a kind of character who is made into a demon by other characters. At the same time, such characters as Honor possess sexual energies that allow them to enslave their victims. In this novel, everyone is enslaved. Martin is lucky in his relationship to one of his enslavers.

Scholes, Robert. *Structuralism in Literature*. New Haven, Conn.: Yale University Press, 1974.

Brief remarks in Chapter 6. Martin must make an existential leap past his Freudian fear to read Honor's love. Scholes sees this leap as paralleling Murdoch's own progress from existentialism to structuralism.

Siegel, Carol. *Male Masochism: Modern Revisions of the Story of Love*. Bloomington: Indiana University Press, 1995.

Modern male masochism causes men to suffer for giving over what they think is their birthright to dominate women. Male writers make such sacrifices cathartic. In *A Severed Head*, Murdoch parodies this behavior. Honor, by means of the shock of incest, forces Martin out of his masochistic role with Palmer and Antonia and into a new, realistic, and terrifying world.

Smithson, Isaiah. "Iris Murdoch's *A Severed Head*: The Evolution of Human Consciousness." *Southern Review* 11 (1978): 133-153.

In his complex argument, Smithson reads this novel in light of Erich Neumann's ideas about the development of both human consciousness and individual consciousnesses. He distinguishes stages of development and the symbols by which these stages have been expressed. The ego begins totally absorbed in the whole of the unconscious, as symbolized by the Great Mother; it painfully separates itself (symbolized by a fight with a dragon or a descent to an underworld) until it becomes independent (symbolized by the hero) and capable of distinguishing opposites.

In *A Severed Head*, Martin begins in childlike stasis; Antonia and Georgie (and others) act as his Great Mother. Honor is a Great Mother too, as well as its opposite, the Terrible Mother. For Martin to emerge from his unconscious, he has not one but three dragon-fights or underworld descents with Honor: at the train station, in the dining room with the Samurai sword, and in the cellar. Martin is changed by these encounters. He values, then loves Honor; he begins to understand himself, to leave the past behind, and to assert himself. In loving Honor, he accomplishes the ultimate task: he frees the princess and unearths the treasure. Psychically, he finds his own soul.

Souvage, Jacques. "The Novels of Iris Murdoch." *Studia Germanica Gandensia* 4 (1962): 225-252.

A mix of Freudian nightmare and drawing-room comedy. Souvage reads the novel, especially its severed head/Medusa symbol, in an exclusively Freudian way. Honor Klien, like Medusa, is both horrible and fascinating to Martin.

Spear, Hilda D. *Iris Murdoch*. New York: St. Martin's Press, 1995.

In Chapter 3, Spear groups this novel with others that display the strength of the ties of marriage and religion. Although the setting is mainly London, most scenes occur in closed rooms; even outdoor scenes do not display full daylight. Rooms, especially those of Antonia and Georgie, are filled with significant detail. Murdoch's farcical plot shows characters are tied to each other in complicated ways, yet struggling to be free. Honor Klein is the central character, the severed head/Medusa-like prophetess who seems to decree that Martin's love for her is doomed. Yet at the end, in a scene full of light and after Martin sees that his earlier roles were false, he and Honor do get together. A valuable and succinct analysis.

Todd, Richard. *Iris Murdoch*. London: Methuen, 1984.
In very brief comments in Chapter 3, Todd groups this novel with five others from the early 1960's which have alienated some readers and puzzled critics. Martin is a deluded narrator in the Henry James tradition. In its symmetry, the plot is also Jamesian. Todd comments on the way repeated acts may mean different things to different characters.

_____. *Iris Murdoch: The Shakespearean Interest*. New York: Barnes & Noble Books, 1979.
This novel resembles a Shakespearean comedy in the way its characters shift their attachments. Its comic ending escapes being arbitrary because the reader is convinced that Martin has come to love Honor.

Turner, Jack. *Murdoch vs. Freud: A Freudian Look at an Anti-Freudian*. New York: Peter Lang, 1993.
In Chapter 3 of this crude look at Murdoch's relation to Freud, Turner says that the author makes use of Freud openly in this novel. In all of its sexual variations, Murdoch appeals to the reader's id. At the same time she is expressing her own desires (possibly homosexual) and hostilities.

_____. "Murdoch vs. Freud in *A Severed Head* and Other Novels." *Literature and Psychology* 36 (1990): 110-121.
An earlier version of a chapter in the author's *Murdoch vs. Freud*.

Whiteside, George. "The Novels of Iris Murdoch." *Critique: Studies in Contemporary Fiction* 6 (Spring, 1964): 27-47.
This novel is a romantic comedy, almost a farce. Some loves of the four ordinary people are protective, some abject. Enter two

Gods, Palmer the Apollonian and Honor the Dionysian, whose powers are enhanced by being both foreign and associated with exotic professions. Martin's abject love makes Honor into a castrating goddess. At the end, their union is not ideal, for Martin is still abject.

Widmer, Kingsley. "The Wages of Intellectuality . . . and the Fictional Wages of Iris Murdoch." In *Twentieth Century Women Novelists*, edited by Thomas F. Staley. Totowa, N.J.: Barnes & Noble Books, 1982.

Behind this version of a drawing-room comedy lie both the ideas of D. H. Lawrence about erotic dark gods and the plot of the classic French novel, *Les Liasons Dangereuses*. Among the comic and complex web of sexual connections, betrayals, and ironies, Martin is almost heroic as he discovers Honor Klein, a representative of these transforming dark gods.

Wolfe, Peter. *The Disciplined Heart: Iris Murdoch and Her Novels.* Columbia: University of Missouri Press, 1966.

In Chapter 7, Wolfe interprets this novel in a unique and challenging way (with many references to other critics). Although the characters in this novel are self-regarding, their lives show the interrelationships that psychoanalysis ignores. It is Antonia and Palmer's affair, and Martin's acquiescence, that precipitates the troubles of all the characters. Most of the characters are fraudulent as they put civilized masks on their behavior. But Murdoch alludes to the Aries/Aphrodite/Hephaestus myth as well as to Nietzsche's ideas about power when she shows how savage these characters really are. The masks of convention are destroyed by a unique character in British fiction: Honor Klein. Honor exudes sexual power; she stands against fraud and for wisdom and control.

Yet Martin is the novel's central character. The novel's greatest irony is that Martin is a first-person narrator who does not seem to know he tells the story of his own moral development from a mild and empty man to the a man who can acknowledge his dark forces and quest for Honor's love like a medieval knight. But the novel's conclusion is not neatly organized. Honor is not only a principle but a human being; she seems to need Martin's love. Wolfe suggests that Martin's development may not be over, that Honor does not represent his last stage.

An Unofficial Rose, 1962.

Baldanza, Frank. *Iris Murdoch*. New York: Twayne, 1974.
In his Chapter 7, Baldanza's analysis divides characters by generation. Among the adolescents, Miranda is clearly a figure of power; under her mask of innocence, she plots viciously. Penn seems weak until he falls in love and becomes violent. Elderly lovers fair somewhat better. Emma Sands is the novel's "alien god" figure; she derives much of her sadistic power from the mystery others see in her. Because Mildred doggedly pursues him, Hugh finds himself paired off with her at the end. The middle-aged entanglements of Randall, his wife Ann, and her suitor Felix are more sensational and less satisfactory.

Baldanza also classifies the characters by Murdoch's categories of artists (who desire formal perfection) and saints (who accept imperfection and formlessness). Randall, who creates and loves roses, is an artist, and so to varying degrees are Miranda, Hugh, Lindsay, and Emma. The saints are the bumbling, inarticulate, long-suffering Ann and the gentlemanly Felix. Baldanza thinks in this novel Murdoch introduces several new elements. She may suggest that the suffering of saints has redemptive qualities. In the story's sprawling form, Murdoch takes us into the consciousness of almost all of the main characters.

Bove, Cheryl K. *Understanding Iris Murdoch*. Columbia: University of South Carolina Press, 1993.
In Chapter 3, Bove's discussion is judgmental. The immature and selfish Randall is unattractive. Emma Sands, though attractive, is wicked. Ann, seen as an ideal by some, is indecisive; Bove judges her harshly for what she does *not* do.

Byatt, A. S. *Degrees of Freedom: The Novels of Iris Murdoch*. New York: Barnes & Noble Books, 1965.
In Chapter 7, Byatt sees this novel's themes as the relation of perfection to the real world (a harmony visualized in Hugh's Tintoretto) and the conflict of freedom and marriage. She thinks

the novel suffers because its rapacious characters (Randall, Emma, Lindsey, Miranda) are not well done. Randall is a self-centered man who yearns for freedom; Emma is inscrutable and not fully realized. Of the good characters, Ann shows how goodness exists in the ordinary world. She resembles Maggie Verver of *The Golden Bowl* by Henry James as analyzed by John Bayley, Murdoch's husband. Though she has the chance, Ann does not break free, and she ends the novel in a state of simplicity and unconsciousness. In this she resembles Hugh, though he regrets that he did not break free of his wife when he had the chance. Both Ann and Hugh seem to accept the inscrutable nature of reality.

_____. *Iris Murdoch*. Harlow, Essex, England: Longman Group, 1976.

In *An Unofficial Rose* Murdoch tries to emulate nineteenth century English novelists by creating, not symbolic figures, but free and even formless characters who find they must work out their own unpredictable destinies. The mysterious and shapeless Ann provides a contrast to both the Tintoretto painting and to a perfect rose.

Byatt, A. S., and Ingnês Sodré. *Imagining Characters: Six Conversations about Women Writers*, edited by Rebecca Swift. London: Chatto & Windus, 1995.

In Chapter 5, Byatt and Sodré, a psychoanalyst, discuss *An Unofficial Rose* in a rambling conversation that does not always yield clear ideas. They compare this novel to Jane Austen's *Mansfield Park*. In much of their talk, they seem to regard Murdoch's characters as real people, distinguishing "bad" and dangerous ones (like Randall and Lindsey) from "good" ones like Ann. She is deficient in spirit and held in by convention, which is not necessarily a virtue. Her relation to Randall is sadomasochistic. Hugh is a better person than Ann. He is selfish, but he did truly love Emma, and he tried not to hurt Fanny. Mildred is stronger and has moments of true lucidity; because she makes a moral decision against her own selfish interests, Byatt thinks she can be rewarded by the novel's comic machinery.

The two critics disagree about Douglas Swann, but agree that Miranda is "bad." She may not be believable, but her dolls are certainly symbolic; Byatt suggests they suggest Medusa's head in their watchfulness. Randall is not entirely believable; he seems compelled by a demon. Emma is bad, but we know she has suffered. Byatt sees many fairy tales behind this novel: Ann is "Sleeping Beauty" and pricks her finger; Emma is the wicked witch in "Rapunzel." The critics discuss Emma, *Villette*, and the German dagger at length. Both the Tintoretto painting and the roses are symbolic. Randall resembles Adam in Eden as he names the plants; Nancy is either Eve or the serpent.

Conradi, Peter. *Iris Murdoch: The Saint and the Artist*. New York: St. Martin's Press, 1986.
In Chapter 3, Conradi divides characters in a usual way. Randall is an artist who wants form and style; Ann is a kind of formless saint. She is the "unofficial rose," a phrase from a Rupert Brooke poem. (Conradi also sees the influence of Henry James and Jane Austen on this novel.) Characters who think they can act freely find out that they are not so free. Male characters seem generally weak as they pursue their dreams. Female characters range from the passive Ann to the energetic, tough, clear-sighted Emma.

Dipple, Elizabeth. *Iris Murdoch: Work for the Spirit*. London: Metheun, 1982.
In Chapter 3, Dipple discusses Ann as a figure of unconscious good: she is ineffective and defeated, and she seems to renounce happiness. As her husband complains, she lacks form. Yet even if she is somewhat unattractive, she gives the reader an idea of goodness. In Chapter 5, Dipple groups this with Murdoch's first ten novels and calls it one which focuses upon character. Dipple thinks this novel is unsuccessful for many reasons. It moves too slowly; its contrasts, such as good versus evil, are too simple; Ann is simply too colorless. Emma Sands is a muted version of Murdoch's enchanter-figure, while Miranda is the nastiest of Murdoch's demonic children.

Emerson, Donald. "Violence and Survival in the Novels of Iris Murdoch." *Transactions of the Wisconsin Academy of Sciences, Arts, and Letters* 57 (1969): 21-28.
In this comparatively unsensational novel, the violence is muted: selfishness, hatred, deception. Many characters survive in various

fashions. Hugh will have a brief interval of freedom; Ann endures in ignorance.

German, Howard. "The Range of Allusions in the Novels of Iris Murdoch." *Journal of Modern Literature* 2 (September, 1971): 57-85.

The allusions in this novel are drawn from Northern European folklore, Near Eastern legends, and Finno-Ugric and Siberian myths. Literary sources suggesting the characters' fantasy lives include Maurice Maeterlinck's *The Blue Bird*, J. M. Barrie's *Peter Pan*, and William Shakespeare's *The Tempest*. Reinforcing the novel's realistic side are allusions to works by Rupert Brooke (in the novel's title and epigraph), by Jane Austen, and by Henry James (in particular to *The Golden Bowl*).

Gordon, David J. *Iris Murdoch's Fables of Unselfing*. Columbia: University of Missouri Press, 1995.

In Chapter 5, Gordon notes that in this novel Murdoch writes high comedy in the manner of Henry James, comedy in which clever females get the better of less clever males. Murdoch's real problem is with Ann, a woman whose loyalty to her husband is involuntary. How do you make such a good character interesting?

Goshgarian, Gary. "Feminist Values in the Novels of Iris Murdoch." *Revue des Langues Vivantes* 40 (1974): 519-527.

Murdoch has feminist concerns. Specifically, many of her novels show men constructing fantasies about women; in particular, men exalt them as goddesses. Randall fantasizes about Lindsey and hopes she will bring him freedom and salvation. When he wakes from his myth, he wishes he were back with Ann.

Griffin, Gabriele. *The Influence of the Writings of Simone Weil on the Fiction of Iris Murdoch*. San Francisco: Mellen Research University Press, 1993.

Griffin notes that this novel presents the usual Murdoch contrast of male selfishness and female selflessness.

McDowell, F. P. W. "`The Devious Involutions of Human Character and Emotions': Reflections on Some Recent British Novels."

Wisconsin Studies in Contemporary Literature 4 (Autumn, 1963): 339-366.

This novel has too many characters and lacks intensity. Its theme is the difficulty of calculating one's moral responsibilities to oneself and to others. Hugh and Randall both fail. Hugh fails from cowardice, Randall because he has no sense of the transcendent. Is Ann a coward too? Perhaps duty is her calling.

Maes-Jelinek, Hena. "A House for Free Characters." *Revue des Langues Vivantes* 29 (1963): 45-69.

Murdoch characters do not live by conventional morality but strive for freedom. Hugh, who has learned little in a long life, thinks selling his Tintoretto will at least make Randall free. He is wrong; Randall is not strong enough to break completely with Ann. Ann, in turn, refrains from immoral acts, but only because of inertia. Paradoxically, selling the painting makes Hugh feel free. Maes-Jelinek praises this novel for the depth of its characters.

Obumselu, Ben. "Iris Murdoch and Sartre." *ELH* 42 (Summer, 1975): 296-317.

Randall's character is thin compared to the heroes of nineteenth century novels. Ann submits to contingency, but she does little. Lindsey is simply a focus of fantasy.

Pondrom, Cyrena N. "Iris Murdoch, An Existentialist?" *Comparative Literature Studies* 5 (December, 1968): 403-419.

Though Murdoch agrees with Sartre that the contingent world threatens human freedom, this novel diverges from the practice of existentialist novelists. Murdoch sets this novel in the ordinary world in which human beings are barred from freedom by many conditions and forces. Some of the limits on freedom come from characters not knowing the truth.

Punja, Prem Parkash. *The Novels of Iris Murdoch: A Critical Study.* Jalandar, India: ABS Publications, 1993.

In Chapter 4, Punja cites Ann as a figure of unconscious goodness; she is truthful, pious, helpful, and ineffective. Though she is exploited by people like her husband, she survives. In Chapter 5,

Punja contrasts three extramarital affairs in which one partner seems ready to do anything to possess his or her sexual object.

Rabinovitz, Rubin. "Iris Murdoch." In *Six Contemporary British Novelists*, edited by George Stade. New York: Columbia University Press, 1976. The first part of this essay is a reprint of Rabinovitz's pamphlet *Iris Murdoch* (New York: Columbia University Press, 1968).

The theme of mastery and enslavement or enchantment is central to this novel. Many characters feel they are free, only to find they are slaves. Randall leaves home to be free, but is enslaved by Lindsey, who had been enslaved to Emma, who even as master had not been free. Only Hugh, by avoiding enslavement to Emma and by seeing his dead wife clearly, becomes free. The opposite of all these neurotic people is the conventional Ann, who cannot break accepted patterns to accept Felix's love.

Ryan, Marjorie. "Iris Murdoch: *An Unofficial Rose.*" *Critique* 5 (Winter, 1963): 117-121.

Ryan identifies the theme of this novel as the clash between conventional people and those rebellious spirits who desire experience and mystery. Murdoch shows that even though the real world is messy, people try to give form to their lives. By the end of the novel, wild impulses have subsided, quests have failed, and characters try to simplify matters to accord with their own wishes. Ryan praises this novel for blending the symbolic, the comic, and the realistic.

Spear, Hilda D. *Iris Murdoch*. New York: St. Martin's Press, 1995.

In Chapter 3, Spear groups *An Unofficial Rose* with others that display the strength of the ties of marriage and religion and makes very brief comments on it. This novel is less complicated and hence less farcical than *A Severed Head*. It displays life's cycles and ends on a melancholy note.

Stettler-Imfeld, Barbara. *The Adolescent in the Novels of Iris Murdoch*. Zürich: Juris Druck & Verlag Zürich, 1970.

This novel's two adolescents emerge from childhood differently. Penn is forced to begin growing up by leaving his childhood home in Australia to live with the Perronets. He is shocked by the crises in the adult world and by death. Then he falls hopelessly in love with Miranda. By turns, he feels manly and lustful; he idealizes her and is tormented by her. He decides to act. His invasion of Miranda's bedroom produces a mixed effect, but he learns from it that Miranda is a violent and willful person and that his love has been a illusion. He then returns, a more mature young man, to Australia.

The mysterious Miranda seems childish, especially in her devotion to her odd dolls. But without others noticing very much, her parents' problems hasten her maturation. So does her silent love for Felix, which metamorphosed from a childish admiration. Nobody understands. She tries to escape by idealizing her dead brother and by remembering childish happiness with Felix. She acts symbolically through her dolls, and when she outgrows them, she destroys them. She does what she can to prevent her mother's marrying Felix and succeeds. She sees a future of living with her father as bleak.

Todd, Richard. *Iris Murdoch*. London: Methuen, 1984.
In very brief comments in Chapter 3, Todd groups this novel with five others from the early 1960's which have alienated some readers and puzzled critics by their excess of passion and obvious symbolism. Murdoch's usual plot device of repeated actions here occurs over generations in the same family. Todd detects the influence of Henry James in the novel's multiple centers of consciousness and in its emphasis on the power of money. However, the influence of Shakespeare appears to be growing: Murdoch provides a subplot.

Weatherhead, A. Kingsley. "Backgrounds with Figures in Iris Murdoch." *Texas Studies in Literature and Language: A Journal of the Humanities* 10 (Winter, 1969): 635-648.
In Murdoch's early novels, characters (often defined by their environment) fall under the spell of powerful enchanters and eventually reject them. This novel is filled with rejections of enchanting persons and objects. Hugo sells his enchanting Tintoretto; Lindsay despoils Emma's room; Mildred knocks over Miranda's dolls; Randall realizes Lindsay is not so enchanting as he once thought.

Whiteside, George. "The Novels of Iris Murdoch." *Critique: Studies in Contemporary Fiction* 6 (Spring, 1964): 27-47.
Both Randall and Hugh are abject lovers who see their love objects as moon goddesses. Both become disillusioned. Whiteside objects that though Murdoch mocks the young people in the novel, she does not mock the adults.

Wolfe, Peter. *The Disciplined Heart: Iris Murdoch and Her Novels.* Columbia: University of Missouri Press, 1966.
In Chapter 8, Wolfe says that in its depth of characterization and of human relations this novel resembles those of Henry James. The country settings may be arid and genteel, but the characters' erotic desires are selfish and antisocial. Murdoch's picture of human relations challenges both sociologists and Freud. Emma has become a lonely, self-centered, second-rate artist. Wolfe sees Miranda as a juvenile version of Emma. Randall, however devoted he once was to the beauty of his flowers, is immature; he learns too late that Lindsey is not ideal. Ann is mindlessly and conventionally good, a representative of negative Christian virtues. But when Hugo selfishly sells his Tintoretto, many ordered relationships break apart; for his part, he enters a new, more flexible time of life. The novel ends on a promising note with Hugh and Mildred at sea.

The Unicorn, 1963.

Allen, Diogenes. "Two Experiences of Existence: Jean-Paul Sartre and Iris Murdoch." *International Philosophical Quarterly* 14 (June, 1974): 181-187.
Allen compares Roquentin's nausea in *La Nausée* to Effington's reactions in the bog scene in *The Unicorn*. Effington experiences first the death of the self, then a sense of something outside of the self, then love of the world. Effington's vision does not last, but Murdoch recognizes the possibility of a person's growth toward perfection. Allen prefers Murdoch's way of describing the human task.

Backus, Gary. *Iris Murdoch: The Novelist as Philosopher, the Philosopher as Novelist;* The Unicorn *as a Philosophical Novel.* New York: Peter Lang, 1986.

Backus discusses in detail the novel's literary and philosophical backgrounds, as well as previous criticism. In Chapter 11, Backus provides a useful summary of the novel's plot, a map, a list of places, a list of main characters, and a chronology (with weather reports). Chapter 12 gives an exhaustive chapter-by-chapter commentary occasioned by the actions in that chapter. Backus does not summarize his reading of the novel.

Baldanza, Frank. *Iris Murdoch.* New York: Twayne, 1974.

In Chapter 8, Baldanza describes the "gothic" elements in this novel: Hannah the imprisoned lady; Marian, a governess-like young woman; evil enslavers like Peter and Gerald; the castle and its sexual atmosphere; the gloomy surrounding territory; even the novel's style. He defines two forces. Peter and Gerald are evil because of their sensual and alcoholic indulgence and because they enslave Hannah. Max, the philosopher is their good opposite. In between are Hannah, Effington, and Marian. Marian is mainly a narrative device, a reasonable observer who cannot say at the end what she has learned. Effington has a religious vision when he is lost in a bog, but the effects soon wear off. Hannah is at the novel's center. She is saintly in a way. Baldanza sees her approach to God as involving the sort of welcome affliction defined by the French philosopher Simone Weil, a state of mind that leads to the denial of the self. On the other hand, Hannah's suffering may be her atonement for what she did to her husband or may be the sign of her enslavement to him and to his lover Gerald. The novel's pervasive sexuality (both heterosexual and homosexual) underlines Hannah's dark side. What seems holiness to others may really be her using her power to deceive them. Baldanza does a good job in sorting out a confusing novel.

Bove, Cheryl K. "Americas and Americans in Iris Murdoch's Novels." In *Encounters with Iris Murdoch*, edited by Richard Todd. Amsterdam: Free University Press, 1988.

In Murdoch's novels, the United States is regularly associated with evil people, such as Peter Crean-Smith.

_____. *Understanding Iris Murdoch.* Columbia: University of South Carolina Press, 1993.

In Chapter 8, Bove points out the many ways in which this work is a Gothic novel. Although Hannah could be the unicorn of the title, Bove thinks Denis is a better candidate: he is Christ-like, chaste, and clear-sighted, and he is a healer as well. Bove has an interesting discussion of the power of imperfect suffering (in such characters as Hannah) and its victims.

Byatt, A. S. *Degrees of Freedom: The Novels of Iris Murdoch.* New York: Barnes & Noble Books, 1965.

Byatt's argument in Chapter 8 is intricate. Even though this novel's characters are flat, its allegory is intriguing. The novel's physical landscape combines intractable fact with mythical suggestions; its characters' speeches are more philosophical than usual, especially when they talk about Hannah. The ideas of Simone Weil have influenced Murdoch here, and Byatt quotes them extensively. Byatt offers many alternative explanations for Hannah's suffering and predicament. Can she be explained as suffering from neurotic hysterical fantasies? Should we view her as Freud views the isolated primitive king? Do her sufferings come from within, or are they imposed from without? Is she a witch or a vampire? Should she be an object of Platonic contemplation? Does she suffer from the burden of sin? Or from her distance from God's love? If so, this love is one of God's perfection, a love that omits the love of real human beings. Perhaps Hannah is ultimately ambiguous. In Chapter 9, Byatt says that the events in this novel cannot bear the full weight of significance Murdoch places on them.

_____. *Iris Murdoch.* Harlow, Essex, England: Longman Group, 1976.

In *The Unicorn* and other novels written during the same years, Murdoch shows how many actions are driven by psychological forces the actors may not understand. Several characters try to escape their enslavement; Effingham has a brief vision of spiritual freedom.

_____. "'The Omnipotence of Thought': Frazer, Freud and Post Modernist Fiction." In *Passions of the Mind: Selected Essays*. London: Chatto & Windus, 1991.
The section of this essay that deals with *The Unicorn* recapitulates Byatt's argument in *Degrees of Freedom*, though with a small change in emphasis.

Cavaliero, Glen. *The Supernatural and English Fiction*. New York: Oxford University Press, 1995.
In Chapter 6, Cavaliero discusses how Murdoch mixes naturalistic detail and bizarre yet explicable happenings and with inexplicable, preternatural events. The events of this novel are interpreted in many ways: mythologically, psychologically, ideologically. Murdoch's point is that all interpretations here are relative. The imagination projects the patterns it desires (as Effingham does in the bog), yet no interpretation is definitive. To think that an interpretation *is* definitive is to be literal-minded and to narrow life's possibilities.

Charpentier, Collette. "The Critical Reception of Iris Murdoch's Irish Novels (1963-1976) I: *The Unicorn*." *Etudes Irlandaises* 5 (December, 1980): 91-103.
A plodding and detailed survey, without much interpretation, of the reviews of this novel. Many reviewers find the novel without humor, though Gothic and grotesque. Many do not specify the novel's setting, but several place it in Ireland.

Conradi, Peter. *Iris Murdoch: The Saint and the Artist*. New York: St. Martin's Press, 1986.
In Chapter 5, Conradi notes the many similarities this novel has to *The Bell*: the remote enclosed settings, the spiritual environment with Platonic hints, the innocent outsiders who set out on rescue missions. In this novel, Effingham's near-death experience in the bog is a vision of the positive sublime. Murdoch is being ironic in giving such a vision to such a silly man. Conradi comments on the atmosphere at Gaze Castle. It is a purgatorial world, full of empty and confused symbols: Hannah is both Christ and an enchantress. Its inhabitants live in sadomasochistic relations of sexual feudalism. In contrast, at the end Denis walks away

with his dog into a pure world, and Marian returns to the real world renewed by her experiences.

Cosenza, Joseph A. "Murdoch's *The Unicorn*." *Explicator* 50 (Spring, 1992): 175-177.

Most critics say because the unicorn is a Christ-symbol, it refers to Hannah. But it fits Denis Nolan much better: he is male; he is associated with wild animals; he is a thirty-three-year-old virgin. After Marian seduces him, he suffers so that others will not.

Detweiler, Robert. *Iris Murdoch's* The Unicorn. New York: Seabury Press, 1969.

A lucid and valuable discussion of the novel from a broadly Christian point of view. This novel's Gothic setting enables Murdoch to free the action from realistic detail. It is a semiallegorical fiction drawing upon three medieval sources, all of which have both religious and sexual aspects: the unicorn legend, the Sleeping Beauty myth, and the courtly love tradition. Murdoch does not use these materials precisely. Rather than creating characters who participate in myths, she evokes myths that are revealed only imperfectly, sometimes even in parody, in the individualistic characters.

In all these sources and in the novel, there are imprisonments. Hannah seems imprisoned by guilt; her sufferings, which do not always seem so terrible, have become a way of life for her and for the people around her. Like the unicorn or the courtly lady, Hannah has the power to create devotion on others. She is the center of the substitute Gaze religion. But does she really suffer? She does not love anyone. Or if she does suffer, could it be that the suffering itself gives meaning to her life, that her situation has become a way of life, that she does not want to escape? Detweiler, in a reference to Kierkegaard, calls her suffering a paralysis of the will.

But Hannah's way of life is shattered when her husband is expected to return. Gerald's rape (if it is rape) is an ugly equivalent of the prince's kiss. Hannah becomes free and human, but a human without relation to any other. Detweiler speculates on what her killing Gerald and herself means. An affirmation of freedom? More likely, a giving up, a gesture the opposite of the Kierkegaardian leap of faith. Detweiler thinks that evil in this novel results from refusing to accept human responsibilities. Even after Hannah's suicide, characters like Marian and Effingham leave without making any genuine loving commitment. They leave, that is, without doing the one thing that can make a free life possible. Denis comes the closest. His love for Hannah is real, even though he betrays that love with Marian.

Dipple, Elizabeth. *Iris Murdoch: Work for the Spirit*. London: Metheun, 1982.

In Chapter 3, Dipple says that Hannah's spirituality anticipates Carel's evil vision in *The Time of the Angels*. In Chapter 5, she considers this novel among Murdoch's first ten, classes it as a religious story, and briefly notes the elements of its gothic atmosphere.

In Chapter 9, Dipple cites this novel and *The Sea, The Sea* as works in which Murdoch deals with magic. If Murdoch thinks the magic of fiction distracts readers from reality, magic in Murdoch's novels must have a higher function than simple enchantment. Even though Dipple thinks this novel is confusing, she sees Hannah at the center, functioning both as a realistic human being and as an image on which other characters project their individual magical fictions. Dipple divides these characters in several ways. The good (Denis and Max) see Hannah as emblematic of the soul yearning to be free of the world. The evil and powerful (Peter and Gerald) see Hannah as someone on which to inflict suffering. Most of the minor characters of the household see Hannah as related to the divine, but the novel destroys their visions, and her death leads to their deaths. Two major characters (Marian and Effingham) are also neither good nor evil but come from the outside. Both return to the real world touched only lightly by their experience. Nevertheless, Effingham has had the novel's only pure vision: when he is near death in the bog, he sees that the extinction of self leads to pure love. But this vision fades, and he is reduced to Freudian babble.

Dunbar, Scott. "On Art, Morals and Religion: Some Reflection on the Work of Iris Murdoch." *Religious Studies* 14 (December, 1978): 515-524.

This essay is mainly a discussion of *The Sovereignty of the Good*. In *The Unicorn*, Effingham's ego is laid aside in the bog.

Ganner-Rauth, H. "Iris Murdoch and the Brontë Heritage." *Studies in English Literature* 58 (1981): 61-74.
Treats the influence of the Brontës on this novel and on *The Sacred and Profound Love Machine*. Although resemblances to *Jane Eyre* are at first most obvious, Ganner-Rauth thinks *Wuthering Heights* has a stronger influence. Both novels have a locked-up lunatic who once tried to murder her husband. Marion resembles Lockwood.

German, Howard. "The Range of Allusions in the Novels of Iris Murdoch." *Journal of Modern Literature* 2 (September, 1971): 57-85.
Most of the allusions here are to literature: Mme. de La Fayette's *La Princess de Clèves*, Jocelyn Brooke's *The Scapegoat*, *The Oresteia* and Jean-Paul Sartre's version *The Flies*, and Gothic novels, in particular Sheridan Le Fanu's *Uncle Silas*. Murdoch also seems to allude to surrealist paintings.

Gerstenberger, Donna. *Iris Murdoch*. Lewisburg, Pa.: Bucknell University Press, 1975.
In Chapter 1, Gerstenberger notes that the setting is Ireland-like and that the guilt is typically Anglo-Irish. The characters' ideas about reality create the novel's world; Hannah is almost entirely defined by others. Effingham's epiphany in the bog is formulated out of what he has been using his fantasies to avoid thinking about. Marian is freed by accepting the separateness of other people.

Gordon, David J. *Iris Murdoch's Fables of Unselfing*. Columbia: University of Missouri Press, 1995.
In Chapter 5, Gordon calls this novel a critique of spiritual suffering, Christian suffering in particular. Hannah's sorrow seduces other characters, who in turn use it to enhance their own sense of self. When Hannah dies, they easily turn to other erotic pursuits. Gordon thinks the novel is too long and generally ineffective.

Goshgarian, Gary. "Feminist Values in the Novels of Iris Murdoch." *Revue des Langues Vivantes* 40 (1974): 519-527.
Murdoch has feminist concerns. Specifically, many of her novels show men constructing fantasies about women, in particular

exalting them as goddesses. Real women are, however, not goddesses, but human beings. Effingham thinks he loves Hannah, but his love is really his fantasy about her. He calls her by many different epithets. Because so many people mythologize her, Hannah is really an outcast and can escape only by death.

Green, Arthur. "The Worlds of Iris Murdoch." *The Iris Murdoch Newsletter*, no. 10 (December, 1996): 1-6.
The setting is County Clare, with its great cliffs. The dangerous Scarren resembles "the Burren."

Grigson, Geoffrey. "A Captured Unicorn." In *The Contrary View: Glimpses of Fudge and Gold.* London: Macmillan, 1974.
A disparaging review. Grigson locates the novel's setting in Burren, County Clare, Ireland. Murdoch's characters seem drawn from women's magazines, then animated by Disney with a touch of Irish whimsy. Her style is inflated, and her dialogue banal. The symbols are pretentious and vulgar.

Hebblethwaite, Peter. "Out Hunting Unicorns." *The Month* (October, 1963): 224-228.
An impressionistic review of *The Unicorn* from a religious perspective. Gaze Castle is a prison, and its gloomy surroundings suggest a fairy-tale. If characters cannot escape by land, they may be able escape to God. Denis plays the role of Christ is saving Effingham and Marian, though he is also an imperfect man. Hannah combines many roles: priestess, nun, prisoner, and even imprisoner, when she functions as a false image of God for other characters.

Heusel, Barbara. "An Interview with Iris Murdoch." *University of Windsor Review* 21 (Winter, 1988): 1-13.
Even though the novel does not explicitly say so, it is set in County Clare, Ireland, where there are black cliffs and limestone deserts.

_____. *Patterned Aimlessness: Iris Murdoch's Novels of the 1970s and 1980s.* Athens: University of Georgia Press, 1995.
In Chapter 9, Heusel identifies Effington's vision in the bog as a moment in the soul's journey from Plato's cave into the sun.

Heyd, Ruth. "Interview with Iris Murdoch." *University of Windsor Review* 1 (Spring, 1965): 138-143.

Murdoch characters often project their longings and fears on other people, such as Hannah. Murdoch says that Hannah started out to be a redeeming figure; when she took on a life of her own, she became unsuitable.

Johnson, Deborah. *Iris Murdoch*. Bloomington: Indiana University Press, 1987.

In Chapter 3, Johnson groups this novel with others whose plots are particularly harsh and patriarchal and which provide a vision of hell. Allusions to Tennyson underline how women are turned into figures in a myth. In Chapter 5, Johnson says Murdoch undermines the realism of the usual fictional ending by having Effingham close the story simply by closing his eyes.

Kane, Richard C. *Iris Murdoch, Muriel Spark, and John Fowles: Didactic Demons in Modern Fiction*. Rutherford, N.J.: Fairleigh Dickinson University Press, 1988.

In his chapter on this novel, Kane finds that Gaze Castle is home to a number of characters trapped in various versions of a legend concerning Hannah. Some elements of this legend are that she will die if she leaves the castle and that something violent is about to happen, for it has been seven years since the beginning of her imprisonment. The castle's inhabitants are locked in demonic ways as defined by Kane: a demonic relationship is one in which each party has a fantastic and distorted view of the other. The story's many mirrors are symbols of the self-centeredness necessary to such fantasies.

Kane surveys each of the main characters: Gerald (a truly demonic and sexy man), Denis (a man of primitive vitality), Max (a thinker who will not act), and Hannah herself, whose vague portrait allows her to be viewed in ways as different as Pure Good or Circe. A similar ambiguity is part of the legacy of the unicorn symbol: does it represent Christ or a demon? The outsiders are different. Marion, a Romantic and a modern liberal, begins to learn from her mistakes. Effingham, an egotist who enjoys playing a part in the myth of courtly love, is "politely demonic" and does not learn. He is an unlikely person to receive the vision of the bog, and he forgets it soon afterwards.

Kennard, Jean E. "Iris Murdoch: The Revelation of Reality." In *Number and Nightmare: Forms of Fantasy in Contemporary Fiction*. Hamden, Conn.: Archon Books, 1975.
While Effingham fantasizes about Hannah, he also realizes the real person is not like his fantasies. Both houses, Hannah's and Max's, are the centers of webs of fantasy and theory that must be broken.

Kuehl, Linda. "Iris Murdoch: The Novelist as Magician/The Magician as Artist." *Modern Fiction Studies* 15 (Autumn, 1969): 347-360. Reprinted in *Contemporary Women Novelists*, edited by Patricia Meyer Spacks. Englewood Cliffs, N.J.: Prentice-Hall, 1977.
In a famous attack, Kuehl calls this novel a grotesque joke.

McDowell, F. P. W. "'The Devious Involutions of Human Character and Emotions': Reflections of Some Recent British Novels." *Wisconsin Studies in Contemporary Literature* 4 (Autumn, 1963): 339-366.
The grotesque predominates in this novel. Its meanings are obscure, perhaps because Murdoch is confused. Hannah is at the center, seen only through the eyes of others. Many of the novels images refer to her: princess, sleeping beauty, golden idol, enchantress, figure of doom. Her significance lies in her guilt and her suffering. Max supplies one key to the novel when he quotes Aeschylus on learning by suffering. Marian moves from detachment to involvement, from innocence to experience. But at the end, what has she learned? What does the reader learn?

Martin, Graham. "Iris Murdoch and the Symbolist Novel." *British Journal of Aesthetics* 5 (July, 1965): 296-300.
In this novel, Murdoch tries to free truths from Christian moral censoriousness. Unlike Lawrence and Forster, she does not generalize; she embeds her ideas in individual characters. Effingham has a transcendent experience in the bog, but he is not an allegorical figure. He is all too human and forgets what happened.

Obumselu, Ben. "Iris Murdoch and Sartre." *ELH* 42 (Summer, 1975): 296-317.

This work does not make sense as a realistic novel. Even as a parable, it is contradictory.

Pearson, Carol, and Katherine Pope. *The Female Hero in American and British Literature*. New York: R. R. Bowker, 1981.

In their discussion of the female hero myth, the authors call Hannah both a sleeping beauty and a princess who cannot be rescued from her castle. Hannah represents the traditional woman in a patriarchal society, confined at home, constrained by the guilt she feels because of her rage at her husband. She is a supreme egotist, controlled by others but also controlling, both victim and victimizer. She may understand her own plight. Marian is the female hero. She tries to understand why Hannah voluntarily lives in oppression, she tries to set Hannah free, and she escapes heroically when Hannah's spell is finally broken. An illuminating reading.

Phillips, Diana. *Agencies of the Good in the Work of Iris Murdoch*. Frankfurt: Peter Lang, 1991.

In Chapter 4, Phillips finds that this novel emphasizes love's negative sides: obsession and sadomasochism. Phillips asks questions about Hannah from many perspectives. Is she the captive of her husband and her own obsessions? If so, can she be saved? (Marion thinks so.) Is she a spiritual being purifying herself through suffering? If so, should anyone interfere? Or does she enjoy wielding power over others, like a master over her slaves? (Many other relationships have suggestions of master and slave, medieval lord and vassal.) Phillips charts the reader's changing response to these possibilities; whatever the truth, she thinks Hannah is a tragic figure. When the spell is broken and all the various egotisms are exposed, Hannah faces only death. Phillips then discusses two pairs of characters: the spiritual Max and Dennis and the rational Effingham and Marian. She ends the chapter by pointing out illuminating parallels between this novel and *The Bell*.

Pondrom, Cyrena. "Iris Murdoch: *The Unicorn*." *Critique: Studies in Modern Fiction* 6 (Winter, 1963): 177-180.

This novel is less ironic than most of Murdoch's other works. Its points are that symbols are ambiguous and that the truth about another person cannot be known. Hannah cannot sustain her image as a sufferer; she can be both saint and demon. Marian and Effingham come from practical London and do not understand these things. There is no grace in the world of this novel; characters are full of guilt, and their attempts to love are not successful.

Punja, Prem Parkash. *The Novels of Iris Murdoch: A Critical Study*. Jalandar, India: ABS Publications, 1993.
In Chapter 3, Punja documents *The Unicorn*'s Gothic heritage, calling the novel both preposterous and a parody. It is not the usual Gothic novel of character, but one of myth and allegory. Its characters believe in superstitions and still have the religious feelings (such as Hannah's guilt) appropriate to Gothic ages.

Rabinovitz, Rubin. "Iris Murdoch." In *Six Contemporary British Novelists*, edited by George Stade. New York: Columbia University Press, 1976. The first part of this essay is a reprint of Rabinovitz's pamphlet *Iris Murdoch* (New York: Columbia University Press, 1968).
Medieval romances and their later Gothic versions lie behind this novel. As usual in Murdoch, all characters are so imprisoned in their fantasies that they cannot truly see or love other people. Hannah exemplifies Weil's ideas about guilt and suffering: suffering is self-centered and leads to guilt which leads to self-hatred and violence. Weil's idea of Até or the transfer of suffering explains many of the novel's chains of events: one character suffers; he or she therefore hurts another; that person for no rational reason then inflicts suffering on yet another, and so on.

Rose, W. K. "An Interview with Iris Murdoch." *Shenandoah* 19 (Winter, 1968): 3-22. Reprinted as "Iris Murdoch, Informally" in *London Magazine* 8 (June, 1968): 59-73.
Murdoch says that this novel differs from most of her other works because a religious idea is central.

Scholes, Robert. "Iris Murdoch's Unicorn." In *The Fabulators*. New York: Oxford University Press, 1967. Reprinted in *Fabulation and Metafiction*. Urbana: University of Illinois Press, 1979.

In the past, allegory revealed divine order; for contemporary writers like Murdoch, allegory reveals the order imposed by the human mind. Scholes's lengthy comments on *The Unicorn*, especially on the opening paragraphs, demonstrate how Murdoch slowly teaches the reader how to read her allegory by sorting out its various worlds. First there is the "real" world of Marian and Effingham, a world of liberal values and self-development. Then there is Gaze's world of romance and Christian feudal values. In contrast, Riders is the center of classical Platonic values. Everyone tries to understand Hannah, but she is a symbol of the twentieth century: an elusive Christ figure who may also suggest Circe. The novel's message is relativity. The two outsiders who come to Gaze fare differently: Marian is touched by Gaze's problems, while Effingham remains aloof and ultimately unaffected.

Spear, Hilda D. *Iris Murdoch*. New York: St. Martin's Press, 1995.
In Chapter 3, Spear groups *The Unicorn* with others that display the strength of the ties of marriage and religion. Gaze Castle, located perhaps in Ireland, provides another of Murdoch's closed communities. The novel has Gothic trappings (including many repetitions of the number seven) and a significant core. Marian and Effingham are catalysts/outsiders, who view Hannah without understanding her. Hannah herself resembles both a cursed, enchanted figure of Gothic romance, like Tennyson's Lady of Shalott, and Christ. She is an unusual Gothic lady, for she does not wish to be rescued. As Christ she embodies truths about suffering, expiation of guilt, and redemption from which the outsiders can learn when her spell is over. As a real woman, she suffers really.

Sullivan, Zohreh Tawakuli. "The Contracting Universe of Iris Murdoch's Gothic Novels." *Modern Fiction Studies* 23 (Winter, 1977-1978): 557-569. Reprinted in *Critical Essays on Iris Murdoch*, edited by Lindsey Tucker. New York: G. K. Hall, 1992. In this valuable essay, Sullivan treats *The Unicorn* briefly but tellingly. Hannah is both spellbound and one who binds by spells. To avoid real life, others project the fantasies of ideals and of order upon her; when their faith wanes, Hannah dies. Effingham and Marian show the inadequacies of contemporary moral and romantic perspectives. Dennis is a Christ figure; he inherits Hannah's pain.

Todd, Richard. *Iris Murdoch*. London: Methuen, 1984.
In brief comments in Chapter 3, Todd groups this novel with five others from the early 1960's which have distressed critics, in this case by its Gothic trappings. The meaning of the novel's central symbol, the unicorn, seems not to be fixed but bestowed by the different characters, particularly the two centers of consciousness, Marian and Effingham. The latter's experience in the bog is "pseudo-metaphysical." Todd summarizes comments by Robert Scholes and by Murdoch herself.

Turner, Jack. *Murdoch vs. Freud: A Freudian Look at an Anti-Freudian*. New York: Peter Lang, 1993.
In Chapter 4 of this crude attack on Murdoch, Turner describes this novel as progressing from the romantic delusions that Hannah is Christ to the shock that she is actually a castrator and a killer. Hannah is a debased Christ; Effingham's name is a rude joke, and his vision is unscientific. Murdoch's private fantasies operate here as usual.

Weatherhead, A. Kingsley. "Backgrounds with Figures in Iris Murdoch." *Texas Studies in Literature and Language: A Journal of the Humanities* 10 (Winter, 1969): 635-648.
In Murdoch's early novels, characters (often defined by their environment) fall under the spell of powerful enchanters and eventually reject them. Here Effingham's failure to respond to Hannah's appeal leads to violence.

Whiteside, George. "The Novels of Iris Murdoch." *Critique: Studies in Contemporary Fiction* 6 (Spring, 1964): 27-47.
A romantic tragedy satirically treated. Hannah is the enchanter, the object of love, but unlike many such figures in Murdoch's novels, she enjoys her role. The idea she seems to embody, that suffering brings a person closer to reality, is a masochistic religious fantasy, a fantasy which is ultimately shown to be the abject love of evil. The problem in this novel is that the outsiders Marian and Effingham are taken in. There is nobody to break the

spell until Hannah realizes Gerald has tricked her, and she kills him.

Widmer, Kingsley. "The Wages of Intellectuality . . . and the Fictional Wages of Iris Murdoch." In *Twentieth Century Women Novelists*, edited by Thomas F. Staley. Totowa, N.J.: Barnes & Noble Books, 1982.
A brief analysis. Effingham mistakes Hannah for the Unicorn or Christ. His enlightenment in the bog cannot last. A grotesque Gothic melodrama.

Winsor, Dorothy A. "Solipsistic Sexuality in Iris Murdoch's Gothic Novels." *Renascence* 34 (Autumn, 1981): 52-63. Reprinted in *Iris Murdoch*, edited by Harold Bloom. New York: Chelsea House, 1986.
Murdoch uses Gothic material to explore the relation between inner sexual fantasy and outer reality. Here the primitive setting is appropriate to a story of primitive sexuality. Gerald seems the typical Gothic male. Other characters are typically repressed, especially Hannah, whose repression is masochistic. Neither she nor any of the other characters succeed in transforming passion into healthy sexuality.

Wolfe, Peter. *The Disciplined Heart: Iris Murdoch and Her Novels.* Columbia: University of Missouri Press, 1966.
In Chapter 9, Wolfe analyzes this novel's web of personal relations and sets Murdoch's ideas against Sartre's. Her characters indulge their romantic needs for symbolism, synthesis, and visions of perfection to create the world of Gaze Castle. The setting is grim and isolated. At the center is Hannah, the focus of their needs, and yet a person in her own right who accepts her role. Wolfe calls Hannah the author's "allegorical refutation of religious devotion." Her suffering brings no knowledge. The system that focuses its gaze (as in Gaze Castle) is a barrier to true freedom to see the world as it is. In his bog experience, Effingham briefly does understand the real world's fullness. Although all the characters are responsible for the violence at the end of the novel, Marian may be less so. Wolfe finds the ending ambiguous, both in its meaning and in the motivations of the characters.

The Italian Girl, 1964.

Baldanza, Frank. *Iris Murdoch*. New York: Twayne, 1974.
> In Chapter 8, Baldanza divides this novel into four main sections and discusses two themes to be found throughout: Lydia's destructive oedipal influence and the vision of female characters as both virgin and temptress. In Chapters 3-7, Edmund interviews other characters and gets conflicting stories. In Chapters 8-13, Edmund conducts more interviews which reveal both men and women as possessed by demons who lead them through self-indulgence and violence into monstrous sexual complications. Chapters 14 through 17 provide a climax of reversals and revelations in which many characters begin to face the truth. In Chapters 18-21, Edmund conducts four more interviews (with David, Otto, Isabel, and Maggie) in which the reader can see how these characters have begun to change. Finally Edmund too begins to change. As he talks to Maggie, love awakens.

Bove, Cheryl K. *Understanding Iris Murdoch*. Columbia: University of South Carolina Press, 1993.
> In Chapter 8, Bove classifies this as a Gothic work and calls it Murdoch's least successful novel. Its theme centers on oedipal conflicts, and Edmund's change of mind is not believable.

Bronzwaer, W. J. M. *Tense in the Novel: An Investigation of Some Potentialities of Linguistic Criticism*. Gronigen, the Netherlands: Wolters-Noordhoff, 1970.
> This book is written for the specialist, but Bronzwaer makes his seemingly narrow linguistic investigations relevant to Murdoch's deepest concerns. In Chapter 4, Bronzwaer applies his theories to this novel. Edmund employs its system of tenses to distinguish his two roles: that of narrator and that of a character in the story. Edmund the narrator writes from the perspective of his hard-won wisdom. The reader must be alert to which "I" is speaking.
>
> One fruitful ambiguity occurs when Edmund's knock on his mother's door can be seen as a knock on the door of his childhood, a search for self-knowledge. Bronzwaer then asks a series of important questions about Murdoch's fiction as represented by this novel and answers them in the affirmative. Murdoch's symbols are not confusing and lead the reader to transcendent meanings.

Her mysterious characters are not simply wayward, and her melodramatic plots are not pointless; both reflect the density and opacity of life. Her novels embody, not just an escape, but a real challenge to logical positivism. Whatever its literary merits, *The Italian Girl* is a coherent statement on these issues.

Conradi, Peter. *Iris Murdoch: The Saint and the Artist*. New York: St. Martin's Press, 1986.
Conradi has only scattered references to this novel. He notes that Edmund only gradually becomes able to see the Italian girl as a real person.

Dipple, Elizabeth. *Iris Murdoch: Work for the Spirit*. London: Metheun, 1982.
In Chapter 5, Murdoch groups this with Murdoch's other novels of trickery. She think it is a failure, an unintended parody of her own style.

Ganner-Rauth, H. "Iris Murdoch and the Brontë Heritage." *Studies in English Literature* 58 (1981): 61-74.
The Levkins resemble Emily Brontë's demon children.

German, Howard. "The Range of Allusions in the Novels of Iris Murdoch." *Journal of Modern Literature* 2 (September, 1971): 57-85.
Most of the literary allusions in this novel are to works by Johann Wolfgang von Goethe: *Wilhelm Meister's Apprenticeship* and *Faust*, though there are some allusions to poems by Gerard Manley Hopkins. There are also allusions to Vaslav Nijinsky and Auguste Rodin, as well as to some African myths. The novel contains many references to animals, some of which suggest Eugène Ionesco's *Rhinoceros*.

Gordon, David J. *Iris Murdoch's Fables of Unselfing*. Columbia: University of Missouri Press, 1995.
In Chapter 1, Gordon says that Murdoch characters who, like Edmund, want to set people free are really only pseudo-healers. In Chapter 3, Gordon discusses the structural irony of this novel's first-person narration.

Griffin, Gabriele. *The Influence of the Writings of Simone Weil on the Fiction of Iris Murdoch.* San Francisco: Mellen Research University Press, 1993.
Griffin refers to this novel several times. It contains the usual Murdoch contrast between male selfishness and female unselfishness. Weil stresses the need for roots; David and Elsa are uprooted characters. Murdoch impels the reader's attention by having characters do unexpected things, like Edmund's falling in love. The novel's happy ending implies the possibility of moral self-improvement.

Halio, Jay. "A Sense of the Present." *Southern Review* 2, n.s. (Autumn, 1966): 952-966.
After much difficulty Edmund awakens, not only to his identity but also to the possibilities of the present moment. The book ends with some sort of fulfillment for many of its characters, especially for Maggie.

Hoffman, Frederick J. "The Miracle of Contingency." *Shenandoah* 17 (Autumn, 1965): 49-56. Reprinted as "The Italian Girl" in *Iris Murdoch*, edited by Harold Bloom. New York: Chelsea House, 1986.
Although this novel does not have a conventional plot, it illustrates important Murdoch themes. Edmund slowly learns about what one person morally owes to another. At the beginning, he is a man of hate, of disgust, and of fixed positions. By the end, he has begun to love and also to acknowledge the imperfect human condition.

Johnson, Deborah. *Iris Murdoch.* Bloomington: Indiana University Press, 1987. Chapter 1 reprinted in *Critical Essays on Iris Murdoch*, edited by Lindsey Tucker. New York: G. K. Hall, 1992.
In Chapter 1, Johnson explains that Edmund's male quest is undermined by his erotic self-deception. In Chapter 2, she shows how there is a female presence in Edmund's first-person male narrative (though Murdoch is not always in control of his tone). His misogynistic male judgments are undercut because they are so often wrong.

Mettler, Darlene D. *Sound and Sense: Musical Allusion and Imagery in the Novels of Iris Murdoch*. New York: Peter Lang, 1991.
In Chapter 5, Mettler points out that when Isabel plays music by Wagner and Sibelius, their romanticism reinforces suggestions of her chaotic nature.

Punja, Prem Parkash. *The Novels of Iris Murdoch: A Critical Study*. Jalandar, India: ABS Publications, 1993.
In Chapter 3, Punja describes the unusual and vaguely Gothic atmosphere of this novel. We find midnight scenes, odd dreams, and sexual irregularities.

Rabinovitz, Rubin. "Iris Murdoch." In *Six Contemporary British Novelists*, edited by George Stade. New York: Columbia University Press, 1976. The first part of this essay is a reprint of Rabinovitz's pamphlet *Iris Murdoch* (New York: Columbia University Press, 1968).
This novel provides a clear example of the self-centered blindness Murdoch is always against. The Narraway family employed a series of maids they referred to as "the Italian girl" without seeing these women as individual human beings. Readers find this and many other Murdoch themes in this novel, though expressed without their earlier vitality.

Rose, W. K. "An Interview with Iris Murdoch." *Shenandoah* 19 (Winter, 1968): 3-22. Reprinted as "Iris Murdoch, Informally" in *London Magazine* 8 (June, 1968): 59-73.
The Oedipus myth is central. Murdoch does not think this novel is very successful.

Spear, Hilda D. *Iris Murdoch*. New York: St. Martin's Press, 1995.
In Chapter 3, Spear groups this novel with others that display the strength of the traditional ties of marriage and religion. In an very brief comment, Spear says this novel is Murdoch's least successful because its mythic meanings are not integrated with its realistic characters.

Stettler-Imfeld, Barbara. *The Adolescent in the Novels of Iris Murdoch*. Zürich: Juris Druck & Verlag Zürich, 1970.

Flora's entrance into adolescence is complicated by adults. She blames her pregnancy on the indifference of her parents, and she is ultimately disappointed by a father-substitute, Edmund. She must get over her faith in adults. Her acts allow her to mature: she gets an abortion, she blurts out secrets, she talks to her father, and she throws stones at those who have betrayed her. Her acts also shake Edmund and Otto out of their stupor.

Todd, Richard. *Iris Murdoch*. London: Methuen, 1984.
In very brief comments in Chapter 3, Todd groups this novel with five others from the early 1960's which have not pleased all critics. In its preponderance of dialogue, this novel resembles drama. Edmund's fastidiousness gradually disappears as he is drawn into a messy and contingent world. Todd thinks it is Murdoch's least effective novel.

Wolfe, Peter. *The Disciplined Heart: Iris Murdoch and Her Novels*. Columbia: University of Missouri Press, 1966.
In Chapter 10, Wolfe treats this novel briefly. Edmund is an indecisive, repressed man who seems to seek humiliation. In the course of the story he becomes more directed toward others. At the end, he and the rest of the characters freely choose their individual futures. The novel suffers being too short; it does not develop sufficiently the characters of Otto and Maggie. It suffers too from the distractions of farce and melodrama.

The Red and the Green, 1965.

Baldanza, Frank. *Iris Murdoch*. New York: Twayne, 1974.
In Chapter 9, Baldanza treats this novel briefly. Although set in an "historical" time, it is not really focused on history. Its central theme concerns how energies are deflected. Pat's sexual energies inflame his patriotism, his violence, and ultimately his drive to suicide. His promiscuous Aunt Millie seems his opposite, especially when three potential lovers collide at her home. But she is equally obsessed by her love for Pat himself. Baldanza also sees Andrew's pursuit of a career in the cavalry as an example of the deflection of his homosexual attraction for Pat. Barney's energies are religious. They were once deflected into love for Millie, but

now are to be found in his self-indulgent memoir and in his thoughts during two religious services. Although Baldanza thinks the novel is not unified, he thinks Murdoch makes Barney's pitiable condition believable and moving.

Berthoff, Warner. "Fortunes of the Novel: Muriel Spark and Iris Murdoch." *Massachusetts Review* 8 (Spring, 1967): 301-332.
Murdoch shows the tangle of family relationships, the messiness of life. For the first time in her career, she gives her story a historical dimension. But the events of the Easter Rising serve mainly to intensify the personal experience of her characters. In Pat's case, history requires his life. Berthoff is eloquent in describing what he thinks are the novel's finest characters, Millie and Barney.

Bove, Cheryl K. *Understanding Iris Murdoch*. Columbia: University of South Carolina Press, 1993.
In Chapter 7, Bove says this novel's themes resemble those of James Joyce's *Dubliners*. She emphasizes Irish problems and Andrew's initiation into sex.

Bradbury, Malcolm. "'A House Fit for Free Characters': Iris Murdoch and *Under the Net*." In *Possibilities: Essays on the State of the Novel*. London: Oxford University Press, 1973.
Bradbury illustrates the tension between the individuality of characters and their place in a novel's scheme by the episode in which the four individual male characters come to Millie's house. All of them and Millie taken together suggest something about the situation of Ireland. Bradbury asks if this pattern destroys the characters' contingency.

Burgess, Anthony. *The Novel Now: A Student's Guide to Contemporary Fiction*. London: Faber & Faber, 1967.
Burgess complains that Murdoch does not catch the flavor of Dublin talk or the excitement of the time. The novel lacks a big hero.

Cahalan, James M. *Great Hatred, Little Room: The Irish Historical Novel*. Syracuse, N.Y.: Syracuse University Press, 1983.

This novel is more concerned with sex than other novels on the Easter Rising; most male characters are sexually frustrated, mainly by Millie. Cahalan is most interested in comparing this novel to those by other Irish writers, such as Liam O'Flaherty and Walter Macken. Compare to them, Murdoch's treatment of historical events is not conclusive and her characters are not compelling.

Charpentier, Collette. "The Critical Reception of Iris Murdoch's Irish Novels (1963-1976) II: *The Red and the Green (1)*." *Etudes Irlandaises* 6 (December, 1981): 87-98.
    The continuation of a survey of which began with reviews of *The Unicorn*. Most reviewers agree that *The Red and the Green* is a historical novel and accept as accurate Murdoch's physical descriptions of the island and of Dublin. They seldom mention religion. Reviewers often think the private story parallels the public one. Many, however, agree with Christopher Ricks that the bedroom farce detracts from the novel, for it demeans Irish history. Chapentier ends with some interesting comparisons between Murdoch's two Irish novels.

Conradi, Peter. *Iris Murdoch: The Saint and the Artist*. New York: St. Martin's Press, 1986.
    In Chapter 5, Conradi illustrates the positive sublime by Barney's brief vision in the Dominican chapel.

DeSalvo, Louise A. "'This Should Not Be': Iris Murdoch's Critique of English Policy Towards Ireland in *The Red and the Green*." *Colby Library Quarterly* 19 (September, 1983): 113-124.
    Murdoch's novel not only attacks British policy towards Ireland, but by implication it attacks British imperialism in general and American aggression in Vietnam as well. The British try to dominate Ireland, as Andrew and Millie attempt to dominate Frances and Barney. Frances (a nationalist, a Marxist, and a feminist) resists. Pat resists Millie's domination, but is dominated by his obsession about Ireland. Murdoch's point concerns both international and personal relations: it is impossible to love when subjugated. When subjugated, men become impotent and women powerless; they may not even have the energies to rebel. Suffering corrupts the sufferer.

Dipple, Elizabeth. *Iris Murdoch: Work for the Spirit.* London: Metheun, 1982.

In Chapter 5, Dipple calls this novel a partial failure. As in *The Italian Girl*, Murdoch imposes her design too forcibly on her material. Millie as a would-be artist contrasts with Kathleen, a dreary saint-like figure. Pat Dumay is the romantic hero, but readers are not sure why other characters find him so fascinating. The epilogue does not fit with the body of the novel.

German, Howard. "The Range of Allusions in the Novels of Iris Murdoch." *Journal of Modern Literature* 2 (September, 1971): 57-85.

To establish the Irish background and some of the themes of this novel, its allusions are mainly to works by Irish authors: Oliver St. John Gogarty, George Moore, W. B. Yeats, James Joyce, and Jonathan Swift. The Gogarty and Moore allusions cluster about Barney. There are also many animal images.

Gerstenberger, Donna. *Iris Murdoch.* Lewisburg, Pa.: Bucknell University Press, 1975. Chapter 2 on *The Red and the Green* is reprinted in *Iris Murdoch*, edited by Harold Bloom. New York: Chelsea House, 1986.

In comparison to Yeats's poem "Easter 1916," Murdoch's novel fails as an evocation of a specific historical time. In presenting many perspectives on its events, the novel is distanced, not involved. Gerstenberger discusses the many meanings of the title. The novel's characters can be divided into the sterile English and the passionate Irish. Among the latter, Millie displays sexual frustration; Pat is the idealist; Barney shows what Pat might have become if he had lived and lost his purpose. For many reasons, Gerstenberger thinks the epilogue is a failure.

Gordon, David J. *Iris Murdoch's Fables of Unselfing.* Columbia: University of Missouri Press, 1995.

In Chapter 5, Gordon mentions this novel briefly. Pat is its most interesting character: a brave fighter who, like an artist, scorns the mediocre. Mainly the novel is just melodrama.

标记

Griffin, Gabriele. *The Influence of the Writings of Simone Weil on the Fiction of Iris Murdoch*. San Francisco: Mellen Research University Press, 1993.

Griffin refers to this novel several times. Griffin thinks Murdoch differs from Weil in their attitudes toward politics and social issues. Weil had strong political and social views. In this novel, after some simple history lessons, the political side becomes personalized, absorbed by personal metaphors and myths. As usual in Murdoch, truly good individuals like Kathleen are devoid of theory.

Halio, Jay. "A Sense of the Present." *Southern Review* 2, n.s. (Autumn, 1966): 952-966.

Unlike some other critics, Halio stresses that this novel is about politics and history. The fratricidal fighting within the family groups mirrors the sociopolitical incest of Anglo-Irish relations and is perhaps caused by it. Even though attempts by family members to protect innocence do not work, they are valuable. Similarly, the rebels may have been foolish, but they were better off for having tried.

Kemp, Peter. "The Fight Against Fancy: Iris Murdoch's *The Red and the Green*." *Modern Fiction Studies* 15 (Autumn, 1969): 403-415.

Murdoch's insistence on the importance of getting past patterns to the contingent is at odds with her novels. In this novel, her usual grouping of characters around an idea is replaced by arranging them around an event. The parallels are obvious: Irish suffering and the Easter rebellion reflect Jesus' suffering and his resurrection. The different characters display an organized spectrum of attitudes toward the uprising. Only Barney breaks free from the degradation of a patterned life to a kind rebirth of self-knowledge.

Kershner, R. B. "A French Connection: Iris Murdoch and Raymond Queneau." *Eire-Ireland: A Journal of Irish Studies* 18 (Winter, 1983): 144-151.

In spite of the subject matter of this unsatisfactory novel, Murdoch seems distant from Ireland's troubles. Her status as an Irish writer is therefore questionable. *The Red and the Green* may owe much, not to history, but to a novel by the non-Irishman Raymond

Queneau, *On est toujours trop bon avec les femmes.* It too deals
with the Easter Rebellion, but with Joycean wit in the service of
violent farce. It too has a strong, lustful woman who survives.
Murdoch's relation to the Irish rebellion is thereby ironic and
devious. Her debts to Yeats are similar. At the end, Frances
seems to respond to revolution in a Yeatsian way, but her commitment is also undercut by farce.

Leitch, Thomas M. "To What is Fiction Committed?" *Prose Studies* 6
(September, 1983): 159-175.
The philosopher John Searle used the opening sentence of this
novel to illustrate the difference between speech acts in journalism
(real assertions) and in fiction (not serious assertions). Leitch
argues with Searle that novels (as a particular species of fiction)
make particular kinds of serious assertions in the form of hypothe-
ses about human nature. Leitch says that readers read *The Red
and the Green* in many ways: as a novel, as an historical novel, as
a novel by Iris Murdoch. He analyzes the novel's opening words
in detail to suggest what expectations they awake in the reader.

McCabe, Bernard. "The Guises of Love." *Commonweal*, December 3,
1965, 270-273.
McCabe complains that Ireland is only a backdrop for farce.

Phillips, Diana. "The Complementarity of Good and Evil in *A Fairly
Honorable Defeat.*" In *Encounters with Iris Murdoch*, edited by
Richard Todd. Amsterdam: Free University Press, 1988.
Murdoch's comments on this paper contain a reference to *The Red
and the Green*. She points out that the novel was written before
the IRA's violence began again; she could not have written it at a
later date. She defends her mixture of frivolous people and great
events.

Punja, Prem Parkash. *The Novels of Iris Murdoch: A Critical Study.*
Jalandar, India: ABS Publications, 1993.
In Chapter 5, Punja discusses Barney as a man whose deep and
lasting love for Millie has bad effects. In Chapter 6, he shows
how politics affects personal relations.

Rabinovitz, Rubin.   "Iris Murdoch."   In *Six Contemporary British Novelists*, edited by George Stade. New York: Columbia University Press, 1976.   The first part of this essay is a reprint of Rabinovitz's pamphlet *Iris Murdoch* (New York: Columbia University Press, 1968).

The Irish setting is not important, for readers of this novel find the usual Murdoch personalities, enslaved by sex and money. Murdoch adds something new: the slavery of political fanaticism. Frances is the only character capable of love.

Ricks, Christopher. "A Sort of Mystery Novel."   *New Statesman* 70 (October 22, 1965): 604-605.

The weaknesses of Murdoch's style can be seen in repeated phrases like "a sort of." Her characters are abstractions. This novel demeans Irish history.

Rome, Joy. "A Respect for the Contingent." *English Studies in Africa* 14 (March, 1971): 87-98.

Frances represents the good of Ireland, Millie all that is wrong. Andrew, Pat, and Barney—each tries to construct his separate salvation, only to have it undermined by another. They fail to realize that they must discard their own concepts to discover contingent reality. The novel combines realism and allegory.

Sage, Lorna. *Women and the House of Fiction: Post-War Women Novelists*. New York: Routledge, 1992.

In Chapter 3, Sage calls *The Red and the Green* the first of Murdoch's mature novels, for not only does it have many characters and a sprawling plot, but its descriptions of Dublin are well done. Her characters live in a convincing muddle of local and contingent detail.

Scanlan, Margaret.   "Fiction and the Fictions of History in Iris Murdoch's *The Red and the Green*." *CLIO: A Journal of Literature, History, and the Philosophy of History* 9 (Spring, 1980): 365-378.

This novel is not only about history but about how literature relates to history. It relates to Joyce's *Ulysses* in many ways: Barney is like Bloom (and a bit like Stephen); Pat the revolutionary is very much like Stephen the artist in that both try to impose forms on reality; there are many parallel incidents. There are many allusions to Yeats as well, especially to "Easter, 1916." When Murdoch alludes to Joyce and Yeats, her point is that modernist writers, whose aim is to produce unified works of art, falsify real events, and these falsifications in turn effect real events. For example, Yeats's poem glamorized rebellion and violent death. Far from being an anticlimax, this novel's epilogue shows that literary works like Yeats's influence people in later times. Even though his British father is without illusions about the Spanish Civil War, Frances's son is going off to Spain with her encouragement. In sum, politics and art can contaminate each other. Scanlan offers Picasso's *Guernica* as a model, for it memorializes conflict without glamorizing it. An important article.

_____. *Traces of Another Time: History and Politics in Postwar British Fiction*. Princeton, N.J.: Princeton University Press, 1990. Chapter 1 is a revised version of her article "Fiction and the Fictions of History in Iris Murdoch's *The Red and the Green*."

Sheed, Wilfrid. "Iris Murdoch: *The Red and the Green*." In *The Morning After: Selected Essays and Reviews*. New York: Farrar, Straus & Giroux, 1971.
Murdoch usually explores a private world. In this novel, she tries to emerge into a real place and time. But her characters have no real connections to either Ireland or England; they resemble the plastic people from previous Murdoch novels. Sheed objects to Aunt Millie, both as a character and as a symbol.

Spear, Hilda D. *Iris Murdoch*. New York: St. Martin's Press, 1995.
Even though this appears to be an historical novel, Spear groups it in Chapter 3 with others that show the entanglements of love and the strength of marital and of religious ties. This novel has Murdoch's most complicated set of family relationships. Three characters display the wide range of its values: Millie (evil and destructive), Barney (typically Irish, torn between the spirit and flesh), and Pat (the true lover of his brother and Ireland). The epilogue shows Murdoch's unfortunate tendency to tie up the threads of her plots.

Stettler-Imfeld, Barbara. *The Adolescent in the Novels of Iris Murdoch*. Zürich: Juris Druck & Verlag Zürich, 1970.
   The innocent Andrew enters adolescence late. He tries to live in the past, but is forced to recognize both that the Ireland of his childhood is no more and that love involves sex. He fails at love three times. His obsession with his cousin Pat leads to his humiliation; he is rejected by Frances; and he cannot consummate the sexual act with Millie. His acts affect nobody but himself. These humiliations lead to self-knowledge, as the result of which he returns to soldiering and, before dying in action, fights valiantly.

Todd, Richard. *Iris Murdoch*. London: Methuen, 1984.
   In very brief comments in Chapter 3, Todd groups this novel with five others from the early 1960's which have alienated some readers. Todd thinks that the escapades of Murdoch's characters compromise the seriousness of the historical events she describes. Todd thinks J. G. Farrell's *Troubles* (1970) does a better job.

Weatherhead, A. Kingsley. "Backgrounds with Figures in Iris Murdoch." *Texas Studies in Literature and Language: A Journal of the Humanities* 10 (Winter, 1969): 635-648.
   In Murdoch's early novels, characters (often defined by their environment) fall under the spell of powerful enchanters and eventually reject them. In this novel, however, the enchantment of Ireland and of political action may never be completely rejected. Other enchantments are also powerful. Aunt Millie enchants many. Weatherhead argues that Pat can be understood as someone who violently rejects his own body for the Irish cause.

The Time of the Angels, 1966.

Baldanza, Frank. *Iris Murdoch*. New York: Twayne, 1974.
   In Chapter 9, Baldanza praises this novel for its unity, even though it is repellent (and perhaps dangerous). At the center is Father Carel's "God is dead" philosophy: good is an illusion; only evil, power, and chance are real. The angels of the title exist only as thoughts that enslave humanity. Marcus and Nora are weak counterforces of secular morality. They cannot save Carel's victims (Muriel, Eugene, and Pattie), who helplessly grope about

for love.   Baldanza points out many parallels with earlier
Murdoch novels.

Bove, Cheryl K. *Understanding Iris Murdoch*. Columbia: University
of South Carolina Press, 1993.
In Chapter 8, Bove formulates this Gothic novel's question: without a belief in God, where is morality to be found? Carel lives in
a wasteland and is a corrupt version of a "fisher king." The
subterranean labyrinth of a nearby subway and its rumblings are
symbolic. Elizabeth is the secluded maiden of the plot, but she is
not the innocent girl that Gothic conventions call for.

Byatt, A. S. *Degrees of Freedom: The Novels of Iris Murdoch*.
Expanded ed. London: Vintage, 1994.
In Chapter 10, Byatt praises Murdoch for writing the kind of
novel which shows that contemplating a concept has moral
consequences. Carel thinks only power, pain, and chance are real;
Byatt sets his ideas in the context of Nietzsche's thought and of
death-of-God theology. At the novel's center, Muriel spies on her
father and Elizabeth, yet Byatt does not think these characters can
carry the weight of Murdoch's meaning. Eugene and Pattie are
more satisfactory characters.

_____. *Iris Murdoch*. Harlow, Essex, England: Longman
Group, 1976.
Murdoch depicts how actions are driven by psychological forces
that the actors may not understand. Carel briefly escapes from
these forces into a totally negative vision. Byatt criticizes
Murdoch for mixing Pattie's detailed individuality with her
symbolic role.

Conradi, Peter. *Iris Murdoch: The Saint and the Artist*. New York:
St. Martin's Press, 1986.
In Chapter 6, Conradi pairs this novel with *The Nice and the
Good*; both show how spiritual forces scatter in a world without
God. In this novel, the atmosphere is Gothic, apocalyptic,
suffocating; it is filled with boxes and enclosed spaces like the
isolated rectory. The spiritual forces are almost all negative.
Three liberal humanist outsiders try to get into the rectory, but
with little success. Carel Fisher's vision is the negative sublime, a

parody of Murdoch's own ideas. Yet he is human, and the reader understands that he is driven by guilt. His death, like that of the Fisher King, promises fertility in the modern wasteland.

Dipple, Elizabeth. *Iris Murdoch: Work for the Spirit*. London: Metheun, 1982.

In Chapter 3, Dipple analyzes this novel at length. Three intellectuals provide different responses to a world without God. The Bishop knows that even though the old mythology is dead, humans have transcendent yearnings for something beyond mere morality. He conceives of a mystical vision of emptiness. Marcus is a rationalist, an ordinary man who wants the empty myths to remain as a defense against meaninglessness. Carel is truly evil. The death of God has freed the angels; chaos now reigns. In an act of supreme egotism, Carel himself will become God.

Dipple discusses Carel's and the novel's many versions of the Trinity, some blasphemous parodies, some representing forces that will bring Carel down. Foremost among these are Eugene's Russian icon of the Trinity, Anthea as a symbol of wisdom, and Pattie as a symbol of the good earth, of mankind's yearning for sainthood. In Chapter 5, Dipple categorizes this as one of Murdoch's early novels with a religious focus. As opposed to the abstractly allegorical nature of some others, *The Time of the Angels* is more realistic: its characters have their own freedom and believability. Pattie is a fine creation, a woman who is repeatedly seduced by evil, but who still yearns for the good.

Emerson, Donald. "Violence and Survival in the Novels of Iris Murdoch." *Transactions of the Wisconsin Academy of Sciences, Arts, and Letters* 57 (1969): 21-28.

The world of this novel is intense and enclosed; its characters are concerned with God, suffering, and evil. Appropriately, violence is nasty and routinely associated with the evil Carel. Even though some characters are alive at the end, Muriel and Pattie cannot be said to have survived.

Ganner-Rauth, H. "Iris Murdoch and the Brontë Heritage." *Studies in English Literature* 58 (1981): 61-74.

Murdoch's statement about Pattie that "she was Carel" echoes Catherine's statement that "I am Heathcliff."

German, Howard. "The Range of Allusions in the Novels of Iris Murdoch." *Journal of Modern Literature* 2 (September, 1971): 57-85.

This novel's most important literary allusions are to the lives and works of Vladimir Nabokov, Graham Greene, and André Gide.

Gordon, David J. *Iris Murdoch's Fables of Unselfing.* Columbia: University of Missouri Press, 1995.

In Chapter 3, Gordon classifies Marcus as one of a kind of Murdoch character who tries to play a role he or she cannot sustain. In the case of Platonists like Martin, Murdoch sees to it that they are humiliated. In Chapter 5, Gordon says that, even though this novel has a serious purpose (in this case, to explore the nature of evil), it is too self-conscious and too lurid. Readers do not feel Carel's despair.

Griffin, Gabriele. *The Influence of the Writings of Simone Weil on the Fiction of Iris Murdoch.* San Francisco: Mellen Research University Press, 1993.

In Chapter 3, Griffin discusses this novel at length with regard to Weil's notion of the void: an empty vision, a spiritual achievement which can only be experienced at rare moments. Carel's rejection of God implies the void. But he goes wrong in both Weil's and Murdoch's terms by dreaming of the unity that has disappeared in the void. The novel offers two choices for belief. Carel chooses to believe in evil and hence accepts his role as a powerful father figure. Marcus chooses good. For him, the void is an ethical problem. He too wants structure. His solution to the problem in morals in a godless world is like Murdoch's in *The Sovereignty of Good.* He is harmless and gullible. Leo is discussed as well. In Chapter 4, Griffin relates Pattie's fondness for rhythmic language to Weil's concerns.

Johnson, Deborah. *Iris Murdoch.* Bloomington: Indiana University Press, 1987.

In Chapter 3, Johnson treats this novel with others in which a harsh, quick-moving, and patriarchal plot protects the reader from too great contact with real, yet culturally induced, female misery. Echoes of Tennyson suggest how women are made into creatures of myth. Muriel realizes that she has colluded in Elizabeth's imprisonment. In Chapter 5, Johnson says the ending of this novel undermines conventional realism: the final image of Carel's house seems to fade away.

Kaftan, Robert A.   "Doubt and the Self: Two Murdoch Priests." *Christian Century*, October 25, 1978, 1101-1104.
Treats Carel's isolation, his loss of faith, and his despair. Carel replaces God with egotistic self-consciousness.

Kennard, Jean E.   "Iris Murdoch: The Revelation of Reality."   In *Number and Nightmare: Forms of Fantasy in Contemporary Fiction*. Hamden, Conn.: Archon Books, 1975.
Marcus is a fool separated from reality by his philosophical theories. Carel's isolated household is this novel's restrictive web. Inside, Muriel is bound by her fantasies about Elizabeth. Pattie's instincts are against theory and fantasy, and Muriel breaks out after this novel's revelation scene, the moment she sees Elizabeth in bed with her father. The cherry cake at tea is one of Murdoch's miraculous objects.

Majdiak, Daniel.   "Romanticism in the Aesthetics of Iris Murdoch." *Texas Studies in Literature and Language: A Journal of the Humanities* 14 (Summer, 1972): 359-375.
Despite her anti-Romanticism, Murdoch is a romantic in some ways. This is her most demonic novel. Pattie shows the influence of Romanticism in that her life parallels that of Blake's "Little Black Boy" from the *Songs of Innocence and Experience*. She also plays earth to Carel's Urizen; when she surrenders to Carel, she gives up all hope. Even though the major characters cannot respond to the Russian icon's beauty, the novel suggests that art can provide some kind of salvation in a world dominated by Satan.

Mettler, Darlene D. *Sound and Sense: Musical Allusion and Imagery in the Novels of Iris Murdoch*. New York: Peter Lang, 1991.
As fog surrounds Carel's house, Tchaikovsky's music plays within it. Mettler finds that specific works, especially ballet music, are heard precisely when they can furnish parallels to the plot, some of which are more exact than others. Elizabeth is *The Sleeping Beauty*; Pattie is sometimes labeled the sugarplum fairy from *The*

Nutcracker. The *1812 Overture* suggests Eugene's flight from Russia, as the *"Pathétique" Symphony* prefigures Carel's death. *Swan Lake* provides the most parallels: Carel is like Rothbart; Elizabeth is the Swan Princess.

Miles, Rosalind. *The Fiction of Sex: Themes and Functions of Sex Differences in the Modern Novel*. London: Vision Press, 1974.
Pattie is an excellent study of the psychology of service.

Punja, Prem Parkash. *The Novels of Iris Murdoch: A Critical Study*. Jalandar, India: ABS Publications, 1993.
In Chapter 3, Punja finds this novel to be truly Gothic in its many elements. The Gothic atmosphere dominates the novels characters, who play their roles in the Gothic pattern. Carel is both god and demon. Punja shows how various characters can be arranged into trinities (perhaps parodies of the Christian Trinity). The trinity on the Russian icon may have the last word, for when it returns to the house, real miracles begin to happen.

Rabinovitz, Rubin. "Iris Murdoch." In *Six Contemporary British Novelists*, edited by George Stade. New York: Columbia University Press, 1976. The first part of this essay is a reprint of Rabinovitz's pamphlet *Iris Murdoch* (New York: Columbia University Press, 1968).
This is a novel about ethical alternatives in a godless world. Carel takes the self-centered Satanic alternative as influenced by Nietzsche and Heidegger. He practices his theory, and, on the principle of Até, his evil spreads. The other alternative is a weak humanism; its representatives are Norah, the Bishop, and Marcus, who by the end approaches a Platonic understanding of love.

Rice, Thomas. "Death and Love in Iris Murdoch's *The Time of the Angels*." *Critique* 36 (Winter, 1995): 130-144.
This is not only a novel but simultaneously a philosophical allegory which depends on Murdoch's conception of the relation of love and death. Carel's isolated rectory is an emblem for modern man's isolation in a world in which God is dead. Four characters try to live without the things that once supported their structures of belief; Rice calls their situations oedipal conflicts. Pattie represents the mixed human soul of the average reader.

Although her world collapses when she learns of Carel's incest, she escapes to the purgatory of Africa. Muriel (the artist) is not so lucky. When she sees Carel's incest, her god ceases to exist, and she can experience only a love *of* death. Eugene loses his beloved icon, but becomes reconciled to a view which combines both love and death. Marcus the philosopher comes to a similar conclusion after Carel destroys his earlier faith that it was possible to attain the Good.

Carel makes several mistakes. He makes an absolute distinction between good and evil (Murdoch believes in a continuum), and he can only conceive of evil. The novel's title may mean more than Carel's interpretation: St. Thomas speaks of the kind of time that angels live in, which is not human time.

Rose, W. K. "An Interview with Iris Murdoch." *Shenandoah* 19 (Winter, 1968): 3-22. Reprinted as "Iris Murdoch, Informally" in *London Magazine* 8 (June, 1968): 59-73.
Murdoch says that this novel differs from most of her other works because in it a metaphysical idea is central.

Sinfield, Alan. "Varieties of Religion." In *Society and Literature, 1945-1970.* New York: Holmes & Meier, 1983.
In his survey of religious life in Britain after World War II, Sinfield refers briefly to this novel as evidence of the contemporary debate within the Church of England.

Spear, Hilda D. *Iris Murdoch.* New York: St. Martin's Press, 1995.
In Chapter 4, Spear groups this depressing novel with five others in which Murdoch contrasts ineffective good people with the true demonic evil that proceeds from independent, lonely, rational existential man. Here Carel is the demonic force, an elusive, dark, yet potent power that binds other characters together and inspires their love. He is a priest who believes not only that God is dead, but also that satanic figures like himself are now free to spread evil. Pattie and Eugene have their brief moments of hope blighted by Carel, but after Carel's suicide only Pattie is free. Images of dark then give way to images of light. Murdoch's philosophical concerns illustrate the concerns of the essays she was writing at the time. In addition, they illuminate some farcical episodes, as when Marcus descends into the hellish coal hole.

Sullivan, Zohreh Tawakuli.   "The Contracting Universe of Iris
   Murdoch's Gothic Novels." *Modern Fiction Studies* 23 (Winter,
   1977-78): 557-569.   Reprinted in *Critical Essays on Iris
   Murdoch*, edited by Lindsey Tucker. New York: G. K. Hall, 1992.
   In this Gothic novel, the powerful isolated enchanter, Carel, not
   only enslaves and corrupts others, but he destroys himself. His
   spells immobilize and dehumanize; this is the meaning of the
   novel's many cocoon images.   The rectory provides a demonic
   parody of the healthy family, healthy love, and healthy sex. The
   only character to escape is Pattie, who not only recognizes evil but
   devotes her life to service.

_____.   "Iris Murdoch's Self-conscious Gothicism: *The Time of
   the Angels*." *Arizona Quarterly* 33 (Spring, 1977): 47-60.
   Murdoch uses the conventions of Gothic fiction to suggest a
   parallel between the spiritual crises of the late eighteenth century
   and today.   The rectory is a descendant of the Castle of Otranto.
   The people without, like Marcus and Norah, are analogous to the
   villagers who attack the castle in Frankenstein movies.   Within,
   the six characters are symmetrically arranged.   In other novels,
   the isolated hero may be comic; here the demonic Carel is
   horrifying as he denies the human and contingent and affirms
   both the abstract and his will to dominate.   Murdoch associates
   him with Leverkuhn, Thomas Mann's Faustus figure, with Hitler,
   and with the philosopher Martin Heidegger.
       Balancing Carel is the radiant figure of light, Eugene Peshkov,
   a man who has lost faith in God but not his love and humanity.
   Carel has two mistresses: the black Pattie who is his good angel
   and the white Elizabeth, his daughter and bad angel.   As Carel
   shows spiritual corruption, so Elizabeth (Murdoch's ultimate
   demon-child) displays physical corruption.   Muriel inherits evil;
   she is Carel's victim.   Leo inherits nothing and manifests inexplicable evil, the sort that Marcus and Norah, the well-meaning
   outsiders, cannot understand.

Todd, Richard. *Iris Murdoch*. London: Methuen, 1984.
   In very brief comments in Chapter 3, Todd groups this novel with
   five others from the early 1960's which have alienated some
   readers and puzzled critics.   Here the ideas behind the novel are

more interesting than the novel itself. Carel is more a symbol than a real character.

Widmer, Kingsley. "The Wages of Intellectuality . . . and the Fictional Wages of Iris Murdoch." In *Twentieth Century Women Novelists*, edited by Thomas F. Staley. Totowa, N.J.: Barnes & Noble Books, 1982.
Widmer thinks that this novel is too intellectual. Since God is dead, angels are free to be evil: existential ideas in a Gothic plot.

Winsor, Dorothy A. "Solipsistic Sexuality in Iris Murdoch's Gothic Novels." *Renascence* 34 (Autumn, 1981): 52-63. Reprinted in *Iris Murdoch*, edited by Harold Bloom. New York: Chelsea House, 1986.
Murdoch's use of Gothic material is most pessimistic in this novel. Carel, the novel's Gothic hero, is totally sadistic. His rectory is almost totally isolated, and its inhabitants live without God and without love.

The Nice and the Good, 1968.

Ashworth, Ann M. "'Venus, Cupid, Folly, and Time': Bronzino's Allegory and Murdoch's Fiction." *Critique: Studies in Contemporary Fiction* 23, No. 3 (1981): 18-24.
The ways Paula Biranne responds to Bronzino's painting in the National Gallery are significant. When she looks at it early in the novel, she sees it through her ex-husband Richard's eyes: Time is a lecher. She does not notice Deceit and Truth. In contrast, this novel makes the point through the career of John Ducane that Truth is all-important. Paula and Richard learn that—and more. When they meet in front of the picture toward the end of the novel, they see not only Deceit and Truth, but Jealousy.

Baldanza, Frank. *Iris Murdoch*. New York: Twayne, 1974.
In Chapter 10, Baldanza reprints a slightly condensed version of his *Modern Fiction Studies* article.

_____. "*The Nice and the Good*." *Modern Fiction Studies* 15 (Autumn, 1969): 417-428. Reprinted in *Iris Murdoch*, edited by Harold Bloom. New York: Chelsea House, 1986.

Baldanza describes this novel's plot as more open and diffuse than that of many of Murdoch's earlier works. It is divided into two strains. The story of Radeechy's suicide and its aftermath displays the seamier sides of sex and sustains John Ducane's pervasive anxiety. The more important strain involves the couplings and uncouplings of lovers as Murdoch displays the often conflicting forces of lust and a love than transcends lust without denying it. In general, characters in this novel must come to terms with the past in order to live in the present. Baldanza in particular praises Murdoch's handling of the reconciliation of Paula and Richard before a painting in the National Gallery. At the center of the novel is John Ducane, whose moral progress is revealed in stages, culminating with his vision of forgiveness when he thinks he might drown and with his helping to unite many of the couples at the end of the novel.

Bove, Cheryl K. "Americas and Americans in Iris Murdoch's Novels." In *Encounters with Iris Murdoch*, edited by Richard Todd. Amsterdam: Free University Press, 1988.

In Murdoch's novels, the United States is regularly associated with evil people, such as Eric Sears.

_____. *Understanding Iris Murdoch*. Columbia: University of South Carolina Press, 1993.

In Chapter 4, Bove explicates many aspects of love in the Bronzino painting. She focuses on three characters who have some sense of the good: Willy, Theo, and Ducane. Theo despairs at his distance from the good and learns to live without expectation. Ducane at first strives to be good but knows he has evil aspects. By his brush with death, he learns to stop judging and to love and forgive.

Byatt, A. S. *Degrees of Freedom: The Novels of Iris Murdoch*. Expanded ed. London: Vintage, 1994.

In Chapter 11, Byatt provides brief but insightful comments. The characters find the world both horrible and beautiful; most of them try to distinguish the nice (pleasures that feed the ego) from the good (unselfish love). Byatt praises Ducane, whose confusions and struggles are made real to the reader. She applauds the absence of myth and symbolic figures; ideas here are in the minds of the characters.

Cavaliero, Glen. *The Supernatural and English Fiction*. New York: Oxford University Press, 1995.

In Chapter 6, Cavaliero provides a brief but illuminating discussion of this difficult subject. He finds the key to Murdoch's use of the paranormal in Chapter 17 of this novel, where she speaks of the mysterious agencies of the human mind. The novel ends with a transcendent epiphany, when the children see a flying saucer.

Conradi, Peter. *Iris Murdoch: The Saint and the Artist*. New York: St. Martin's Press, 1986.

In Chapter 6, this novel is paired with *The Time of the Angels* as works in which multiple spiritual forces are dispersed after the death of God. But the mood here is entirely different. The earlier novel *ended* with the death of a satanic figure; this one *opens* with the death of Radeechy. *The Nice and the Good* notices "good" people who strive for ideals, but its main business is with "nice" people. At the center are the selfish and hedonistic Grays. Their Dorset home is a place of warmth, sun, love, sex, multiplicity, and the marvelous (including mermaids and flying saucers). The Biranne twins are infinitely curious about the world's multiplicity, which is also the point of many collections and lists made by other characters. As in Shakespearean comedies and romances, there are displaced persons in the court world of Dorset, people like Paula and Mary who need to exorcise the past before they can be happy. Conradi discusses the effects of associating people with animals. Duncane remains a shadowy figure. After two descents into something like hell (Radeechy's cellar and Gunnar's cave), he returns to everyday life and joins that happy people in the world of the "nice."

Dipple, Elizabeth. *Iris Murdoch: Work for the Spirit*. London: Metheun, 1982.

In Chapter 2, Dipple calls Theo one of three characters in the novels who are almost saints. By the final scenes of the novel, he has shed his ego and his illusions about life, yet he continues to live in it. As a "good" person, he is better than merely "nice" and comfortable ones. In Chapter 5, Dipple argues that in *The Nice and the Good* realistically human characters act with freedom, rather than, as in her earlier novels, being forced into Murdoch's overall allegorical frames. The novel contains an element of an old-fashioned mystery story.

Uncle Theo is good, but not a complete saint. Other characters live mainly unthinking lives in a muddled world. Ducane is the best of them, a man who yearns to be both good and just. Murdoch uses a major work of visual art (this time a Bronzino picture from the National Gallery) to pass judgment on the acts of the novel; its allegory shows love being destroyed by time. In the course of the novel, Ducane learns this and more; the woman he marries has also learned a lesson, in her case about giving up the past. Despite the chilling implications of its Buddhist-like theme, this novel is not gloomy. Dipple restates this idea in Chapter 6: although a character may glimpse the Good, he or she changes very little. When healthy persons embrace life, they do so in less than full knowledge.

Gordon, David J. *Iris Murdoch's Fables of Unselfing.* Columbia: University of Missouri Press, 1995.

In Chapter 3, Gordon describes Murdoch's typical charismatic power-figure. Theo is the opposite, a good man who has a negative charisma. In Chapter 4, Gordon reads this novel as a tragicomedy. Even though the evil Radeechy sounds a sinister note, the majority of the characters are, if not good, nice. Murdoch distributes their fates accurately and charitably. In Chapter 6, Gordon places this novel as the first in Murdoch's "major phase." The Gothic Radeechy story suggests her previous novels, but halfway through *The Nice and the Good*, Murdoch dismisses it and moves into a new kind of novel. From now on, evil will not only be located in a demonic figure, but will be found within central characters like Ducane.

Griffin, Gabriele. *The Influence of the Writings of Simone Weil on the Fiction of Iris Murdoch.* San Francisco: Mellen Research University Press, 1993.

Griffin refers to this novel several times. Jessica shows contradictions in her personality when she writes several versions of a

letter. From this novel on, Murdoch more and more describes
only a white, educated, middle-class society.

Johnson, Deborah. *Iris Murdoch*. Bloomington: Indiana University
Press, 1987.
In Chapter 3, Johnson comments on how Mary's love is weakly
communicated in the clichés of magazine romances. In Chapter
4, Johnson gives a feminist reading to several analogues of Plato's
cave: Gunnar's Cave (a source of wisdom for Pierce in his rite of
passage) and even the flying saucer. In Chapter 5, Johnson says
the ending of this novel undermines that of traditional novels by a
Shakespearean distancing note.

Kennard, Jean E. "Iris Murdoch: The Revelation of Reality." In
*Number and Nightmare: Forms of Fantasy in Contemporary
Fiction*. Hamden, Conn.: Archon Books, 1975.
Ducane's pursuit of Pierce into the sea cave provides another of
Murdoch's "technical scenes," passages whose precise details
make readers realize how remarkable the world is.

McEwan, Neil. "Iris Murdoch's Contemporary World." In *The
Survival of the Novel*. Totowa, N.J.: Barnes & Noble Books,
1981.
Murdoch's novels depend on the tension between traditional and
contemporary elements. *The Nice and the Good* has many of the
ingredients of a Victorian novel: gentlemen, ladies, a Jamesian
style. Yet this world is unsettled by more contemporary elements:
suicide, erotic and sadistic cult practices, and absurd complications in the love plot.

Marget, Madeline. "The Water is Deep: Iris Murdoch's `Utterly
Demanding Present.'" *Commonweal*, June 14, 1991, 399-402.
When Ducane is immersed in water (a pervasive Murdoch symbol), he promises himself to do good and to love. His change is
both symbolic and realistic.

Mettler, Darlene D. *Sound and Sense: Musical Allusion and Imagery
in the Novels of Iris Murdoch*. New York: Peter Lang, 1991.
Willy Kost retreats from life into the order of Mozart. but finds
that Mozart can be liberating too. Kate and Octavian present

parallels to Mozart's *The Abduction from the Seraglio*. The cuckoo's song provides a comment on several relationships; when the bird changes its song and leaves, relationships change as well.

Packer, P. A. "The Theme of Love in the Novels of Iris Murdoch." *Durham University Journal* 38 (1977): 217-224.
Packer praises Murdoch's rendering the complexities of many varieties of love, especially the scene in which Mary Clothier realizes she loves Ducane.

Punja, Prem Parkash. *The Novels of Iris Murdoch: A Critical Study*. Jalandar, India: ABS Publications, 1993.
In Chapter 4, Punja distinguishes nice people from good people. Kate is nice, for she avoids hurting others and helps others when it does not involve sacrifice. Ducane is a thoughtful man who achieves true goodness when he saves Pierce in the cave: he acts without self-interest. Other good characters are Mary, Willy, and Theo.

Rabinovitz, Rubin. "Iris Murdoch." In *Six Contemporary British Novelists*, edited by George Stade. New York: Columbia University Press, 1976. The first part of this essay is a reprint of Rabinovitz's pamphlet *Iris Murdoch* (New York: Columbia University Press, 1968).
This novel may look like a spy story, but it is really about moral distinctions. Murdoch distinguishes between ordinary "nice" people and people like Ducane who become truly good. With so many characters falling in and out of love, their emotions are not always sufficiently explained.

Rippy, Frances Mayhew. "Katabasis in Vergil and Murdoch." *The Iris Murdoch Newsletter*, no. 10 (December, 1996): 9-11.
A famous *katabasis*, or a descent into the underworld, occurs in Book 6 of *The Aeneid*. In *The Nice and the Good*, Vergil's story is echoed in Chapter 26, Ducane's descent into old air-raid shelters, and in Chapters 34 and 35, which cover the Gunnar's cave episode. Murdoch departs from Vergil when she adds a Christian element: Duncane, once intent on justice for Biranne, is convinced by his cave experience to love and forgive. The differences in

descents is mirrored in the difference in dogs: Vergil's Cerebus is nasty; Mingo's warmth saves Duncane and Pierce.

Spear, Hilda D. *Iris Murdoch*. New York: St. Martin's Press, 1995.
In brief comments in Chapter 4, Spear groups this novel with five others in which good people contest with evil ones. In this case, the evil character, Radeechy, dies at the beginning on the story, and the evil he has engendered does not prosper. Ducane's strange goodness touches many lives and ensures a happy ending.

Stettler-Imfeld, Barbara. *The Adolescent in the Novels of Iris Murdoch*. Zürich: Juris Druck & Verlag Zürich, 1970.
Pierce and Barbara were close as children. Pierce is pushed from childhood when he feels sexual passion for her, but is rejected by a newly independent Barbara. They are examples of children who change in a world that does not. Pierce retreats into a childish world of pebbles and shells but then is impelled by his frustrations, first to many small destructive acts and then to suicide in the sea cave. In the cave, he realizes he does not want to die and struggles to escape. This experience frees him from his obsession. After he is rewarded by Barbara, he feels ready to go on with life, clear-headed but not fully mature.

Todd, Richard. *Iris Murdoch*. London: Methuen, 1984.
In brief comments in Chapter 4, Todd says that, in its descriptions and tone, this novel shows a return to the virtues of *The Bell*. When Ducane uses his power, not to ruin Biranne, but to persuade him to go back to his wife, we see an analogue to Murdoch the novelist: she sees now that a novelist must resist too neatly ordering her material. Even so, this novel ends with Shakespearean neatness. Todd discusses the complexities of Ducane's situation and the novel's complex web of motifs.

_____. *Iris Murdoch: The Shakespearean Interest*. New York: Barnes & Noble Books, 1979.
In Chapter 5, Todd explores parallels between Shakespearean power figures, especially the Duke in *Measure for Measure*, and John Ducane. (Radeechy is a parody of a power figure.) Ducane's power is limited (the power of art is needed to reconcile Biranne and Paula), and he joins in the final resolution. Ducane appears

to be a power figure who realizes that the problem is how to use power for good without exploiting other people.

Bruno's Dream, 1969.

Baldanza, Frank. *Iris Murdoch*. New York: Twayne, 1974.
In his dense and valuable Chapter 11, Baldanza analyzes this novel's spectrum of love relationships. There is the sensual love of Will and Adelaide, as well as that of Danby. There is the aged Bruno's yearning for forgiveness, from his dead wife and from his son Miles. Miles's own emotions have been shocked into atrophy, but they come alive in his love for Lisa. Lisa herself reciprocates, but neither of them will enter an adulterous relationship. Lisa's spiritual love is shown to be basically sexual when she makes do with Danby. Miles's supposedly shallow wife Diana is the character who, in her care for Bruno, ultimately experiences the most spiritual of states, a pure love based on the renunciation of the self. Bruno too dies in a state of love, in the certainty of forgiveness. Baldanza thinks that the character Nigel may be too allegorical for readers to believe, but (especially in Chapters 3 and 23) he shows Murdoch's focus on the nature of spiritual love.

Beams, David W. "In Defense of *Bruno's Dream*." *The Iris Murdoch Newsletter*, no. 10 (December, 1996): 6-9.
Beams asserts the profundity of this novel by showing how prominently Schopenhauer and Indian religions figure in its ideas and metaphors.

Bove, Cheryl K. *Understanding Iris Murdoch*. Columbia: University of South Carolina Press, 1993.
In Chapter 8, Bove notes Bruno's oppressive house and the novel's many different kinds of love. Except for Diana's caring for Bruno, most of these loves are selfish, most of all Lisa's hedonistic commitment to Danby.

Byatt, A. S. *Degrees of Freedom: The Novels of Iris Murdoch*. Expanded ed. London: Vintage, 1994.
In Chapter 12, Byatt calls this novel a meditation on the effect of death on a person's sense of life. Bruno's dying consciousness is

finely rendered. Other characters either muddle along or fall in love, and love like death intensifies the consciousness. Byatt regrets that this is one of Murdoch's highly patterned novels and therefore one of her less convincing and moving ones. Its pattern involves webs of symbols: Indian deities, spiders, and the Thames.

Conradi, Peter. *Iris Murdoch: The Saint and the Artist.* New York: St. Martin's Press, 1986.
In Chapter 4, Conradi thinks that the characters of this novel at first lead lives that are unenlightened, unconscious, erotic, and repetitious. But in this novel, those that move away from such lives do not necessarily choose an ascetic existence. Although Diana, once a hedonist, chooses pain and devotion to Bruno, her sister Lisa moves from saintliness to a kind of advanced hedonism. Both Nigel and Danby are good as well as hedonistic.

_____. "Platonism in Iris Murdoch." In *Platonism and the English Imagination*, edited by Anna Baldwin and Sarah Hutton. New York: Cambridge University Press, 1994.
Bruno's dying is set against a symbolic cityscape of energy and death.

Dipple, Elizabeth. *Iris Murdoch: Work for the Spirit.* London: Metheun, 1982. Chapter 4 is reprinted as "*The Black Prince* and the Figure of Marsyas" in *Iris Murdoch*, edited by Harold Bloom. New York: Chelsea House, 1986.
In Chapter 4, Dipple calls Miles a precursor of Bradley Pearson in *The Black Prince*. Both are egocentric writers who try to perfect their gifts but produce little. Miles, however, is more purely negative. In Chapter 6, Dipple contrasts this novel to *The Nice and the Good*, for here Murdoch shows us several characters who can change by breaking through to see reality clearly. Not Miles, for he remains egocentric. Lisa may seem saintlike at first but chooses the world.

In contrast, her sister Diana moves in the opposite direction when she develops a real love for Bruno. Dipple admires Murdoch's depiction of Danby, a character who seems to move outside of the novel's framework. He is an ordinary sensual man, a drinker and a womanizer. But he seems to glimpse the good. He feels responsibility for Bruno, and his love for Gwen and later

Lisa shows the positive influence of erotic love. Bruno himself changes. Murdoch shows the steps in his dying, his memories, and his guilt. His reconciliation with Miles is only partially satisfactory, but Lisa helps him to realize that his dying wife did not curse him and that the divine lives in daily occurrences. Minor characters like Nigel and Will provide parallels and comic relief.

Fletcher, John. "Iris Murdoch, Novelist of London." *International Fiction Review* 17 (Winter, 1990): 9-13.
Many of the places in London mentioned in this novel are ones which Murdoch lived near at one time.

Gerstenberger, Donna. *Iris Murdoch.* Lewisburg, Pa.: Bucknell University Press, 1975.
In Chapter 1, Gerstenberger notes that critics have been confused by this novel's mixed moods, by Nigel's strangeness, and by what seems the playfulness of the ending. Many characters are threatened by death, but most live on in improbable ways.

Gordon, David J. *Iris Murdoch's Fables of Unselfing.* Columbia: University of Missouri Press, 1995.
In Chapter 6, Gordon sees her rendition of Bruno's dying as something new in Murdoch's novels. Despite Lisa's good advice, Bruno cannot forgive himself until the end. The rest of the novel is not so successful.

Griffin, Gabriele. *The Influence of the Writings of Simone Weil on the Fiction of Iris Murdoch.* San Francisco: Mellen Research University Press, 1993.
Griffin discusses this novel in great detail. In Chapter 2, she uses Weilian terms to discuss several characters' attempt to achieve selflessness. Lisa begins the novel as a fictional version of Weil herself. She is selfless, mediating, sexless. But she faces the possibility of sexual love. Miles pursues Lisa for selfish reasons. He thinks he needs her love to write again; when she turns him down, she serves equally well as his angel. Danby is also selfish, but more worthy. His marriage ended when the saintly Gwen died; he pursues Lisa for the same reason he loved Gwen: he needs help from the outside to improve. Sexually awakened, Lisa chooses marriage, love, and laughter with Danby. Her change

from saint to sexual woman is hard for many people to accept. In the course of the novel, Diana changes in the opposite way. She ends as a spiritual person, loving the dying Bruno, learning from his death about the death of the self. Murdoch has taken over Weil's spiritual hierarchies in this novel. Women occupy the highest position; women and men mingle in the middle; the lower rank is made up of men only: Miles, Nigel, and Will.

In Chapter 5, Griffin explains how Murdoch turns her and Weil's ideas into fiction by concentrating on the presentation of Nigel, a male Weil-like character. He is hard to pin down. Other characters see him only through their own egos; his replies to them are evasive. At first, readers see him only through the subjective reactions of these characters. Then readers learn about him from the omniscient narrator. He is a mystic and has a mystic experience; Griffin examines Murdoch's portrayal of that experience in great detail. How should reader judge him? His acts produce some good results, yet by dubious means. Griffin thinks Murdoch wants readers to see him as flawed, as a man in the grip of a personal fantasy, as an egotist who enjoys playing God and manipulating people. In other chapters, Griffin notes that Nigel's dotty aunt provides a touch of the "uncanny," and that Lisa at the beginning resembles other Murdoch "good" characters in her asexuality.

Hall, William F. "*Bruno's Dream*: Technique and Meaning in the Novels of Iris Murdoch." *Modern Fiction Studies* 15 (Autumn, 1969): 429-443.

Murdoch's earlier novels show a contest between the forces of form/masculinity/consciousness and those of contingency/femaleness/unconsciousness. Here both worlds exist simultaneously. At the heart of this novel, Hall finds many parallels with Indian creation myths. Nigel, the mystic, shows *the way* to Lisa, Diana, and Danby. At one pole of existence is Nigel and his eastern consciousness. At the other is Bruno, who represents the dying consciousness of western civilizations. Will and Adelaide are so prosaic that their story is not informed by any mythic significance.

Johnson, Deborah. *Iris Murdoch*. Bloomington: Indiana University Press, 1987.

In Chapter 5, Johnson says Murdoch undermines any claims the novel may have to realism by Lisa's improbable union with Danby. Diana's love for Bruno is qualified by the worldliness of Will and Adelaide.

Kennard, Jean E. "Iris Murdoch: The Revelation of Reality." In *Number and Nightmare: Forms of Fantasy in Contemporary Fiction*. Hamden, Conn.: Archon Books, 1975.
Bruno is at the center of this novel's web, which as usual contains a pair of twins, Nigel and Will.

Kermode, Frank. "Iris Murdoch." In *Modern Essays*. London: Collins/Fontana, 1971. Reprinted as "Bruno's Dream" in *Iris Murdoch*, edited by Harold Bloom. New York: Chelsea House, 1986.
Even though Murdoch says she is against novelists who pattern their stories too strongly, readers sense a myth is concealed beneath the surface of this work. Kermode evokes the contents of this myth.

Marget, Madeline. "The Water Is Deep: Iris Murdoch's `Utterly Demanding Present.'" *Commonweal*, June 14, 1991, 399-402.
Another symbolic use of water: it takes Bruno's stamp collection away but leaves him with spirituality.

Martz, Louis. "Iris Murdoch: The London Novels." In *Twentieth Century Literature in Retrospect*, edited by Reuben A. Brower. Cambridge, Mass.: Harvard University Press, 1971. Reprinted in *Iris Murdoch*, edited by Harold Bloom. New York: Chelsea House, 1986.
Murdoch's love of the particularities of London is Dickensian. Characters are classified by their love of place. Bruno in particular is limited in his love. Danby, on the other hand, not only loves his house and garden but is lovable in himself.

Packer, P. A. "The Theme of Love in the Novels of Iris Murdoch." *Durham University Journal* 38 (1977): 217-224.
Packer describes Murdoch's rendering the complexities of many varieties of love, especially Diana's love for the dying Bruno. Her

love is one that demands nothing. It transforms her feelings and leads to a vision of the Good. Eloquent praise.

Phillips, Diana. *Agencies of the Good in the Work of Iris Murdoch*. Frankfurt: Peter Lang, 1991.

In Chapter 5, Phillips says this novel centers on the close relation of love and death. Nigel provides some eastern wisdom even though his character is self-centered and does not inspire confidence. Danby is an ordinary man who can live with muddles. He is morally superior to Miles, a rationalist who at first cannot face the reality of death. Like other major characters, Danby has his moment of understanding, but cannot sustain it. We know the women, Lisa and Diana, mainly at first from the men's perspectives. Diana begins as a superficial and romantic woman. When her world is shattered, she gradually becomes able to give selfless loving attention to Bruno and, in a sense, shares his death.

For Phillips, the novel's message is that death can teach the living that love encompasses and even transcends death. Bruno begins as a guilt-ridden, lonely man who, much like the spiders he studies, lurks in the labyrinth of the self. As he faces his death, he slowly understands that his concerns are futile and that his wife forgave him at the moment of her death. Phillips sees the progress of Adelaide and Will as Murdoch's ironic pandering to readers' desires for patterned endings.

Punja, Prem Parkash. *The Novels of Iris Murdoch: A Critical Study*. Jalandar, India: ABS Publications, 1993.

In Chapter 5, Punja discusses Lisa as the center of the love relationships in this novel.

Rabinovitz, Rubin. "Iris Murdoch." In *Six Contemporary British Novelists*, edited by George Stade. New York: Columbia University Press, 1976.

Most of this novel's characters project their fantasies on their lovers and are ultimately disappointed. The dying Bruno serves them as a *memento mori* and a litmus test of compassion. One character who seems compassionate at first is Nigel, but it becomes clear that all he wants is power. Miraculously at the end, Nigel is reformed; miraculously too, most other characters are changed and are happy. Rabinovitz thinks that these changes are not believable.

Sizemore, Christine Wick. *A Female Vision of the City: London in the Novels of Five British Women.* Knoxville: University of Tennessee Press, 1989.
Murdoch sees London as a labyrinth. This early novel is Dickensian in its affection for London, yet it is not sentimental. The dangerous labyrinth is redeemed by Diane's love for Bruno. The benign vision of London life is symbolized by the towers of the Lots Road power station; although they are ugly, they provide light and protection.

Spear, Hilda D. *Iris Murdoch.* New York: St. Martin's Press, 1995.
In Chapter 4, Spear groups this novel with five others in which Murdoch, echoing moral essays she was writing at the time, contrasts good people with evil ones. Will and Nigel are sometimes evil, though Nigel also stands for selfless love and performs more and more good acts. The heart of the novel is Bruno's dream, his self-centered memories and the many people who have done evil to him. As he dreams of his pointless life, he worries that soon he will be no more than a dream. The convolutions of the loves of the novel's other characters lead to Diana's caring for Bruno. His approaching death enables her to accept death and to realize that love has existed.

Thomson, P. W. "Iris Murdoch's Honest Puppetry." *Critical Quarterly* [Manchester, U.K.] 11 (Autumn, 1969): 277-283.
Critics misunderstand this novel because when they try to read it as realism, they find characters who lack credible psychological dimensions. But the novel depends on ritual and myth. For example, Nigel is not intended to be psychologically believable. He is an angel of Love and Death; he alters people's attitudes and interprets Bruno's dream. The pattern of what happens to Bruno and the other widowers (Miles and Danby) is significant: they rediscover something they lost. In short, the events of this novel are extravagant and not probable from a realistic point of view, but they support the novel's essential pattern.

Todd, Richard. *Iris Murdoch: The Shakespearean Interest.* New York: Barnes & Noble Books, 1979.
In Chapter 3, Todd discusses this novel with relation to Murdoch's attempt to rival Shakespeare in presenting death with a consolation that is not false. At one point, Murdoch seems to admit that it cannot be done. Yet Bruno's death is artistically satisfying without giving any false consolation. As he dies, not only does he realize his life cannot be redeemed, but he realizes that his dead wife Janie must have known the same thing. Therefore, she must have forgiven him, not cursed him. Bruno, like Lear, dies in joy.

_____. *Iris Murdoch.* London: Methuen, 1984.
In very brief comments in Chapter 4, Todd discusses critical opinion. He thinks Murdoch has patterned this novel too rigidly.

A Fairly Honorable Defeat, 1970.

Baldanza, Frank. *Iris Murdoch.* New York: Twayne, 1974.
In Chapter 12, Baldanza treats this novel briefly (and unsatisfactorily) as an example of a group of long, somewhat disorganized novels in which Murdoch draws upon earlier devices. Julius is in the tradition of powerful, satanic, manipulative characters. Tallis Browne is the saint. The novel's good people seem like puppets as Julius manipulates and destroys them. Leonard represents an extreme of cynicism. The only stable relationship turns out to be a homosexual one. Baldanza thinks that Murdoch's melodramatic plots strain the reader's credulity.

Bigsby, Christopher. "Interview with Iris Murdoch." In *The Radical Imagination and the Liberal Tradition: Interviews with English and American Novelists*, edited by Christopher Bigsby and Heide Ziegler. London: Junction Books, 1982.
Murdoch calls Tallis her only saint. Julius is the devil in person.

Bove, Cheryl K. "Americas and Americans in Iris Murdoch's Novels." In *Encounters with Iris Murdoch*, edited by Richard Todd. Amsterdam: Free University Press, 1988.

In Murdoch's novels, the United States is regularly associated with violent forces and evil people. In this novel, Julius's nerve gas research is subsidized at an American college.

_____. *Understanding Iris Murdoch*. Columbia: University of South Carolina Press, 1993.
In Chapter 4, Bove discusses how this novel's allegory is communicated through fully realized characters. Tallis is Christlike, but also human in his muddle. Julius is satanic, but he has understandable human motivations. Morgan shows the dark side of the soul. In Simon and Alex, Murdoch wanted to show a happy homosexual couple.

Brans, Jo. *Listen to the Voices: Conversations with Contemporary Writers*. Dallas: Southern Methodist University Press, 1988.
In an interview titled "Virtuous Dogs and a Unicorn," Murdoch defends Tallis's dirty kitchen in *A Fairly Honorable Defeat*. Tallis is Christlike; it takes the devilish Julius to clean it up. In the character of Julius, the reader sees that the devil can suffer and that the devil does not recognize Christ immediately.

Burling, Valerie. "*A Fairly Honorable Defeat*: Jeux Formels. In *Rencontres avec Iris Murdoch*. Caen, France: Centre de Recherches de Littérature et Linguistique des Pays de Langue Anglaise de l'Université de Caen, 1978. [In French.]
The novel is a series of formal variations on the theme of love. Julius, like Shakespeare's Prospero, casts a spell over Rupert and Morgan, thinking he can later dissolve the enchantment. But matters get out of control, with tragic consequences. The real dramatist is offstage: Murdoch herself.

Byatt, A. S. *Iris Murdoch*. Harlow, Essex, England: Longman Group, 1976.
Byatt's favorite among Murdoch's later novels. It makes both the reader and its characters pay attention to what other people are like. Good examples of characters who do this are Simon and Alex.

Conradi, Peter. *Iris Murdoch: The Saint and the Artist*. New York: St. Martin's Press, 1986. Chapter 7 is reprinted in *Critical Essays on Iris Murdoch*, edited by Lindsey Tucker. New York: G. K. Hall, 1992.

In Chapter 5, Conradi notes that Morgan experiences both the positive and negative sublimes in quick succession. In Chapter 7, the novel is analyzed in detail as the first of Murdoch's mature works. Evil and Good are sharply contrasted, and evil inflicts the defeat noted in the book's title. Julius is the Satanic character, and he destroys the Foster marriage to prove a generalization: depending on their own needs, people will attach themselves to almost anyone. Metaphors of machines and puppets underline Julius's theories, as do visions of the negative sublime by such characters as Leonard and Morgan.

Nevertheless, the novel qualifies these ideas in several ways. There are good characters. Tallis is a type of Christ or holy fool who acts out his goodness and love. Murdoch also dramatizes the suffering that betrayal costs characters like Simon and Hilda. In short, Conradi stresses that not only does the novel have its mythic organization (Julius and Tallis seem conscious of their mythic status), but also that its characters are fully developed individuals.

Conradi also stresses the significance of the novel's division. In Book I, the Foster home is a center of happiness, parties, and rituals, though ominously broken at times. Book II shows the acting out of Julius's wager: the destruction of the Foster marriage (and other things) and the dispersal of guests. In the background are many immersions and drownings as well as parallels with Shakespeare's plays (especially *Much Ado About Nothing* and *Cymbeline*) and operas (especially Mozart's). Murdoch ends the story like a Victorian novelist by distributing appropriate fates: Julian is in Paris attending an opera which demonstrates the triumph of evil.

Dipple, Elizabeth. *Iris Murdoch: Work for the Spirit*. London: Metheun, 1982.

In Chapter 2, Dipple says Tallis is almost a saint. In the novel's allegorical scheme, Tallis is Christ who opposes Julius's Satan. (Tallis's father is an embittered God, and his dead sister the Holy Spirit.) Yet because the real Tallis's ineffectual character does not fully support its allegorical mission, readers sense that Murdoch is showing real human unmythological good as comparatively weak.

Tallis acts with understanding and self-knowledge, but without theorizing.

In Chapter 3, Dipple calls Julius an evil artist: self-indulgent, charismatic, demonic, manipulative. She discusses Simon and Axel with relation to the myth of Apollo and Marsyas. In Chapter 6, Dipple provides an extended comparison of Julius and Tallis. The defeat of Rupert, a moderately good man, seems "fairly honorable" to both of them, but in different ways. Peter is a destructive adolescent. Morgan can sense the good but is hopelessly greedy and egotistic. Axel criticizes Rupert's Platonic theories and describes the impermanence of love. Only Simon has doubts about Julius; he seems weak but shows real strength and is rewarded. Dipple identifies and analyzes many symbols: the hedgehog, dead birds, puppets, and drowning.

Dollimore, Jonathan. "The Challenge of Sexuality." In *Society and Literature, 1945-1970*. New York: Holmes & Meier, 1983.
In his survey of attitudes toward sex since World War II, Dollimore notes Murdoch's treatment of homosexuality in *A Fairly Honorable Defeat*. A homosexual couple's love stands the test of time, whereas a bourgeois marriage does not. But Dollimore thinks homosexuality is irrelevant; it is simply love that gives Simon and Axel their strength.

Fletcher, John. "Iris Murdoch, Novelist of London." *International Fiction Review* 17 (Winter, 1990): 9-13.
Many of the locations in this novel are real places in Kensington, Mayfair, and Notting Hill.

_____. "Rough Magic and Moral Toughness: Iris Murdoch's Fictional Universe." In *The British and Irish Novel Since 1960*, edited by James Acheson. New York: St. Martin's Press, 1991.
Fletcher uses Murdoch's terms to label Rupert as a "nice" man trying to be a "good" one. Morgan is neither nice nor good, but an egocentric fantasist. Tallis is legitimately good, but can achieve only small successes. Julius is really evil, but he wins the reader's respect for his suffering and his moral toughness.

Gordon, David J. *Iris Murdoch's Fables of Unselfing*. Columbia: University of Missouri Press, 1995.

In Chapter 1, Gordon cites Tallis as a man to whom freedom is
obedience. In Chapter 3, Rupert is identified as one of a number
of Murdoch characters who try to take on a role which they cannot
sustain. Because he is a Platonist, Murdoch has him humiliated
and killed. Juilus, the power figure, is an artist-figure as well. In
Chapter 6, Gordon praises this novel as showing an integration of
realistic story and characters with symbolic myth. Gordon notes
how Morgan, torn between husband and lover, has a vision of innocent love with Peter. Yet finally her actions are incoherent and
less credible than Murdoch would have wished. Rupert is often
brilliant as a pseudo-Platonist; the homosexual marriage of Alex
and Simon is well done.

Griffin, Gabriele. *The Influence of the Writings of Simone Weil on the
Fiction of Iris Murdoch*.   San Francisco: Mellen Research
University Press, 1993.
Griffin refers to this novel several times. In Gothic tales, women
are often imprisoned; Simon is the only man imprisoned in a
Murdoch novel. This novel makes the usual distinction between
selfish and selfless characters, but Griffin notes that the selfless
character (Tallis) is male and that one of the selfish characters
(Morgan) is female.

Hoskins, Robert. "Iris Murdoch's Midsummer Nightmare." *Twentieth
Century Literature* 18 (July, 1972): 191-198.
Murdoch shows Shakespeare's influence, not only in making
many allusions to his plays, but also in incorporating extended
parallels.   Hoskins demonstrates his thesis by comparing this
novel to *A Midsummer Night's Dream*. Although many comparisons are not exact, the rough parallels are: Rupert and Hilda are
Theseus and Hippolyta; Julius combines Oberon and Puck, while
Morgan is Titania; Alex and Simon are like the lovers, and at
times so are Morgan, Rupert, and Hilda. Rupert, who is asinine
like Bottom in his pretensions to virtue, is also the Bottom who
sleeps in Titania's (Morgan's) arms; unlike Bottom, he awakens to
a nightmare. Although the tragedy of Pyramus and Thisbe is
played for laughs in Shakespeare, its tragic side shows in the fate
of Rupert (Bottom/Pyramus). Rupert's self-centered theorizings
are defeated, but Murdoch does not want readers to think that
Julius's cynicism is an acceptable alternative.

Kennard, Jean E. "Iris Murdoch: The Revelation of Reality." In *Number and Nightmare: Forms of Fantasy in Contemporary Fiction.* Hamden, Conn.: Archon Books, 1975.

In her novels, Murdoch often uses characters like Julius who come from Eastern Europe to suggest knowledge of primitive and instinctive humanity. Characters like Rupert who construct theories are seen as fools. Julius is at the center of a web of fantasy and secrecy until Simon breaks free by pushing him into the swimming pool. Hilda's wrestling with the telephone provides this novel's "technical scene," a passage whose detail is so precise as to make readers realize how remarkable is the world.

Mettler, Darlene D. *Sound and Sense: Musical Allusion and Imagery in the Novels of Iris Murdoch.* New York: Peter Lang, 1991.

Many operas are mentioned in this novel, and some offer revealing parallels. Julius resembles the title character of Mozart's *Don Giovanni,* and he probably enjoys the evil power displayed in Monteverdi's *L'Incoronozione di Poppea.* The song Simon hums from Mozart's *The Marriage of Figaro* suggest his effeminacy. Both Morgan here and Leonore in Beethoven's *Fidelio* dress in men's clothes, but for opposite reasons.

Packer, P. A. "The Theme of Love in the Novels of Iris Murdoch." *Durham University Journal* 38 (1977): 217-224.

Packer praises Murdoch's rendering the complexities of many varieties of love, especially that of Simon and Alex. Simon brings about change by his loving and daring. Packer calls this one of Murdoch's fullest explorations of a love relationship.

Phillips, Diana. *Agencies of the Good in the Work of Iris Murdoch.* Frankfurt: Peter Lang, 1991.

Chapter 6 is an expansion of Phillips's paper in *Encounters with Iris Murdoch,* and has the same title. Julius the demonic and Tallis the Christlike contend for the human soul, as symbolized by Morgan. Murdoch not only presents these characters as symbols but also gives them histories to make them believable as a human beings. Julius had been at Belsen. Tallis's sister had been raped and murdered. Morgan, who lives in a series of delusions and is the cause of pain to many, is granted a moment of revelation, one she cannot translate into everyday life. Phillips pairs the two brothers Rupert and Simon, two moderately good men. But Rupert is destroyed by his inadequacies, and Simon is saved because he is capable of selfless love. Phillips concludes with a discussion of this novel's versions of Murdoch's typical device: a trial by water.

_____. "The Complementarity of Good and Evil in *A Fairly Honorable Defeat*." In *Encounters with Iris Murdoch*, edited by Richard Todd. Amsterdam: Free University Press, 1988.
In her paper, Phillips says that this novel embodies the struggle between good and evil in the characters of the Tallis and Julius. Tallis is pushes a cart through the street as Christ carried the cross to Calvary. Julius is demonic in his ability to enslave and manipulate. But neither are simply symbols; both are motivated and human. Julius's plot to demonstrate humanity's self-centeredness is at the center of the novel. Rupert is an easy victim, for his Platonic theory is shallow and his goodness is not humble. Phillips analyzes Chapter 21, in which Julius cleans Tallis's kitchen, at some length. In it, the encounter between Julius and Tallis becomes one between evil and good. Much seems to remain unspoken; the devilish Julius seems to want a sign of forgiveness. At the end, Julius seems to have won. But Tallis exists, and the much-patronized Simon has resisted Julius and found love with Alex. Phillips does not think the ending is depressing.
After the paper, Murdoch commented that although Julius is the devil, Tallis is not Christ but a very good, spiritual being. Julius does not recognize this until the kitchen scene. They then show the sympathy of two spiritual beings in a human environment. To continue the allegory, Leonard can be seen as a decrepit God the Father, one appropriate to an age when the belief in a personal God has faded. Such allegorical readings are justified, as well as more realistic readings. Murdoch thinks that perhaps Morgan is not a successful character; she should have been odder. Julius is both a supernatural force and a pitiable human, like Jesse Baltram in *The Good Apprentice*. Murdoch thinks that young writers need not be experimental; the traditional novel still lives.

Punja, Prem Parkash. *The Novels of Iris Murdoch: A Critical Study*. Jalandar, India: ABS Publications, 1993.

In Chapter 4, Punja sees Rupert as a man whose ego causes him to fail to be good. Tallis is weakly good, a shabby and unappreciated person who saves another's life in a restaurant. In him, Murdoch tries to present a good man without any Miltonic mythology. In Chapter 5, Punja says this novel presents are particularly cynical view of human love as Julius corrupts Rupert and Hilda. Julius cannot touch the love of Axel and Simon.

Rabinovitz, Rubin. "Iris Murdoch." In *Six Contemporary British Novelists*, edited by George Stade. New York: Columbia University Press, 1976.

Julius is a survivor of Belsen, whose evil began the chain of evil (on the Até principle) that makes him a Satanic destroyer. In opposition, Rupert fails; his Platonism is flawed by its lack of metaphysics. Tallis is a good man who does good work; he is both a holy fool and a Job figure. In the end, when Tallis is still unhappy and Julius is unrepentant, the best the reader can conclude is that there is no easy victory for goodness. Some readers will be indignant. The novel is flawed by too many sudden turns of plot and by Murdoch's reliance on such melodramatic devices as stolen letters and broken telephones.

Ramanathan, Suguna. *Iris Murdoch: Figures of Good*. London: Macmillan, 1990.

In her introduction, Ramanathan uses this novel to illustrate Murdoch's ideas of the Good. Tallis is the figure of Good here. In his discussion with Rupert, Julius makes a strong attack on goodness, an attack which cannot be answered on his terms. Julius does not recognize the selfless love that is not based on need or power.

Spear, Hilda D. *Iris Murdoch*. New York: St. Martin's Press, 1995.

In Chapter 4, Spear groups this novel with five others in which Murdoch contrasts ineffective good people with the true demonic evil that proceeds from independent, lonely, rational existential man. Tallis is the principal good character: Christlike, but confused and easily bettered. Rupert too is not a fit defender of the good. Julius is the satanic, self-centered, powerful, manipulative, and ultimately triumphal figure of evil. Spear describes the novel's atmosphere (the oppressive heat of summer) and notes many Shakespearean parallels. The happy ending of the Alex/ Simon subplot strikes an uncharacteristic note.

Stevenson, Randall. *The British Novel Since the Thirties.* Athens: University of Georgia Press, 1986.
Stevenson notes that even though Julius argues that novelists can never create interesting and successful good characters, Murdoch's creation of Tallis refutes this claim.

Swinden, Patrick. *Unofficial Selves.* New York: Barnes & Noble Books, 1973.
In Chapter 7, Swinden says that each character in this novel sees herself or himself as the central character in a drama with Shakespearean patterns and sees other people as taking minor roles. Julius, a watcher of others, understands this and thinks that behind the fantasies of language and the maneuvers of life there is really nothing of meaning, that people can move in and out of roles easily, breaking any relationship. He is also a plotter; he treats human beings a puppets. Rupert, a systematizer of ideas, disagrees, and so does Morgan, a structuralist. But even though Julius seems to win in the end, his ideas do not. Julius does not understand that relationships like marriages have reality. Rupert was right about the Good, though he did not embody it. Tallis does embody good, and Julius is powerless against him.

Todd, Richard. *Iris Murdoch.* London: Methuen, 1984.
In brief comments in Chapter 4, Todd notes that this novel has many Shakespearean analogues. The diabolical enchanter figure, Julius, attempts to order reality and does succeed in destroying the Foster marriage. By showing Julius's psychosomatic disorders, Murdoch dramatizes the price that enchanters pay. In contrast, the Christlike Tallis lives with messiness. In Simon and Alex, Murdoch shows a relationship, in this case a homosexual one, that Julius cannot destroy.

_____. *Iris Murdoch: The Shakespearean Interest.* New York: Barnes & Noble Books, 1979.
In Chapter 2, Todd sees *Othello* in some of this novel's patterns: Julius as Iago, both Rupert and Axel as Othello. In Chapter 4, Todd feels that Murdoch validates the conventional comic ending

by the convincing and successful love of Axel and Simon. In Chapter 5, Todd sees parallels between Shakespearean power figures and Julius. Most characters are betrayed by laziness or vanity into defeat. Simon shows his strength when he pushes Julius into the pool; Tallis is strong, but cannot help himself.

Turner, Jack. *Murdoch vs. Freud: A Freudian Look at an Anti-Freudian.* New York: Peter Lang, 1993.
In Chapter 5 of this attack on Murdoch, Turner says that this novel vindicates Freud's ideas. Julius is pure id, and the reader enjoys his triumphs. He resembles Murdoch in that both enjoy manipulating people. Murdoch's own oedipal fantasies appear. She needs the novel's comedy and its references to religion to avoid the tragedy of the truth.

Watrin, Jany. "Iris Murdoch's *A Fairly Honorable Defeat.*" *Revue des Langues Vivantes* 38, No. 1 (1972): 46-64.
Watrin reviews the characters of this novel one by one to show how each is motivated by egotism and vanity and how each tries to impose his or her pattern on the world. Because the world is messy, they are all doomed to defeat. These defeats are honorable, however, because the characters fulfill themselves. The one exception to this generalization is Tallis. He can see reality; he can see other people as they are and accept them; he can act and love. As usual, some of Murdoch's philosophical digressions detract from the narrative. But this novel blends formal symbols with its naturalistic story very well. Such symbols include animals (the hedgehog symbolizes Rupert's blindness to reality), rooms as traps, and water that suggests unpredictability. Morgan sees herself as an eagle, but she is more like a pigeon in the Underground.

Widmer, Kingsley. "The Wages of Intellectuality . . . and the Fictional Wages of Iris Murdoch." In *Twentieth Century Women Novelists*, edited by Thomas F. Staley. Totowa, N.J.: Barnes & Noble Books, 1982.
Morgan is a parody of a romantic moralist. Rupert is killed by his moral pretensions. The novel seems false and confused because it gives the satanic Julius the best arguments.

An Accidental Man, 1971.

Baldanza, Frank. *Iris Murdoch*. New York: Twayne, 1974.
> In Chapter 12, Baldanza treats this novel briefly. Murdoch here employs some new devices. Letters to and from many marginal characters add a note of farce. The events of this novel are precipitated, not by the usual powerful manipulator, but by accident. The accidental man himself is the failure, Austin. The central theme is that of the Good Samaritan. Matthew and Garth are both tormented because they have both witnessed incidents in which they have not come to another person's aid. Even though Ludwig has been convinced by the shallow Gracie not to help is fellow creatures, he too feels guilt when he thinks he may have caused Dorina's death. Even so, *An Accidental Man* is one of a group of long, somewhat disorganized novels in which the author draws mainly upon earlier devices.

Bove, Cheryl K. *Understanding Iris Murdoch*. Columbia: University of South Carolina Press, 1993.
> In Chapter 7, Bove discusses this novel briefly. She concentrates on Austin, Matthew, Garth, and Ludwig. In their immaturity, many characters resemble Peter Pan, and one of them comes upon that figure's statue in Kensington Gardens.

Conradi, Peter. *Iris Murdoch: The Saint and the Artist*. New York: St. Martin's Press, 1986.
> In Chapter 3, Conradi briefly evokes the cast of comic and pitiful characters. He contrasts the novel's Good Samaritans to one object of their charity: Austin, a man who has brought bad luck on himself by his own will.

Dipple, Elizabeth. *Iris Murdoch: Work for the Spirit*. London: Metheun, 1982.
> In Chapter 3, Dipple cites Dorina's speech before her death as showing how characters yearn for the Christian God in a Godless age. In Chapter 7, Dipple analyzes this novel at length. It has the largest number of characters of any Murdoch novel up to its time; Murdoch here creates several large party scenes and uses batches of letters extensively. All of these mediocre characters yearn for ideals, many of which have roots in childhood traumas. The

novel seems to say that all yearnings of this sort will fail. The spiritually unfocused Dorina yearns for a spiritual haven, but dies. Matthew, a failed Buddhist, wants to save his brother Austin; Dipple calls him a mediocre artist who is wrong to try to impose his own design. Garth has been shocked into realism, but is corrupted by literary success. Austin is the one demonic character: selfish, self-pitying, and destructive; his fantasies are childish. Dipple says that Murdoch's judgment is severe: the futile acts of these mediocre people are set against the backdrop of a futile war.

Gordon, David J. *Iris Murdoch's Fables of Unselfing.* Columbia: University of Missouri Press, 1995.

In Chapter 1, Gordon cites Matthew as a kind of Murdoch character who wishes to set people free; such characters are only pseudo-healers. In Chapter 3, Matthew is also identified as the kind of person who adopts a role he cannot sustain, and is therefore chastised. In Chapter 4, Gordon discusses in detail this novel's attempt to represent contingency. In Chapter 6, Gordon praises the scene rendered wholly in unattributed dialogue. Murdoch scorns Austin as a man whose vanity leads him to selfish suffering. After Dorina's death, he becomes less self-centered.

Hague, Angela. *Iris Murdoch's Comic Vision.* Cranbury, N.J.: Associated University Presses, 1984. This chapter is reprinted in *Critical Essays on Iris Murdoch,* edited by Lindsey Tucker, New York: G. K. Hall, 1992.

In Chapter 3, Hague uses Northrop Frye's comic theory imaginatively and writes lucidly on how this novel is a comedy. When Murdoch emphasizes contingency and accident, she seems to struggle against any kind of form, even comic form. But all the accidents in this novel are integrated into a very complex comedy, one that mingles various tones and structures. In Frye's terms, both Austin and Ludwig are comic heroes, though of different sorts: Austin emerges victorious over his world, whereas Ludwig leaves it. Blocking figures include Gracie's father and the U. S. government, while Dorina is the novel's scapegoat. Its pervasive ironic tone is made possible by the apparent absence of any narrative judgment in the epistolary chapters and in many passages rendered by dialogue only. The ending has many elements Frye identifies as festive: marriages and pregnancies. But it is mainly ironic and dark. Ludwig remains in prison, and an unsatisfactory society is still in control.

Hardy, Barbara. *Tellers and Listeners: The Narrative Imagination.* London: Athlone Press, 1975.
In Chapter 4, Hardy says that Murdoch is in the tradition of Aldous Huxley in creating stylized, public talk in this novel. Her collective voice is not random but has a regular rhythm.

Heusel, Barbara. *Patterned Aimlessness: Iris Murdoch's Novels of the 1970s and 1980s.* Athens: University of Georgia Press, 1995.
In Chapter 5, Heusel provides a brilliant analysis of this "open" novel in light of Bakhtin's theories. *An Accidental Man* is truly dialogic. Its characters have separate voices and pursue their separate dramas incidental to the main thrust of the novel. Their multiple letters and stichomythic dialogues create a pattern, but it is a centerless pattern reported by a narrator who is on their level. Heusel discusses Murdoch's use of Shakespeare's *The Tempest* and T. S. Eliot's *The Waste Land.*

Jefferson, Douglas W. "Iris Murdoch and the Structures of Character." *Critical Quarterly* 26 (Winter, 1984): 47-58.
Most of Murdoch's characters develop machine-like from one basic obsession. Here Austin's egotistical self-pity is the result of a childhood event in which his hand was damaged.

Johnson, Deborah. *Iris Murdoch.* Bloomington: Indiana University Press, 1987.
In Chapter 3, Johnson says that this novel's fast-moving plot deflects attention from the very real female misery of Dorina and Charlotte. The allusions to Tennyson in describing Charlotte suggest that she is being "textualized"—that is, turned into a figure of myth.

Martindale, K. M. "Contingency and Goodness in Iris Murdoch's *An Accidental Man* and Wittgenstein's *Tractatus.*" *CEA Critic: An Official Journal of the College English Association* 42 (Winter-Summer, 1986-1987): 139-148.
Martindale discusses Murdoch's understanding of Wittgenstein's ideas about the separation of ethical decisions from the world of

facts and her disagreements with some of them. He finds that these ideas can illuminate some of the choices made by the two of the "accidental" men of this novel, Austin and Ludwig. They can illuminate some of the decisions made by Garth and Matthew as well.

Miles, Rosalind. *The Fiction of Sex: Themes and Functions of Sex Differences in the Modern Novel.* London: Vision Press, 1974.
In Chapter 5, Miles says the Mrs. Carberry is not successful as a portrait of a working-class woman. Murdoch's satire in this novel covers a wide range of characters; the author views her creations with a mixture of laughter and love.

Punja, Prem Parkash. *The Novels of Iris Murdoch: A Critical Study.* Jalandar, India: ABS Publications, 1993.
In Chapter 6, Punja discusses religion, morality, and politics in this novel. Both World War II and the Vietnam War influence the characters. In a world full of accidents, people act as if they could be in control; hence many characters blame themselves for Dorina's death or console themselves in other ways. Others have even shallower morals, as shown by their exchange of witty letters. Because he suffers from so many accidents, Austin represents every human being. Only Mrs. Carberry is traditionally religious, but both Dorina and Matthew are spiritual. Dorina longs to escape to a heaven, and Matthew once hoped to be accepted as a Buddhist.

Rabinovitz, Rubin. "Iris Murdoch." In *Six Contemporary British Novelists*, edited by George Stade. New York: Columbia University Press, 1976.
This novel presents only standard Murdoch characters and perfunctory analyses of ethical questions.

Scanlan, Margaret. "The Machinery of Pain: Romantic Suffering in Three Works of Iris Murdoch." *Renascence: Essays on Value in Literature* 29 (Winter, 1977): 69-85.
Scanlan sees this novel (and *The Sacred and Profane Love Machine*) as Murdoch's critique of standard Romantic notions about love and suffering. Here is a wide variety of suffering and a wide variety of moral choices. Murdoch's treatment of Austin's

suffering is convincing, as he progresses from a largely imaginary injury, through simple selfishness and the kind of suffering that inspires women's pity, to emerging as a destructive monster, blind to reality. Matthew and others show that contemplation of suffering does not make one a better person.

Murdoch fails with Ludwig. His suffering over his decision to return to the United States does not convince for two reasons. Readers are simply told about (and not shown) his realization that he must return home; Gracie, who seems to symbolize the pleasure principle, becomes so distasteful that Ludwig's departure cannot represent renouncing a great love. Scanlan thinks that *The Sacred and Profane Love Machine* renders these problems more fully, but she complains that neither novel provides a positive model of ways to transcend the problems it dramatizes.

Spear, Hilda D. *Iris Murdoch*. New York: St. Martin's Press, 1995.
In Chapter 4, Spear makes a very brief comment in which she groups this novel with others in which Murdoch contrasts the goodness of ineffective people to the demonic evil that proceeds from existential man. When Murdoch uses so many letters for the first time, she links this work with the novels of the past.

Todd, Richard. *Iris Murdoch*. London: Methuen, 1984.
In brief comments in Chapter 4, Todd notes that accidents and contingency play larger than usual roles in this novel. A failure to intervene can function much like an accident. Todd also notes Murdoch's innovations, such as the groups of comic letters which appear from time to time. When one of these letters reports a death which could have been rendered tragically, Todd thinks that Murdoch says that life is comic and absurd, not tragic. Todd also notes that this novel also explores the moral issues connected to the Vietnam War.

_____. *Iris Murdoch: The Shakespearean Interest*. New York: Barnes & Noble Books, 1979.
In Chapter 3, Todd discusses this novel as another attempt by Murdoch to rival Shakespeare in presenting death with a consolation that is not false. The point of the novel is its accidents; it gains form by its repetition of patterns. This patterning is what gives the novel coherence without offering consolation.

The Black Prince, 1973.

Arnold, David Scott. *Liminal Readings: Forms of Otherness in Melville, Joyce and Murdoch*. New York: St. Martin's Press, 1993.
Chapter 5, which deals primarily with *A Severed Head*, has an excellent analysis of this novel's point of view. Bradley, like Martin Lynch-Gibbon, is an unlikable, egotistic male first-person narrator who moves toward freedom through making risky commitments to love. Both offer naïve narration mixed with some autobiographical retrospection. Unlike Martin, Bradley tries to explain his method before he begins.

Baldanza, Frank. *Iris Murdoch*. New York: Twayne, 1974.
In Chapter 12, Baldanza treats this novel briefly (and unsatisfactorily) as an example of a group of long, somewhat disorganized novels in which Murdoch draws upon earlier devices. His best discussion is of Bradley's love and its consequences for his art. Baldanza thinks that Bradley's storytelling method of moment-to-moment narration is a departure for the conservative Murdoch. By including the forewords and afterwords, she shows her discomfort with this method. Baldanza makes brief suggestions about how the various works of art mentioned in the novel (especially *Hamlet*) relate to the central story.

Bigsby, Christopher. "Interview with Iris Murdoch." In *The Radical Imagination and the Liberal Tradition: Interviews with English and American Novelists*, edited by Christopher Bigsby and Heide Ziegler. London: Junction Books, 1982.
Murdoch says that a good novelist maintains authority even when her characters are free. Here, the reader knows when to believe Bradley and when not. The postscripts are simply playful.

————. "The Uneasy Middleground of British Fiction." *Granta* 3 (1980): 137-149.
This novel looks experimental, but Murdoch is playing with experiment. In Bigsby's interview with her, Murdoch resisted a postmodern reading.

Biles, Jack I. "An Interview with Iris Murdoch." *Studies in the Literary Imagination* 11 (Fall, 1978): 115-125. Reprinted in *British Novelists Since 1900.* New York: AMS Press, 1987.
Some of Bradley's opinions about *Hamlet* are accurate, but some are crazy. Murdoch seems to say that the effect of the appendices is to convince the reader there is no way to be sure what really happened.

Bove, Cheryl K. *Understanding Iris Murdoch.* Columbia: University of South Carolina Press, 1993.
In Chapter 4, Bove discusses Loxias, Apollo, and Titian's painting. In Murdoch's terms, Bradley is a crystalline author, Arnold a journalistic one. Bove focuses on Bradley's failings: he is naïve and self-centered; he fails to understand Rachel and to honor his pledge of love to her; he is responsible for his sister's suicide. Eventually, he loses his illusions.

Brooks-Davies, Douglas. *Fielding, Dickens, Gosse, Iris Murdoch, and Oedipal* Hamlet. New York: St. Martin's Press, 1989.
The author uses the perspective of psychoanalysis to probe the character of Bradley and the underlying meaning of this novel. Bradley and Apollo represent the male mind, which for millennia has denigrated women. Bradley finds women frail and silly. He fantasizes a male-centered theory of creation by which sex with Julian brings him closer to the Black Eros god, but this intercourse is really a rape. He had a chance to break out of his male pattern of hatred, but he failed. At the end, he is not enlightened; he is a failure. The other voice in the novel is Murdoch, the female creator. The novel is a woman's revenge for oppression and suppression of the feminine, and Bradley is the scapegoat. Murdoch discloses, even through a male narrator, the mystery of the woman as artist. The Apollo-Marsyas myth is told from a male perspective; Marsyas's song is really that of female freedom and creativity.

Byatt, A. S. *Degrees of Freedom: The Novels of Iris Murdoch.* Expanded ed. London: Vintage, 1994.
In Chapter 13, Byatt asks and then clarifies many questions she thinks the novel itself asks about Bradley's love for Julian and his (and Murdoch's) ideas about art. Bradley's own novel seems to be

an act to dominate and possess Julian, but at the end Bradley gives that up. Frances Marloe's name combines elements of two supposed authors of Shakespeare's plays. Byatt thinks he most resembles Mephistopheles in Christopher Marlowe's *Doctor Faustus*.

_____. *Iris Murdoch*. Harlow, Essex, England: Longman Group, 1976.
Byatt points out parallels with *Under the Net*.

_____. "People in Paper Houses: Attitudes to `Realism' and `Experiment' in English Postwar Fiction." In *The Contemporary English Novel*, edited by Malcolm Bradbury and David Palmer. New York: Holmes & Meier, 1980.
In her survey, Byatt treats Murdoch's *The Black Prince* at some length as an example of a novel concerned about truth-telling in fiction. In Murdoch's own terms, Arnold Baffin is a journalistic novelist, whereas Bradley thinks he is a crystalline one. But Bradley's own story is journalistic. In Bradley's description, Shakespeare combines both approaches to fiction.

Cohan, Steven. "From Subtext to Dream Text: The Brutal Egoism of Iris Murdoch's Male Narrators." *Women and Literature* 2 (1982): 222-242. Reprinted in *Men and Women*, edited by Janet Todd. New York: Holmes & Meier, 1981.
Like other of Murdoch's first-person male narrators, Bradley finds it difficult to understand other people. The postscripts not only show other people from their own perspectives, but demonstrate *their* egotistical self-centeredness.

Conradi, Peter. *Iris Murdoch: The Saint and the Artist*. New York: St. Martin's Press, 1986.
In Chapter 8, Conradi's excellent discussion focuses on the love theme in this novel (which he values very highly). Because the postscript writers' accounts are so consistent with the egotisms they display in Bradley's story, Conradi, like Murdoch herself, calls the postscripts a joke.
   At the heart of this analysis are the novel's many references to *Hamlet*, the most important of which is Bradley's analysis for Julian. (Conradi reassures confused readers that it *is* complex.)

Bradley begins with a Freudian interpretation echoing that of
Ernest Jones. It makes sense, as do Freudian interpretations of
many relationships in Murdoch's/Bradley's novel itself. Bradley
often warns the reader that commonplace Freudian explanations,
like those offered by the foolish Francis, are not to be taken as
truth; current Freudian clichés diminish reality. In fact, the
second part of Bradley's reading of *Hamlet* is Neoplatonic. The
Black Prince here is the Neoplatonic Dark Eros, the force behind
Marsyas as he risks and suffers flaying by Apollo in the myth.
(Conradi has reason to think these are Murdoch's own opinions.)

The novel contains many horrors to cause suffering, especially
to women betrayed in love, but it presents Bradley's flaying in
most detail. In fact, in Conradi's opinion, Murdoch's rendition of
Bradley experiencing love is unrivaled in literature. Even though
his love is ultimately an illusion, it is shown to have valuable
effects. As sexual love opens Bradley to the knowledge that
someone else (here, Julian) exists, so after he suffers from the
destruction of his love, Bradley can experience a deeper loss of
self. But although this change is real, it is cloistered. Bradley is
never tested in the world outside his prison. (Chapter 10 provides
a good discussion of this novel's point of view.)

_____. "Platonism in Iris Murdoch." In *Platonism and the
English Imagination*, edited by Anna Baldwin and Sarah Hutton.
New York: Cambridge University Press, 1994.
In this novel Murdoch employs Plato's conception of Eros in all its
ambiguity and power. Bradley is impelled by love into the contingent world. The Marsyas myth expresses his fate: Bradley is
flayed into truth. Murdoch seems to say that good art is all that
matters.

Dipple, Elizabeth. *Iris Murdoch: Work for the Spirit*. London:
Metheun, 1982.
In Chapter 3, Dipple discusses the artist in Murdoch's fiction.
Both Bradley and Arnold are bad artists, though in opposite ways.
Bradley reveals that he knows the difficulty of being a great artist
in his analysis of *Hamlet*: like Marsayas in the myth, Shakespeare
must suffer a loss of self. Through love, Bradley himself must
undergo this process.

In Chapter 4, Dipple expands on these ideas in a long and even more brilliant analysis of this novel, which she calls Murdoch's greatest through 1980. Dipple explains that Bradley narrates his story in two voices. His primary voice is of a man experiencing the events of the story and commenting on art. He is, in terms Murdoch derives from Plato, a mediocre artist. Although he is not a naïve weaver of fantasies like Arnold, his cynical reliance on purity masks his failure to write. His literary criticism is likewise self-serving. In life, his struggles to avoid involvement and to begin to write are comic, though he begins to sense a transformation is approaching. This transformation, he thinks, will come through the dark god Eros, though its actual occurrence through his love for Julian takes him by surprise. Though he is transformed by love, his human imperfections lead to his downfall and trial.

As Bradley tells his story in his primary voice, readers sense (and are often confused by) his secondary voice, one allied with Loxias/Apollo in his foreword, a voice that understands the ultimate truth of the story of Apollo and Marsyas, the necessity of suffering to attain wisdom and the Good. This is the Bradley who has been tried (flayed) and imprisoned, the man who is writing the story of his life. He occasionally interrupts his narrative to speak directly to the reader; usually he signals this direct speech by addressing his "dear friend" Apollo. The character of Bradley in the story sometimes understands what Bradley the author knows, notably in his remarks on *Hamlet*, but not usually. Dipple speculates on the multiple suggestions of the novel's title.

_____. "Iris Murdoch and Vladimir Nabokov: An Essay in Literary Realism and Experimentalism." In *The Practical Vision: Essays in English Literature in Honor of Flora Roy*, edited by Jane Campbell and James Doyle. Waterloo, Ontario: Wilfred Laurier University Press, 1978.
A brilliant article in which Dipple compares *The Black Prince* to Nabokov's *Lolita* in order to argue that both novels combine realistic and unrealistic elements in ways that comment on the function of art. Dipple notes the many similarities between the works: Both contain a romance between a young girl and an older man, and both frame the central story by other voices. Murdoch does not play games with language in a Nabokovian manner.

Dipple sees Bradley's remarks on *Hamlet* as central to Murdoch's ideas about art. Bradley's story, like that of the mythical Marsyas, shows him creating a work of art out of pain, a work that celebrates not only his love for Julian but also the horrors of Priscilla's life. Dipple thinks the postscripts by the four characters call Bradley's authority into question, but that they are resolved by P. Loxias's final word.

Fletcher, John. "Rough Magic and Moral Toughness: Iris Murdoch's Fictional Universe." In *The British and Irish Novel Since 1960*, edited by James Acheson. New York: St. Martin's Press, 1991.
In spite of this novel's complex ironies, Fletcher focuses on one fact: in her postscript Julian says she once loved Bradley. Her admission proves that Bradley is telling the truth and Rachel is a liar.

Fogarty, Margaret E. "The Fiction of Iris Murdoch: Amalgam of Yeatsian and Joycean Motifs." In *Literary Interrelations: Ireland, England and the World II: Comparison and Impact*, edited by Wolfgang Zach and Heinz Kosok. Tübingen, Germany: Gunter Narr, 1987.
Murdoch's essential Irishness is suggested by parallels between this novel and Yeats's poetry. In both, there are references to silence and secrets, as well as to arrows and similar implements. The novel's balloons and kites recall Yeats's "The Balloon of the Mind." Not convincing.

Gordon, David J. *Iris Murdoch's Fables of Unselfing*. Columbia: University of Missouri Press, 1995.
In Chapter 2, Gordon discusses how eros can lead to the Good. The heart of the novel is Bradley's love for Julian; Loxias validates Bradley's perspective. In Chapter 3, Gordon discusses Bradley's first-person narration, which purports to be both a vision and reportage.

Griffin, Gabriele. *The Influence of the Writings of Simone Weil on the Fiction of Iris Murdoch*. San Francisco: Mellen Research University Press, 1993.
In Chapter 5, Griffin provides an uncharacteristically narrow discussion of how Murdoch tries to demonstrate how Bradley's

consciousness works as it attempts to achieve the detachment necessary to see reality. According to Griffin, though Bradley believes in paying attention and knows that the ego distorts reality, he fails utterly by the standards of both Weil and Murdoch. He is self-centered; he has an aversion to life and its messy details; he will not see any woman as having a separate reality. He lacks self-knowledge; he is not an artist. Marloe is right when he says Bradley is homosexual.

Falling in love with Julian should encourage him to attend to reality; his progress in love resembles the progress of a religious experience. But it only makes him more self-centered; he feels like a God creating his beloved. He turns Julian into an abstraction. Toward the end of the novel, he invokes spurious gods created by his fantasies. Griffin says that in prison Bradley has some sort of mystical experience. She discusses Bradley's comments on *Hamlet* and the parallels between Murdoch's own career and those of both Bradley and Arnold. In other chapters, Griffin notes that Murdoch uses the ambiguities of this novel's multiple endings to undercut the reader's sense that life is tidy. Bradley's love for Julian is one more example in Murdoch's novels of someone expressing needs through love, but not seeing the reality of the beloved.

Hague, Angela. *Iris Murdoch's Comic Vision.* Cranbury, N.J.: Associated University Presses, 1984.

In Chapter 4, Hague elaborates upon Northrop Frye's ideas about comedy to illuminate this novel. Francis is the comic buffoon, while Arnold is both the *alazon* or impostor figure and the blocking father. Bradley combines the roles of *eiron*, buffoon, scapegoat, and comic hero. Bradley is an *eiron* in his detachment and continual mockery and self-mockery. Even the seriousness of Bradley's love is made comic by the glee and detachment with which he describes it. Murdoch plays with conventional concepts in that Bradley the young lover is ten years older than the father who blocks his desires. Although the novel ends with the lovers apart, Bradley still celebrates love in the story he writes. The authors of the postscripts reveal themselves to be foolish persons.

Heusel, Barbara. "Can We Tell the Good Art from the Bad? Iris
   Murdoch's *The Black Prince* and *The Sea, The Sea.*" *University
   of Dayton Review* 19 (Summer, 1988): 99-107.
   In this novel and in *The Sea, The Sea*, artist protagonists confront
   Murdoch's central contrast between bad art that uses its formal
   pattern to console and good art that shows life's contingency and
   does not console. In both cases, Murdoch mixes elements. In this
   novel, Bradley frames his report of contingent experiences with
   his consolatory postscript. The opposite is true in *The Sea, The
   Sea*. There, Charles has consolatory fantasies about re-creating
   his childhood dream, but they are framed by sections that recognize contingency and do not console.

_____. *Patterned Aimlessness: Iris Murdoch's Novels of the 1970s
   and 1980s*. Athens: University of Georgia Press, 1995.
   In Chapter 6, Heusel sees this novel not only as a successful
   experiment with the Bakhtinian carnivalesque, but as essentially
   postmodern. Bradley is seldom the mouthpiece for Murdoch's
   own views, especially when he talks about love. The postscripts
   are truly postmodern. They (especially Francis Marloe's reflections, which Heusel discusses at length) call into question everything Bradley has said. The reader is led to wonder if P. Loxias is
   simply a product of Bradley's imagination. In Chapter 8, Heusel
   discusses how central characters in four novels try to create
   patterns in the face of life's determinism. In *The Black Prince*,
   Bradley has structured his life as a civil servant, but knows he
   must escape his routines if he is to be an artist. Heusel also sees
   his struggle as attempting to break out of his egotism. With P.
   Loxias's help, Bradley finally realizes that artists create through
   suffering.

Johnson, Deborah. *Iris Murdoch*. Bloomington: Indiana University
   Press, 1987. Chapter 1 reprinted in *Critical Essays on Iris
   Murdoch*, edited by Lindsey Tucker. New York: G. K. Hall, 1992.
   In Chapter 1, Johnson explains how a female author undercuts
   Bradley's male oedipal quest by showing that it conflicts with
   Julian's own oedipal regard for her father. In Chapter 2, Johnson
   discusses at length the complex relation Murdoch has with this
   novel's male narrator. Sometimes she undercuts his assumptions
   to suggest the real horrors his language masks, and sometimes

she transgresses the usual boundaries of gender to partially reveal herself. In Chapter 5, Johnson contrasts Bradley's postscript (which is not conclusive) to Loxias's (which is very conclusive). In both cases, Murdoch does not provide a usual realistic ending.

Kenyon, Olga. *Women Novelists Today: A Survey of English Writing in the Seventies and Eighties*. New York: St. Martin's Press, 1988.

Kenyon focuses with indignation on two rejected women, Priscilla and Rachel, whose potential has been repressed by their husbands.

Lamarque, Peter. "Truth and Art in Iris Murdoch's *The Black Prince*." *Philosophy and Literature* 2 (Fall, 1978): 209-222.

An essay on how art conveys truth, using *The Black Prince* as an example. Lamarque is not concerned with simple true statements or with statements we accept as true within a fiction, but with a kind of truth art only can convey. This novel's first-person narrator adds to the problem: how can we tell when Murdoch is speaking through Bradley and when not? Bradley himself warns that what he says will not always be selfless. Lamarque thinks that, though readers tend to believe Bradley much of the time, they suspect Bradley's self-centered fantasies take over when he talks about his progress toward creating a great work of art. When Bradley falls for Julian, love at first makes him selfless and reliable, but soon desire and jealousy make him unreliable. As he falls in love, Bradley fails as an artist. The novel shows how difficult it is to be selfless. It also shows something about the particularity of great art when it documents the way one small act (like Bradley's kissing Rachel) can have many chains of consequences. Lamarque thinks that, although Bradley is not a very attractive character, we sympathize with his struggles. The attention that Murdoch demands of the reader is what all of us need in the real world.

Mettler, Darlene D. *Sound and Sense: Musical Allusion and Imagery in the Novels of Iris Murdoch*. New York: Peter Lang, 1991.

Most often, music suggests disorder to Bradley; he dislikes Igor Stravinsky's *Firebird* for that reason. The plot of the opera Bradley attends, Richard Strauss's *Der Rosenkavalier*, offers many parallels to his situation. While he is at the opera house, he comments on how powerfully such music affects him. At the end, Bradley escapes from disorder into captivity; in prison he enjoys the ordered music of Mozart.

Nussbaum, Martha C. "Love and Vision: Iris Murdoch on Eros and the Individual." In *Iris Murdoch and the Search for Human Goodness*, edited by Maria Antonaccio and William Schwelker. Chicago: University of Chicago Press, 1996.

Nussbaum contrasts Murdoch's allegiances to Dante's and Plato's concepts of the relation of sexual love to the Good. *The Black Prince* provides Murdoch's clearest example of Platonic love. The egotistic, envious, emotionally sterile Bradley is stripped of his anxieties by sexual passion, by his love for Julian. It gives him joy and leads to virtuous acts. For example, it is for Julian's sake that Bradley conceals the true facts of her mother's murdering her father. Bradley's Platonic love is imperfect: Julian complains he does not really see her, and their lovemaking seems impersonal. Julian's postscript echoes Dante when she says that erotic love can make only bad art. But she is repudiated at the end by Apollo himself. In some of Bradley's last thoughts about Julian, Nussbaum also finds traces of an Aristotelian love, which does not imply any ascent to the Good.

Orr, Christopher. "Iris Murdoch's Critique of Tragedy in *The Black Prince* and *A Word Child*." *The Bulletin of the West Virginia Association of College English Teachers* 4 (1977): 10-18.

Orr asks why Murdoch says absolute morality is better served by comedy than by tragedy. Orr looks at this novel and *A Word Child* from an Aristotelian perspective. *The Black Prince* fits Aristotle's definition of a tragedy, and readers experience something of a purgation at Bradley's rise and fall. Yet Bradley says his life is not tragic, and Murdoch subverts any tragic feelings by her postscripts. In contrast, although *A Word Child* has tragic ingredients, its reader experiences no catharsis. To Murdoch, imposing a tragic meaning on life is exaggerating the human place in the universe. Comedy gives a clearer picture.

Phillips, Diana. *Agencies of the Good in the Work of Iris Murdoch*. Frankfurt: Peter Lang, 1991.

In Chapter 7, Phillips discusses the relation of Bradley's and Arnold's ideas about art to Murdoch's own. She distinguishes between the Bradley who experiences the novel and the Bradley who writes about these experiences. One can argue that although Bradley colors his account, Loxias's postscript validates his account. But Phillips's main argument runs counter to her that of her earlier paper: The postscripts by the other characters make readers doubt him and, for that matter, Loxias. Perhaps Bradley did kill Arnold. Perhaps, rather than an account of a man who has been purified by love and art, Bradley is simply a mediocre writer and a failure as a man.

_____. "The Complementarity of Good and Evil in *A Fairly Honorable Defeat.*" In *Encounters with Iris Murdoch,* edited by Richard Todd. Amsterdam: Free University Press, 1988.
Murdoch makes very important comments on *The Black Prince* in an informal discussion of another novel. In creating a complicated frame for this novel, she does not try to mystify her readers by inspiring wildly different interpretations. Bradley Pearson mainly tells the truth. When he does not (as when he finds secret clues in Julian's messages), the reader can easily tell. She did not intend for readers to think Bradley killed Arnold. Because their short postscripts reveal each author's private reasons to distort their accounts, they do not invalidate Bradley's longer story. Julian's admission that she did love Bradley does validate Bradley's story, and readers should believe that.

Piper, William Bowman. "The Accommodation of the Present in Novels by Murdoch and Powell." *Studies in the Novel* 11 (Summer, 1979): 178-193.
This novel is a prime example of how Murdoch shows important events in a vivid present. It suffers from containing too many puzzles and from the obvious necessity of making Bradley too old for Julian.

Punja, Prem Parkash. *The Novels of Iris Murdoch: A Critical Study.* Jalandar, India: ABS Publications, 1993.
In Chapter 4, Punja says that Bradley treats his sister callously and that he has love-hate relationships with Christian, Arnold,

and Rachel. Bradley's great love is Julian; it transforms him. For Julian, it is an infatuation, and she realizes her mistake.

Rabinovitz, Rubin. "Iris Murdoch." In *Six Contemporary British Novelists*, edited by George Stade. New York: Columbia University Press, 1976.
A brief note. Murdoch's evocation of Bradley's psyche is good, and her passages about his love are moving. But she throws everything away by her twists of plot. When Arnold apologizes for writing so many novels, Rabinovitz thinks Murdoch is answering her critics.

Slaymaker, William E. "Myths, Mystery and the Mechanisms of Determinism: The Aesthetics of Freedom in Iris Murdoch's Fiction." *Papers on Language and Literature: A Journal for Scholars and Critics of Language and Literature* 18 (Spring, 1982): 166-180. Reprinted in *Critical Essays on Iris Murdoch*, edited by Lindsey Tucker. New York: G. K. Hall, 1992.
Characters in Murdoch's novels have even less freedom than that she defines in her philosophical works. Bradley and P. Loxias agree that human beings cannot help creating stories, myths, and fantasies. Bradley admits he has been propelled by energies and fantasies of love. His theories about *Hamlet* reflect his own obsessions. The postscripts show that his whole story is an exercise in fantasy.

Spear, Hilda D. *Iris Murdoch*. New York: St. Martin's Press, 1995.
In Chapter 5, Spear groups this novel with three others in which Murdoch makes her readers more conscious than before that a story is being told. These novels mix elements of thriller and mystery stories with a concern for the power of love to redeem or destroy. In discussing this novel, Spear speculates on the significance of the title and unconvincingly attempts to divide the action into three parts. She sees Rachel as triumphant, even though the reader does not believe her version of events. The center of the novel lies in Bradley's journey of self-discovery and the many discussions of the nature of art.

Stewart, Jack F. "Art and Love in Murdoch's *The Black Prince*." *Research Studies* 46 (June, 1978): 68-78.

A difficult and valuable discussion of Bradley's *Hamlet* tutorial and his postscript, in which Stewart claims Bradley synthesizes existential and Platonic ideas. Bradley's love moves him from the contingent world to the world of universals, yet Bradley is not deluded. In the end, Bradley has moved almost beyond the self and possesses a Shakespearean negative capability. He also learns that no one can possess another human soul.

Sturrock, June. "Good and the Gods of *The Black Prince*." *Mosaic: A Journal for the Comparative Study of Literature and Ideas* 10 (Summer, 1977): 133-141.

The idea of a dark god develops slowly through the story. At first it seems only a figure of speech, but in his discussion of *Hamlet* Bradley talks openly of a Black Eros that is connected to art as well as love. With Julian, the timid Bradley seems propelled by this Black Eros in works of art (Julian as Hamlet, *Der Rosenkavalier*) to make violent love. He knows that this love opens up the way to art, and he is also aware that the Black Eros is only the agent of a greater and unnamed God. But in the middle of the novel, Bradley's loving attention is focused upon Julian; he is blinded to Patricia's needs. Sturrock equates the unnamed God with the real name of the editor P. Loxias: Apollo Luxius, the Sun God, the God of Truth. It is only after he is imprisoned that Bradley can come close to Apollo. The novel's weakness is that because the illuminated Bradley is imprisoned, it cannot show how such a person might demonstrate his loving attitude toward real people. This is not the novel's only weakness: it has too much comedy, and it is ultimately too pessimistic. Even though this article comes to debatable conclusions, it makes many good points.

Todd, Richard. *Iris Murdoch*. London: Methuen, 1984.

In brief comments in Chapter 4 (based in part on his article "The Plausibility of *The Black Prince*") Todd says that Murdoch here approaches the postmodern novel. The editorial apparatus makes readers doubt the story at every turn. When readers note Bradley's footfetishism and his harsh sexual treatment of Julian, they may also wonder how much they can trust what he says. Bradley and Arnold are versions of Murdoch's usual contrast of pure saint and messy artist. Todd also remarks that if Loxias plays Apollo to Bradley's flayed Marsyas, Bradley may be said to flay Arnold.

_____. *Iris Murdoch: The Shakespearean Interest.* New York: Barnes & Noble Books, 1979.
In Chapter 2, Todd discusses how Bradley's ideas about *Hamlet* are probably close to Murdoch's own. To Bradley, *Hamlet* is the kind of work he admires, one that is both a masochistic revelation and a superb formal artistic achievement.

_____. "The Plausibility of *The Black Prince.*" *Dutch Quarterly Review of Anglo-American Letters* 8, no. 2 (1978): 82-93.
One of Bradley's problems is his footfetish. Fetishes in Murdoch are obsessions that interfere with clear attention to the real world and hence cloud judgment. For this and other reasons, Bradley must be considered an unreliable narrator. Todd goes into detail on the complexities of Bradley's reactions to Julian, which include more than his fetish. Bradley may be aware of his problem, but to Murdoch self-knowledge is not enough.

_____. "The Presence of Postmodernism in British Fiction: Aspects of Style and Selfhood." In *Approaching Postmodernism,* edited by Douwe Fokkema and Hans Bertens. Amsterdam: John Benjamins, 1986.
Todd calls Murdoch a postmodern writer. The editorial apparatus of *The Black Prince* challenges the main text, and Murdoch seems to refer to her own concerns as a novelist in the figure of Arnold Baffin and in Bradley's theories about *Hamlet.*

Wheeler, Michael. "The Limits of Hell: Lodge, Murdoch, Burgess, Golding." *Literature and Theology: An International Journal of Theory, Criticism, and Culture* 4 (March, 1990): 72-83.
People may not believe in a literal hell anymore, but many writers of recent times use the language of hell to describe experiences in the here and now. In *The Black Prince,* Bradley at first uses traditional sacred language to describe his love for Julian, but soon his words verge toward the demonic. The language of hell describes both physical desire and the loss of his love. After such suffering, it is easy for Bradley to embrace a kind of hell in his prison. In contrast to Sartre, who defined hell as other people,

Murdoch implies hell is the *absence* of other people, who hold forth the possibility of love.

Widmer, Kingsley. "The Wages of Intellectuality . . . and the Fictional Wages of Iris Murdoch." In *Twentieth Century Women Novelists*, edited by Thomas F. Staley. Totowa, N.J.: Barnes & Noble Books, 1982.
This novel resembles Nabokov's *Lolita* in its ironies. Its ugly world of destructive obsessions is without justice.

Wolfe, Peter. "'Malformed Treatise' and Prizewinner: Iris Murdoch's *The Black Prince*." *Studies in the Literary Imagination* 11 (Fall, 1978): 97-113. Reprinted in *British Novelists Since 1900*, edited by Jack I. Biles. New York: AMS Press, 1987.
Wolfe concentrates on Bradley's failings. He fails his relatives. He is wrong not to tell Julian of Priscilla's death. When she discovers his deception, she loses trust in him because he has not trusted her to give him comfort. Arnold's discovery of the pair is a just retribution. At the end, Bradley's self-defeating acts are suicidal. As a writer, he aimed at a cold and formal perfection. Now in his life he creates a satisfying tragic pattern with himself as martyr and saint. Wolfe finds such an act mean-spirited, an act born of self-contempt and contempt for others.

The Sacred and Profane Love Machine, 1974.

Allen, Brooke. "The Drawing-room Comedy of Iris Murdoch." *New Criterion* 15 (September, 1996): 66-73.
In the last part of this novel, Edgar becomes a mouthpiece for Murdoch's ideas.

Bove, Cheryl K. *Understanding Iris Murdoch*. Columbia: University of South Carolina Press, 1993.
In Chapter 7, Bove looks at this novel briefly. Although Harriet is saintlike and selfless, female power is also a theme. Bove finds the ending morally unsatisfying.

Conradi, Peter. *Iris Murdoch: The Saint and the Artist*. New York: St. Martin's Press, 1986.

In Chapter 9, Conradi comments that Monty's fictional creations, the fat Magnus and the thin Milo, represent his two *alter egos*. It is Blaise who divides himself between sacred and profane loves. Harriet, the sacred wife, lives for love alone. When objects to love are stripped from her, she dies; Murdoch has her killed by terrorists. Emily represents profane, probably masochistic love. Her son Luca first brings the sacred and profane worlds together, suggesting that to Murdoch both kinds of love are degrees of the same Eros. Conradi notes that most men in the novel are weak, dominated by their mothers. He also notes that the novel has many dreams and much haunting. The ending in which the virtuous Harriet is gunned down while the unpleasant Blaise and Emily are together provides a comment of notions of poetic justice.

_____. "Platonism in Iris Murdoch." In *Platonism and the English Imagination*, edited by Anna Baldwin and Sarah Hutton. New York: Cambridge University Press, 1994.
Murdoch thinks psychologists encourage self-centeredness. Blaise reduces experience to formulae.

Dipple, Elizabeth. *Iris Murdoch: Work for the Spirit*. London: Metheun, 1982.
In Chapter 7, Dipple analyzes this complex novel at length, including the many ways its title applies to the story. On the surface, the novel is about Blaise's sacred love for his wife Harriet and his profane love for his mistress Emily. As befitting his role as a psychologist, Blaise's version of profane love is exclusively sexual. In another sense, Blaise is essentially profane, whereas Monty, the novel's other central character, is allied with the sacred. Although he is an artist who may be capable of real creation, and although he is associated with dreams and psychic energies and phenomena, Monty fails each sacred test as he failed in his marriage. He continues his mediocre life, writing more mediocre novels.

The novel does have characters who are good. Harriet begins as a loving wife. As she is repeatedly betrayed, she constructs a succession of myths that will give her consolation. Her death allows her one last saintly act and functions as the horrible realization of the wishes of Blaise and Emily. Dipple analyzes several paintings and several myths that lie behind the action. The myth of Actaeon, his hounds, and Diana is particularly important, especially to explain the significance of Harriet's dogs. What hope there is left at the end of the novel resides in Edgar.

Ganner-Rauth, H. "Iris Murdoch and the Brontë Heritage." *Studies in English Literature* 58 (1981): 61-74.
Treats the influence of *Wuthering Heights* on this novel and on *The Unicorn*. The scene in which Harriet sees Luca from her bedroom window resembles two scenes in Emily Brontë's novel. There are many other resemblances. Luca is like a visitor from another world.

Gordon, David J. *Iris Murdoch's Fables of Unselfing*. Columbia: University of Missouri Press, 1995.
In Chapter 6, Gordon speculates that the motive for this novel was Murdoch's annoyance with psychoanalysis, for its promising beginning gives way to a coarser, more cynical tone. Harriet changes into a monster; her saving Luca is not so much admirable as grotesque.

Griffin, Gabriele. *The Influence of the Writings of Simone Weil on the Fiction of Iris Murdoch*. San Francisco: Mellen Research University Press, 1993.
Griffin refers to this novel several times. Blaise is a typical Murdoch character who begins by seeing the world only in terms of his own needs, but begins to learn that it has no real pattern and that other people exist. This novel also makes Murdoch's usual contrast of male selfishness and female selflessness.

Jefferson, Douglas W. "Iris Murdoch and the Structures of Character." *Critical Quarterly* 26 (Winter, 1984): 47-58.
Many Murdoch characters develop in a machinelike way from one basic impulse or obsession. Here, given Blaise's sexuality, his agony is inevitable: he is torn between his need for Harriet (his pure wife) and his desires for Emily. Because Harriet develops, she is a satisfying character; Emily is less so.

Lloyd, Genevieve. "Iris Murdoch on the Ethical Significance of Truth." *Philosophy and Literature* 6 (1982): 62-75.

Lloyd is mainly concerned with Murdoch's philosophical ideas about a transcendent Good and a unitary Truth. She turns to this novel to show how these ideas work out differently in fiction than they do in philosophy. Although it may seem that Blaise lives in two worlds, each of which embodies different truths, these truths are really false creations of his selfish mind. Harriet seems to embody selfless love until her love is revealed as a will to dominate. But Murdoch's ideals do not disappear; Edgar recommends humility to David. Lloyd wants to use the complications of her novels to refine Murdoch's philosophy.

Nussbaum, Martha C. "Love and Vision: Iris Murdoch on Eros and the Individual." In *Iris Murdoch and the Search for Human Goodness*, edited by Maria Antonaccio and William Schwelker. Chicago: University of Chicago Press, 1996.
Nussbaum analyzes this novel to discern Murdoch's responses to Plato's and to Dante's ideas about sexual love. At first glance, this novel seems Dantean. Blaise's love for Emily leads him to unconvincing rationalizations. His love blinds him to Emily's pain. Monty's story seems to make the same point: his love for Sophie causes his intense jealousy, an emotion that distorts his view of everything else. Yet Nussbaum argues that the novel has a Platonic side. The love and Blaise and Emily has a kind of glory and freedom that his inhibiting love for Harriet did not. Toward the end of the novel, the narrator intrudes with a passage rich in Platonic imagery that validates this view. In Monty's case, his egotistic behavior masked a real love. Although Murdoch thus echoes Plato, she also shows that Plato is too simple.

Punja, Prem Parkash. *The Novels of Iris Murdoch: A Critical Study*. Jalandar, India: ABS Publications, 1993.
In Chapter 4, Punja sees Harriet as an unassertive and trusting character who is consciously good. After she learns about Blaise's infidelity, she first tries to be saintly, then begins to act like an ordinary person. When she dies protecting Luca, she again shows her goodness.

Rabinovitz, Rubin. "Iris Murdoch." In *Six Contemporary British Novelists*, edited by George Stade. New York: Columbia University Press, 1976.

A brief note. Blaise is a stereotype: a psychiatrist who needs a psychiatrist. The novel is too melodramatic, and Murdoch ties up the plot in an unlikely fashion.

Scanlan, Margaret. "The Machinery of Pain: Romantic Suffering in Three Works of Iris Murdoch." *Renascence: Essays on Value in Literature* 29 (Winter, 1977): 69-85.

Scanlan thinks this novel is a more successful critique of Romantic notions about love and suffering than *An Accidental Man*, for it shows more complexities and dramatizes them better. Blaise's and Emily have a "great love," albeit a depraved, sadomasochistic one. Murdoch's judgment is clear when she shows that their love causes them to suffer and causes suffering to others, notably to Harriet and their children. Blaise is particularly blameworthy, for he is greedy, deceptive, and totally self-centered; he is a moral failure. Even so, he is only a fallible human being, not a monster like Austin in *An Accidental Man*. Harriet may seem like a nice woman, but she too is self-centered. Monty suffers real grief and tries to escape his selfishness, but fails. Only Edgar is clear-sighted. Scanlan complains that neither novel provides any positive model of ways to transcend the problems it dramatizes.

Siegel, Carol. *Male Masochism: Modern Revisions of the Story of Love.* Bloomington: Indiana University Press, 1995.

This novel is full of sadomasochistic characters, but in the end they all become conventional.

Slaymaker, William E. "The Labyrinth of Love: The Problem of Love and Freedom in the Novels of Iris Murdoch." *The Bluegrass Literary Review* 1, (1980): 39-44.

In *The Sovereignty of the Good*, Murdoch called the human psyche a machine. It uses energy and acts according to a limited number of patterns; it lives in fantasy, asserts itself, and avoids pain. This description fits the psyches of most characters in this novel. Blaise in particular is a profane love machine; in a labyrinth of relationships, he is a minotaur who devours love. In her essay, Murdoch describes sacred love, which requires a person to escape from fantasy and accept reality. No one in this novel makes this kind of escape. Harriet comes the closest, for she loves and forgives. Yet she is not without her own needs.

Spear, Hilda D. *Iris Murdoch*. New York: St. Martin's Press, 1995.
In Chapter 5, Spear groups this novel with three others in which Murdoch focuses on the power of love to redeem or destroy. In this novel, the good characters do not survive.

Todd, Richard. *Iris Murdoch*. London: Methuen, 1984.
In brief comments in Chapter 4, Todd says this novel is on the surface less serious than some of its predecessors. Murdoch's point is that both fantasies and accidents exert power on the real world.

_____. *Iris Murdoch: The Shakespearean Interest*. New York: Barnes & Noble Books, 1979.
In Chapter 4, Todd says this novel parodies the conventions of Shakespearean comedy. He uses Harriet's arbitrary but convenient death to prove his point.

Turner, Jack. *Murdoch vs. Freud: A Freudian Look at an Anti-Freudian*. New York: Peter Lang, 1993.
In Chapter 6 of this attack on Murdoch, Turner compares this novel to trashy best-sellers. It is unrealistic and manipulative, a failure. In it, Murdoch attacks Freud through Blaise, whose views in actuality are great oversimplifications of Freud's ideas.

Updike, John. "Topnotch Witches." *The New Yorker*, January 6, 1975, 76-81.
Though erotic love is at the center of this novel, Updike praises Murdoch's precise rendering of flora and fauna. He also praises her invention of characters, though he complains that they are not memorable. She resembles not Shakespeare but Prospero; she is an enchantress who captivates readers while they are on her island.

Winsor, Dorothy A. "Iris Murdoch's Conflicting Ethical Demands: Separation Versus Passivity in *The Sacred and Profane Love Machine*." *Modern Language Quarterly: A Journal of Literary History* 44 (December, 1983): 394-409. Reprinted in *Critical Essays on Iris Murdoch*, edited by Lindsey Tucker. New York: G. K. Hall, 1992.

Murdoch's essays call behavior moral when a person recognizes the separateness of others. The novels, however, see such acts as being almost impossible to perform, for almost every character is trapped in childish, selfish fantasies in which one merges with other persons either by dominating them or submitting to them.

Winsor discusses the main characters of this novel in light of these insights. David tries to escape his childish merging with his parents only to become like most other adults, persons who are driven to dominate through sex. Blaise not only is shaped by fantasy but also imposes fantasies on others; he tries to submit, but fails. Emily both submits and controls. Harriet tries to control by passiveness; she becomes more and more aggressive, but seems to attain wisdom only as she approaches her death. Monty defends himself against both his mother and Blaise. He tried to love his wife as a separate person, but he failed because of his jealousy. Although Edgar sees the others clearly, he is weak.

A Word Child, 1975.

Bove, Cheryl K. *Understanding Iris Murdoch*. Columbia: University of South Carolina Press, 1993.
In Chapter 7, Bove says that this novel shows the effects of the lack of love. Hilary's skill with words is mechanical and thus ultimately useless. He compartmentalizes his acquaintances and travels in circles. Hilary treats women badly; his immaturity is emphasized by his meetings by the statue of Peter Pan. By the end of the novel, he has learned remorse.

Cohan, Steven. "From Subtext to Dream Text: The Brutal Egoism of Iris Murdoch's Male Narrators." *Women and Literature* 2 (1982): 222-242. Reprinted in *Men and Women*, edited by Janet Todd. New York: Holmes & Meier, 1981.
Hilary is one of a succession of Murdoch's first-person male narrators who try to impose their routines on the world and to dominate women. Hilary's fantasies about women are particularly brutal as he tries to destroy their identities. He learns he cannot control events, and his sister resists his fantasies about her.

Conradi, Peter. *Iris Murdoch: The Saint and the Artist.* New York: St. Martin's Press, 1986.
Conradi makes only passing references to this novel.

Dipple, Elizabeth. *Iris Murdoch: Work for the Spirit.* London: Metheun, 1982.
In Chapter 7, Dipple characterizes Hilary Burde as an egotistical, destructive, narrow, and negative man, one who still suffers from guilt for killing Anne. He is the "word child" because of his un-productive obsession with languages and his childish behavior. (Anne's husband Gunnar is similarly warped.) Hilary cruelly enslaves his sister Crystal, almost preventing her from marrying. Crystal and Arthur are humble good people. Hilary ultimately is shocked from his insensitivity to others by Crystal's confessions and Clifford's suicide. The novel ends on a somewhat positive note: Hilary's future seems open. Dipple analyzes how literary works provide significant background to the story, especially J. M. Barrie's *Peter Pan* and T. S. Eliot's *Four Quartets.*

Fletcher, John. "Iris Murdoch, Novelist of London." *International Fiction Review* 17 (Winter, 1990): 9-13.
Real places in London play important roles in this novel: the Circle Line (part of the Underground), Whitehall and the Guards Memorial, a fountain in Kensington Gardens, and St. Stephen's Church in Gloucester Road.

Gordon, David J. *Iris Murdoch's Fables of Unselfing.* Columbia: University of Missouri Press, 1995.
In Chapter 1, Gordon identifies Kitty as a pseudo-healer, one who claims to set people free. He discusses this novel's first-person, unreliable narration in Chapter 3. The reader senses Hilary's compulsive nature in his staccato sentences; he condemns himself repeatedly. Even so, he seems to stand outside the novel. In Chapter 4, Gordon discusses how this novel attempts to represent contingency. The story seems to be tragic, but Hilary realizes it was silly for him to have suffered so much. Murdoch seems to push an interpretations of events with which many readers may not agree.

Griffin, Gabriele. *The Influence of the Writings of Simone Weil on the Fiction of Iris Murdoch.* San Francisco: Mellen Research University Press, 1993.

Griffin refers to this novel several times. Hilary's love for his sister exemplifies what Murdoch and Weil would call obsessive love, an expression of a need. Because of his insecurities and failures, Hilary needs to control Crystal, and he almost destroys her. This novel shows the usual contrast between male selfishness and female selflessness. Murdoch gets the reader's attention by using sexually ambiguous names like Hilary. Her "good" characters are usually androgynous or homosexual, like Christopher.

Hawkins, Peter. *The Language of Grace: Flannery O'Connor, Walker Percy, and Iris Murdoch.* Cambridge, Mass.: Cowley Publications, 1983.

Murdoch does not believe in God. But even in this novel where a first-person narrator seems totally unreligious, she uses a religious vocabulary to discuss human mysteries. Hilary is a limited, self-centered, and arid person who develops a personal mythology: only a woman can save him. Yet at the end, he has the beginning of a religious experience in a church once attended by T. S. Eliot. Crystal is a representative of the Good; Gunnar learns forgiveness from her.

Heusel, Barbara. "Iris Murdoch's *A Word Child*: Playing Games with Wittgenstein's *Perspectives.*" *Studies in the Humanities* 13 (December, 1986): 81-92.

Heusel argues that Wittgenstein is a strong influence both on Murdoch's view of life and on the way she writes fiction. Wittgenstein argues that language is a game and that mysteries cannot be explained by words, only shown by comparisons and juxtapositions. Hilary is concerned with words, but in only a very superficial way. Because he knows many languages, he can shield himself from other people and from his own neuroses. He uses his knowledge as a point of stability in his life; it feeds his ego and dilutes his pain. Heusel explains how Hilary has developed a different way to use language for many different situations, but not for intimacy. Murdoch plays language games with her reader when she presents long unattributed conversations.

_____. *Patterned Aimlessness: Iris Murdoch's Novels of the 1970s and 1980s.* Athens: University of Georgia Press, 1995.
In Chapter 3, Heusel notes that both Wittgenstein and Murdoch agree that studying languages is one good way to get different perspectives, to escape the categories of a particular culture. In contrast, Hilary (the word child) studies languages, not to communicate and understand others, but to control his violent tendencies, to fight his fears, to wall himself off from others, to deprecate other people, and to give order to his life. In Chapter 8, Heusel discusses how central characters in four novels are free to create their own mythical patterns in the face of life's determinism. In this case, the determinism is Freudian; Hilary's loves repeat cyclical oedipal patterns. He strives to counteract these cycles by imposing obsessive orders; he learns languages and observes a strict weekly routine. The end of the novel offers little closure, but Hilary may be growing slightly less self-centered.

Howard, Catherine E. "'Only Connect': Logical Aesthetic of Fragmentation in *A Word Child.*" *Twentieth Century Literature: A Scholarly and Critical Journal* 38 (Spring, 1992): 54-65.
Howard provides a detailed but strained point-by-point comparison between this novel and E. M. Forster's *Howard's End*. By the end of *A Word Child*, Hilary is beginning to realize the truth of Forster's famous phrase "only connect."

Jefferson, Douglas W. "Iris Murdoch and the Structures of Character." *Critical Quarterly* 26 (Winter, 1984): 47-58.
Most of Murdoch's characters develop machinelike qualities from one basic impulse or obsession. Here Hilary's deprived youth has made him compulsive; he orders his life and his sister's. It has also rendered him unable to love.

MacPhail, Fiona, and Jean-Louis Chevalier. "*A Word Child* ou L'Héautontimorouménos." In *Rencontres avec Iris Murdoch*. Caen, France: Centre de Recherches de Littérature et Linguistique des Pays de Langue Anglaise de l'Université de Caen, 1978. [In French.]
Charles Baudelaire's poem "L'Héautontimorouménos" helps explain Hilary's self-torture. By becoming and expert on words and languages, Hilary escapes the prison of his obscure origins.

In his guilt over Gunnar's wife's death, he refuses to use words in normal ways. Later, he fills out meaningless forms and engages in superficial conversations. His immersion in routine is symbolized by his endless rides on the London Underground's Circle Line. An escape from this second prison seems to occur when, after he is implicated in Kitty's death, he finally talks to Gunnar. His possible rebirth takes place at Christmas.

Orr, Christopher. "Iris Murdoch's Critique of Tragedy in *The Black Prince* and *A Word Child*." *The Bulletin of the West Virginia Association of College English Teachers* 4 (1977): 10-18.
Orr asks why Murdoch says absolute morality is better served by comedy than by tragedy. Orr looks at this novel and *The Black Prince* from an Aristotelian perspective. *The Black Prince* fits Aristotle's definition of a tragedy, and readers experience something of a purgation at Bradley's rise and fall. Yet Bradley says his life is not tragic, and Murdoch subverts any tragic feelings by her postscripts. In contrast, although *A Word Child* has plenty of error and punishment, we soon see that Hilary's quest for a cathartic release from his guilt is self-deceiving and self-protective. When Kitty dies, his quest actually results in doubling his guilt. He has gained nothing from his ordeal, and the reader, despite this novel's tragic ingredients, experiences no catharsis. To Murdoch, imposing a tragic meaning on life is exaggerating the human place in the universe. Comedy gives a clearer picture.

Piper, William Bowman. "The Accommodation of the Present in Novels by Murdoch and Powell." *Studies in the Novel* 11 (Summer, 1979): 178-193.
Piper shows how Murdoch uses the past tense to make present actions vivid. He praises this novel for its intensity and its coherence.

Punja, Prem Parkash. *The Novels of Iris Murdoch: A Critical Study*. Jalandar, India: ABS Publications, 1993.
In Chapter 6, Punja sees Hilary as an example of British educational policy, by which poor children from illiterate backgrounds can win their way to a kind of Oxford education. Hilary's narrowness causes disastrous effects.

Schaumburger, Nancy E. "The Conversion of Hilary Burde in *A Word Child*." *Iris Murdoch News Letter*, no. 6 (Summer, 1992): 3-4.
How will Hilary continue to live with his guilt at the end of this novel? Schaumburger argues that because he is beginning to forgive and feels he is forgiven, he will settle for living with his sister in domesticity.

Sizemore, Christine Wick. *A Female Vision of the City: London in the Novels of Five British Women*. Knoxville: University of Tennessee Press, 1989.
Murdoch sees London as a labyrinth. In this pessimistic novel, the literal details of London are particularly vivid, and the figurative labyrinth has at its center the Minotaur of egotism and selfishness. Hilary, fixated on his guilt for Anne's death, lives in this labyrinth, moving in circles underground when possible and avoiding any boundaries of experience. Symbolically, he avoids his minotaur; he avoids attachments to other human beings. Like other of Murdoch's male characters, Hilary thinks of London as organized around landmarks, in his case Big Ben. The novel ends with the hint he may have faced his minotaur and may be receiving forgiveness.

Spear, Hilda D. *Iris Murdoch*. New York: St. Martin's Press, 1995.
In Chapter 5, Spear groups this novel with others in which Murdoch makes her readers more conscious than before that a story is being told. These novels mix elements of thriller and mystery stories with a concern for the power of love to redeem or destroy. In this novel, love outside of marriage is not only destructive, but without joy.

Todd, Richard. *Iris Murdoch*. London: Methuen, 1984. Part of Chapter 4 is reprinted as "*A Word Child*" in *Iris Murdoch*, edited by Harold Bloom. New York: Chelsea House, 1986.
Todd points out that Hilary's problems (he comes from a lower-class, loveless, and illiterate background) reflects contemporary debates about education. Todd also reflects on many of the mysteries surrounding his relationship to Gunnar.

_____. *Iris Murdoch: The Shakespearean Interest*. New York: Barnes & Noble Books, 1979.

In Chapter 3, Todd compares the effect of this novel's ending to Lear's final entrance with Cordelia in his arms. Shakespeare does not offer any false consolations in his ending, and neither does Murdoch with regard to Hilary's fate.

Henry and Cato, 1976.

Bove, Cheryl K. "Americas and Americans in Iris Murdoch's Novels." In *Encounters with Iris Murdoch*, edited by Richard Todd. Amsterdam: Free University Press, 1988.
In Murdoch's novels, the United States is regularly associated with shallow people and low academic standards, such as those at the college where Henry teaches. Russ and Bella do not really know each other; they abandon Henry. In a reply to this paper, Murdoch defends Russ and Bella: they had to take new jobs; their farewell was affectionate.

_____. *Understanding Iris Murdoch*. Columbia: University of South Carolina Press, 1993.
In Chapter 7, Bove calls Henry a man who finds truth too horrible to bear; he therefore decides to live a mediocre life. Brendan's Platonism echoes Murdoch's own.

Brooks-Davies, Douglas. *Fielding, Dickens, Gosse, Iris Murdoch, and Oedipal* Hamlet. New York: St. Martin's Press, 1989.
The author touches on the oedipal patterns in this novel. Gerta, a Gertrude figure, prefers both Henry's father and his elder brother to Henry himself.

Byatt, A. S. *Degrees of Freedom: The Novels of Iris Murdoch*. Expanded ed. London: Vintage, 1994.
In Chapter 14, Byatt very briefly praises this novel for having intelligent characters who discuss important moral problems. Cato wants to help the destitute, but cannot handle real savagery. Byatt finds the love story satisfactory.

Conradi, Peter. *Iris Murdoch: The Saint and the Artist*. New York: St. Martin's Press, 1986.

In Chapter 9, Conradi sees this novel as telling two stories that move in opposite directions. Cato starts off comparatively happy, but becomes more and more unhappy as he cruelly loses both his faith and his beloved Beautiful Joe. Henry returns to England to destroy his home supposedly to promote social good; Murdoch makes clear his motives are really more oedipal. He is deflected from his task by Colette and becomes a contented man. Conradi thinks that Brendan and Gerta, both realists, perform similar functions.

Dipple, Elizabeth. *Iris Murdoch: Work for the Spirit.* London: Metheun, 1982. Chapter 8 is reprinted in *Critical Essays on Iris Murdoch*, edited by Lindsey Tucker. New York: G. K. Hall, 1992. In Chapter 2, Dipple identifies Brendan Craddock as one of a handful of Murdoch characters who approach sainthood. In an important passage, Craddock speaks for Murdoch herself as he explains Cato's spiritual problem and prescribes moving beyond egotism. By the end of the novel, Craddock has moved beyond Christian images and leaves for India. In Chapter 8, Dipple compares this novel to *The Bell*. Both have sacred and profane characters, here Cato and Henry. Unlike the orthodox and rigid James of the earlier novel, Brendan is more profound and understands change. Unlike Michael of *The Bell*, Brendan does not despair, but moves away from Christian images to live in India. His knowledge is reflected in the works of art which Dipple explains are behind the novel's action: Max Beckmann's *Departure* and Titian's *The Death of Actaeon*. In Titian, the divine Diana proceeds with indifference to Actaeon's human suffering. (Women in this novel are not ambitious, yet female figures have powerful mythic roles.)

Cato and Henry both desire some kind of transcendence, and both suffer failure. Cato's religious conversion is egotistical and shallow; his world falls apart after Beautiful Joe dies. Henry is also egotistical, as well as neurotic and destructive. In his desire to give away his money, he ignores the pain he will cause many other people. In the end, he knows he has failed, that he will only be a mediocre, though happy, person. Henry's eventual wife, Colette, learns when she is imprisoned that her girlish love for Henry has changed. Dipple cannot accept the happy ending of the novel. Because of the profundity of Murdoch's religious insights in this novel, the happy marriage of Henry and Colette can only be read as ironic.

Gordon, David J. *Iris Murdoch's Fables of Unselfing.* Columbia: University of Missouri Press, 1995.
In Chapter 3, Henry is seen as a typical Murdoch character who adopts a role he cannot sustain. Gordon also sees structural irony in having two characters undergoing different, though incomplete, ordeals. In Chapter 6, Gordon calls this novel unambitious and effective. The reader sees the foolishness of both main characters, but Murdoch does not mock them. Both have their ordeals, and Henry comes through gracefully. At the end, Murdoch implies that Cato has begun his spiritual journey.

Griffin, Gabriele. *The Influence of the Writings of Simone Weil on the Fiction of Iris Murdoch.* San Francisco: Mellen Research University Press, 1993.
Griffin refers to this novel several times. Cato's love for Joe is an example of an obsession in which the lover does not see the other person clearly.

Heusel, Barbara. *Patterned Aimlessness: Iris Murdoch's Novels of the 1970s and 1980s.* Athens: University of Georgia Press, 1995.
In Chapter 9, Heusel illustrates Murdoch's spatial imagination by reproducing diagrams of landscapes from this novel.

Kaftan, Robert A. "Doubt and the Self: Two Murdoch Priests." *Christian Century*, October 25, 1978, 1101-1104.
Cato replaces Christ with Beautiful Joe, God with egotistic self-consciousness. The novel shows his blindness, isolation, and self-deception.

Loades, Ann. "Iris Murdoch: The Vision of the Good and the *via negativa*." *Universities Quarterly: Culture and Education in Society* 40 (Winter, 1986): 147-155.
Loades uses several of Murdoch's novels, *Henry and Cato* in particular, to propose that readers would rather share Henry's fate than suffer with Cato in ways that Murdoch seems to think are necessary to begin to approach the Good.

McEwan, Neil. "Iris Murdoch's Contemporary World." In *The Survival of the Novel*. Totowa, N.J.: Barnes & Noble Books, 1981.
Some critics call Murdoch old-fashioned, but her novels depend for much of their effect on the tension between traditional and contemporary elements. Here the initial situation could come from a Victorian novel, but the characters act in an un-Victorian way. For example, Cato converts to Catholicism, and Henry not only will sell the house he has inherited but also will take up with his brother's mistress.

Mettler, Darlene D. *Sound and Sense: Musical Allusion and Imagery in the Novels of Iris Murdoch*. New York: Peter Lang, 1991.
In Chapter 5, Mettler points out that Bach's formality allows Lucius to escape the disorder of his world.

Punja, Prem Parkash. *The Novels of Iris Murdoch: A Critical Study*. Jalandar, India: ABS Publications, 1993.
In Chapter 6, Punja finds the novel provides two alternatives: Henry's upper-class compromises and Brendan's priesthood. Brendan is a real priest, for he has come though frustrations and change. Cato is at best a provisional and self-indulgent priest.

Ramanathan, Suguna. "The Concept of Good in Four of Iris Murdoch's Later Novels." *Heythrop Journal* 28 (1987): 388-404.
An earlier version of her arguments in *Iris Murdoch: Figures of Good*.

_____. *Iris Murdoch: Figures of Good*. London: Macmillan, 1990.
In Chapter 2, Cato symbolizes possibilities. His religious experiences are genuine, but too intense to last. He cannot control his love for Beautiful Joe and ends in despair and failure: his old belief is gone, though he still has his crucifix. Brendan Craddock is the most traditional of Murdoch's figures of good. He moves toward simplicity by giving up his friendship with Cato and his intellectual life. Although his beliefs become almost Buddhist, he remains within the Christian Church. Faith to him is abandoning the desire for human security; God is a recognition by reason of something greater than reason. Ramanathan analyzes well the

appearance of a kestrel, a bird that is both a sign of the Holy Spirit and an actual predatory creature.

Sage, Lorna. "The Pursuit of Imperfection." *Critical Quarterly* 19 (Summer, 1977): 61-68. Reprinted as "The Pursuit of Imperfection: *Henry and Cato*" in *Iris Murdoch*, edited by Harold Bloom. New York: Chelsea House, 1986.

Sage argues that this is a novel about the importance of imperfection which is itself imperfect. Both Cato and Henry try to impose patterns on life. Both are defeated by people who not only will not be imposed upon but who act on their own. Both must settle for imperfect and provisional illusions: Cato has his crucifix, and Henry has his love for Colette. They must also live in real but limited places; hell is conceived of as the empty nonplace in which Cato is imprisoned. The novel's world is filled with characters who imperfectly understand each other. (Lucius Lamb is a touching example of a man with in intense inner life who lives almost unnoticed by others.) But even though a critic might wish for Murdoch to be consistent and to render the inner life of even more of her characters, Murdoch does not strive for such perfection. Even if Murdoch thereby tries to deflect criticism, Sage manages to register some complaints.

Snape, Ray. "*Henry and Cato* and the `Intelligence' of Iris Murdoch." *The Durham University Journal* 78 (June, 1986): 327-333.

Most reviewers and critics collude when they write about Iris Murdoch: they say she is an intelligent novelist. Snape disputes these assertions. Her lack of intelligence is demonstrated in this novel in many ways. She does not render Cato's conversion in convincing detail; she is not interested in the real Paddington where Cato goes; Beautiful Joe is unconvincing. The same can be said for Stephanie, and Murdoch's treatment of Henry's wealth is not serious. She has an unappealing preoccupation with clothes.

Spear, Hilda D. *Iris Murdoch*. New York: St. Martin's Press, 1995.

In Chapter 5, Spear groups this novel with others in which Murdoch makes her readers conscious that a story is being told. These novels mix elements of thrillers and mystery stories with a concern for the power of love to redeem or destroy. In her useful discussion of this novel, Spear points out that the title characters follow opposite courses. The "good" convert Cato indulges himself in a selfish infatuation that leads to murder. He counsels greed, he eventually loses his faith, and he ends in desolation. The "bad" Henry tries to do good even though he does not believe in God. He responds to love and chooses happiness.

Todd, Richard. *Iris Murdoch*. London: Methuen, 1984.
In brief comments in Chapter 5, Todd notes how this novel has parallel strands, the Henry plot and the Cato plot. Todd argues that Murdoch puzzles the reader about the characters' motivations in order to communicate their mystery and independence.

The Sea, The Sea, 1978. Awarded the Booker Prize.

Bigsby, Christopher. "Interview with Iris Murdoch." In *The Radical Imagination and the Liberal Tradition: Interviews with English and American Novelists*, edited by Christopher Bigsby and Heide Ziegler. London: Junction Books, 1982.
James is a lost soul, a demonic spiritual being. He loves Charles. When James comes to say good-bye, he finds he has to use magic to save Charles. Murdoch says James did in a sense walk on water. This action sets James free; he escapes from his spell and, the reader is to believe, dies.

Bove, Cheryl K. *Understanding Iris Murdoch*. Columbia: University of South Carolina Press, 1993.
In Chapter 5, Bove finds that the power of illusion is at the heart of this novel. Charles, the man of the theater, has used its illusion as a tool for his egotism. James, the Buddhist, realizes that, even though he uses spiritual magic for the good, it has impeded his own spiritual progress. Under his influence, Charles seems to make progress until a young woman tempts him back to his egotistic life.

Byatt, A. S. *Degrees of Freedom: The Novels of Iris Murdoch*. Expanded ed. London: Vintage, 1994.
In Chapter 15, Byatt notes that the presence of a first-person male narrator is a sign that self-delusion and that wish fulfillment will be one of the novel's themes. Byatt finds Charles more likable

than other such narrators, perhaps because he pays such precise attention to the details of his life, particularly culinary details. Murdoch's earlier imprisoned ladies in *The Unicorn* and *The Time of the Angels* is echoed here by Charles's imprisoning the very ordinary Hartley. Both Charles the theatrical director and James the Buddhist have magical powers which they find hard, like Prospero, to renounce. Byatt asks how well in a seemingly realistic novel do the magical tricks and sea-serpents work. Her answer is "not quite."

Cavaliero, Glen. *The Supernatural and English Fiction*. New York: Oxford University Press, 1995.

In Chapter 6, Cavaliero discusses how Murdoch mixes naturalistic detail and bizarre yet explicable happenings and with inexplicable, preternatural events. Charles's vision of the sea monster suggests the reciprocal nature of spiritual and physical experience. This, to Cavaliero, is the essence of the supernatural. James's magical powers are more dangerous than useful. In general, although Murdoch acknowledges supernatural powers may be evil, they are most often a force for good.

Cohan, Steven. "From Subtext to Dream Text: The Brutal Egoism of Iris Murdoch's Male Narrators." *Women and Literature* 2 (1982): 222-242. Reprinted in *Men and Women*, edited by Janet Todd. New York: Holmes & Meier, 1981.

Charles is a particularly destructive example of Murdoch's first-person male narrators, men who attempt to impose their fantasies on the world, particularly on its women. Even when Hartley resists, Charles is blind. This novel differs from others which use this kind of narration, in that Murdoch's judgment is explicit, not implicit. This judgment is rendered when Charles's account of the past shows that he was always domineering and violent, and when he begins to see the truth.

Conradi, Peter. *Iris Murdoch: The Saint and the Artist*. New York: St. Martin's Press, 1986.

In Chapter 10, Conradi calls this Murdoch's greatest novel. He cites as the source of the title a poem by Paul Valéry to which Murdoch refers in earlier novels. As Charles tells his story as a diary, readers sense his self-deception. When he retires to his

seaside house, Charles thinks that, like Prospero in Shakespeare's
The Tempest, he can leave his previous life, theatrical and personal, behind him. But he does not change, and he still must pay
for his sins. He is still tyrannical, possessive, manipulative, and
greedy. He is an immature child/man who, perhaps because of an
adolescent love trauma, cannot commit himself to another person.
Women love him. They cast themselves and him in roles, he as
tyrant and they as victims. When Charles meets Hartley, his early
love, he cannot understand her masochistic ties to her husband
and must control her. After he is persuaded to release her from
imprisonment, his recovery to some kind of sanity is helped by
two disasters, his escape from the whirlpool and the drowning of
Hartley's son.

If Charles is Murdoch's artist figure in this novel, Charles's
cousin James is its saint. He possesses a Buddhist spiritual
detachment and performs tricks of spiritual magic. He seems to
love Charles. Conradi attempts to explain the mystery of this
somewhat unsatisfactory character. Conradi also discusses two of
the novel's most pervasive images. Boxes and enclosures literally
enclose and imprison the characters; in another way, they suggest
Charles's obsession and its sources in his unconscious mind. The
ultimate unimportance of his obsession is made clear by Charles's
views of the magnitude of the heavens and by the sea itself.
Conradi brilliantly evokes the magic of Murdoch's descriptions of
the sea and says that it is more than a symbol: huge, destructive,
unpredictable, indefinable. Similarly, other comparisons (as to
the theater and to pictures in the National Gallery) are suggestive
but cannot be interpreted simply. The ending of the novel is
satisfactory: Charles begins to recover from his obsession and
admits his mortality.

Dipple, Elizabeth. *Iris Murdoch: Work for the Spirit*. London:
Metheun, 1982.

In Chapter 9, Dipple cites this novel and *The Unicorn* as works in
which Murdoch deals with magic. In a detailed analysis, Dipple
describes the egotistical Charles Arrowby as he tries to imitate
Shakespeare's Prospero and make his life into an art object. In his
diary he will shape the formlessness of reality into a story in
which he will rid himself of his competitive adult years and
restore the innocence of his adolescence. Yet from the very first

page, his narrative is interrupted, first by a sea monster, then by his sighting of Hartley, his long-lost love. His attempt to transform her fails (Dipple writes appreciatively of Hartley's ordinary virtues), and he must finally admit defeat. Part of Murdoch's commentary on Charles's doomed attempts comes through symbols and parallels with literary works (Shakespeare, Valéry, Marcel Proust) and paintings; Dipple analyzes all of these brilliantly.

At the end, the defeated Charles seems able to see the world somewhat clearly and refuses to end his novel with any sort of artistic closure. In spite of the novel's focus on Charles, Dipple thinks he is only its ostensible subject. As the novel progresses, the attentive reader realizes that his Buddhist cousin James is at the novel's heart. Unlike Charles, James is not naïve; he knows how people endow objects and persons (like Hartley) with spiritual powers they do not really possess. Like Charles, James too fails. He succumbs to the temptation to intervene in the world and dies a failure.

Gordon, David J. *Iris Murdoch's Fables of Unselfing*. Columbia: University of Missouri Press, 1995.
In Chapter 2, Gordon makes clear that Charles's love is not one that leads to the Good. In Chapter 3, Gordon notes that this is the first novel in which Murdoch shows *good* magic. Gordon comments on Charles the narrator in both chapters. He is both the egotistical victim of an illusion and the narrator that makes that clear. In Chapter 6, Gordon considers how Titus's death is the end of a chain of causes that are not psychological. Similarly, James calls Charles's strong emotions concerning Hartley, not the evidence of deep psychological problems, but of egotism based on an illusion.

Griffin, Gabriele. *The Influence of the Writings of Simone Weil on the Fiction of Iris Murdoch*. San Francisco: Mellen Research University Press, 1993.
In Chapter 2 (which concerns the Weilian idea of selflessness), Griffin discusses this novel at length because its central character is so obviously selfish from beginning to end. Griffin sees the key to Charles's behavior in his attachment to his mother. What he wanted from the young Hartley and all his subsequent women is a

return to a infantile paradise, a sinless world. As a result, he sees all women as simply refuges, none of them as individual, separate persons. When he meets Hartley again, his obsession leads to various excesses which Griffin explains with reference to Freud. His cousin James, a man who has learned something about self-lessness through Buddhism, teaches him and rescues him (symbolically) from drowning in his own ego. But even though Charles has moments of vision and selflessness, he ends the novel still striving for self-knowledge, affirming that he can only live by pursuing self-satisfaction. In a later chapter, Griffin points out that Charles's descriptions of food are examples of "attention."

Hague, Angela. *Iris Murdoch's Comic Vision*. Cranbury, N.J.: Associated University Presses, 1984.
In Chapter 5, Hague again uses the comic theories of Northrop Frye to gain valuable insights into a Murdoch novel. Charles, the central character and narrator, is an *alazon*: a deluded impostor. In addition, Murdoch casts him as both the youthful hero questing for his princess (in this case the aging Hartley) and the aged Fisher King needing rejuvenation. Murdoch draws on romantic comedy in this novel, for Charles in his move to the seaside tries to enter the innocent world of romance. In this plot, Titus is a scapegoat; Rosina is the evil witch; James is both a helper and a benevolent and wise magician; and Gilbert is both a buffoon and another helper.
The novel takes on aspects of Frye's fifth and sixth phases of comedy, for it contains elements of the magical and the occult and its perspective is often one of looking down on the action. But Murdoch also inverts these conventions. Charles is seen to be an egotistical manipulator, a theatrical director who now tries to make drama out of real people who, like Hartley, do not wish to play their parts. Murdoch's power figure here becomes risible. The end of the novel is puzzling, for Charles seems to repent and then to mock everything that has gone before.

Heusel, Barbara. "Can We Tell the Good Art from the Bad? Iris Murdoch's *The Black Prince* and *The Sea, The Sea*." *University of Dayton Review* 19 (Summer, 1988): 99-107.
In this novel and in *The Black Prince*, Murdoch presents central characters who are artists and who illustrate her central contrast

between bad art that consoles by means of its formal pattern and good art that shows life's contingency and does not console. In both cases, Murdoch mixes elements. In *The Black Prince*, Bradley frames his report of contingent experiences with a consolatory postscript. The opposite is true in this novel. Charles has consolatory fantasies about re-creating his childhood dream, but they are framed by sections that recognize contingency and do not console.

_____. *Patterned Aimlessness: Iris Murdoch's Novels of the 1970s and 1980s*. Athens: University of Georgia Press, 1995.
In Chapter 3, Heusel shows how Murdoch mixes Wittgenstein's and Plato's ideas about human illusions. Charles thought if he went to the seaside he could shed his egotism, but from the beginning he follows his narrow egotistic perceptions. He distorts what he sees and further distorts it when he writes. Yet he begins to move out of his Platonic cave when he pays some attention to inner voices and when he is assaulted from without by monsters. Heusel explains Murdoch's symbolism: Charles's mind is the cave, the sea his unconscious, and the phallic monster his egotism.

Charles's progress from the cave is derailed, however, when he meets the real Hartley again. He cannot see her clearly; he does not listen to her; he becomes the prisoner of his illusions, denials, and rationalizations. As a result, he releases evil forces that hurt other people, even causing Titus's death. In Chapter 8, Heusel discusses how central characters in four novels try to create patterns in the face of life's determinism. In this novel, Charles directs the narrative: he digresses; he records his patterning of his daily activities. He himself alludes to moving out of Plato's cave. Nevertheless he is dominated by his obsessions with Hartley and James.

Jefferson, Douglas W. "Iris Murdoch and the Structures of Character." *Critical Quarterly* 26 (Winter, 1984): 47-58.
Most of Murdoch's characters develop machinelike qualities from one basic impulse; here Charles's obsession is with his youthful love. But Charles is unpleasant, self-absorbed, stupid, garrulous, and embarrassing. His obsession is unconvincing, and the novel is a failure.

Johnson, Deborah. *Iris Murdoch*. Bloomington: Indiana University Press, 1987.
In Chapter 2, Johnson shows how Charles's misogynistic first-person narration is comically undercut by the female author. He unconsciously reveals his fear of the feminine in his descriptions of objects. In Chapter 4, Johnson says that Charles is uncertain of the meaning of the cave myth. Is he moving to the light or to the center of the earth? Which is illusion, and which truth? In Chapter 5, Johnson cites the inconclusive closure of this novel as evidence that Murdoch resists traditional endings.

Kenyon, Olga. *Women Novelists Today: A Survey of English Writing in the Seventies and Eighties*. New York: St. Martin's Press, 1988.
A narrow perspective: one abandoned women (Rosina) has her vindication. Another (Hartley) is shown to be morally superior to Charles, the man who is romantically obsessed with her.

Khanna, Urmilla. "Iris Murdoch and Shakespeare." *Yearly Review* [University of Delhi] (December, 1991): 17-28.
Shakespeare's Sonnet 144 lies behind the love triangle of Lizzie, Gilbert, and Charles.

Mettler, Darlene D. *Sound and Sense: Musical Allusion and Imagery in the Novels of Iris Murdoch*. New York: Peter Lang, 1991.
Mettler's analysis of music in this novel is revealing. Charles values control; he hates vocal music because from an early age it has suggested to him the emotions and sexuality he cannot control. Yet people from his past visit him and fill his cottage with song. Titus is associated with an Italian street song used to count children out of a game; it suggests how people are dropping out of Charles's life. The melody of "Greensleeves" was the song of his chaste young love with Hartley; later he realizes the applicability of its secular words.

Moss, Howard. "Narrow Escapes: Iris Murdoch." *Grand Street* 6 (Autumn, 1986): 228-240.
This rambling review-essay contains valuable criticism. Charles Arrowby is a monster/magician who creates a drama in which all the other characters are forced to participate. He is in thrall to a

childhood romance and is determined to re-create it by projecting ideal qualities on an ordinary middle-age woman. He eventually learns that what he called love is really his need to control. Murdoch gives a sense of a world beyond Charles: his house, Shruff End, is inhabited by ghosts of the past; magical sea serpents lurk in the ocean.

Oates, Joyce Carol. "Sacred and Profane Iris Murdoch." In *The Profane Art: Essays and Reviews.* New York: E. P. Dutton, 1983.
In this chapter, Oates reviews this novel and makes many references to other Murdoch works. Murdoch's novels are filled, not with human beings, but ideas. In her best novels, she is even-handed when she shows these ideas doing battle; the winner is the one most in tune with the impersonal universe. Although this is a pessimistic view, it does not exclude comedy, and Murdoch's mission is to protect her readers from despair. In this novel, Charles is an egotist who will impose his fantasy of love on Hartley. Not only is it hard to believe that a person could act like this, but readers must suffer though his garrulous first-person narration. The supernatural elements are not convincing either. Oates is disappointed that Charles is happy at the end.

Punja, Prem Parkash. *The Novels of Iris Murdoch: A Critical Study.* Jalandar, India: ABS Publications, 1993.
In Chapter 3, Punja calls this a Gothic novel because of its mysterious and even demonic atmosphere. The novel has many unexplained mysteries, particularly James's magic powers and the sea monster. Charles fails to explain the monster in the novel; Punja cannot explain it either.

Ramanathan, Suguna. "The Concept of Good in Four of Iris Murdoch's Later Novels." *Heythrop Journal* 28 (1987): 388-404.
An earlier version of her arguments in *Iris Murdoch: Figures of Good.*

_____. *Iris Murdoch: Figures of Good.* London: Macmillan, 1990.
In Chapter 3, Ramanathan treats Charles's first-person journal (the novel itself) as a Buddhist document, a long, delusive, occasionally hilarious revelation of his preoccupation with the self.

The sea of the title may suggest the indifferent sea of unordered experience in which Charles exists, a sea full of demons and whirlpools. Charles's self-centered mind falsifies reality in accordance with Buddhist ideas: he sees an imaginary Hartley, not the real woman. James is overtly a Buddhist, and his development follows traditional Buddhist steps. He falters when he uses magic powers, but that is Murdoch's way of dramatizing the mind's power. James continues to grow along Buddhist lines and dies well. Ramanathan disagrees with Elizabeth Dipple about the postscript. There we see that even though Charles still lives in the world, he has subtly changed for the better.

Spear, Hilda D. *Iris Murdoch*. New York: St. Martin's Press, 1995.
In Chapter 6, Spear groups this long novel with others which are deeply concerned with philosophy, religion, and mysticism as well as with psychological domination. Here Charles is a naïve and somewhat unreliable first-person narrator; he tells the reader he is a happy, successful man, but really he is deeply distressed. His obsession with Hartley is a doomed attempt to recapture the only pure love he has known. The saintly James is the moral center of the novel, a man who strives for the Platonic Good. He saves Charles twice and tells him the truth about his obsession: that Charles's role as a brokenhearted lover is only an attempt to console himself for his spiritual emptiness. James's supposed death enables Charles to understand himself. A succinct and valuable treatment of this complex novel.

Sullivan, Zohreh Tawakuli. "Women Novelists and Variations on the Uses of Obscurity." *South Carolina Review* 16 (Fall, 1983): 51-58.
Even though in many ways this is a realistic novel, it is postmodern as well. The changeable Charles is not a consistent nineteenth century character, and his story depends on his illusions and neuroses. Murdoch is postmodern as she explores the role fictionality plays in real life.

Todd, Richard. *Iris Murdoch*. London: Methuen, 1984.
In brief comments in Chapter 5, Todd sees Charles and James as examples of Murdoch's usual contrast of artist and saint. That Charles is a first-person narrator, and not necessarily a reliable

one, enables Murdoch to preserve some mysteries and to introduce seemingly supernatural events.

Tucker, Lindsey. "Released from Bands: Iris Murdoch's Two Prosperos in *The Sea, the Sea*." *Contemporary Literature* 27 (Fall, 1986): 378-395. Reprinted in *Critical Essays on Iris Murdoch*. New York: G. K. Hall, 1992.

A very interesting and informative article. Both Shakespeare's *The Tempest* and Buddhist ideas inform this novel (which has Gothic trappings as well). Charles is a kind of Prospero; he is a master of theatrical tricks and seems to enchant his friends. (Tucker notes how they also resemble characters in *The Tempest*.) But he is not truly creative. As a director, he enjoys power; his friends enchant themselves. Charles is actually an enchanted man, for he plays Ferdinand to Hartley's Miranda. The novel's true Prospero is James, and his mission is to save Charles by his own kind of tricks. Tucker explains Buddhist concepts of the stages of spiritual illumination and shows how they apply to James and begin to apply to Charles. When James saves Charles from the sea, he is initiating Charles's spiritual rebirth as well. The two men end differently. Reports of James's death suggest he died well in Buddhist terms. Although Charles recovers from illness into a state of illumination, the novel's postscript suggests that his understanding has faded.

Turner, Jack. *Murdoch vs. Freud: A Freudian Look at an Anti-Freudian*. New York: Peter Lang, 1993.

In Chapter 7 of this attack on Murdoch, Turner says that here Murdoch, probably unconsciously, uses writing as therapy, for her concerns are distributed among many characters. Turner analyzes the symbolism of how various houses are arranged, Charles's house in particular.

Nuns and Soldiers, 1980.

Bove, Cheryl K. *Understanding Iris Murdoch*. Columbia: University of South Carolina Press, 1993.

In Chapter 5, Bove interprets this novel's title: its characters are alienated like nuns, but soldier on. She praises the Count for his idealism and love and censures Gertrude for her egotism and flirtatiousness. The most important characters are Anne and Tim. Anne, whose assertiveness is admirable and whose vision of Christ is unnerving to some, sets human love aside and devotes her life to service. Tim also makes spiritual progress, but not so much. After several epiphanies and near-death experiences, he accepts his blessing in his marriage to Gertrude.

Brooks-Davies, Douglas. *Fielding, Dickens, Gosse, Iris Murdoch, and Oedipal* Hamlet. New York: St. Martin's Press, 1989.
The author notes many parallels with *Hamlet*. Guy dies, and Gertrude remarries quickly.

Byatt, A. S. *Degrees of Freedom: The Novels of Iris Murdoch.* Expanded ed. London: Vintage, 1994.
In Chapter 15, Byatt praises Murdoch for showing great understanding of love while placing it in the larger (and nastier) world. She also praises Murdoch's surprising changes of pace and her characters. Anne and the Count make a pessimistic pair; he has no Poland, and she has no God. Her vision of Christ is hardly comforting. In contrast, Gertrude and Tim are happy egoists. Byatt gives Tim his due as one who simply perceives.

Cavaliero, Glen. *The Supernatural and English Fiction.* New York: Oxford University Press, 1995.
In Chapter 6, Cavaliero provides a brief but very illuminating discussion of this difficult subject. Murdoch mixes naturalistic detail both with bizarre yet explicable happenings and with inexplicable, preternatural events. One example of such an event is Anne's talk with Jesus in *Nun's and Soldiers*; she could be said to have imagined it, except that it leaves a real mark on her.

Conradi, Peter. *Iris Murdoch: The Saint and the Artist.* New York: St. Martin's Press, 1986.
In Chapter 11, Conradi makes brief comments on this work. In the background are stories by Henry James and Petronius. This novel once again shows that in Murdoch's world the secure self-love of well-born people has value, but not the greatest value.

_____. "Useful Fictions: Iris Murdoch." *Critical Quarterly* 23 (Fall, 1981): 63-69.

A suggestive, informal essay. Conradi here defines Murdoch's somewhat melodramatic mode as "operatic realism." Guy, a Jew with godlike certainties, is dying, much as God himself is dying. People from various cultures gather in his home. In the world that is left after he dies, these people undergo ordeals, reversals, and testings. They fall in love, long for justice, and are sometimes happily surprised. Conradi contrasts the mystical, selfless religion that Anne strives for with useful fictions such as family and Providence. These fictions are created by love and by artists; most of the characters need them to survive. This novel itself is a useful fiction.

Cuneen, Sally. "The Post-Divine Comedy of Iris Murdoch." *The Christian Century*, May 20, 1981, 27-31.

This novel shows how characters' self-centeredness can obscure reality for them. Philosophy, literature, and religion often help them to be self-centered. Anne's vision of Christ is dry and not consoling; she must continue to seek.

Dipple, Elizabeth. *Iris Murdoch: Work for the Spirit.* London: Metheun, 1982.

Dipple devotes Chapter 10 to an extended analysis of this novel. Its real center lies in Anne and the Count, alien characters who may yearn for a place in the world, but who can only be satisfied by renunciation. Dipple emphasizes Anne's vision of Christ, a figure who challenges her but offers no redemption. Most of the novel, Dipple complains, is given over to less admirable characters who desire not the Good, but happiness. Daisy is a marvelous contrast to the cold Anne. Gertrude resembles her namesake in *Hamlet*, for, after the death of an admirable man, she tries to find happiness with an inferior being. Dipple praises how Murdoch reveals the selfishness in Gertrude's psyche. Tim is also deeply flawed, a man always associated with the muddle of the world. Yet when he gives up Daisy, he improves. At the end, his experience of the sublime in the landscape of France connects him to some aspects of the Good. His salvation from the tunnel is a parody of the Christian story. Dipple feels that his and Gertrude's

happiness at the novel's close may be ironic; Murdoch may wish
to satisfy the desires of her more conventional readers.

Gordon, David J. *Iris Murdoch's Fables of Unselfing*. Columbia:
University of Missouri Press, 1995.
In Chapter 3, Gordon succinctly details the structural ironies of
this novel, explaining who are the nuns and who the soldiers. In
Chapter 6, Gordon emphasizes the force of Gertrude and Tim's
romantic love; Murdoch's ironies never completely undercut it,
even when she shows Anne moving away from human love.

Griffin, Gabriele. *The Influence of the Writings of Simone Weil on the
Fiction of Iris Murdoch*. San Francisco: Mellen Research
University Press, 1993.
Griffin refers to this novel several times. The Count is an
example of rootlessness, a sad condition. In Murdoch's novels,
good, selfless characters like Anne are not sexually active; they
are often paired with selfish characters like Gertrude.

Guerin, Caroline. "Iris Murdoch—A Revisionist Theology?: A Comparative Study of Iris Murdoch's *Nuns and Soldiers* and Sara
Maitland's *Virgin Territory*." *Literature and Theology: An International Journal of Theory, Criticism, and Culture* 6 (June,
1992): 153-170.
Guerin compares Murdoch's novel to Maitland's avowedly
feminist one. She thinks that many aspects of a feminist consciousness can be found in Murdoch's work, but despite the two
novels' parallels and neat contrasts, Murdoch's is not exclusively
feminist. Anne's friendship with Gertrude is marked not by
lesbianism, but by rivalry. Anne leaves the convent not to find
what she has been missing sexually, but to pursue Truth in her
own way. She finds it when Christ visits her kitchen (even
though her love of Christ is mixed with her love of the Count).
She learns how vulnerable human beings are, but this does not
bring despair. Guerin thinks what Christ tells Anne is that the
patriarchy has hidden the true feminist message of Christianity.

Hauk, Gary S. "Moral Transcendence in Iris Murdoch's *Nuns and
Soldiers*: Apropos of Theocentric Ethics." *Christianity and
Literature* 40 (Winter, 1991): 137-156.

Hauk finds that James Gustafson's *Ethics from a Theocentric Perspective* illuminates this novel. Like Gustafson, Murdoch is interested in how identities are formed, how persons are located inside and outside of groups, how individuals survive in a hostile world, and how dogma is insignificant in the face of mystery and death. Tim and Daisy suffer from deceit, failure, and sloth; Tim seems to have no fixed identity. The Count's burden is his utter separation from his Polish home; he is narrow, and he knows it. Both the Count and Anne are limited by their earlier choices. None of the characters really change; they settle for getting by. Perhaps for Tim, Gertrude, and the Count, their lowered expectations are healthy. Anne ultimately does not seek happiness, but hopes to continue her slow process of transformation. She will live secretly according to her religious ideas—a true saint in Murdoch's world. Meeting Christ in her kitchen produces real effects. All these ideas and others resemble Gustafson's.

Heusel, Barbara. "Iris Murdoch's *A Word Child*: Playing Games with Wittgenstein's *Perspectives*." *Studies in the Humanities* 13 (December, 1986): 81-92.
The dying Guy Openshaw is the one Murdoch character who seems to understand Wittgenstein. He can go beyond logic to look at reality; he explores language from multiple perspectives.

_____. *Patterned Aimlessness: Iris Murdoch's Novels of the 1970s and 1980s*. Athens: University of Georgia Press, 1995.
In Chapter 3, Heusel shows how Murdoch (like Wittgenstein) desires to evoke life's mystery, not by analysis, but by thought-provoking, playful juxtapositions. What is the message that Guy wanted to communicate? Heusel analyzes Guy's speeches to show how different phrases can mean many different things in different contexts. She focuses on Guy's dying references to "the upper side of the cube" and "the white swan." In Chapter 7, she cites Anne as an example of a fully drawn female character. Trying to decide what to do, Anne listens to many of her own voices: those of religion, unselfish love, romantic love, confession, and pain. In Chapter 8, Heusel compares Tim to three characters from other Murdoch novels and finds, in terms of Plato's myth, he moves farthest out of the cave and into the sun. His near-drownings were

the result of innocence; he is more lovable than the others; his fate is more hopeful.

Johnson, Deborah. *Iris Murdoch*. Bloomington: Indiana University Press, 1987.
In Chapter 4, Johnson says the circular pool is another cavelike symbols of female creativity. Tim respects the pool; Gertrude bathes in it.

Kenyon, Olga. *Women Novelists Today: A Survey of English Writing in the Seventies and Eighties*. New York: St. Martin's Press, 1988.
Kenyon considers this novel unusual because Murdoch creates three strong women characters. Daisy in particular is praised for her strength, her free spirit, and her ideas about art.

Mettler, Darlene D. *Sound and Sense: Musical Allusion and Imagery in the Novels of Iris Murdoch*. New York: Peter Lang, 1991.
Murdoch uses references to three operas for comic and satiric effects. Usually Murdoch's parallels make comic juxtapositions between an opera's formulaic story and Murdoch's muddled plot, one that reflects the contingencies of life. Guy's relatives in the novel's opening scenes reflect the greedy death watchers in Giacomo Puccini's *Turandot*. Giuseppi Verdi's *Aida* dramatizes the love of two women for one men; Daisy and Gertrude love Tim. Tim sees himself and Daisy as Papageno and Papegena from Mozart's *The Magic Flute*. Tim does resemble Papageno in many ways, but it is Gertrude who, like Papegena, changes into a desirable woman.

Moss, Howard. "Narrow Escapes: Iris Murdoch." *Grand Street* 6 (Autumn, 1986): 228-240.
Moss treats this novel briefly. He praises the magic of its Provençal house, but he finds Murdoch's Jewish characters dull. The scene in which Anne talks to Jesus is Murdoch's worst.

Punja, Prem Parkash. *The Novels of Iris Murdoch: A Critical Study*. Jalandar, India: ABS Publications, 1993.
In Chapter 4, Punja says that Guy is good because of his generosity and that the Count is good because of his unselfish love

for Gertrude. Anne aims for the unattainable good by loving other people. She rejects her love for a single individual (the Count), because she thinks that romantic love is madness.

Ramanathan, Suguna. "The Concept of Good in Four of Iris Murdoch's Later Novels." *Heythrop Journal* 28 (1987): 388-404. An earlier version of her arguments in *Iris Murdoch: Figures of Good*.

_____. *Iris Murdoch: Figures of Good*. London: Macmillan, 1990.
In Chapter 4, Ramanathan first discusses the similarity of Murdoch's ideas to those of Julian of Norwich: both acknowledge the magnetic pull of a transcendent force. Most of the chapter deals with Christ's appearance to Anne Cavidge, an isolated scene based closely on Julian. Christ is not a dream, though he exists only in a human being's capacity for selfless seeing and love. He rejects the role of savior and tells Anne she will have to save herself. Ramanathan lists how Murdoch's Christ differs from the traditional one: he is not emotional or sentimental; he does not inspire rapture in Anne as he did in Julian; there is no suggestion of redemptive suffering or atonement. What Christ does is awaken Anne's loving human heart. Yet natural explanations do not explain everything, not Anne's wound or the stone Christ may have left behind.

_____. "Murdoch's Use of *Hamlet* in *Nuns and Soldiers*." *Hamlet Studies: An International Journal of Research on The Tragedie of Hamlet, Prince of Denmark* 16 (Summer-Winter, 1994): 88-94.
Murdoch rewrites Shakespeare's story to make it closer in spirit to his late plays. Ramanathan lists ways *Hamlet* is in the background of this novel. There are not only many verbal allusions, but many parallel situations: Gertrude and Guy resemble Gertrude and the elder Hamlet; the Count plays Hamlet himself, and Anne, the former nun, resembles Ophelia in some ways. But Murdoch changes the story from one of revenge to one of love and reconciliation. The Count is only an informally adopted son. Although Gertrude's love for Tim is erotic, their union in the south of France is seen as good. Tim may have his faults, but he is not a Claudius.

Scanlan, Margaret. "The Problem of the Past in Iris Murdoch's *Nuns and Soldiers*." *Renascence: Essays on Value in Literature* 38 (Spring, 1986): 170-182. Reprinted in *Critical Essays on Iris Murdoch*, edited by Lindsey Tucker. New York: G. K. Hall, 1992. Although this is not a historical novel, its central characters have differing relations to their personal histories. The passive Count feels himself determined by Poland's tragic history. Tim is without a sense of history; he cuts himself off from the past and lives for the feeling of beginning again in the present. In fact, he is rebaptized twice by nearly drowning. Gertrude, like Tim, shucks off the past and is happy. Scanlan calls her a survivor. Anne's return to the secular world is not happy. Though she briefly yearns for timeless moments of love, she commits herself to a vision of an historical Christ who lived and suffered in historical time. All Murdoch's characters forget and rewrite the past, and she forces her readers to do the same with their interpretations of the novel itself. Scanlan offers many ways of reading the novel's title.

_____. *Traces of Another Time: History and Politics in Postwar British Fiction*. Princeton, N.J.: Princeton University Press, 1990. Chapter 5 is a revised version of her article "The Problem of the Past in Iris Murdoch's *Nuns and Soldiers*."

Sizemore, Christine Wick. *A Female Vision of the City: London in the Novels of Five British Women*. Knoxville: University of Tennessee Press, 1989. As usual, Murdoch sees London as a labyrinth, but London here is not so vivid as in *A World Child*. The city—its pubs and its public places—is charming and pleasant. The weather is milder than usual. Perhaps because Murdoch spends more time in the minds of female characters, the novel itself is not so pessimistic. *Nuns and Soldiers* offers two ways out of human problems. Anne walks the streets of the city in search of selflessness. Her vision of Jesus conflicts with human love, and in the end she embarks on a life of service. Tim, who also walks London's streets and sits on park benches, has a different kind of mystical vision, one that helps him to lose his egotism and regain Gertrude's love. Like Tim, Gertrude also achieves happiness through human love.

Spear, Hilda D. *Iris Murdoch*. New York: St. Martin's Press, 1995.
In Chapter 6, Spear groups this long novel with five other long novels which are deeply concerned with philosophy, religion, and mysticism as well as with psychological domination. Very brief comments.

Todd, Richard. *Iris Murdoch*. London: Methuen, 1984.
In very brief comments in Chapter 5, Todd notes parallels with *Hamlet* in this less than satisfactory novel. Many elements in the story read like self-parody. It has more of a sense of history than most Murdoch novels.

The Philosopher's Pupil, 1983.

Bove, Cheryl K. "Americas and Americans in Iris Murdoch's Novels." In *Encounters with Iris Murdoch*, edited by Richard Todd. Amsterdam: Free University Press, 1988.
In Murdoch's novels, the United States is regularly associated with bad scholarship, such as that of the ambitious Steve Glatz.

_____. *Understanding Iris Murdoch*. Columbia: University of South Carolina Press, 1993.
In Chapter 6, Bove notes that even though Ennistone's magical waters are healing for most, they are an inferno for others. The central character is Rozanov, a mediocre philosopher whose egotism leads him to cut himself off from everyone, including his granddaughter Hattie and his former pupil George. George, a violent man obsessed with gaining his teacher's attention, changes into a quiet and perhaps broken man. Two religious figures are important. Father Jacoby mixes various religious trappings; he believes in spiritual forces but not in God. William Eastcote, a Quaker with a simple faith, does good; the novel amplifies his death, suggesting that Murdoch approves of his selflessness.

Conradi, Peter. *Iris Murdoch: The Saint and the Artist*. New York: St. Martin's Press, 1986.
In Chapter 3, Conradi explains that the philosopher Rozanov espouses absolute ideas that Murdoch does not endorse. George tries to kill Rozanov because he cannot live up to Rozanov's

perfectionism. In Chapter 5, Conradi identifies Tom as someone who suffers from the negative sublime. In Chapter 10, Conradi sees water in this novel as a symbol of Eros. In very brief remarks in Chapter 11, he calls attention to one source: Dostoevski's *The Brothers Karamazov*. In Murdoch's novel, George symbolically murders his father when he attacks his teacher, an old philosopher who finds his work too hard. Conradi thinks this novel is not completely successful because it contains too many disparate elements.

_____. "Iris Murdoch and Dostoevsky." In *Encounters with Iris Murdoch*, edited by Richard Todd. Amsterdam: Free University Press, 1988.
Murdoch, like Dostoevsky, worries that the decline of religion will result in moral anarchy. George, who resembles Kirilov in *The Devils*, wants to act out the idea of going beyond morality. In a discussion, Murdoch agrees that her narrator "N" is Dostoevskian and hints that "N" may be Sir Ivor Sefton.

Dipple, Elizabeth. *The Unresolvable Plot: Reading Contemporary Fiction*. New York: Routledge, 1989.
In Chapter 9, Dipple discusses this novel as typical of Murdoch's later work. Here are the ingredients of a conventional novel: a detailed evocation of place, believable characters, and a narrator interested in shaping his material to a satisfying conclusion. But Murdoch is experimental as well. The novel often questions the accuracy of reading, its characters are opaque, and its meaning ambiguous. The title speaks of one pupil, but besides George, there are many others who learn different things: Father Jacoby, Hattie, Stella, Steve.

Gordon, David J. *Iris Murdoch's Fables of Unselfing*. Columbia: University of Missouri Press, 1995.
In Chapter 1, Gordon speculates the Rozanov kills himself partly out of his frustration with philosophy. In Chapter 4, Gordon discusses how this novel represents contingency, in particular George's motives for trying to kill his wife. In Chapter 6, Gordon asks: who really is the philosopher's pupil? Although George is the obvious candidate, Father Bernard is a better one. He receives

Rozanov's unspoken message, and Gordon summarizes its implications.

Griffin, Gabriele. *The Influence of the Writings of Simone Weil on the Fiction of Iris Murdoch.* San Francisco: Mellen Research University Press, 1993.

Griffin mentions this novel in references scattered throughout her study. George's obsession about Rozanov is based purely on his own needs. The novel's opening description of violent rain shows how Murdoch makes details reflect the mental state of a character. Father Bernard is one of many religious figures in Murdoch's fiction who (like Murdoch and Weil) do not believe in a personal God, but who take Christ seriously. Murdoch's novels show a growing hostility to feminists; this novel shows no female bonding. On the other hand, very masculine men like George lack moral integrity. Rozanov is a typical Murdoch father figure, who mainly reflects the needs of those who are obsessed with him. Many fathers and father figures like Rozanov die in Murdoch novels; their deaths signal the end of some illusions. Rozanov is also one of many Murdoch men who write or are writing great books; these men are seldom capable of responding to other people.

Haffenden, John. *Novelists in Interview.* London: Methuen, 1985.

In this interview, Murdoch says that at the center of this novel is not philosophy, but the pupil-teacher relationship. Rozanov is a study of how power is misused and of how power figures are isolated. Although George the pupil is a man obsessed, Rozanov acts wrongly toward him. As a philosopher, Rozanov shows a particular kind of despair, that born of a wish to see everything. Even though it is inconclusive, his discussion with Father Bernard is central to the novel because it bears upon the other characters. Stella is not a successful character. The Slipper House should not be compared to Prospero's island: Murdoch emphatically denies any specific parallels with *The Tempest.*

Heusel, Barbara. "An Interview with Iris Murdoch." *University of Windsor Review* 21 (Winter, 1988): 1-13.

Murdoch resists Heusel's attempt to read Bakhtinian meanings into this novel. George is half-mad, under the common delusion that his teacher continues to think about him. Murdoch took the name of Rozanov from that of a painter. Her use of a narrator resembles Dostoevsky's in *The Possessed*.

_____. *Patterned Aimlessness: Iris Murdoch's Novels of the 1970s and 1980s*. Athens: University of Georgia Press, 1995.
This book treats this novel in detail. In Chapter 2, Heusel says that Rozanov's death at the hand of a pupil recalls the death of a real philosopher, Moritz Schlick. In Chapter 6, she analyzes this novel's mixture of styles, voices, and genres in light of Bakhtin's theories of the carnivalesque. In its low comedy, Tom is the carnival king who endures ritual death and is revived. Rozanov is the old king who is dethroned and dies but is not revived. He figures as a scapegoat, and his death reinvigorates the community. Heusel emphasizes Murdoch's parody of newspaper reports. In Chapter 9, Heusel notes the resemblance of the waterworks to ancient structures such as the Roman baths at Bath. The society at the Bath Institute is carnivalesque in its mingling of all sorts of people. The baths themselves are womblike; Tom's exploration of them is sexual. Heusel reproduces several of Murdoch's floor plans of the Institute.

Johnson, Deborah. *Iris Murdoch*. Bloomington: Indiana University Press, 1987.
In Chapter 2, Johnson looks at the elusive relation of the female author to N., the limited and garrulous male narrator. She thinks Murdoch's presence can be discerned in the gap (which increases as the novel goes on) between N's interpretations and the real significance of the events he reports. In Chapter 4, Johnson points out that the spa's underground recesses is another cavelike symbol; Tim's descent is a magical act. George on the other hand shows a more orthodox interpretation of the Platonic myth: he wants perfect truth and is almost blinded.
     In Chapter 5, Johnson says that pairing up Hattie and Tom so improbably and so neatly suggests that life is not this way: many female concerns are ignored. Johnson also provides an important discussion of the ending of this novel in relation to its central symbol. The Ennistone baths built on Roman foundations symbolize the forces of eros and fecundity through time and the efforts of civilizations to control them. The delightful babies that

swim in them are associated with their opposite, the cerebral and unhappy Rozanov, in that his body returns to the waters after his death. The end of the novel provides, not usual closure, but a sense of the flux of organic life.

Kenyon, Olga. *Women Novelists Today: A Survey of English Writing in the Seventies and Eighties.* New York: St. Martin's Press, 1988.
Kenyon dislikes this novel because its women are stereotypes who let themselves be used by men.

Khanna, Urmilla. "Iris Murdoch and Shakespeare." *Yearly Review* [University of Delhi] (December, 1991): 17-28.
Khanna sees echoes of Shakespeare's Sonnet 20 in the friendship of "Emma" and Tom.

Marget, Madeline. "The Water is Deep: Iris Murdoch's `Utterly Demanding Present.'" *Commonweal*, June 14, 1991, 399-402.
Symbolic water is everywhere, even though Ennistone's baths (modeled on Bath's baths) are realistic. All residents bathe, and most are rewarded by contentment or at least that possibility.

Mettler, Darlene D. *Sound and Sense: Musical Allusion and Imagery in the Novels of Iris Murdoch.* New York: Peter Lang, 1991.
A fictional musical play named "The Triumph of Aphrodite" helps unify the themes of this novel. Aphrodite's triumph combines with Roman history to suggest the presence of pagan sexuality in Ennistone to oppose the town's staid Quakerism. Music is more explicitly present in the countertenor voice possessed by Emma. Even though he tries to keep his talent a secret, thinking it is somehow sinister, he sings out over the chaos at Slipper House and calms the rioters.

Moss, Howard. "Narrow Escapes: Iris Murdoch." *Grand Street* 6 (Autumn, 1986): 228-240.
A rambling review-essay which contains some excellent Murdoch criticism. Rozanov is a monster/magician who inspires devotion in many and who tries to dictate his granddaughter's life. George's demand for recognition is no stronger than Rozanov's will to deny it. Yet Rozanov does love. He discovers that his life

as a dispassionate intellectual is undermined when he gives in to his emotions. Alex's "Slipper House" is a magical place, filled with human associations. It is also haunted by foxes, and Moss is brilliant when he evokes what these animals suggest: an alien, natural, animate, and mysterious world.

Punja, Prem Parkash. *The Novels of Iris Murdoch: A Critical Study.* Jalandar, India: ABS Publications, 1993.
In Chapter 5, the relationships Punja treats are ones of teacher and pupil. In Father Bernard's relation to Hattie, there is real teaching and learning. Emma's teachers try to force him to choose between their subjects. George's relation to Rozanov is one of obsessed pupil to powerful and indifferent teacher; it shows the pain that can result when a teacher withdraws his attention.

Ramanathan, Suguna. "The Concept of Good in Four of Iris Murdoch's Later Novels." *Heythrop Journal* 28 (1987): 388-404.
An earlier version of her arguments in *Iris Murdoch: Figures of Good.*

_____. *Iris Murdoch: Figures of Good.* London: Macmillan, 1990.
In Chapter 5, Ramanathan sees William Eastcote, a Quaker, as this novel's character who strives for the Good. She analyzes his speech to a Quaker meeting, which shows in its grammar and in its ideas that he is close to attaining an innocent and peaceful state of contemplation. He often figures as a Christ figure, and his death suggests atonement to some. He presents a contrast to the other tortured characters in the novel. Gabriel is good, but her sympathetic gushes of love imply need. In spite of being a philosopher (or perhaps because of it), Rozanov has neglected his heart. In spite of suspicions that he has been deluded, he acts heartlessly, especially to George. He lies and manipulates; he is driven by his love of power, not by virtue. Pitiable George is driven by an obsession. After Eastcote's death, he seems to have changed, like the man from Plato's cave who has seen the sun (the Good) too directly. Father Bernard's attempt to unself himself parodies Eastcote's achievement; yet at the end, he has made some progress. Murdoch's overall tone is both "sad and affectionate"

toward her character's capacity for good and evil—and for absurdity.

Spear, Hilda D. *Iris Murdoch*. New York: St. Martin's Press, 1995.
In Chapter 6, Spear groups this long novel with five other long novels which are deeply concerned with philosophy, religion, and mysticism as well as with psychological domination and obsession. Very brief comments.

Todd, Richard. *Iris Murdoch*. London: Methuen, 1984.
In brief comments in Chapter 5, Todd notes Murdoch's departures from her usual practices. The background is a spa town close to London. The cast of characters is very large. The narration is in the first person by "N," a nameless figure who knows more than most third-person narrators. Todd thinks this method of narration allows Murdoch to order her story without surrendering its many mysteries.

Updike, John. "Baggy Monsters." *The New Yorker*, November 14, 1983, 188-205.
Updike reviews this novel with Umberto Eco's *The Name of the Rose*. He praises it and particularly likes The Bath Institute, where citizens swim and stand about, nearly naked figures that resemble those on "one of Dante's penitential terraces." The baths rumble, like "the earth's subconscious." Tom descends into their forbidden heart like a knight errant into a dragon's cave. Yet even with all this symbolism, the baths remain a marvel of Victorian plumbing.

Walsh, Harry. "Stylization and Parody on Dostoevskian Themes." *Rocky Mountain Review of Language and Literature* 45 (1991): 217-229.
Walsh distinguishes a Russian novelist's stylistic emulation of Dostoevski from Murdoch's parody. In this novel, Murdoch creates a travesty by applying aspects of Dostoevskian highly dramatic struggles of good and evil to unworthy provincial English characters. Murdoch's narrator N. resembles the Russian's narrator G. in *The Devils*; the novels have similar beginnings. Both George and Rozanov seem possessed by demons in the Russian manner. (Rozanov's name is the same as a disciple of

Dostoevski's.) The teacher-pupil relation of George and Rozanov resembles that of Stavrogin and Verkhovensky, except that in the Russian novel the pupil rejects the teacher. George mentions a suicide in a Dostoevski novel. There are also other significant parallels, including insect imagery and references to disease. Not very convincing.

The Good Apprentice, 1985.

Bloom, Harold. "Introduction." In *Iris Murdoch*. New York: Chelsea House, 1986.
   Behind the social comedy, Murdoch is an original religious writer, a bitter Platonist. In his progression from hell to purgatory, Edward meets many figures who should guide him, but who do not. The pastoral idyll at Seegard turns out to be hollow. Edward is the novel's only good person, and his journey of self-purgation reminds Bloom of Freudian ideas. Bloom admires this novel, though he thinks that both Murdoch's blend of realism and fantasy and her authorial intrusions are not entirely successful.

Bove, Cheryl K. *Understanding Iris Murdoch*. Columbia: University of South Carolina Press, 1993.
   In Chapter 7, Bove helps readers sort out this novel's complicated relationships by focusing on its two quests for maturity. Stuart, a Platonist, withdraws from the world and cannot return until a vision in an Underground station enables him to take his place. Edward, propelled by guilt into a search for his father's love, painfully develops a concern for others.

Brooks-Davies, Douglas. *Fielding, Dickens, Gosse, Iris Murdoch, and Oedipal* Hamlet. New York: St. Martin's Press, 1989.
   The author notes the pattern of *Hamlet* in this novel. Jesse the father seems both dead and not dead; Edmund is the haunted, Hamlet-like son.

Byatt, A. S. *Degrees of Freedom: The Novels of Iris Murdoch*. Expanded ed. London: Vintage, 1994.
   In Chapter 17, Byatt briefly evokes the mythic power of this novel. Stuart's saintly quest is compared to Edward's journey to the

underworld in search of his father. Jesse, who appears as a fertility god, lives in a magical and dangerous earthly paradise decorated in an Arts and Crafts style. Both Edward and Stuart have moments of illumination (Stuart when he sees a mouse in the Underground). Edward sees his life as shaped both by chance and by a dramatic order. Byatt compares this novel to Shakespeare's *A Winter's Tale*.

Conradi, Peter. "Platonism in Iris Murdoch." In *Platonism and the English Imagination*, edited by Anna Baldwin and Sarah Hutton. New York: Cambridge University Press, 1994.
Murdoch usually scorns psychiatrists, but McCaskerville is an exception, perhaps because he is moving toward Buddhism.

Dipple, Elizabeth. *The Unresolvable Plot: Reading Contemporary Fiction*. New York: Routledge, 1989.
In Chapter 9, Dipple says that this novel is about illusion and about the impossibility of understanding the world. Stuart tries to find the truth by withdrawing. Edward, like the prodigal son or Cain, quests in the world. He is helped to pass from guilt to awareness by the magic of Seegard. This is the house of his enchanter/father Jesse; it seems like something from a legend, except that it is literally dirty, the parody of a pastoral setting. This novel is both old-fashioned in its realistic characters and experimental in the ambiguity of its message.

Gordon, David J. *Iris Murdoch's Fables of Unselfing*. Columbia: University of Missouri Press, 1995.
In Chapter 3, Gordon sees Murdoch behind Edward's facing the problem of the tension between art and magic and between accident and connectedness. In Chapter 6, Gordon notes how the story is based on the cycle of seasons. He praises its simple structure in which all begins with Edward's act and consequent suffering. Jesse is the novel's magician. Gordon calls Stuart an apprentice saint, a man who tries to keep his innocence in the adult world. Edward's healing takes a long time. He looks outward toward what is mysterious, especially toward his father. Finally he receives proof of his father's love. The book ends in various joys.

Griffin, Gabriele. *The Influence of the Writings of Simone Weil on the Fiction of Iris Murdoch.* San Francisco: Mellen Research University Press, 1993.

In Chapter 3, Griffin discusses the influence on this novel of Weil's concept of the void: a moment of spiritual nothingness beyond God. The only truly otherworldly godlike figure is Mark in the moment before his death. The novel's other characters ask how to act in a godless world. Thomas knows the void and, though he is attracted to the death of the self, elects to help other through the theory of psychoanalysis. When his detachment is shattered by his wife's infidelity, he copes by forgiving her in a priestlike way. Murdoch suggests that both analyst and priest are fillers of the void.

Stuart is a Weil-like figure. He knows the void and wants to do good without the help of a god, an institution, a theory, or a father figure. Like Carel in *The Time of the Angels*, he knows the absence of God, but he does not despair. He wants to *be* a void, and almost succeeds. But he finds that in the world his good acts have consequences (like Midge's falling in love with him) that are not always good. He becomes a teacher and a morally mature person.

Edward describes his situation is Weilian terms: he is like a stalled airplane needing energy to buoy him up. He looks to Harry, but his stepfather is an inadequate father figure. He seeks his real father, Jesse, whose forgiveness begins to heal him; at the same time he sees that Jesse is decaying. He is forgiven by the sister of the man he had caused to die, and he also ends by helping others. Midge has a vision as well; at the insistence of males, she gives it over to return to an ordinary life (Griffin seems to disapprove). Griffin also notes how Murdoch tries to upset her readers' ideas of reality by the uncanny (Ilona dances above the ground) and how Murdoch reinforces some stereotypes: single women like May are bitter; women, like the Baltrams, bond only with reference to a man; masculine men like Harry are limited.

Heusel, Barbara. "An Interview with Iris Murdoch." *University of Windsor Review* 21 (Winter, 1988)" 1-13.

At the end of the novel, Stuart is the only good apprentice.

Jones, Alan. "Apprenticed to Goodness: The Modern Passion Play." *Studies in Formative Spirituality* 9 (Fall, 1988): 37-53.
An article on Christian spirituality and morals which speaks of God's comic drama. He cites *The Divine Comedy* as a work of literature that reflects this drama, and he uses *The Good Apprentice* to provide some examples of how it works. Each of the novel's characters is in hell or in purgatory. Stuart is an apprentice to goodness and as such resembles the flayed Marsyas. Midge and Harry are having an affair, and their obsessions wear them out. Harry wants Midge to be his goddess; when he is disappointed, his lust turns to despair. Neither can see the otherness of the other person. Edward is in a timeless hell, but he has two advantages: he is forced to recognize the sufferings of others, and he has Thomas to be (Dante-like) his guide.

Kenyon, Olga. *Women Novelists Today: A Survey of English Writing in the Seventies and Eighties.* New York: St. Martin's Press, 1988.
Kenyon likes the vitality of the women in this novel. Its central question is how human beings can communicate and can judge their actions.

Khanna, Urmilla. "Iris Murdoch and Shakespeare." *Yearly Review* [University of Delhi] (December, 1991): 17-28.
McCaskerville is Prospero-like when he contemplates giving up his power over others.

Johnson, Deborah. *Iris Murdoch.* Bloomington: Indiana University Press, 1987.
In Chapter 5, Johnson discusses ways in which in the endings of her novels Murdoch undermines the usual sorts of neat conclusions. In this novel, she refuses to sum up and lets her readers make their own interpretations.

Lundin, Roger. "Murdoch's Magic: The Consolations of Fiction." *Christian Century*, May 18, 1988, 499-502.
Lundin makes brief but telling comments on the toast to good things offered at the end of the novel.

Moss, Howard. "Narrow Escapes: Iris Murdoch." *Grand Street* 6
    (Autumn, 1986): 228-240.
    Here are Murdoch's usual themes (the search for Good, forgive-
    ness) and her usual magical landscapes. Edward Baltram is a
    hero straight from a nineteenth century novel, a young man like
    David Copperfield.

Phillips, Diana. "The Complementarity of Good and Evil in *A Fairly
    Honorable Defeat.*" In *Encounters with Iris Murdoch*, edited by
    Richard Todd. Amsterdam: Free University Press, 1988.
    Murdoch comments in passing that in this novel Jesse Baltram is
    viewed by some characters as a magician, a supernatural being,
    and by others as a harmless old man. Both views have merit.

Punja, Prem Parkash. *The Novels of Iris Murdoch: A Critical Study.*
    Jalandar, India: ABS Publications, 1993.
    In Chapter 4, Punja finds three characters of goodness in this
    novel. Stuart tries to help Edward and Midge, but he is often
    misinterpreted because he lacks practical wisdom. Thomas also
    tries to help Edward and takes Midge back. Ursula's goodness is
    more practical and wise. She understands both Edward and
    Stuart.

Ramanathan, Suguna. *Iris Murdoch: Figures of Good.* London:
    Macmillan, 1990.
    Stuart Cuno is "the good apprentice." He is a figure of good who
    is beginning his journey. He carries purification one step beyond
    previous figures: though he feels the pull of various Western
    traditions, he has no religious beliefs. In relying only on intuition,
    he resembles the philosopher George Moore. He resembles Christ
    as well and produces a Christlike effect on Midge, a Magdalene
    figure. Stuart the good is opposed by Jesse, a Merlin-like man
    who represents artistic energy, and by his Seegard community.
    The world of Seegard is amoral, demonic, beautiful, magical, yet
    decaying. Murdoch presents the antithesis as ambiguous: art has
    its attractions, and Stuart doubts when he sees a mouse happy in
    the Underground. Thomas McCaskerville understands and envies
    Stuart.

Simon, Irène. "A Note on Iris Murdoch's *The Good Apprentice*." *English Studies* 68 (February, 1987): 75-78.

Murdoch alerts her readers to look in this novel for resemblances to the parable of the Prodigal Son. In many ways, Edward does resembles the prodigal and Stuart the elder son of the Bible story. But the parallels are not exact. Edward prospers, not so much because his father forgives him for his sin, but because he comes to love his father so much.

Spear, Hilda D. *Iris Murdoch*. New York: St. Martin's Press, 1995.

In Chapter 6, Spear groups this long novel with five other long novels which are deeply concerned with philosophy, religion, and mysticism as well as with psychological domination. This novel's title is ambiguous, for Edward is a guilty young man; at best he is an apprentice trying to become good. Edward's sin brings on depression (which parallels his half brother Stuart's sufferings) in which he cannot believe he can be forgiven. Edward grasps at a hint from a seance; he has guides like Stuart and his Uncle Thomas (an enchanter), who sends him to Seegard. Here he finds a way of life which Spear says resembles William Morris's kind of socialism. He finds the love of his sisters. But he still needs to find his father (a second enchanter), and when he does he is absolved from sin, yet bound to his father. The climax is complex and mystical; Edward is released from his self-centeredness. At the end, Edward's apprenticeship ends. He has come to terms with his past and will try to be good. A provocative analysis of a complex novel.

Turner, Jack. "Iris Murdoch and the Good Psychoanalyst." *Twentieth Century Literature* 40 (Fall, 1994): 300-317.

Apparently written before Turner's book *Murdoch vs. Freud*, this article makes the same arguments. Murdoch is afraid to look too deeply into Freud, for she is afraid he might undermine her own philosophy.

_____. *Murdoch vs. Freud: A Freudian Look at an Anti-Freudian*. New York: Peter Lang, 1993.

In Chapter 8 of this attack on Murdoch, Turner makes his usual points: Murdoch is working out her own sadomasochistic problems and expressing her oedipal fantasies. Yet this is her best novel because at its center is Thomas McCaskerville, an ethical, wise, and sympathetic man. And at times Murdoch undermines her usual didacticism and seems to lampoon Stuart, a man devoted to the Good. Even so, Murdoch denigrates Freud by having McCaskerville drift away from Freudian orthodoxy.

The Book and the Brotherhood, 1987.

Bove, Cheryl K. "New Directions: Iris Murdoch's Latest Women." In *Critical Essays on Iris Murdoch*, edited by Lindsey Tucker. New York: G. K. Hall, 1992.
In this and other late novels, Murdoch tells the story through many different centers of consciousness. As a result, her female characters are stronger here than in some earlier male-dominated novels. Rose is a victim who subordinates herself to Gerard throughout the novel; her strength is that she understands what is happening. On the other hand, Tamar is at first a total victim, but then after her religious conversion, she gets power. Unfortunately, power makes her hard-hearted.

_____. *Understanding Iris Murdoch*. Columbia: University of South Carolina Press, 1993.
In Chapter 8, Bove emphasizes Tamar's role. She illustrates women's social situation; her religious conversion is wrongly egotistical. Jenkin is a good man who does good works. Crimond is a demonic absolutist whose lifework is motivated by ego and whose book will be read by only a few. Its best effect is to release Gerard's creativity.

Byatt, A. S. *Degrees of Freedom: The Novels of Iris Murdoch*. Expanded ed. London: Vintage, 1994.
In Chapter 18, Byatt identifies Crimond as this novel's version of Murdoch's demonic enchanter. The brotherhood, as represented by Gerard, is mired in confused, liberal, bourgeois ideas that cannot stand up to Crimond's, just as they cannot do much about Tamar or Jenkin. Yet minor characters survive, though humility and magic, as do precisely observed things like the human body, snails, and a parrot.

Colley, Mary. "Iris Murdoch—The `Good' Novelist." *Contemporary Review* 261 (December, 1992): 319-322.

In this novel (as in others), Murdoch does not introduce her characters gently, but demands and gets total participation as the reader meets many important characters in the first scene. Like Trollope, Murdoch often shows different people in different places at the same time.

Dipple, Elizabeth. "The Green Knight and Other Vagaries of the Spirit; or, Tricks and Images for the Human Soul; or, the Uses of Imaginative Literature." In *Iris Murdoch and the Search for Human Goodness*, edited by Maria Antonaccio and William Schweiker. Chicago: University of Chicago Press, 1996.

This novel's conclusion (the couples' happiness, Gerard's plans to write a book) is an ironic parody of happy endings. Most of the characters are egocentric and helplessly idle, moral flotsam. They are paralyzed, unable to commit themselves to the present or any course of action. The books central antagonism is between Jenkin and Crimond. Jenkin is a character of potential good, a man who is not egocentric, who tries for perspective, and who attempts to act. Crimond is a man of potential for much evil and destruction, yet who wishes to create.

Gordon, David J. *Iris Murdoch's Fables of Unselfing*. Columbia: University of Missouri Press, 1995.

In Chapter 3, Gordon sees Jenkin as the opposite of a typical Murdoch charismatic power-figure; Jenkin is benign and has a negative charisma. Gerard is a typical Murdoch character who adopts a role he cannot sustain; like other Platonists of this sort, he is humiliated. In Chapter 7, Gordon sees this novel as the beginning of Murdoch's late phase, one in which she is interested in the possibility of a spiritual figure who can give her age what it requires. These novels suffer because readers are not fascinated by these figures, in this case Crimond. What his book is about is left vague. Gordon suspects Murdoch's real concerns are not political, but religious. The rest of the characters are a sad bunch of liberal intellectuals who are incapable of loving; Gerard is particularly foolish.

Griffin, Gabriele. *The Influence of the Writings of Simone Weil on the Fiction of Iris Murdoch.* San Francisco: Mellen Research University Press, 1993.

Griffin makes scattered references to this novel throughout her study. By its indeterminate ending, Murdoch wishes to insist on the unpredictability of life. Its middle-aged women live in a Victorian world in which women have no life apart from a man, and no male characters give them the validation that they crave. Murdoch engages the readers attention by long conversations in which the speakers are hard to identify. Often, Murdoch's married couples remain yoked together, even when, like Jean and Duncan, they are separated. She uses instances of the "uncanny" (like Lily and Gulliver's snails) to upset a reader's limited conceptions of reality. Father McAlister is an typical example of a clergyman who does not believe in God. Crimond is a typical father figure, and Duncan is typically obsessed by him.

In her conclusion, Griffin discusses the direction Murdoch's work has taken. Her work does not explore political or social issues like the unemployed (Gulliver) or teenage girls getting abortions (Tamar). The few attempts at female bonding are failures. Groups do not cohere well enough to perform significant actions. The violent Crimond destroys the brotherhood in a primitive way by taking one of the group's women with him.

Khanna, Urmilla. "Iris Murdoch and Shakespeare." *Yearly Review* [University of Delhi] (December, 1991): 17-28.

Khanna sees the love triangle of Shakespeare's Sonnet 144 behind the early Rose-Gerard-Sinclair relation. The confusions of Shakespearean comedy can be seen when both Jenkin and Crimond love Rose while Gerard declares his love for Jenkin.

Levenson, Michael. "Liberals in Love." *New Republic*, June 6, 1988, 40-44.

A discerning review. The theme of this novel seems to be that liberalism is dying; its center will not hold. The three pivotal characters represent three alternatives. To the Platonist Gerard, the world is mixed up, but the True and Good are still somewhere above. The Marxist Crimond is really a godless, sexy, and amoral adventurer; he is his own God. The humble Jenkin is closer to Murdoch's heart. But liberalism and Marxism are not the center of this novel. Love is. It creates melodrama in Murdoch's fiction as it emphasizes that other people exist. In this novel, Murdoch creates a great diversity of "free" characters who wander about to find diverse fates. Her political allegory metamorphoses into a "miasma" of common life and love.

Levenson is eloquent on Murdoch's own dream. Murdoch shows moments (as one between Jenkin and Gerard) when characters are able to project themselves onto other characters and understand each other. But Levenson wonders if there can be such moments outside of fiction? Murdoch seems to wish that life could be more like her novels. Readers might wish that they could be known and loved by a novelist who dreamed them into being.

Lundin, Roger. "Murdoch's Magic: The Consolations of Fiction." *Christian Century*, May 18, 1988, 499-502.
Many characters in this novel are attracted to the legacy of Christianity, but feel guilty because they have no right. They live by a set of liberal ideas located between the extremes of Legquist (Christianity is fantasy) and Crimond (the bourgeois world must be destroyed). What is needed is magic, a web of words. Fiction is therapy. The unbelieving Father McAlister supplies Christian words to Tamar, and they seem to change her. Religion becomes therapy too.

Meyers, Jeffrey. "An Interview with Iris Murdoch." *Denver Quarterly* 26 (Summer, 1991): 102-111.
Murdoch remarks that this novel grew out of her interest in Marxism and her observation of the ways people change after their university days. The novel is about the way people are defined by the way their opinions differ.

Newman, Charles. "Leftists in Love." *The New York Times Book Review*, January 31, 1988, 1, 26-27.
Newman praises this novel for being about politics, ideas, and the British nation without being political, ideological, or provincial. Newman thinks Crimond is a fascinating creation, weak in his dependence on Jean, but strong in the force and clarity of his deterministic views. In this he is out of place in the Brotherhood, members of which lack discipline and rigor. Even so, Murdoch

shows a world in which ideas are transmitted not in the abstract,
but by individual personalities. When Gerard prepares to reply to
Crimond's book, we see a true brotherhood, a group held together
by their responding to ideas and by their literacy. By the end of
the novel, the forces of love and contingency begin to work
against Crimond's determinism.

Ramanathan, Suguna. *Iris Murdoch: Figures of Good.* London:
    Macmillan, 1990.
    In Chapter 7, Ramanathan see Jenkin Riderhood as a figure of
    good. Even though neither the reader or the novel's other charac-
    ters recognize it at first, he resembles Christ, not in his suffering
    (he dies quickly) but in his humility, his love, and his willingness
    to help others. Ramanathan sets Jenkin in the novel's world, one
    which has no focal point, no shared morality, no coherence. Two
    characters present two alternatives. Crimond, who is strong, sexy,
    and manipulative, expresses an extreme Marxist view. Gerard,
    who is cultivated, sensitive, well-meaning, and vain, espouses
    liberal values. Jenkin's third way is Murdoch's vision of a good
    man in contemporary life: he is humble and loving; he acts out
    religious values without having religious faith and hope.

Spear, Hilda D. *Iris Murdoch.* New York: St. Martin's Press, 1995.
    In Chapter 6, Spear groups this novel with five other long novels
    which are deeply concerned with philosophy, religion, and
    mysticism as well as with psychological domination. In brief
    comments, Spear says this novel suffers because Crimond's
    attraction is not believable.

Spice, Nicholas. "Thatchercraft." *London Review of Books*, October
    1, 1987, 8-9.
    In comparison to Ian McEwan's anti-Thatcherite *The Child in
    Time*, Murdoch's novel is out of date. Its opposing forces speak of
    class differences. Crimond, the leftist intellectual who speaks
    with clarity, comes from Scotland and from the lower classes. His
    opponents, most of the rest of the characters, are English, well-
    educated, leisured people with muddled ideas. The novel itself
    speaks of class for it deals with lofty issues, never with lowly ones,
    and never with lowly diction. Murdoch's scrutiny spares nobody,
    except perhaps Jenkin. Most of the characters are obsessed by

Crimond (who can be see as mean and pathetic). So is Murdoch herself; she cannot make up her mind about him. The novel is anachronistic and seems to understand its own anachronism.

Thomas, Jo. "To Know Secret Thoughts." *The New York Times Book Review*, January 31, 1988, 26.
A very brief interview in which Murdoch says *The Book and the Brotherhood* is about Marxism.

Towers, Robert. "The Way We Live Now." *The New York Review of Books*, March 31, 1988, 36-37.
This novel can be read as an allegory of contemporary Britain and of the whole late capitalist world. Its characters talk too much; it is too prolix. But Towers praises the effect of several scenes: the skating party and the attempt at vehicular suicide.

The Message to the Planet, 1989.

Bove, Cheryl K. "New Directions: Iris Murdoch's Latest Women." In *Critical Essays on Iris Murdoch*, edited by Lindsey Tucker. New York: G. K. Hall, 1992.
Murdoch's female characters are stronger here than in some earlier male-dominated novels. At first Irina seems helpless, but she becomes powerful without losing her perceptiveness. Maisie, who resembles Murdoch herself, is outspoken and assertive without being egotistical. Only Franca seems a victim. Although she is enraged by how her husband treats her, she returns to him. Even though many readers object to her return, it may be justified in that she knows what she is doing.

_____. *Understanding Iris Murdoch*. Columbia: University of South Carolina Press, 1993.
In Chapter 8, Bove identifies Marcus as an intellectual demon figure. When he heals Patrick, some say he shows how spirituality can degenerate into magic. Others think Marcus really does have a spiritual message for the world. The cause of his death is debated, as is its meaning. Although Ludens thinks Marcus has a message, he can only give his own Murdoch-like advice: act for the good.

Broyard, Anatole. "In the Emergency Ward of the Mind." *The New York Times Book Review*, February 4, 1990, 3, 28.
    Although he is puzzled, Broyard appreciates this novel. Marcus brings Patrick back to life by refusing to be nauseated by him.

Colley, Mary. "Iris Murdoch—The `Good' Novelist." *Contemporary Review* 261 (December, 1992): 319-322.
    As elsewhere, Murdoch does not introduce her characters politely, but demands and gets her readers' total participation as they quickly meet many important characters. Like Anthony Trollope, Murdoch often shows different people in different places at the same time.

Dipple, Elizabeth. "The Green Knight and Other Vagaries of the Spirit; or, Tricks and Images for the Human Soul; or, the Uses of Imaginative Literature." In *Iris Murdoch and the Search for Human Goodness*, edited by Maria Antonaccio and William Schweiker. Chicago: University of Chicago Press, 1996.
    Dipple comments at length on Ludens's dream about Leonardo giving him a picture of a bicycle and telling him he can ride it if he tries hard enough. This dream applies to Ludens's desire to get from Vallar a coherent book-like message for the planet. Ludens misinterprets Vallar at every turn. Vallar's message seems to be that there is no message, but we can ride one anyway if we try. Vallar, like other Murdoch heroes in her late novels, is a man who can be read either as an evil force or as a suffering old man. He has a magnetic energy that causes others to create illusions.

Gordon, David J. *Iris Murdoch's Fables of Unselfing*. Columbia: University of Missouri Press, 1995.
    In Chapter 7, Gordon says that Marcus Vallar is not a credible character and that the novel is very thin. Murdoch strives for meaning, yet fears it is an illusion.

Griffin, Gabriele. *The Influence of the Writings of Simone Weil on the Fiction of Iris Murdoch*. San Francisco: Mellen Research University Press, 1993.
    Griffin makes several references to this novel in her study.

Heusel, Barbara. *Patterned Aimlessness: Iris Murdoch's Novels of the 1970s and 1980s.* Athens: University of Georgia Press, 1995.
In Chapter 2, Heusel says that Murdoch gives Marcus many of Wittgenstein's characteristics. In Chapter 3, Heusel shows how Murdoch (like Wittgenstein) desires to evoke life's mystery, not by analysis, but by thought-provoking, playful juxtapositions. What is the message that great thinkers like Marcus may want to communicate? That all is accidental? Marcus's phrases have different meanings in different contexts. One possible message is that (as in *Under the Net*) it is painful to go under the patterned net of ordinary thought in order to glimpse the reality underneath. In Chapter 7, Heusel discusses Franca, who, unlike many other trapped Murdoch women, has a chance to choose freedom and power. She chooses to fail. Murdoch shows the progress of her friendship with a powerful woman, Maisie, and their womanly conversation.

Ramanathan, Suguna. *Iris Murdoch: Figures of Good.* London: Macmillan, 1990.
In Chapter 8, Ramanathan sees Marcus not so much as good but as holy. People around him view him that way, especially after he raises Pat from the dead. Ludens, his chief disciple, is a loving, ordinary soul who wants Marcus to leave a written text for mankind. But Marcus is interested in holiness. Murdoch asks how such a man can relate to the ordinary world of Ludens; the answer seems to be that Marcus must be separate. Marcus's compassion for human suffering leads him to concentrate on the Holocaust; his identification with its victims is so intense that he appears to will his own death. The novel also stresses the dangers of technology to morality and religion.

Sinclair, Clive. "Is There Anybody Out There? *The Times Literary Supplement*, October 20, 1989, 1149.
Vallar resembles Wittgenstein, Canetti, Prospero, Lear, and Shylock. He is also like Aslan, Lord of C. S. Lewis's Narnia, a kind of Christ. Vallar is also human—and mad. What is the message? Sinclair speculates that, because of all its detail, the novel itself may be a message for beings from another planet.

Spear, Hilda D. *Iris Murdoch*. New York: St. Martin's Press, 1995.
    In Chapter 6, Spear groups this long novel with five other long
    novels which are deeply concerned with philosophy, religion, and
    mysticism as well as with psychological domination.

Sutherland, John. "Shakespeare the Novelist." *London Review of
    Books*, September 28, 1989, 26-27.
    This novel's five central characters represent five modes of
    thought. Ludens is an historian; Gildas is a musician and former
    priest; Patrick is a poet; Jack is an artist; and Marcus is a philoso-
    pher and a mathematician. Ludens works hard to find Marcus's
    message, but neither he nor Sutherland can do so. As usual,
    Murdoch renders physical processes wonderfully, in this case
    getting a divan down a flight of stairs.

Sturrock, June. "Murdoch's Leach Gatherer: Interpretation in *The
    Message to the Planet*. *English Studies in Canada* 19
    (December, 1993): 457-469.
    In this novel, Murdoch investigates the problem of interpretation
    by parodying not only Wordsworth's "Resolution and Independ-
    ence" but Lewis Carroll's parody of that poem. In Wordsworth, an
    old leech-gatherer tells the poet about his life, but the poet hardly
    hears him (the point of Carroll's parody). Instead, Wordsworth's
    imagination transforms the old man into a symbol; the poem
    celebrates the power of the imagination. Murdoch describes the
    same process from a different perspective. In his obsessed desire
    to extract a message from Marcus the philosopher, Ludens cannot
    hear what Marcus the real man says and see what he is. Ludens is
    not alone, for other characters interpret Marcus as artist, healer,
    monster, or sphinx. Ludens is blind, not only to Marcus the man,
    but to his own situation, his search for a father and his jealousy of
    his half brother. Finally, Marcus's message is only meaningless
    babble, Murdoch's way of saying that everything is contingent,
    uninterpretable. The Ludens/Marcus relationship can be seen in
    Jack and Franca as well, except that she willingly plays roles in
    Jack's fantasies.

The Green Knight, 1993.

Dipple, Elizabeth. "The Green Knight and Other Vagaries of the Spirit; or, Tricks and Images for the Human Soul; or, The Uses of Imaginative Literature." In *Iris Murdoch and the Search for Human Goodness*, edited by Maria Antonaccio and William Schwelker. Chicago: University of Chicago Press, 1996.
Peter Mir, like Crimond of *The Book and the Brotherhood* and Vallar of *The Message to the Planet*, is a character outside the range of our perception, a good magician veiled from us by the narrator. His antagonist, Lucas Graffe, seems to be an evil magician. The three sisters are three fairy princesses living in their castle in Hammersmith before being plucked from it by Life. Mir's life suggests many parallels: he can be seen as Christ, as a scapegoat, as the bringer of the apocalypse and the millennium. He exists at the boundaries of the real world and the spirit world. After Mir's death, Moy enters the sea as fearlessly as Gawain and seeks death as a kind of pagan baptism. Moy sees what Mir sees, yet is at home in the world and loves all beings. Her suffering is a kind of spiritual yearning. Bellamy comically represents the vagaries of the human spirit. He wants a vision; he wants to serve Mir. He desires the world to be energized by Mir's spirit, but must make do with less than that.

Gordon, David J. *Iris Murdoch's Fables of Unselfing*. Columbia: University of Missouri Press, 1995.
In Chapter 3, Gordon sees Bellamy as a typical Murdoch character who takes on a role he cannot sustain. Mir, like other power figures, has connections to Eastern Europe. In Chapter 7, Gordon finds this novel more attractive than the two that preceded it. Its characters are likable, as is the dog. Moreover, the good magician, Mir, is not so repellent as are Crimond and Vallar. Mir faces the bad magician, Lucas, and their talk goes over the heads of Bellamy and Clement. But the story does not work on the literal level as well as it does on the symbolic. The last third of the novel is best, for people think that there may be a good force that can help them.

Martin, Priscilla. "*Sir Gawain* and *The Green Knight*." *Iris Murdoch News Letter*, no. 9 (Autumn, 1995): 11-12.

When a character, Clement, tries to discover similarities between the story in which he is living and the late medieval poem, he finds magicians and beautiful maidens but not much more. For Martin, both works begin by emphasizing justice and restitution and move on to emphasize mercy and reconciliation. Peter, like the Green Knight himself, turns out to be benevolent (though not in a specifically Christian way). Neither work is tragic; in both, characters return home from their quests with a new humility.

Shippey, Tom. "In a Magic Circle." *The Times Literary Supplement*, September 10, 1993, 20.
Its title implies that this novel's genre will be social realism. Parallels to the fairy-tale-like *Gawain and the Green Knight* abound, for a character returns from the dead to challenge and liberate an upper-class society. But they do not add up. The novel also fails on the literal level: many episodes (like the crime and the trial) are not believable. A *deus ex machina* arrives from Texas, but his plan to do business by fax shows that Murdoch does not understand how business is done. Shippey says these realistic details are important to the moral fable but does not say why.

Simon, Linda. "The Mugger Who Came Back From the Dead." *The New York Times Book Review*, January 9, 1994, 7.
As in *Sir Gawain*, a mystical character appears among a group of people and acts as a catalyst. Many characters believe that Mir can relieve their desolation.

Spear, Hilda D. *Iris Murdoch*. New York: St. Martin's Press, 1995.
In Chapter 7, Spear discusses *The Green Knight* at considerable length. She finds it somewhat puzzling. Lucas resembles Julius in *A Fairly Honorable Defeat*. He is both attractive and evil; he learns nothing from Peter Mir's death and at the end abducts Aleph. Clement, who is the good brother, strives for truth and understands that Peter has saved his life. In Peter, the novel's layers of mythology converge: he resembles both the Green Knight (seemingly murdered, he returns for justice) and Christ (he dies to save Clement). His conversion from Old Testament morality echoes Paul's on the road to Damascus.
    Other characters display similar patterns. Bellamy James lives a religious quest. Moy begins as an innocent, untried girl to

whom every thing is alive and holy; she resembles Leda when she wrestles with a swan; her powers leave her as she experiences unrequited love; at the end, she seems to be able to face the future. Spear stresses the novel's theatrically potent scenes, but warns that readers should not expect answers to the questions it raises. A very valuable discussion.

Spice, Nicholas. "I Hear, I See, I Learn." *London Review of Books*, November 4, 1993, 25-26.

These characters send out social signals to contemporary British readers, even if the novel itself ignores social questions. And even though Murdoch includes a token lower-class man, Rathbone, the novel has no social implications. Its themes are universal. It seems to be an allegorical fairy tale; some characters recognize how certain events suggest *Gawain and the Green Knight*. Lucas's clubbing of Mir is an evil act by an evil man, but it releases a flow of action that liberates. As Murdoch points out in her *Metaphysics as a Guide to Morals*, evil can unlock good. (The two books should be read together.) Murdoch *almost* finds a middle way between realism and allegory.

Jackson's Dilemma, 1995.

Allen, Brooke. "The Drawing-room Comedy of Iris Murdoch." *New Criterion* 15 (September, 1996): 66-73.

Allen sees *As You Like It* behind this novel, with Benet as Jacques. When everyone is paralyzed by the cancellation of the wedding, Jackson takes action and eventually sorts matters out. Jackson is a supernatural and vaguely religious figure; he seems to be undergoing some sort of redemptive suffering. The novel is puzzling and ultimately silly. Murdoch is past her prime.

Dipple, Elizabeth. "Fragments of Iris Murdoch's Vision: *Jackson's Dilemma* as Interlude." *Iris Murdoch News Letter*, no. 9 (Autumn, 1995): 4-8.

Murdoch has written a kind of Shakespearean comedy as a novel. She parodies aspects of many of his comedies, especially their happy endings; her situations seem drawn from a romantic fairy-land. Jackson may be an angel: he has no history, no specific age;

he is a messenger, and he can create visions. But what can angels (or Shakespeare) do in the present? Very little, Murdoch seems to say. Even angels seem not to know how to act.

Leithauser, Brad. "The Good Servant." *The New York Times Book Review*, January 7, 1996, 6.
    The promise of fairy-tale romance gives way to the reality of a psychological thriller. On the edge of the drama, yet also at its center, is Jackson. Perhaps he is the agent of divine intervention, for he helps bring about many happy endings. Leithauser berates Murdoch for sloppy writing.

Rowe, Anne. "Review of Critical Reception of *Jackson's Dilemma*." *Iris Murdoch News Letter*, no. 9 (Autumn, 1995): 8-9.
    The reception of this novel in the British press ranged from rude to ecstatic. Rowe notes ten specific reviews.

Sage, Lorna. "Among Entities." *The Times Literary Supplement*, September 29, 1995, 25.
    The apparent center of this "mystic farce" lies in two decent men, Edward and Martin, surrounded by eccentrics. The real story is Jackson's, who tries to persuade others to accept the world as it is. Jackson is an enabler or midwife as he hastens the novel's happy endings, most notably his own reconciliation with Benet, who had been reading Heidegger all his life.

Bibliographical Studies.

Begnal, Kate. *Iris Murdoch: A Reference Guide*. Boston: G. K. Hall, 1987.
    This guide features an annotated list of writing about Murdoch up to 1983. The list include book reviews and is arranged by year. Begnal's brief introduction surveys Murdoch criticism.

Bove, Cheryl K., and John Fletcher. *Iris Murdoch: A Descriptive Primary and Annotated Secondary Bibliography*. New York: Garland, 1994.
    The standard bibliography. It is exhaustive, lucid, invaluable. The list of works by Murdoch includes translations and juvenilia.

The list of works about Murdoch includes, besides books and articles, dissertations and theses, allusions, radio and television programs, reviews, and biographical and bibliographical sources. Bove and Fletcher also list manuscripts and letters and their whereabouts.

Culley, Ann, and John Feaster.   "Criticism of Iris Murdoch: A Selected Checklist." *Modern Fiction Studies* 15 (Autumn, 1969): 449-457.
Includes many reviews and notes from popular publications in the United States and the United Kingdom.

Todd, Richard. "Bibliography." In *Encounters with Iris Murdoch*, edited by Richard Todd. Amsterdam: Free University Press, 1988.

Tominga, Thomas T., and Wilma Schneidermeyer. *Iris Murdoch and Muriel Spark: A Bibliography*. Metuchen, N.J.: Scarecrow Press, 1976.
A full list of writings by and about Murdoch to 1975. The list of critical works mixes reviews in newspapers and popular magazines with articles in academic journals. For many articles, the authors note which Murdoch work is discussed.

Widmann, R. L. "An Iris Murdoch Checklist." *Critique: Studies in Modern Fiction* 10 (Spring, 1968): 17-29.
In this list which extends through *The Time of the Angels*, Widmann notes editions, translations, and reviews of Murdoch's works as well as books and articles about her.

Other Works

Central to the study of Murdoch's novels is her article "Against Dryness" (*Encounter* 16, January, 1961) and reprinted in *The Novel Today*, edited by Malcolm Bradbury (Manchester: Manchester University Press, 1977). Also valuable is "Existentialists and Mystics: A Note on the Novel in the New Utilitarian Age" in *Essays and Poems Presented to Lord David Cecil*, edited by W. W. Robson (London: Constable, 1970). Murdoch's major philosophical works are *Sartre: Romantic Rationalist* (Cambridge: Bowes & Bowes, 1953),

The Sovereignty of Good over Other Concepts (London: Cambridge University Press, 1967), *The Fire and the Sun: Why Plato Banished the Artists* (Oxford: Clarendon Press, 1977), *Acastos: Two Platonic Dialogues* (London: Chatto & Windus, 1986), and *Metaphysics as a Guide to Morals* (London: Chatto & Windus, 1992). *Existentialists and Mystics: Essays on Philosophy and Literature* (London: Chatto and Windus, 1997) is a collection of essays written between 1950 and 1986. *A Year of Birds* (Tisbury, England: Compton Press, 1978) contains her poetry. Besides dramatizing several of her novels, she has written and published a libretto (*The Servants*, 1980) and two plays: *The Three Arrows and The Servants and the Snow* (1973).

Barbara Pym

General Studies

Ackley, Katherine Anne. *The Novels of Barbara Pym.* New York: Garland, 1989.

This is not a study of individual novels but a discussion of Pym's world. The first chapter gives a useful overview of Pym's writings, including those posthumously published. Ackley emphasizes the importance of unmarried women, food, clothes, and eavesdropping. She notes that the novels generally end inconclusively, though they imply that something is about to happen. Subsequent chapters treat specific themes in evocative detail. Male-female relations are often ridiculous, partly because most men are self-centered. Women sometimes think that female friends are second-best and are catty about them, but Pym shows that satisfying female friendships are possible, particularly between sisters and between married women. Mothers often blight their children's lives. Pym's heroines are independent, but often lonely. The novels generally depict a world in change, but even the most tragic ones suggest affirmations of life. Ackley's last chapter discusses what Pym implies about the dangers and the powers of literature. Because Ackley has provided no index, comments on specific novels are difficult to find.

_____. "Proving One's Worth: The Importance of Marriage in the World of Barbara Pym." In *Joinings and Disjoinings: The Significance of Marital Status in Literature*, edited by JoAnna Stephens Mink and Janet Doubler Ward. Bowling Green, Ohio: Bowling Green State University Popular Press, 1991.

Pym's women, living in a pre-liberation world, are pre-occupied with men and have learned to define themselves by their relations to them. Unmarried women rank low. Married women have higher status, though Pym shows how dull their marriages are. Widows have the best position: all the status of marriage without having husbands to bother with. But even though spinsters look dowdy and put themselves down, Pym emphasizes that her unmarried heroines possess intelligence, self-knowledge, and resilience.

Allen, Orphia Jane. *Barbara Pym: Writing a Life*. Metuchen, N.J.: Scarecrow Press, 1994.

A comprehensive survey of Pym's novels and what critics have written. Allen's thesis is that Pym "wrote her life" in her novels. Both in their superficial details and deeper themes, the novels grow directly out of the life. In addition, Pym addresses feminist issues; her deflation of feminine myths is at the heart of her comedy. Part I relates the details of Pym's life to her writing. Part II treats the novels with reference to Pym's most basic concerns: love, the Church, and literature. Part III provides an extensive summary of the scholarly and critical work on Pym under three categories. The first is "Bibliography, Biography, and the Creative Process." Under "Themes," Allen considers mainly the relations between the sexes. Under "Narrative Technique," Allen reviews the comparisons critics have made between Pym and other novelists. She summarizes more briefly ideas on Pym's satire, her use of trivial details, her comic techniques and irony, and her narrative structures and points of view. Part IV provides an extensive bibliography, especially of reviews. No index.

Bachelder, Frances H. "The Importance of Connecting." In *The Life and Work of Barbara Pym*, edited by Dale Salwak. Iowa City: University of Iowa Press, 1987.

An affectionate tribute to Pym. Bachelder discusses why readers enjoy Pym's work and emphasizes Pym's positive ideas (about life being a glass of blessings). Bachelder calls attention to some strange moments, especially in *A Few Green Leaves*.

Bayley, John. "Where, Exactly, is the Pym World?" In *The Life and Work of Barbara Pym*, edited by Dale Salwak. Iowa City: University of Iowa Press, 1987.

A short, appreciative essay. Ordinary criticism cannot explain Pym's novels. Whereas modernist novels present themselves as witty extensions of their authors, Pym's are unself-conscious. Everyone lives in two worlds: the everyday trivial one and the mental one in which romance, despair, yearning, and loneliness are possible. Pym's secret is that she presents these worlds simultaneously.

Benet, Diana. "The Language of Christianity in Pym's Novels." *Thought: A Review of Culture and Ideas* 59 (December, 1984): 504-513.

In Benet's simplified account, Pym's novels show an Anglican Church out of touch with its times. Church members often talk in pious clichés and quote inappropriate hymns. The clergy's sermons are either confused or too high-brow for their audiences. The Church has become at best a social institution. In itself, it does little to help the only real Christians about, the "excellent women" who perform daily charities. *A Few Green Leaves* provides Pym's most optimistic view of the Church's possible effectiveness.

_____. *Something to Love: Barbara Pym's Novels.* Columbia: University of Missouri Press, 1986.

A lucid and useful introduction to Pym's work. Benet does not deal with style or employ dazzling critical theories, but gives straightforward, balanced, and sympathetic accounts of the characters and themes of the novels. In her introduction, Benet surveys Pym's achievement and idiosyncrasies. Though two novels are written in the first person, most present an omniscient irreverent and playful narrator. The cast of characters, usually limited to a small circle centering on a church, typically includes clergymen, anthropologists, and spinsters. Women are central and usually grow in assertiveness and self-knowledge. Although early male characters are shallow, later men are more fully drawn. Benet summarizes Pym's themes: the division of people into observers and participants, the need to love, the range of objects for that love, and the possibility of unsuitable attachments. Three chapters deal with individual novels. Each chapter concludes with a brief overview of one phase of Pym's career; the last also provides an excellent summary of Pym's achievement.

Bowman, Barbara. "Pym's Subversive Subtext." In *Independent Women: The Function of Gender in the Novels of Barbara Pym*, edited by Janice Rossen. New York: St. Martin's Press, 1988.

An important article on Pym's narrator and her heroines. Bow-man takes Mildred and her first-person narration of *Excellent Women* as an example of Pym's heroines. (Belinda in the third-person narration of *Some Tame Gazelle* would yield similar insights.) Bowman analyzes the complex ironies that go on in selected passages from *Excellent Women*. Mildred expresses conventional thoughts out loud, thoughts in harmony with the dominant (primarily male) culture, but then adds ironic comments that subvert that culture.

These ironies are not revolutionary; Mildred and others like her rarely challenge authority. The interaction here is made even more complex by another voice, what Bowman calls the narrator of the novel and what other critics would call "the implied author" or simply "Pym." Bowman shows how many aspects of Mildred's female subordination fit in with the theories of a contemporary psychologist. Mildred's language expresses her subordination as well; many of her statements are indefinite or negative. Men of the dominant culture are much different; they are competitive and complacent.

Bradham, Margaret C. "Barbara Pym's Women." *World Literature Today* 61 (Winter, 1987): 31-37.
Pym's true subject is the Pym Woman, a middle-aged spinster leading an unexciting life, usually as an "excellent woman" about a church, as a minor professional, or as an office worker. These women are usually unmarried and thus are thought to be inferior to married women. They are perhaps too self-centered; they secretly seek romance and would like to be loved and needed. But they remain unfulfilled and lonely, even if they are actually married. (If a marriage is implied for a major character at the end of the novel, Pym means to downgrade this attachment.) Most of these women conclude that people do not get what they want in life, but even so they continue to be open to possibilities. Pym sympathizes with her heroines, but is not sentimental.

Brothers, Barbara. "Women Victimized by Fiction: Living and Loving in the Novels by Barbara Pym." In *Twentieth Century Women Novelists*, edited by Thomas F. Staley. Totowa, N.J.: Barnes & Noble Books, 1982.

Like other feminists, Pym attacks both the myths that have imprisoned women and the novelists who have perpetuated these myths. Many of her characters, female as well as male, believe that romantic love is the only proper fulfillment for a woman; that the alternative is to be a spinster and give your life over to service; indeed, that women are meant to serve men, whose work is noble; and that women should not be given a serious education. Some of Pym's characters discover these myths are false. Pym herself is under no illusions. She is a subversive writer.

_____. "Love, Marriage, and Manners in the Novels of Barbara Pym." In *Reading and Writing Women's Lives: A Study of the Novel of Manners*, edited by Barbara Brothers and Bege K. Bowers. Ann Arbor, Mich.: University Microfilms International Research Press, 1990.

Two hundred years ago, the romantic love plot attacked the out-moded class system. Victorian ideas are no longer suited to the modern world in which women work outside the home and have the option not to marry. Pym's plots subvert the importance of romantic love and the system of Victorian manners. In Pym, married women are *not* fulfilled by sacrifice, and women have jobs. But Victorian attitudes persist in the workplace, where women are often required to perform wifely tasks. Brothers analyzes *Jane and Prudence* in light of these ideas. She also remarks that Pym's men are not so bad as many critics have said.

Burkhart, Charles. "Barbara Pym and the Africans." *Twentieth Century Literature: A Scholarly and Critical Journal* 29 (Spring, 1983): 45-53.

An early version of Chapter Three of the author's *The Pleasure of Miss Pym*.

_____. "Glamourous Acolytes." In *Independent Women: The Function of Gender in the Novels of Barbara Pym*, edited by Janice Rossen. New York: St. Martin's Press, 1988.

Burkhart surveys the homosexual men in Pym's novels and finds that many are gourmets. Of the major figures, Piers of *A Glass of Blessings* is likable, and Ned in *The Sweet Dove Died* is hateful. Even so, after the problems Pym's women have with straight men, most homosexual men provide welcome solaces.

_____. *The Pleasure of Miss Pym*. Austin: University of Texas Press, 1987.

A chatty, uncluttered appreciation. Burkhart thinks Pym is the finest English writer of high comedy in the twentieth century. He evokes her work under several chapter headings. In "Miss Pym and the World," he describes her life, her virtues, and how the world responded to her work. In "Miss Pym and the World of Her Novels," he discusses their settings and how Pym deals with such matters as class, love, and food. He finds her literariness limiting, but admires her manipulation of point of view. In "Miss Pym and the Africans," he shows that, although Pym made fun of anthologists, she also saw how their methods could apply to life in England.

In "Miss Pym and the Comic Muse," he characterizes Pym's voice as simultaneously joyous and ironic, a voice one might hear at tea time. Her style runs to declarative sentences and to adverbs rather than adjectives. Burkhart provides many passages that are comical in a variety of ways. "Miss Pym and Men and Women" surveys the varying forms such relations can take. In "God and Miss Pym," Burkhart says that, although it is hard to see behind the religious trappings that fill the novels, he thinks that Pym had a strong private religion. Burkhart sees some of its quality in the hope that many readers sense behind all of her work. The last section of Chapter Two is a survey of individual novels.

Byatt, A. S. *Passions of the Mind*. New York: Random House, 1992.

A negative view. In her short review of *An Academic Question*, Byatt calls the revival of interest in Pym not just pretentious but unhealthy. Pym is praised because it is not proper to criticize a female author much in favor with female readers. Americans may be fascinated by Pym as an example of entropy. She should not be considered along with such authors as Iris Murdoch or Muriel Spark—or even Fay Weldon. According to Byatt, she should be classified with such modest talents as Angela Thirkell and Dorothy Sayers.

Calisher, Hortense. "Enclosures: Barbara Pym." *New Criterion* 1 (September, 1982): 53-56.

Calisher places Pym's fiction in the tradition of cozy novels by Angela Thirkell and E. F. Benson.

Cooley, Mason. *The Comic Art of Barbara Pym.* New York: AMS Press, 1990.

An analysis of the novels in order of composition. Cooley's introduction defines Pym as a comic novelist and includes even *Quartet in Autumn* under that definition. Colley notes the many tones in Pym's comedy, from farce, to hilarity, to satire, to elegiac detachment. Instead of conventional romantic comedy, Pym gives us ironic comedy in which heroines are rewarded, not with Prince Charming, but with a recovery of cheerfulness, a change of heart. In these heroines, Pym has transformed a stock figure of fun, the old maid, into a serious and usually admirable central character. Cooley devotes a chapter to each novel. For each, he sums up the novel's unique qualities; often he provides detailed and revealing analyses of specific passages. In his very interesting final chapter, Cooley searches for the secret of Pym's distinctive literary voice; he finds it in her mixture of fact and fantasy and in her tilting the weight of traditional balanced sentences toward uncertainty.

Cotsell, Michael. *Barbara Pym.* New York: St. Martin's Press, 1989.

Cotsell deals with Pym's published and unpublished work and speculates interestingly on the relation of her personal life to her fiction. In his introduction and first chapter, Cotsell generalizes about Pym's fictional comic world and its central female characters; although these women experience rejection and loneliness, they are seldom without good humor and hope. Cotsell sees Pym's early romance with Henry Harvey not only as the great rejection of her life but as part of her literary debate with modernism. In her case, she both imitates and parodies the fiction of Aldous Huxley, Ivy Compton-Burnett, and Elizabeth Bowen. Cotsell thinks that by employing the perspective of anthropology later in her career, Pym creates some of the distancing of modernism.

In Chapters 1 and 2, Cotsell provides valuable discussions of Pym's early unpublished works. He charts her growing awareness of and detachment from the conditions of the present and a growing attachment to the details of a past social order. He divides her published novels somewhat arbitrarily, but in his excellent discussions of them he often cites early drafts to show how Pym shaped her fictions. In the beginning of Chapter 5, Cotsell contrasts Pym's implicit view of language with that of nineteenth century realists and finds it resembles Wittgenstein's.

In Chapter 6, he summarizes her critical reception as illustrated in the contemporary reviews he cites in his bibliography.

Crosland, Margaret. *Beyond the Lighthouse: English Women Novelists in the Twentieth Century.* New York: Taplinger Publishing, 1981.
Brief comments on Pym in Chapter 10. Readers find the goodness in the novels comforting.

De Paolo, Rosemary. "You Are What You Drink." *The Barbara Pym Newsletter* 2 (December, 1987): 1-5.
What Pym characters drink reveals both character and class. Drinking alcohol suggests freedom; men expect to be offered strong drink, and excellent women avoid it. Drinking tea in the evening is for members of the working classes; at all times tea is comforting, but tea drinkers have narrow expectations. Ovaltine is a tea substitute. Coffee (especially instant coffee) is to be avoided.

Doan, Laura L. "Pym's Singular Interest: The Self as Spinster." In *Old Maids to Radical Spinsters: Unmarried Women in the Twentieth-Century Novel.* Urbana: University of Illinois Press, 1991.
When she was twenty-four years old, Pym proclaimed herself an independent spinster. Then she wrote novels to reconcile herself to her situation. But how could she present spinsterhood as a choice rather than a necessity? How could she make spinsters interesting in fiction? Her solutions: portray marriages as unfulfilling and show spinsters rejecting suitors. (Doan analyzes *Crampton Hodnet, Some Tame Gazelle,* and *Jane and Prudence.*) Pym also embodies her concerns in her style. Even when she seems to affirm conventional ideas (such as "women should marry"), her ironies subvert them. Pym gives her female characters their choice of life and gives her spinsters many of life's good things with the exception of sex. Pym and her spinsters regard that as unpleasant.

_____. "Text and the Single Man: The Bachelor in Pym's Dual-Voiced Narrative." In *Independent Women: The Function of*

Gender in the Novels of Barbara Pym, edited by Janice Rossen. New York: St. Martin's Press, 1988.
Pym's world has two kinds of bachelors: those single by choice (often homosexuals) and those available for marriage. The latter, including many curates and vicars, are viewed as objects by Pym's women, even though they are selfish and unfeeling. The bachelors resemble spinsters, in that they have dull jobs and are often effeminate, irritable, and nosy. Unlike spinsters, however, they do not reveal what Doan calls a double voice; we do not hear them, as we hear Mildred in *Excellent Women*, speak in a dutiful public voice while harboring subversive, individualistic reservations. Their selfishness may disrupt a spinster's world, but they should be pitied.

Dobie, Ann B. "The World of Barbara Pym: Novelist as Anthropologist." *Arizona Quarterly: A Journal of American Literature, Culture, and Theory* 44 (Spring, 1988): 5-18.
When Pym's characters settle for less than they wanted, they do so with a dignity supported by the rituals of society. Pym resembles an anthropologist as she observes these rituals, which govern such matters as church affairs, dress, and food. Food literally makes life go on, and food rituals give order to life. What is more, these rituals feed the soul. Food can be a metaphor for the dreams that sustain men and women; when food is shared, it becomes a metaphor for love.

Epstein, Joseph. "Miss Pym and Mr. Larkin." *Commentary*, July, 1986, 38-46.
A charming, appreciative essay comparing Pym to the poet Philip Larkin. Both display middle-class, undoctrinaire common sense of a sort that has grown unfashionable, especially among American authors. They write as grown-ups. Both write of loneliness. Pym is not a usual feminist, but she implies that women are superior to men, who appear in her novels as bumbling and selfish, but amusing.

Everett, Barbara. "The Pleasures of Poverty." In *Independent Women: The Function of Gender in the Novels of Barbara Pym*, edited by Janice Rossen. New York: St. Martin's Press, 1988.

Everett points to the heart of Pym's work when she asks how Pym transformed herself from a keeper of diaries into a novelist. The change came when Pym the diarist begins to communicate various tones, a mixture of romantic hope and idealism with ironic dispassionateness and an appreciation of everyday pleasures. Everett compares her to Cervantes as a writer of "romantic anti-romances."

Ezell, Margaret J. M. "`What Shall We Do With Our Old Maids?':, Barbara Pym and the Woman Question." *International Journal of Women's Studies* 7 (November/December, 1984): 450-465.
Ezell sets Pym's novels against Victorian views on the problems of unmarried women in society. They were looked down upon. The only roles deemed appropriate were those which resembled the duties of married women: teachers and caregivers. One hundred years later, the spinster is better off, but society still looks down on her and restricts her roles. Like Charlotte Brontë's before her, Pym's novels may be read as a protest against this situation. Pym notes the antagonism between married and single women and satirizes the rituals of a society in which a married woman is still honored more than a single woman who supports herself.

Findlayson, Iain. "An Interview with Barbara Pym." *Literary Review*, February 23, 1980, 2-5.
In an interview shortly before her death, Pym reflects on her career as a novelist, especially about the years in which she could not find a publisher. After considerable prodding, Pym comments on Cyril Connolly's *Enemies of Promise* and calls Martin Amis the "archetypal young writer."

Fisichelli, Glynn Ellen. "The Novelist as Anthropologist—Barbara Pym's Fiction: Fieldwork Done at Home." *Papers on Language and Literature: A Journal for Scholars and Critics of Language and Literature* 24 (Fall, 1988): 436-445.
Pym's two worlds of literature and anthropology overlapped, for Pym was a meticulous observer of details. Among other things, she observed social changes and even anthropologists themselves. Yet she was primarily a novelist. Like Catherine, the writer in *Less Than Angels*, she used details to tell about common humanity and not, like an anthropologist, to lay bare the secrets of a culture.

Gordon, Joan. "Cozy Heroines: Quotidian Bravery in Barbara Pym's Novels." *Essays in Literature* 16 (Fall, 1989): 224-233.
Gordon finds value in Pym's world, its daily activities and its cozy heroines. Pym values humility, community, and even a kind of modest miracle. Gordon makes valuable comments on the appropriateness of Pym's style to these values and makes more extensive comments on *Quartet in Autumn, The Sweet Dove Died*, and *A Few Green Leaves*.

Graham, Robert J. "Cumbered With Much Serving: Barbara Pym's *Excellent Women*." *Mosaic: A Journal for the Interdisciplinary Study of Literature* 17 (Spring, 1984): 141-160. Reprinted in *"For Better or Worse": Attitudes Toward Marriage in Literature*, edited by Evelyn J. Hinz. 2d ed. Winnipeg: University of Manitoba Press, 1985.
The novels ask if it is better for a woman to marry or not. Pym's married women do not fare well: marriage gives them no intellectual stimulation, and their husbands patronize them. In *Jane and Prudence*, Jane is bored; Ianthe of *An Unsuitable Attachment* seems to marry for passion only. On the other hand, spinsters in the early novels, though they think about marriage, have their own cozy comforts. Graham thinks that Leonora in *The Sweet Dove Died* returns happily to her earlier self-sufficient life. Pym's last two novels continue the debate. Spinsters have little comfort in *Quartet in Autumn*, but the novel ends on a faintly optimistic note. Even though *A Few Green Leaves* ends with the suggestion the spinster Emma will marry, Graham concludes that Pym thinks the single life can be fulfilling.

_____. "The Narrative Sense of Barbara Pym." In *The Life and Work of Barbara Pym*, edited by Dale Salwak. Iowa City: University of Iowa Press, 1987.
Even though Pym's novels may seem artless, they are crafted with artistry. In her notebooks we see her method: she observes daily life closely, then writes, then revises. Graham shows that Pym's detached observer/narrators often begin a chapter with an observation to be developed. The daily activities she describes soon become universalized. Her usual theme is that life is a series of losses, and she builds it slowly as she supplies readers with background information bit by bit. Her method is also gradual as she

builds up the meaning of words like "excellent" and "suitable."
She characteristically qualifies her assertions with adverbs like
"almost" and "too."

Groner, Marlene San Miguel. "Barbara Pym's Allusions to Seven-
    teenth Century Poets." *Cross-Bias: Newsletter of Friends of
    Bemerton* 11 (1987): 5-7.
    Groner identifies Pym's many allusions to English metaphysical
    poets and comments on them.

Halperin, John. "Barbara Pym and the War of the Sexes." In *The Life
    and Work of Barbara Pym*, edited by Dale Salwak. Iowa City:
    University of Iowa Press, 1987.
    A plodding survey of the battle of the sexes in four Pym novels.
    Halperin concludes that Pym shows no satisfactory relationship.
    Though Pym's women can sometimes be calculating and overbear-
    ing, they are usually strong and admirable. Men, on the other
    hand, are usually heartless, selfish, and dull. Halperin treats *Jane
    and Prudence*, *Less Than Angels*, *A Glass of Blessings*, and *The
    Sweet Dove Died*.

Heberlein, Kate Browder. "Barbara Pym and Anthony Trollope:
    Communities of Imaginative Participation." *Pacific Coast
    Philology* 19 (November, 1984): 277-296.
    Heberlein makes a good case for comparing the two writers. In
    their novels, calm surfaces hide energetic and ironic depths.
    Pym's endings may be more casual, but reading a number of Pym's
    novels produces an effect like reading the chronicles of Trollope's
    Barsetshire. This effect is heightened by both novelists when they
    have characters carry over from novel to novel. (Heberlein makes
    a definitive list of Pym's overlapping characters.) Both authors
    also depend on literary allusions, though they introduce them
    differently. Both are pluralistic in that they let various kinds of
    people have their say; they are not strongly judgmental. These
    qualities are admirable because they build communities.

_____. "Thankless Tasks or Labors of Love: Women's Work in
    Barbara Pym's Novels." *The Barbara Pym Newsletter* 2 (June,
    1987): 1-5.

Though in her own employment she preferred the thankless tasks of helping men and carrying out domestic duties, Pym's attitude toward women's work ranges from ambivalent to positive. Even Pym's professional women like Miss Clovis are willing to serve. All Pym's women prefer serving men whom they like or love, even if their affections are not reciprocated. In her last novel, *A Few Green Leaves*, men are more selfish and helpless than ever. But Pym's work makes a feminist statement. Women are exploited, even though in most ways, they are men's equals, if not their superiors; cultural factors may influence women's subservient behavior. One occupation in particular is enhanced by a woman's unique talents of attention and observation: that of the novelist. Pym serves her readers by enlivening the everyday world.

Hills, C. A. R. "The Bubble, Reputation: The Decline and Rise of Barbara Pym." *Encounter* 68 (May, 1987): 33-38.
Hills tells the Pym story and asks why she is great. Her realistic world is quietly distorted to produce comic and even hilarious effects, a way for Pym heroines to triumph over loneliness. The early novels can be called "high-spirited," the later novels more "astringent." The novels are not overtly religious, but they communicate the traditional virtue of humility and a sense that this life is incomplete.

Holt, Hazel. "The Home Front: Barbara Pym in Oswestry, 1939-1941." In *Independent Women: The Function of Gender in the Novels of Barbara Pym*, edited by Janice Rossen. New York: St. Martin's Press, 1988.
Pym's literary executor strings together quotations from Pym's diaries for the years after she left Oxford. These notes provided material for her novels.

_____. *A Lot to Ask: A Life of Barbara Pym*. New York: Dutton, 1991.
A biography by Pym's close friend and literary executor. Holt provides many quotations from Pym's diaries and notebooks, but she says she has avoided material that she used in editing Pym's "autobiography," *A Very Private Eye*. Background information about individual novels can be found throughout, and it is well indexed.

_____. "The Novelist in the Field: 1946-74." In *The Life and Work of Barbara Pym*, edited by Dale Salwak. Iowa City: University of Iowa Press, 1987.

Pym wrote many novels while employed as an editor at the International African Institute in London. The office life which Holt describes is reflected in *Jane and Prudence*, *Less Than Angels*, and *Quartet in Autumn*. Holt reports that although Pym had little serious interest in either anthropology or Africa, the Institute provided many real-life anthropologists upon whom to base characters in her fiction.

_____. "Philip Larkin and Barbara Pym: Two Quiet People." In *Philip Larkin: The Man and His Work*, edited by Dale Salwak. Iowa City: University of Iowa Press, 1989.

The story of their friendship told mainly by quotations from their letters.

Kane, Patricia. "A Curious Eye: Barbara Pym's Women." *South Dakota Review* 24 (Summer, 1986): 50-59.

Kane divides Pym's women into observers (like Dulcie in *No Fond Return of Love*), manipulators, and typists. Kane finds women typing for men everywhere in Pym's novels, but by "typists," she really means "excellent women" who will serve men by typing, making indexes, and the like. Manipulators are divided into ineffectual ones like Jane in *Jane and Prudence* and nasty ones like Leonora in *The Sweet Dove Died* and Sophia in *An Unsuitable Attachment*. Kane is severe on Sophia, calling her destructive and selfish.

Kapp, Isa. "Out of the Swim with Barbara Pym." *The American Scholar* 52 (Spring, 1983): 237-242.

Pym's novels are very different from those of contemporary America. They have little action; their settings are confined. Pym's philosophy is particularly hard for Americans to accept. Pym thinks women should serve men, even though men are the weaker sex. Pym boosts women's morale by her own detachment and strength. A generous and affectionate essay with many oversimplifications.

Kaufman, Anthony. "Barbara Pym (1913-1980)." In *Essays on the Contemporary British Novel*, edited by Hedwig Bock and Albert Wertheim. Munich: Max Hueber, 1986.
A survey of Pym's themes and characters, especially "excellent women." Kaufman wonders how such ostensibly ordinary females can be so observant.

Keener, Frederick M. "Barbara Pym Herself and Jane Austen." *Twentieth Century Literature: A Scholarly and Critical Journal* 31 (Spring, 1985): 89-110.
Keener uses his running comparison of Pym to Austen as the occasion for writing an entertaining and useful overview of Pym's work. His appreciations of three novels are memorable: *A Glass of Blessings*, *No Fond Return of Love*, and *A Few Green Leaves*.

Kennard, Jean E. "Barbara Pym and Romantic Love." *Contemporary Literature* 34 (Spring, 1993): 44-60.
Pym undercuts notions of romantic love in many ways, but belonging to a community of anthropologists is no consolation. Better alternatives are life's daily joys and the subdued sort of marriage Mildred seems to look forward to in *Excellent Women*. The best consolation is the Christian community as implied in that novel and even in *Quartet in Autumn*.

Larkin, Philip. "The Rejection of Barbara Pym." In *The Life and Work of Barbara Pym*, edited by Dale Salwak. Iowa City: University of Iowa Press, 1987.
This is the introduction to the first publication of *An Unsuitable Attachment* in 1982. Larkin makes critical comments and tells the story of the novel's rejection and Pym's eventual rediscovery.

_____. "The World of Barbara Pym." *The Times Literary Supplement*, March 11, 1977, 260.
Larkin's appreciative evocation of Pym's early novels, written soon after her rediscovery. Pym's novels impart a sense of loneliness without self-pity. They speak to women, but "no man can read them and be quite the same again."

Larson, Edith S. "The Celebration of the Ordinary in Barbara Pym's Novels." *San Jose Studies* 9 (Spring, 1983): 17-22.

Pym celebrates the force of ordinary experiences in offering support in a sad world. Drinking tea is a symbol for all such mundane activity. Larson discusses *Some Tame Gazelle*, *Less Than Angels*, and *Quartet in Autumn*.

Liddell, Robert. *A Mind at Ease: Barbara Pym and Her Novels*. London: Peter Owen, 1989.
Liddell was a friend of Pym in her Oxford days. Much of this study is given over to rambling and often snobbish remarks on individual novels. At the end of Chapter 5, Liddell generalizes about marriages in "the canon" and finds that, though most are humdrum, they are not to be considered as bad. In Chapters 3 and 10, he makes valuable contributions to Pym criticism. He defines Pym's first major phase (from *Excellent Women* to *An Unsuitable Attachment*) as "the canon." This group of hopeful and spirited novels is populated by middle-class and middle-aged people set against a placid background in which the Anglican Church is everywhere. In Chapter 10, Liddell denigrates academic critics and says the Pym's value lies in the playful fantasy that readers find in her most memorable heroines (Mildred, Jane, Catherine, Wilmet, Dulcie) and a few men (Rocky, for example).

_____. "A Success Story." In *The Life and Work of Barbara Pym*, edited by Dale Salwak. Iowa City: University of Iowa Press, 1987.
Liddell writes to correct the impressions some critics have of Pym. Pym's life was a success. It is a mistake to assume that unmarried women must always be "frustrated." Pym's frustrations were more literary than anything else. She was an "excellent" woman and a quietly religious one.

_____. "Two Friends: Barbara Pym and Ivy Compton-Burnett." *London Magazine*, n.s. 24 (August-September, 1984): 59-69.
Liddell remembers his friendship with Pym and discusses her virtues.

Little, Judy. "Humoring the Sentence: Women's Dialogic Comedy." In *Women's Comic Visions*, edited by June Sochen. Detroit: Wayne State University Press, 1991.
Women often use the patriarchal language, but simultaneously subvert it by irony and mimicry. Little uses a brief example from

Excellent Women to show how Pym uses language this way. At the end, when Mildred says she will submit to Everard's requests, he says it will be a "nice change" for her. When she agrees, she repeats these words ironically.

_____. "Influential Anxieties: Woolf and Pym." *Virginia Woolf Miscellany* 39 (Fall, 1992): 5-6.
A brief note suggesting that at the back of her mind Pym often had Virginia Woolf's idea that a woman needs "a room of [her] own."

Lively, Penelope. "The World of Barbara Pym." In *The Life and Work of Barbara Pym*, edited by Dale Salwak. Iowa City: University of Iowa Press, 1987.
A short, evocative, and appreciative essay. Lively finds the battle between men and women at the heart of Pym's novels, a battle in which women are at least moral victors. Lively thinks *A Quartet in Autumn* is Pym's best.

Long, Robert Emmet. *Barbara Pym*. New York: Frederick Ungar, 1986.
Chapter 1 is an evocative and very readable summary of Pym's life and career. In subsequent well-written and useful chapters, Long treats the other novels in groups of two or three. One of Long's themes is that, no matter what they may seem to say, Pym's novels never end happily. In his conclusion, Long provides an excellent discussion of the usual comparison between Pym and Jane Austen. Long also enumerates Pym's limitations as a novelist. In spite of them and in spite of her narrow range, Long values Pym highly. He notes why feminists do not honor her (her women too passively accept their subordinate roles) and speculates that Pym may have influenced Anita Brookner.

Lyles, Jean Caffey. "Pym's Cup: Anglicans and Anthropologists." *Christian Century*, May 21, 1986, 519-523.
Pym's novels give a charming sense of the petty details of Anglican parish life, almost as if an anthropologist was at work. The novels imply that, though the local churches are flawed, they form necessary communities.

McGuirk, Carol. "Drabble to Carter: Fiction by Women, 1962-1992."
    In *The Columbia History of the British Novel*, edited by John
    Richetti. New York: Columbia University Press, 1994.
    Many women writers of this era share a number of traits. Like the
    others, Pym's early life was disrupted by World War II. Like the
    others, Pym distances herself from both from mass culture and
    high culture. Pym's evocations of Jane Austen imply she is a part
    of traditional English culture, but her echoes mainly make satiric
    points. Like the others, Pym's novels are not dramatic; they are
    often uneventful and end awkwardly; they center on women,
    especially women in competition. Pym does not always show
    assertive women as winning; she denies victory to Wilmet in *A
    Glass of Blessings* and to Leonora in *The Sweet Dove Died*.

Malloy, Constance. "The Quest for a Career." In *The Life and Work
    of Barbara Pym*, edited by Dale Salwak. Iowa City: University of
    Iowa Press, 1987.
    A good biographical summary, emphasizing Pym's lifelong persis-
    tence in writing. Especially interesting on the years 1963-1977.

Moseley, Merritt. "A Few Words About Barbara Pym." *Sewanee
    Review* 98 (Winter, 1990): 75-87.
    Moseley tells the Pym story, lists her novels' typical ingredients,
    and speculates on why readers like her so much. Pym not only
    creates an imaginative world, she sees that world with a clear and
    unsentimental eye. Moreover, her tone is always perfect. She and
    her heroines have a fine eye for what is suitable and what is not.
    Unsuitabilities make for comic incongruities.

Moseley, Merritt, and Pamela J. Nickless. "Pym's Homosexuals."
    Barbara Pym Newsletter 5, no. 1 (1990): 5-8.
    Pym's male homosexuals often resemble "excellent women" and
    often function as noncombatants in the war between men and
    women.

Nardin, Jane. *Barbara Pym*. Boston: Twayne, 1985.
    The first full-length guide to Pym's life and works. In Chapter 2,
    Nardin explains how Pym has adapted traditional literary models.
    Pym treats both dull and unlikely characters with respect, even
    during their solitary meals and their poetic reveries. Nardin

interestingly explains that Pym does not create patterns which develop her themes fully. It is appropriate therefore than her novels have open-ended conclusions. In Chapter 3, Nardin discusses some of Pym's main thematic concerns: love, the relations of men and women, religion, literature, and science. She also discusses Pym's increasing dismay at social changes in England. In her last two chapters, Nardin discusses most of the individual novels. Perhaps because this was the first guide to Pym, it is sometimes overly schematic in its analyses.

Oates, Joyce Carol. "Barbara Pym's Novelistic Genius." In *The Life and Work of Barbara Pym*, edited by Dale Salwak. Iowa City: University of Iowa Press, 1987.
In a brief note, Oates says we value Pym most for her personal voice. Her favorite Pym novel is *A Glass of Blessings*, followed by *Jane and Prudence*.

Phelps, Gilbert. "Fellow Writers in a Cotswold Village." In *The Life and Work of Barbara Pym*, edited by Dale Salwak. Iowa City: University of Iowa Press, 1987.
Phelps, a novelist and critic, lived near Pym in her Oxfordshire village during her last years, and he recounts many affectionate memories. Phelps recalls Pym saying that, even though she was tempted, she included no direct portraits of villagers in *A Few Green Leaves*.

Pym, Barbara. "Finding a Voice: a Radio Talk." In *Civil to Strangers and Other Writings*, edited by Hazel Holt. New York: E. P. Dutton, 1988.
Essential. Recorded on February 8, 1978. Pym distinguishes between what an author says and (what may be more important) the voice in which he or she says it. *Quartet in Autumn* is about the problems of aging, but when she wrote it she was most concerned with the comic and ironic voice with which she told the story. She would like to be recognized by her voice, her style. Pym tells about her career as a novelist in order to suggest how a distinctive voice is developed. Pym thinks that, when her novels were rejected in the 1960's, it was probably too late to change her voice.

_____. *A Very Private Eye: An Autobiography in Diaries and Letters*, edited by Hazel Holt and Hilary Pym. New York: E. P. Dutton, 1984.
An invaluable illustrated compilation of Pym materials. References to the individual novels are scattered through the text and indexed.

Pym, Hilary, and Honor Wyatt. *The Barbara Pym Cookbook*. New York: E. P. Dutton, 1988.
A curiosity. Recipes, for the most part for dishes mentioned in the novels, and appropriate quotations. No recipe for a macaroni cheese.

Radner, Sanford. "Barbara Pym's People." *Western Humanities Review* 39 (Summer, 1985): 172-177.
Beneath the surface of Pym's work, Radner senses one story: "a self-denying mother feeds her ungrateful baby son." Pym's men are unvaryingly childish and demanding. (Pym's novels have almost no children, for that role is occupied by adult males.) Pym's "excellent women" compete among themselves to give selfless service to these men. Occasionally we meet a "failed excellent woman," one who knows her gifts are not good enough. Pym's comedy lies in seeing adults act out such childish games.

"Reputations Revisited." In *The Times Literary Supplement*, January 21, 1977, 66-68.
The tributes by Philip Larkin and Lord David Cecil that led to Pym's rediscovery. Cecil particularly admires *Excellent Women* and *A Glass of Blessings*.

Rossen, Janice, ed. *Independent Women: The Function of Gender in the Novels of Barbara Pym*. New York: St. Martin's Press, 1988.
An important and specialized collection of articles recorded separately here. Rossen's introduction summarizes the articles and shows how they address specific questions: How did Pym become a novelist? What attitudes did she have toward men, specifically toward homosexual men? What were Pym's most important literary influences? What was she like as a person?

_____. "Love in the Great Libraries: Oxford in the Work of Barbara Pym." *Journal of Modern Literature* 12 (July, 1985): 277-296. Reprinted as Chapter 2 in *The World of Barbara Pym*. New York: St. Martin's Press, 1987.

Oxford meant to Pym a heady mixture of study and romance. In an enjoyable essay, Rossen surveys Pym's personal diaries to show how the undergraduate Barbara chose to be a flirt as well as a student of literature. This real-life mixture is reflected in *Some Tame Gazelle, Crampton Hodnet, Jane and Prudence*, and *No Fond Return of Love*.

_____. "On Not Being Jane Eyre: The Romantic Heroine in Barbara Pym's Novels." In *Independent Women: The Function of Gender in the Novels of Barbara Pym*. New York: St. Martin's Press, 1988.

Charlotte Brontë's novel lies behind much of Pym's work. Even though Mildred in *Excellent Women* says she is not like Jane Eyre, Pym's heroines do resemble Brontë's in many ways: they are plain women, not rich, and often they must tear themselves or be torn from the men they love. But, as Rossen points out, Pym's heroines do not end up, as Jane did, in bliss with the handsome romantic hero they love. Pym's women console themselves by adopting a comic perspective, with reading English poetry, and with seeking out cozy comforts. Pym's men are not like Brontë's, either. Whereas Rochester was decisive and desirable, Pym's men are his opposite. Rossen discusses *Excellent Women* and *The Sweet Dove Died* at length.

_____. "The Pym Papers." In *The Life and Work of Barbara Pym*, edited by Dale Salwak. Iowa City: University of Iowa Press, 1987.

Pym's papers (including such items as drafts of novels and stories, diaries, notebooks, and correspondence) repose appropriately in the Bodleian Library of Oxford University. Rossen provides a lucid overview and commentary.

_____. *The World of Barbara Pym*. New York: St. Martin's Press, 1987.

An important and valuable study. Rossen analyzes Pym's themes, tying them to aspects of her life. In Chapter 1, Rossen discusses the literary influences on Pym's style: Jane Austen, Anthony

Trollope, Charlotte M. Yonge, John Betjeman, Aldous Huxley, and especially Ivy Compton-Burnett. Her many literary allusions come from the range of English literature, but Pym's use is often ironic and funny. Often the allusions trivialize their subject or help measure what a given character is lacking. Although Pym's prose is full of detail, such details are not so much sensual as full of ritual significance. Rossen sums up by praising Pym's charm. Chapter 2 reprints Rossen's article "Love in the Great Libraries."

In Chapter 3, Rossen discusses spinsters, people largely ignored by other novelists, and ties this discussion to Pym's own life. Spinsters have limited their lives. They do not marry because men are vain and selfish, or gay, or otherwise unattainable. Nevertheless, the spinsters seem committed to unrequited love. They are often pictured eating solitary meals in their kitchens, thinking of men. They often give gifts to men, but to little effect. They face the prospect of leading lives of solitude. But in her novels (as in her life), Pym creates a persona for solitary middle-aged spinsters: a woman who can accept and even cherish her unrequited loving, who creates her own cozy domestic world (sometimes with a female companion), and who can view the world and her place in it with ironic detachment.

Chapter 4 deals with the Anglican Church. In Pym's old-fashioned world, the Church is always present. Although her characters do not debate theological questions, we see them in the daily rounds of religious life. Pym does not seek to reform or to satirize harshly. Rossen thinks she treats the Church in its physical and spiritual sides as a metaphor for English culture in general: cozy, solid, and comforting. Pym does give voice to objections to the Anglican Church and dramatizes many of its challenges: agnosticism, rationalism, paganism, aestheticism, science, and Roman Catholicism. On the other hand, English literature functions in tandem with the Church in many characters' spiritual lives. In fact, many characters derive their ideas about life from literary works.

In Chapter 5, Rossen surveys Pym's treatment of anthropology. Pym's easy assumptions about the superiority of English culture changed as she grew older. Rossen defines Pym's central subject as the same as that of anthropology: life in a community. Her method is also similar. She and her characters try to interpret the significance of the rituals of daily life, especially those relating to food and clothing. Anthropologists themselves and their narrow and competitive communities are often the targets of Pym's amused observation.

In Chapter 6, Rossen discusses several Pym's heroines as they relate to Pym's personal life. In Belinda of *Some Tame Gazelle* and in Mildred of *Excellent Women*, Pym gives us prototypes for Pym's artist/observer. Both are mild, modest, apologetic, self-conscious and self-mocking "excellent women" who lead constricted lives, often subservient to more powerful people (usually male). But these women are observers who see beneath the surface of life, witnessing the ridiculousness of events and communicating their visions with irony. Their tone is one of muted resentment, often seeming to mask real anger. Often they have few other characters with whom to confide; the reader is drawn in to fill the role of confidant. In this respect, Rossen also discusses Catherine of *Less Than Angels* and Wilmet of *Glass of Blessings*. The final chapter is devoted to *A Few Green Leaves*, which Rossen sees as both affirmative and disillusioned.

Rowse, A. L. "Miss Pym and Miss Austen." In *The Life and Work of Barbara Pym*, edited by Dale Salwak. Iowa City: University of Iowa Press, 1987.
A leading historian compares Pym to Jane Austen. Both were observant women without illusions; both were Anglicans who told little about the life of the spirit. Whereas Jane Austen wrote of a settled, hierarchical society in which young women looked to marriage, Pym records a world that is much different. The certainties of the past are crumbling; London shows signs of bombing and is a mixture of races and classes. Pym's women yearn for love more than marriage. Pym the novelist is more interested in clothes and food than was Austen, and she accepts a very much wider range of sexual activity. Rowse celebrates them both.

Rubenstein, Jill. "Comedy and Consolation in the Novels of Barbara Pym." *Renascence* 42 (Spring, 1990): 173-183.
Usually for Pym, what happens at church is a source of comedy: clergymen who are either egotists or bumblers, excellent women, superficial worshipers. But by implication Pym asks if the decaying institution can ever be a source of real spirituality and consolation. The answer seems to be usually *no*, but sometimes

yes. Rubenstein describes three women who do get some sort of awakening from their association with the Church: Jane of *Jane and Prudence*, Sophia of *An Unsuitable Attachment*, and Wilmet of *A Glass of Blessings*.

_____. "'For the Ovaltine Had Loosened Her Tongue': Failures of Speech in Barbara Pym's *Less Than Angels*." *Modern Fiction Studies* 32 (Winter, 1986): 573-580.
Rubenstein uses several theories to try to illuminate Pym's work. The most convincing theory contrasts two kinds of speakers. One, usually male, speaks factually and unimaginatively. The other, always a woman, uses her imagination to transform facts into satisfying fictions. Conversations between these types are difficult and usually comic.

Saar, Doreen Alvarez. "Irony from a Female Perspective: A Study of the Early Novels of Barbara Pym." *West Virginia University Philological Papers* 33 (1987): 68-75.
Underneath their charming surface, Pym's novels make a strong criticism of how society treats women. This effect is produced by ironies of different sorts. Sometimes characters are ironically aware of the self-deceptions of other characters; sometimes only the reader is aware of a character's own self-deception. Like all ironists, Pym depends on her audience. In order to catch the ironies, Pym's audience must be aware of the injustices women suffer and should have a working knowledge of English literature.

Sadler, Lynn Veach. "The Pathos of Everyday Living in the Novels of Barbara Pym." *West Virginia University Philological Papers* 31 (1986): 82-90.
At the heart of Pym's novels is her description of pathetic people, often spinsters or older people, leading drab lives. But no matter what has caused them to be pathetic, their lives have value. Pym shows them coping with their loneliness with faith and hope; their integrity and dignity enables them to shape their lives and win a kind of happiness.

_____. "Spinsters, Non-Spinsters, and Men in the World of Barbara Pym." *Critique: Studies in Modern Fiction* 26 (Spring, 1985): 141-154.

Most of Pym's spinsters could have married; they chose spinster-hood. Pym's treatment of women breaks with that in most fiction. Her women are usually employed. Even though they are aware of society's limitations, they often take on masculine roles. Their friendship with other women is a recurrent theme. Sadler mis-reads the ending of *The Sweet Dove Died.*

Salwak, Dale. *Barbara Pym: A Reference Guide.* Boston: G. K. Hall, 1991.
A list of Pym's works and an annotated list of writing about her arranged by year of publication. Annotations are useful but brief.

_____, ed. *The Life and Work of Barbara Pym.* Iowa City: University of Iowa Press, 1987.
An important collection of nineteen essays, many of which are by nonacademic writers. Most treat Pym's life as well as her work. The essays are listed separately here.

Schofield, Mary Anne. "Well-Fed or Well-Loved? Patterns of Cooking and Eating in the Novels of Barbara Pym." *University of Windsor Review* 18 (Spring-Summer, 1985): 1-8.
The anthropologist Claude Lévi-Straus thinks that cooking raw foods is an essential process of civilization. Often when women cook for men it is a symbol of the female's civilizing power. Schofield argues that not only do Pym's females never cook for themselves, but also when they do provide food for men, they seldom cook nourishing meals and seldom establish a satisfying relationship. She cites telling examples from *Excellent Women, No Fond Return of Love, An Unsuitable Attachment,* and *The Sweet Dove Died.* Schofield sometimes forces her examples, but he theory explains a lot about the meals in the novels.

Schultz, Muriel. "The Novelist as Anthropologist." In *The Life and Work of Barbara Pym,* edited by Dale Salwak. Iowa City: University of Iowa Press, 1987.
A detailed survey of Pym's attitudes toward anthropology and her comparisons of anthropologists and novelists. Schultz is convinc-ing when she argues that Pym thinks that contemporary anthro-pology is in many ways sterile and inaccurate. Although novelists resemble anthropologists in many ways, they do not dehumanize

their subjects.   Schultz pays particular attention to *Excellent Women*, *Less Than Angels*, *No Fond Return of Love*, and *A Few Green Leaves*.

Shapiro, Anna.   "The Resurrection of Barbara Pym."   *Saturday Review*, July-August, 1983, 29-31.
A positive overview with some inaccuracies.   Pym makes everything ridiculous; her women seem to be priests in drag.

Smith, Robert.   "How Pleasant to Know Miss Pym."   *Ariel* 2 (1971): 63-68.   Reprinted in *The Life and Work of Barbara Pym*, edited by Dale Salwak.   Iowa City: University of Iowa Press, 1987.
One of the only appreciative articles written during Pym's dark days.   Smith praises Pym's enchanted closed world and her new kind of heroine, the "excellent woman."   The Church is everywhere, but her treatment of religion is reserved.   Smith hopes Pym will publish more novels.

_____.   "Remembering Barbara Pym."   In *Independent Women: The Function of Gender in the Novels of Barbara Pym*, edited by Janice Rossen.   New York: St. Martin's Press, 1988.
Reminiscences of a friend.   Interesting reflections on Pym's religion.

Snow, Lotus.   "Literary Allusions in the Novels."   In *The Life and Work of Barbara Pym*, edited by Dale Salwak.   Iowa City: University of Iowa Press, 1987.
Literary allusions and references are everywhere in Pym novels, except for *Quartet in Autumn*.   Pym sometimes alludes to Elizabethan poets (mainly Shakespeare) and Romantic poets (mainly Wordsworth and Keats).   But most of her references are to Donne and other metaphysical poets and to Victorians, such as Tennyson and Arnold.   Indeed, Matthew Arnold seems to be Pym's favorite.   The novelists she most alludes to are Austen, Trollope, Charlotte Brontë, and Charlotte M. Yonge.

_____.   *One Little Room an Everywhere*.   Orono, Maine: Puckerbrust Press, 1987.
This book reprints Snow's essay on "Literary Allusions" and reprints portions of "Trivial Round," as noted below.   In addition,

Snow compares Pym to Jane Austen and discusses Pym's allusive use of proper names, male/female relationships, and her recurring characters.

_____. "The Trivial Round, the Common Task: Barbara Pym's Novels." *Research Studies* 48 (1980): 83-93.
Pym and her characters often focus on the trivial details of ordinary people's lives. Snow divides these women into types. They are either spinsters—excellent women who are courageous, useful, and loving—or the kind of woman whom men select to love. Snow's categories are blurred, but this is an enjoyable survey.

Strauss-Noll, Mary. "Love and Marriage in the Novels." In *The Life and Work of Barbara Pym*, edited by Dale Salwak. Iowa City: University of Iowa Press, 1987.
Strauss-Noll surveys the attitudes toward marriage expressed by Pym and her characters. Though most female characters yearn for marriage, they have few illusions about what married life is like. Although Pym portrays men as selfish, dull, and lazy, Strauss-Noll insists that her tone is light and teasing. (The amused detachment of Pym the author did not come easily for Pym the woman.) A woman's ideal state is to be a widow with children; failing that, she should be a spinster who has settled into a comfortable state of unrequited love, like Belinda in *Some Tame Gazelle*.

Updike, John. "Books: Lem and Pym." *The New Yorker*, February 26, 1979, 115-21. Reprinted in *Hugging the Shore*. New York: Alfred A. Knopf, 1993.
Updike praises Pym for showing that people can choose to be solitary. He also praises Pym's exact and discriminating sense of moral issues and finds that novels like *Quartet in Autumn* are marvelously harmonious.

Watson, Daphne. *Their Own Worst Enemies: Women Writers of Women's Fictions*. London: Pluto Press, 1995.
In Chapter 2, Watson treats both Anita Brookner and Pym. Americans like Pym because of her quaint village settings. Watson likes Pym because in the course of her novels written over many years she chronicles a changing England. Watson also likes

her ironic, judgmental wit, though its effect is often blunted by
hopeful notes at the ends of novels. Pym's heroines are exploited,
condescended to by men and dependent on them, and unlucky in
love—just like Pym in real life. *The Sweet Dove Died* is Pym's
best novel because its bleak vision is not compromised by
sympathy. Like Brookner, she appeals to a middle-class audience.
Her characters are one-dimensional. Like Brookner's heroines,
they are "weak, exploitative, insensitive, vain, self-important."
They waste themselves pursuing men when they could have had
rewarding relationships with women.

Weld, Annette. *Barbara Pym and the Novel of Manners*. New York:
St. Martin's Press, 1992.
In her first chapter, Weld analyzes the traditions of the novel of
manners: a limited society with stable codes of manners is upset
by an irritant; the complications are finally resolved by the central
character, and harmony reigns once again. The narrator is often
ironic, and the world is comic in tone; nuances of words, actions,
and dress count for a lot; some characters verge on stereotypes. In
later chapters, Weld discusses Pym's individual novels as novels
of manners and provides much additional comment as well; she
uses manuscript sources to describe how Pym shaped her story. In
Chapter 4, she discusses Pym's style as an example of good
manners and lists some words for which Pym has special
meanings. Part of Chapter 5 analyzes Pym's use of foreign settings in unpublished material to suggest the erotic and decadent.

Whitney, Carol Wilkinson. "'Women Are So Terrifying These Days':
Fear Between the Sexes in the World of Barbara Pym." *Essays in
Literature* 16 (Spring, 1989): 71-84.
Whitney divides Pym's women into two categories besides the
familiar one of "excellent women." "Formidable women" are
independent and not looking for men. They have adopted masculine characteristics and interests. Esther Clovis, who appears in
several novels, is an excellent example. More prominent are the
"terrifying women." They are terrifying to men because they act
forcefully to secure a husband. Their actions form the basis for
the fear between the sexes that is a constant Pym theme. Allegra
Gray in *Excellent Women* is this type's most unpleasant example.

Whitney uses these distinctions to comment at length on *No Fond Return of Love*.

Widmayer, Richard A. "The Varied Portrait of Barbara Pym: A Review of the Post-1985 Critical Explosion." *Rocky Mountain Review of Language and Literature* 41 (1987): 241-245.
A frank and incisive survey of early books on Pym. Critics are divided between those who see Pym as a pleasant and humorous writer and those who view her as darker and more serious. *A Very Private Life* did little to help view Pym as a serious novelist.

Wilson, A. N. *Penfriend from Porlock*. New York: W. W. Norton, 1989.
This essay on Pym is a conflation of reviews of *A Few Green Leaves* and *An Unsuitable Attachment*. Wilson searches for the right way to praise Pym, a novelist he admires.

Wyatt-Brown, Anne M. *Barbara Pym: A Critical Biography*. Columbia: University of Missouri Press, 1992.
Although Pym herself often avoided introspection, a biographer should probe an artist's life and works. Wyatt-Brown does. Pym's inhibitions made her life sad, but her difficulties were the source of her creativity. Individual novels are discussed in detail.

_____. "Creativity: Defense Against Death." In *Proceedings of the Ninth International Conference on Literature and Psychology*, edited by Federico Periera. Lisbon: Inst[itute] Superior de Psicologia Aplicada, 1993.
Wyatt-Brown incorporates material from *Barbara Pym: A Critical Biography* into a short survey of her life with emphasis on the recognition she received in her later years. The calm and philosophical tone of *A Few Green Leaves* shows that Pym has used her sense of creative accomplishment to achieve a kind of peace before she died.

_____. "Ellipsis, Eccentricity and Evasion in the Diaries of Barbara Pym." In *Independent Women: The Function of Gender in the Novels of Barbara Pym*, edited by Janice Rossen. New York: St. Martin's Press, 1988.

In a detailed and interesting essay, Wyatt-Brown first connects
Pym's own character and her publisher's shortcomings to the
difficulties she faced as a novelist. Wyatt-Brown then speculates
on how Pym's childhood contributed to her later personal disappointments and to incidents in her novels.

_____. "From Fantasy to Pathology: Images of Aging in the
Novels of Barbara Pym." *Human Values and Aging Newsletter* 6
(January-February, 1985): 5-7.
From the beginning, Pym wrote as an outsider, and many of her
heroines were not young. In fact, *Some Tame Gazelle* is a fantasy
about how people in their fifties and sixties would live in an
idealized village. Neither ill-health or economic problems matter
to them. But as Pym herself aged, she became more pessimistic
about the fate of older people, especially older women. *The Sweet
Dove Died* has an aging, bitter heroine. By the time of *Quartet in
Autumn*, Pym could face the fears of aging and could note its
compensations. Letty finds that she has power to decide about her
future. Pym shows that old people have the capacity to change.

_____. "Late Style in the Novels of Barbara Pym and Penelope
Mortimer." *Gerontologist* 28 (December, 1988): 835-839.
The author contrasts two novelists in how they adjusted to old age.
In her childhood, Pym learned to try to rise above feelings of disappointment. Because she was hurt so deeply as a young woman,
she theorized in *Some Tame Gazelle* that old people learn to
abandon their passions and dreams. Her other early novels show
her converting unpleasantness into fiction. Only after a series of
personal shocks was she able to write an novel that expressed her
real pain—*Quartet in Autumn*. She saw old age as a time of deprivation and came to value the courage and independence of the
old. This urgency is missing from *A Few Green Leaves*, which
Wyatt-Brown sees as her serene swan song.

Wymard, Eleanor B. "Secular Faith in Barbara Pym." *Commonweal*,
January 13, 1984, 19-21.
In Pym's early novels, characters shy away from the big questions
about life, whereas in the later novels some of them do face life's
terrors. In either case, Pym often shows us people keeping chaos
away by daily, often domestic, rituals. These rituals are often

private (a spinster's lonely meal), but are communal as well (friends have a cup of tea or meet for lunch). In Pym's novels, faith in life's purpose comes, not from the Church, but from human nature through secular rituals. Wymard cites as an example Wilmet's feeling of rebirth at the end of *A Glass of Blessing*.

Criticism of Individual Novels

[Dates of composition and revision are supplied in brackets if they are significantly different from those of publication.]

Some Tame Gazelle, 1950. [1935-1950]

Ackley, Katherine Anne. *The Novels of Barbara Pym*. New York: Garland, 1989.
Useful discussions of this novel's themes are scattered throughout this book. No index.

Allen, Orphia Jane. *Barbara Pym: Writing a Life*. Metuchen, N.J.: Scarecrow Press, 1994.
In Part 1, Allen points out that Pym's humor in this novel as well as many of its details are drawn from Pym's own life. In Part 2, Allen shows how this novel treats the large issues Pym was always concerned about: the inadequacy of romantic love, the Church (especially its insensitive clergymen), and literature. Pym's allusions are usually ironic.

Benet, Diana. *Something to Love: Barbara Pym's Novels*. Columbia: University of Missouri Press, 1986.
In her second chapter, Benet treats Pym's first four novels, comic stories which center on women's need to love. In this novel the conventional romantic plot is transformed into a muddle of entanglements of older men and older women. Benet discriminates among the characters' relations and points out how they illustrate one of Pym's usual themes: how unsuitable most attachments are. Even so, Belinda's love for Archdeacon Hoccleve is memorable. It is long-lasting and sincere, and without illusion. In the end, it is sisterly love that proves most satisfying. An intelligent and detailed overview.

Burkhart, Charles. *The Pleasure of Miss Pym*. Austin: University of
    Texas Press, 1987.
    Pym transforms Oxford friends and places them in a fantastic and
    unchanging imaginary village.

Cooley, Mason. *The Comic Art of Barbara Pym*. New York: AMS
    Press, 1990.
    A detailed and appreciative analysis. The novel's village setting is
    a timeless golden world; the account is embellished by many
    literary allusions. Cooley contrasts the sisters' styles and says the
    Archdeacon is Pym's finest comic character. He explains how the
    novel's comedy is based on subtle social distinctions and a ribaldry
    unique in Pym's works. The happy ending is the reverse of the
    usual romantic one. It depends, not on the sisters getting married,
    but on their rejecting their suitors. At the end, they are happy
    because nothing has changed.

Cotsell, Michael. *Barbara Pym*. New York: St. Martin's Press, 1989.
    Cotsell treats this novel in Chapter One. Though it has strong
    autobiographical Oxford roots, it establishes the imaginative
    world of most Pym novels: a church-focused community, at the
    center of which is a single woman disappointed in love. Even so,
    Some Tame Gazelle was considerably revised in the fifteen years
    between composition and publication. Pym made it less witty in a
    Huxley-like way and more sentimental and domestic. Cotsell
    argues that in the contrast between the Archdeacon (who repre-
    sents Pym's beloved Henry Harvey) and Belinda (who resembles
    Pym herself), Pym continues a real-life debate between Harvey's
    modernism and Pym's odd postmodernism.

Graham, Peter W. "Emma's Three Sisters." *Arizona Quarterly: A
    Journal of American Literature, Culture, and Theory* 43 (Spring,
    1987): 39-52.
    Very forced comparisons with the Austen novel. Count Bianco is
    like Robert Martin, Mr. Mold is like Frank Churchill, and so
    forth.

Larson, Edith S. "The Celebration of the Ordinary in Barbara Pym's
    Novels." *San Jose Studies* 9 (Spring, 1983): 17-22.

Pym celebrates the force ordinary experiences may have to offer support in a sad world. Pym celebrates without any irony the impromptu tea party give by Miss Liversidge.

Liddell, Robert. *A Mind at Ease: Barbara Pym and Her Novels.* London: Peter Owen, 1989.
In Chapter 1, Liddell tells us that he read early versions of this novel when it was more like a serial letter addressed to him and to Henry Harvey, with whom Pym was in love. He read its revisions; Bishop Grote was an addition of the late 1940's. He confirms that the Archdeacon is a telling caricature of Harvey which Pym probably wrote to cure herself of her love. Liddell himself appears as Nicholas Parnell, a librarian. He admires the novel's aura of comfort and moderate happiness.

Long, Robert Emmet. *Barbara Pym.* New York: Frederick Ungar, 1986.
In Chapter 2, Long calls this novel a blend of genres: Victorian courtship novel, pastoral, drawing-room comedy. It has conventional rituals and conventional characters, many of which are eccentric caricatures. Its form is classically symmetrical, each character balancing another. As in Victorian novels, the balance of the community is upset by the arrival of intruders. This novel's concerns are domestic. The relations among women are most important; Long thinks the tacit communication between the Bede sisters is the finest thing in the novel. Even though many women have romantic fantasies, the life here is genteel and repressed. We see these fantasies and repressions most in Belinda's mind. Long wonders whether the joy she finds in daily tasks makes up for her deprivation and loneliness.

Nardin, Jane. *Barbara Pym.* Boston: Twayne, 1985.
In Chapter 4, Nardin sees the plot of this novel as one that turns a Jane Austen plot upside down. Here the women are older, not young; the men who arrive from the outside are rejected, not married. A marriage concludes the novel, but what is celebrated is the pleasures of the sisters living a single life. The novel shows Belinda slowly realizing that she is truly happy as she is, living with an affectionate sister. She and Harriet also have the very real

pleasures of detached, unrequited, and unfulfilled love—a love preferable to marriage.

Rossen, Janice. "Love in the Great Libraries: Oxford in the Work of Barbara Pym." *Journal of Modern Literature* 12 (July, 1985): 277-296.
In real life, Oxford meant to Pym a heady mixture of study and romance. In this novel, Pym takes a somewhat apologetic and ironic look at her former self.

_____. *The World of Barbara Pym*. New York: St. Martin's Press, 1987.
References to this novel are scattered throughout this study. Chapter 2 repeats Rossen's article "Love in the Great Libraries." In Chapter 3, Belinda and Harriet are spinsters who have achieved a pleasant, though perhaps schoolgirlish and immature, life together. They continue to yearn for men and give them gifts. But when they both reject offers of marriage, they show they have chosen spinsterhood. The youthful Pym seems to have foreseen her own future. Chapter 4 sketches and Anglican Church background for this and other novels: the petty disputes, the unsuitable sermons, the jumble sales. In Chapter 5, Rossen notes that it was after she began to work with anthropologists that Pym revised this novel to make much of an African bishop. Chapter 6 begins with an analysis of how the humble and self-deprecating Belinda comes to enjoy a quite triumph over her rival Agatha. In Chapter 7, Rossen uses this early novel as a foil to Pym's last work.

Weld, Annette. *Barbara Pym and the Novel of Manners*. New York: St. Martin's Press, 1992.
In Chapter 3, Weld shows how this novel, even though it is somewhat pastoral and its characters can verge on caricatures, is a novel of manners. The villagers have a code of proper conduct, based in part on the importance of maintaining everyone's dignity. Violators like Bishop Grote are frowned upon. Details of food and clothing have a great deal of significance. The narrator views the scene with ironic humor, often communicated through literary allusions.

Wyatt-Brown, Anne M. *Barbara Pym: A Critical Biography*. Columbia: University of Missouri Press, 1992.
A psychological investigation of Pym's life and work. In Chapter 2, Wyatt-Brown describes Pym writing the early versions of this novel as an attempt to escape her life at Oxford; she could not control real life, but she could control her fictional world. Pym's detached tone was necessary to hide her deep emotions. Later, as she revised, she made Belinda less servile. When Pym again revised the novel after World War II (as described in Chapter 3), she was happier, and her tone became more content. She gave Belinda more joy in daily life; she gave the Bishop experiences she had learned from her job at the African Institute. Most important, Belinda's relation with Harriet reflected Pym's joy in living with her sister Hilary as well as her anxieties that Hilary might remarry. Wyatt-Brown thinks that Pym's novels suffer from her own inhibitions about sex.

_____. "Late Style in the Novels of Barbara Pym and Penelope Mortimer." *Gerontologist* 28 (December, 1988): 835-839.
In her childhood, Pym learned to try to rise about feelings of disappointment. Because she was hurt so deeply as a young woman, in *Some Tame Gazelle* she theorized that old people learn to abandon their passions and dreams.

Excellent Women, 1952.

Ackley, Katherine Anne. *The Novels of Barbara Pym*. New York: Garland, 1989.
Useful discussions of this novel's themes are scattered throughout this book. No index.

Allen, Orphia Jane. *Barbara Pym: Writing a Life*. Metuchen, N.J.: Scarecrow Press, 1994.
In Part 1, Allen relates the novel's setting in London and the presence of anthropologists to Pym's own residence and her job. Part 2 shows how Pym deals with her major themes of religion and literature. The Anglican Church is related both to the Learned Society of anthropologists and to Roman Catholicism. Allen

thinks that the recurrent images of bathrooms are symbols of the
Roman Catholic Church.

Benet, Diana. *Something to Love: Barbara Pym's Novels.* Columbia:
University of Missouri Press, 1986.
In her second chapter, Benet treats *Excellent Women* with Pym's
other early novels, comic stories which center on a women's need
to love. Mildred and others experience unsuitable attachments.
But will Mildred remain a combination of observer and "excellent
woman," a spinster who derives satisfaction from selflessly
serving other's needs? Or will she become an assertive "good
woman" who has a life of her own? Gradually Pym answers these
questions as Mildred learns from Allegra Gray and the Napiers
about assertiveness and love. She is corrupted from being an
excellent woman, but she gains a story of her own. A lucid and
useful summary of the novel's characters and themes.

Bixler, Frances. "Female Narrative Structure in Barbara Pym's
Excellent Women." *Barbara Pym Newsletter* 5, no. 2 (1991): 2-6.
Using a base of contemporary theory, Bixler thinks that Pym had
difficulty structuring her stories in the usual female narrative
pattern.

Bowman, Barbara. "Pym's Subversive Subtext." In *Independent
Women: The Function of Gender in the Novels of Barbara Pym*,
edited by Janice Rossen. New York: St. Martin's Press, 1988.
Bowman analyzes the complex ironies that go on in selected passages. Mildred expresses many conventional thoughts out loud,
thoughts consistent with the ideas of the dominant (primarily
male) culture, but then adds ironic comments that subvert that
culture. These ironies are not revolutionary; Mildred challenges
authority only three times in this novel. The interaction is made
even more complex by what Bowman identifies as the narrator of
the novel—what some critics would call "the implied author."
With the help of the contemporary psychologist Jean Baker
Miller, Bowman defines many more characteristics of Mildred's
subordinate and female attitudes. Mildred takes on acceptable,
but not worthy roles; she deprecates herself; she hides her
intelligence from males; she feels guilty when she thinks she does
not give enough; she tries to please members of the dominant

culture.   Bowman sees subordinate tendencies in Mildred's language; her statements are often indefinite or negative.

Burkhart, Charles. *The Pleasure of Miss Pym*. Austin: University of Texas Press, 1987.
In Chapter 2, Burkhart evokes why Mildred responds to the charms of the Napiers.

Cooley, Mason. *The Comic Art of Barbara Pym*. New York: AMS Press, 1990.
Cooley's generalizations about postwar London are not convincing, nor is his attempt to make Mildred symbolic of Britain at the end of its empire. He is on firmer ground when he calls this novel the first of Pym's artistic maturity and Mildred the first typical Pym heroine: an intelligent, lonely, sad, ladylike, churchgoing spinster. She is an "excellent woman," though Cooley's definition of that term is thin. Though the London of this novel is drab, it has vitality, and Mildred is not passive. Cooley sees a pattern in her behavior. She is curious, and she approaches; she is fearful, and she retreats. Although she likes the role of observer, at heart she desires to connect with other people. As is usual in Pym's work, people arrive from the outside and disrupt the novel's world; the Napiers, Allegra Gray, and the anthropologists, in particular Everard Bone. For all her skill as an observer, Mildred misreads many signals, especially from Everard. The novel ends, not with any immediate marriage, but with Mildred feeling much less superfluous than before. Cooley says the theme of the novel is that the melancholy of loneliness can be overcome.

Cotsell, Michael. *Barbara Pym*. New York: St. Martin's Press, 1989.
In Chapter 3, Cotsell says that this novel, along with the three others published between 1952 and 1958, may represent Pym's finest work. Even though these novels contain Pym's first references to anthropologists (reflecting her postwar job), they are less obviously autobiographical than before. Cotsell makes a useful analysis of this novel's varied setting: wartime destruction, modern institutions, and Victorian remnants. He describes the origins of the novel, but spends most space evoking Mildred's character, a mixture of self-deprecating wit, repression, vulnerability, and desire. The object of this desire, Rocky, is a stereotype, but aware

of it.   Cotsell makes a brief reference to contemporary literary
theory to explain Mildred's function.

Doan, Laura L.   "Text and the Single Man: The Bachelor in Pym's
Dual-Voiced Narrative." In *Independent Women: The Function of
Gender in the Novels of Barbara Pym*, edited by Janice Rossen.
New York: St. Martin's Press, 1988.
Doan uses Mildred's initial response to illustrate a woman's
capacity to utter dutiful expressions, yet have subversive thoughts.
In contrast, though Pym's bachelors are somewhat spinsterish in
their habits, they are (like William Caldicote) single-minded in
their selfishness. As a bachelor/clergyman, Julian has difficulty
reconciling sex with celibacy.

Ezell, Margaret J. M.   "'What Shall We Do With Our Old Maids?':
Barbara Pym and the Woman Question." *International Journal of
Women's Studies* 7 (November/December, 1984): 450-465.
One consequence of the preference society still gives to married
women is that there are often tensions between them and single
women. One example is Helena's treatment of Mildred.

Griffin, Barbara. "Private Space and Self-Definition in Barbara Pym's
Excellent Women." *Essays in Literature* 19 (Spring, 1992): 132-
143.
As Mildred must fight to preserve her living space against the
Napiers and Winifred, so she must protect her psychic space as
well. She does this by cultivating three voices. The first is dutiful
and unironic. Though other people often hear this voice, it is not
simply a public voice; Mildred talks to herself this way.   Her
second voice is more resistant and is often heard almost
simultaneously with the first. It can be ironic, amused, fatigued,
resentful; it can mock the conventions of excellent women.

Mildred's third voice is private, fanciful, and lyric (as when she
speculates on medieval shopping lists or on organists from East
Sheen). Other characters do not hear it, and it does not influence
events. Nevertheless, it gives Mildred a inviolate private space.
Griffin's argument illuminates the novel's ending.   No matter
what other novels say, Mildred is not now married to Everard.
She, like contemporary feminists, understands that women are
pulled in two directions: to turn away from others and become

independent or to move toward others and become subservient. In her, readers see a female character resisting being forced to make these choices.

Liddell, Robert. *A Mind at Ease: Barbara Pym and Her Novels.* London: Peter Owen, 1989.
In Chapter 4, Liddell says he thinks this novel is the best of Pym's early work. He finds it contains much detail from ordinary life, particularly about cooking and cleaning up afterward.

Long, Robert Emmet. *Barbara Pym.* New York: Frederick Ungar, 1986.
In Chapter 2, Long's analysis brings out Pym's clear organization. Against a background of a diminished England, Mildred leads a repressed and limited life. She participates in two distinct worlds, her local church and the Learned Society. The marginal and enervated qualities of each are made clear by parallel scenes: the church's pitiful jumble sale and the marvelously comic meeting of the society. Her life is complicated as well by Allegra and Rocky, two intruders who eventually seek her help. Pym makes a sharp contrast between Mildred's men: the eccentric Everard, her actual suitor, is the antithesis of the dashing Rocky, the man she fantasizes about. Long finds the novel's ending ambiguous. Will Mildred's future life be a full one, or be just as bleak as before?

Nardin, Jane. *Barbara Pym.* Boston: Twayne, 1985.
In Chapter 4, Nardin analyzes two sides to Mildred's character. On one hand, Mildred is a conventional, conscientious spinster content to do good works. On the other, she likes food, displays humor and irony, and falls for Rocky. Even though she will marry Everard Bone, she has not escaped her condition. Bone is selfish and sexless; her marriage will be a kind of servitude.

Radner, Sanford. "Barbara Pym's People." *Western Humanities Review* 39 (Summer, 1985): 172-177.
Beneath the surface of Pym's work, Radner finds one story: "a self-denying mother feeds her ungrateful baby son." Pym's men are unvaryingly childish and demanding, like the church workers or even Everard. Women like Mildred and Allegra compete

among themselves to serve these men.   Pym's comedy lies in
seeing adults act out such childish games.

Rossen, Janice. "On Not Being Jane Eyre: The Romantic Heroine in
    Barbara Pym's Novels." In *Independent Women: The Function of
    Gender in the Novels of Barbara Pym*. New York: St. Martin's
    Press, 1988.
    Even though Mildred says she is not like Jane Eyre, she resembles
    Brontë's heroine in many ways: both are plain women who do not
    expect to be loved, neither is rich, and both are torn from the men
    they love. But the novels end differently. After discussing several
    feminist critiques of the two endings, Rossen concludes that Pym's
    ending is meant to form a contrast with Brontë's. Mildred does
    not end marrying a romantic hero, but may possibly marry
    Everard Bone, a character who corresponds to St. John in *Jane
    Eyre*.

_____. *The World of Barbara Pym*. New York: St. Martin's Press,
    1987.
    References are scattered throughout this study. In Chapter 1,
    Rossen points out that Mildred uses literary quotations both to
    imply what she is and what she is not. Chapter 3 often refers to
    Mildred, Pym's archetypical spinster. She may appear pitiful as
    she prepares her lonely meals in her kitchen, yet she often enjoys
    her solitude, rejecting other women who may want to stay with
    her. Nevertheless, even though she thinks she is simply a spin-
    ster, she experiences strong feelings for the men who enter her
    life. She cooks for them, does dishes, and even proofreads. Pym
    unsentimentally shows Mildred deluding herself about Rocky for
    awhile.
       Chapter 4 treats this novel at length as an example of how the
    Church figures in Pym's fiction. It lies behind the action of the
    novel, specifically in showing parish life. Mildred is a believer
    and an active church worker. Unlike other religious characters,
    she tells us that she entered a church to meditate. But, like others
    believers in Pym, she is reticent when it comes to talking about
    spiritual matters. In Chapter 5, Rossen shows the role anthropol-
    ogy plays in this novel. Mildred gets to know Helen (a career
    women very unlike her) and Everard, the dispassionate profes-
    sional who is attracted to her. Rossen also discusses how food is

treated as a ritual in the story. (She is one of the only critics to try to make sense of Mrs. Bone.)

The first half of Chapter 6 is devoted to Mildred as Pym's quintessential voice. Mildred presents herself as meek, self-conscious, and apologetic. She tries not to admit her deep passions. She feels inferior to others and defers to superior authority. Yet her tone is one of muted resentment, sometimes suggesting real anger at her humiliations and constrictions. Even though she has no real confidant in the novel, she can tell her thoughts to the reader. In the end, she triumphs as an observer who sees the ridiculousness of others and achieves an ironic acceptance of her lot. Her lot may include marriage to Everard, and Rossen explains how this relationship is prepared.

Schofield, Mary Anne. "Well-Fed or Well-Loved? Patterns of Cooking and Eating in the Novels of Barbara Pym." *University of Windsor Review* 18 (Spring-Summer, 1985): 1-8.
When women cook for men, it can be a symbol of the female's civilizing power. When Mildred makes a meal for herself, it is meager. When she actually provides food for a man, it is uncooked lettuce and cheese. She does not cook nourishing meals and does not establish a satisfying relationship.

Schultz, Muriel. "The Novelist as Anthropologist." In *The Life and Work of Barbara Pym*, edited by Dale Salwak. Iowa City: University of Iowa Press, 1987.
In her survey of Pym's treatment of anthropology, Schulz shows how Pym distinguishes in this novel between two generations of anthropologists, the older amateurs and the young not-so-likable scientists.

Weld, Annette. *Barbara Pym and the Novel of Manners*. New York: St. Martin's Press, 1992.
In Chapter 4, Weld tells why this work is a novel of manners. It is centered on a limited community, organized around a church, with a definite hierarchy, definite delegations of labor, and codes of religious behavior. Mildred has a strong sense of propriety and is embarrassed by references to bathrooms. Intruders (the Napiers, Allegra Gray) must be dealt with. Mildred notes that other communities, like the anthropologists, have different codes.

Wyatt-Brown, Anne M.   *Barbara Pym: A Critical Biography*.
    Columbia: University of Missouri Press, 1992.
    When she wrote this novel, Pym was confident of her abilities and
    happy with her life with her sister (Chapter 1).   Mildred was
    created out of this state of mind. In Chapter 3, Wyatt-Brown says
    the early charters show Mildred in a kind of Eden; later chapters
    show her fall. Wyatt-Brown draws a parallel between Pym's own
    loss of innocence and Mildred's. The difference is that from the
    beginning Mildred is more aware of the way men act than Pym
    was in real life.   Mildred shows her awareness by subversive
    asides and reflections.   Wyatt-Brown thinks Pym intends for
    readers to see Mildred's fate as dreary. At the end of the novel she
    is solitary, but the emotions that Rocky has awakened make it
    impossible for her to retreat back to being merely a spinster.

Jane and Prudence, 1953.

Ackley, Katherine Anne.   *The Novels of Barbara Pym*. New York:
    Garland, 1989.
    Useful discussions of this novel's themes are scattered throughout
    this book. No index.

Allen, Orphia Jane.   *Barbara Pym: Writing a Life*.   Metuchen, N.J.:
    Scarecrow Press, 1994.
    In Part 1, Allen discusses the relation of this novel to *Crampton
    Hodnet* and speculates that Pym's own worry about being
    unmarried is reflected in what happens to its female characters.
    In Part 2, Allen writes that Pym supplements her usual treatment
    of unfulfilled spinsters with many married female characters, who
    are even worse off. Her treatment of religion shows evidence of
    the attractions the Roman Catholic Church had for Pym. Pym's
    literary allusions are more profound, as she worries about happy
    endings and about her own place in English literature.

Benet, Diana. *Something to Love: Barbara Pym's Novels*. Columbia:
    University of Missouri Press, 1986.
    In her second chapter, Benet treats Pym's first four novels, stories
    which center on women's need to love. She gives this novel an
    intelligent and sympathetic reading, pointing out that despite their

differences the two women have much in common. Both Jane and Prudence have active imaginations which dwell on the relations between the sexes and upon the way they see themselves. Prudence sees herself as the heroine of tragic romances, and that is the way her life goes on. Although she imagines Fabian Driver to be a romantic hero, he is really tacky and shallow and is easily captured by the plain but unromantic Jessie Morrow. Jane tries to fulfill the role of helpmeet for her clergyman husband, but fails at every turn because of her sloppy housekeeping and irreverent and inappropriate fancies. In the world of this novel, the promises of female characters are not fulfilled and their imaginations do not serve them well.

Brothers, Barbara. "Love, Marriage, and Manners in the Novels of Barbara Pym." In *Reading and Writing Women's Lives: A Study of the Novel of Manners*, edited by Barbara Brothers and Bege K. Bowers. Ann Arbor, Mich.: University Microfilms International Research Press, 1990.
Brothers discusses this novel in light of her general thesis: Pym's novels subvert Victorian attitudes. Both women mix fantasy and reality; both are uncertain about how to live their lives; each one pities the other. Pym's men are not so bad as they have been painted. Jane and Prudence often try to imagine what men really want.

Burkhart, Charles. *The Pleasure of Miss Pym*. Austin: University of Texas Press, 1987.
In Chapter 2, Burkhart explains why Jane is his favorite Pym character.

Cooley, Mason. *The Comic Art of Barbara Pym*. New York: AMS Press, 1990.
With this novel, Cooley tells us that Pym begins to establish interconnections: characters developed in one novel appear later in minor roles. Readers accept these coincidences because the worlds of clergy, academics, and anthropologists are connected in real life. Men in this novel can, as usual, be divided into dull husbands or weak bachelors. As in *Some Tame Gazelle*, two women are central. Jane looks at life from a literary perspective. Not only does she see herself as Jane Austen's Emma when she

tries to make matches, her conversation proceeds so much by verbal associations that ordinary people are baffled. Prudence casts herself as the heroine of romantic tragedy. She thinks she loves the vain philanderer Fabian Driver, but when he is captured by the unromantic Jessie Morrow (from *Crampton Hodnet*), she quickly begins to think of another man. (Fabian has been as much a prisoner of his fantasies as she is of hers.) At the end, neither Jane nor Prudence have changed: they continue to enjoy their literary fantasies.

Cotsell, Michael. *Barbara Pym*. New York: St. Martin's Press, 1989.
In Chapter 3, Cotsell says that this novel, along with the three others published between 1952 and 1958, may be Pym's finest work. Even though these novels make anthropological references (reflecting Pym's postwar job), they are less obviously autobiographical than before. Cotsell calls *Jane and Prudence* Pym's funniest novels. Much of the talk about food is funny because of its sexual undertones. Prudence and Fabian are amusing in their pursuit of stereotyped romance. Cotsell is best when he treats the lovable Jane, who fantastic imagination sometimes erupts in embarrassing talk. It is Jane's comforting and loving relation with her curate husband that provides the center of the novel's values, particularly in a kitchen scene which blends both pagan and Christian elements. Cotsell finds Pym's dispute with modernism reflected in Jane's and Prudence's taste in literature.

Doan, Laura L. "Pym's Singular Interest: The Self as Spinster." In *Old Maids to Radical Spinsters: Unmarried Women in the Twentieth-Century Novel*. Urbana: University of Illinois Press, 1991.
Pym wishes to show spinsters in a good light. In this novel, Prudence not only has more fun than Jane but also is better off in the end.

Halperin, John. "Barbara Pym and the War of the Sexes." In *The Life and Work of Barbara Pym*, edited by Dale Salwak. Iowa City: University of Iowa Press, 1987.
This novel is an attack on men. Women are generally in charge; a woman's love is capable of making something out of a man. Men

are heartless and selfish (especially when it comes to food). They do not like intelligent, energetic women.

Liddell, Robert. *A Mind at Ease: Barbara Pym and Her Novels.* London: Peter Owen, 1989.
In Chapter 5, Liddell discusses some details that signal class distinctions and lavishes praise on Jane for her exuberance, charm, and goodness. She may resemble Pym's mother.

Long, Robert Emmet. *Barbara Pym.* New York: Frederick Ungar, 1986.
In Chapter 3, Long discusses how Pym developed this novel out of the as-yet-unpublished *Crampton Hodnet*. Both are works which show the deflation of romantic illusions. As Fabian Driver himself is a Victorian stereotype, so his garden is an ironic version of the gardens of romance. Prudence is equally narcissistic. Jane and her vicar husband are the triumphs of the novel, especially Jane with her wonderful flights of fancy. In spite of their vivacity, both Jane and Prudence are isolated and limited; despite their moderate happiness at the end, the reader must think the future is unpromising.

Nardin, Jane. *Barbara Pym.* Boston: Twayne, 1985.
In Chapter 4, Nardin says this novel deals with women's disappointments, from the opening scenes at their Oxford reunion to what happens to both Prudence and Jane. Prudence is vain, and she meets more than her match in the superbly vain Fabian Driver. They do not marry because each one bores the other. At the end, the reader wonders if Prudence may begin to suspect that she is fated to repeat these disillusioning affairs. Jane, on the other hand, is very aware of her failures as a scholar, as a mother, and as a clergyman's wife. At the end, she does have a comfortable relation with her husband and has made some improvement. Pym here sees most men as vain and selfish.

Radner, Sanford. "Barbara Pym's People." *Western Humanities Review* 39 (Summer, 1985): 172-177.
Beneath the surface of Pym's work, Radner senses one story: "a self-denying mother feeds her ungrateful baby son." Pym's men are unvaryingly childish and demanding. Yet Pym's "excellent

women" compete among themselves to give selfless service to
these men, usually (as in this novel) giving them the best food.
Occasionally we meet a "failed excellent woman" like Jane, who
feels guilty about not being able to serve her husband well enough.
Pym's comedy lies in seeing adults act out such childish games.

Rossen, Janice. "Love in the Great Libraries: Oxford in the Work of
Barbara Pym." *Journal of Modern Literature* 12 (July, 1985):
277-296.
Real-life Oxford memories lie behind this novel, for Jane observes
that after some years no one of her Oxford contemporaries has
fulfilled her promise. Female characters often think of themselves
as reliving the lives of women from novels.

_____. *The World of Barbara Pym*. New York: St. Martin's Press,
1987.
References to this novel are scattered throughout this study. In
Chapter 1, Rossen points out that Prudence Bates's name is an
ironic echo of Austen's Miss Bates in *Emma*. It is Jane's style that
is literary; her flights of fancy often fall flat on her unliterary
audience. Chapter 2 reprints Rossen's article "Love in the Great
Libraries." In Chapter 3, Rossen deals with this novel's two
spinsters. Prudence eats well when she eats alone, showing she
thinks highly of herself. Her defense against loneliness is to have
a succession of affairs. Jessie Morrow is very much a social
inferior, almost a Jane Eyre figure. She plans to entice the man
she desires and succeeds. Chapter 4 deals with Pym and the
Anglican Church. Jane is a woman who derived her notion of
what a vicar's wife should be from Victorian fiction and then has
difficulty living up to it. Rossen provides valuable historic background on the relation between "high church" Anglicanism and
Roman Catholicism. In Chapter 5, Rossen shows that Pym had an
anthropologist's eye when she depicted many daily rituals, especially ones relating to food and cosmetics.

Rubenstein, Jill. "Comedy and Consolation in the Novels of Barbara
Pym." *Renascence* 42 (Spring, 1990): 173-183.
The Church is a source of comedy for Pym, but a few characters
do get some sort of consolation from religion. The incompetent

Jane fails to sense God in her drawing room, but in a sense she succeeds because she knows enough to look for Him there.

Weld, Annette. *Barbara Pym and the Novel of Manners*. New York: St. Martin's Press, 1992.
In Chapter 4, Weld compares this novel to the tale of the country mouse (Jane) and the city mouse (Prudence). Pym contrasts them by comparing their manners with regard to many things, including clothes, cooking, food, drink, and reading material. Pym is an appropriately ironic narrator.

Wyatt-Brown, Anne M. *Barbara Pym: A Critical Biography*. Columbia: University of Missouri Press, 1992.
In Chapter 3, Wyatt-Brown traces the characters in this novel to their sources in Pym's life. Pym made the male figures much weaker persons than their counterparts in earlier novels in revenge for the pain particular men caused her in real life. Both Jane and Prudence have personal sources as well, though these are more complex. Unlike other women novelists of this age, Pym does not dissect the institution of marriage, for she had no personal experience of it.

Less Than Angels, 1955.

Ackley, Katherine Anne. *The Novels of Barbara Pym*. New York: Garland, 1989.
Useful discussions of this novel's themes are scattered throughout this book. No index.

Allen, Orphia Jane. *Barbara Pym: Writing a Life*. Metuchen, N.J.: Scarecrow Press, 1994.
In Part 1, Allen shows how this novel makes extensive use of what Pym learned through her job at the International African Institute. In Part 2, Allen argues that in this novel, Pym makes her most explicit statement about what her kind of novel can do. The novel first contrasts the objective vision of anthropologists with the fanciful view of Catherine, a writer of romances. (Clergymen and religion are somehow allied with anthropology in this novel.) Catherine moves toward a more realistic kind of fiction in two

stages marked by two of the important male characters. Tom's
disillusionment with anthropology and his death symbolize the
sterility of the objective ideal. Alaric's burning his notes and his
hopes to write fiction suggest an ideal for Catherine the novelist:
to achieve a mean between the excesses of objectivity and fantasy.

Benet, Diana. *Something to Love: Barbara Pym's Novels*. Columbia:
University of Missouri Press, 1986.
In her third chapter, Benet treats this novel along with three
others from the middle of Pym's career. In these novels, we see
Pym treating male characters more fully and showing both men
and women making fulfilling choices. Benet impressively sorts
out the many characters and issues of this novel. She sees the
anthropologist Tom Mallow as central; he is an observer of life,
and his profession underscores this trait. Tom and other anthropologists observe tribal customs in Africa; likewise there are
tribelike communities in the suburbs of London and in the
country. Tom is alienated from both, as is his lover Catherine.
Although the novel explores gender differences, the problems of
detachment and alienation are most important. In the end, many
characters escape (at least to some extent) from the alienation that
tormented them. Deirdre marries a good man; Catherine finds a
community in the suburbs; she rescues Alaric by helping him burn
the notes that had made him dysfunctional.

Bowman, Barbara. "Pym's Subversive Subtext." In *Independent
Women: The Function of Gender in the Novels of Barbara Pym*,
edited by Janice Rossen. New York: St. Martin's Press, 1988.
Pym's heroines have an ironic attitude toward the dominant
culture. Because Deirdre is too young to have such ironies, she is
not a full-fledged heroine.

Burkhart, Charles. *The Pleasure of Miss Pym*. Austin: University of
Texas Press, 1987.
In Chapter 2, Burkhart says this novel shows a greater range and
greater objectivity than Pym's earlier fictions. The essential story,
one of lost love and painful detribalization, is sad.

Cooley, Mason. *The Comic Art of Barbara Pym*. New York: AMS
Press, 1990.

Less Than Angels differs from other Pym novels in that it has no nurturing community, neither a village nor an urban parish, to sustain its characters. Whether they living in central London, the suburbs, or in the country, most of the characters are loveless and alone. Even though she briefly has a live-in boyfriend (something new in Pym's world), Catherine is lonely. Like other Pym heroines, she consoles herself with her work, with her curiosity, and with her energetic and playful imagination.

Others are equally alone. Suburban people do not know their neighbors, and, except for Elaine, country people live in separate worlds. But anthropologists are the most alienated. Cooley describes their world well: it is full of activity, competition, irritability, greed, and indifference. Tom is its chief figure. He seeks detachment above all; when he dies, nobody cares very much. Alaric is also alienated, but his detachment is a kind of defense that can be broken down. In this novel, Pym occasionally reflects on a novelist's craft. Catherine writes romantic pot-boilers, and Pym reflects that an omniscient narrator can take readers where she wants them to go.

Cotsell, Michael. *Barbara Pym*. New York: St. Martin's Press, 1989.
In Chapter 3, Cotsell says that this novel, along with the others published between 1952 and 1958, may be Pym's finest work. Even though these novels reflect Pym's postwar job by their many references to anthropologists, they are less obviously autobiographical than before. Cotsell gives this novel a very interesting symbolic reading. The setting is cruel and modern. There are few churches, but there is much petty competition among professional anthropologists. Under the surface, life has real violence. The novel's title refers to its vision of human beings as placed somewhere lower than angels, but not far above the violence the anthropologists study in Africa. Cotsell also reads the central conflict in a personal way. Tom the anthropologist succeeds in detaching himself from human feelings and from the women who love him. Catherine, not a modernist but a writer of old-fashioned romances, embodies the female strength Tom lacks. After Tom dies, Catherine rescues another anthropologist, Alaric, from his isolation.

Halperin, John. "Barbara Pym and the War of the Sexes." In *The Life and Work of Barbara Pym*, edited by Dale Salwak. Iowa City: University of Iowa Press, 1987.
Pym's treatment here of the war between the sexes is more moderate than elsewhere. Her women are sometimes tactless; Catherine observes they sometimes overwhelm a man. Yet men unthinkingly make use women as usual.

Larson, Edith S. "The Celebration of the Ordinary in Barbara Pym's Novels." *San Jose Studies* 9 (Spring, 1983): 17-22.
Pym celebrates the ordinary—drinking tea in particular—to offer support in a sad world. Here Catherine drinks tea to cheer her after discovering Tom's betrayal. Mabel and Rhoda's suburban world offers ordinary comforts.

Liddell, Robert. *A Mind at Ease: Barbara Pym and Her Novels.* London: Peter Owen, 1989.
In Chapter 6, Liddell calls anthropology a jargon-filled academic discipline. It is his opinion that some academics have used anthropology to replace the extensive literary background that was possessed by educated people in the past. Tom moves from the old world to the new world; even so, he is never completely "detribalized." Liddell distinguishes detached anthropological observation from the more personal investigations made by Catherine in this novel, by Dulcie in *No Fond Return of Love*, and by Pym herself.

Long, Robert Emmet. *Barbara Pym.* New York: Frederick Ungar, 1986.
In Chapter 4, Long sees the isolation of women as the theme of this novel. Men are isolated as well—Tom, in particular. Anthropologists in general are isolated from normal society in their sterile pursuits. But it is Tom who disappoints many women, especially those who assemble after his death. Catherine is the most fully drawn. Pym compares her rescue of Alaric to Jane Eyre's saving Rochester in Charlotte Brontë's novel and implies they will marry. For the first time Pym adds a note of acceptance: isolation is a normal condition for both men and women.

Nardin, Jane. *Barbara Pym*. Boston: Twayne, 1985.
In Chapter 2, Nardin evokes Rhoda Wellcome nicely. In Chapter 4, she treats this novel in detail. Pym here for the first time implies that anthropologists and novelists are similar in how they observe human life. In fact, all her characters are observers, from Rhoda and Mabel to Catherine to the professional anthropologists. Pym depicts the amusing rituals of many social groups, especially those rituals having to do with courtship and sex. For all their training, anthropologists seem unaware of the rituals of their own profession. Catherine is more self-conscious about such matters, so when she meets Alaric, a man who cannot conform to the rituals of his group, she is able to rescue him. Even though Pym's distinction between the harsh objectivity of the social sciences and the humanity of literature is not so sharp here as in *A Few Green Leaves*, Alaric resembles Emma in that novel when he thinks he will turn from anthropology to writing fiction.

Rossen, Janice. *The World of Barbara Pym*. New York: St. Martin's Press, 1987.
In Chapter 3, Rossen analyzes Catherine as a very independent spinster. Even though Tom lives with her, Catherine will say nothing about their sexual relationship. Much of Chapter 5 is devoted to this novel. Anthropologists are targets for satire, especially when they question their work and when they draw odd conclusions about English behavior. Yet sometimes an anthropological perspective yields insights into the meaning of actions at home. A example of both insight and absurdity involves the observations of the foreigner Jean-Pierre Rossignol. In Chapter 6, Rossen discusses Catherine, a writer who resembles an anthropologist in her observant nature, yet who knows she alters the facts when she turns them into romantic stories. Catherine matures when she begins to try to tell the truth in her fiction.

Rubenstein, Jill. "'For the Ovaltine Had Loosened Her Tongue': Failures of Speech in Barbara Pym's *Less Than Angels*." *Modern Fiction Studies* 32 (Winter, 1986): 573-580.
Rubenstein uses several theories to try to illuminate Pym's work. The most convincing theory contrasts two kinds of speakers. One, usually male, speaks factually and unimaginatively. The other, always a woman, uses her imagination to transform facts into

satisfying fictions. Conversations between these types are always difficult and usually comic. She shows that *Less Than Angels* provides a series of failed communications, particularly in conversations between women.

Schultz, Muriel. "The Novelist as Anthropologist." In *The Life and Work of Barbara Pym*, edited by Dale Salwak. Iowa City: University of Iowa Press, 1987.
In this novel, Pym makes a detailed case against anthropologists. They are patronizing. They impose their own patterns on the life they observe. In their scientific detachment, they dehumanize their subjects and have no concern for them. Their work is sterile and unreadable. Perhaps they should study contemporary England. Catherine, the writer of fiction, forms a contrast to the dehumanized anthropologist, Tom. By the end, she knows that Alaric is a lonely man and rescues him.

Weld, Annette. *Barbara Pym and the Novel of Manners.* New York: St. Martin's Press, 1992.
In Chapter 4, Weld discusses this work as a novel of manners. The primary community here that of the humorless and hierarchical anthropologists. Pym stretches the code of this kind of novel by making more open references to sex and by allowing a major character to die a violent death.

Wyatt-Brown, Anne M. *Barbara Pym: A Critical Biography.* Columbia: University of Missouri Press, 1992.
In Chapter 4, Wyatt-Brown explains the personal reasons that enabled Pym to make this book seem more optimistic than her earlier works, especially in her tolerant rendering of suburbia. Nevertheless, Pym's own personal pain shows in her portraits of Alaric and Catherine.

A Glass of Blessings, 1958.

Ackley, Katherine Anne. *The Novels of Barbara Pym.* New York: Garland, 1989.
Useful discussions of this novel are scattered throughout. No index.

Allen, Orphia Jane. *Barbara Pym: Writing a Life*. Metuchen, N.J.: Scarecrow Press, 1994.

Allen has little to say about this novel in Part 1, but in Part 2 she draws parallels with Jane Austen's *Emma*. Like Emma, Wilmet has many illusions and moves toward knowledge. Pym's religious concerns are symbolically rendered when Father Ransom is able to resist the temptations of Roman Catholicism by the love of the good Anglican Mary Beamish. The romance theme here has two aspects. Even though romantic dreams are doomed, stable relationships (even between homosexuals) are possible and valuable.

Benet, Diana. *Something to Love: Barbara Pym's Novels*. Columbia: University of Missouri Press, 1986.

In Chapter 3, Benet treats this novel along with three others in which men are given equal treatment and in which some men and some women have happy endings. Here although Benet sees many subtle parallels and variations, the elegant, lonely, and snobbish Wilmet is central. The novel is the story of her search for purpose both in her church and in romance. At first, Wilmet feels out of place among the dull people at church. In her pursuit of romance, she settles on the elegant Piers, who turns out to be homosexual. Wilmet is capable of learning. She learns forgiveness at church, and after Piers tells her she cannot love other people, she changes. She and her husband move toward one another as they plan a new home, she becomes part of her church community, and she realizes how devoted Piers's lover Keith really is. The book's climax is at a coffeehouse where Wilmet realizes that she belongs to many worlds and that she wants to help others feel they belong as well.

Burkhart, Charles. *The Pleasure of Miss Pym*. Austin: University of Texas Press, 1987.

In Chapter 2, Burkhart surveys this novel's characters.

Cooley, Mason. *The Comic Art of Barbara Pym*. New York: AMS Press, 1990.

This novel's central concern is the unfolding of the mind of the narrator, Wilmet Forsyth, a vain and idle, but imaginative and curious upper-class London woman. Because she is bored, Wilmet tries to understand lives outside her limited circle by

interpreting their actions and judging them as well. The novel is
the story of how she is forced to revise her interpretations and of
the admirable resilience she shows in adjusting to new circum-
stances. Wilmet learns that married men make passes at women
not their wives, that plain and even elderly women do have erotic
futures, and that handsome wastrels cannot be redeemed on her
terms. Cooley makes a fine analysis of one conversation in which
he shows that other characters share Wilmet's powers of tolerance,
resilience, and what could be called Christian charity.

Cotsell, Michael. *Barbara Pym*. New York: St. Martin's Press, 1989.
An important analysis. In Chapter 3, Cotsell says that this novel
may be Pym's most charming and delightful. Cotsell charts how
subtly Wilmet's development is revealed in her first-person
narration. Three things contribute most to Wilmet's change.
Wilmet's involvement with the Church leads to her spending
time at a religious retreat where she comes to self-knowledge.
Golden memories of Italy eventually inspire Wilmet and her
husband to rekindle their love. And her mother-in-law Sybil
engineers some of Wilmet's progress. Costell calls this a joyous
romantic comedy in the Shakespearean tradition. Cotsell also
compares this novel to Jane Austen's *Emma*. In both there are
many relations and causes that their heroines do not understand
and that are likewise missed by first-time readers.

Fergus, Jan. "*A Glass of Blessings*, Jane Austen's *Emma* and Barbara
Pym's Art of Allusion." In *Independent Women: The Function of
Gender in the Novels of Barbara Pym*, edited by Janice Rossen.
New York: St. Martin's Press, 1988.
The title is deceptive, for this article is about much more than
Pym's allusions to *Emma*. Fergus points out interesting broad
parallels with Austen's novel and insists on many that are only
marginally convincing. Pym's point may be the great distance
between Emma's world and Wilmet's. Fergus is brilliant when
she compares Emma's straightforward repentance and reward
with what happens to Pym's heroine. Wilmet's regeneration and
ultimate happiness takes place at the retreat house and later at
Keith's coffee bar. Wilmet is partially unconscious of her
reconciliation of pagan and Christian, flesh and spirit. Pym
communicates the nature of this reconciliation by symbols (the

compost heap, the swarm of bees) and by allusions to authors other than Austen, mainly Andrew Marvell and T. S. Eliot. Wilmet is rewarded by a new understanding with her husband, an unlikely Mr. Knightly figure. Fergus thinks this is Pym's happiest ending.

Halperin, John. "Barbara Pym and the War of the Sexes." In *The Life and Work of Barbara Pym*, edited by Dale Salwak. Iowa City: University of Iowa Press, 1987.
Men are not valued in this novel. Men, though tyrannical, are weak; marriage is a dead end. On the other hand, women sometimes get a sadistic pleasure from treating them badly.

Liddell, Robert. *A Mind at Ease: Barbara Pym and Her Novels.* London: Peter Owen, 1989.
In Chapter 7, Liddell has little to say about this novel. He praises Wilmet's subtle discovery of Piers's homosexuality by comparing it to Emma's discoveries in the Jane Austen novel. At the end, Wilmet has improved herself somewhat, but perhaps that makes her less interesting.

Long, Robert Emmet. *Barbara Pym.* New York: Frederick Ungar, 1986.
In Chapter 4, Long praises this novel for many things. Though the novel contains less satire and less caricature than other Pym works, Wilf Bason and Keith are wonderful comic characters. Long traces patterns of mainly Christian symbolism and echoes of T. S. Eliot, Henry James, and Jane Austen. He shows that Pym organizes many events around opposite tendencies: high and low social positions, the sacred and the profane, Christian and pagan. Wilmet is at the center, and the novel is about her progress. She begins as a rich, elegant, lonely, unsatisfied wife who yearns after the handsome Piers. Through her involvement with him, with his lover, and with many finely drawn characters associated with the Church, Wilmet is gradually changed. She recognizes that the categories she thought within are not absolute, that all of life can be accepted. Many characters receive blessings at the end of this novel. Although Wilmet herself does not find the love she yearns for, she now understands life and accepts it. Her isolation is not so great as before.

Nardin, Jane. *Barbara Pym*. Boston: Twayne, 1985.

In Chapter 4, Nardin describes Wilmet as a self-centered woman who dreams of romantic love and who misinterprets much of what goes on about her. Gradually she learns various truths. Gradually, too, she develops friendships with other women and experiences a renewal of her marriage. At the end, she has not changed very much on the surface, but she knows she is happy. Nardin points out how much her mother-in-law does for Wilmet without her being aware of it.

Rossen, Janice. *The World of Barbara Pym*. New York: St. Martin's Press, 1987.

References to this novel are to be found throughout this book. In Chapter 1, Rossen notes that Wilmet uses a literary comparison to define herself: she cannot interpret details as Virginia Woolf might have done. In Chapter 3, Rossen shows how Wilmet, though married, resembles Pym's usual spinsters. Wilmet tries to suppress her emotions. When she cannot, she weaves fantasies about a man she cannot have and is humiliated by his rejection of her. Chapter 4 deals at length with the presence of the Church in this novel. Even though it is threatened from all sides (by rationalism, paganism, aestheticism, and Roman Catholicism), it has a calm and pervasive presence. English literature provides a counterpoint to belief. In Chapter 6, Rossen analyzes Wilmet's change. Like Jane Austen's Emma, Wilmet is mistaken about everyone else's motives. She must learn, among other things, that Piers does not love her. Rossen dislikes the way Pym makes Wilmet end up an apparent winner. Wilmet does not deserve victory, for she is unfeeling, cold, selfish, obtuse, and basically unsympathetic.

Rubenstein, Jill. "Comedy and Consolation in the Novels of Barbara Pym." *Renascence* 42 (Spring, 1990): 173-183.

The Church is a source of comedy for Pym, but a few characters do get something from religion. Wilmet does not know she craves spiritual help until Piers upbraids her for her snobbery. Her religious feelings then deepen.

Weld, Annette. *Barbara Pym and the Novel of Manners*. New York: St. Martin's Press, 1992.

In Chapter 4, Weld shows that Pym and her heroine Wilmet are discerning in matters of food, dress, and houses. Although the ironic narrative voice in this novel is one appropriate to the novel of manners, it is less satiric than usual here. Some things are not mocked; some people are genuinely devout and forgiving.

Wyatt-Brown, Anne M. *Barbara Pym: A Critical Biography*. Columbia: University of Missouri Press, 1992.
In Chapter 4, Wyatt-Brown explains that this novel has many sources in Pym's personal experience. Like Pym, Wilmet finds she must give over her romantic fantasies. Piers, Keith, and others are based on Pym's compulsive spying into other people's lives. Pym's inspiration was flagging; the theme of the novel is failure.

No Fond Return of Love, 1961.

Ackley, Katherine Anne. *The Novels of Barbara Pym*. New York: Garland, 1989.
Discussions of this novel's themes are scattered throughout this book. No index.

Allen, Orphia Jane. *Barbara Pym: Writing a Life*. Metuchen, N.J.: Scarecrow Press, 1994.
In Part 1, Allen points out that Dulcie's detective work is based on Pym's own. In Part 2, Allen notes parallels with novels by Jane Austen and Henry James and Pym's greater-than-usual self-consciousness about the role of the novelist. The love theme is more darkly rendered in this novel. Marriage is not desirable. At the end, Dulcie can have a relationship with either of the Forbes brothers, but turns them down. Allen does not think she will fall for Aylwin's invitation at the end.

Benet, Diana. *Something to Love: Barbara Pym's Novels*. Columbia: University of Missouri Press, 1986.
In Chapter 3, Benet treats this novel along with others in which men are treated sympathetically and in which many people find fulfillment. This novel shows how people create self-images, either positive ones, like the vain Aylwin Forbes, or negative ones,

like Dulcie Mainwaring. It also shows how people create false images of others, and Benet explores these confusions in detail. For example, other characters see Dulcie in various ways, but the reader knows more about her: her ironic humor, her compulsive prying into the lives of other people, her wild imaginings. Benet ties Dulcie to the author herself, and suggests that Pym went out of her way to give her female characters romantic fulfillments.

Burkhart, Charles. *The Pleasure of Miss Pym*. Austin: University of Texas Press, 1987.
In Chapter 2, Burkhart finds this novel unsatisfactory, mainly because Dulcie is too prying and sentimental and because Aylwin is not convincing.

Cooley, Mason. *The Comic Art of Barbara Pym*. New York: AMS Press, 1990.
Although on the surface suburban London life is ordinary, underneath there are peculiarities that verge on madness. Characters here come closer to caricatures than in most other Pym novels. Dulcie, this novel's spinster heroine, has a curiosity that becomes almost a mania. Her zest for detective work implies that her curious mind is more important than her wounded heart. Alwyn is handsome and attractive enough to be a romantic hero, but he has unheroic sides. Unlike situations in romantic fiction, it is he who faints and Dulcie who revives him.

Cotsell, Michael. *Barbara Pym*. New York: St. Martin's Press, 1989.
In Chapter 4, Cotsell groups this novel with *An Unsuitable Attachment*, *The Sweet Dove Died*, and the posthumous *An Academic Question* as representing a falling off of Pym's artistry and then the beginning of new achievement. Like many other critics, Cotsell finds *No Fond Return of Love* to be flawed. Aylwin's has little charm; the women display no real friendship; most characters and situations are not well-developed. The novel lacks Pym's usual texture of descriptions and allusions. Dulcie is probably too much like Pym herself; the novel becomes a working out of her fantasies. Cotsell is particularly critical of Pym's attempts to be fashionably self-reflexive about fictionality. Cotsell forces this novel into his pattern.

Liddell, Robert. *A Mind at Ease: Barbara Pym and Her Novels.* London: Peter Owen, 1989.

In Chapter 8, Liddell notes that Dulcie the investigator resembles Pym herself. The novel is inferior, in part because readers cannot take Dulcie seriously as a moral agent.

Long, Robert Emmet. *Barbara Pym.* New York: Frederick Ungar, 1986.

In Chapter 5, Long shows how this novel covers much of Pym's usual ground: spinsters serving weak men. There are many parallel characters. But if Dulcie, like other heroines, is an observer of life, she is Pym's most energetic detective. The novel also has more than its share of eccentric families and places to live: Mrs. Beltane's establishment, Mrs. Williton's home, The Eagle House Private Hotel. Long points out that the scenes at Eagle House and the nearby Castle are an odd mixture of social comedy and Victorian gothic romance. At the end, Dulcie resembles Cinderella, but as usual the happy ending is ironic. There is little promise of real fulfillment for any of the characters.

Rossen, Janice. "Love in the Great Libraries: Oxford in the Work of Barbara Pym." *Journal of Modern Literature* 12 (July, 1985): 277-296.

Dulcie's cleaning woman questions the value of a literary education. Devotion to a literary employer can affect some women.

_____. *The World of Barbara Pym.* New York: St. Martin's Press, 1987.

References to this novel occur throughout this study. In Chapter 1, Rossen thinks Dulcie's literary allusions are often lost on her audience; her speeches thus resemble soliloquies. Chapter 2 reprints Rossen's article "Love in the Great Libraries." In Chapter 3, Dulcie is a typical Pym spinster when she works alone in her kitchen trying not to think of Aylwin and later when she knows her academic skills will attract him. Dulcie is the most energetic example of how Pym women play detective to discover what a man they desire is like. In Chapter 5, Rossen notes two occasions when servants violate the rituals of class distinctions. In Chapter 6, Rossen says that Pym creates Dulcie as another artist/observer and emphasizes the importance of this figure by appearing herself, thinly disguised.

Schofield, Mary Anne.   "Well-Fed or Well-Loved? Patterns of Cooking and Eating in the Novels of Barbara Pym." *University of Windsor Review* 18 (Spring-Summer, 1985): 1-8.

Women cooking for men can be a symbol of a civilizing power, usually a woman's. When Dulcie eats alone or when Viola hosts Dulcie, the meal is uncooked. Sedge, a male, cooks for Viola and civilizes her. When Dulcie does cook food for a man, she denigrates her abilities. Perhaps because it fits her thesis, Schofield thinks that Dulcie will not marry Aylwin.

Schultz, Muriel. "The Novelist as Anthropologist." In *The Life and Work of Barbara Pym*, edited by Dale Salwak.   Iowa City: University of Iowa Press, 1987.

In her survey of Pym's anthropologists, Schulz cites Señor MacBride-Pereira as a comic example of a foreign observer confused by what he sees.

Weld, Annette. *Barbara Pym and the Novel of Manners*. New York: St. Martin's Press, 1992.

In Chapter 4, Weld shows that this comic novel of manners has inclinations toward farce. It is full of characters and full of action, intrigue, whispering, eavesdropping. At the same time, characters worry about the usual questions of dress, food, and cosmetics. Pym provides everything in triplicate—three settings, three families, three main characters. It is appropriately an especially self-conscious novel (people often compare themselves and others to fictional characters) and a self-referential one (Pym herself appears briefly). Even so, Dulcie sometimes touches a note of more serious feeling.

Whitney, Carol Wilkinson. "'Women Are So Terrifying These Days': Fear Between the Sexes in the World of Barbara Pym." *Essays in Literature* 16 (Spring, 1989): 71-84.

Whitney divides Pym's women into two categories besides the familiar one of "excellent women." A "formidable woman" is not looking for a man; she adopts masculine characteristics and interests. The "terrifying woman" terrifies men because she acts forcefully to get a husband. This terror forms the basis for the fear between the sexes that is a constant in Pym's novels and is especially important in this one. The Forbes brothers are both terrified. Neville flees to his mother when pursued. Because Aylwin fears both formidable women and terrifying women, he marries the girlish Marjorie and is infatuated with an actual girl, Laurel. Dulcie is fearful as well. In her pain after Maurice broke their engagement, she begins to transform herself into the familiar Pym figure of an excellent woman. She is generous; she is an observer; she carries out her detective work. But her affection for Aylwin enables her to assume the formidable woman role and tell him he should marry an older woman like herself.

Wyatt-Brown, Anne M. *Barbara Pym: A Critical Biography.* Columbia: University of Missouri Press, 1992.
In Chapter 4, Wyatt-Brown says this novel reflects Pym's unhappy life. The female characters' problems are Pym's own, even though Pym may not have been completely aware of them. Later chapters are based on Pym's personal fantasy. Dulcie's detective work and her trip to the Eagle Hotel are based on Pym's actual trip to a seaside hotel to spy on two neighbors. Wyatt-Brown finds the ending unconvincing.

Quartet in Autumn, 1977.

Ackley, Katherine Anne. *The Novels of Barbara Pym.* New York: Garland, 1989.
Useful discussions of this novel's themes are scattered throughout. Ackley thinks this novel is Pym's masterpiece. No index.

Allen, Orphia Jane. *Barbara Pym: Writing a Life.* Metuchen, N.J.: Scarecrow Press, 1994.
In Part 1, Allen connects Pym's advancing age and her health problems to this novel's refrains of aging and death. The novel also shows Pym's knowledge of how offices work. In Part 2, Allen shows how Pym bends her usual love theme: this novel shows a succession of failures to make any kind of connection. The Church is no longer responsible for the characters' loneliness, and

the welfare state cannot help either. Letty is the only reader among the four.

Benet, Diana. *Something to Love: Barbara Pym's Novels.* Columbia: University of Missouri Press, 1986.
In her last chapter, Benet discusses Pym's last novels and finds their central characters not only are loveless, but also do not recognize that they need love. This novel is a particularly bleak story about four very lonely people. The figure of the Good Samaritan is embodied in representatives of the welfare state and in individuals who are prompted to become Samaritans themselves, or dissuaded from becoming one. Two of the novel's central figures (Letty and Edwin) have ways of dealing with their loneliness, and after Marcia's death the remaining three seem stirred into some kind of new life.

Burkhart, Charles. *The Pleasure of Miss Pym.* Austin: University of Texas Press, 1987.
In Chapter 2, Burkhart wonders how one author could write two novels so different as *Some Tame Gazelle* and this one. *Quartet in Autumn*'s bleak setting, its suffocating routine, and its characters' approach to death are the opposite of the earlier novel's ingredients. If the Archdeacon is Pym's greatest comic creation, Marcia is her most tragic. The novel (as Pym said) has its comic touches and can be called a comedy. Yet Burkhart thinks it finally becomes something more than comedy.

Cooley, Mason. *The Comic Art of Barbara Pym.* New York: AMS Press, 1990.
Cooley sets this novel against the unsettling events of Pym's later life. In it, Pym takes earlier themes to extremes. Its four main characters are old, insignificant, and lonely; their work is dull and useless. Only Letty, this novel's excellent woman, has sufficient self-consciousness to feel lonely. Except subconsciously, they do not yearn to make contact with others. In fact, they arrange their lives to avoid contact. Marcia takes refusal the farthest and starves herself. Only at the end do the three survivors seem to establish some connection. Cooley emphasizes the importance of recurring images in conveying Pym's meanings, especially various references to human hair. *Quartet in Autumn* may be the most

grimy and dark of Pym's novels, but, citing a remark by Pym herself in support, Cooley stresses that the novel's tone is essentially comic.

Cotsell, Michael. *Barbara Pym*. New York: St. Martin's Press, 1989.
In Chapter 5, Cotsell cites manuscript evidence in establishing that this novel is a product of Pym's own hospital experience. The world of the novel is contemporary England. The days of empire are past; the well-meaning but impersonal welfare state is here. The novel is also about the old age of its central characters, four people who do not make human contact and who do not seem to have the energy to do so. The death of Marcia, whose hospital experiences resemble Pym's, is the novel's central event. Somehow it manages to bring the others closer together and to give them glimmers of hope.

Doan, Laura L. "Text and the Single Man: The Bachelor in Pym's Dual-Voiced Narrative." In *Independent Women: The Function of Gender in the Novels of Barbara Pym*, edited by Janice Rossen. New York: St. Martin's Press, 1988.
Norman is a typical Pym bachelor, for he is spinsterish in his habits and selfish. Edwin, a widower, is not nearly so insensitive. The Reverend David Lydell is an example of a selfish clergyman/bachelor.

Gordon, Joan. "Cozy Heroines: Quotidian Bravery in Barbara Pym's Novels." *Essays in Literature* 16 (Fall, 1989): 224-233.
Pym values humility, community, and even a kind of modest miracle. In this novel, Letty shows humility and even charity. Pym's style suits her subject.

Kennard, Jean E. "Barbara Pym and Romantic Love." *Contemporary Literature* 34 (Spring, 1993): 44-60.
The best consolation Pym offers is a sense of Christian community, implied here by the way three survivors draw closer after Marcia's death. Letty invites the two men for a day in the country.

Larson, Edith S. "The Celebration of the Ordinary in Barbara Pym's Novels." *San Jose Studies* 9 (Spring, 1983): 17-22.

Pym usually celebrates ordinary experiences for offering support in a sad world. Except for Letty, characters find less support in this novel than in others.

Liddell, Robert. *A Mind at Ease: Barbara Pym and Her Novels.* London: Peter Owen, 1989.
In Chapter 12, Liddell judges this to be Pym's finest novel. It is also the saddest, lacking almost all coziness. It is unique in that it is about, not the old, but people who are aging, people on both sides of retirement. Pym draws a world much different from that in her early novels. Marcia is Pym's only true tragic heroine, but all four central characters have the virtues of independence. No matter how bad things are, they do not whine about injustice and do not lean on social workers.

Long, Robert Emmet. *Barbara Pym.* New York: Frederick Ungar, 1986.
In Chapter 6, Long praises Pym's blend of sympathy and detachment in her treatment of the four major characters of this atypical novel. Unlike Pym's earlier characters, they are old and eccentric. They have little to show for their lives, and, though some are capable of yearning, they are solitary. New too is the background against which these lives are now lived: the welfare state, new generations, social change. Long thinks the reunion lunch is a failure, but after Marcia's death there are rays of hope.

Maitre, Doreen. *Literature and Possible Worlds.* London: Pembridge Press for Middlesex Polytechnic Press, 1983.
In Chapter 4, Maitre uses this novel as an example of a realistic novel which forces its readers to contemplate aspects of the real world of which they may not have been aware.

Nardin, Jane. *Barbara Pym.* Boston: Twayne, 1985.
In Chapter 5, Nardin describes London as a place in which the characters lack personal relations; they never eat together. The novel shows them making some progress. The four have lunch; Edwin helps Letty get a room; Letty gains some confidence and hope. Most symbolically, the death of Marcia moves the three remaining characters to have lunch together.

Pym, Barbara. "Finding a Voice: a Radio Talk." In *Civil to Strangers and Other Writings*, edited by Hazel Holt. New York: E. P. Dutton, 1988.

Although this novel is about the problems of aging, Pym says that when she wrote it she was most concerned with the comic and ironic voice with which she told the story.

Radner, Sanford. "Barbara Pym's People." *Western Humanities Review* 39 (Summer, 1985): 172-177.

Beneath the surface of Pym's work Radner senses one story: "a self-denying mother feeds her ungrateful baby son." Pym's men are unvaryingly childish and demanding. Pym's "excellent women" give selfless service to these men. Edwin's wife is a perfect example, for she died putting a shepherd's pie into the oven.

Rossen, Janice. *The World of Barbara Pym*. New York: St. Martin's Press, 1987.

A few references are scattered throughout this study. In Chapter 3, both Letty and Marcia resemble other Pym spinsters when they prepare solitary meals. Marcia is different in that she ultimately does not prepare such meals and starves. Letty, the surviving spinster, asks the question implicit in Pym's novels: can deprivation be a positive state? Chapter 4 explains how in this novel, even though one character enjoys its festivals, the Church is in decline. Letty is embarrassed by the flamboyant, un-Anglican Christianity of her Nigerian neighbors. In Chapter 7, Rossen groups this work with other late novels and finds that they are darker in tone, that they focus and aging and death, and that they show lives that have not realized their potential.

Snow, Lotus. "Literary Allusions in the Novels." In *The Life and Work of Barbara Pym*, edited by Dale Salwak. Iowa City: University of Iowa Press, 1987.

This novel is unique among Pym's works in that it has few literary allusions. Perhaps because the characters here are not well-educated, none of them derive any consolation from poetry.

Stetz, Margaret Diane. "*Quartet in Autumn*: New Light on Barbara Pym as a Modernist." *Arizona Quarterly: A Journal of American Literature, Culture, and Theory* 41 (Spring, 1985): 24-37.

An excellent article in which Stetz demonstrates that in this novel Pym's intentions and her techniques are more modernist than is usually recognized. That is, they are much like those of Virgina Woolf in *Mrs. Dalloway*. Like Woolf, Pym is interested not in events but in consciousness. Like Woolf, she emphasizes this interest by showing many events not as consecutive, but as simultaneous; they are linked by associations, repetitions, and motifs. Pym's patterns of images, like those of death and falling, work upon the reader's subconscious. The characters themselves are revealed, not just by their actions, but by our sense of their inner life of memory and fantasy. Both novels end with a sense that the world is in flux.

Weld, Annette. *Barbara Pym and the Novel of Manners*. New York: St. Martin's Press, 1992.
In Chapter 5, Weld calls this a novel of manners: its characters are defined, perhaps more realistically than in Pym's other novels, by their clothes, their food, their income, and where they live. In another sense, manners are seen to be deteriorating. Characters make few connections and have few communal meals. Those who remain establish a kind of community in a meal at the end of the novel.

Wyatt-Brown, Anne M. *Barbara Pym: A Critical Biography*. Columbia: University of Missouri Press, 1992.
In Chapter 6, Wyatt-Brown explains that Pym wrote and revised this novel as she was experiencing great changes in her life: she had a mastectomy and then a stroke. She retired and moved to the country. London was changing; friends were dying. Pym as usual avoided introspection. In this novel, Pym wrote of her own problems, especially her experiences of retirement, in Letty; she specifically projected her fear of aging on Marcia; references to death are everywhere. Yet her own retirement was pleasant, and in the novel's final version she hit a more positive tone.

_____. "From Fantasy to Pathology: Images of Aging in the Novels of Barbara Pym." *Human Values and Aging Newsletter* 6 (January-February, 1985): 5-7.
From the beginning, Pym wrote as an outsider, and many of her heroines were not young. As Pym herself aged, she became more

pessimistic about the fate of older people, especially older women. By the time of *Quartet in Autumn*, Pym could face the fears of aging and could note its compensations. Letty finds that she has power to decide about her future. Pym shows that old people have the capacity to change.

_____. "Late Style in the Novels of Barbara Pym and Penelope Mortimer." *Gerontologist* 28 (December, 1988): 835-839.
In her childhood Pym learned to try to rise about feelings of disappointment. In her early novels, she converted unpleasantness into fiction. Only after a series of personal shocks was she able to write an novel—*Quartet in Autumn*—that expressed her real pain. She now saw old age as a time of deprivation and valued old people's courage and independence.

The Sweet Dove Died, 1978. [1963-1969]

Ackley, Katherine Anne. *The Novels of Barbara Pym*. New York: Garland, 1989.
Useful discussions of this novel's themes throughout this book. No index.

Allen, Orphia Jane. *Barbara Pym: Writing a Life*. Metuchen, N.J.: Scarecrow Press, 1994.
In Part 1, Allen sees Pym's own experiences with a younger man behind this novel. In Part 2, she elaborates: cats, caged or otherwise, are symbols for male homosexuals like James. Leonora clearly reflects Pym's concern for older women like herself. Phoebe, whose untidiness suggests sexual love, sees James clearly as a man looking for a mother in Leonora.

Benet, Diana. *Something to Love: Barbara Pym's Novels*. Columbia: University of Missouri Press, 1986.
In her last chapter, Benet finds the central characters of Pym's last novels are not only loveless and lonely, but do not fully recognize that they need love. The frigid Leonora, for example, is moved by the bisexual James to the beginnings of real passion. But when he leaves her for Ned, she is able to control her suffering. When he asks to be taken back into a real but imperfect relationship, she

rejects him and finds satisfaction only in the perfection of flowers
or objects of art. Benet comments perceptively on the significance
of Leonora's fruitwood mirror and on revealing parallels with
other characters.

Burkhart, Charles. *The Pleasure of Miss Pym*. Austin: University of
Texas Press, 1987.
In Chapter 2, Burkhart praises Pym for creating a heroine we do
not like but come to pity. Leonora may be cold cruel and humorless, but she has courage to go on living.

Cooley, Mason. *The Comic Art of Barbara Pym*. New York: AMS
Press, 1990.
Although this is Pym's least lovable novel, Cooley thinks it may
be her best. What it lacks in geniality, it gains in compression
and force. Its central characters are studies in narcissism, the
passive James, the cold and power-hungry Ned, but most of all
Leonora. Like other Pym heroines, she is intelligent and lonely,
but she is also cold, self-centered, and ruthless. She is almost
without passion. Many minor characters provide a contrast to her
because they are capable of some sort of love. The intrigues of the
novel remind Cooley of Restoration comedy at its most bitter.
Although the intrigues are brutal and immoral, they are also
amusing and even provoke sympathy. Leonora ends the novel
lonely and miserable, but her heart can be broken.

_____. "*The Sweet Dove Died*: The Sexual Politics of Narcis-
sism." *Twentieth Century Literature: A Scholarly and Critical
Journal* 32 (Spring, 1986): 40-49.
An early version of Chapter 10 of the author's *The Comic Art of
Barbara Pym*.

Cotsell, Michael. *Barbara Pym*. New York: St. Martin's Press, 1989.
In Chapter 4, Cotsell groups this novel with *No Fond Return of
Love, An Unsuitable Attachment*, and the posthumous *An
Academic Question* as works showing a falling off of Pym's
artistry and also, in this case, a kind of achievement. At Philip
Larkin's suggestion, she revised her first draft to concentrate on
Leonora. The result is a bleak work of great compression. The
mood of the novel is set by Pym's including blatant and even nasty

homosexuals and by excluding her usual rich allusiveness and references to the Church. The mood is appropriate to the self-centered and loveless Leonora. She is a woman who likes her own elegant image and equally elegant objects of art; she tries to avoid friendship, love, and sex in any form. When she is defeated in her one passion, she at least can triumph by not taking him back. But her victory is hollow, and she must look forward to an lonely old age. Cotsell thinks the novel is marred by its coldness; the characters are not vivid enough for us to care for.

Gordon, Joan. "Cozy Heroines: Quotidian Bravery in Barbara Pym's Novels." *Essays in Literature* 16 (Fall, 1989): 224-233.
Gordon finds value in Pym's world, its daily activities, its cozy heroines, and their values of humility and community. In this novel, on the other hand, Leonora has no humility. She is so egocentric she can form no community with anyone else. She leads a lonely and empty life. Gordon points out how Leonora's way of talking about herself as "one" is a sign of her selfishness.

Graham, Robert J. "Cumbered With Much Serving: Barbara Pym's *Excellent Women*." *Mosaic: A Journal for the Interdisciplinary Study of Literature* 17 (Spring, 1984): 141-160. Reprinted in *"For Better or Worse": Attitudes Toward Marriage in Literature*, edited by Evelyn J. Hinz. 2d ed. Winnipeg: University of Manitoba Press, 1985.
Graham thinks that when Leonora rejects James, she returns to the self-sufficient life she had led before she met him.

Halperin, John. "Barbara Pym and the War of the Sexes." In *The Life and Work of Barbara Pym*, edited by Dale Salwak. Iowa City: University of Iowa Press, 1987.
This novel shows sexual warfare at its most complex and most ferocious. Men, as usual, are selfish; here they are also brutal. Women try to entrap men and treat other women badly.

Liddell, Robert. *A Mind at Ease: Barbara Pym and Her Novels*. London: Peter Owen, 1989.
In Chapter 11, Liddell says that Pym made this darker than her earlier novels because she wanted to write something that was not

"cozy." This novel is better than its predecessors, but suffers because it shows no kind of life that a reader could desire.

Long, Robert Emmet. *Barbara Pym*. New York: Frederick Ungar, 1986.
In Chapter 5, Long provides much valuable biographical background material. He finds *The Sweet Dove Died* unique among Pym's novels. It is neither cozy or comic; it has only four main characters; none are likable, including the manipulative and sexless Leonora. It has an unusual texture of symbolic images and allusions, particularly to Henry James. Most important, it is disagreeable: Ned is Pym's nastiest character, and Leonora her most hollow. Long sees a climax of the novel in the Keats House scene, where Leonora momentarily seems to sympathize with another human being. Finally, he thinks that for many reasons the novel is not successful. Long is discerning in his treatment of complex material.

Nardin, Jane. *Barbara Pym*. Boston: Twayne, 1985.
In Chapter 5, Nardin places Leonora in the tradition of Prudence from *Jane and Prudence* and Wilmet from *A Glass of Blessings*: they are all women whose beauty is a barrier to their being able to love. Not only is Leonora's narcissism self-destructive, she is a perfectionist in other matters. As such, she fears aging and death, loves beautiful objects, and is fascinated by a beautiful youth, James. Leonora is ruthless and frigid. The nasty Ned, who steals James's affections, is Leonora's male counterpart in all but sexuality. Other female characters (Meg and Liz) do have emotions and thus provide a contrast to Leonora. Nardin is perceptive when she analyzes why Leonora rejects James in the end. Leonora refuses the pain and indignity of love; besides, after being rejected by Ned, James is damaged goods. Leonora ends this grim novel with little self-knowledge.

Rossen, Janice. *The World of Barbara Pym*. New York: St. Martin's Press, 1987.
References to this novel are scattered throughout this study. In Chapter 3, Rossen points out that Leonora is like other Pym spinsters in several ways: although she protects her own solitude, she has admirers. When she is attracted to a man, she gives him gifts,

in this case a place to live. The object of Leonora's love, too, is unattainable: James is both gay and very young. This novel's particular emphasis is that Leonora lost her love because she tried to possess him. In Chapter 7, Rossen groups this work with *Quartet in Autumn* and finds they are darker, urban novels, in which England is seen to be changing. Both focus on the approach of death; Leonora is particularly sensitive to aging. They both show lives that do not realize their potential.

_____. "On Not Being Jane Eyre: The Romantic Heroine in Barbara Pym's Novels." In *Independent Women: The Function of Gender in the Novels of Barbara Pym*. New York: St. Martin's Press, 1988.
Charlotte Brontë's novel lies behind much of Pym's work. Although Leonora Eyre's name may reflect both Brontë's and Beethoven's brave heroines, she is much different. Pym's plot reverses, and even parodies, the earlier plots at many points.

Schofield, Mary Anne. "Well-Fed or Well-Loved? Patterns of Cooking and Eating in the Novels of Barbara Pym." *University of Windsor Review* 18 (Spring-Summer, 1985): 1-8.
Women cooking for men can be a symbol of the female's civilizing power. Leonora's tins of lobster and her exotic meals do not nourish any man.

Watson, Daphne. *Their Own Worst Enemies: Women Writers of Women's Fictions*. London: Pluto Press, 1995.
In Chapter 2, Watson argues that this novel is Pym's best. In other novels, the judgments made by Pym's wit are marred by hopeful notes. Here the shallow and nasty Leonora is given no sympathy. The novel's vision is bleak, never pathetic.

Weld, Annette. *Barbara Pym and the Novel of Manners*. New York: St. Martin's Press, 1992.
In Chapter 5, Weld treats this novel briefly. Characters are defined by their manners. Phoebe is hopelessly middle class. Leonora is higher on the social scale and defined by the objects she possesses. Pym tried here to produce a different sort of novel—bleaker, more probing in its pyschology—from the one

that had been rejected in 1963. Weld provides many details of its
extensive autobiographical sources.

Wyatt-Brown, Anne M. *Barbara Pym: A Critical Biography*.
    Columbia: University of Missouri Press, 1992.
    In Chapter 5, Wyatt-Brown sees this novel as a symptom of Pym's
    continuing depression and a product of her relationship with a
    young antique dealer. Leonora is a complex character, but Pym's
    own fear of introspection makes it impossible for her to probe her
    character's psyche deeply enough.

A Few Green Leaves, 1980.

Ackley, Katherine Anne. *The Novels of Barbara Pym*. New York:
    Garland, 1989.
    Useful discussions of this novel's themes are scattered throughout
    this book. The end of Chapter 6 deals with the role of the past.
    No index.

Allen, Orphia Jane. *Barbara Pym: Writing a Life*. Metuchen, N.J.:
    Scarecrow Press, 1994.
    In Part 1, Allen speculates that Pym's terminal cancer caused her
    to reflect on death in this novel and to summon up motifs from
    her earlier novels. In Part 2, Allen plays down the importance of
    romantic love in the novel but emphasizes the contrast between
    the consolations of physician/scientists and the Anglican Church.
    The literary theme echoes that of *Less Than Angels*: Emma moves
    away from anthropology to consider becoming (like Catherine
    Oliphant) a novelist like Pym herself, one who combines the
    magic of art with realistic autobiographical details.

Benet, Diana. *Something to Love: Barbara Pym's Novels*. Columbia:
    University of Missouri Press, 1986.
    In her last chapter, Benet discusses Pym's last three novels. The
    central characters of this novel are lonely but do not recognize
    that they need to love. Tom and Emma are both detached from
    the present, he as a clergyman obsessed by the past, she as a
    modern woman, an anthropologist observing the village. But
    unlike the other two late novels, this one is cheerful and comic.

From the first, Emma in particular desires to be involved with the community and wants to love. Although her brief affair with Graham Pettifer is unsatisfactory, it reawakens her. Tom is liberated by his sister's departure and by discovering the medieval ruins he had fantasized about. They can look to the future with some hope of fulfillment. Benet touches upon the parallels and contrasts provided by minor characters, especially the trendy Dr. Martin Shrubsole and his manipulative wife Avice.

Burkhart, Charles. *The Pleasure of Miss Pym*. Austin: University of Texas Press, 1987.
In Chapter 2, Burkhart sees in this novel a partial return to the Pym of old. Even so, the village reminds us that most of the old ways have passed.

Cooley, Mason. *The Comic Art of Barbara Pym*. New York: AMS Press, 1990.
Pym's last novel is not dark or bitter like *The Sweet Dove Died* or *Quartet in Autumn*, but serene and comic. Its setting is not the pastoral and timeless village of *Some Tame Gazelle* but a real English village of the 1970's. Each of the characters evokes some side of village life, which is a mixture of the old (most valued by middle-class newcomers) and the new: the welfare state, television aerials, junk. Doctors have replaced clergymen as the village's most important persons. The passing of the old is reflected by the presence of death throughout the book; only one character dies, but Tom the clergyman meditates on shrouds and often walks in the cemetery. The central character is Emma, a modern woman. She is an anthropologist; her new affair with an old lover is almost without passion; she is unsentimental and un-literary. But a symbolic few green leaves still bloom in this gray world. An old governess returns; a pious village woman polishes the church's lectern; Emma feels some real affection for Tom. The old order may be passing in many ways, but Pym's mood is not bitter.

Cotsell, Michael. *Barbara Pym*. New York: St. Martin's Press, 1989.
Cotsell sets this novel in the context of earlier ones. Like *Quartet in Autumn*, it evokes contemporary England in convincing detail. Like many others, it is set in an English village. But the old village ways are no more; their remnants are of interest only to

antiquarians. Cotsell thinks Pym's narration is an attempt to do something new. This novel's story line is not forceful; the events of the village seem simply to happen. Some events, like Miss Lickerish's death, point to deeper concerns, but nothing ever really comes of them. People like Daphne have yearnings, but they are not fulfilled. Emma, an anthropologist who wants only to observe the village, is at first indifferent to literature. The main action of the novel is her growing desire to become involved in village life and even to write a novel.

Doan, Laura L. "Text and the Single Man: The Bachelor in Pym's Dual-Voiced Narrative." In *Independent Women: The Function of Gender in the Novels of Barbara Pym*, edited by Janice Rossen. New York: St. Martin's Press, 1988.
Adam Prince is a typical Pym bachelor; he is spinsterish in manners and selfish. He has given up worship of God for worship of food.

Gordon, Joan. "Cozy Heroines: Quotidian Bravery in Barbara Pym's Novels." *Essays in Literature* 16 (Fall, 1989): 224-233.
Gordon approves of Emma's discovery of Pym's values of humility and community. Gordon also thinks this novel shows a kind of miracle, not a sensational one or one connected to any sort of metaphysics, but one that shows itself in daily life.

Liddell, Robert. *A Mind at Ease: Barbara Pym and Her Novels.* London: Peter Owen, 1989.
In Chapter 13, Liddell sees in the gentleness and cheerfulness of this novel the happiness Pym found during her last years in a West Oxfordshire village. It serves as an epilogue to her work.

Long, Robert Emmet. *Barbara Pym.* New York: Frederick Ungar, 1986.
In Chapter 6, Long defines the tone of Pym's last novel as composed and low-keyed. The novel shows the web of relations in village life set against the progression of the seasons and the background of its past. An awareness of death is always present. The social changes of modern England are in the background as well. Old rituals fade; automobile junkyards spring up. The major characters are isolated and repressed. Still, there are some

positive notes at the end. Miss Vereker returns and miraculously finds a medieval village. Emma sees hope in her life.

McGuirk, Carol. "Drabble to Carter: Fiction by Women, 1962-1992." In *The Columbia History of the British Novel*, edited by John Richetti. New York: Columbia University Press, 1994.
Pym echoes Jane Austen to make satiric points. Tom may correspond to Mr. Knightly in this Emma's story, but he has none of the authority of the Austen hero. Although the past may be wonderful, it is inert.

Nardin, Jane. *Barbara Pym*. Boston: Twayne, 1985.
In Chapter 5, Nardin observes that village life now is much different from that described in Pym's early novels. She divides the story's characters into two groups. Most ordinary people and scientists are satisfied with the way things are. Others like Tom, the clergyman, and the older gentry flee the present and become preoccupied with the past. (Daphne flees not in time but in space, first to Greece and then to Birmingham.) The center of the novel is Emma's journey from being part of the first group (she is an anthropologist and has an affair with another anthropologist) to joining the second. Nardin analyzes parallels with Jane Austen's novels, particularly *Emma* and *Mansfield Park*. The novel ends happily with Emma and Tom together, with the triumph of literature and religion. Nevertheless, Nardin thinks that any triumph that rejects the modern would does not ring completely true.

Rossen, Janice. *The World of Barbara Pym*. New York: St. Martin's Press, 1987.
References to this novel are scattered throughout. In Chapter 3, Rossen sees the governess Miss Vereker as a representative spinster of an earlier era. The Misses Lee and Grundy show how even ill-tempered spinsters can live together. Emma is the central spinster. She is independent and has an affair with an unattractive man; everybody expects her to marry someone. Chapter 4 focuses on Tom and his church. Tom himself is in the tradition of the scholar/priest. Even though attendance is down, church services have a role at important events like death. And church festivals and the building itself (including its furnishings) have a positive role in some people's lives.

Chapter 7 treats *A Few Green Leaves* as Pym's summing up and justification for a large audience. Although Pym's earlier village setting has been somewhat modernized here, this novel's themes are Pym's usual ones. Yet the tone is different. It is not so bleak as *The Sweet Dove Died* or *Quartet in Autumn*, and its comedy seems warmer than that of her early novels. Even so, Rossen detects a note of melancholy behind the action. Emma is only one of this novel's spinsters, and the prospect of aging is more important than in the earlier works. Like earlier heroines, Emma changes. She abandons anthropology for literature and will marry Tom, the priest. But both Emma and Tom are so introspective that the reader is not asked to feel the elation usual at the end of a comic novel. Rossen thinks that in this novel Pym is presenting herself both as an author and as a person who has rallied in face of rejection to present a modest and dignified face to the world.

Schultz, Muriel. "The Novelist as Anthropologist." In *The Life and Work of Barbara Pym*, edited by Dale Salwak. Iowa City: University of Iowa Press, 1987.
In her survey of Pym's treatment of anthropology, Schulz sees this novel as Pym's summation. Emma does observe interesting things in the village, especially how the influence of the gentry and the Church have almost disappeared. Emma also realizes that though novelists resemble anthropologists in that they are curious and observant, they are superior in that they do not dehumanize. She may change careers.

Weld, Annette. *Barbara Pym and the Novel of Manners*. New York: St. Martin's Press, 1992.
In Chapter 5, Weld comments briefly. Pym adds contemporary variations to her usual novel of village manners.

Wilson, A. N. *Penfriend from Porlock*. New York: W. W. Norton, 1989.
Wilson praises this novel for combining Pym's early comic with her later tragic modes.

Wyatt-Brown, Anne M. *Barbara Pym: A Critical Biography*. Columbia: University of Missouri Press, 1992.

In Chapter 7, Wyatt-Brown ties the warmer tone of this novel both to Pym's success as a writer and her knowledge of her impending death. Pym takes up many of her earlier themes and creates new versions of old types of characters. Emma is in a sense Pym's heir; her rescue by her mother enacts one of Pym's fantasies. Pym views the action with a detached sympathy, a sign that Pym had accepted the natural cycle of birth and death. Wyatt-Brown points out that Pym gives two specific examples of old people. Miss Lickerish dies a calm death; her funeral becomes a satisfying village ritual. Miss Vereker's return to the village is heroic and ultimately rescues Tom from his obsession.

_____. "Creativity: Defense Against Death." In *Proceedings of the Ninth International Conference on Literature and Psychology*, edited by Federico Pereira. Lisbon: Inst[itute] Superior de Psicologia Aplicada, 1993.
Even though Pym knew she was dying as she wrote this book, its emphasis is not on death. Village life is vigorous, and the main characters are not old. Miss Vereker is an "elderly sleeping beauty" who releases Tom from his bondage to the past. The calm and philosophical tone of *A Few Green Leaves* shows that Pym has used her sense of creative accomplishment to achieve a kind of peace before she died.

_____. "Late Style in the Novels of Barbara Pym and Penelope Mortimer." *Gerontologist* 28 (December, 1988): 835-839.
In *Quartet in Autumn*, Pym expressed real pain and showed old age as a time of deprivation. This urgency is missing from *A Few Green Leaves*, which Wyatt-Brown sees as her serene swan song.

An Unsuitable Attachment, 1982. [1960-1965]

Ackley, Katherine Anne. *The Novels of Barbara Pym*. New York: Garland, 1989.
Useful discussions of this novel's themes are scattered throughout this book. No index.

Allen, Orphia Jane. *Barbara Pym: Writing a Life*. Metuchen, N.J.: Scarecrow Press, 1994.

In Part 1, Allen notes that in this novel Pym extends her sympathies to a good male character, Rupert Stonebird. In Part 2, Allen
identifies two strains of imagery in the novel: animals and the
bundle of lemon leaves Sophia finds in Italy. The animals
(mainly cats) stalk each other, but are also very wary of other
animals and humans. Likewise men and women stalk and are
wary; they find communication difficult. Women are wary of
other women; clergymen and anthropologists both find it hard to
communicate. Pym seems to reflect that novelists can do things
better: they can unwrap the bundle of lemon leaves to reveal what
is essential.

Benet, Diana. *Something to Love: Barbara Pym's Novels*. Columbia:
University of Missouri Press, 1986.
In her third chapter, Benet treats this along with the three other
published novels from the middle of Pym's career. Like the
others, this novel treats male characters as seriously as female
ones. Rupert Stonebird may be Pym's most sympathetic man; in
his decency and shyness, he resembles an excellent woman. Benet
analyzes in detail the propensity of characters to use their imaginations to create false and stereotypical pictures of other people,
pictures that are eventually shattered. And, as the title indicates,
the novel rings changes on the theme of unsuitable attachments,
particularly Ianthe's for her lower-class coworker and the vicar's
wife for her cat. But attachments thought to be unsuitable may
prove to be real love.

Burkhart, Charles. *The Pleasure of Miss Pym*. Austin: University of
Texas Press, 1987.
In Chapter 2, Burkhart finds the most obvious unsuitable attachment, that of Ianthe to John, unconvincing. In contrast, Sophia is
fascinating. When she visits her aunt in the south of Italy, an
epiphany occurs. But, Burkhart asks, what does it mean?

Cooley, Mason. *The Comic Art of Barbara Pym*. New York: AMS
Press, 1990.
Cooley treats this novel in its order of composition—after *No
Fond Return of Love*. He concurs with Philip Larkin that the
novel, though enjoyable, is not one of Pym's best: its strands do
not cohere; John is not fully drawn. As usual, Cooley sums up the

novel well. Characters drift against a churchish background; the central women like the novel do not possess Pym's usual exuberance and irony. Cooley analyzes a passage to show how Pym here subordinates comedy to realism. Ianthe, the only Pym heroine to have a wedding, discovers what may be the novel's theme: that Eros cannot be ordered, that love is where one finds it. Cooley admires the episode in which a number of the characters visit Italy. They do not experience the romantic awakenings that usually happen in fiction. In fact, Sophia finds that her aunt's situation with her Italian lover is not attractive at all.

Cotsell, Michael. *Barbara Pym*. New York: St. Martin's Press, 1989.
In Chapter 4, Cotsell groups this novel with *No Fond Return of Love*, *The Sweet Dove Died*, and the posthumous *An Academic Question*. They represent both a falling off of Pym's artistry, perhaps because Pym found she could not write well about adult love, and then the beginning of new achievement. Cotsell finds that the elements of this rather somber novel are disconnected. The evocation of the urban mixture of peoples is interesting, but the Rupert/Penelope romance is not. The symbolism of the Italian lemons (which seems to be where Pym began to imagine the story) may tells us something about Sophia's alienation from her life as a curate's wife, but it does not seem to apply to Ianthe and John's love affair. Cotsell thinks Ianthe is a well-developed character and explains that Pym made her love John to show how her old-fashioned virtues can be opened to modern life. But like other critics, he does not think Pym was able to imagine what the lower-class John was like.

Doan, Laura L. "Text and the Single Man: The Bachelor in Pym's Dual-Voiced Narrative." In *Independent Women: The Function of Gender in the Novels of Barbara Pym*, edited by Janice Rossen. New York: St. Martin's Press, 1988.
Pym's women (like Ianthe) often have a capacity to utter dutiful expressions, yet have subversive thoughts. In contrast, though Pym's bachelors are somewhat spinsterish in their habits, they are (like Mervyn) single-minded in their selfishness. Although Mark is married, he is bachelor-like. Rupert is an odd mixture for Pym. He resembles a confirmed bachelor, yet he takes on the status of an object for several women. He is somewhat spinsterish and he

is somewhat selfish like other bachelors, yet he begins to have feelings for others.

Ezell, Margaret J. M. "'What Shall We Do With Our Old Maids?': Barbara Pym and the Woman Question." *International Journal of Women's Studies* 7 (November/December, 1984): 450-465.
One consequence of the preference society still gives to married women is that there are often tensions between them and single women. One example is the ill-feeling between Ianthe and Sophia.

Kane, Patricia. "A Curious Eye: Barbara Pym's Women." *South Dakota Review* 24 (Summer, 1986): 50-59.
In discussing Pym's manipulative characters, Kane singles out Sophia as the most disagreeable. Sophia tramples on other people, is selfish, and loves only her cat.

Larkin, Philip. "The Rejection of Barbara Pym." In *The Life and Work of Barbara Pym*, edited by Dale Salwak. Iowa City: University of Iowa Press, 1987.
In this introduction to the first publication of *An Unsuitable Attachment* in 1982, Larkin says the novel's major fault is that the attachment between Ianthe and John is not fully enough developed. He thinks Pym is self-indulgent when she includes the reappearances of many characters from her earlier books. He likes much of the novel, particularly Faustina and Sophia's unsuitable attachment to her.

Liddell, Robert. *A Mind at Ease: Barbara Pym and Her Novels.* London: Peter Owen, 1989.
In Chapter 9, Liddell regards this novel as the last of Pym's first phase, "the canon." He finds it flawed, especially in pairing Ianthe off with John. But it has elements that could have been profitably explored, especially The Reverend Mark Ainger and his wife Sophia. In Chapter 10, Liddell wishes Pym had rewritten the novel with Sophia as the heroine.

Long, Robert Emmet. *Barbara Pym.* New York: Frederick Ungar, 1986.

In Chapter 5, Long calls this another courtship novel dominated by the repressive atmosphere of British life. All the central characters are isolated and unhappy. Ianthe tries to break out, but her romance with John seems sexless. Like many other critics, Long thinks the romance is incompletely realized. The only creatures who seem free are Sophia's aunt in Italy and the cat, Faustina.

Rossen, Janice. "On Not Being Jane Eyre: The Romantic Heroine in Barbara Pym's Novels." In *Independent Women: The Function of Gender in the Novels of Barbara Pym.* New York: St. Martin's Press, 1988.

Like Jane Eyre, Pym's heroines are often plain, loving, and unloved, but they usually do not marry the handsome hero. In this novel, Ianthe *does* marry the handsome John, but her love is compared to a kind of sickness.

_____. *The World of Barbara Pym.* New York: St. Martin's Press, 1987.

References to this novel are scattered throughout this study. In Chapter 1, Pym's shows her literary influences when Ianthe thinks of herself as an Elizabeth Bowen heroine, but not good enough to be a Jane Austen one. In Chapter 3, when Ianthe prepares herself a solitary meal, she shows she values herself highly. Rossen treats this novel at length as a study of singleness, for many characters are alone and lonely. Penelope is Pym's angriest unmarried woman. Even Sophia, a married woman, must dote on her cat Faustina. Although Ianthe and John marry, they face much opposition. Chapter 4 treats the Church. The Anglican clergyman worries about the influence of Roman Catholicism when he and his parishioners visit Rome, and one character (Rupert) tells of recovering his childhood faith.

In Chapter 5, Rossen notes that Rupert is the only character who is an anthropologist. He laments how little anthropologists are understood by the general public. Like the professional he is, he has learned how to blend in with his surroundings, the better to make observations. Pym shows her anthropological observation when she comments on the ritual significance of Ianthe's brandy and Penelope's extravagant clothes. In Chapter 7, Rossen discusses the impact the rejection of this novel had on Pym herself.

The melancholy note of Pym's later novels is anticipated by
Sophia.

Rubenstein, Jill. "Comedy and Consolation in the Novels of Barbara
    Pym." *Renascence* 42 (Spring, 1990): 173-183.
    The Church is mainly a source of comedy for Pym, but a few
    characters do get some sort of consolation from religion. Sophia
    is an unsatisfied, scheming clergyman's wife, but learns humility.

Schofield, Mary Anne.   "Well-Fed or Well-Loved? Patterns of
    Cooking and Eating in the Novels of Barbara Pym." *University of
    Windsor Review* 18 (Spring-Summer, 1985): 1-8.
    Women cooking for men can be a symbol of the female's civiliz-
    ing power. Oddly, though Ianthe can cook meat, she allows
    herself to be cooked for.

Weld, Annette. *Barbara Pym and the Novel of Manners*. New York:
    St. Martin's Press, 1992.
    In Chapter 5, Weld discusses how Pym uses foreign locales to
    suggest the erotic. She points out how Pym satirizes the manners
    of the English characters in Italy and how John's manners set him
    apart from Ianthe.

Wilson, A. N. *Penfriend from Porlock*. New York: W. W. Norton,
    1989.
    Wilson has high praise for this novel. He admires the courage of
    its characters and Pym's use of food throughout.

Wyatt-Brown, Anne M.   *Barbara Pym: A Critical Biography*.
    Columbia: University of Missouri Press, 1992.
    In Chapter 5, Wyatt-Brown explains that in middle-age Pym did
    not find new creativity. For the most part, this novel lamely
    follows her earlier practices. One exception is that, probably
    because of her friendships with men, Pym now is able to extend
    her sympathies to them.

Crampton Hodnet, 1985. [1939-1940]

Ackley, Katherine Anne. *The Novels of Barbara Pym*. New York: Garland, 1989.
Useful discussions of this novel's themes are scattered throughout this book. No index.

Allen, Orphia Jane. *Barbara Pym: Writing a Life*. Metuchen, N.J.: Scarecrow Press, 1994.
In Part 1, Allen shows how Pym writes about her own experiences when she describes many of the female characters.

Benet, Diana. *Something to Love: Barbara Pym's Novels*. Columbia: University of Missouri Press, 1986.
In her second chapter, Benet treats this novel along with Pym's first three published books as comic yet serious treatments of women's need to love. This novel displays some of Pym's usual themes: the unsuitability of many emotional attachments and the problems raised by romantic passions. Unfortunately, in Benet's opinion, *Crampton Hodnet* is not well written. The strands of the plot do not illuminate one another; some characters change inexplicably; others are developed, then dropped; the tones of the novel are inappropriately mixed.

Bowman, Barbara. "Pym's Subversive Subtext." In *Independent Women: The Function of Gender in the Novels of Barbara Pym*, edited by Janice Rossen. New York: St. Martin's Press, 1988.
Pym's heroines have an ironic attitude toward the dominant culture. Barbara Bird is too young to have such ironies and thus is not a full-fledged heroine.

Burkhart, Charles. *The Pleasure of Miss Pym*. Austin: University of Texas Press, 1987.
A weak novel, but with humor for Pym lovers.

Cooley, Mason. *The Comic Art of Barbara Pym*. New York: AMS Press, 1990.
Cooley's affectionate analysis of Pym's youthful creation defines North Oxford as a magical world which mixes conventional Victorian comic oppressiveness, romantic reveries, and jazz-age

youth. Into this world come outsiders: a curate and two attractive undergraduates. Romance develops. When it subsides, North Oxford remains the same. Although Jessie Morrow is a figure of Victorian dependency, she has a mind of her own like later Pym heroines. Only Stephen Latimer seems to feel any real passion.

Cotsell, Michael. *Barbara Pym*. New York: St. Martin's Press, 1989.
Cotsell treats this novel briefly in Chapter 2. Pym's fascination with the Victorian past is strong in this novel, set among the imposing Victorian houses of North Oxford. Because the bitter spinster Miss Morrow is the principal narrator of this novel, its range and tone are limited. Cotsell identifies the influence of John Betjeman in some of Miss Morrow's reflections.

Doan, Laura L. "Pym's Singular Interest: The Self as Spinster." In *Old Maids to Radical Spinsters: Unmarried Women in the Twentieth-Century Novel*. Urbana: University of Illinois Press, 1991.
Pym makes readers know that her spinsters have chosen to be single. Jessie Morrow may look like a stereotypical dull spinster, but in reality she is an admirable clear-headed woman who rejects Stephen because she wants true love or nothing.

_____. "Text and the Single Man: The Bachelor in Pym's Dual-Voiced Narrative." In *Independent Women: The Function of Gender in the Novels of Barbara Pym*, edited by Janice Rossen. New York: St. Martin's Press, 1988.
Pym's women have a capacity to utter dutiful expressions, yet have subversive thoughts. In contrast, though Pym's bachelors (like Edward) are somewhat spinsterish in their habits, they are (like Stephen Latimer) single-minded in their selfishness.

Liddell, Robert. *A Mind at Ease: Barbara Pym and Her Novels*. London: Peter Owen, 1989.
In Chapter 2, Liddell says he thinks Pym would not have wanted this novel to be published. Liddell remarks on the influence the novelist Ivy Compton-Burnett had on Pym and documents how this novel was quarried for characters in later works.

Long, Robert Emmet. *Barbara Pym*. New York: Frederick Ungar, 1986.
In Chapter 3, Long expresses his admiration and affection for this view of Oxford life. Long points out the similarities in the novel's male suitors: they all are weak, and they all tell lies. Maude Doggett is the central character, but her employee, Jessie Morrow, adds the novel's dark note. She is one of Pym's spinsters; she views others with clarity. Even though Oxford will go on from year to year without essentially changing, the novel implies at the end that Jessie's emotional life will decay.

Rossen, Janice. "Love in the Great Libraries: Oxford in the Work of Barbara Pym." *Journal of Modern Literature* 12 (July, 1985): 277-296.
In real life, Oxford to Pym meant a heady mixture of study and romance. The world of this novel is much more inhibited than that Pym describes in her diaries.

_____. *The World of Barbara Pym*. New York: St. Martin's Press, 1987.
Chapter 2 is a reprint of Rossen's article, "Love in the Great Libraries." A few references to *Crampton Hodnet* appear elsewhere in this study.

Weld, Annette. *Barbara Pym and the Novel of Manners*. New York: St. Martin's Press, 1992.
In Chapter 3, Weld admits this novel verges upon farce in several ways, but maintains it is a novel of manners. Miss Doggett is the guardian of proper behavior, and the novel shows the subtle distinctions of food and clothing Pym made in her Oxford years.

Wyatt-Brown, Anne M. *Barbara Pym: A Critical Biography*. Columbia: University of Missouri Press, 1992.
In Chapter 2, Wyatt-Brown ties the tone of this novel to Pym's fears and disappointments. Her failed relationship with a younger man colors her treatment of Simon and his father. Her personal fears for the future are mirrored in Jessie Morrow; her sexual inhibitions are mirrored in Barbara Bird. In general, her personal pessimism lies behind this novel's harsh satire against marriage and romance. Only a mother's love is valued.

An Academic Question, 1986. [1965-1972; assembled from drafts]

Ackley, Katherine Anne. *The Novels of Barbara Pym*. New York: Garland, 1989.
Some references to this novel's themes are scattered throughout this book. No index.

Allen, Orphia Jane. *Barbara Pym: Writing a Life*. Metuchen, N.J.: Scarecrow Press, 1994.
Brief remarks in "The Wilderness Years" section of Part 1.

Burkhart, Charles. *The Pleasure of Miss Pym*. Austin: University of Texas Press, 1987.
In Chapter 2, Burkhart says this posthumous novel suffers from not having been thoroughly revised by Pym herself.

Byatt, A. S. *Passions of the Mind*. New York: Random House, 1992.
Byatt dislikes this novel, saying it communicates self-regarding self-pity. Pym is overvalued.

Cotsell, Michael. *Barbara Pym*. New York: St. Martin's Press, 1989.
In Chapter 4, Cotsell groups this posthumous novel with others that show a falling off of Pym's artistry. Pym here tried to write a kind of story that would be popular with contemporary readers.

Rossen, Janice. *The World of Barbara Pym*. New York: St. Martin's Press, 1987.
References to this novel are scattered throughout.

Weld, Annette. *Barbara Pym and the Novel of Manners*. New York: St. Martin's Press, 1992.
In Chapter 5, Weld says that this novel does not succeed because in most episodes Pym deserts her favorite genre, the novel of manners.

Wyatt-Brown, Anne M. *Barbara Pym: A Critical Biography*. Columbia: University of Missouri Press, 1992.
Wyatt-Brown treats this work briefly in Chapter 5 and calls it a failed attempt to write in a current mode. While writing it, Pym was growing older and had a serious operation. As a result, her

interest in romantic love declined. She shifts some attention and sympathy to older characters, but is not yet engaged with them.

Civil to Strangers and Other Writings, 1988. [1935-1941]

Ackley, Katherine Anne. *The Novels of Barbara Pym*. New York: Garland, 1989.
References are scattered throughout. No index.

Allen, Orphia Jane. *Barbara Pym: Writing a Life*. Metuchen, N.J.: Scarecrow Press, 1994.
In Part 1, Allen describes how in her early unpublished fiction, Pym wrote about the details of her own life.

Rossen, Janice. *The World of Barbara Pym*. New York: St. Martin's Press, 1987.
References to Pym's early work are to be found throughout this study. In Chapter 3, Rossen analyzes the role of spinsters in these early writings.

Weld, Annette. *Barbara Pym and the Novel of Manners*. New York: St. Martin's Press, 1992.
In Chapter 3, Weld discusses these writings briefly.

Wyatt-Brown, Anne M. *Barbara Pym: A Critical Biography*. Columbia: University of Missouri Press, 1992.
Brief references to these works can be found throughout.

Bibliographical Studies

Berndt, Judy. "Barbara Pym: A Supplemental List of Secondary Sources." *Bulletin of Bibliography* 43 (June, 1986): 76-80.

Myers, Mary H. "Barbara Pym: A Further List of Secondary Sources." *Bulletin of Bibliography* 48 (March, 1991): 25-26.

_____. "Barbara Pym: A Supplement to a Further List of Secondary Sources." *Bulletin of Bibliography* 49 (March, 1992): 81-82.

Peterson, Lorna. "Barbara Pym: A Checklist, 1950-1984." *Bulletin of Bibliography* 41 (December, 1984): 201-206.

Salwak, Dale. *Barbara Pym: A Reference Guide.* Boston: G. K. Hall, 1991.
A list of Pym's works and an annotated list of writing about her arranged by year of publication. Annotations are useful but brief.

Other Works

Pym wrote a number of short stories, only a few of which were published in her lifetime. Four of these are collected in *Civil to Strangers and Other Writings*, edited by Hazel Holt (New York: E. P. Dutton, 1988). That volume also includes edited versions of four unpublished novels, one of them unfinished. One of her two radio plays was broadcast by the BBC in 1950. Many of her other papers were edited after her death by Hazel Holt and Hilary Pym and form a kind of autobiography, *A Very Private Eye: The Diaries, Letters, and Notebooks of Barbara Pym* (New York: E. P. Dutton, 1984).

Index

Index

About the Author

George Soule was born in Fargo, North Dakota, and was educated at Carleton College, Corpus Christi College of Cambridge University, and Yale University. He taught at Oberlin College and the University of Wisconsin at Madison before he returned to Carleton. There he became Professor of English and served as the Chair of the English department from 1980 to 1983. He edited an anthology of drama, *The Theatre of the Mind* (1974), and has taught and published articles on William Shakespeare, James Boswell and Samuel Johnson, William Wordsworth, and contemporary British fiction. In 1990, he was the senior champion on the television program *Jeopardy*. He retired in 1995 and lives in Northfield, Minnesota, with his wife Carolyn.